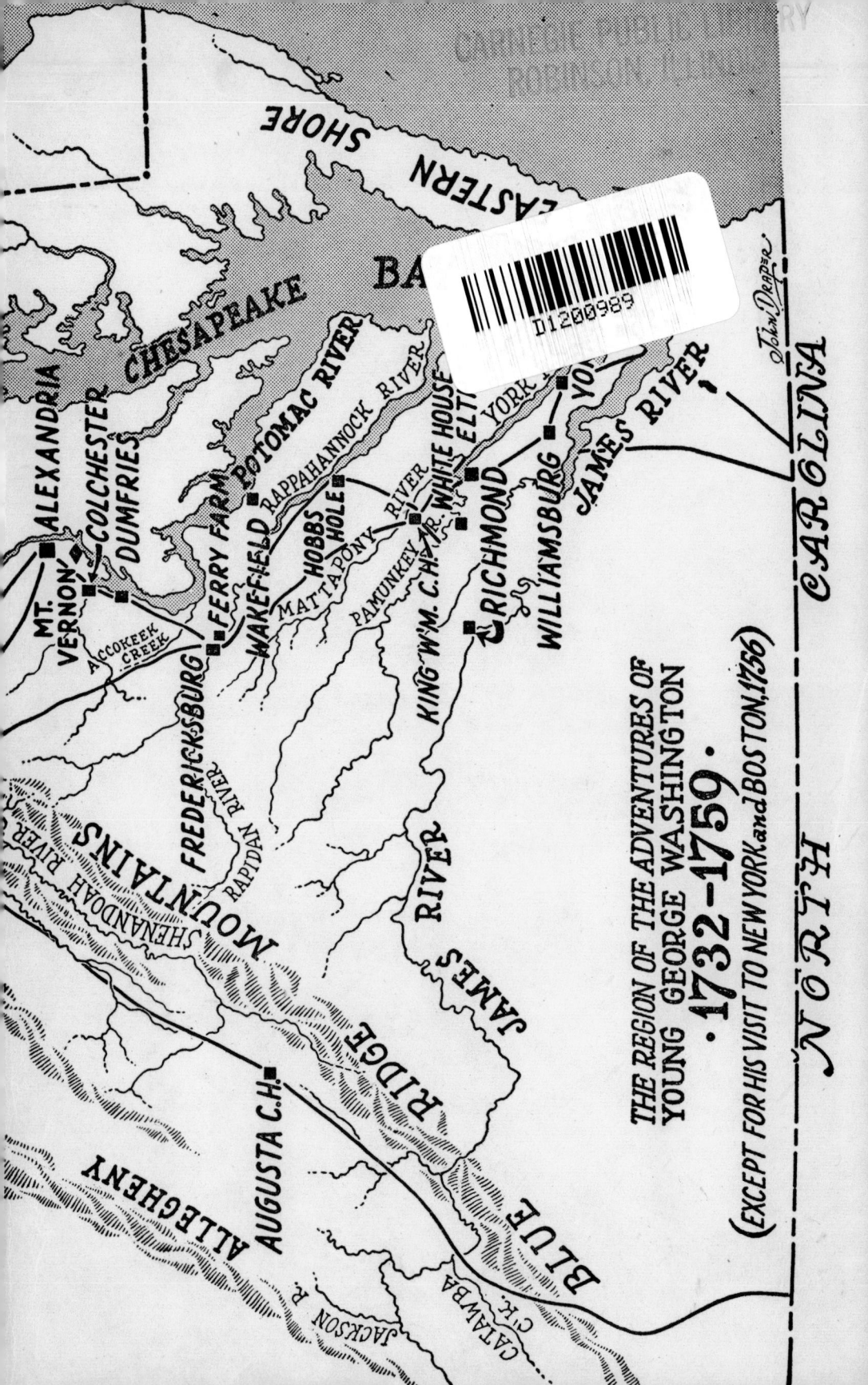

EASTERN SHORE

CHESAPEAKE BA

John Draper

CAROLINA

POTOMAC RIVER

RAPPAHANNOCK RIVER

ALEXANDRIA

COLCHESTER

DUMFRIES

MT. VERNON

FERRY FARM

WAKEFIELD

HOBBS HOLE

MATTAPONY

ACCOKEEK CREEK

FREDERICKSBURG

RAPIDAN RIVER

PAMUNKEY RIVER

MATTAPONY RIVER

KING WM. C. H.

YR. WHITE HOUSE

ELT

YORK

YO

RICHMOND

WILLIAMSBURG

JAMES RIVER

SHENANDOAH RIVER

MOUNTAINS

JAMES RIVER

BLUE RIDGE

ALLEGHENY

AUGUSTA C.H.

JACKSON R.

CATAWBA CK.

NORTH

THE REGION OF THE ADVENTURES OF
YOUNG GEORGE WASHINGTON
·1732-1759·

(EXCEPT FOR HIS VISIT TO NEW YORK and BOSTON, 1756)

GEORGE WASHINGTON

BOOKS BY DOUGLAS SOUTHALL FREEMAN

———

GEORGE WASHINGTON

LEE'S LIEUTENANTS

THE SOUTH TO POSTERITY

R. E. LEE

———

CHARLES SCRIBNER'S SONS

Augustine Washington and Mary Ball was Married the

Sixth of March, 17 30/31

George Washington Son to Augustine & Mary his Wife was Born

y 11th Day of February 1731/2 about 10 in the Morning & was Baptized the 5th of April

following M. Beverley Whiting & Capt. Christopher Brooks Godfathers and

Mrs. Mildred Gregory Godmother

Betty Washington was Born the 20th of June 1733 about 6 in y Morning

Departed this life, the 31 of March 1797 at 4 oclock

Samuel Washington was Born y 16 of Nov. 1734 about 3 in y Morning

Jane Washington Daughter of Augustine and Jane Washington

Departed this Life Jany 17th 1734/5

John Augustine Washington was Born y 13th of Jany about 2 in y Morn 1735/6

Charles Washington was Borne y 1st Day of May about 3 in y Morn 1738

Mildred Washington was Born y 21st of June 1739 about 9 at Night

Mildred Washington Departed this Life Oct. y 23d 1740 being thursday about 12 a Clock at Noon Aged 1 Year & 4 Months

Augustine Washington Departed this Life y 12th Day of April 174 aged 19 Years —

THE RECORD OF WASHINGTON'S BIRTH

Entries, by an unknown hand, in the family Bible, of the births and deaths of the children of Augustine and Mary Ball Washington. The date of George Washington's birth was entered as Feb. 11, 1731/32 "Old Style." By the British Calendar corrected in 1752, the date was Feb. 22, 1732, "New Style."

From the original at Mount Vernon, reproduced by permission of the Regents.

GEORGE WASHINGTON

A BIOGRAPHY

By

Douglas Southall Freeman

VOLUME ONE

YOUNG
WASHINGTON

NEW YORK
CHARLES SCRIBNER'S SONS
1948

TO

THE BEST LOVED

CONTENTS

CONTENTS

APPENDICES

ILLUSTRATIONS

INTRODUCTION

No SOONER was this work taken in hand than the dimness of the background of George Washington's life became apparent. It was manifest that the establishment of powerful families, the eager provision of new plantations for younger sons, and the steady advance of settlement up the Valley of the Potomac River were related to the ease with which favored individuals could procure patents of land under the Fairfax proprietary. For a full history of the grant and lease of that domain between the Potomac and the Rappahannock, one looked in vain. It consequently became necessary to study the events that made the region of Washington's birth an *imperium in imperio*. That inquiry was all the more essential because one agent of the proprietary, Col. William Fairfax, had as much personal influence on the life of young George Washington as the land system itself had on the society in which the boy lived. When the story of the proprietorship was written, it was so formidable in bulk that it could not be permitted to burden the opening chapters of this biography, but it had to be summarized there and it seemed to be entitled to publication as an appendix. There can be no understanding of young Washington without some knowledge of the Fairfaxes and their landholdings.

At the next stage of this study, it was obvious that the nearer background had likewise to be set in sharper detail. Young George was touching daily a colonial life that had its classes, its institutions, its usages, and its distinctive government. He was riding, surveying, visiting and talking with men whose conversation was of vestries and County Courts, of Governor and Burgesses, of Council and General Court, of tobacco inspection and London exchange, of indentured servants and new cargoes of slaves. One could find in the pages of Bruce and of Wertenbaker an account of Virginia life in the seventeenth century, but from the removal of Alexander Spotswood as Lieutenant Governor in 1722 to the outbreak of the French and Indian War, there were shadows and silence. Traditionally it was a period during which "nothing happened." The uncomfortable feeling developed that one was on unfamiliar ground, and that one did not know how Washington or his contemporaries would act in situations that were certain to develop in the course of the narrative, though the participants regarded their various steps as so much a matter of course that they made no record.

One thus had the alternative of remaining uneasy or else of making a detailed survey of the Virginia of Washington's youth. The choice could be none other than the one represented by Chapter IV of the first volume of the present work. The biography is halted there, at the time of the death of Augustine Washington, father of George, who not long thereafter had a rapid and perhaps an explosive emergence into adolescence. It seemed proper to describe, as of that approximate date, the Virginia that he saw around him when his stream of consciousness became continuous. Although a hurried reader may not have patience for the minutiae there set down of Virginia life in 1740–50, one has to confess that only when one had finished that study did one feel "at home" in the society and among the institutions that shaped Washington's life.

There appeared to be no limit to the new material on the Virginia background, other than that of surviving court orders and extant correspondence. On most phases of colonial activity in Washington's boyhood and youth, it would easily have been possible to multiply examples and amusing illustrations until Chapter IV became in itself a volume as large as this. The search for new information on the uprearing of the boy himself was disappointing. In the court records of Westmoreland was found the document which shows that Washington's birthplace was, at the outset, a simple habitation. A sifting of Joseph Ball's Letter Book yielded much information that may illuminate some of the characteristics of his half-sister, Washington's mother. Scattered letters and contracts made it possible to reconstruct most of the essential facts concerning the Principio Iron Furnaces, in which Augustine Washington was a stockholder and doubtless a most provoking and dilatory one, in the eyes of his associates. Wills, orderbooks and inventories yielded a fairly clear picture of the various neighborhoods in which the boy lived. Here and there were scraps that added to known fact, but did not enlarge it substantially. In the end, the boy was no more a personality than any other lad of the same period.

This was disquieting. It seemed for a time to indicate that the sources had been exhausted by previous investigation and that anything further on the life of Washington would be interpretation only. The next stage of inquiry was a surprising, almost a bewildering reversal. From the time Washington began to make money, he preserved a record vastly more informative and human than most of his diaries, which often are tediously dull. His unpublished papers in various depositories, notably in the Library of Congress, demonstrated once again that nearly as much of the life of a man is set down in the letters addressed to him as in those written by him. A great store of collateral and informative material was found in literary remains of his contemporaries—Adam Stephen, for example. The period of the French and Indian War yielded so much, especially from Canadian transcripts and the letters of Col. Henry Bouquet in the British Museum, that a somewhat formidable part of the task became that of selection.

Still more surprising was the mass of unused fact in printed sources. For the years covered by the first and second volumes of this work, Fitzpatrick's edition of the *Writings of Washington* added little of importance to what had been published in Worthington C. Ford's edition; but the riches of other collections, even of such familiar works as the correspondence of Horatio Sharpe or the letters of Robert Dinwiddie, scarcely seemed to have been tapped. The amount of new incident was considerable. Obscure facts could be clarified and important incidents elaborated from some of the printed works. The bulk of these sources may have discouraged thorough examination in the past. Undeniably, much of their content is hard reading, but it is rewarding.

The third surprise of the inquiry covered by these two volumes was that of the extent to which the personality of young Washington has been ignored, one even might say, suppressed, by all writers except Rupert Hughes and two or three others. Apparently there have been two orthodox approaches to the youth of Washington—one forward through Weems and the other backward from Gilbert Stuart and John Marshall. If Weems were followed, Washington was a cross between a prig and a paragon. When seen through the eyes of the Chief Justice or those of the Rhode Island painter, he was so awesome and reserved a figure that he never could be credited with a youth.

These distortions are difficult to understand, because Washington was excessively candid in talking about himself in youth. Although surviving letters written before he was twenty-three years of age are comparatively few in number—Fitzpatrick found thirty-five only— some of them are remarkable for self-revelation. How, for example, could even a hero-worshipper fail to concede the boyishness and the emotional violence of a humiliated ex-officer of twenty-two and a half who could write, "I am always ready and always willing to do my country any service that I am capable of but never upon the terms I have done, having suffered much in my private fortune, besides impairing one of the best of constitutions"? Between the time Washington succeeded to the command of the Virginia Regiment in June, 1754, and the date he returned his commission about the end of 1758, he resigned once and threatened to do so at least six times. Was this the conduct of a young man so mature in his patriotism that he would bear all things, endure all things? Why was it deemed necessary to put on a verbal pedestal a young Colonel who asked a friend in the regular army to recommend him to his new commander not as one who hoped for military preferment, "but as a person who would gladly be distinguished in some measure from the *common run* of provincial officers, as I understand there will be a motley herd of us"?

Truth is, the George Washington sketched in the last chapter of the second volume of this work was a rapidly developed young man of complicated character—moral, just, patient, amiable and able to win the affection of his Captains and Lieutenants, but at the same time humorless, ambitious, persistent to positive obstinacy, acquisitive, suspicious of rivals and extraordinarily sensitive. Within this fundamental antithesis of qualities, there were conflicts, gradations and contradictions. Scarcely a doubt can remain that he was in love with the wife of a neighbor and friend. Although he told her so after he had become engaged to another woman, the discretion of Sally Fairfax and her character and his own saved them from any sort of scandal. His desire to make money was gratified but, even after marriage, his increase of property was cancelled in part by overready compliance with friends' requests for loans. Again, supersensitive though he was to everything that seemed to him to threaten his place in public esteem, he rallied most quickly when he was most sternly rebuked. An emergency always made him forget his bruised pride. He was, in a word, an immensely vital and definitely emotional young man. His responses were certain where his code of principles was involved. In other things, he was an unpredictable son of a self-seeking generation of a century in which raw realism and artificial manners were strangely mingled. When he lost the first race for the Ohio, and learned that the French were in possession of the ground that later became Fort DuQuesne, he voiced an appeal for "the heroic spirit of every free-born Englishman to attest the rights and privileges of our King." Thereafter, he was in his twenty-seventh year and had given up hope of military advancement before he wrote again of service to his King and country, without including a reference of some sort to the public esteem he sought to win or was in danger of losing. The patriot emerged slowly.

Two generations ago this statement would have been considered defamation. The integrity of the United States was assumed, for some reason, to presuppose the flawlessness of Washington's character and vice versa. Complete faith in him, *a juventute,* was part of the creed of loyalty. To what extent this reflected national pride, gratitude and ideals, and in what proportions, who can say? Acceptance of Parson Weems's fables seems to have kept Americans from realizing that to proclaim perfection was to deny growth. Refusal to admit that Washington needed to develop with the years and to overcome weakness was the surest way of all to deprive his life of inspirational value. Few emulate what they cannot hope to duplicate. Youth, conscious of its failings, is suspicious of other youth supposed to have none. Where complete virtue does not create skepticism, it arouses resentment. This is understood now. More Americans will be relieved than will be shocked to know that Washington sometimes was violent, emotional, resentful—a human being and not a monument in frozen flesh.

The later years of the twenty-seven described in the first and second volumes of this work covered the education and development of a soldier as well as of a man with characteristics sharply cut. When Washington rode wearily home from Fort DuQuesne in December, 1758, he had all the training he possessed when he was made commander in 1775 of the military forces subject to the Continental Congress. Between the time he resigned in the belief that colonials could get no recognition in the regular military establishment of Britain, and the day he hesitantly accepted the burdensome duty Congress imposed, he gave little thought to military affairs. He did not follow closely, though he had interest in, the final campaigns of the French and Indian War. As far as is known, he read few books, if any, on tactics, strategy or military organization during the sixteen years and a half he resided at Mount Vernon as a planter whose public service compassed nothing larger than membership in the House of Burgesses. For close to two decades he wrote nothing that echoed soldierly study. What he was when he concluded his service under Forbes, he was when he began the desperate game against Gage and Howe in front of Boston.

For these reasons it has been necessary to review in detail, near the close of Volume II, the scope of Washington's instruction. The conclusion is that he had no training in strategy beyond that which an alert young officer would absorb while acting as aide to a commanding General and, subsequently, while serving at a post where there was abundance of time for discussing military subjects with men whose experience was, if anything, more limited than his own. His acquaintance with tactics was somewhat wider. It included a sufficiency of drill, simple maneuver and march. Washington shared, as all men know, in the bloody action of the Monongahela, but he commanded no troops there. Later, in common with other provincials, he was credited with more than he accomplished in that battle. As a field commander, he had in the early summer of 1754 about a week of hide-and-seek, surprise attack and hopeless defence that ended in the surrender of his small force. Subsequent to that, his only combat was a blundering, costly exchange of fire with some of his own men near Loyal Hannon. The remaining, greater part of Washington's schooling as a soldier was in those things an impatient officer most disliked, the collection and custody of supplies, correspondence with officials, endless hard travel, the maintenance of discipline, and the punishment of those who defied it.

The whole of this was commonplace training of the sort that usually leads a man to resign himself to routine or else to resign his commission. Besides these discouragements, another and a worse had to be faced by Washington: He, a young, high-spirited man, anxious to do the right and ambitious to win honor, was subjected to a harassing fire of ignorant and jealous misrepresentation. His report of January, 1754, on the French plans for an advance to the Ohio, was regarded by some as part of an unworthy scheme to further the interests of a land company. Defeat at Fort Necessity was attributed to a desire to snatch a victory before reenforcements arrived to share the glories of the field. The next year Washington's officers were denounced in print as "drunken debauchees." A call for help sent out by him during a ghastly Indian raid was distorted into a shameful conspiracy to get an enlarged command. He even was suspected of treasonable communication with the enemy.

These things, except the last, of which he was unaware, were good because they were bad. They were still better because they were part of an endless, day-by-day struggle with every sort of inadequacy, human and material. To keep his feeble little Regiment on the frontier, Washington had to develop patience, ingenuity, persistence, skill in making much of little, and—what was hardest of all for a man of his extremely sensitive nature—a determination never to let malignity frustrate him.

Not all his lessons were easily learned or completely mastered; but when his schooling was done he could have told himself, had he so much as considered the possibility of future military service, that nothing he could be called upon to do after 1758 could be more difficult than what he had undergone. Perhaps the pitiful meagreness of America's resources in weapons and in trained men discouraged him less in 1775 because he remembered what had been achieved in conditions even more adverse in 1755 after Braddock's defeat. Again and again, in reading of Washington's woes in trying to organize an effective force to defend Virginia, one is apt to pity the young Colonel, and one doubtless would incline the more to that feeling if Washington had not himself complained so loudly and had not so often threatened to quit. Just when one is about to exclaim of some mistreatment, "What an outrage!" one reflects and says instead, "What a preparation!"

In the period of Washington's training in 1754–58 for the war he was to wage almost twenty years later, he had far less of political schooling than in the years 1759–75, which are described in Volume III. He had been elected Burgess for the first time about five months before he resigned his command of the First Virginia Regiment. Nothing more than a political apprenticeship was to his credit then, but it had been excellent as far as it had gone. Washington had learned how to deal with legislative committees and how to win the good opinion of the political elders who dominated the councils of the Colony. Close relations with Col. William Fairfax and with Speaker Robinson had carried him behind the screen of office. If Washington failed to hold the good opinion of the man who had the largest power in Virginia, Governor Dinwiddie, that was no less valuable than success would have been, because it showed him what were the subjects concerning which a proud executive was most apt to be stubborn, insistent or irascible. More broadly, the realities of Virginia political life taught Washington that respect and candor were indispensable in dealing with lawmakers, and that their good will, once merited and won, was not withdrawn quickly from a man they trusted. At twenty-seven, having stood before committees, and having seen the Burgesses through the eyes of a commander dependent on legislators for supplies of every sort, he is, at the end of Volume II, about to look at military men and their appeals from inside the House.

The privilege of studying young Washington, man, soldier and prospective legislator, has been attended by no special problem of presentation, other than the familiar one that inheres in the organization of so large a body of source material. It has seemed best to confine the narrative to the passing event and neither to refer to later occurrences in the life of Washington nor to make comparisons with them. The aim has been to portray him, year by year, through each new experience, as if nothing were known and nothing were certain about his future. If this has excluded some analogies that might be interesting, it likewise has saved one from an overready assumption of cause and effect. When one does not anticipate, one is less apt to theorize.

Washington did not live in a vacuum. Probably at no stage of his life, and certainly not in the years covered by these volumes, was he so much the master of the scene, so unchallengeably superior to his environment that he was uninfluenced by those around him. Some of the seniors of Williamsburg political life may have shaped permanently his convictions on certain aspects of government. The aptitudes, the peculiarities and the limitations of his military subordinates determined later the scope and form of many of his plans. For these reasons, and on the broad and familiar principle that every man is the better understood if his friends are, it has seemed desirable to sketch several members of Washington's immediate family, some of the leaders of colonial life, and a considerable number of his companions-in-arms. Unfortunately, in a few instances, materials are so meagre that one cannot put muscles and skin on the bare bones of dates and titles. Still other individuals whose names often were connected with Washington's actually meant so little to him that it has not appeared worth the reader's time to delineate them.

It was an interesting society—Lawrence Washington fighting vainly against consumption; old Governor Dinwiddie secretly ambitious to be a Colonel; Lord Fairfax shunning women, buying fashionable clothes and never wearing them, enjoying solitude, and now friendly, now moody; Col. William Fairfax counselling George sagely and then fairly pursuing him in an effort to get a commission for a spoiled son; Christopher Gist who knew the art of the forests and knew, also, when to aid and when to leave Washington alone; Half King with his irrepressible hatred of France and his ineradicable love of making speeches; Andrew Montour with paint on his face and trinkets in his ears but finely appareled and speaking readily French, English and the languages of the natives; Peter Hog who "went to seed" at a remote post; Adam Stephen, attractive and a warm friend, but a good hater, too, and not able to stand up against the self-assertive John Dagworthy—all these and many besides were of breath and blood. In the background were the reluctant militia and the German frontier settlers who seemed to Washington perversely unwilling to speak English, which some of them probably did not understand. There, too, on the stage but in the shadows, were the venders of rumor, the gossips and bitter men of suspicious, jealous mind who invariably put the harshest, most discreditable construction on everything the vigorous, ambitious Washington did.

Much the most exacting of all the sketches that had to be undertaken in these two volumes was that of Mary Ball Washington, George's mother. She has a tall monument in a lovely Virginia town. Her home is preserved there. A college has been named after her. Traditions concerning her represent an extraordinary combination of probability, absurdity and fancy. Instead of trying to ascertain how much of the mother was in the son, some have been disposed to transfer all the virtues of the son to the mother. Verbal pictures of the Roman matron, ready to sacrifice even her first-born for her country, clash strangely with such homely stories as the one long cherished in Fredericksburg that she was exceedingly frugal in using a leg of mutton, which she enjoyed greatly, and that she unhesitatingly would take the cold joint from the dish at table, would hold it to her nose, and would sniff to ascertain if it still was fit to eat.

A student could ask for nothing more fascinating than to take the meagre references to Mrs. Washington and to put them together in an effort to discover the real personality that lies behind the scraps of paper. It is believed that she can be recaptured, in the end, and that her character can be illustrated by evidence that is consistent if by no means ample. By the time George is twenty-seven, at the end of the second volume, the reasons for his lack of warm affection for his mother begin to appear. Although he believed that ample provision was made for her, she constantly was asking for something more—for a present from her half-brother to her daughter, for timber with which to erect a house, for butter and a servant from the frontier, for money whenever George came to visit her. All this was shockingly contrary to the very fundamentals of the strict rule of pay and be paid, according to which Washington lived. As his code similarly enjoined filial duty, he supplied her with what she asked, if he possibly could do so, and he tried always to show patience toward her, but he did not wish to be with her and he seldom gave her his confidence, if ever he did. There always was deference but always distance.

This much is plain and manifestly dates from a time later than that during which she began to display in somewhat exaggerated form a mother's natural and familiar desire to keep her son from danger. In treating the transition from her anxiety to her acquisitiveness and from that to the chronic confusion of being a "poor manager," the one difficulty is that of determining when the changes occurred. There is danger that Mary Washington may be assumed to have in 1758 the fully developed complaining state of mind that was hers in 1781. To his immense embarrassment Washington then had to insist on repeal if, as he feared, an act had been passed by the General Assembly of Virginia to award her a pension because she was said to have lamented the burden of her taxes. It is not likely that the strange progression in her attitude toward money matters can be traced with precision but the effort can at least be made. If, at the last, there is disillusionment concerning her, there is compensation in that the reasons for Washington's avoidance of her are apparent. They are reasons that constitute an entirely human, understandable explanation of what otherwise might appear to be a man's imperial disdain of the woman who bore him.

Of the lesser questions of presentation, the most puzzling perhaps was that of how to deal with traditions and myths of Washington's boyhood and youth. It seemed illogical to say that Weems, McGuire and G. W. P. Custis had no determinable foundation for some of the stories they told, and then to print what one had rejected as spurious or had branded as dubious. A less unsatisfactory arrangement appeared to be that of applying the tests of historical probability and then of classifying the traditions as valid, probable or manifestly untrue. Those traditions that appear to rest on fact—such as the boy's absence at the time of his father's death and the story of the altercation with William Payne in 1755—are included in the text. Where there seems a reasonable possibility that a tradition is well based, it may be mentioned in a footnote; if it is believed to be wholly fictitious it is placed with the myths in Appendix I–7 of Volume I. It may disappoint some readers to find no more about the myth of the cherry tree than a two-line note to the effect that the period covered by the narrative on that page presumably is that to which the myth of the hatchet and the cherry sapling belonged, but it is better to disappoint than to deceive. Needless to say, historical students may not accept one man's conclusion that this story is true and that false. The standard is as frail as judgment is feeble.

Somewhat akin but less perplexing was the question of how to present a considerable body of information regarding Washington's various neighbors on Pope's Creek, in the country between the Potomac and the Rappahannock, around Ferry Farm, in the Chotank district and, finally, in the Belvoir-Mount Vernon-Alexandria area. Washington's social life was influenced by some of these families. The historical setting would have neither color nor vitality if it omitted those with whom Washington romped as a boy or, as a man, played cards, hunted or dined. To hurl all these names at the reader in a single chapter on Washington's neighbors would be, of course, first to confuse, then to bewilder, and finally to bore. The device adopted, in the end, has been the simple one of introducing each of the neighborhoods at the period during which Washington became familiar with it. This has left to Volume III a detailed account of the families and estates between Mount Vernon and Alexandria. Washington knew most of these neighbors from the time he was 15 or 16, but, with the exception of John Carlyle and James Craik, they were not friends with whom he spent much time until after he married and came to live permanently at Mount Vernon in 1759.

A third minor perplexity has been that of how to label inference as distinguished from manifest fact. During the years covered by the first and second volumes of this work, Washington gradually improved as a writer, but he still was wordy and sometimes vague. Occasionally one has to guess at his meaning. In the records, moreover, are many gaps that have to be bridged by inference. Where the employment of this historical process may affect conclusions of any importance, a footnote has been inserted as a direct reminder; but where matters of small consequence were involved, it seemed pedantic and needlessly burdensome to the reader to ask him to observe that four might be the sum of two and two, rather than of three and one. The mildest signpost of the probable, as set off from the known, was the use of "apparently," "doubtless," "it seems," or "no doubt." These monitory words are embarrassingly few in the English language and they are employed with tedious frequency in this work. Acknowledgment is made of this in all humility, but the alternative was the worse fault of failing to draw the line between fact and what one believed to be fact. With respect to some issues, it has been necessary to enter a blunt caveat because the evidence is disputable or contradictory.

Along with these questions of treatment, four that concerned style had to be answered. The first was that of the name by which to call Washington. This is not as trivial as it seems. Some of the adulatory biographers of the nineteenth century apparently would have been pleased to style Washington "the General" from the time he was ten. It manifestly so offended their sense of the proprieties to speak of him as "George" that they did so reluctantly and rarely. "George" he must be in these pages as long as he was a boy. The question really is, when should that name be dropped? The reasonable rule seemed to be to mention him as "George" until he reached the age when most of those around him were apt to refer to him as "Washington" or as "the Colonel." His patronymic or one or another of his titles is used increasingly after 1754, but the transition is made at the latest date in references to him when he was among the members of his family or with those who still called him by his first name. There is deliberate repetition of the adjective "young" in connection with his name because this seemed the easiest way of entering the reminder that the exploits and the opinions described in the text were those of a man who was developing a maturity of judgment and an ability of command far beyond the average of his years.

What should be done about the punctuation and spelling of Washington's letters and those of certain of his correspondents? Faithful and scholarly editors to whom America has become indebted for many published collections of source material have made it their rule in recent years to follow the original precisely. This is as it should be; but when a quotation is made in a biography or other historical work, archaic spelling and punctuation often turn the thought of a reader from what is said to the manner in which it is said. Sometimes, even, spelling that does not conform to modern usage may induce a vague ridicule of the men who "did not know how to spell." In order that the reader may not be brought to a halt by odd misspelling or by awkward punctuation, the modern form of all words and the current usages of punctuation have been employed in the present work with these three exceptions: First, if the punctuation leaves the meaning in the least doubt, the original is reproduced or else the doubt and the correction are mentioned in a footnote; second, in a few instances where Washington's punctuation reflected his emotion, it has been preserved; third, several letters presented such incredible examples of eighteenth-century phonetics that they have been inserted as a *divertissement*.

If Washington here is required, so to say, to make concession to more modern spelling and less painful punctuation, it seemed reciprocal to make the general vocabulary of this work conform to the English of

his day. Many hundred quotations from his letters and orders and from
the papers of his contemporaries had to be inserted in these pages: it
appeared both incongruous and anachronistic to introduce or to follow
those leisured polysyllables with comment or narrative in the clipped
style of the mid-twentieth century. This does not mean that words have
been excluded altogether from these pages because they were not
used in Washington's youth, though it has to be confessed that the
priceless *Modern English Dictionary* has been consulted endlessly to
check words and verbal phrases of doubtful age. The aim has been
merely to avoid too great a contrast between the English usage of
1750–60 and the idiom of two centuries later.

One effort, if one only, has been made at the exact duplication of the
language of Washington's day. That has been with respect to military
terminology. As American, French and British soldiers and sailors of
1754–61 and of 1775–81 had to be quoted and cross-examined, it seemed
certain that confusion would be produced if their testimony was in
approved military terms of their age and the critique in the accepted
technical language of an entirely different tactical era. It is hoped that
in every instance the reader's attention is directed in a footnote to the
first employment in the text of a military term that is different from
the corresponding one of current usage, unless the older words are self-
explanatory.

This procedure, though manifestly desirable, is across a field of some
obscurity and of many pitfalls. Apparently the period of the War of the
Austrian Succession and of the Seven Years' War was one in which
military terminology ceased to be slavishly French and became temporarily polyglot. One cannot always be sure when new phrases appeared. For example, "line of supply" seemed the correct term to
apply to the route of Braddock or that of Forbes from a general base.
"Line of communication," according to early dictionaries, referred to
communication-trenches only; but there is a letter of 1758 in which
Col. Henry Bouquet spoke of a "line of communication" precisely in
the modern sense. Occasionally, but not often, the absence of a current
military term from the vocabulary of the eighteenth-century soldier
creates some awkwardness, as, for instance, when one is barred from
using "logistics" though the alternative phrase cannot well be com-
pressed into less than half a dozen words. In these instances it has
seemed appropriate to mention the corresponding twentieth-century
term in the footnote, but it appeared necessary to adhere in the text to
the language of Washington's age.

Many of these unfamiliar terms in the text are interesting reminders of differences in tactics. As concerns strategy, there is little conflict of terminology in these two volumes, both because the strategic considerations were not large in the Southern expeditions of the French and Indian War and also because Washington had little to do with such strategy as was involved. The great concerns of 1754–58 in Virginia and in Pennsylvania were four imperatives: Get the men and equipment, organize adequate supply, procure Indian help, avoid surprise.

In the foreword to *R. E. Lee,* the remark was made that long labor was repaid through the privilege of living, as it were, in the company of a great gentleman. That is equally true of an intensive study of Washington. He, too, from his youth up, was a great gentleman and—it may surprise some readers to be told—he has been a more interesting young man to study because he was so much more complex in character than Lee. It has been a sufficient reward of the years, in fact, to discover how different young George Washington was from the traditional picture.

His times, too, were interesting. A twentieth-century student who has conducted his researches in the mid-Victorian age is apt to be excited when first he makes the acquaintance of eighteenth-century Americans. They resemble those among whom one lives at present far more than the conspicuous men of the nineteenth century seem akin in spirit to their grandsons of today. Manners were ponderously formal in 1750 if there were any manners at all. In nearly everything else the stream of daily adventure then had much of the course and current one knows in this generation. One may ask, indeed, whether the nineteenth century was not a lake through which American life passed, rather than a part of the river itself. It was a muddy, bloody lake, to be sure, but it was different from the age that emptied into it and no less different from the century into which the eighteen-hundreds flowed. Washington's youthful contemporaries were frank and little disposed to conceal their ambition or to curb their temper. Religion had small place in the life of most of them. One has no great difficulty in understanding why they made contentious captains and quarrelsome soldiers. They were undisciplined and perhaps for that reason were willing to do new things in new ways.

Their records supply titles for a larger bibliography than it seemed necessary to include in Volume II and then to print again in the selected but somewhat extensive bibliography in the final volume of this work. Consequently, the principal manuscript sources are listed but only the more important collections of printed source material and a few score of the many secondary authorities. In every initial citation of a book, it is hoped that the reference is sufficiently full to meet most bibliographical needs. Reference may be facilitated by the short-title index. Two general rules have been applied in the use of secondary authorities: First, on large questions of British imperial policy, colonial institutions and military operations with which Washington had no connection, standard authorities such as Andrews, Beer, Bruce, Gipson, Osgood, Parkman and Wertenbaker have been followed. It seemed as superfluous as it was time-consuming to review again the evidence those distinguished masters had analyzed. Second, where authorities quote sources not previously consulted in this study, the citation of the source carries with it a reference to the authority. This admittedly has encumbered some notes, but it has seemed the only means by which proper acknowledgment could be made to those writers whose research had uncovered fact which, though verified subsequently, might readily have been overlooked.

To make detailed acknowledgment of the endless courtesies received from these and other writers, from librarians and archivists everywhere, and from generous individuals will be the final and most gratifying privilege of this study. Mention of seven names cannot be deferred for inclusion in the last volume. For several years, Raymond B. Fosdick, President of the Rockefeller Foundation, and the late Jackson Davis, Vice-President and Director of the General Education Board, kept insisting that a detailed life of Washington was needed, until at length they convinced a doubting student who now has them, above all others, to thank for a much-enjoyed adventure. As it was manifest that extensive research would be required in Britain, in France, and perhaps in other countries, as well as in the United States and in Canada, Devereux C. Josephs, then President of the Carnegie Corporation, and R. M. Lester, Secretary, most generously procured from the sympathetic trustees of that Foundation ample funds for travel and investigation. These grants being payable through an institution of learning, President Isaiah Bowman and the interested trustees of Johns Hopkins graciously consented to have the Treasurer of that University, Henry S. Baker, act as disbursing agent, a duty he has discharged with the greatest thoughtfulness.

By a happy combination of circumstance, Dr. Gertrude R. B. Richards was procured as principal research assistant. Her sound historical judgment and her mature scholarship have been supplemented by endurance, imaginative resourcefulness in seeking new channels of information, and that most blessed of all qualities in any sort of protracted, exhausting research—an enthusiastic sense of humor. If this story is lightened at intervals by some lively episode, it probably was uncovered by Miss Richards; and if some long-sought fact has been found in a source one scarcely would have thought of consulting, Miss Richards's ingenuity often is to be credited. She has had, of course, no hand in writing any of the narrative that appears over another name, nor has she been responsible for the use of any of the major, printed sources, such as Burnett, Force, Fitzpatrick, Hamilton, the *Virginia Magazine of History and Biography,* the *Journals of the Continental Congress* and other works that could readily be purchased or borrowed from a library. Hers has been the burden of consulting the printed sources that could not be transported or microfilmed, and hers the assignment of examining personally the manuscripts in most of the archives. She likewise has selected the assistants who have labored in the foreign depositories.

Every phase of this study has been a delight—the man, the setting, the diversity of Washington's companions, the age in which he lived. In writing of Gen. R. E. Lee and of the Confederate States of America, one felt always the pervasion of tragedy and, after 1862, the faster approach of the trampling horsemen. For Lee and for most of his lieutenants it was a drama of ill-fortune nobly borne and, in that way, a triumph of character over catastrophe, but it was drama played in the twilight. With Washington, the atmosphere is that of dawn. Disaster never is without hope. Battles may be lost but the war will be won. Even when the men themselves grow old, the nation still is young.

DOUGLAS SOUTHALL FREEMAN

Westbourne,
Richmond, Virginia,
May 28, 1948.

GEORGE WASHINGTON

CHAPTER I

AN AMBITIOUS LANDED SOCIETY
(1640–1722)

It was amazing how the early settlers between the Potomac and the Rappahannock Rivers in Virginia progressed. They had not come in any considerable number to "the Northern Neck," as they called the long peninsula, until 1640 and after. A few were what one of their early historians styled "gentlemen of good descent";[1] most of them were small farmers, artisans, clerks, tradesmen or adventurous younger sons of the middle classes who believed they would have a better chance in the new world than they could hope to win in the old.[2] They possessed little money with which to buy slaves, farm animals and tools, and they received no help from government except "headrights" of fifty acres for each immigrant. Some did not trouble themselves about land titles. Without any formality, they took vacant woodland, cleared fields and planted crops.

Many paid with their lives for their enterprise. Mortality among the seventeenth-century pioneers was disheartening. "Bloody flux," typhoid and perhaps yellow fever slew hundreds in their first year of settlement. Malaria weakened those who survived the other diseases. Indians raided the scattered farms. Rebellion swept the countryside in 1676. Storms destroyed crops. In spite of everything, the families increased fast and with no loss of vigor. Slaves became more numerous, the livestock multiplied, the tobacco grown on expanding plantations crowded yearly the holds of a larger fleet. The second generation began to buy luxuries from England and enjoyed larger leisure. Men of the third generation considered themselves aristocrats. Within seventy-five years, a new and

---

[1] Hugh Jones, *The Present State of Virginia*, (New York, 1865, reprint of the edition of 1724, cited hereafter as Jones, *Virginia*), p. 23.

[2] The complete lack of information concerning the antecedents of most of the early settlers of Virginia was the subject of two admirable notes, presumably by W. G. Stanard, in the *Virginia Magazine of History and Biography*, v. 15, p. 217 ff, and v. 18, p. 339. In accordance with the abbreviations used in E. G. Swem, *Virginia Historical Index*, this publication is cited hereafter as *V*. The number of the volume precedes the initial.

highly prosperous landed society had been organized, where, in 1640, there had been forest or emptiness.

It was a closely knit society, too. Short-lived men and women married early and begot sons and daughters who found wives and husbands on nearby plantations. Soon kinship was so confused that the colonials devoted no inconsiderable part of their conversation to determining and unraveling it. Had there been a college of heralds in Virginia, its members would have grown rich. A few sons of Ishmael were shunned;[3] but by 1730 the majority of the long-seated proprietors were kin or, as they politely phrased it, were "connected by marriage." Robert Carter, for example, by his two successive wives, had twelve children, whose union and descent must have taxed the memory even of their contemporaries. Thomas Gerrard, an early settler,[4] by his first marriage had three sons and five daughters. One of these daughters had three husbands in turn and another daughter accepted five.[5] Gerrard's second marriage was to Rose Tucker. She already had a daughter, Sarah Tucker, who became the wife of the prosperous immigrant William Fitzhugh. After the death of Thomas Gerrard, his widow, Rose, contracted a third marriage, with John Newton,[6] who had himself been married twice previously and had several sons.[7] Equally typical and no less complicated was the kinship of the Turbervilles, of the Bushrods and Corbins, of the Steptoes, of the Ashtons, of the Lees, and bewilderingly, of the McCartys.[8]

Where relationship was general and the dominant class of society so nearly unified, Thomas Gerrard, John Lee, Henry Corbin and Isaac Allerton symbolized even more than they executed in an interesting paper to which they set their hands Mch. 30, 1670. At that period, when boundaries often were uncertain, the law required a periodic

[3] A typical instance is that of Richard Cole and his wife, whose slander of their neighbors is described in *infra*, p. 18.

[4] His patent of 1000 acres on Nomini River, Oct. 18, 1650, appears in *Va. Land Office Records*, v. 2, p. 249. These papers are cited hereafter as *L.O. Records*. Those relating to the Northern Neck after 1692 are abbreviated as *L.O. Records, N.N.* In addition, *the Patent Books* can be identified as *L.O. Records, Patents*. For this particular item, see also Eubank, *The Northern Neck of Virginia* (cited hereafter as *Eubank*), p. 61.

[5] For Anne and Frances Gerrard, see p. 18–19.

[6] See *William and Mary Quarterly*, series I, v. 4, p. 36. For the reason given *supra*, n. 2, this quarterly is cited hereafter as *W*. The number of the volume precedes the initial; the number of the series follows; then the page is given. The citation in this instance consequently is 4 *W* (1) p. 36.

[7] Through one of the lines of these younger Newtons, there was a union with the Eskridge family, the branches of which spread endlessly. See 33 *V* 301 and 7 *W* (1) p. 97.

[8] A few of these typical connections, which are much too detailed and tedious to be listed here, are sketched in Appendix I.

"processioning" of each parish to mark the property lines.[9] To simplify this, the Westmoreland neighbors covenanted not only to set their own boundaries clearly [10] but also to provide a meeting place for friendly celebration. At the junction of Allerton's lands with those of Gerrard, the four friends agreed to construct a Banqueting House where "each man or his heirs yearly according to his due course [will] make a Hon'ble treatment fit to entertain the undertakers thereof, their wives, misters and friends yearly." [11]

In this closely knit society, primogeniture was favored. A wealthy father usually left much of his land and most of his slaves and his animals to his oldest son. As late as 1749, for instance, when Thomas Lee [12] made his will, he bequeathed his eldest son 100 Negroes above ten years of age, his second son fifty, his third son forty and his youngest son thirty.[13] Daughters seldom received as much as their brothers inherited.[14]

Devises of this sort were expected and accepted, but the father of a younger son of twenty-one who married the seventeen-year-old daughter [15] of a neighbor was as unwilling as were the girl's parents to have the newly-married couple descend to the level of "inferior planters." [16] Provision had to be made for them to climb back quickly to the scale of living of their class. For this purpose, some of the paternal estates in the lower part of the Northern Neck sufficed. Various branches of the Lee family held large, separate tracts that could be divided into self-sustaining plantations.[17] Robert Carter's home estate,

10 See their agreement of Mch. 30, 1670 in 9 *Westmoreland Deeds and Wills,* 344–45.

11 *Ibid.* Because he wanted this land in 1744, George Lee, grandnephew of John Lee, had the agreement entered of record, Mch. 27, 1744, on motion before the County Court of Westmoreland (*ibid.*). Included in the record is the deposition of Thomas Lee concerning the origin of the Banqueting House.

12 President of the Ohio Company and junior agent of the proprietary, whose many activities are spread across Virginia colonial history for a generation.

13 Will of Feb. 22, 1749; 11 *Westmoreland Deeds and Wills,* 311. By act of the previous year, slaves had ceased to be real estate and had become chattels personal. See W. W. Hening, *Statutes at Large* [of Virginia] v. 5, p. 432, (cited hereafter as *H*).

14 All Thomas Lee's bequests of land to his sons were in tail male.

15 This appears to have been the average age of a girl at marriage, subsequent to 1725, or approximately that date.

16 For the use of this term by Governor Dinwiddie, see *infra*, Chapter IV.

17 The exact acreage of Lee holdings in 1722 is almost impossible to ascertain. For the extent of properties when the family was in full flower, see *Lee of Virginia,* 70. The earliest grants to the first Richard Lee are listed in 4 *L.O. Records,* 375. Cf. *Lee of Virginia,* 52, and *Eaton,* 57. As late as the time of Gen. R. E. Lee, there was a certain resentment in the family that the second Richard Lee, who died in 1714, failed to enlarge the estate. Information on Richard Lee II appears in *The Official Letters of Alexander Spotswood* (cited hereafter as *Spotswood's Letters*), v. 1, p. 179; in *Lee of Virginia,* 74 ff; and in Louis B. Wright, *The First Gentlemen of Virginia* (cited hereafter as *Wright*), p. 212 ff.

Corotoman, contained 8000 acres and more.[18] In Northumberland, before the end of the seventeenth century, John Mottrom had patented 3700 acres,[19] Peter Presley 4150,[20] and Peter Knight 7600.[21] Estates of this size were the exception and were not held long. Some names, conspicuous in the late seventeenth century, disappeared in the eighteenth. Other planters held to their fathers' holdings, but their sons received divided property that did not suffice for the lavish living of more than one large family. The rent roll of Westmoreland in 1740 was to show 199 proprietors. Seventy-seven of these owned 300 acres or more, but eleven only of the seventy-seven had over 1000 acres.[22]

Happily for the perpetuation of the new society, there was abundance of unoccupied land at and above "the freshes," the upper stretches of the rivers where fresh water ran into the brackish tidal streams. This land was to be had by the payment of annual quit rents. Except during one brief period, all unclaimed fields, hills and woodlands South of the Rappahannock could be "patented" directly from the Crown, through the Governor and Council. Between the Rappahannock and the Potomac, new acreage had to be sought from the Proprietors or their agents.

In the autumn of 1649, eight months after the execution of his father, Charles II had bestowed on seven favorite companions in exile that part of Virginia "bounded by and within the heads" of these two rivers, Potomac and Rappahannock,[23] an area of about 1,000,000 acres by minimum calculation. Beneficiaries of the patent had been empowered

[18] The patents taken out by his father, Col. John Carter, along Corotoman Creek, 1653–68, covered 11,970 acres (3 *L.O. Records*, 88, 4 *ibid.*, 507; 5 *ibid.*, 345, and 6 *ibid.*, 136. For the location and description of the estate and house, see 32 *V* 19, and *Eubank*, 97. In addition to the frontier lands patented in 1724–31, Robert Carter acquired Ripon Hall from the heirs of Edmund Jenings, the 6000 acres of Nomini from the Spencers, and the Lloyd estate in Richmond County (32 *V* 18). In spite of the extreme length of his will, printed in 5 *V* 408 ff, 6 *V* 1 ff, Robert Carter did not avoid a dereliction of many eighteenth-century Virginians. These testators usually would be explicit concerning the area of unimportant frontier lands but would be content to refer to their interesting home estate as "The place where I live," or words of similar vagueness. In Carter's case, Corotoman was mentioned as part of his "Lands in Lancaster County" and as the "Great Tract I now live on" (5 *V* 409, 413) but the acreage is not given anywhere in the will.

[19] 2 *L.O. Records*, 247; 3 *ibid.*, 64; 5 *ibid.*, 482.

[20] *Ibid.*, 186; 5 *ibid.*, 547; 6 *ibid.*, 11.

[21] 5 *ibid.*, 64, 452; 6 *ibid.*, 11. In considering early grants, it is desirable to remember that many of them lapsed for non-settlement or were forfeited because they were abandoned. Cf. 2 H 56, 136–37; 3 *ibid.*, 314.   [22] *Eaton*, 9.

[23] Moncure D. Conway pointed out in his *Barons of the Potomac* (cited hereafter as *Conway's Barons*), p. 9, that the Rappahannock was especially the highway of the tobacco trade. For a description of the Potomac, *c.* 1775, see Smyth, *A Tour in the United States of America* (cited hereafter as *Smyth*), v. 2, p. 146. The legislative acts for the creation of the earliest Counties of the Northern Neck will be found in 1 H 240, 337, 352, 374, 381, 427. Detailed tables of the origin and subsequent division of the Counties are printed in M. P. Robinson, *Virginia Counties*.

to exercise what were substantially feudal rights and to "give, grant, or by any other way or means sell or alienate" lands within the proprietary. The grant was in perpetuity; the annual rent was a few pounds only. One or two of the Proprietors came to the Colony, probably to survey and develop this Northern Neck; but as Virginia surrendered to the Parliamentary Commissioners, Mch. 22, 1652, Charles's act of bounty was not recognized.

After the Restoration, the patent was enrolled in 1661 and was upheld in all its terms by the King. Various amendments subsequently were made in some of its provisions; compromises between Colony and Proprietors and between Proprietors and tenants became necessary; the proprietary itself continued and influenced the settlement of Virginia in these six major respects: [24]

1. Those who had settled on the Northern Neck before the establishment of the proprietary, and some who ignorantly or defiantly established themselves there after 1749, refused to recognize any obligation to pay quit rents to the owners.

2. The Proprietors sought to increase their authority and to extend their domain for their own enrichment.

3. These efforts of the Proprietors led to numerous clashes between them and the colonial government and, for a time, to a rivalry between the proprietary and the Colony in the issuance of patents.

4. After a single Proprietor came into control of the vast estate, he usually remained in England, but he placed the management of the Northern Neck in the hands of agents or lessees, who emulated him in seeking larger profits. Some of these representatives of the Proprietor developed ambitions of their own to create extensive family "manors" within the proprietary.

5. The system was one under which wealthy planters who had the money with which to pay quit rents and the slaves to develop farms could increase their holdings and provide for themselves and for their families estates of large potential value.

6. Development of the western part of the proprietary was retarded

[24] As a detailed history of the Northern Neck proprietary has not been published, it has seemed desirable to sketch this important part of the background of George Washington. A somewhat extended account of the grant of 1649 and of the men who had an interest in its various changes and transfers will be found in Appendix I–1. Readers who have the patience to examine it will realize how many of the opportunities of the youth of Washington sprang from the proprietary. What follows in the text is a brief epitome of the relationship of the proprietary to the settlement of Virginia prior to 1723. Those who consider it too long for their time or too detailed for their interest will find the remainder of this chapter summarized on p. 14.

circumstantially, by changes of policy, by disputes over the boundary and by the danger of Indian raids; but, all in all, opportunity was offered the rich to get richer and to perpetuate a society of land estates at the same time that small farms could be sold profitably to immigrants and indentured servants who had little money.

One verb told the story of the proprietorship for almost a century: it was grab, grab, grab. The rest was detail, always interesting and sometimes amusing but detail only.

Through the effort of the colonial government, the early settlers who had no grant from the Proprietors won these terms in 1669: The Proprietors agreed to recognize all patents issued without their consent for Northern Neck lands before Michaelmas, 1661, provided the beneficiary was in actual possession of the land as of May 8, 1669. Patent holders had, moreover, to pay regularly in future the quit rent of two shillings per 100 acres.[25] In all other respects, the Northern Neck was to be subject to the same taxes and administration as the remainder of the Colony. This validation of all grants made prior to Michaelmas, 1661, was accepted by the settlers, or by their sons, as merely a vindication of their rights and not as part of a contract that provided for the subsequent payment of annual quit rents. They seldom could be induced to meet the Proprietors' terms. At length, a diligent agent, William Fitzhugh, set out to convince the planters that the Proprietors' demand was lawful. By subtlety of persuasive art, or by the offer of minimum condonation for delinquent quit rents, Fitzhugh induced the second Richard Lee to acknowledge the obligation and to covenant to discharge it. Progressively, after 1700, other planters followed Lee's example and, with much of reluctance and still more of delay, paid for the use of the land they regarded as in every essential their own. By 1710, argument on this score ended, though many tenants were chronically behind in their quit rents.

In the second development of the proprietary—the effort to get more land and more power—the beneficiaries of the original grant were cunning, persistent and successful. An attempt on the part of Lord Culpeper and Lord Arlington to extend the proprietary to all unpatented land in Virginia was frustrated, but, in 1688, just before the flight of James II, the wily Culpeper procured a renewal of the grant of the Northern Neck in perpetuity. Its boundaries were set between the Potomac and the Rappahannock, from the "first heads or springs" of

[25] As will be explained in n. 26, "fines" were imposed at one period for acreage in excess of 100.

the two rivers, instead of "within the heads" of those streams, as originally provided in 1649.

This change in description apparently escaped all notice in the Colony at the time. It probably was unknown when, in 1689, the principal Proprietor, Lord Culpeper, died and left his interests in the Northern Neck to his daughter. The next year, 1690, she married Thomas, fifth Lord Fairfax, a collateral descendant of the parliamentary General who had been Cromwell's most renowned lieutenant. Fairfax in 1693 procured a confirmation of the grant that had been renewed for Culpeper in 1688, and subsequently he made various changes in the management of the property.

An aggressive agent of his began, after 1702, to contest with the colonial authorities the ownership of the land between "the first heads or springs" of the rivers. The proprietary, according to the agent, extended from the headwaters of the farthest branch of the Potomac across the mountains to the most remote spring that fed the main stream that formed the Rappahannock. On the death of the fifth Lord Fairfax, who left as his heir a son of sixteen, the controversy over the boundaries of the Northern Neck was suspended, but it was not ended. The possibility, the probability even, remained that Lord Fairfax or his agents could issue favorable grants to vast, rich lands the Governor had pronounced royal domain.

Some aspects of the rivalry between crown grants and patents from the Proprietors had to do with the quit rents paid and the requirements for "planting" and "seating" new lands; [26] but, as respects the magnitude

[26] Outside the Northern Neck, under a law of 1666 (2 H 244, a statute that is a model of brevity and clarity) a patented tract was "seated" when the owner built a house on it and kept stock there for one continuous year; the land was "planted" when one acre was cleared, tended and given a crop of any sort. If either of these things was done, and the quit rent was paid, the patent was valid; but if the property was neither seated nor planted within three years after the patent was issued, the land reverted to the Crown. After Dec. 1, 1714, the law (4 H 37 ff) prescribed an initial fee of 10 *s.* per 100 acres. When this was paid a patent for crown lands would be issued. Subsequent quit rents on the land were to be 1 *s.* per fifty acres, with the proviso that three of every fifty acres had to be under cultivation within three years. Where this was not done or quit rents were three years in arrears, the property would revert to the King. Generous provision, not of importance in this connection, was made concerning "barren" land. By an act of 1748, even three years' non-payment of quit rent was not sufficient basis for the reversion of property unless suit were entered in the General Court (5 H 418–19. Cf. H. D. Farish, ed., Hartwell, Blair and Chilton, *The Present State of Virginia,* 1697, cited hereafter as *Hartwell, Blair and Chilton,* p. 19). An act of 1705 provided, further, that a "house" built on patented land had to be at least twelve by twelve feet and of the usual construction (3 H 307, amended in 1710; *ibid.,* 517). Previously a "shed" could have been a "house." On the Northern Neck, a patentee agreed to pay 2 *s.* yearly for 100 acres. Above 100, "fines" began. For every 100 acres in excess of 100 and under 600, the "fine" was 5 *s.* Beyond 600, the charge was 10 *s.* per 100 acres. No requirement for "seating" was set forth in the Proprietor's patents. All that was demanded of the tenant was that he tender the quit rents. In event the rents were not paid for two years, the Proprietor could cancel the patent. (Typical grants of 1690 *et seq.* appear in *L.O. Records, N.N.,* v. 1, p. 4 ff.) Occasionally, as with the Brent Town grant, a flat quit rent of 2 *s.* per 100 acres, with no "fines," was allowed.

of grants, the Land Office of the Colony did not adhere permanently to a policy essentially different from that which made it possible for the agents and lessees of the proprietary to grab avidly and often.

This, the fourth development of the proprietary, began soon after the fifth Lord Fairfax in 1693 named George Brent and William Fitzhugh as his agents. These two men were ambitious to be great landed proprietors on their own account. Brent had been one of a group of four who in 1686–87 had received 30,000 acres on which they proposed to settle religious refugees from Europe.[27] Fitzhugh had acquired his widespreading Bedford estate[28] and had taken the first steps toward patenting approximately 22,000 acres that were to constitute Ravensworth.[29] While agents, Fitzhugh and Brent were their "own best customers" in patenting some of the finest of Fairfax's lands, for which, so far as is known, they paid quit rents on the same terms as other lessees.[30] Death cut short their speculation and led to the appointment in 1702 of Robert Carter of Corotoman as agent. Carter, already the owner of a large landed estate, had been vehement in his denunciation of the policy of the Proprietor and, in 1695, had led a legislative protest against the course of the Proprietor's agents in exacting, as he alleged, quit rents double those of 2 s. per 100 acres the King required.[31] Furthermore, said Carter, it was possible for a man to "hold 50,000 or more acres of land by a secure title . . . without so much as actually seating or building upon any part of it."[32]

Now that Carter had opportunity of patenting the fairest lands he found in the proprietary, he reversed his position. Although his first concern was the better collection of the quit rents, he soon granted

[27] The history of this Brenton or Brent Town is given succinctly in Fairfax Harrison, *Virginia Land Grants* (cited hereafter as *Va. Land Grants*), p. 70, and in the same author's *Landmarks of Old Prince William* (cited hereafter as *Landmarks*), p. 177 ff.

[28] See *infra*, p. 226. Bedford is described by Fitzhugh in 1 *V* 395. William Fitzhugh's specific bequests of land, according to his will, were 49,583 acres (2 *V* 276).

[29] *Landmarks*, 187; 2 *L.O. Records, N.N.* 14.

[30] Fairfax Harrison, in *Landmarks*, 239, mentioned the possibility that the Proprietor may have "waived composition or quit rents" in the patents issued his agents, but of this Mr. Harrison found no hint in surviving records. For later provisions concerning an agent's right to lease unpatented land, see *infra*, p. 10.

[31] In *Va. Land Grants*, 128, the statement is made that double quit rents were not demanded in the Northern Neck. Actually, in *L.O. Records, N.N.*, v. 2, Maxwell Brown agreed to pay 4 s., 6 d. (142), and John Hornby assumed like obligation, (*ibid.*) while Peter Hammon covenanted to pay 3 s. (*ibid.*, 144). A grant to Thomas Dodson at 2 s. (*ibid.*, 143) is sandwiched between one to John Howlitt at 6 s. (*ibid.*, 144) and one to Thomas Salisbury at 6 s. (*ibid.*, 151). All these grants were in March, 1695.

[32] *Journal of the House of Burgesses* (cited hereafter as *Journ. H.B.*), 1695–1702, entry of May 9, 1695, p. 26. Apparently this protest, though approved by the House of Burgesses, was not accepted by the Council. See *Landmarks*, 240.

almost 13,500 acres in the name of two associates and had this land transferred to him. Close to 1000 acres were added later in the name of one of his sons.[33] If he felt that he needed justification for this, he could have found it in the fact that the Governor and the General Assembly conditionally were approving larger grants from the royal domain. By an act of 1701, the lawmakers provided that a company could patent at one time as many as 30,000 acres of land if it would keep a specified number of men there for the defence of the frontier.[34] A statute adopted four years later left it within the power of an owner of numerous slaves to procure a single patent for a maximum of 4000 acres.[35]

Before Carter had grabbed half the land his keen eye and his soaring ambition coveted, the death of the fifth Lord Fairfax was followed by still another change of policy. The trustees of the youthful sixth Lord were persuaded they could make more money and escape much trouble by leasing the proprietary for about £425 per annum to a colonial of some distinction, Edmund Jenings, who named as his deputy Thomas Lee, an able man of 21 years. Jenings was feeble and, for a time, resided in England, with the result that the management of the proprietary during the first part of the lease was almost entirely in the hands of Lee. He did much to improve the system of entering grants in the land books of the proprietary and, like Carter and Brent and Fitzhugh, he feathered his own nest while guarding the Proprietor's eggs. In particular, he patented what he considered to be the most valuable land on the Potomac, a stretch of the southern bank of the river, near the falls, where he thought a city would rise at the head of navigation.[36]

Unfortunately for the plans of the ambitious Lee, his principal, Edmund Jenings, fell behind on payments not long before the expiration of the lease of the proprietary. Another death in the Fairfax family in 1719 led to a change of counsellors and to the reappointment of Robert Carter as agent. Carter's status now was substantially changed in two particulars: First, he became lessee as well as agent, and as he was paying £450 per annum for the use of the proprietary, he determined to get the most for his money. In his new agreement was inserted definite authorization by the Proprietor to grant unpatented

[33] *Landmarks*, 198.
[34] 3 *H* 204 ff.
[35] Act of 1705, 3 *H* 304, amended by act of 1710, *ibid.*, 517.
[36] *Landmarks*, 147–49.

lands.[37] There need be no limit to Carter's land speculation now except the ability to pay the quit rents. His right of acquisition could not be challenged.

Robert Carter, in the second place, had attained to even higher distinction after the termination of his first agency. Although he had acquired no new offices,[38] he had gained in renown and in power.[39] His very name had the clatter of outriders and the rumble of a coach and six. "King" Carter he was styled, and during his last years he was as regal in his manner of living as the resources of the Colony permitted; but he knew all the details of his affairs, even to the capabilities of individual workers on his plantations.[40] He wanted his money's worth of these men's toil and of all else that was his.[41] No waste of labor would be countenanced by him in a Colony that needed every hand.[42] Although "King" Carter was as strong in his dislikes [43] as in his loves and his loyalties, he was a realist, clear-headed and courageous, in all his business affairs.[44] Proud, he was pious; lordly, he led more than one protest in which the interest of the small farmer was relatively greater than his own. Now—agent, lessee, Councillor, the richest, most powerful man in the Northern Neck—he was free to share to the utmost in the new trend toward farther-spreading estates of rich, virgin soil.

Nor was it his opportunity alone. His family and cousins might share and, after them, his intimates, his friends and men of his society. The fathers of some of these worthies, and in a few instances their grandfathers, had sensed the wealth that lay in vast forests and in rich bottom lands then trodden by wild animals only. Several alert families, such as the Lees, for example, had begun to acquire land upstream after the

37 The only reference to this provision does not exclude the possibility that it was in the first lease also. See John, Charles and Landon Carter to Alderman Perry, n.m., 10, 1736: "If his Lordship is pleased to let me have a lease for £500 per annum with the same power of granting unpatented land that my Father had, I am willing to serve him . . ." Carter-Plummer MSS, p. 9. For this interesting collection of letters, see the Bibliography, Vol. II of this work.

38He was Burgess in 1691–92 and in 1695–99, Councillor in 1699–1732, Speaker of the House for the sessions of 1696–99. Later he was Trustee and Rector of the College of William and Mary, President of the Council, 1726–32, and acting Governor, 1726–27.

39 Cf. John Custis to "Dr. Mad":, 1727 [?], n.m., n.d., concerning a vacancy in Council: ". . . it is thought it will be [filled by] some of Colonel Carter's relations—he presiding over us at present." (Custis MS Letter Book, No. 42.)

40 See Letters of Robert Carter, 1720–29, edited by Louis B. Wright, letter of July 14, 1720, p. 21–22. This collection is cited hereafter as Carter Letters.

41 Cf. Carter Letters, 11.

42 Ibid., 21.

43 E.g., ibid., 8.

44 Note, for example, his comment on the South Sea Bubble (ibid., 39), and his attitude toward losses (ibid., 79): "All I can say is that we must haul in our horns and live as we can afford."

compromise of 1669 concerning titles;[45] but the "seating" of the "freshes" had been slow. Above the falls of the Potomac, few patents, if any, had been taken out prior to 1709.[46]

During their five active years, Jenings and Lee had issued patents for 164,000 acres above Potomac Creek, which then was, roughly, the dividing line between the old settlements and the new. The total assigned by the two agents equalled almost 70 per cent of the entire acreage, 235,000, that had been patented in that region during all the previous history of grants there. At that, from 1649 through 1721, approximately 400,000 acres would have been the maximum figure for all grants, royal and proprietary, between Potomac Creek and Goose Creek, the first stream above the Little Falls of the Potomac.[47] Two-thirds of this acreage was patented during the agency of Edmund Jenings.[48] Probably the greater part of these grants were below the falls. Now, for those who had the influential friends, the money and the slaves, the opportunity was immense—an opportunity, in fact, of creating the colonial equivalent of the revered and profitable manors "at home."[49] This seemed positively—the pious might say providentially—ordained for those who already had carved noble estates from the wilderness.

No poor man could do what was required. In an earlier generation, William Fitzhugh had said that the opening of a new plantation cost almost 30,000 lbs. of tobacco.[50] The best start usually was made by sending skilled indentured servants to build the necessary structures

45 The patent of Nicholas Spencer and John Washington opposite Piscataway is mentioned, *infra*, p. 21. Much the most informative of all the early "upstream" movements on the Potomac by a single family is that of the Lees. It is too long a story to be recorded here, but the development may be traced in the "headrights" of the family (*Lee of Virginia*, 53 ff); in the grants to the first Richard Lee (4 *L.O. Records*, 139, 372); in the will of this Richard (*Lee of Virginia*, 61); in the will of his son Richard II (*ibid.*, 79); and in the will of a typical Lee of the next generation, Thomas (11 *Westmoreland Deeds and Wills*, 311). The economic progress of the first Henry Lee is equally informative. Cf. *Lee of Virginia*, 131. Illustrative of a still earlier development was the case of John Hallowes, one-time carpenter and indentured servant, as set forth in *Eaton*, 46.

46 The grant of Feb. 2, 1709, to Daniel McCarty of 2993 acres (*L.O. Records, N.N.*, v. 3, p. 248), is believed to be the first above the falls. Tithables in Stafford County represent the best index to the "seating" of the "freshes." In 1692, there were 317 tithables in the county (1 *Calendar Virginia State Papers*, cited hereafter as C), p. 68. Established figures for the specified years are as follows: for 1698, 697 (*Calendar State Papers, Colonial: America and West Indies*, cited hereafter as *Cal. Am.* & *W.I.*, an. 1701, no. 635–6); for 1699, 708 (*ibid.*); for 1702, 828 (1 *V* 371); for 1722, 1503 (*Va. Historical Register*, cited hereafter as *R*, p. 19); for 1723, 1554 (*ibid.*, 67); for 1726, 1800 (*ibid.*, 74).

47 The exact acreage, computed directly from the Land Books, is 399,779; but this figure assumes that the existing records are complete.

48 That is, according to *L.O. Records, N.N.*, v. 5, approximately 164,000 acres.

49 For the argument on the fallacy of too strict an application of the term "manor," see the note in *Landmarks*, 249.

50 Letter of Jan. 30, 1680–81 to Nicholas Hayward, 2 *V* 23.

on the chosen site.[51] For the opening of the forest and the cultivation of the land, the Negro slave was satisfactory under competent overseers. In fact, new plantations were needed to afford work for the multiplying servants. "I have . . . often inculcated to you," Robert Carter subsequently wrote his English agent, ". . . how much the lands were overstocked with slaves, how impossible it was to make tolerable crops with them and how absolutely necessary it was to find more lands for the better half of these slaves." [52] Their labor, their shelter and their subsistence were the heavy initial cost. After they were "seated," the luxurious crops of well-chosen new grounds paid the quit rents.

How small they seemed when tobacco was bringing a good price! Even if the "fines" were added, £23, 2 s. a year were all a man had to pay to hold 5000 acres of Northern Neck land as securely as if it were his in fee. It was as simple to get good tobacco land from the royal government as from the Proprietor of the Northern Neck and at the same annual quit rent of 2 s. per 100 acres, but there was this difference: As tobacco was a bulky, heavy crop intended for shipment overseas, it was grown most economically close to navigable streams. The best land had been "taken up" early in the seventeenth century along all the deep rivers in those parts of Virginia where patents could be issued by the Governor. In the proprietary, much good land remained: most of it was close to the falls of the Potomac and the Rappahannock or above them, but there would be roads, canals, development and an endless flow of Pennsylvania Germans who wanted to buy small farms.

So—grab, grab, grab. There was one obstacle only. Many of the more fertile meadows and river bottoms were in regions claimed by the Indians or else they were unpleasantly close to the routes the savages traveled from North to South.[53] If the redmen could be persuaded to remain West of the mountains, there would be still greater opportunities for settlement and for the acquisition of wealth within the proprietary, which Robert Carter was striving more vigorously than ever to extend to the first "heads or springs" of the boundary rivers. Long disputes and an appeal to the Crown might be necessary before Carter could be sure the western lines of the proprietary would be those for which he contended. A possible bargain with the Five Nations to keep at a distance from the border settlements held a high prospect of early

[51] *Ibid.* Often these indentured servants became small proprietors on their own account and established families that later achieved distinction. Cf. *Landmarks,* 108.
[52] Letter of Apr. 15, 1729; *Carter Transcripts,* 181, VHS. See *infra,* Appendix I–1.
[53] For the route followed by the Six Nations East of the Blue Ridge, see *Landmarks,* 454 ff.

profit because the Indians were far nearer and were more easily persuaded than was his Royal Highness, George I. The natives, in fact, were never averse to any barter that gave them arms, ammunition and liquor.

For these reasons, every powerful planter who had ambition for western lands heard with joy of a new phase of the sixth great development in the history of the proprietary—that an Indian delegation had come to Williamsburg in October, 1721, and had agreed to the basic terms of a treaty. The next May, the General Assembly of Virginia approved the preliminaries and prescribed the penalties for violation of the terms of the treaty.[54] No member of the Five Nations was to come South of the Potomac or "pass to the eastward of the great ridge of mountains"; Indians tributary to Virginia were not to cross the Potomac or proceed beyond the range. Exception could be made by written license or passport only; disregard of the covenant was punishable with death or transportation to the West Indies and sale into slavery. Most significantly, nothing in the agreement limited the movements of white men or set western boundaries to Virginia. The pact was to come into effect when ratified by the Five Nations at a conference Governor Spotswood was to hold with them at Albany, New York.

In anticipation of full and prompt acceptance of the treaty, some of the wealthy Virginia colonials descended on the colonial capital for the patent of lands that would be secure for settlement when the Indians no longer descended on the frontier. Before he set out for Albany, Spotswood himself had his personal agents patent 68,000 acres of land South of the Rapidan.[55] Another speculator took up 12,000 acres nearby; two partners procured a patent for 24,000 acres in a most desirable location; a man of high station, Gawin Corbin, received 18,000.[56] Some of these grants were for parts of the disputed land Carter alleged to be within the proprietary, and were not exclusively within the region South of the Rappahannock, where the Governor had exclusive authority, under the King, to issue patents. Lines did not halt speculators. Wherever there was good land, access to a tobacco market, and measurable security against the Indians, there was a patentee and usually one who already owned a large estate.[57]

[54] 4 H 103–04.   [55] Landmarks, 224, 227.   [56] Ibid., 228.
[57] Fairfax Harrison observed (Landmarks, 421) that the names of down-the-river planters are often encountered in connection with large grants in Fairfax County. A photostat of c. 1746 in VSL bears this out. Twenty-eight "absentee landlords" of Prince William and Fairfax are listed; twenty-seven were well-known residents of the lower Northern Neck.

"King" Carter's actions bespoke his belief that the great day of opportunity had come. Due signing of the Indian treaty at Albany in
September, 1722, did not make him obligate himself for poor lands
because someone else might want them. For that matter, in selecting
deliberately, he stood to lose nothing to preemptors because, as agent
and lessee, he could deny to others any tract he might be considering
for himself. He picked carefully but regally. During 1724 he patented
for his children and grandchildren almost 90,000 acres.[58] In the seven
years that followed, he transferred to his family or to his own list of
holdings 118,000 acres of excellent, well-located land.[59] On a somewhat smaller scale, several of his sons emulated his example.[60]

Every planter of means had his opportunity. A new era had begun
for the descendants of those who settled on the Northern Neck in the
middle of the seventeenth century. The first comers—to summarize—
had squatted, had acquired "headrights" or had patented land cheaply
from the Crown. When they had found they were in a proprietorship,
they had protested; but, after the agreement of 1669 for the confirmation of their titles, they acquiesced gradually in the payment of the
moderate annual quit rent of £3, 7 s. per 1000 acres. As these colonials
multiplied and intermarried, the more intelligent and aggressive of
them prospered on the growing of tobacco by their fecund slaves.
Primogeniture was usual, but wealthy parents undertook to acquire
lands on which their daughters and their numerous younger sons could
live in affluence. Proprietor, agent, lessee, tenant—all sought wider
fields, new plantations. As settlement moved westward up the boundary
rivers, ambitions were shaped for larger and still larger estates, which
could support a new landed aristocracy and, if divided and resold, could
serve humbler settlers and small farmers.

There was to be a new manorial, almost a new feudal age in Virginia.
To them who had, more was to be given. From the expenditure of
little, much was to be gained. More than forty years after the Treaty
of Albany the magnitude of that opportunity of gaining wealth was
recalled to the mind of a confused debtor. How, he was asked, had
"the greatest estates we have in this Colony" been accumulated? "Was
it not by taking up and purchasing at very low rates the rich back
lands which were thought nothing of in those days . . . ?" [61]

---

[58] *Landmarks,* 241–42.   [59] *Ibid.,* 244–45.
[60] To name one only, George Carter later received 10,000 acres or more from his father's
estate, but acquired so much land on his own account that, when he died, his executors offered
21,000 unneeded acres for sale (6 *V* 15; *Va. Gazette,* May 9, 1745).
[61] George Washington to John Posey, June 24, 1767; *Writings of George Washington,* ed.
John C. Fitzpatrick (cited hereafter as *G. W.*), v. 2, p. 459.

CHAPTER II

THE RISE OF THE WASHINGTONS
(1657–FEBRUARY, 1732)

IN EVERY PART of the story of the development of the Northern Neck, from the days of the Commonwealth to the immense new opportunities that seemed to be opened by the Treaty of Albany, men named Washington had a modest share. The first to arrive there was John Washington, aged about 25, who came early in 1657 [1] as mate and voyage partner in the ketch *Sea Horse of London*. Washington was the son of an English clergyman, an M.A. of Brasenose College, Oxford, who had been ousted from his parish by the Puritans in 1643 on the charge, probably false, that he was "a common frequenter of ale houses" and was "oft drunk." [2] John, the son, had received decent schooling and, on making the voyage to Virginia, he saw possibilities of self-advancement on the Northern Neck.

Circumstance favored him. When the time came for the ketch to start home with a cargo of tobacco she ran aground on a shoal in the river. Before she could be floated off, a heavy winter storm hit and sank her. All her tobacco was ruined, but there was a chance she could be raised. Washington went to work with the others and helped in getting her above water. Doubtless during the time he was sharing in this task he made new friends, among them Nathaniel Pope, a well-to-do Marylander, residing in Virginia, [3] who had a marriageable

[1] Perhaps in December, 1656; see 1 *Hoppin*, 147.

[2] A brief outline of the English ancestry of Washington, based on *Hoppin*, will be found in Appendix I–4. Somewhat less detailed than *Hoppin*, but fuller on Washington's parents and generation is Worthington C. Ford, *The Washington Family*. This appears in v. 14 of Ford's edition of *The Writings of George Washington* (cited as *Ford*) and was published separately.

[3] Nathaniel Pope appeared in Maryland prior to 1637 and served in 1642 as a member of the legislature of that Colony. He was in Maryland as late as 1646 (18 *W* (2) p. 443), but by 1651 was patenting land in Westmoreland ("Mr. Pope's Cliffs," later Stratford; *Eaton*, 65). He must have been prosperous because, in 1652, he was seeking a tutor for his brood (9 *V* 332). His four children were Anne, Thomas, who became a merchant (d. May 1, 1741; see 9 *Westmoreland Deeds and Wills*, 198), Nathaniel, a mariner, and Margaret, who married William Hardidge (see an interesting love letter to her, May 8, 1669, in 4 *W* (1) p. 81). The will of Nathaniel Pope, May 16, 1659, will be found in 1 *Westmoreland Deeds and Wills*, 115. His deed to Anne, mentioned *infra*, is in *ibid.*, 88. The records spell her name both Anne and Ann.

daughter Anne. For this or other persuasive reasons, John Washington prevailed on Edward Prescott, the master and part owner of the *Sea Horse* to release him from further service on the ketch in order that he might remain in Virginia. When the work on the vessel was complete and departure was a matter of a few days only, Washington demanded payment of his wages. Prescott countered with an assertion that Washington owed him money and had responsibility for part of the damage done the vessel. Arrest and imprisonment were threatened. Nathaniel Pope promptly offered to go Washington's bond in beaverskins, and befriended him in every way he could. The litigation that followed because of these counter-claims left John Washington in a mood to seek revenge on Prescott,[4] but, more immediately, he had to settle a different and gentler issue with Anne Pope. She and her father both approved him. The father, in fact, was so hearty in his blessing of the union that when his daughter married Washington, he gave her 700 acres of land[5] and lent John £80 or more,[6] with which to get a start.

The next autumn a son was born to Anne and John Washington, a son whose coming softened the spirit of the young father, though he still wished to square accounts with his former skipper. Washington learned in September, 1659, that Prescott was back in Chesapeake Bay and had landed in Maryland. By some of Prescott's sailors, Washington was told, also, that on the new voyage to Virginia, a witch had been hanged on the ship. Immediately John filed a complaint with the Maryland authorities, who promptly arrested Prescott on a charge of murder and notified Washington to appear with his witnesses. This was a perfect opportunity of avenging the wrong John thought the shipmaster had done him, but, as it chanced, the date fixed for the trial was close to the time set for the christening of the infant. Washington consequently wrote the court: "I am sorry that an extraordinary occasion will not permit me to be at the next provincial court. . . . Because then I intend my young son baptized. All the company and the Gossips being already invited. Besides in this short time witnesses cannot be got to come over . . ." He sought a postponement and, failing to procure it, chose to have his son baptized in preference to seeing his

---

[4] All the known documents are printed in 1 *Hoppin*, 147 ff. They do not show the outcome of the suit, if there was one.

[5] May 11, 1659; 1 *Westmoreland Deeds and Wills*, 88.

[6] 1 *Hoppin*, 153–54. The date of the marriage of John Washington and Anne Pope is not known but is assumed to have been prior to December, 1658.

enemy hanged.[7] Prescott went free, for lack of evidence against him.

The next spring, Nathaniel Pope died and in his will, though bequeathing no more property to Anne, he cancelled the debt of £80 due him by John Washington.[8] Fortune continued to favor Washington. Thus, by the time the patent to the Northern Neck was being confirmed to the Proprietors in England, John Washington was established in Virginia. He then was about 29 years of age, was full of energy, and was resolved not to be content with the moderate estate the success of Nathaniel Pope and his own luck in marriage had assured him. Promptly he began to acquire more land by importing servants whose "headrights" he could claim. On his own account or in partnership with his brother-in-law, Thomas Pope, he "brought over," first and last, sixty-three persons or more, for each of whom he and Pope jointly were allowed fifty acres.[9] John's own share of this was approximately 1820 acres. By purchase, by original patent, and by taking up grants of deserted land, he yearly added to his holdings until by about 1668 he had been owner of considerably more than 5000 acres, on part of which he was growing tobacco. In acquiring this land he was not able to emulate the great planters and patent large tracts under a single grant. Most of his early holdings were gained little by little, here a hundred acres or two, there a like stretch of forest, and another and another.[10] He sought and gained in succession an ascending order of profitable offices and court appointments. As early as 1661, he was Coroner. Later, he was trustee of estates, guardian of children, and Justice of the County Court.[11] The honorific position of vestryman was his, also.[12] His family increased with his honors and his acres. By 1668, Anne Washington had borne him five children.[13]

[7] The records, including the first letter known to have been written in Virginia by a member of the Washington family, appear in 1 *Hoppin*, 151 ff.

[8] 1 *Hoppin*, 282.

[9] Known grants of this nature were: Sept. 4, 1661, to Washington and Pope, 1200 acres, same date, one-half interest in fifty acres; 1663, June 24, "headrights" of 600 acres for twelve persons; Mch. 23, 1664, acreage of 195 for importing four persons; 1664, June 1, apparently 400 acres to John Washington as his "dividend" for the transportation of twenty-two persons.

[10] First and last he owned 10,000 acres, the details of which will be found in 1 *Hoppin*, 156–83. The known records are as follows: 4 *L.O. Records*, 342, 352; 5 *ibid.*, 38, 49, 6 *ibid.*, 183, 349, 615; *Westmoreland Orders*, 1662–64, p. 25; 1 *Westmoreland Deeds*, 226, 261–62, 295, 382; *ibid.*, 126; *Westmoreland Deeds and Patents*, 1665–77, p. 73, 77, 80, 176; *Minutes of the Council and General Court of Colonial Virginia* (cited hereafter as *Council Minutes*), p. 278.

[11] See the extracts from court records, etc., in 1 *Hoppin*, 167, 170–71, 173. For his service as Burgess and as Lieutenant Colonel of militia, see *infra*, p. 20, 23 ff.

[12] He was made vestryman of Appomattox Parish, July 3, 1661 (*Westmoreland Deeds*, 1661–62, p. 47; 1 *Hoppin*, 167).

[13] It is probable that one or more of them did not survive infancy. Three of them only, Lawrence, John and Anne, were alive at the time of their father's death.

In that year, Anne herself died. She was lamented, no doubt, but not so poignantly that John refused to seek a second wife to share in the management of his farms and in the rearing of his children. The lady of his choice was Anne Gerrard,[14] who previously had married Walter Brodhurst and, after his death in the winter of 1658–59,[15] had been the wife of Henry Brett. She was distinctly a business woman,[16] and was credited with transporting to Virginia at least two persons for whom she was allowed "headrights." [17]

Before the death of Brett,[18] she and her sister Frances, who was then the wife of John Appleton, somehow acquired the ill will of Richard Cole and his wife Anna. The Coles were of a type not frequent in Virginia. Richard had come to Maryland as an indentured servant and soon displayed an excess of self-confidence and of arrogance.[19] As he accumulated land, he likewise added venom. Governor Berkeley was a particular object of his hatred. Cole's brother soon was coming over as Governor, said "Dick," and would "kick His Honour from his place." [20] Mrs. Cole was scarcely less notorious. In 1664, she had been committed to the custody of the Sheriff "upon suspicion of the murder of Rose Parker." [21] Of this charge, Anna Cole must have been acquitted if brought to trial, and she did not have her tongue bridled by her experience. Husband and wife not only remained on the Northern Neck, but also felt free to go to the homes of some of the leading planters.

Evidently Cole looked on Thomas Gerrard and the Gerrard girls as enemies, and he had no words too harsh for them. Cole said openly that Dr. Gerrard used his servants to steal hogs, that "he was a base fellow and a whore master and that he would be with a Negro woman or an Indian woman when he wished." [22] As for the daughters, Cole

[14] Daughter of Thomas Gerrard by his first wife, Susannah Snow, daughter of Justinian Snow, one of the early Marylanders. Thomas Gerrard's second wife was Rose, widow of John Tucker, whose daughter married the immigrant William Fitzhugh, of Bedford. See 4 *W* (1) p. 36, and *supra*, p. 2.
[15] For some incidents of his career, see 4 *W* (1) p. 31. His will was probated Feb. 12, 1659; *Westmoreland Deeds, Wills and Patents*, 1653–59, p. 121. An inventory, Apr. 19, 1661, is in *Westmoreland Deeds and Wills*, 1661–62, p. 48.
[16] See *Westmoreland Deeds and Wills*, 1661–62, p. 48, for suits to which she was party. *Vide* also *Westmoreland Orders*, 1662–64, p. 30, 34.
[17] *Westmoreland Orders*, 1662–64, p. 33. Allotments of this sort to women rarely are found in Virginia court records.
[18] The settlement of his accounts, after the marriage of his widow to John Washington, bore date of Nov. 3, 1670 (*Westmoreland Deeds and Patents*, 1665–77, p. 99).
[19] 4 *W* (1) p. 30.
[20] *Westmoreland Deeds, Wills and Patents*, 1653–59, p. 1.
[21] *Westmoreland Orders*, 1662–64, p. 35.
[22] *Westmoreland Deeds and Patents*, 1665–77, p. 24.

charged that the two of them had spent the night in the company of a man, with the candle out, while Frances's husband was away from home. It was the trick of a whore, said Cole; Anne Gerrard Brett, he went on, was keeping a bawdy house; Frances Appleton, sister of Anne, was herself whoring.[23] In the same disgusting strain, Cole alleged to James Coldstream that Frances was the mistress of the Governor, who was paying her money.[24]

The Gerrards were not of a sort to take these charges quietly. A son of Dr. Gerrard returned the fire of the accusers and denounced Mrs. Cole as of the profession she attributed to his sisters.[25] Mrs. Appleton asserted that she would have a warrant issued against Mrs. Cole. The retort was that Frances would be foolish to stir, because "the more she stirred the more she would stink."[26] In tones as amazing, Mrs. Cole wrote Susan Gerrard, the girl's mother, of the allegation young Gerrard had made concerning the virtue of Mrs. Cole. The letter did not lack point:

Madam, I was lately informed that at court your son did much abuse me and called me whore. I do conceive he might have found one nearer home for I never complained of my husband's disabilities or wished the boat might sink under him when he went to Maryland as others have done. Your daughter Appleton reports that if I go to any house in the country but Col. Spencer's, Maj. Allerton's or Capt. Lee's I shall be kicked out. They are all houses of Qualitey, and that will hers never be as long as she is mistress of it. I have not yet meeted with her or any other, but please to advise her now to cease her discourses of me or I shall desire Mr. Appleton to ask her who that was that lay upon the bed a whole night with Mr. Pitts in the dark when her husband was at York. My authors are good and persons of quality. I should have enlarged but am somewhat indisposed by some fever and am constrained to end abruptly.

Madam, yours
Anna Cole.[27]

In the face of this, the decision of the Gerrards was to place the slanderous charges and the libel of Mrs. Cole's letter before the County Court. This was done Oct. 28, 1668. Unchallenged witnesses made depositions of what they had heard the Coles allege. When the matter thus was brought into the open, nobody apparently credited it. John

[23] Ibid., 25.   [24] Ibid., 26.
[25] Ibid., 26.   [26] Ibid., 25.
[27] Court entry of Oct. 28, 1668; ibid., 26.

Washington certainly did not. He was one of the Justices before whom the filthy charges were laid, and subsequently he was not deterred from wooing Anne Brett after the death of her second husband.[28] John Washington himself had not escaped altogether the wrath of the Coles, but he had been denounced for nothing worse than being an "ass Negro driver." Cole professed an intention of bringing Washington before the Governor and Council as a companion of the "caterpillar fellows" who, said Cole, "live on my bills of exchange." [29]

Had Cole been less slanderous and more realistic, he might have described John Washington, at the time of marriage to Anne Brett, as an agent and attorney,[30] as a Collector of the tobacco tax,[31] as a miller on Rozier's Creek, as a member of the House of Burgesses,[32] as a Lieutenant Colonel of militia, and, after the union with the widow Brett, as the owner of a court house, a prison, a shop and an ordinary. This singular combination of property represented his wife's bequest under the will of her first husband who had erected the structures and had rented them to the County.[33] Washington granted a lease on the ordinary but prudently reserved the use of the other buildings.[34] He was equally careful in all his business transactions. The General Assembly decided, for example, that certain lands patented by him in Richmond and Westmoreland Counties should be included in those assigned to Nanzatico Indians. John Washington perforce acquiesced, but he prevailed upon the House of Burgesses to direct that if the Indians left the property, it should revert to him.[35]

His greatest coup was a singular one. In 1657, Henry Vincent had patented from the royal government 500 acres on the south side of the Potomac "in the freshes opposite [the Indian town of] Piscataway and a little below." [36] Other settlers were equally desirous of getting what

[28] The tattered and mutilated *Westmoreland Deeds and Patents*, 1665–77, do not show how the depositions against Thomas and Anna Cole were introduced, or what action was taken on them.

[29] *Westmoreland Deeds and Patents*, 1665–77, p. 1. Cole's will and self-penned epitaph appear in *ibid.*, 185. After his death, his widow married Thomas Kirton, who was Lord Culpeper's agent for patenting Northern Neck lands. See *Eaton*, 56, where the later history of 1350 acres of Cole's land is traced.

[30] Cf. *Westmoreland Deeds and Patents*, 1665–77, p. 43, 64; *ibid.*, 64.

[31] *Journ. H.B.*, 1659–93, p. 501.

[32] He is listed as a Burgess of 1666 (2 H 250; *Journ. H.B.* 1659–93, p. 32, 36, 37, 89); and he was again a member of the House in 1667 (*ibid.*). His committee assignments indicate that he was a respected and perhaps a conspicuous Burgess but scarcely a leader.

[33] 4 *W* (1) p. 41.

[34] *Westmoreland Deeds and Patents*, 1665–77, p. 49. Cf. 1 *Hoppin*, 180 ff. The lessee of the tavern was Lewis Markham, ancestor of John Marshall.

[35] *Journ. H.B.*, 1659–93, p. 41, entry of Nov. 5, 1666.

[36] 4 *L.O. Records*, 181.

appeared to be excellent land in this region. That same year, at least half-a-score grants of 300 to 2600 acres had been made there or on nearby Doeg Island.[37] As some of these tracts were not "seated" within the meaning of the law,[38] the land reverted to the Crown. By 1660, new patents were being issued by the Governor to planters or speculators who promised to place families in residence at "the freshes." [39] The most notable beneficiary of this was Col. Richard Lee the first, who in 1663, was confirmed in 4000 acres previously patented on or near Little Hunting Creek by three individuals.[40] This grant was "headrights" for eighty persons; but Colonel Lee apparently was no more· successful than his predecessors in settling the land.

It happened that Lee's tract adjoined property owned by Thomas Speke, husband of the Frances Gerrard who later was the victim of the Coles. After Speke died in 1659, Frances married Valentine Peyton and when he, too, succumbed, she made John Washington her attorney in 1665.[41] As Frances's sister Anne married Washington, it is entirely possible Frances acquainted him with the fact that the desirable land of Richard Lee on Little Hunting Creek had not been settled. In any event, John Washington entered into a bargain with Nicholas Spencer, Secretary of the Colony and, next the Governor, probably the most powerful man in Virginia. Together, they had Lee's tract surveyed in April, 1669, by Major John Alexander.[42]

[37] It must not be assumed that all of these, or any specific number of the grants of 1657, were for lands later incorporated in the Spencer-Washington grant that subsequently became Mount Vernon. Descriptions are so vague that it is not possible, in the absence of surveys, to state what land was covered by most of the grants. General location only is known. The following patents of 1657 are recorded: (1) Jan. 27, 1657, 1000 acres to William Wildey, reissued Nov. 20, 1657, to Thomas Broughton, 4 L.O. Records, 181, 216, 244; (2) Mch. 22, 1657, 1000 acres on Doeg Island to Nicholas Jernew, ibid., 232; (3) June 15, 1657, 2500 acres to Robert Clerke, ibid., 259; Jan. 4 and July 15, 1657, five grants totaling 2600 acres, headrights included, to James Wood, ibid., 74, 171, 173, 176; July 15, 1657, 1000 acres to Robert Castleton, ibid., 172; (10) Sept. 7, 1657, 650 acres to Thomas Broughton, reissued Sept. 16, 1657, to Henry Vincent, ibid., 156, 286; (11) n.d., 1000 acres to John Walker, ibid., 331. See n. infra.

[38] See infra, Appendix I-1.

[39] A definite case in point is that of 650 acres on Little Hunting Creek, patented Sept. 16, 1657 by Henry Vincent and repatented Oct. n.d., 1660 by Capt. Peter Jenings (4 L.O. Records, 286, 452, 485). Grants of 500 acres, Oct. 15, 1660, and of 1000 acres, Sept. 10, 1663, to Peter Jenings and to Mathew Kemp were reissues. See ibid., 452, 485.

[40] These men were John Walker, Robert Ca[stleton?], and Robert Clarke [previously Clerke], all of whom had been patentees of 1657. The word "confirmed" in the text is used because the recorded patent in ibid., 447—the entry listing the previous patentees—bears date Nov. 26, 166 [sic]. It is preceded by a patent of Sept. 20, 1661 and is followed by a similar document of Nov. 26, 1660. In the margin is the notation that this patent was renewed by order of the General Court, Mch. 26, 1663, and was granted to Colonel Lee the same day by Governor Berkeley. Cf. Lee of Virginia, 58 n. 1, 63, 80.

[41] Hoppin, 184. Her third husband, Capt. John Appleton, is believed to have died not long after Sept. 21, 1675 when, as a friend, he witnessed the will of John Washington (1 Hoppin, 208).   [42] Landmarks, 49.

This date either was singularly fortunate or else Spencer had fore-knowledge of what was about to occur in England. The revised charter of the proprietary, issued by the Crown in 1669, provided that all land grants issued in the Northern Neck, prior to Michaelmas, 1661, would be validated if the grantee was in actual possession of the land on May 8, 1669.[43] Washington and Spencer may have had the survey made in April in order to make immediate application in event Colonel Lee failed to complete the formality of actual possession.[44] The two con-testants of Lee's title did not procure immediately a patent of their own, but they laid their plans to get it. At length, March 9, 1674/75, Spencer and Washington procured directly from Lord Culpeper, then Pro-prietor, a patent for Lee's 4000 acres and for an additional 1000 acres that adjoined.[45]

Although the quit rents were 4 s. per 100 acres, and "seating" was required within three years, this patent placed Washington's fortunes at their highest. Of a county levy of 36,000 pounds of tobacco in 1673, he received more than 10,000 for his public service.[46] A parish was named after him;[47] his friends and neighbors included the most success-ful of the planters along the Potomac, though, of course, this swift rise was bought at a continuing price of jealousy and backbiting. In addition to the slander of the Coles, he and Anne had to endure an attack by Clement Spilman who, in manner unknown, "did out of malicious principles and dangerous corruption endeavor to take away and defame the good name and fame" of the two. Washington believed in the power of the law, and in this case as in that involving Richard and Anna Cole, he brought the accuser before the court. Spilman asked forgiveness and agreed to pay the costs of the action.[48]

The strangest of all John Washington's experiences was now to begin. Early in September, 1675, he received from Green Spring, the

[43] See Appendix I–1. The statement in the text is taken almost verbatim from the summary in *Landmarks*, 49–50.   [44] *Ibid*.

[45] *L.O. Records, N.N.*, 5, p. 207. The grant was not recorded in court until 1677 (*L.O. Records, N.N.*, 6, p. 615). Fairfax Harrison (*Landmarks*, 50) was of opinion that this patent may have been the basis of litigation between 1669 and 1675. Harrison thought, also, that the grant in person by Lord Culpeper, the active Proprietor, may have been influenced by his kin-ship to Spencer. For the descent of the title to John Washington's part of this land, see *infra*, p. 36. Richard Lee, who still had possession in 1673 (*Lee of Virginia*, 80), bequeathed the entire 4000 acres to his daughter as if he still regarded his title valid. No record of any final adjustment between the Lees and Washingtons has been found.

[46] Sept. 7, 1673; *Westmoreland Deeds and Patents*, 1665–77, p. 168. Cf. *ibid.*, 501, and *Journ. H.B.*, 1659–93, p. 84.

[47] It extended "from Upper Machodock to the foot of the westernmost side of Pope's Cliffs" (*Westmoreland Orders*, 1662–64, p. 31). For details, see *infra*, p. 50.

[48] *Westmoreland Deeds and Patents*, 1665–77, p. 45.

home of Governor Berkeley, a copy of a startling order in Council. This set forth, under date of August 31, that the Doeg Indians from Maryland had made forays into Virginia and had committed three murders, for the punishment of which the Governor of Maryland had agreed to permit forces from South of the Potomac to enter that Colony. Washington and Major Isaac Allerton accordingly were ordered to assemble the militia officers of the Northern Neck, to make inquiry and to demand satisfaction from the Indians. If the two commanders thought it "requisite and necessary," they were to raise a "fit number of men" in the Northern Neck and were to proceed against the Indians.[49]

Washington did not take this lightly. According to his practice with all important public papers, he had the order in Council made a matter of record,[50] and he proceeded to make his will.[51] With surprising promptness he and Allerton assembled some of the other militia officers and set out for the Indian fort on the north bank of the Potomac about fifteen miles above Washington's and Spencer's tract at the "freshes." [52] The Virginians arrived on the 25th of September and found that a force of Indians had been in a bloody fight at nearby Hinson's plantation and then had been driven into a crude fort where they were under siege by Major Truman's Maryland militia. A quick examination made Washington realize that the refuge could be captured easily. Some of its occupants, foreseeing their doom, already had come out to parley. Five were standing nearby under a guard of two files of soldiers.

Why, asked the Virginians, were the Indians being held? The answer was that the savages had attempted to get away. No intimation was given that the redmen had come from the fort as emissaries to seek terms of peace. Washington then explained that he and Allerton had instructions to treat with the natives before undertaking to punish them. Major Truman did not appear to object to this. With his consent, a stronger cordon was thrown around the five prisoners. Then, through an interpreter, Washington accused the savages of their crimes in Virginia. All of the savages denied responsibility. The murders, they

[49] Text in 1 *Hoppin*, p. 189–90.
[50] *Westmoreland Deeds and Patents,* 1665–77, p. 231–32.
[51] It is dated Sept. 21, 1675. See *infra*, p. 29.
[52] The Indian fort is believed to have been within the confines of the present city of Washington. Thomas Mathews in his MS narrative, quoted in 1 *Hoppin*, 189, said that Governor Berkeley sent Washington and Allerton with 200 men; but what is known of the mission does not indicate that any large number of Virginians were employed.

said, had been committed by the Senecas, not by them. As this exchange continued slowly and awkwardly, Major Truman became more
and more impatient. Several times he interrupted to ask, "Gentlemen, have you done? For I resolve to say nothing until you have
done."

"When we have done," Washington answered, "we will give you
notice."

He went on with his accusations, but at length, despairing of getting
either confession or satisfaction from the Indians, Washington and
Allerton "bade them defiance" and turned them over to Truman, who
at once began a new indictment through his interpreter, John Shanks.
After some vain attempts to get an admission of guilt from the
prisoners, Truman cried out to Washington, who had withdrawn a
short distance, "Are not these impudent rogues to deny the murders
they have done, when their Indians lie dead at Mr. Hinson's plantation
being killed in a fight there?"

Washington spoke up: "It would be very convenient to carry
them up thither and to show them their Indians that are there
buried."

"And so I will," Truman replied.

The rest is a matter of conflicting evidence. A Marylander, Capt.
John Allen, subsequently made deposition that Truman sent a small
scouting party to Hinson's the next morning to see if the Indians had
plundered the house and whether any ammunition remained there.
On the return of these men, argument was renewed over the disposition of the captives. Washington is alleged to have said, "What
[why] should we keep them any longer? Let us knock them on the
head; we shall get the fort today." To this, said the Captain, Truman
objected, but "was overswayed by the Virginia officers." After a brief
discussion, Allen testified, the bound Indians were led off and were
killed by blows on their skulls. Some of the Virginians later swore,
on the contrary, that after the Indians were carried to Hinson's and
were shown the bodies of their companions who had been killed there,
Allerton asked what was to be done with the savages, who remained
under colonial guard.

"I think they deserve the like," said Truman.

"I do not think so," Allerton replied. With no further exchange of
words, according to the Virginia version, the Marylanders marched the
savages off some 500 yards and slew them. This, said two witnesses,

"much amazed and startled us and our commanders, being a thing that was never imagined or expected of us." [53]

Shortly after, the expedition was disbanded. The Virginians returned home, but the whisper pursued them that they had been party to the murder of Indians who had left the fort to arrange a surrender. The public conscience was stirred. Governor Berkeley was quoted as saying of the Indians, "If they killed my father and my mother and all my friends, yet if they had come to treat of peace, they should have gone in peace." [54] The Virginians who had visited the fort asserted that the Marylanders had killed the Indians; the Marylanders insisted that the savages had been slain by the Virginians or by unidentified persons at the instance of Colonel Washington.

Besides his concern over this charge, John Washington had the distress of illness at home. In a short time Anne Brett Washington died.[55] As it chanced, her sister Frances about the same time lost her husband, John Appleton, who had witnessed the signing of John Washington's will. In accordance with the quick accommodation of the times, a prompt marriage of the bereaved Colonel and the weeping widow seemed in order, but Frances was no ingenue in such a matter. She had been born in Maryland, it would appear, prior to the migration of her father, Dr. Thomas Gerrard, to Virginia.[56] While quite young, Frances had married Thomas Speke, who, it will be recalled, had owned land next to the tract that Washington and Spencer subsequently patented when Richard Lee failed to seat it. After Speke's death about 1660,[57] Frances soon accepted as her second husband Valentine Peyton, who had been a planter or land speculator or both, from about 1654.[58] It was after his death, presumably in 1665, that Frances named her

[53] The greater part of the deposition of Allen, from *Proceedings of the Assembly of Maryland*, v. 2, p. 482, is reprinted, slightly condensed, in 1 *Hoppin*, 191. Hoppin should be given fullest credit for discovering and making public many entirely unknown facts. Virginia testimony is in *Westmoreland Deeds and Patents*, 1665–77, p. 287–8. Nothing is known of the date and circumstances of the return of Washington and of Allerton to their own Colony.

[54] 1 *Hoppin*, 191.

[55] The date is not known but it was subsequent to Sept. 21, 1675, when Washington made his will, and it was some time prior to the agreement of May 10, 1676, mentioned *infra*, p. 26. So far as is known, Anne Brett Washington, who must not be confused with Anne Pope Washington, had no children by her last husband. She had two sons by her first husband, Gerrard and Walter Brodhurst II.

[56] The date of her birth has not been established.

[57] See his patents, Sept. 16, 1651, of 1000 acres on the northwest side of Nomini River, including Cedar Island, and of 900 acres, also on the northwest side, where his land was divided from that of Walter Brodhurst, who was the first husband of Anne Gerrard, Frances's sister (2 *L.O. Records*, 337). The will of Thomas Speke is in 1 *Westmoreland Deeds and Wills*, 103. It is possible that his son Thomas, executor of his will, was born of an earlier marriage.

[58] He was a son of Henry Peyton of Nomini. Valentine Peyton's land patents of 2600 acres on Aquia Creek are in 3 *L.O. Records*, 272, 351; 4 *ibid.*, 426.

"trusted and beloved friend" John Washington as her attorney,[59] but she did not require his services long. John Appleton, appearing wishfully, became Frances's third mate.[60] By the time he had ended his days and Frances Gerrard-Speke-Peyton-Appleton had dried her tears, she had acquired sufficient experience to know that a wife should prepare to be a widow. Consequently, before she agreed to take her fourth husband and to be the third wife of John Washington, she insisted on a definite jointure: First, John Washington was to deed to trustees of her choice 500 acres of land on a specified stream and was to give bond of 30,000 pounds of tobacco for the purchase of an equivalent tract in the event she did not like the property set aside for her; second, Colonel Washington was to assign to her, as of the date of his death, one-third of the profits of his grist mill at the head of Rozier's Creek,[61] with the explicit proviso that Washington should not alienate the equity during his lifetime; third, the prospective fourth husband of Frances was to provide by will that eight "good Negroes" should be her property at his demise; finally, if Frances predeceased John Washington, then, within six months, he was to pay £100 sterling to her son, Gerrard Peyton.[62] To these stiff terms, John Washington duly subscribed, May 10, 1676, in the presence of Frances's brother, Justinian Gerrard, and of another witness.

The marriage probably followed almost immediately, but its pleasure was interrupted by Bacon's Rebellion, the worst disaster that swept Virginia after the massacre of 1622. Nathaniel Bacon, a fiery, well-born young settler, who was twenty-nine years of age in 1676, led a protest against the laxity of Governor Sir William Berkeley in combating Indian raids. With a company of determined men, Bacon struck several heavy blows at the savages and thereby won the support of nearly all the owners of small farms in exposed regions. He was less successful in plans for reforming the government of the Colony, which he and his followers considered partial to the ruling coterie and oppressive of the element that was extending settlement. In dealing with Bacon in 1676, Governor Berkeley acted on the premise that the leader of the new faction was a personal rival and a political rebel, against whom deception was a permissible weapon. Although the Governor had twice to

---

[59] 1 *Westmoreland Deeds and Wills*, 260.

[60] He was appointed Sheriff of Westmoreland, Aug. 31, 1671; *Westmoreland Deeds and Patents*, 1665–77, p. 98. For his inventory, see *ibid.*, 267.

[61] For the location of the mill, which is believed to have been built in 1662, see *Eaton*, 43.

[62] The text of this jointure, from *Westmoreland Deeds and Patents*, 1665–77, p. 274 ff, is printed in 1 *Hoppin*, 185.

retreat from Jamestown to the country between Chesapeake Bay and the Atlantic Ocean, he rallied the large proprietors and did not for a moment abandon the task of putting down the "rebellion." Young Bacon, in turn, maintained that Berkeley had fled and that the new government represented the King and had authority to issue orders in the royal name.

When the uprising spread to Westmoreland, Bacon sent repeated orders to Col. John Washington, who apparently ignored them. Washington, in fact, may have gone to the "Eastern Shore" to join Berkeley.[63] In October, 1676, word reached Bacon's lieutenant in Westmoreland, Stephen Mannering, that John Washington's overseers were using a sloop, and perhaps more than one, to carry food and tobacco from his Virginia plantations across the Potomac to Maryland. Mannering was preparing at the moment to set out on an expedition against the Indians and consequently could not go in person to Washington's farms. In his place, Mannering sent a party of "rebels" under Daniel White, with instructions to impress all of Colonel Washington's stores, to seize his small craft, and to prevent any further shipment to the Maryland shore.[64] White obediently proceeded to Washington's place on Mattox Creek and to the other large tract of the Colonel's at Round Hill. Washington was not there. In his absence, the "rebels" stopped all removal of food and tobacco and then apparently established themselves on the plantation as a guard. They probably ate and drank and perhaps did some plundering in ignorance of the fact that Bacon himself had died that month in Gloucester County.

While the insurrectionists enjoyed the unwilling hospitality of John Washington's home, their comrades surrendered a few at a time or else slipped away from their camps and returned to their farms. The great planters reasserted themselves quickly. Berkeley recovered power and began with heavy hand to punish the "rebels." One day that autumn, William Armiger and a group of "Loyalists" quietly approached the Washington plantation, where seven or more of Bacon's adherents were stationed. Although the garrison had no less than fourteen loaded guns and all the advantage of shelter from which to fire, they either had lost heart or else had ceased to exercise vigilance.

[63] No positive evidence of this exists; the inferential evidence is that of Washington's absence from home in October. Bacon's orders to Washington, which probably were similar to those sent other Justices and County militia commanders, will be found in 1 *Hoppin,* 195 ff.

[64] The text of White's orders is given in 1 *Hoppin,* 198. It was through the diligent search of Mr. Hoppin that the interesting documents on John Washington's part in Bacon's Rebellion were brought to light.

By a quick descent, Armiger captured seven of the men and their entire store of weapons.[65]

Washington himself soon returned and, with his usual regard for the remedies of the law, proceeded to institute suit for the damage done him. Daniel White was put under bond to keep the peace and to make good the loss he had inflicted.[66] Mannering, too, was bonded but was not silenced. He had the effrontery, while still under penalty, to visit the plantation and to talk with Armiger, in Mrs. Washington's presence, of the manner in which the place had been recovered. When Armiger said that seven men and fourteen loaded weapons had been captured, Mannering broke out: "God damn me, were I here with fourteen men, I would uphold the house from 500 men, or else die at their feet."

"You are a fool!" said Armiger.

"I am bound to the peace," Mannering stormed, "and dare not challenge you." He stamped his foot and glared. "I do not challenge you—but come out, if you please."

Mrs. Washington spoke up: "If you were advised by your wife, you need not have come to this pass."

"God damn my wife," answered Mannering, "if it were to [be done] again, I would do it again." [67]

This spirit on the part of some of the ex-rebels did not interfere with the collection by John Washington of damages. The Colonel was not too severe in pressing Daniel White, who by his own profession was a "poor man" and had to "labor hard for [a] living." [68] Compromise was made with White, but from the County of Westmoreland Washington received ultimately about 9500 pounds of tobacco for services performed and expenses sustained.[69] In addition he was paid 6000 pounds of tobacco and £80 cash by the Colony.[70] Careful as he was in collect-

[65] This seems the one reasonable interpretation of the depositions of Armiger and of John Deery, July 26, 1677, as printed in 1 *Hoppin*, 199. A careful analysis of these confused papers does not indicate that Frances Washington had a part in this coup or that she even was on the plantation when Armiger and his men came. Misunderstanding has arisen because Mannering's remarks and Mrs. Washington's wifely observation are assumed to have been made at the time of Armiger's appearance. Actually, the conversation was some months later. One of the depositions specifically states that the talks were of events that had occurred "in the time of Bacon's Rebellion."

[66] See White's petition to Nicholas Spencer, presiding Justice, July 24, 1677, in 1 *Hoppin*, 200–01.

[67] Armiger's deposition of July 26, 1677. The conversation is in the third person, but it is so detailed that no error is risked in changing it back to the first person. See 1 *Hoppin*, 199.

[68] White's petition, *loc. cit.*

[69] Proceedings of Aug. 14, 1677, printed in 1 *Hoppin*, 202.

[70] *Journ. H.B.*, 1659–93, p. 84; *Winder Transcripts*, v. 2, p. 281; see also 1 *Hoppin*, 202. Immediately prior to Bacon's Rebellion, tobacco was 12 *s.* per cwt.

ing, he had to pay part of his own bill, so to say, by meeting his share of the stiff tax levied to cover the cost of "raising forces . . . for suppressing the late rebellion."[71]

The inquisitor knocked at John Washington's door before the tax collector did. In June, 1677, by order of the colonial government. Nicholas Spencer and Richard Lee began to collect testimony concerning the alleged murder of the Indians in October, 1675. John Washington either received no summons as a witness, or else stood on his rights and refused to testify against himself.[72] Those of his companions whose depositions subsequently were taken in Westmoreland County unanimously absolved him and put the blame on Truman's Marylanders.[73]

This was John Washington's last vindication against slander that had pursued him. On Aug. 14, 1677, he attended a conference regarding the levy to pay for the suppression of Bacon's rising. Nearby, as the committee sat down at Captain Beale's house, was an acquaintance of Washington's who bore the name William Ball. If the two shook hands, they could not have imagined what the mingling of their blood was to mean in the next century.[74]

Eleven days after the two men met, John Washington sat in a court at his own residence. A month later, Sept. 26, 1677, his colleagues were performing the sombre duty of admitting his will to probate.[75] Interment was on his own plantation, by the side of Anne Pope Washington and close to the graves of two children who had died in infancy. If the directions expressed in his will were carried out, the other funeral costs did not exceed 400 pounds of tobacco.

John Washington's will divided his landed property among his three children, Lawrence, John and Anne. In accordance with customary primogeniture, Lawrence inherited the largest share of the land and

---

[71] Proceedings of Aug. 14, 1677, *supra*, n.

[72] It is almost certain that if he had made a deposition, he would have had it recorded along with those mentioned in the next note.

[73] See the depositions of John Gerrard, Daniel Lisson and Capt. Robert Massey in 1 *Hoppin*, 192–94.

[74] For William Ball, grandfather of Mary Ball, mother of George Washington, see the Ball genealogy, Appendix I–5.

[75] *Westmoreland Deeds and Patents*, 1665–77, p. 349, 366. A convenient text is in W. C. Ford, *The Washington Family*, 77 ff, printed also in W. C. Ford, ed., *The Writings of George Washington*, v. 14, p. 391 ff. The authoritative text, with notes of the errors in other versions, will be found in 1 *Hoppin*, 205–07. Needless to say, the season of Washington's death and the known time limits of his illness suggest that his malady was typhoid fever or dysentery. In *Westmoreland Orders*, 1676–89, p. 100, is the court order, Nov. 25, 1677, for the delivery to Frances of the eight Negroes due her under prenuptial agreement. For the appointment on Jan. 3, 1683, of men to divide the estate, see *ibid.*, 269.

the mill on Rozier's Creek. Provision for a third interest in the mill had duly been assigned Anne Brett Washington when the will was drawn during her lifetime. The same clause of that document protected the life-interest given Frances Appleton Washington under the prenuptial agreement. Personal property was distributed equally among the three children and the widow. To Lawrence Washington, John's brother, 4000 pounds of tobacco were bequeathed,[76] though, as it befell, Lawrence died months before John did.[77] With as few court orders as possible where a prenuptial agreement existed, the will of John Washington was executed.[78]

John's eldest son and principal heir, Lawrence Washington, was born in September, 1659, on the farm his grandfather had given his mother, Anne Pope, on her union with John Washington.[79] Apparently the boy was schooled in England, with which John the immigrant never had lost contact.[80] Soon after his father's death, Lawrence was back in Virginia and was taking up some of the public duties his parent had discharged. He was Justice of the Peace before he reached his majority;[81] at twenty-five he was a Burgess;[82] thereafter came service as Sheriff.[83] His interest in the increase of his property seems to have been small, perhaps because his compensation from public office was adequate. As far as is known, he added only some 440 acres to his patrimony[84] and he failed to develop the plantations he inherited. He did not marry until he was approximately twenty-seven—an age of mature bachelorhood in Virginia—but then he found in Mildred Warner a wife of character and of established position. Mildred's father, who died about four years prior to her marriage, was Augustine Warner of Gloucester, Speaker of the House of Burgesses and a member of the Council. Her mother, born Mildred Reade, was a granddaughter of a French Walloon, Nicholas Marteau, who had settled in Virginia in 1620.[85]

With Mildred, in all probability, Lawrence Washington made an-

---

[76] In view of the detailed treatment given the first American Lawrence Washington, great-granduncle of George Washington, in 1 *Hoppin*, 130–38, it has not seemed necessary to review his career, which was far less active than that of his brother, John, the direct ancestor of George Washington.

[77] His will, printed in 1 *Hoppin*, 137–38, was probated June 7, 1677.

[78] *Westmoreland Orders*, 1676–89, p. 100, 269.

[79] 1 *Hoppin*, 224.

[80] John Washington's will contained three references to money he had in England.

[81] 1 *Hoppin*, 224.   [82] *Ibid.*

[83] *Ibid.*, 234.   [84] *Ibid.*, 237, 240.

[85] 1 *Hoppin*, 229.

other visit to England in 1686. He could afford this, because life was easier for him than it had been for his father. Economically he began at a higher level; socially he went further. Old duties and new were resumed on his return from England, but it was for a few years only. Not long after Mch. 11, 1698, when he was in his thirty-eighth year, Lawrence died.[86] His father, it will be remembered, was born in 1631 or close to that year, and had been buried in 1677, presumably aged forty-six. Rev. Lawrence Washington, father of John, had a life span of fifty-one years (1602–1653). A total of ninety-six years had compassed three generations.

At the time of his death, Lawrence Washington had three children, John, Augustine and Mildred. The oldest of the three, John, was then almost seven years of age. Augustine was three;[87] Mildred was an infant. Provision for them was not lavish but was adequate. John was given the home tract and other desirable lands; Augustine was to have a total of approximately 1100 acres when life tenancy of about 700 of it was terminated. Mildred received the 2500 acres which had been her grandfather Washington's share of the 5000 he and Nicholas Spencer jointly had patented at the "freshes" of the Potomac. Like his father before him, Lawrence stipulated that his personal property be divided equally into four parts for his wife and the three children. During their minority, or until their marriage before they became of age, John, Augustine and Mildred were to "remain under the care and tuition of their mother," who was to have "the profits of their estates" in order to pay for their support and schooling.[88]

Mildred Washington probably remained a widow longer than was customary, but in the spring of 1700 she married George Gale, who seems to have been a temporary resident of the Colony. On May 16, 1700, with the consent of John Washington, one of her husband's executors, Mildred entered into an arrangement whereby she was empowered to devise her rights, under Lawrence's will, as she saw fit.[89] When stripped of legal terms, this meant that she was free to turn over to her second husband the considerable property left her by her first

[86] Except in respect to his scholarship, concerning which little is known, Lawrence Washington's place in the history of his family is similar to that of the second Richard in the annals of the Lees in Westmoreland.

[87] Although no documentary evidence exists, Augustine Washington almost certainly was born in 1694.

[88] The text is in 2 *Westmoreland Wills*, 133, and is printed in Ford, *The Washington Family*, 82 ff, and in 1 *Hoppin*, 239–40.

[89] See the extract from her will in 1 *Hoppin*, 244.

mate. George Gale made the most of this. In the autumn of 1700, he took his wife, her children and some of their possessions and migrated to England.[90] Mildred was pregnant at the time and, following her arrival at White Haven, Cumberland, was stricken with a serious malady. A few days after her child was born, she made her will, Jan. 26, 1701, and bequeathed £1000 to Gale. The balance of her estate she divided among him and her children. Care of the three young Washingtons was entrusted to the husband.

Upon her demise, George Gale duly filed bond for the proper custody of the children and sent the boys to Appleby School, Westmoreland, about fifty miles from White Haven.[91] There they might have remained, to be reared as young Englishmen, had not questions been raised across the Atlantic. When word of Mildred Washington Gale's death reached Virginia, and the terms of her will became known, some of the Washingtons disputed the validity of Mildred's action. They insisted that Lawrence had left to his three children estates of value, in which Gale had no legal interest. Moreover, by Lawrence's will, the income from the children's holdings had been assigned their mother during her lifetime: could she pass on that income to Gale during the minority of beneficiaries? John Washington, Lawrence's cousin and executor, put the question to counsel. The opinion of the lawyer was that Mildred's interest in her children's estates ended with her death. She could not bequeath the property, the income, or the custody of the children to her husband. Gale, said the attorney, could not claim the *droit de garde* from the executors of Lawrence Washington.

On the basis of this, John Washington entered complaint against Gale in Westmoreland County, Virginia,[92] Apr. 13, 1702, and demanded the return of the orphans and of their property.[93] As a result, within slightly less than twenty-four months, they were in the custody of the court and under the care of John Washington.[94] Young Augustine's schooling in England consequently was cut short. It did not cover the whole of the four calendar years between his own sixth and ninth birthdays, but it must have been a profitable time for him and it probably was pleasant as well.[95]

[90] All these facts appear in the summary of the petition of John Washington, executor, Apr. 13, 1702, *Westmoreland Orders*, 1698–1705, p. 157.   [91] 1 *Hoppin*, 244.
[92] It is remarkable that the boys were then in Westmorland, England.
[93] *Westmoreland Orders*, 1698–1705, p. 157.
[94] 3 *Westmoreland Deeds*, 369, printed in 1 *Hoppin*, 244. Recordation was Sept. 3, 1705.
[95] The assurance of this is in the fact that when he had sons of his own, he sent two of them to the school he had attended. See *infra*, p. 46.

Augustine's home for the next few years was with his cousin, John Washington, the executor to whose diligence may be due the fact that Augustine grew up as a Virginia planter and not as a resident of White Haven. This John Washington—"of Chotank"—was a son of the immigrant Lawrence, brother of the first John. A prosperous man of station, John "of Chotank" served as Undersheriff of Westmoreland County and later as Sheriff and Justice of Stafford County.[96] He proved less vigilant in keeping the accounts of his youthful cousins than he had been in recovering their estate from George Gale. In consequence, the property of John, Augustine and Mildred was thrown into disorder and was confused with that of their guardian. After John reached his majority in 1712, he went into court several times, over a period of two years, in repeated efforts to get a settlement from his Chotank cousin.[97] Doubtless by consent, differences between the accounts of John the executor and John the heir were left by the court to four leading men of the county as referees. Even then, another year passed without complete agreement on all items. Final adjustments probably were made out of court.[98]

During this litigation, new guardianship was provided for the younger children,[99] but this was not required long for Augustine because, in 1715, he came of age. Gus, as he was called by his friends, was blond, of fine proportions and great physical strength and stood six feet in his stockings.[100] His kindly nature matched his towering strength. Together, they made it easy for him to select a wife from among the numerous daughters of the well-to-do planters of Westmoreland. The girl who filled his eye returned his affection. Not long after he was twenty-one, he was married, in 1715 or 1716, to Jane Butler,[101]

[96] H. R. McIlwaine, ed., *Executive Journals of the Council of Colonial Virginia* (cited hereafter as *E. J.*), v. 3, p. 448. A glimpse of "John of Chotank" is given in his letter of June 22, 1699, to his half-sister in England, Mary Washington Gibson, 1 *Hoppin*, 133, with quotation from Ford, *The Washington Family*, 25. An extract will be found in Chap. VI, *infra*, p. 224. "John of Chotank" married Mary, daughter of Robert Townsend (*Westmoreland Orders*, 1690–98, p. 63).

[97] *Westmoreland Orders*, 1705–21, p. 198, 199, 203, 210, 222.

[98] *Ibid.*, 222, 236.

[99] *Ibid.*, order of May 27, 1713, p. 212. Strangely enough, one of the three guardians served in like capacity for Jane Butler, and another acted for Mary Ball. The third guardian was John, brother of Augustine and Mildred.

[100] G. W. P. Custis, a grandson of Mrs. George Washington, wrote Charles Brown in 1854 that Robert Lewis, a grandson of Augustine, had found one person only who remembered ever to have seen George Washington's father. This person was a "Mr. Withers of Stafford, a very aged gentleman." (11 *N.E. Hist. and Gen. Reg.*, 4). Mr. Withers's description is the one used here; it is a feeble authority to quote, but there is no other.

[101] The traditional date of the marriage is Apr. 30, 1715, 8 *Tyler's Quarterly* (cited hereafter as *T*), p. 87, but this is not established firmly.

then sixteen or seventeen,[102] and the daughter of Caleb Butler, lawyer and planter. Jane's mother was Mary Foxhall, who prior to her union with Butler, had buried three husbands.[103] Caleb Butler himself had died when Jane was about ten years of age but he had made provision for her under his will, which had stipulated that her name be changed from Jenny to Jane.[104] The early marriage of the widow Butler to Rev. John Bagg, her fifth adventure, had been followed soon by her death. Jane then had been temporarily under the guardianship of her step-father, but he soon was replaced by Joseph Bayley, her father's surviving trustee.[105]

With Jane's lands and other property to supplement his own holdings, Augustine began his married life as proprietor of more than 1740 acres.[106] Like his father and his grandfather, he soon became a Justice of the Peace and took his seat on the bench of the County Court;[107] unlike Lawrence but in the energetic spirit of the immigrant John, he began forthwith to trade in land and to have his measure of contention over bequests and the interpretation of wills.[108]

Augustine was in the first heat of this acquisition of new land when the reappointment of Robert Carter as agent of the proprietary was followed by the Treaty of Albany. Not only the "King" himself, but also George Turberville, Mann Page, who was Carter's son-in-law, Charles Carter, Robert Carter, Jr., George Eskridge and others of like station and speculative temper, took out patents for large acreage.[109] All the talk was of new plantations and sale to small farmers. It was an intoxicating time. Washington did not venture as far westward as these rich planters did, nor could he hope to equal the size of the tracts they acquired, but he caught so much of the speculative spirit that he extended himself to the limit of his means and perhaps beyond his resources.[110]

[102] Born Dec. 24, 1699; 14 V 443.
[103] Eaton, 47.
[104] For Caleb Butler's will, see 4 Westmoreland Deeds and Wills, 192. Various directions for the administration and division of the estate will be found in Westmoreland Orders, 1705-21, p. 156, 170, 211.
[105] Ibid., 211, 223.
[106] The Hill tract, mentioned in 1 Hoppin, 240, was covered by three patents of 1659-61 to a total of 600 acres (Eaton, Plate 2), but no record has been found of the acreage purchased by Augustine Washington.
[107] He took the oath July 25, 1716, Westmoreland Orders, 1705-21, p. 288.
[108] Ibid., 288, 304; 6 Westmoreland Deeds and Wills, 34.
[109] L.O. Records, N.N., A. 165 patents covering 188,995 acres in 1723-26.
[110] Some of his deeds and leases of 1726 and of the following years suggest the possibility of devices to raise money for new transactions. See Westmoreland Orders, 1721-31, p. 131, 375; 8 Westmoreland Deeds, 226.

First in interest to Jane and Augustine was the purchase in 1717 of land to add to the farm John the immigrant had acquired between Pope's and Bridges Creeks on the south bank of the Potomac.[111] Five years later, Augustine was prepared to build a new residence on the enlarged tract. For a site he chose good ground on the west side of Pope's Creek, about three-quarters of a mile from the point where that stream empties into the Potomac. Approximately a mile and an eighth to the Northwest were the family burying ground and, presumably, John Washington's last habitation.[112]

For the building of the new house, Augustine hired David Jones, who was to be assisted, no doubt, by slaves and perhaps by indentured servants in the employ of Washington. Apparently, Jones came to live on property of Augustine's and near enough for certain small borrowing of supplies to take place between his family and Washington's. From time to time, particularly in 1722-23, Augustine made advances to Jones, or paid in tobacco or money for materials and supplies. Unfortunately Jones was engaged in building Round Hill Church, it would appear, at the same time he was erecting Augustine Washington's dwelling. For this or other reason, the contractor fell behind with his work and died in 1725. Augustine then had to complete the residence by separate arrangement and at a cost of 500 pounds of tobacco. When he computed the advances he had made Jones for the house, for the church and for a small poplar table, he found Jones in his debt for 2761½ pounds of tobacco and almost £18 cash.[113] To recover this, Washington entered suit against Jones's estate in March, 1726, when the building still was unfinished.[114]

The structure, finally occupied in 1726 or 1727, was not given a name and was not known until years later as Wakefield. It must have been a simple abode, because Jones's total charges for his part of the work were to have been only 5000 pounds of tobacco, which was 1000 pounds less than the contract price for Round Hill Church. In contrast, the

[111] 6 *Westmoreland Deeds,* 240. This was 150 acres of the "Abbingdon grant," the remainder of which Augustine bought Sept. 5, 1734. See 8 *ibid.,* 246.

[112] The most convenient, accurate map is on Plate 8 of the *George Washington Atlas,* edited by Lawrence Martin. A rough plat as of Aug. 24, 1742, will be found in 9 *Westmoreland Deeds,* 279. For a summary of arguments concerning the sites of John and Augustine Washington's homes, see 8 *T* 74, 76, 85, 219, 225, 231.

[113] Virtually all that has been ascertained in the present research, concerning the erection of this house, appears in Augustine Washington's account against the estate of David Jones. (*Westmoreland Records and Inventories,* 1723-46, p. 24, a document printed as Appendix I-6 in the present volume.) While the evidence afforded by the account is entirely inferential or circumstantial, most of the conclusions to be drawn from the paper are explicit.

[114] *Ibid.* and *Westmoreland Orders,* 1721-31, p. 113.

FIRST PATENT OF NORTHERN NECK PROPRIETARY

The original of the document reproduced on the opposite page is a parchment 21½ by 15½ inches engrossed carefully on both sides. Bearing the royal seal, it is signed on the front, in the upper left-hand corner, "Charles R." It is "*Additional Charter* 13585 of the British Museum," the first grant of the proprietary of the Northern Neck of Virginia, the region between the Potomac and the Rappahannock Rivers.

When Charles II issued this patent at St. Germaine-en-Laye, Sept. 18, 1649, he doubtless reflected that he was giving to seven of his companions in exile a reward that might some day be a rich one. Its value, like his crown, depended upon his restoration to the throne of England. Even after the King returned to London in 1660, the most conspicuous of the beneficiaries, John Lord Culpeper (Colepeper), so little esteemed his share in the proprietorship of the Northern Neck that he did not mention it in his will. In time, his son, Thomas Lord Culpeper, acquired the interest of most of the other sharers in the grant, and, at his death, passed the property to his daughter Catherine, who married a collateral descendant of Cromwell's renowned second-in-command, General Lord Fairfax. Through this marriage the rights became known as the Fairfax Proprietary.

On the legal basis of this grant, as amended, there developed by 1750 in the valleys of the boundary rivers a society so opulent and so enviable that it aroused the ambition of many Virginians and, among them, of a younger son of a dead planter and ironmaster, Augustine Washington. Associated already with names renowned and notorious, this grant became a spur to the career of George Washington.

Charles R

Charles the Second

Anno Dm. 1632, 1635, 1639.

Mr Trafford (now Vicar of Gillingham in Kent)
in these years, Bursar.

Tutors   Scholler   The Bursar demands of

Mr Lawrence Washington	Pitt	09 . 05 . 00 $\frac{1}{4}$	Caution money at Mr Washington to account
now Parson of Purleg in Essex) for	Himselfe	03 . 17 . 10 $\frac{1}{2}$	Mr Washington to account
Mr Wm Dutchfield (Bach) for	D. Holland	00 . 02 . 06 .	
Mr Arthur Bricke, dd for	D. Marbury	08 . 03 . 06 $\frac{1}{2}q^a$	must give $\frac{2nd}{2}$
	D. Egerton sen:	02 . 00 . 07 . 06 q^a at 5	
	D. Egerton jun:	01 . 18 . 08 . 06 q^a	
	Mr Worrall of Warrington	00 . 19 . 09 . 06 q^a to be put to account	
Mr Richardson, jun: for D. Carter	✶✶✶✶	02 . 08 . 01 . 05	Mr Richardson must account $\frac{1}{4}$ $\frac{1}{4}$ pag. 43
Chr: Coke (now Vicar of Drayton Salog) for	Taylor	00 . 00 . 08 q^a	
Mr Richardson sen: for Wood		00 . 25 . 01 . $0\frac{1}{2}q^a$ lost	

"MR. WASHINGTON TO BE SUED"

When Lawrence Washington, M.A., Fellow of Brasenose College, Oxford, married and resigned his fellowship in 1633, he left the University without settling his own indebtedness or the account of the student, Pitt, whom he was tutoring. His own bill was 17s 10d only; but Pitt's "battels"—the amounts due for board and provisions—were £9, 5s.

After the college Bursar, Trafford, left to become vicar of Gillingham, Kent, an official went over the records and set down in tabular form the debtors and their various obligations on the Bursar's books. Opposite the name of Lawrence Washington, whose residence and ministerial function were known, was written "Mr. Washington to be sued." If action was taken, the result

was not recorded on this original account, which is here reproduced by the permission of the Governing Board of Brasenose College, granted Apr. 28, 1948.

Among the records of the same college is the autographed resignation in Latin of Lawrence Washington as Fellow. In translation it reads: "I, Lawrence Washington, an accepted Fellow of the College of Brase Nose, resign into the hands of the Master and Principal all rights and interest which I now have, have had, or may have from the said community, and this I do freely, spontaneously and of my own will, to which I now affix my hand and seal."

He was George Washington's great-great-grandfather.

price of Pohick Church, where Augustine later served as vestryman, was 33,500 pounds of tobacco.[115] In all probability, the original dwelling on Pope's Creek subsequently was enlarged. It perhaps was rebuilt; [116] but when a celebrated son of that stock subsequently spoke of the "ancient mansion seat" of Augustine, he could not have intended to convey the idea subsequently implied in American use of the word, that the residence was a great manorial home.[117] The term "mansion house" was to be employed in a nearby parish about ten years later with reference to a dwelling not larger than twenty-four by twenty-four feet.[118]

For that matter, Augustine Washington had too many uses for his money to build extravagantly.[119] One of several reasons he did not lavish money on his Pope's Creek home was the opportunity offered him of damming Pope's Creek and of building a mill there. No difficulty with neighbors was to be anticipated because of lowering the water at their landings. The creek was not navigable; [120] a mill there might take profitable toll of many planters.[121]

Next, a bargain seemed to be offered Augustine in the 2500 acres of land that represented Grandfather John Washington's share of the land patented at the "freshes" of the Potomac opposite the Indian village of Piscataway. John the immigrant had bequeathed this to his son Lawrence, Augustine's father; Lawrence had arranged for the amicable division of the entire tract of 5000 acres with the heirs of Nicholas

115 See *infra*, p. 53. To judge by the fines the court of Westmoreland County imposed at this time in terms of cash or tobacco, the price was 10 *s.* per cwt. *Westmoreland Orders,* 1721–31, p. 37. Jones's price consequently was £25. Pohick cost £167, 10 *s.*

116 In Moncure D. Conway, *Barons of the Potomack and the Rappahannock,* 55—a book of widely diversified interest—is a description of the ruins of the stout foundations when they, relatively speaking, were untroubled. It is possible that the tradition of the early burning of the birthplace of Washington is well-founded and that the footings seen by Conway were those of a later and larger building.

117 32 *G. W.,* 29.

118 See Philip Slaughter, *History of Truro Parish,,* 12, entry of April, 1737. Needless to say, this was general English usage of the eighteenth century. "Mansion" then meant primarily a place of abode.

119 For Mr. Hoppin's views on the possible resemblance of Wakefield to other Northern Neck homes, see 8 *T* 222. The size and elegance of Wakefield are one of the subjects concerning which some writers on Virginia history have been sensitive to an amusing degree. Much the same feeling has been displayed in describing private libraries, carriages and equipage. See *infra,* p. 126 and 152.

120 All the maps indicate that small boats only could be used in the creek. The mill, which was in operation as late as 1865, must not be confused with the one erected by John Washington, about 1662, at the head of Rozier's Creek (*Eaton,* 43).

121 For the relation of grist mills to the advance of the frontier, see *infra,* p. 105. As John Pope had erected a mill in 1713 on the creek that bore his name, it is entirely possible that Augustine rebuilt this.

Spencer and had left his holding to his daughter Mildred,[122] who first had married one of the Lewises and, second, Roger Gregory of King and Queen County.[123] Mildred and her husband were willing to sell the "Little Hunting Creek Tract," as it had come to be known, for £180 sterling. Augustine thought the property worth that much then and worth still more in the future. On May 17, 1726, the agreement was signed.[124] By this purchase, Augustine advanced his landed interests to a point within twenty-four miles, as the river ran, of the Great Falls of the Potomac, then the dividing line between the old and the new settlements.

The improvement of the Pope's Creek property and the purchase of the Little Hunting Creek tract were by no means the end of Gus Washington's enterprises. He bought more agricultural land to cultivate or to resell in the sociable region of Potomac shore known as Chotank.[125] More particularly, he began to share in the development of ore-bearing lands and iron furnaces. These were the backward children of colonial industry [126] and they never had thriven; but they had the attention of several companies of adventurous Marylanders and Virginians, who would not permit themselves to be discouraged. In rivalry, "King" Carter and Thomas Lee were hunting for mineral lands near the Little Falls of the Potomac; [127] Alexander Spotswood already was operating a furnace; William Byrd soon was to be interested.

The solid results, in a sense both metaphorical and real, had been achieved in Maryland. There, as early as 1718, at what later became the Principio Iron Works,[128] John Farmer had produced and had sent to England three and a half tons of the metal.[129] England was then at odds with Sweden, whence came the greater part of the island's best iron. To replace this, colonial furnaces were encouraged. The Principio

---

[122] See *supra,* p. 21, and his will in 1 *Hoppin,* 240. For the division, see the original document at Mount Vernon, with a plat of the tract.

[123] 1 *Hoppin,* 163.

[124] In *Birch Cat.* 663, items 46, 47, 52 and 53 suggest that the transfer was not actually made until Oct. 18–19, 1726. No record exists in the books of Prince William or of Westmoreland. Either the original deed or a contemporary copy is in the Library of Congress among the *Papers of George Washington.* It is interesting to note that the price of what later became Mount Vernon was slightly less than 1 *s.* 5 *d.* per acre.

[125] 6 *H* 514; *Stafford Deeds,* 1722–28, p. 430. A description of Chotank will be found *infra,* p. 224.

[126] For its relationship to the economic life of the Colony, see *infra,* p. 145.

[127] *Landmarks,* 422.

[128] The Principio partnership in England is said by E. C. May, *Principio to Wheeling* (cited hereafter as *May*), p. 44, to date from Mch. 7, 1720.

[129] *May,* 13.

partners did their utmost to supply the needed iron and to reap a coveted profit, but they did not have in John Farmer a man of requisite vigor and ability. To spur or to succeed him, they sent to Maryland an experienced ironmaster, John England.[130]

Either John England's wide prospecting or Augustine Washington's own search brought to light what appeared to be rich iron deposits on land patented in part by Washington along Accokeek Creek, which lies between Potomac and Aquia Creeks and near Marlborough Point, about eight miles Northeast of Fredericksburg. England was eager to use this ore. By January, 1725, he reached an informal agreement with Augustine who was to receive a share in the Principio works as his compensation. This preliminary bargain seemed to John England to be so advantageous to Principio that he was anxious the partners across the Atlantic sign at once to bind Washington. In urging on them promptness and legal care, England suggested that they send the Virginian "a small present of wine" as evidence of their approval.[131] Augustine, for his part, quickly acquired on Accokeek 349 acres that were desired for the enlargement of the mining enterprise.[132]

Apparently his good fortune in finding ore on his land had a curious effect on Augustine. In his early land transactions there had been no evidence either of haste or of doubt, of recklessness or of overcaution. If his trading had not been bold or brilliant, it could not have been considered foolish. He seemed to know his own mind and to trust his own judgment or that of elders who did not mislead him. Now that the possible gains were larger, he developed a strange, almost baffling attitude toward the venture in iron. He would neither quit the undertaking nor conclude an agreement to advance it. If he did not haggle, he hesitated; and if he did not hesitate, he was apt to procrastinate.

The English Quakers who owned the Principio works could not determine whether Augustine was uninterested or merely unbusinesslike, but they supported John England. By late autumn, 1725, their agent had full authorization to build the ironworks on Washington's land, to

---

130 William Byrd ("Progress to the Mines," *Writings,* Bassett, ed., 374) quoted a report that England could neither read nor write, but surviving papers are well written in what apparently is his autograph. His letters of Apr. 3, 25, 27, July 1, 9, Sept. 11, 12, 25, 1723, Jan. 13, Jan. n.d. 1723-24, Nov. 9, 1725 (*Principio MSS.* Md. H.S.) explain many of the details of the ironmaster's work. Another interesting letter, William Chetwynd to John England, Feb. 9, 1723, O. S., is in the *Principio Papers,* Emmett Collection, N.Y. Pub. Lib.
131 Letter of Jan. 5, 1725 to the Principio Company; 11 *Penn. Mag.,* p. 193.
132 *L.O. Records, N.N.,* A, p. 143.

allow the owner one-sixth or two-twelfths interest, according to the number of partners, and to make "an absolute bargain" with Washington.[133] In the face of all urging, Augustine hung back for months but finally accepted a limited contract in a form that justified John England in beginning actual expenditure for an iron furnace.[134] The British partners insisted subsequently that this agreement provided for the transfer to them of the immediate site and of the adjacent woodland, mine and waters. In return Augustine was to have an interest of two-twelfths in the furnace, which the other partners were to erect without cost to him. After construction was finished, Washington was to pay his pro rata of all expenses.[135]

If Gus Washington signed such a contract and correctly understood its provisions, he soon decided that he could make a better, more inclusive bargain. He must have procured an "order," as it was styled, for a tract of an additional 396 acres on Accokeek [136] Run and for 4360 acres on Deep Run and the branches of Aquia Creek.[137] Then, on the 24th of July, 1726, he made this strange bargain with John England, who acted on behalf of the Principio Company: Washington leased the concern a tract of 1600 acres for 1000 years, with the understanding that the other partners would erect a furnace on the land and would bear all expenses, including repairs, until the first blast had been made. One-sixth of the iron from this furnace was to go to Washington. He was to pay for one-sixth of the expense of erecting buildings at the furnace, with the proviso that if the total exceeded £120, he was not liable for any more than his share of the original sum. Further, Gus was to assume his one-sixth of the cost of repairs to the furnace after the first blast, and proportionately of supplies, charcoal and other needed materials. In the event operations were stopped, Washington

---

[133] William Chetwynd and others to John England, MS, Sept. 15, 1725; L. W. Smith Collection, *Principio Papers;* same to same, MS, Sept. 19, 1725, Md. H.S.

[134] In *May,* 44, the date is given as Mch. 2, 1726, but the terms are not printed. The date of the actual "first charge" on account of the new works appears in the opening statement on the ledger, reproduced in *ibid.*, 144. A blank space on the ledger folio shows that the man who made the entry, in 1728 or later, did not have before him, even then, the date of Washington's final contract. The list of partners, as of November, 1726 (Br. Mus. Add. MS 29600, F. 10) included the name of John English but not that of Augustine Washington.

[135] Ledger note *supra.*

[136] The name is spelt Accotick in the document but this stream must not be confused with Accotink.

[137] *L.O. Records, N.N.,* A, 219, 220. These patents are dated Aug. 16, 1726, nearly a month subsequent to the contract about to be mentioned in the text. Consequently, Washington would have been leasing lands he did not possess unless, prior to the new contract, he had procured an "order" for the lands. Such a procedure was not unusual. It was one of the issues in the controversy over the "pistole fee," for which see *infra,* p. 171.

was not to be liable for any part of the loss. The next provision was the oddest: during the entire life of the lease, not more than 100 tons of iron were to be dug without the permission of Washington. That was equivalent to saying that after 100 tons had been brought to the surface, Washington could demand a revision of the contract.[138]

This appeared to be an excellent bargain for the young Virginian. The cost of a completed furnace would not be less than £700.[139] None of this would Gus be called upon to provide. His liability for structures at the furnace would not exceed £20. That sum and the use of the land and woods represented the total he would have to adventure before the first blast. If all went well, he would have one-sixth of the profits, which would be close to £5½ per ton at the furnace or £3 to £4 per ton in England.[140] When, with Augustine's consent, the furnace had run 100 tons of pig iron, his part of the anticipated profits would be at least £50, or more than enough to cover his costs. After that, with the furnace and buildings standing on his land, he would be able to make still better terms.

Nothing was said in this contract regarding the satisfaction of Lord Fairfax's claim to one-third of the ore brought to the surface, a claim that subsequently was regarded as an obstacle to the development of the industry [141] in that part of Virginia. Nor was any provision made for the purchase of slaves to dig the ore and to perform other labor. Was Augustine liable for any part of this cost? [142] Either he did not consider that he was, or else he did not have the ready money to meet his payments. John England, with a twelfth interest, was of like mind or circumstance. Neither man paid anything for the purchase of slaves and for other charges prior to Mch. 31, 1728.[143]

This state of affairs was one and perhaps the prime reason why Augustine Washington determined in the summer of 1729 to go to

138 *Stafford Deeds,* 1722–28, p. 524. The indenture used the words "iron dug," not "iron ore." It consequently is difficult to say whether the tonnage was of ore or pig iron. Cf. "Abstract of Writings Relating to Iron Works in America" *LC.*

139 Byrd, "Progress to the Mines," *Writings,* ed. Bassett, 362. In this familiar narrative of the second William Byrd will be found a somewhat sketchy account of the methods then employed at Virginia blast furnaces.

140 The Principio accounts of August, 1727, in 11 *Penn. Mag.,* 192, show an over-all cost of £4, 5 s. 9 d. per ton and a sales price of £10 per ton. William Byrd, *op. cit.,* 346, 349, 363, listed the costs of production, freight, etc., and quoted the estimates of net profit given in the text. His figures were for 1732, but there is no reason to assume any substantial difference in production costs of 1727. According to what was told Byrd, freight was 7 s. 6 d. and the English impost was 3 s. 6 d. per ton but the *Complete View of the British Customs,* ed. 1729, v. 2, p. 110, gave examples that show a duty of 41 s. per ton.

141 See *infra,* Chapter IV.   142 See the opening Ledger statement, n. 134 *supra.*
143 *Ibid.*

England and to deal directly with his partners. He left the Potomac sometime after May 28 [144] and made the long voyage across the Atlantic. If, in dull days aboard ship, he took occasion to review his career, he had reason to be gratified. At 35 years of age, he had a wife and three children, Lawrence, Augustine and Jane.[145] He was not rich, but he was prospering and was discharging the duties and holding the offices that usually fell to a gentleman of the County. To his service as Justice of the Peace [146] was added occasional work as executor of estates.[147] By 1724 he had become church warden; [148] in March, 1727, he had been appointed Sheriff,[149] a position that paid a minimum of 1080 pounds of tobacco per annum.[150] Like his grandfather, he had unpleasantness along with success. In 1722 he suffered the embarrassment of having to go into court to confess that, through mistake or oversight, he had omitted from his list the names of twenty-one "tithables" on whom he should have paid taxes.[151] After appointment as church warden, Augustine had the continuing annoyance of a succession of suits by Rev. Lawrence De Butts, who insisted that Washington and other parishioners were denying him rights and perquisites as minister. [152] In spite of these vexations and occasional reverses, Washington was established and, it would appear, was financially stronger every year.

Such was Augustine's state when he arrived in England. His strange attitude toward a new bargain kept him a long time there. Before he started home, he named an agent in England and drew up a formal contract with his partners. In order that Nathaniel Chapman, a capable

144 In an entry concerning Francis Ash of St. Mary's County, Md., June 5, 1728, there is a line in *Westmoreland Orders*, 1721–31, p. 74, to the effect that Augustine Washington was going to England, but he was in court November 27 (*ibid.*, 238), and was there, also, May 28, 1729 (*ibid.*, 267). He consequently must have deferred his voyage until 1729. He brought action in Westmoreland, Aug. 28, 1729 (*ibid.*, 289), but of course need not have been present in person for this.

145 The first child, Butler, born 1716, had died in infancy. According to 1 *Hoppin*, 245, Lawrence was born in 1718, Augustine in 1719–20, and Jane in 1722.

146 Cf. *Westmoreland Orders*, 1721–31, p. 11.

147 E.g., the estate of Robert Vaulx, 7 *Westmoreland Deeds*, 252.

148 *Westmoreland Orders*, 1721–31, p. 66.

149 *Ibid.*, 151.

150 Plus fees for special services. Cf. *ibid.*, 235. There long has been a tradition that "Capt." Augustine Washington was a shipowner and carried on maritime trade. Nothing in surviving court records, in his will or in his inventory suggests that this tradition has any basis of fact. Augustine's title probably was in the militia, or was the honorary one often given a Justice of the County Court. In fact, it would appear, strangely enough, that after a Justice had served for a number of terms he might be styled Major.

151 *Ibid.*, 31. "Tithables" were white males and all Negroes over 16 years of age. See *infra*, p. 184. The annual levy on tithables in Westmoreland was reduced in 1723 from 700 to 500 pounds of tobacco (*Westmoreland Orders*, 1721–31, p. 31).

152 *Ibid.* et passim. See particularly the agreement of Mch. 26, 1729, p. 250 to settle the controversy by arbitration out of court.

manager at Accokeek, might be sent to Maryland to direct the Principio
Works, Augustine agreed to take charge of the furnace in Virginia,
provided the resident founder could produce the quality of iron desired
there. Washington promised, further, to have the property at the
furnace appraised and to give bond for its safe return on the termination
of his contract.

When Augustine reached Pope's Creek on the 26th of May, 1730, he
had the worst shock of his life: his wife, Jane Butler, had died the
preceding November 24.[153] This left him with the care of three
children. It was impossible for him to have them remain at home in
the care of the slaves, during the long periods he had to be at the
furnace; it was equally impossible for him to take the two boys and the
little girl to live at the ironworks. He consequently had to abandon
the contract to manage the enterprise, though he went to the furnace
and did what he could to keep it in order until John England could
return. Unfortunately he delayed a month and a half in reporting
to his partners what had happened and then he irritated them by
failure to say flatly that he could not carry out his bargain.[154] This did
not lead to an estrangement. Instead, a new, limited agreement was
made. Chapman remained at Accokeek; Augustine undertook to dig
the ore with his own laborers and to deliver it at the furnace for 20 s.
per ton of iron produced. A supplementary arrangement covered the
hauling of the finished iron six miles to a landing on the Potomac.[155]
Other disputed matters of contract were deferred.

One thing that could not be deferred by the father of three young
children on a plantation in Westmoreland was the finding of a new
mother for them.[156] Augustine looked about, visited and, on Mch. 6,
1731, married a healthy orphan of moderate height, rounded figure,

153 In a letter of George Washington's, May 2, 1792 (32 G. W., 28), the date is set down
as Nov. 24, 1728, but the inscription on her tombstone gives the year as 1729. Cf. 14 V 443.
It will be noted that the statement of Jane Butler Washington's death during the absence of
Augustine in England implies that his visit certainly was later and probably was longer than
has been assumed; but on this point the new evidence offered in John Wightwick's letter of
Oct. 2, 1730, to John England (MS, Md. H.S.), appears to be conclusive. This letter reads in
part: ". . . we have letters from him [i.e., Augustine Washington] of the 10th of July, in
which he says that upon his arrival to his great grief he found his Wife was dead." While it
is not explicitly stated that Augustine's arrival was from England, the inference to that effect
is plain.
154 It may be, of course, that he did this on advice of counsel.
155 Byrd, op. cit., 374. The information Byrd had of this agreement was given him second
hand in 1732 but it was conveyed in a fashion that obviously left no doubt in his mind
of its accuracy.
156 The matter-of-fact succession of wives is illustrated by the copy of Matthew Hale's Contemplations mentioned in 1 Schroeder, Life of Washington, 19. On the title page is Jane Butler
Washington's signature. Below it is Mary Ball Washington's name,

and pleasant voice, Mary Ball, aged 23.[157] Mary was the daughter of
Joseph and of Mary Johnson Ball, and in the extent of her property
holdings represented a triumph over the familiar tragedy that befell
many families when the father was stricken while his children still
were young.[158]

Joseph Ball, born in England about 1649, had come to Virginia as
a young man to join his father, William Ball, who had migrated during
the period of the Commonwealth. By the time Joseph Ball was approaching his sixtieth birthday, he had reared a family, had lost his wife
and had accumulated numerous undeveloped tracts of land and several
plantations under successful cultivation. He probably had decided in
1707 to marry a widow, Mary Johnson, whose schooling had been so
stinted that, apparently, she could not write her name. The possible
opposition of his son and daughters to such a union may have prompted
Joseph Ball to pursue his plan and at the same time to placate his
protesting children by transferring to them a large part of his estate.
This he did, Feb. 7, 1707, by a formal deed of gift in which he was
careful to preserve the dower rights of a second wife and to make provision for the possible issue of a new union.[159]

After this document was duly acknowledged and recorded, Joseph
Ball and Mary Johnson were married.[160] In 1708 or 1709 [161] a daughter
was born to them and was given the mother's name. When she was
three years of age, her father died. In his will he gave Mary Johnson
Ball something more than her dower rights and to the daughter, Mary,
he left 400 acres of land, near the falls of the Rappahannock River. In
addition, he bequeathed her fifteen cattle, three Negroes and all the
feathers "in the kitchen loft to be put in a bed for her." [162] Under the

[157] The familiar description of her person in G. W. P. Custis, *Recollections and Private
Memoirs of Washington,* (cited hereafter as *G. W. P. Custis*), p. 146–47, may, of course, be
based on the observations of those who did not know her until, in the old Virginia phrase, she
had "stoutened up." Ella Bassett Washington, in her article "Mother of Washington," *Century
Mag.* v. 43, p. 837, is authority for the statement concerning the voice of Mary Washington.
Neither the exact date of Mary's birth nor the place of her marriage is known. Cf. Hoppin in
8 *T* 77. If one guess is as good as another concerning the place of the marriage ceremony of
Augustine Washington and Mary Ball, it may be ventured that the most probable setting was
Sandy Point, the home of Mary's executor and former guardian, George Eskridge or else the
residence of her half sister, Elizabeth Johnson Bonum, then a widow, whose farm was on the
Potomac, near Pecatone.

[158] A brief survey of the Ball genealogy, prior to the birth of Mary Ball, will be found
in Appendix I–5, *infra.*

[159] 9 R. *Lancaster Deeds,* 246.

[160] The date and place are not known, but the language of the deed of gift makes it plain
that the marriage had not occurred at the time the paper was submitted to the court.

[161] Here, again, exact chronology cannot be established, but the weight of evidence is in
favor of the winter of 1708–09 as the time of Mary Ball's birth.

[162] 10 R. *Lancaster Wills and Inventories,* 88.

law, of course, the widow became guardian of Mary, but Joseph Ball the second, son of the testator, and not Mary Johnson Ball, was made executor of the estate.

Within a year, more or less, Mary Johnson Ball found a third husband in Richard Hewes of Cherry Point, Northumberland County.[163] To that pleasant place went the youthful Mary and there, probably, she shaped her first memories of farm and river. Her property rights and those of her mother were not established without some difficulty. Joseph Ball II, the executor of his father's estate, was a litigious young gentleman;[164] Mrs. Hewes and her husband were not inclined to interpret to their disadvantage a single line of the senior Ball's will. Suits between the executor and Mrs. Hewes developed,[165] but before a courteous court could hear all the issues at the convenience of the litigants, Mrs. Hewes was again a widow. In March, 1713, she filed the inventory of her third husband's estate[166] and took over the management of Cherry Point farm. Although she and Joseph Ball composed their differences, Mrs. Hewes continued periodic visits to the bar of justice in an effort to collect debts due her.[167]

By her first marriage, Mary Hewes had two surviving children, a daughter named Elizabeth, and a son John. In time, Elizabeth married Samuel Bonum, who lived across the Yeocomico River.[168] John Johnson remained with his mother and half-sister at Cherry Point, where life flowed quietly until 1721. In that year, first John Johnson and then his mother died. John left Mary a tract of land in Stafford County that had been bequeathed him by his stepfather.[169] Under her mother's will the girl received virtually the whole of Mary Hewes's estate.[170] As Mary Ball was then only twelve years of age, her mother had stipulated

163 The 589 acres of this tract had been patented, Oct. 1, 1668, by Jonathan Hewes (6 *L.O. Records,* 200).
164 See Appendix I–5.
165 *Northumberland Orders,* 1713–19, p. 299 *et passim.*   166 *Ibid.,* 17, 19.
167 *Ibid.,* 1699–1713; *Northumberland Records,* 1718–26.
168 Samuel Bonum, grandfather of this Samuel, appears to have been the first of his name in Virginia. In 1653, he patented land at the mouth of what became known in time as Bonum Creek (*Eubank,* 66; *Eaton,* 46; 3 *L.O. Records,* 18, 46). As the *Westmoreland Records* of 1676–89 attest, he was constantly in litigation of some sort. An inventory of his estate, dated Mch. 28, 1691, appears in 2 *Westmoreland Deeds and Wills,* 39. His daughter Rebecca married George Eskridge (22 *V* 309). Little is known of Samuel Bonum's son, who was father of Samuel Bonum II. Bonum Creek farm, beautifully situated on the Potomac, was sold after the death of Samuel Bonum the second. In 1753 the tract passed to Willoughby Newton, who married Sally Poythress, widow of Richard Lee.
169 For John Johnson's will, see *Northumberland Records,* 1718–26, p. 177. The tract probably was the one subsequently known in the Washington family as the "upper quarter." Mrs. Hewes died early in 1721, before her son's will was probated, and evidently very soon after John's death (19 *Northumberland Orders,* 42).
170 The will is in *ibid.,* 177, and in 8 *V* 284. It was filed for probate simultaneously with that of John Johnson July 19, 1721 (19 *Northumberland Orders,* 42). Inheritance by Mary Ball

that she remain during her minority under the "tutelage and govern-ment" [171] of George Eskridge, who was named as executor also—a choice that was a credit to Mary Hewes as surely as it was a compliment to him. George Eskridge was a lawyer of distinction, a land speculator of skill and a gentleman of character. For most of the legislative terms of three decades, he was Burgess from Westmoreland.[172] Perhaps no man of his day served more frequently in the Northern Neck as executor of large estates, and none served more acceptably. His first wife had been Rebecca Bonum, who was an aunt of the Samuel Bonum whom Mary Ball's half-sister, Elizabeth Johnson, had married. Mary Ball, therefore, was equally welcome after her mother's death, at the Bonum farm or with George Eskridge's three daughters at Sandy Point, his Potomac plantation two miles from the mouth of the Yeocomico.[173]

Either place was comfortable; the society was good though not bril-liant; in her own right the girl had sufficient income for her needs, possessed several riding horses and, no doubt, used often the "good silk plush riding saddle" which her mother's will had directed the executor to purchase for her.[174] So familiar was Mary's love of animals and so friendly her relations with the Bonums that when the husband of her half-sister died in 1726, he left her a "young gray dapple horse." [175] As a young woman of a mind that never was orderly and probably was becoming more and more positive, she lived simply but not meagrely with these kindly Bonums and Eskridges until she married Augustine Washington.[176]

---

of part of the estate of her mother was accidental. Mary Hewes made specific bequest to Mary Ball of a Negro, two horses and various personal effects. The will then provided that the landed property and the remaining personal effects should go to Johnson and, in default of issue, to Mary Ball. As John predeceased his mother and died unmarried, Mary became heiress. Had she died without children, the estate of Mary Hewes would have gone to Elizabeth Johnson Bonum, who received nothing directly in the will except a "suit of white and black callico" that had belonged to her mother.

171 Mary Hewes's will. The convenient text is that of 8 V 284 ff.

172 The sessions are listed by W. G. Stanard in *Colonial Register*, 309. For notices of the life of George Eskridge, see 7 V 434–35; 18 *ibid.*, 153.

173 22 V 309; 8 *ibid.*, 286–87.

174 8 V 285.

175 8 *Westmoreland Deeds and Wills*, 72. Elizabeth Johnson Bonum married James Straughan. Her daughter of this marriage, Elizabeth Straughan, married Charles Haynie. She will appear in these pages later.

176 It would be easy to load these pages with the spurious anecdotes and the dubious traditions of Mary Ball, but the facts set forth in the text are all of any importance that have survived. Internal evidence discredits all except two of the letters attributed to her and published in good faith in W. H. Snowden's *Historic Landmarks of Virginia and Maryland* (cited hereafter as Snowden, *Historic Landmarks*). No proof has been offered for the story that she went to England and met Augustine Washington there. Some actual unpleasant occurrence may underlie the sensational yarn in G. W. P. Custis, 141, that Mary Washington's fear of thunderstorms had its origin in the death by lightning of a friend who was sitting beside her at the dining table. As related, authenticity of the incident is discredited by the statement that the knife and fork in the hands of the stricken friend were melted by the bolt of lightning.

Augustine took her to his home on Pope's Creek, where the servants, the furnishings and the activities of the farm were not different in material degree from those Mary had known at Bonum's and at Sandy Point. Although she had to assume the duties of mother of three children, the two boys either were at Appleby School in England or else were sent there about the time of the marriage. Perhaps it was well for her that she did not have to take them in hand at that particular age. Lawrence, the older of the two, was then about thirteen, or less than ten years younger than his new stepmother. Augustine, the second son, was in his twelfth year.[177] The girl, Jane, was about 9 and consequently of an age with which Mary could deal.

It was not for many months that Mary's thoughts of children were confined to those of her husband's first marriage. By June, 1731, she knew that she was pregnant and that, if all went well, she would be delivered in midwinter. It was a time of interest in a larger world than hers. As 1731 ended and 1732 began, Britishers still talked occasionally of the Duke of Marlborough, who had been dead ten years, and of Joseph Addison, who had come to the end of his days in 1719. Louis XIV, by 1732, had been in his tomb seventeen years. George II, at 49, had been on the throne a single lustrum; his Whig Prime Minister, Sir Robert Walpole, was 56 and, having quarreled in 1730 with Townsend, was almost supreme. Montesquieu was 43 in 1732. Both Bach and Handel were 47. Bach had finished his "Matthew Passion" and was at work on part of his "Mass in B Minor." Handel was to live another decade before he presented "The Messiah." Time was to wait four years for the birth of James Watt, eleven for the infant Lavoisier, and seventeen for Goethe; but everywhere in Western Europe, young men, destined to fame, were enlarging their opportunities. Frederick of Prussia—some day to be called "The Great"—was 20. He had just been permitted by his father to appear in uniform again after a period of disgrace and that year he was to receive a Regiment as Colonel. In Königsberg, an eight-year-old lad named Immanuel Kant was romping gravely. Maria Haydn, wife of an Austrian village wheelwright, was carrying in her womb a child whom she was to name Franz Joseph. That same year, Joshua Reynolds, aged 9, was attending the Plympton grammar school in Devon, where his father was master. William Pitt was 24 and a cornet in the command later renowned as the First Dragoon Guards. One year older than Pitt was Henry Fielding, who was

[177] See *supra*, p. 41, n. 145.

having only moderate success with his own dramas and was translating Molière. A fiery minister of 29, John Wesley, was preaching often and, as he said, "laying a deeper foundation of repentance, saw a little fruit." Samuel Johnson, 23, was burning still with regret that lack of funds had compelled him the previous autumn to leave Oxford without a degree. In Philadelphia, Benjamin Franklin at 26 was beginning to win reputation.

By comparison with the achievements of even the least of these men, it seemed a small thing that at 10 A.M. on the 22nd of February, 1732, Mary Ball was delivered of her first-born child, a lusty boy.[178] The mother recovered promptly; the infant throve. On the 5th of April, probably at the home on Pope's Creek, minister, godparents and neighbors assembled for the christening. After a time, in the familiar usage of the Church of England, the clergyman took the baby in his arms and repeated the words of the ritual: "Name this child."

"George," answered the sponsors.[179]

[178] For the hour of birth, etc., see the entry in the family Bible, reproduced as the frontispiece of Vol. I of the present work. Augustine Washington gave bond, Feb. 23, 1732, for John Shropshire who was licensed to keep an ordinary at his residence near Mattox at the ferry on the main road, but this date doubtless was O.S., whereas George's birth, February 22, is N.S. (see *Westmoreland Orders,* 1731–39, p. 11). For nearly the whole of the month of February, when the court sat, Augustine was present. He was there, also, in April (*ibid.,* 16, 19), and he may have shared in the remonstrance and petition of Westmoreland citizens against the act "for amending the staple of tobacco" (see *ibid.,* 23). On May 31, Augustine was appointed to take a list of tithables in the lower precinct of Washington Parish (*ibid.,* 26). About two months later he again was named a Justice (*ibid.,* 30).

[179] Almost certainly, he was named for George Eskridge. The reason for believing that the christening occurred at home is that Pope's Creek Church was not built until 1742. The only other church, Round Hill, was too far away. Mattox church may have been standing (*Westmoreland Orders,* 1750–52, p. 48) but it had fallen into disuse. The clergyman in the services doubtless was Rev. Roderick McCullough, rector of Washington Parish, 1730–46, but of his actual observance of the rite, there is no record. Nor is the identity of two of the godparents established by anything more than the entry in the family Bible. One of the godfathers, Beverley Whiting, bears the name of a son of Henry Whiting and of Ann Whiting, daughter of Peter Beverley, but there may have been another man of the same name. It is known that a Beverley Whiting was matriculated at Christ Church, Oxford, in 1722. He served as Burgess for Gloucester in 1740–54 (17 *W* (2) p. 124), and died in 1755 (10 *W* (2) p. 51). Capt. Christopher Brooke, the other godfather, bore the name of one of the incorporators of the Virginia Company under the second charter, 1609. See 9 *V* 314, with citation of the list of incorporators (1 *H* 81 ff). It is highly probable that this godfather was Captain of the ship *Cambridge* of London, mentioned in 1729, when his storehouse was plundered by Gloucester slaves who, perhaps significantly, belonged to Mrs. Elizabeth Whiting, of the same surname as the other godfather of George. It might be conjectured, of course, that there was some business connection between Brooke and the Whitings and that the vessel, with Christopher Brooke and Beverley Whiting aboard, was one used by Augustine Washington for the shipment of his tobacco and was in the Potomac at the time George was christened. In those circumstances, if Augustine were a friend of Brooke and of Whiting, it would have been entirely proper for him to have invited them to stand as godfathers. This, be it repeated, is conjecture and is set down with some hesitation because, in the past, plausible guesses regarding obscure incidents of Washington's career have been passed on as established "fact." George Washington's godmother was his aunt, Mildred Washington Gregory.

CHAPTER III

Changing Homes and Fortunes

(February, 1732–April, 1743)

THE GREAT event of the Northern Neck in the year of George's birth was the death on August 4 of "King" Carter. Every person who knew of Carter's wealth and of his part in the development of the "back country" must have talked for days of his obsequies, his will and his children's fortune. He had done well by them and not ill by the Proprietor. During his second lease, 1720–32, Carter had issued between Potomac and Goose Creeks, along the line of growing speculation and increasing settlement, patents for 600,000 acres. Friends and descendants might assert it was to the Proprietor's interest, rather than otherwise, that a considerable part of this had been acquired by Carter's family and intimates: they were financially responsible; their quit rents would be paid.[1]

To Augustine Washington, the passing of "King" Carter meant little at the time. The young planter was busy both on Pope's Creek and at the Accokeek furnace, which was inconveniently distant from the Washington home in Westmoreland. Nor was the time, financially, one of jubilation for Augustine. He was not "land poor," but he was possessed of many acres that were yielding little. His speculation almost ceased in the early seventeen-thirties either because he found few bargains or else because he lacked the money with which to take advantage of those he saw.[2] He lost something through the death of William Lord;[3] he was not above the performance of many petty duties for the trivial compensation allowed him and William Brown as executors of

---

[1] As shown by the *Land Books* of the proprietary, the patents by volumes and years were as follows: Book A, 1723–26, acreage 188,995; Book B, 1726–29, acreage, 77,956; Book C, 1729–31, acreage, 278,244; Book D, 1731–32, acreage, 55,651. Carter's will, as noted already, was published in 5 *V* 408 ff and 6 *ibid.*, 1 ff.

[2] His recorded transactions of 1732–34 include only a lease of 100 acres to Joseph Lee for £4 a year current money, the purchase of the islands near the mouth of Pope's Creek from his brother John, and an exchange of land with Daniel McCarty and William Aylett. (8 *Westmoreland Deeds*, 175, 245; *Westmoreland Orders*, 1731–39, p. 28.)

[3] *Westmoreland Orders*, 1731–39, p. 68.

the small estate of James Mason;[4] although Robert Washington was official Coroner, Augustine held two inquests for which he received a total of 266 pounds of tobacco.[5]

As George meanwhile came to consciousness and learned to walk, there was a new sister, Betty, with whom to become acquainted.[6] Before she was a year and a half old, another baby arrived, a brother, who was christened Samuel.[7] In addition, there was around George an amazing world of dogs and chickens and pigs and calves, as well as those towering creatures called cows. Soon, too, in front of someone on a horse, he had the breath-taking adventure of going to the mill or visiting neighbors.[8] Among these friends were the Hedges of Twiford. When George went there he may have found delight in the contrasting colors of the different rooms. His elders, no doubt, were more interested in the fine paneling of the dwelling, though the building was nearer a cottage than a "great house" in design.[9]

Across Pope's Creek, down the Potomac, was Longwood, the home of the McCartys, who were close friends of George's parents. The Mc-Carty family had lived there only some fifteen years, but it had resided for a long time on the Northern Neck,[10] and it felt it had a right to

---

4 *Westmoreland Records and Inventories,* 1723–46, p. 138.
5 *Westmoreland Orders,* 1731–39, p. 109.
6 She was born June 20, 1733. See 32 *G. W.,* p. 28.   7 Born Nov. 16, 1734, *ibid.*
8 It is to be regretted that the letter supposed to have been written by Augustine Washington in 1733 to "Mr. Jeffries" cannot be accepted as historical evidence. As quoted in *Conway's Barons,* 56, the letter stated, in effect, that Augustine and Mary were planning to visit James Ball of Bewdley and would take their baby George with them. En route they would visit Jeffries. It was stated, *op. cit.,* that Lawrence Washington of Alexandria had read this paper, which Mr. Conway himself never saw. Some such letter may have been in existence, but the description of its contents is distorted and second-hand. Were there no other internal evidence against the accuracy of the reported contents of the letter, it has to be noted that visiting at so great a distance, especially with a small child, scarcely would have been attempted until the sunshine of May had dried the muddy roads. By that time, Mary Ball Washington was seven and a half months pregnant with Betty and consequently in no condition to travel.
9 Twiford, nearly nine miles from the Washington home, resembles the present memorial house at Wakefield and retains much of the feeling of the early seventeen-hundreds. The house and tract passed from the Hedges to the Fitzhughs; then Twiford became a Beverley home. After about 1815 it was the residence of John Washington Hungerford, whose mother was one of the twelve children of John Washington of Hylton. See *Eubank,* 35, and J. W. Wayland, *The Washingtons and Their Homes,* 329.
10 Charles and Owen McCarty came to Virginia in 1635 (*McCarthy Family,* 2). By 1662 men of the same name were planting between the Potomac and the Rappahannock. Dennis McCarty married Elizabeth Billington, and, among other children, had a son Daniel, born in 1679. This first Daniel married Anne Lee and in 1717 bought the Longwood property from his brother-in-law, Richard Lee, who had acquired it from Nathaniel Pope (6 *Westmoreland Deeds,* 291; *Eubank,* 43). Daniel McCarty the first died in 1724. By a will of unusual interest (8 *Westmoreland Deeds and Wills,* 17 ff), he left his Westmoreland lands to his son Daniel the second. Father and son have been confused often in narratives of the Northern Neck. The second Daniel, who owned Longwood in George Washington's childhood, was Burgess from 1734 until his death in 1744, and was Collector of Potomac River and Colonel of militia. The first and the second of these offices previously had been held by his father (*Eaton,* 40).

the consideration "due gentlemen," as, for example, in such a matter as the diversion of a public road for a season, so that a McCarty wheat-field would not be trampled or nibbled.[11] All this meant nothing to George, but by the time he was four, he may have had ear and partial understanding if any one told him how, years before, woodmen had seen a juice dropping from trees on back-country lands owned by the McCartys. The newcomers tasted some of the juice, which previously had hardened, and they found it sweet. "McCarty's sugar lands" the pioneers called that part of the forest, words to make the mouth of a boy water.[12] Beyond the home of the owners of the "sugar lands" the horizon of the youthful George could not then extend down the river. Perhaps his elders spoke of Stratford [13] below Longwood, of Currioman Bay and of Nomini Creek, but these must have been no more than musical names to the lad.

In the opposite direction from Longwood and Pope's Creek was Mattox Creek. There the ferry was located—in George's eyes a most mysterious contrivance that would carry man or beast to the other side of the stream for thrippence.[14] Farther up the Potomac was Mattox Church in a parish that had for George a natural sound, Washington Parish.[15] George no doubt heard also, then or thereafter, the tale of the man who stole the purple plush cloth from the pulpit of the church and made himself a pair of breeches with it.[16]

[11] *Westmoreland Orders, 1731–39*, p. 11.

[12] The "sugar lands" were on the Potomac near the present boundary of Loudoun and Fairfax (*Beverley*, 108). One is tempted to write more of this interesting family. Anne Lee McCarty's will, probated May 31, 1732, is in 8 *Westmoreland Wills and Deeds*, 169. The will of Daniel McCarty the second, probated May 16, 1744, is in 10 *ibid.*, 28.

[13] The date of the building of the great home of the Lees is doubtful, but Ethel Armes (*Stratford Hall*, 52) was of opinion that construction was begun "about 1721–22" and that the house was "ready for occupancy by 1729–30."

[14] *Eaton*, 4.

[15] See *supra*, p. 22. For the order of May 25, 1664, establishing the parish and fixing its boundaries, see *Westmoreland Orders, 1662–64*, p. 31. The location of the edifice is not precisely known, but it apparently was on the road to the ferry. The first American John Washington left this church copies of the Ten Commandments and one of the King's arms. See his will in W. C. Ford, *The Washington Family*, 75. Rev. John Rozier patented 1450 acres of land on the creek that later bore his name (*Eaton*, 43). Goodwin, in 2 *Colonial Churches*, 303, stated that Rozier held parishes in York and in Accomac. No mention is made of Rozier's ministry in Westmoreland. In 1720–28, the rector of the church was Rev. Lawrence De Butts, already mentioned. See more fully Goodwin, 2 *op. cit.*, 264; *Meade*, v. 2, p. 158. Pope's Creek Church, it may be repeated, was not built till 1742 (*Lee of Virginia*, 124), though a late transcription of a court order of June 1, 1716, concerning the roads adjoining the "mouth" of Pope's Creek, gave "church" for "mouth" and consequently created the impression that a church was there at that early date. No such blunder appears in the original. See *Westmoreland Orders, 1705–21*, p. 282. For the later history of the church, see 2 *Meade*, 162. The extension of the glebe is described in 12 *Westmoreland Deeds*, 35, 40, 45.

[16] See the trial of Robert Alworthy, June 3, 1715, as summarized in *Westmoreland Orders, 1705–21*, p. 270.

Above the church was Mattox plantation. There George's great-great-grandfather, Nathaniel Pope, had established an early warehouse and wharf, and there John Washington, Nathaniel's son-in-law and George's great-grandfather, had built a residence.[17] Close to Mattox farm was Bleak House, the property of Lawrence Butler, a kinsman of the first wife of George's father. A somewhat handsome establishment Bleak House was. As developed later, it had fine furnishings, ample livestock and Negroes in sufficient number for all work.[18]

Lawrence's nearest neighbors, the Marshalls, were not so well-to-do, but they were interesting in their rise. John Marshall, who was the proprietor in George's boyhood, was the son of Thomas Marshall, a carpenter of King and Queen County. By 1728, John had acquired 200 acres of uninviting land that John Washington and Thomas Pope had patented and then had failed to "seat," that is, to occupy and plant. Because this land was back from the river, Marshall was "John of the Forest," a suffix applied, with different given names, to all those who lived in the undeveloped regions away from the verdant bottoms and the ready wharves.[19] John was industrious and fortunate in the breeding of his slaves. When George was 20, Marshall was to die in possession of seventeen Negroes, a liquor still, an herb still, a fiddle and sundry other effects to the total value of £730.[20] What was of immediate interest to George the toddler was the fact that John Marshall's son Thomas was two years older and, by that fact, was someone to whom to look up.[21]

North of Bleak House and not far from the Marshalls was the Monroe tract, which lay along the river between Mattox Creek and Monroe Bay. This and other land had been patented by Andrew Monroe. In George's infancy, part of it was the property of Andrew's grandson, Spence Monroe.[22] His position was one of respect and influence, but

17 *Eaton*, 44. The inventory of the second Nathaniel Pope, May 9, 1719, is in 1 *Westmoreland Deeds*, 115. The will of Humphrey Pope, son of Thomas and perhaps a nephew of this second Nathaniel, Jan. 10, p. 1734, will be found in 8 *ibid.*, 253. In *Westmoreland Orders*, 1731–39, p. 151, under date of Nov. 26, 1734, is Mary Pope's renunciation of Humphrey's will.
18 See the inventory of Lawrence Butler, Oct. 28, 1766, in 4 *Westmoreland Records*, 224. His precise kinship to Jane Butler has not been determined.
19 See 3 *Westmoreland Deeds and Wills*, 232, entry of Mch. 21, 1704, and 8 *ibid.*, 276. See also *Eaton*, 37.
20 His inventory is in 2 *Westmoreland Records*, 207, entry of May 26, 1752. For his will, see 11 *Westmoreland Wills*, 419.
21 A. J. Beveridge, *Life of John Marshall*, v. 1, p. 7.
22 Andrew Monroe the first, immigrant and member of the Westmoreland Commission (2 H 16), patented most of this land (2 *L.O. Records*, 225 and 3 *ibid.*, 169. Cf. *Eubank*, 30). He died in 1668. For his line of descent, see 15 *W* (1) p. 192–95. His son, Andrew Monroe the second, married Eleanor Spence, a daughter of the family that owned Spence's Point, near

the Monroe name and stock were not then renowned on the Northern Neck. For that matter, the Washingtons, though honorable, were not among the most distinguished families of the region.

It was in this friendly little neighborhood of McCartys, Butlers, Washingtons, Monroes, Marshalls and like-minded folk that George experienced the first sorrow of his life: On the 17th of January, 1735, shortly before he was three years old, they told him that his half-sister Jane was dead.[23] Another event of that year led George in a new direction. Augustine, it will be remembered,[24] had purchased in 1726 from his sister Mildred the tract of 2500 acres that had been John Washington's part of the 5000 he and Nicholas Spencer had acquired after the lapse of Richard Lee's patent on Little Hunting Creek, a stream that flowed from the Virginia shore into the Potomac opposite the Indian village of Piscataway. As this property, then called Epsewasson, included land that had never been under the plow, Augustine probably caught anew the spirit that was carrying settlement up the Potomac and he concluded [25] in 1735 that it would be to his advantage to establish his family on his up-river farm.[26] Once he decided to move, he leased

---

Sandy Point of the Potomac. The second Andrew, 1664–1714 (see his will and his inventory of £563 in 5 *Westmoreland Deeds,* 285,293), left four sons—William, Andrew, Spence and James. Of these, William was a militia Captain (*Westmoreland Orders,* 1747–50, p. 203; for a suit against him, see *ibid.,* 1731–39, p. 14). Spence became a joiner and married Elizabeth Jones. Her father kept an ordinary in King George; her brother, Joseph Jones, will appear again as a member of the Continental Congress. Needless to say, Spence Monroe was the father of James Monroe. The will of Spence Monroe, dated Feb. 14, 1774, is in 16 *Westmoreland Deeds and Wills,* 128.

23 The date is given in 1 *Hoppin,* 245. "It is officially recorded," Hoppin wrote, that Jane died in Truro Parish, but he gave no authority for the statement.   24 See *supra,* p. 37.

25 Writing George Washington, Apr. 9, 1792, Hannah Washington stated that Augustine moved to Prince William in 1734 (32 *G. W.,* 28, n. 78), but 1735 seems the more probable though not the certain year.

26 The simple statement in the text is all that the evidence justifies one in making. No tangible basis can be found for the tradition that the move to the property later known as Mount Vernon was made because the death of Jane had convinced Augustine and Mary Washington that they must find a healthier place for the rearing of their children. If Jane had died in summer of dysentery or of malaria, her father might have reasoned, perhaps, that the site on Little Hunting Creek would be less unhealthy; but as Jane died during the season when bronchial complaints were the chief cause of fatal illness, the chances are that influenza or pneumonia was responsible. Her father scarcely could have concluded that the family would be less liable to respiratory diseases at "the freshes" of the Potomac than on Pope's Creek. Besides, instances of removal for reasons of health were few at that late period of the settlement of Tidewater Virginia. Planters already had observed and had applied the little that the sanitation of the age taught concerning unhealthy sites. Augustine's home on Pope's Creek was no worse located, in this respect, than were most of the estates on the Potomac. The other reason that naturally suggests itself as an explanation of Augustine Washington's change of residence is that he might have wished to be closer to the Accokeek iron furnace. This explanation would seem to be barred by the fact that the distance by the most direct route from Hunting Creek and from Pope's Creek to Accokeek is substantially the same. More streams, and wider, had to be crossed in riding from "the freshes" than from Pope's Creek, Westmoreland. Some of the most maddening marshes of the region were South of Epsewasson. In these circumstances, no specific statement of the reason for removal "up the river" can be given.

some of his Westermoreland land [27] and the next year sold 305 acres of it.[28]

On the new site, Augustine Washington probably owned a dwelling that may have been built by his father. It was not large but neither was his household.[29] With Lawrence and Augustine at school in England, the family to be sheltered at Epsewasson consisted of five only—the parents, George, Betty and Samuel. Cabins for the Negroes were erected easily. In accordance with earlier practice on Mattox and on Pope's Creek, Augustine soon built a mill on Doeg Run.[30] This completed the task of making the plantation self-sustaining. If change of domicile involved any hardship, it was in the scarcity of neighbors. Few they were and those, in the main, some miles up the river in the district that later was to have the attractive name Belhaven. Even the nearest road, which ran from the future Belhaven to Fredericksburg, passed so far from the house at Epsewasson that travelers along it could not be seen or be heard.

Thus isolated, the Washingtons had to find their interest in the farm itself, in the church and in the arrival of more children. Mary Washington's fourth baby was a third son, John Augustine,[31] whose christening may have been delayed because of the vacancy in the family's new parish, Truro. Within a short time after he was established on Little Hunting Creek, Augustine was elected to the vestry,[32] an assignment rarely peaceful and not always pious. The parish had been set up Nov. 1, 1732, from the previous Hamilton Parish and had been assigned all of Prince William North of Occoquan and Bull Run.[33] Lacking a regular minister, the vestry had agreed in April, 1733, that Augustine's

27 *Westmoreland Orders, 1731–39*, p. 165.   28 8 *Westmoreland Deeds and Wills*, 303.

29 Concerning few aspects of George Washington's environment has more been reared in words, on scantier foundation of fact, than about the early history of Mount Vernon. Truth is, no written record exists of any structures there prior to the death of Augustine Washington in 1743. The archaeological evidence, admirably summarized by Resident Superintendent Charles C. Wall in 2 *W* (3) p. 173 ff indicates strongly that a small structure, most probably a residence, existed on part of the site of the present building. Mr. Wall thinks this early house was built by Augustine's father, Lawrence. The tradition that the barn at Mount Vernon was erected by Augustine Washington no longer is accepted. See Mr. Wall's remarks in the *Report of the M.V.L.A.*, 1938.

30 Muir, *Potomac Interlude*, 18. The name Doeg later became Dogue.

31 In his list of his family, George Washington wrote that John Augustine was born Jan. 13, 1735; but this was 1735–36 O.S. On the present calendar, the birth of John Augustine was Jan. 24, 1736.

32 Slaughter, *History of Truro Parish*, 9, gave the date as Nov. 18, 1735, but the MS of *Vestry Book* shows the correct date to be November 28. The discovery of Augustine Washington's name in that volume was the first evidence brought to light of his residence at Epsewasson. Previously the assumption had been that he moved directly from Pope's Creek to Ferry Farm, opposite Fredericksburg.

33 4 *H* 367. From Bull Run the line ran westward to the "Indian Thoroughfare of the Blue Ridge."

litigious adversary of Westmoreland, Rev. Lawrence De Butts, was to preach three times a month for one year. As compensation, the clergyman was to receive 8000 pounds of tobacco, half the normal allowance per annum of a resident minister charged with the care of a parish.[34] Contract had been made a few months later with Richard Blackburn [35] to construct a church "at the crossroads near Michael Riggins," on the Potomac path between Occoquan and Pohick Run.[36] This edifice had been completed by the time Augustine became a vestryman,[37] but something no less exciting to the flock lay ahead. John Colville, a member of the vestry, who was about to sail for England, was entrusted by his colleagues in September, 1734, with the duty of procuring a "discreet and godly member of the Church of England" as rector.[38] Colonel Colville either was a failure in this mission or else was slow in discharging it. As late as August, 1736, the parish was without a spiritual guide. Augustine Washington then recommended that a resident of the parish, Dr. Charles Green, proceed to England, qualify himself for holy orders and, if approved by the Bishop of London, become minister of Truro. Green was reputed to be well educated and was, in addition, a practicing physician.[39] As both he and the vestry were agreeable, this arrangement was approved, but when Green was licensed by the Governor and Council to act temporarily as minister, pending approval from England, he maintained that Lord Fairfax and not the Governor had the presentation of the parish. For this he was summoned before the Council but, on apologizing, was excused later. Green left for England.[40] He had not long been gone when Rev. John Holmes appeared. This gentleman subsequently was described by Dr. Green as "an itinerant preacher without orders," [41] but he must have pleased the parishioners. They listened gladly to his sermons and soon asked him to serve as their minter,[42] a progression of confidence and enthusiasm that must have been the subject of talk in every household of the neighborhood.[43]

[34] MS *Truro Vestry Book*, 2.

[35] Subsequently the architect of Mount Vernon.

[36] MS *Truro Vestry Book*, 2. On the basis of newly discovered evidence, Fairfax Harrison in 36 *V* 180, elaborated the statement he had made in *Landmarks*, 286, concerning the location of this church, the predecessor of the more renowned Pohick Church which is still (1948) standing on a different site.

[37] It is quite probable, though it cannot be stated positively, that this was the first church ever attended by George Washington.   [38] MS *Truro Vestry Book*, 8.

[39] See Wyndham B. Blanton, *Medicine in Virginia in the Eighteenth Century* (cited hereafter as *Blanton*), 298.

[40] MS *Truro Vestry Book*, 12; 4 *E. J.*, 407, 413.

[41] *Ibid.*, 11.   [42] *Ibid.*, 11, 12.

[43] Green's subsequent comments on "the levity of the members of the vestry" in making contradictory agreements for a minister appear in *ibid*.

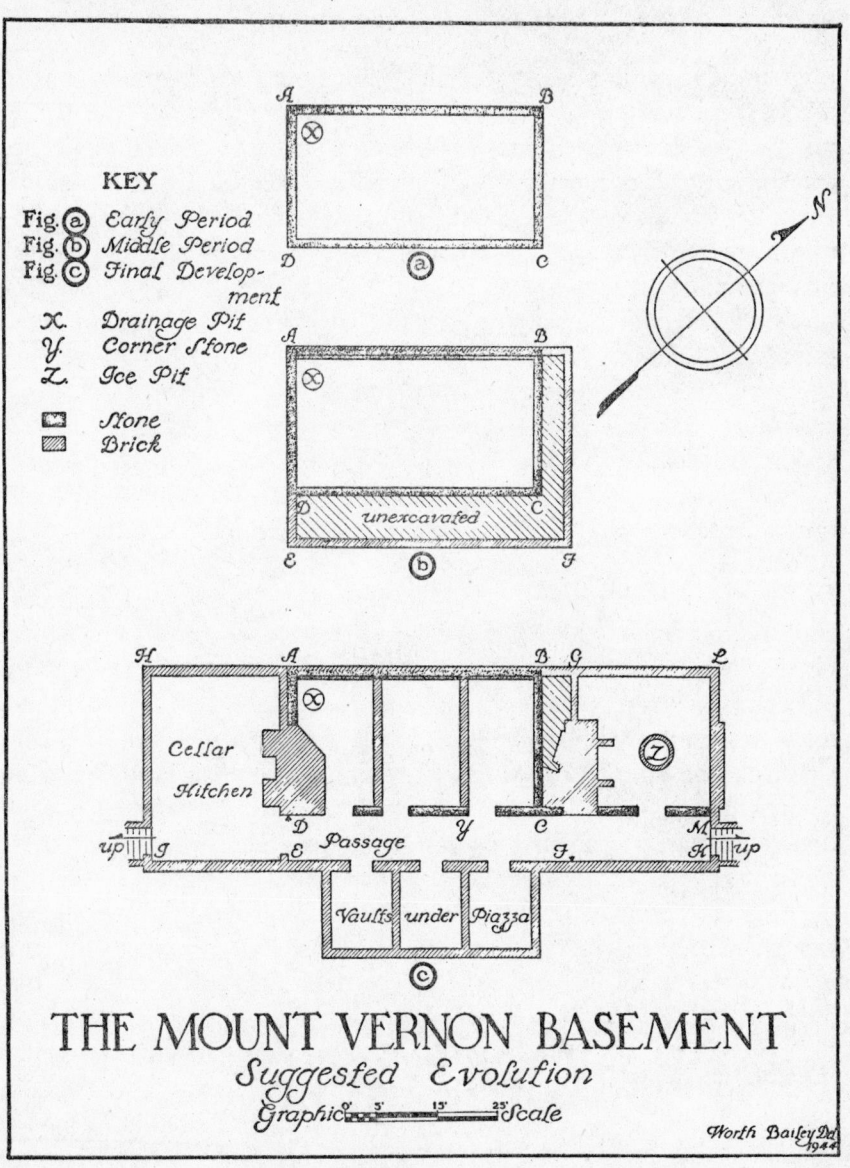

KEY

Fig. (a) Early Period
Fig. (b) Middle Period
Fig. (c) Final Develop-
              ment
    X.   Drainage Pit
    Y.   Corner Stone
    Z.   Ice Pit

    ☐   Stone
    ▨   Brick

THE MOUNT VERNON BASEMENT
Suggested Evolution
Graphic Scale

Worth Bailey Del
1944

How Mount Vernon Was Enlarged

These drawings show the foundations of Mount Vernon at three successive periods of development. It is believed that the rectangular walls of the basement, as shown in drawing "a," are
those of the house at Epsewasson to which, in 1735, Augustine Washington brought his wife,
his three-year-old son George and two younger children. (After the original by Worth Bailey,
archivist at Mount Vernon, to illustrate the article by Superintendent C. C. Wall entitled "Notes
on the Early History of Mount Vernon," published in the *William and Mary Quarterly*,
series 3, volume 2, p. 173 ff.)

Before Holmes became rector in Truro Parish, Augustine Washington was faced with a serious and more personal dilemma. The iron works on Accokeek probably had been for some years under the general care of John England, who had been living meagrely nearby. Augustine Washington had continued and fulfilled his contract to dig and deliver the ore for the blast, and then to transport the iron to the river.[44] In this way, no doubt, he contributed to the good reputation enjoyed by "England's iron furnace," as it was called. The owners of that property were believed to be willing to approve any expenditure that would make the furnace more profitable,[45] but, in general, the Virginia iron industry was not prosperous. Operators of colonial furnaces were not permitted under British law to export bar iron. Nor were they allowed to make iron castings, such as pots, firebacks and andirons, though actually some of the founders did manufacture and sell these articles.[46] Conditions imposed by the home government were so hampering that Governor Gooch in 1737 doubted whether any of the furnaces would be kept in blast if the proprietors could find other work.[47]

At Accokeek, Gus Washington's contract, yielding him 20 s. for every ton of finished iron he laid on the Potomac wharf,[48] still was an acceptable one so long as his slaves were under diligent overseers; but unless his experience was different from that of almost all his contemporaries, the difficulty was in procuring regular direction by competent men of character and intelligence. Accokeek was thirty miles from Epsewasson,[49] with several streams and entrapping marshes in between. The distance was enough to discourage frequent journeys but not so great, perhaps, as to deter Washington from attempting to keep in touch with the enterprise while residing at home.[50] In 1735, the death of John England, manager of the iron furnace,[51] probably forced

44 Cf. Byrd, *Writings,* ed. Bassett, 374. The authority for the meagreness of John England's establishment is the inventory of his personal property, for which see *infra,* n. 51.

45 Byrd, *loc. cit.*

46 Governor Gooch to the Board of Trade, Sept. 12, 1733; 2 *Gooch MSS,* 334. A description of this important collection of transcripts, dealing with Virginia in the period of Washington's youth, will be found in the Bibliography, Vol. II.

47 Same to same, June 20, 1737, *loc. cit.,* 475. Other comment on the iron industry will be found in *ibid.,* 341, 554. It is not known whether Lord Fairfax at this date was claiming one-third of the ore brought to the surface; see *infra,* Chap. IV, p. 145.

48 Byrd, *loc. cit.*   49 See *supra,* p. 52, n. 26.

50 As reference appears in 1736–37 to Augustine Washington and Co. (*King George Orders,* 1735–51, p. 92), it is entirely possible that Augustine had at Accokeek prior to that year some unidentified partner, perhaps Nathaniel Chapman.

51 His inventory was entered of record Dec. 5, 1735 (*King George Wills,* 1721–44, p. 200). Its total of £14, 14s, suggests that the death may have occurred shortly before that date, because no long time would have been required to prepare the inventory of so small a property.

Augustine to take a larger part in the management of the property. This proved to be a task as hard to discharge from Epsewasson as it had been when Augustine lived on Bridges Creek. England's death, moreover, raised a question concerning the future of the work at Accokeek. It was profitable to a reasonable degree but it was not making the partners rich. Although much had been spent on the furnace, there was no assurance that the deposits of ore were large enough to support indefinite operation.[52] Could it be continued; should it be suspended? Where could an experienced and diligent ironmaster be hired? How was the quality of the product to be maintained?

For an answer to these questions, Augustine concluded that it would be necessary to consult his partners overseas. In 1736 or during the first wintry months of 1737, he left the family at Epsewasson and went again to Britain.[53] When he returned in the early summer of 1737, he had much news for the household. In the first place, he had signed on the 15th of April a contract by which he was allowed a twelfth of the whole Principio enterprise in place of his two-twelfths previous interest in the profits of the Virginia furnace.[54] Next, Augustine was able to report that he had seen his sons, Lawrence and Augustine,[55] familiarly "Austin," who were at Appleby. The other part of Augustine's story was grim. Homeward bound, he had as his traveling companion Capt. Hugh French, a man of the upper social class; but the greater part of the ship's company consisted of convicts, whose service was to be sold in Virginia. Gaol fever [56] broke out among these men. Captain French caught the disease and died of it. Augustine had the distress of witnessing the burial of this friend at sea, though he himself escaped.[57]

[52] Surviving records do not show when it first became apparent that the ore deposit on Accokeek was small and was approaching exhaustion. Nor is there any satisfactory evidence concerning the position of Nathaniel Chapman at the furnace. Inasmuch as he was named as one of Augustine's executors, he manifestly was on the best of terms with Washington and probably was living nearby.

[53] See *supra*, p. 41. As Augustine's name does not appear among those of vestrymen at meetings of 1736 subsequent to July, it may be that he left Virginia during the summer of that year, but this cannot be stated as a fact. The possibility cannot be excluded, either, that he was at Accokeek when absent from meetings. The familiar, established date of his presence in England is fixed by an autograph note in his copy, now in the Boston Athenaeum, of *A Complete View of the British Customs*. This reads: "Augustine Washington his Book bought the 4th of May, 1737 of ye Booksellers under ye Royal Exchange Cost 7 Shillings." The date of his new contract shows that he was in England at least three weeks before he purchased the book.

[54] See an extract from the agreement in *May*, 43-44. The full text is in the *Principio Papers*, Emmett Collection, N.Y. Pub. Lib.

[55] A letter of Richard Yates to Augustine Washington, Oct. 9, 1741, L. W. Smith Coll., *Havemeyer Papers*, shows that Augustine was acquainted with some of the masters of Appleby School.

[56] Modern typhus.   [57] *Va. Gazette*, July 15, 1737.

When Augustine had told of his adventures and inquired what had happened during his absence, he may have heard, among other things, that his accounts had not been well collected. Several suits had been necessary.[58] Augustine learned, also, that Charles Green had reached or soon would arrive in the parish with the blessing of the Bishop of London. In due time, John Holmes relinquished his care of the parish; Dr. Green was accepted as minister.[59] As Augustine had recommended Green, he doubtless was pleased, but he had less time than previously for the affairs of the church. More of the work of the furnace fell to him. On occasion he even had to set an example of manual labor. The Negroes watched and marveled but they could not rival him. As they told it, he could put into a wagon a mass of iron two other men scarcely could lift from the ground.[60] Strong as he was, he could not direct a plantation, look after his other farms and at the same time supervise an iron furnace thirty miles from Epsewasson. If he was to have a continuing personal part in the management of the furnace he had to be closer to Accokeek.

It probably was while Augustine was reasoning toward this conclusion that George made two new acquaintances. One was of a sort no longer to be classed as a surprise. On the 2nd of May, 1738, he had his first look at another brother, who received the name Charles. This boy was the fifth child of Mary Ball and the ninth of Augustine by his two marriages. Of the nine, only two had died [61]—an unusual record in a Colony of hot summers and hosts of flies. George's other new acquaintance of 1738 [62] was his elder half-brother Lawrence who, at 20, returned to Virginia.[63] As a result of his long and careful schooling in England, the young gentleman had grace, bearing and manners that captivated George. The lad quickly made a hero of Lawrence and

58 2 King George Orders, 92, 93, 120.

59 MS Truro Vestry Book, 17. Dr. Green will reappear in these pages. Nothing is known of the circumstances in which Holmes relinquished the parish.

60 G. W. P. Custis in 11 N.E. Hist. and Gen. Reg., 4. Other traditions of the iron furnace on the Accokeek survived. Conway noted (Barons, 103) that in his day the Accokeek Farm still was called "the Furnace." The forest that yielded fuel for the blast was known as "The Woodcutting." For later description of the Occoquan works which could not have differed substantially from those of Accokeek, see Smyth, Tour in U.S., v. 2, p. 177; Ewell, A Virginia Scene, 176; Burnaby, Travels in North America (cited hereafter as Burnaby), 49, 52.

61 Butler and Jane, the first and fourth children of Augustine by Jane Butler. Ibid.

62 It is to this year that Weems assigned the myth of George and the cherry tree, for which see Appendix I–7. The reason for placing the myths and traditions in an appendix is given in the Introduction.

63 A certain doubt attaches both to age and to dates, because no direct evidence of the year of Lawrence's birth or of his arrival in Virginia has been found, but all the circumstantial evidence indicates the return of Lawrence in 1738. It is possible that he was 21 not 20, that year.

began to emulate him. Augustine, for his part, entrusted to his eldest son a part of the management of Epsewasson in order both to train the young man in agriculture and to lighten his own load.

Shortly before the birth of Charles, there had appeared in the *Virginia Gazette* of Apr. 21, 1738, an advertisement that seemed to offer Augustine a means of continuing as a planter and a manufacturer, too. William Strother of King George County, a Justice and a vestryman,[64] had died in the winter of 1732–33 and had left land in Prince William and in King George which his wife was authorized to sell for her benefit.[65] As she took a second husband, John Grant, who had an establishment of his own,[66] she offered for sale the Strother place of about 260 acres, in two tracts, on the left bank of the Rappahannock about two miles below the falls.

This property attracted Augustine. It was within easy riding distance of Accokeek, and it lay in the long belt of country between the land bequeathed Mary Washington by her father and the "upper quarter" given by her half-brother, John Johnson.[67] Moreover, proximity to Fredericksburg held out the possibility of sending the boys to school there. Investigation deepened Augustine's interest and led him on Nov. 2, 1738, to acquire both the tracts for £317 current money.[68] In addition, Augustine leased at £4 per annum, for the life of its owner, Rosewell Neale, 300 acres that adjoined the land he had bought. By December 1, he moved to the new home, which then or thereafter was styled Ferry Farm.[69]

To George, who was nearing his seventh birthday, the journey from Epsewasson doubtless was exciting; [70] the farm itself had to be explored. In the advertisement [71] the residence was pronounced a "very handsome dwelling house," but it probably did not deserve the extravagant adjective.[72] With a nearer approach to accuracy it could have been

---

[64] 2 *Meade*, 186; 2 *King George Orders*, 1726.

[65] His will was probated March 2, 1733 (2 *King George Orders*, 632). The inventory, Apr. 6, 1733, showed twenty-two Negroes and personalty to the total value of £750 (see *King George Inventories*, 1721–44, p. 155).

[66] Part of his inventory, including eleven Negroes, exists, badly mutilated, in 6 *King George Deeds*, 194 ff.   [67] See *supra*, p. 43, 44.

[68] 2 *King George Deeds*, 220, 222. The lease from Neale, Dec. 1, 1738, is in *ibid.*, 272. It will be remembered that King George County then included land which, by a change of boundary, became in 1777 a part of Stafford (9 *H* 244). For the circumstances of Augustine's purchase, etc., see George H. S. King, "Washington's Boyhood Home," 17 *W* (2) p. 265.

[69] Either this or the adjoining Strother tract was known more formally as Pine Grove Farm.

[70] What he saw on part of the same road in 1748 is described *infra*, p. 203 ff.

[71] *Va. Gazette*, Apr. 14, 1738.

[72] In *Conway's Barons*, 71, A. K. Phillips, "venerable citizen" of Fredericksburg, was quoted as saying his father remembered the house as a "plain wooden structure of moderate size and painted a dark red color." The picture published by Lossing is fanciful.

described as a livable residence of eight rooms.[73] Nearby were three storehouses and an adequate number of other outbuildings.[74] The garden was on the North. Eastward, to the rear of the main structure, was a strip of woodland; to the South were open fields, less elevated; on the West was another modest stretch that fell away toward the river. The site was high and fine, but there was an unhappy difference from Epsewasson in the width of the water. Compared with the wide and gracious Potomac, the Rappahannock was a mere creek.

A greater difference, destined to be vexing, was in the roads. At the home on the "river of swans," the only highway—if it deserved the name—was far in rear of the house.[75] Here, on the Rappahannock, the country road came down from the North and forked a short distance Northwest of the residence. One branch ran South a few rods and divided again. If a traveler halted, opened the gate and passed across the large field East of the long rail fence, he was on the way to Stafford Court House; but if he continued South from the gate, and kept the fence and the woods on his left, he would descend to Little Falls Run.

Back at the first fork, a lane ran slightly South of West and then cut South to the gully that led down to the ferry. This lane was unpleasantly close to the house and, having a steep grade, might tempt teamsters to shout and to swear.[76] The ferry-boat itself was fascinating to George, of course, because it was larger and went farther than the one that crossed Mattox Creek, of which George may have had some vague memory. To the adults of the family, the farm ferry was a convenience, but its change, by subscription, to a free ferry in 1745 probably made it something of a nuisance.[77]

Pleasant or unpleasant in this particular, Ferry Farm was home, the third of George's seven years, and it was located opposite something the boy had never seen before, a town. Fredericksburg, on the right bank of the Rappahannock, had been established by act of 1727 on fifty acres of a tract known as the Lease Land, the property of John Roylston and Robert Buckner.[78] The trustees had employed a surveyor the next year to lay out squares [79] for purchasers, who, at the outset, did not

[73] Unless, as seems improbable, some were added during Augustine Washington's occupancy. See *infra*, p. 102 for details of the interior.

[74] *Va. Gazette*, Apr. 14, 1738.   [75] See *supra*, p. 148.

[76] These topographical data appear on George's own survey of Ferry Farm, *George Washington Atlas*, Plate 9.

[77] See *Va. Gazette*, May 2, 1745. This ferry previously had its left-bank landing on the property of Anthony Strother.

[78] 4 H 234.

[79] This surveyor was George Hume. For his career see 38 *V* 100–24, 195–234, 293–98.

prove to be numerous,[80] though the beauty of the setting [81] and its fine relation to a developing tobacco country [82] were appreciated.

When George first saw the town, Fredericksburg possessed a wharf, near which was a quarry. Not more than thirty feet from the landing were the public tobacco warehouses, which had the form of a cross. Farther on, rose the principal stone building of the place, a prison, "the walls of which," according to one traveler, were "strong enough to hold Jack Sheppard if he had been transported there." [83] Stone was available for any number of castles and keeps—there were several quarries besides the one at the wharf—but most of the builders used timber from nearby woodland. Every house, George learned in time, had to be at least twenty feet square; [84] not many exceeded those proportions.

The court of the County had been transferred from Germanna to Fredericksburg the year George was born.[85] Its quarters in 1738 were outdone by a church, which had been built on contract by Col. Henry Willis, third husband of George's Aunt Mildred Washington.[86] It was in the construction of this edifice that the little town had enjoyed its choicest sensation. Rev. Rodman Kenner, a connection of Mary Ball Washington's family, had been appointed rector of the parish in 1729, though the vestry had desired Rev. Lawrence De Butts, who often had made trouble for Augustine Washington in Westmoreland.[87] After Rev. Mr. Keller, came Rev. Patrick Henry,[88] under whom the plans for erecting the church were advanced. Before the structure was completed, Mr. Henry resigned. Soon word was received from Williamsburg that persons in the lower end of the parish disapproved the site chosen by the vestry and wished the church placed elsewhere. Pending a review of their protest, the Governor ordered a suspension of building.[89] The response of the official body of the church, soon called St.

[80] Embrey, *History of Fredericksburg*, 51.
[81] See *Burnaby*, 43.
[82] Cf. the preamble to the act of 1727, 4 H 234.
[83] William Byrd, "Progress to the Mines," *Writings*, ed. Bassett 372–75, from which most of this description of the town is taken.
[84] 4 H 234.   [85] 4 H 364.
[86] See W. Clayton Torrence, "A Virginia Lady of Quality and Her Possessions," 56 V 42. Her first husband was a Lewis of undetermined first name (*Willis Family*, 100); her second was Roger Gregory (1 *Hoppin*, 163). Interesting specifications of the church appear in *St. George's Vestry Book*.
[87] See *supra*, p. 41.
[88] He was uncle of the Revolutionary orator.
[89] *St. George's* (Spotsylvania) *Vestry Book*, Oct. 2, 1733.

George, was a forthright protest: the work had progressed so far that a change of location was impossible.

Not long afterward there appeared in Fredericksburg a clergyman styled the Rev. Mr. Smith, who produced the Governor's recommendation as lawfully qualified to be rector of a parish. The vestry and congregation obediently listened to him preach. When he failed hopelessly, they concluded charitably that he might have been excited. Again he was heard. His incapacity as a preacher then was so manifest that the vestry declined to accept him and so advised the Governor. There was suspense and perhaps some suspicion that His Honor had imposed Mr. Smith on the parish as punishment for disputing his order about the completion of the church. In the end, Smith disappeared.[90] A better-furnished, devout man, Rev. James Marye, had entered upon his duties slightly more than two years before the Washingtons moved to Ferry Farm. Already he was winning the high esteem of the parish.[91]

The town had other celebrities. One of them was the church builder and *pater urbis,* Col. Henry Willis, a stout, blunt gentleman, busy with many things and particularly with the patenting of good land,[92] but negligent in much that concerned his estate. It was said of him that he courted his three successive wives as maids and married them as widows. George's aunt Mildred, who had lost two husbands,[93] wept profusely, the family tradition runs, when she heard that Colonel Willis's second wife, her kinswoman, had died. Her friends were curious: Why was she so distressed over the fate of a cousin? Mildred answered that "the death of her relation was not the sole cause of her grief, though she loved her dearly as they were cousins and bore the same name, but that she knew that old Henry Willis would be down there and she did not know what to do with him."[94] She proved a Cassandra: the Colonel arrived within a month, and within two,

[90] Governor Gooch officially notified the Bishop of London, Apr. 20, 1738, that Mr. Smith had chosen to surrender an unspecified parish rather than face the Commissary's Court (for the court, see *infra,* p. 180. Gooch wrote of Smith: "He was charged with grievous crimes and is such a sot and so weak in mind as in body that he is neither fit nor able to serve a cure." On the 13th of May, 1738, the Governor informed the Bishop that Smith had died the previous day. (2 Gooch MSS, 505, 507.)

[91] Inducted in October, 1735, he served until his death, Jan. 26, 1768. His son of the same name was the next minister of St. George's. See Philip Slaughter, *St. George Parish,* 19 ff.

[92] *Willis Family,* 7; Council Journals in 4 *E.J.,* 134 ff, 220 ff.

[93] See *supra,* p. 37.

[94] Byrd Willis's account of his grandfather, in *Willis Family,* 8.

carried her off as Mrs. Willis.[95] Consequently, George and the other Washington children met a new uncle in the determined gallant whom William Byrd six years previously had described as the "top man of the place."[96]

The second celebrity of Fredericksburg was of a different character and of opposite sex. She was Susanna Livingston, who, during her residence in the town, was first the wife and then the widow of William Livingston.[97] Elsewhere, she is presented in an earlier role, but at Fredericksburg she had a place among first purchasers of lots,[98] and in William Byrd's words, acted "in the double capacity of a doctress and coffee woman." Byrd added, mysteriously, "And were this a populous city she [was] qualified to exercise two other callings."[99] Susanna did not put a low estimate on her service in either of her acknowledged vocations. Doubtless if she had sold more than coffee, the court would have insisted that she take out license for conducting an ordinary and that she adhere to prices the Justices prescribed. No limitations apparently were imposed on the fees she could set as doctress. For "salivating a poor woman," she charged and the parish paid 1000 pounds of tobacco.[100]

Susanna would have been much flattered had she imagined that her combination of callings made her as interesting to posterity as were certain other notables of town—Dr. John Tennent, for example. He was absent in England at the time George came to Fredericksburg, and, present or across the Atlantic, he was a centre of medical contention, but he was regarded by some as a genius who would prove to the world the singular virtues of Virginia snake root.[101] To George, the conspicuous Dr. Tennent could have been no more than a name in comparison with William Lynn, who later was a doctor and apothecary of the town.[102] That worthy was to be a great figure in the eyes of all boys from the time he opened his doors and unshuttered his windows, because, among other delights, he sold white and brown-sugar candy.[103]

95 Her Washington thrift, according to Byrd Willis, saved part of Colonel Willis's estate from ruin (ibid., 100).

96 William Byrd, Writings, ed. Bassett, 373.

97 His will was probated Apr. 1, 1729 (Spotsylvania Wills, A. 93).

98 Spotsylvania Deeds, 1729-34, p. 40. See infra, p. 123.

99 William Byrd, Writings, ed. Bassett, 373.

100 St. George Parish Vestry Book, Oct. 7, 1735, p. 14. Other instances of salivation are included in the references, infra, Chapter IV, p. 137, n. 506, to relief of the poor as a function of the vestry.   101 See Blanton, 119 ff and infra, p. 111.

102 First notice of him in Fredericksburg dates from 1743, but he may have been there earlier. See a sketch in Sons of the Rev. Mag., v. 5, p. 25.

103 For his advertisement of candy and of other wares, see Va. Gazette, Aug. 28, 1746.

Dr. Lynn's offerings were eclipsed twice a year, if only twice. Then the fair authorized by statute was held.[104]

In competition with Fredericksburg, the settlers of King George and of Stafford had proposed to build a town of their own with the gracious old Cornwall name, Falmouth. They had provided for its establishment in the same act that named trustees for Fredericksburg.[105] There were hopes and professions and, for a brief period, a measure of prosperity. A second warehouse was demanded.[106] The church of Brunswick Parish was built there.[107] Beyond this, the town did not progress. As late as 1759, Falmouth was to consist of not more than twenty houses.[108]

Outside the two towns were numerous large plantations. In the County that boasted Fredericksburg as its jewel were some of the Spotswoods and Taliaferros and the numerous and able Thorntons, descendants of William Thornton who had immigrated in 1646.[109] Below Ferry Farm were Strothers and Balls of Mary Washington's line. Across Potomac Creek at Marlborough, lived the young furious attorney John Mercer who practiced in the courts of Spotsylvania and King George,[110] and, more often, in that old Prince William where, for insolence to the Justices, he twice was suspended. With the law he combined much land speculation. When he profited by this, which was not always the case, he put the money into other tracts near Marlborough until, in time, he owned the entire neck between Potomac Creek and the Potomac River.[111]

The spelling of these and other place names of the country around his new home now became a part of George's life. He had his seventh birthday soon after the family established itself at Ferry Farm; that was

104 5 H 104–05. Burnaby (op. cit., 43) wrote that Fredericksburg was "by far the most flourishing town" in that part of Virginia. For references to the town in 1774 see Harrower's diary in American Historical Review (cited hereafter as A.H.R.), v. 6, p. 77.

105 4 H 234. As the boundary line then ran, Falmouth was in King George.

106 2 King George Orders, 179; ibid., 1751–67, p. 14; Va. Gazette, June 5, 1752.

107 The assumption has been that this church was more convenient to the Washingtons than St. George's and that it consequently was the one they attended. This probably was true until the ferry was made free in 1745. After that the Washington family may have crossed the river on occasion to enjoy the larger delights of worship in Fredericksburg. All this is speculative, because the Vestry Book of Brunswick Parish has disappeared. Cf. 17 W (2) p. 40.

108 Burnaby, 44.

109 33 V 35. The will of Col. Francis Thornton, Nov. 11, 1748, is in Spotsylvania Wills, B, 1. Col. John Thornton, Justice of Spotsylvania, Sheriff and Burgess, and adversary of John Spotswood, the County Lieutenant, is sketched in 4 W (1) p. 160. For the other families, see Conway, George Washington and Mount Vernon, xxxiii.

110 2 King George Orders, 101.

111 Landmarks, 369. See also Journ. H.B., 1727–40, p. 66, 71; L.O. Records, N.N., E, 10, 12. The names of numerous friends and of several kinsmen of the Washington family will be found in St. George Vestry Book.

the age at which boys were taught to read and then to write and to cipher.[112] George was in the first stages of this bewildering but rewarding process when he had a new sister;[113] he was progressing in his reading when the Colony, his father, and particularly his brother Lawrence were stirred by news of war with Spain.

On Jan. 11, 1740, the *Virginia Gazette* reported that Admiral Edward Vernon had carried his British warships to Cartagena on the Gulf of Darien, opposite the Isthmus of Panama,[114] had "taken a view of it," had returned to Jamaica, had prepared an expedition, and had gone back to the South American coast to deliver an attack on Cartagena. Three weeks later, the same paper announced that Admiral Vernon had proceeded with seven men-of-war to Porto Bello,[115] in the hope of burning the Spanish ships there.[116] Actually, these accounts reversed the sequence of events. Vernon, then in home waters, received orders,

[112] There is no authentic record whatever of his instructors. Weems's familiar story will be found in Appendix I–7. A measure of credence, though a small measure, must be given the testimony of Rev. Jonathan Boucher who, in 1759–62, was a tutor in Caroline County and subsequently conducted there and in Maryland a small school attended by "Jacky" Custis, George Washington's stepson. Boucher, later an embittered Loyalist, showed the greatest deference for Washington in correspondence about young Custis, but he subsequently wrote that Washington in youth "had no other education than reading, writing and accounts, which he was taught by a convict servant whom his father brought over for a school teacher." (*Reminiscences of an American Loyalist,* 49.) This, of course, was hearsay, about thirty years after George's first schooling. Moncure Conway failed in efforts to identify the convict-teacher as one Hobby who also was sexton of Truro Parish. (See *Barons,* 63 ff.) E. C. McGuire in his *Religious Opinions and Character of Washington,* xv, stated that Hobby was both teacher and sexton, but he, too, offered no evidence to connect the man with the youthful George. The name Hobby was the one used by Weems, *loc. cit.* A reasonable tradition, quoted by Byrd Charles Willis, *op. cit.,* and deserving a place in a footnote rather than in the Appendix on Myths and Traditions, was that George attended a Fredericksburg school, presumably the one Rev. James Marye opened in 1740. There George is said to have occupied himself with ciphering while the other boys played games. Willis went on: ". . . but one ebullition is handed down whilst at that school and that was his romping with one of the largest girls. This was so unusual that it excited no little astonishment amongst the other lads." (Cf. 10 *V* 109–10.) While it is entirely possible that George was taught by a convict servant and then by Rev. James Marye, the stories cannot be accepted otherwise than as unconfirmable traditions which are apt to lose, in frequent retelling, whatever validity they may have had. Augustine Washington had taken the pains and had entailed the expense of sending his two older boys to school in England. Unless, improbably, he had sustained an unknown financial disaster or some unrecorded loss of interest in his children, it is not reasonable to assume that he would have neglected the training of George, his eldest son by his second marriage. In the absence of any evidence, one way or another, it is to be taken for granted that between seven and eleven years of age, George received as good schooling as could be provided at or near his home, from which, as will appear in a different connection, his mother was unwilling he should go.

[113] She was born June 21, 1739, and was named Mildred in honor of her grandmother or of her paternal aunt, Mildred Washington-Lewis-Gregory-Willis.

[114] Cartagena, it scarcely need be explained, is in the present republic of Colombia, which did not become independent until, in 1831, the republic of New Granada, including Panama as well as Colombia, was proclaimed. The name United States of Colombia was adopted in 1906.

[115] This old town is Northeast of the Caribbean entrance to the present-day Panama Canal.

[116] *Va. Gazette,* Feb. 1, 1739–40.

July 19, 1739, to open hostilities against Spain, and on the 23rd he started for the West Indies. By October 19, when war was declared formally, Vernon was at Port Royal, Jamaica, and was ready for action. He descended swiftly on the coast of Panama and boldly assailed the defences of Porto Bello. Finding them feeble, he pressed his attack and within forty-eight hours after his arrival off the town, forced its full surrender. This easy success fired the imagination and fed the pride of Britain.

Vernon himself would have been content, after capturing Porto Bello, to maintain naval superiority in the West Indies, because he did not feel he could conquer Cuba, which he considered the greatest prize of that vast region. The home government was not willing to follow so simple a policy after so shining a victory: Vernon must return to the Caribbean with overwhelming land and naval forces and must "make an attempt upon some of the most considerable of the Spanish settlements." [117] Drake had wrung a ransom from Cartagena in 1585; the French expedition of 1697 had taken £1,000,000 from the place; Vernon decided that as the government gave him a free choice of objectives, he would snatch the same rich prize.

After the first confused reports were set right, Virginians' next news was that 3000 troops for the land expedition to accompany Vernon were to be colonials. All the company officers, except one Lieutenant for each Company, were to be nominated by the Governors of the Colonies that supplied the men.[118] Virginia's quota was to be 400 men.[119] Immediately, every wealthy planter's son who had military ambitions wondered how he could get one of these commissions from Gov. William Gooch or through former Gov. Alexander Spotswood, who had proposed that an American contingent be raised. Spotswood was entrusted with the task of recruiting the men and was given the rank of Major General,[120] but death at Annapolis, June 7, 1740, spared him the pain of saying "No" to some applicants and denied him the pleasure of smiling "Yes" to others. No successor of like rank was named for the

---

[117] Spotswood's instructions of Apr. 5, 1740. See 30 *V* 1.
[118] George II to Gov. William Gooch, Apr. 2, 1740, MS in the Library of the University of Virginia; copy VHS.
[119] 25 *V* 286, n. 7. For the Virginia act to raise levies and recruits, see *Journ. H.B.*, 1727–40, p. 424, 431; 5 *H* 94–96.
[120] In an interesting article on the Cartagena expedition, E. Alfred Jones stated (30 *V* 2) that Spotswood's instructions authorized him to "fill" half the blank commissions sent him. The other half would be "filled" by the Governor.

expedition. The troops were designated the "American Regiment" and were placed under the command of Gooch as Colonel.[121]

Among those who sought Gooch's signature on the King's commission, none was more determined than George's older half-brother.[122] Lawrence had diligent rivals. To procure a captaincy, Richard Bushrod of Westmoreland raised a Company at his own expense.[123] Hugh Rose collected twenty recruits and got at the outset the rank of Ensign only.[124] So far as the records show, Lawrence did no recruiting, but he must have procured the strongest endorsements from influential colonials, because when the Governor announced to the Council, June 17, 1740, the four leaders he had chosen for the Virginia Companies, Lawrence was the first named.[125] Beside him and Bushrod, the fortunate young Captains were Charles Walker and James Mercer, who later became temporary Adjutant.[126]

There was much satisfaction at Ferry Farm over Lawrence's advancement, but, as often happens in war, long delay occurred between the promise of a command and embarkation for foreign service. Although shipping was supposed to be available by Aug. 20, 1740,[127] volunteers were so few that convicts had to be drafted to complete the Virginia quota.[128] In preparation for departure with this strangely mixed force, Lawrence undertook to settle his affairs. He transferred some land to his father and leased to Augustine Senior still other tracts.[129] In return he either received a deed to Epsewasson or had the promise that it should be his when he came back to Virginia.[130] Some lots in which Lawrence had an interest were not fully secured before he had to leave. Nor did he discharge a debt of £100 to William Gooch, the son of the

---

[121] He felt that he was snubbed by General Wentworth. See Gooch to Duke of Newcastle [?], Sept. 16, 1741, 3 *Gooch MSS,* 663. In 1746 Gooch was made Major General.
[122] Cf. John Lewis to Lawrence Washington, June 28, 1742, L. W. Smith Coll., *Havemeyer Papers.*
[123] 30 *V* 8, where the contemporary list of the qualifications of some of the officers is printed.
[124] *Ibid.,* 10. Rose later was made Lieutenant.
[125] 5 *E. J.,* 20 ff. His commission, dated June 9 and delivered July 10, 1740, is at Mount Vernon. For the list of officers, see 2 *Gooch MSS,* 639, transcript of P.R.O., C.O. 5: 1327, f. 138. The Council journal entry of Aug. 6, 1740, mentioned in 30 *V* 18 is scarcely more than a memorandum.
[126] 30 *V* 6. He was a brother of the stormy John Mercer but was not permanently settled in Virginia.
[127] 15 *V* 7; 30 *ibid.,* 18.
[128] 5 *H* 94; *Landmarks,* 164; 30 *V* 256; 44 *ibid.,* 180.
[129] These papers were listed in the *Birch Cat.* 663, items 13 and 15, but their present depository is not known.
[130] Toner (45 *N.E. Hist. and Gen. Reg.,* 164, 202), and Penniman (*George Washington at Mount Vernon*) 14, both stated that Augustine deeded the property to Lawrence in October, 1740. Neither of them quoted any authority.

Governor.[131] It probably was in October, 1740, that Lawrence said farewell and sailed from Chesapeake with his companions in arms.[132]

After Lawrence went away life at Ferry Farm dropped back to its unexciting norm. Only rumor born of rumor mocked the minds of those whose sons had gone. The infant Mildred died Oct. 23, 1740; [133] George continued at school; Augustine probably had more than the usual troubles with the iron furnace. Other such enterprises were closing down or were operating amid continued discouragements.[134] As for Lawrence, he wrote often but the receipt of his letters was uncertain. Summer was approaching, probably, when the family heard that Lawrence had reached Jamaica and then had sailed to Cartagena.[135] While vague snatches of bad news were arriving thereafter, the Washingtons suffered a fire that involved formidable loss; [136] but that soon was made to appear small in comparison with good news received in another letter from Lawrence: He was safe after a disaster that had shamed British arms.

The land forces of Admiral Vernon's expedition of 9000 men had been entrusted to Maj. Gen. Lord Cathcart, but he had died before the fleet had assembled at Port Royal, Jamaica. Command then passed to the senior Brigadier, Thomas Wentworth, a mediocre, inexperienced officer who clashed from the outset with the realistic, vigorous Vernon. The success the Admiral had achieved at Porto Bello had convinced

131 See Lawrence to Augustine Washington, May 30, 1741, *Mag. Am. His.*, v. 2, p. 436–37. The location of the lots is not mentioned, though Lawrence wrote that he intended to "make use of" them for "my dwelling." The fact that Lawrence owed £100 to the son of Governor Gooch of course raises a question whether this was for Lawrence's commission as Captain.

132 A letter from James Blair to the Board of Trade, Nov. 6, 1740 (2 *Gooch MSS*, 648), indicates that departure was in October, but this is not certain.

133 See *supra*, n. 113.

134 Gooch to the Board of Trade, Aug. 27, 1741. The Governor said that one of the four iron furnaces of the Colony was being abandoned. He went on: "and another under the same discouragement is rented out to a single individual for three years who living contiguous to it has the courage to undertake it; the other two [furnaces] are hardly enough to go on." Gooch did not identify the furnaces (3 *Gooch MSS*, 654).

135 A crude check on the time required to hear from Lawrence is offered in the letter written him by Joseph Deane, July 24, 1741. In that communication, Deane acknowledged receipt of one from Lawrence, penned nearly four months previously, Mch. 31, 1741, in the harbor of Cartagena (L. W. Smith Coll., *Havemeyer Papers*). It is reasonable to assume that letters from Cartagena to Virginia were in transit an equal length of time, though the duration of voyages varied greatly. On this basis, information in Virginia would be three to four months behind actual occurrences in the Caribbean.

136 This "late calamity . . . by fire" is mentioned only in a letter of Richard Yates of Appleby School to Augustine Washington, Oct. 9, 1741 (L. W. Smith Coll., *Havemeyer Papers*). Where and when the fire occurred, research has not disclosed, but, by a process of elimination, the property on Little Hunting Creek appears to have been the scene of the fire. The destroyed building may have been a barn or the old residence from which the furniture was saved. If the fire occurred in summer, as the date of Yates's letter suggests, there is, of course, the possibility that it was caused by lightning.

him that Spaniards in a fixed position should be attacked before they had time to prepare for a siege in which they traditionally were stubborn adversaries. As soon, therefore, as Vernon arrived off Cartagena on the 3rd of March, 1740/41, he urged Wentworth to throw troops ashore and to assault immediately. Wentworth disagreed concerning a landing place and then hesitated over the number of troops and the quantity of supplies he would require. It was the afternoon of March 9 when the first boats were grounded, and it was the 13th before Wentworth had on the beaches all his guns and stores.

Vernon kept warning him that delay meant calamity, because the wet season was close at hand and was certain to bring sickness and death. Wentworth was deaf to all counsel except that of his own caution. He did not open fire until March 23 on the northern fort which covered the channel of the "Little Mouth" or Boca Chica, at the southern end of the island of Tierra Bomba. After this fort was reduced, the fleet moved in, the sailors cut the boom of the Boca Chica, and the men-of-war entered the harbor.

The next day, Admiral Vernon was of opinion that the city still could be captured despite the long delays, and in dispatches home he made the mistake of predicting the early fall of Cartagena. Wentworth, on the other hand, continued to debate where and how he should deliver his final assault, and he did not decide until the alarmed Spaniards, working with all the speed of frenzy, had strengthened greatly their positions. When Wentworth at last threw 6600 of his troops against the enemy, he met with a paralyzing repulse. His losses appalled even veterans who had known he would have to pay a heavy "butcher's bill."

Soon the rains reenforced the Spanish guns. Sickness mounted. Yellow fever made its dread appearance. Scores died mysteriously every day. As continued exposure would spell the death of virtually all who had gone ashore, the survivors were reembarked on the 17th of April. A few ships were left to complete the destruction of the forts that had been captured. The remainder of the fleet abandoned the siege, sailed away and returned to Jamaica.[137]

In this unrelieved and undeniable defeat, the convicts in the Ameri-

[137] Perhaps the best brief account of the Cartagena expedition is the one on which the paragraphs in the text are based, namely, the article on Vernon by Sir John Knox Laughton in *DNB*. See also Fortescue, *History of the British Army*, v. 2, p. 60–74. Tobias Smollett's description in *Roderick Random* is cited often but must seldom have been read. It contains little of real value, either in description or in criticism. Smollett, at the time, was surgeon's mate on H.M.S. *Cumberland*.

can Regiment had no interest and little loss, but the volunteers suffered both in pride and in person. General Wentworth distrusted them because they did not bend readily to the discipline demanded of redcoats. As he believed the Americans would not be reliable in action, he permitted only 300 of them to go ashore. The remainder of the volunteers, along with the convicts, the General kept aboard their crowded little vessels—to chafe, to rage and, in hundreds of cases, to succumb to yellow fever. Of the original force,[138] not more than 1300 were destined to see again the shores of English America.[139]

Before the facts were known, many rumors had clashed in contradiction. Admiral Vernon's hopeful statement of the expected capture of Cartagena had been received in England before any news of the defeat was at hand.[140] Premature rejoicing deepened later mourning over the disaster. Among a score of untrue whispers was one that Governor Gooch had denounced the Virginia contingent for cowardice.[141]

Lawrence Washington had been denied a part in the operations ashore. For the period of fighting, he had been among those held on the vessels and he had been given no more exciting task than that of acting as Captain of the Marines on the flagship. His view of the disaster was typically that of the young officer who wished to think that his side had inflicted heavy losses to pay for those it had sustained; but he could not make out a case. In his letter home, after listing the Spanish forts and ships destroyed, he had to admit: ". . . the enemy killed of ours some 600 and some wounded and the climate killed us in greater number. Vast changes we have in each Regiment; some are so weak as to be reduced to two thirds of their men; a great quantity of officers amongst the rest are dead. . . . War is horrid in fact but much more so in imagination. We there have learned to live on ordinary diet; to watch much and disregard the noise or shot of cannon."

When he wrote this from Jamaica, he did not know what the next objective of the fleet and army would be. Although he felt the American Regiment had "not received the treatment we expected," he was resolved to "persevere in the undertaking." If the Regiment was to

138 It is not known how many of the desired 3000 colonials actually had been recruited. Cf. 30 V 2.

139 Ibid.

140 A perplexed commentary on the conflicting news will be found in a letter of Jan. 8, 1742 to William Byrd, 37 V 111.

141 Cf. Jos. Deane to Lawrence Washington, July 24, 1741 (L. W. Smith Coll., Havemeyer Papers). Actually, Gooch supported vigorously his men's claims to half pay.

be put on "the very best footing," as some predicted, he hoped it would not be at the expense of the Colonies; and if recruiting officers were to be sent home, he was anxious to be one of them.[142]

Fortune was not that kind to the young Captain. Months were spent vainly in Cuba, though Vernon did not have strength for a serious attack on that island. Finally, word reached Ferry Farm that the American Regiment had been broken up and that Lawrence had sent the Council of Virginia a memorial in which he had set forth his losses as a claim to the vacant office of Adjutant General of the Colony. Later he brought back to the Old Dominion some of the survivors of the expedition.[143] It was not a triumphant return, nor did he receive immediately the post of Adjutant of Virginia,[144] in succession to Isham Randolph, deceased.[145]

When the veteran of Cartegena came back to Ferry Farm, his full brother was there to welcome him. In June, 1742,[146] Augustine, Jr.— "Austin" to the family—had returned from Appleby, the English school where, it will be remembered, his father and his brother Lawrence also had been instructed.[147] "Austin" had done well in his classes and had dreamed of being a lawyer,[148] but, after reaching his majority, he had sailed for the Rappahannock. This was done, no doubt, at the instance of his father, who wished the well-trained young man to assist in the business of the plantations or of the iron furnace. According to one of his former teachers,[149] "August" had "grown a pretty young fellow." To his half-brothers and sister, he was a pleasant stranger. George soon came to love "Austin," but he found his interest and his admiration

---

[142] Lawrence Washington to Augustine Washington, May 30, 1741, *loc. cit.*
[143] 30 *V* 19.   [144] 5 *E. J.,* 117.
[145] The dates of Lawrence's various moves after the abandonment of the siege of Cartagena are not established, but General Wentworth, then in London, wrote him in a letter of Apr. 1, 1743: "I am favored with yours of Jan. 17, which gives me pleasure as it confirms the account of your safe arrival in Virginia . . ." (30 *V* 19). Wentworth's use of the word "confirms" manifestly indicates that prior to Apr. 1, 1743, he had heard of the return of Washington to the Colony, an event which probably occurred at the end of 1742 or early in January, 1743. There is no foundation whatever in existing records for the charge in Boucher (*op. cit.,* 49) that in "some scrape with a brother officer it was said [Lawrence] did not acquit himself quite as well as he should, and so sold out." Lawrence did not "sell out" but had a status that justified him in seeking half pay after the American Regiment was "broken up." Similarly to be discarded on the strength of Lawrence's own letter of May 30, 1741 (*loc. cit.*) is Conway's statement (*Barons,* 99) that Lawrence Washington probably was second in command to Gooch.
[146] John Lewis to Lawrence Washington, June 28, 1742; L. W. Smith Coll., *Havemeyer Papers.*
[147] See *supra,* p. 32 and 56.
[148] Richard Yates to Augustine Washington, Oct. 9, 1741; L. W. Smith Coll., *Havemeyer Papers.*
[149] Joseph Deane to Lawrence Washington, July 24, 1741; L. W. Smith Coll., *Havemeyer Papers.*

more than ever fixed on Lawrence—on the brother who had seen the
forts of Cartagena, and had heard the cannons roar, and had watched
the battle. Lawrence could talk of transports and ships of the line
and distant countries; Lawrence knew Admiral Vernon, whom he
revered as a great warrior; Lawrence was the man who would direct
the muster and the drill of the militia; in a word Lawrence was more
than ever a hero in the eyes of ten-year-old George!

Augustine, the father, was as proud of Lawrence as George was and,
of course, in larger understanding of Lawrence's excellencies, diligence
and comparative inexperience as a man of business. The head of the
family had not himself been without new honor and new enterprise.
About the time Lawrence had been successful in procuring appointment
as Adjutant General, Augustine had been named a trustee of Fredericksburg [150] which had outgrown its original fifty acres and was enlarging
its borders.[151] Now, as always, Augustine was buying and selling and
trading land.[152] Lawrence, in turn, adhered to the custom of the times
and to the tradition of the family in seeking diligently to collect what
Crown or Colony owed. He pressed for half-pay as a Captain, on account of his services in the Army,[153] and he became more convinced
than ever that large money was to be made through the wise purchase
of land and of slaves. [154]

In study for George, and in business activity for Augustine, for
Lawrence and for "Austin," the winter of 1742-43 passed. With the
coming of spring and the approach of Easter, 1743, George was permitted to go down into the Chotank district of the Potomac to visit
some of his cousins. He was there, in the full enjoyment of the sports
of the farm, when calamity came across the fields. A messenger rode
up with instructions for George to return home at once: his father
was dangerously sick. George set out as soon as practicable. He had
seen little of his father and in later life he was to remember only that
his sire had been tall, fair of complexion, well proportioned and fond of

---

[150] *Papers of G. W.*, LC. The original is in the Fredericksburg Court House.
[151] 5 *H* 197, act of May, 1742.
[152] 2 *King George Orders,* 217, Sept. 7, 1739; 9 *Westmoreland Deeds and Wills,* 260, 281,
Aug. 27, Dec. 3, 1742; *ibid.,* 280, Sept. 27, 1742, Apr. 12, 1743.
[153] See Alexander Wilson to Lawrence Washington, Nov. 6, 1742; L. W. Smith Coll., *Havemeyer Papers.* This evidence refutes the statement in Jared Sparks, *Writings of Washington*
(cited hereafter as *Sparks*), v. 2, p. 422, that Lawrence declined half pay because he could not
conscientiously take the required oath while serving as Adjutant of Virginia. The memorial of
the Virginia officers in England for pay and half pay, Jan. 26, 1743, is in 3 *Gooch MSS,* 716.
[154] See his testamentary provision, *infra,* p. 264, for the investment in this manner, at his
executors' discretion, of the profits from his estate. In the *Birch Cat.* 663, items 13, 15, 30 and 36
were deeds, etc., for some of Lawrence's land transactions of 1738-40.

children; [155] but, of course, it was a deep grief for George when he reached home, to find the family despairing and the great form of Augustine spread out on a bed. The stricken man had made his will and now faced death in content of soul.[156] It was on the 12th of April, 1743, that he died.[157] The next day, in Albemarle County, a man child was born and was christened Thomas Jefferson.

[155] G. W. P. Custis, 129.

[156] Years afterward the tradition was that he thanked God, as he lay dying, that he never had struck a man in anger, "for if I had," he was reported to have said, "I am sure that from my remarkable muscular powers I should have killed my antagonist and then his blood at this awful moment would have lain heavily on my soul." He added; "As it is, I die in peace with all men." (G. W. P. Custis, 1851, in 11 N.E. Hist. and Gen. Reg., 5.) The tradition that George was in Chotank when summoned home was printed (1836) in McGuire, op. cit., xv. Shroeder, writing about 1857 (George Washington, v. 1, p. 17), quoted the tradition that Augustine's gun, then in existence, was long and heavy and was suggestive "of a huntsman of extraordinary size of body and power of arm . . ." Evidently he based this on Weems, 250.

[157] 32 G. W., 28. The cause of death was said to be "gout of the stomach." Concerning this malady Dr. E. C. L. Miller, the distinguished medical lexicographer, wrote under date of June 6, 1946: " 'Gout of the stomach' is described in the Dictionary of Practical Medicine by James Copland in three volumes, (1846) v. 2, p. 42. It was commonly held that as the regular attack of gout receded it tended to go from the foot or toe to some internal organ. It was called retrocedent or displaced gout. 'The stomach is most liable to be so afflicted, severe pain and spasm, with sickness being complained of.' In fact, some went so far as to assert that all ordinary diseases are due to the gout 'striking in.' It recalls the earlier thought of possession by evil spirits."

CHAPTER IV

VIRGINIA DURING THE YOUTH OF WASHINGTON
(1740–1752)

By HIS own wish, the body of Augustine Washington was carried back to the family graveyard on Bridges Creek and was buried there. His will was probated by Lawrence, May 6, 1743.[1] Lawrence, Daniel McCarty and Nathaniel Chapman were the executors. As appraisers, the court named Benjamin Berryman, Anthony Strother, Hancock Lee and Adam Reed.[2] The will itself was devoid of any such confession of faith as had prefaced the last testaments of Augustine's father and grandfather. Usage in such matters was changing. Augustine was content to begin, "In the name of God, Amen" and to proceed with the division of an estate that included seven or more tracts, of a total acreage in excess of 10,000.[3] Slaves numbered at least forty-nine.[4] On Ferry Farm of approximately 260 acres were twenty Negroes of whom seven were able-bodied, eight were of moderate value, and five were not capable of any work.[5] At the quarters[6] were six good Negro hands; in Westmoreland, seven of Augustine's thirteen slaves were able to do a day's work; on the Stafford property were two Negro families, apparently, who probably supplied the drivers and the cooks for the iron furnace. All these properties were well stocked, except for the fact that horses were not numerous. At the Accokeek works were eight steers.

Lawrence, as the eldest son, received much the largest share of his

[1] 2 King George Orders, 333.
[2] Ibid. The text of the will appears conveniently in Ford, The Washington Family, p. 94 ff, and in 9 T 34–38.
[3] This assumes that he had not passed title to Lawrence for Hunting Creek. Known acreage, including that plantation, was 9640, but to this should be added Chotank farm and other property of unascertained area.
[4] In the absence of inventories for some of the farms, the total cannot be determined.
[5] All these statements of the value of the various Washington slaves are based on the appraisal in the inventory of the estate. See King George Inventories, 1721–44, p. 285–91.
[6] These quarters were located on Mary Ball Washington's property below Fredericksburg. See infra, p. 43 ff. As used in Augustine Washington's will "quarters" were a settlement of slaves or of slaves and indentured servants at a distance from their master. Often the word was used in the singular.

father's estate. Everything on Little Hunting Creek was to be his, as was land bought of James Hooe next to Lawrence's property on Mattox Creek. Lawrence was to have, also, Augustine's interest in the iron furnace, subject, first, to the purchase from the profits, of three young slaves for "Austin," and, second, to the payment of £400 to Betty.[7] Half of the debts due Augustine were to go to Lawrence on the assumption by him of a proper share of Augustine's obligations. To "Austin"—Augustine, Jr.—went all the lands in Westmoreland not otherwise bequeathed, together with twenty-five head of cattle, four Negroes and a moiety of the debts due his father, less 50 per cent of the liabilities of the testator.

George received the Ferry Farm,[8] half the Deep Run tract,[9] ten slaves and three lots Augustine had acquired in Fredericksburg. In addition, George was to have his fifth of residual personal property that the father wished to be divided among his wife and her four sons. Samuel, John Augustine and Charles received farms and Negroes besides shares of the personalty. Almost in the language of his own father's will, Augustine wrote that the estates of all these children of his second marriage were to remain in their mother's care during the minority of each of them. Protection of their interest was to be assured in the event their mother remarried. Arrangement was made, also, in a somewhat complicated manner for the transfer of the real estate of any son who had no surviving children. If, for example, Lawrence died without lawful heirs of the body, George was to inherit the land and mill on Hunting Creek [10] unless Augustine preferred that property to the holdings on Mattox Creek. If Augustine chose Hunting Creek in the circumstances set forth, then he was to transfer to George the Mattox plantation.

The widow was to have certain slaves in lieu of dower right in the Negroes as a whole. Besides her fifth of the undivided personalty, and her tenancy of her sons' property during their minority, Mary Washington was given current crops on three plantations and the right of working the Bridges Creek quarter for five years, during which time she could establish a quarter on Deep Run.

A businesslike document the will was. If Augustine had not attained

[7] She received, also, two Negro children.
[8] For a codicil authorizing the sale of part of this property for George's benefit, see *Ford*, 415–16.
[9] Its total acreage was 4360.
[10] Augustine described it merely as "the land and mill . . . lying in the County of Prince William," but he manifestly had forgotten that organization of a new County in 1742 had put this property in Fairfax.

to the goal of the rich planters, who sought to have every male heir maintain the baronial style of the family on a great estate, he had assured a living to all his sons who would make discreet use of what he had left them. So far as eleven-year-old George was concerned, the farm he would receive when he became twenty-one years of age was of moderate size, in a district not particularly fertile.[11] His other property was not valuable. The boy was too young at the time to realize it, but his inheritance was just large enough to raise a question: Would he be lulled into contentment as a planter of the second class, or would he be spurred by what he had to seek more?

Circumstance shaped in a natural manner the first approach to an answer. Lawrence was now seated permanently on Little Hunting Creek [12] and, it was whispered, was courting Anne Fairfax, usually called Nancy, daughter of Col. William Fairfax, cousin and agent of the Proprietor himself! [13] William Fairfax was fifty-two years of age at the time, and, besides acting for His Lordship in the issuance of land grants and the settlement of quit rents, he held office as a Justice, as Burgess and as Collector of Customs for the South Potomac.[14] After a residence comparatively brief on the Potomac he had become, all in all, the most influential man in that part of the Northern Neck. On a "point" of land on the southern shore of the river, below the Hunting Creek property, Colonel Fairfax had acquired a pleasant tract and had built a handsome "great house" which justified the name Belvoir.[15]

[11] George Fitzhugh, writing in 1858, said: "The soil on the Rappahannock is generally light and sandy, better calculated for Indian corn than wheat . . . Wheat and corn are almost the only crops. It is not good grass land generally" (De Bow's Review, new series, v. 1, p. 374). On the plat of his survey of Ferry Farm, 1771, Washington wrote nothing of the fertility of the ground except to say of the northeast field: "Some pretty good land from where the present Field abuts upon the saw pit branch" (George Washington Atlas, Plate 9).

[12] See Richard Yates to Lawrence Washington, Nov. 13, 1743, L. W. Smith Coll., Havemeyer Papers. Yates, a schoolmaster at Appleby, here acknowledged a letter of July 19, 1743, from Lawrence, who had told his former instructor that he had "taken [his] residence" on the Hunting Creek property. The teacher sent a message to Augustine, Sr. in language which makes it plain that Lawrence, writing not more than three months after his father's death, had not mentioned that event to Yates, though the schoolmaster had been acquainted with Augustine.

[13] An inclusive fact-weighted notice of him appears in Landmarks, 340–41.

[14] Beginning April 27, 1741, William Fairfax issued grants dated "In the Proprietor's office," which entry probably means that he then opened his office in Prince William. After July 1, 1741, he used the term "my office in Prince William" (L.O. Records, N.N., E, 300). He previously had been in Westmoreland and then in King George.

[15] If notations in ibid., 299 are correct, part of the Belvoir tract had been granted in 1669 to William Grier and by him had been sold to James Rankin, mariner of London. In 1736, no owner appearing, the tract, which included 1100 acres, reverted to the proprietary. It then was granted Dr. Charles Green who has been introduced already. On Nov. 20, 1741, Dr. Green sold William Fairfax 320 acres between Pohick Creek and Doeg Run for quit rent and £64 (Prince William Deeds, 1740–41, p. 544). Fairfax Harrison stated (Landmarks, 341) that Belvoir had been completed when William Fairfax moved to Prince William in 1741. Either Harrison was mistaken by a year or two in his date of the completion of Belvoir or else the house was not constructed on that part of the estate purchased from Green.

As between the young people, propinquity and mutual attraction did the rest. On July 19, 1743, a little more than two months after Augustine's death, Anne Fairfax became the wife of Lawrence Washington.[16] It was both for Lawrence and for George a fortunate day. To Lawrence it meant alliance with the most powerful interests of the Northern Neck and marriage to a girl who already had valuable lands and before many years was to hold patents for a total of 4000 acres.[17] George, in his turn, found new and desirable associations. Increasingly, after Lawrence's marriage, George visited on Hunting Creek and at Belvoir, where he came under the fine influence of Colonel Fairfax, who loved young men.

George's brother Lawrence, about fourteen years his senior, stood almost *in loco parentis,* and had developed the character his friendly face displayed. He was long of jaw and large of eye. Although his mouth was set too high on his face for comeliness, the curve of his lips was kindly, and his brow was lofty and broad. A thin neck indicated a lack of physical strength; his shoulders sloped.[18] Everything about him suggested a genial approachability and a capacity for making friends. One thinks of him as the person to whom, in a crowd, a stranger would go to make an inquiry.

To Fairfax and to all his seniors, Lawrence was carefully courteous and deferential. Among men of his own age and station, he showed energy, ambition and the urbanity of good schooling. His greatest gifts were social, but they did not make him soft. Less prone to litigation than was his great-grandfather John Washington, he would contend for his rights. In business, his judgment was average, or better, though he sometimes was hasty or careless and was disposed to outrun his re- sources. If he lacked the mathematical mind his younger brother George was beginning to develop, he was genuinely intellectual. His letters, having the grace of his own person, were well reasoned and well written. Lawrence possessed, besides, a good deal of political sense and he had religion without bigotry or pious protestation. Arms were his avocation. He preferred horses to books, apparently, but he had culture and he probably gave the impression of a wider learning than he had mastered. For the enlargement of George's mind and

16 32 *G. W.,* 28; William Beverley to Lord Fairfax, July 27, 1743; 3 *W* (1) p. 235.

17 She had one grant of 1840 acres and another of 1400 and a half-interest in 1900 acres. While her father was land agent, the Fairfax kin of the Proprietor acquired 200,000 acres (*L.O. Records, N.N.,* E, 269, 277, 477).

18 See the portrait attributed to John Wollaston, now at Mount Vernon and reproduced in this Volume.

the polishing of his manners, Lawrence was almost an ideal elder brother.

At Ferry Farm, life had not been stinted or meagre but neither was it opulent or gracious; on Little Hunting Creek, social relations were more polished, and discourse often was of larger subjects. The house itself was perceptibly different from the little dwelling in which George had lived during his father's residence in 1735–38. Lawrence either tore down the structure in which George had spent three years, or else fire [19] had saved Lawrence that trouble. A new residence was rising. It was of the conventional Virginia design [20]—a rectangle cut by a central hall, with two rooms on either side and the same arrangement on the second floor except for an added small "hall room." [21] Beneath the residence were the cellar and walls of the original house.[22] The structure was of wood, not of stone, and it was not of fine interior finish, but it was comfortable and soon was well furnished.[23] In this new house George found delight not only because it was new, but also because its master was his beloved Lawrence. The neighborhood was one of youth and freshness and beauty and activity—the very influences to make George most emulous when he was most impressionable. There was still another stimulus: In honor of the Admiral of the Cartagena expedition, Lawrence styled his home Mount Vernon and, in so doing, unconsciously made the very name a challenge to the imagination of his younger brother. Lawrence talked, too, of war and of the honors and the glories of a soldier's life. It did not seem a distant theme to a boy who lived within two days' ride of the trail the Indians sometimes followed in their raids.

The conversation at Mount Vernon was of lands as well as of armies. Lawrence had the confidence of his father-in-law, and of course knew of the patents issued from Colonel Fairfax's office to speculators who were looking eagerly to the West. Everyone hoped, through the years, that Lord Fairfax would win in the long controversy over the

[19] Cf. *supra*, p. 67.   [20] Cf. *infra*, p. 91.

[21] The plan is sketched admirably in the *Report* for 1938 of the Mount Vernon Ladies' Association, p. 20–21. As Paul Wilstach succinctly put the fact in describing the Mount Vernon of late years: "Detach the present banquet hall on the north and the library on the south, together with the second story thereof, and the developments of the third story, and the original house remains." (*Mount Vernon*, 23.) No data on the date of construction have been found. Conway fixed the time as 1743–44 (*George Washington and Mount Vernon*, lxx), but he cited no authority and probably was doing no more than making a good guess.

[22] See *supra*, p. 53.

[23] It is to be hoped that Lawrence's presumably complete inventory of 1752, which was mentioned in *Birch Cat.* 663 of the sale of Washington relics (*infra*, p. 265), will be found and published.

boundaries of his domain. Hope there was, also, that the Five Nations could be induced to modify the Treaty of Albany and, at the least, to make the Allegheny range and not the Blue Ridge the eastern line they would not cross.[24] If these two uncertainties were resolved favorably, the Shenandoah Valley, which nestled between the Blue Ridge and the Alleghenies, would be open safely to settlers. Much of the region would be in the proprietary. By their knowledge of conditions there and farther westward, William Fairfax and Lawrence Washington might enrich themselves; and if the Indians could be induced to make a larger bargain, the great valley of the Ohio might be tapped.

George, at 11 years of age, doubtless understood some of the talk at Mount Vernon concerning the surveying and patenting of western lands. When he went from Ferry Farm or from Lawrence's home to his brother "Austin's" plantation on Pope's Creek, he found the chief interests of the household to be farming and horses and the life of the river. "Austin," like Lawrence, had found himself a bride of birth and station. This new mistress of the older Washington home on the Potomac was Anne Aylett, one of the four daughters of Col. William Aylett of Westmoreland,[25] former Burgess and a planter of some wealth. In the household of Anne and her husband, George doubtless spent many pleasant weeks, though his mother probably kept him at Ferry Farm during the months of his schooling.[26] He was developing fast, both physically and in knowledge of "ciphering" which soon became his absorbing interest. When in a year or two, he was old enough to look about him with some understanding and discrimination, the result

[24] See *supra,* p. 13.

[25] By his first marriage to Anne Ashton, daughter of Col. Henry Ashton, he had two daughters, Elizabeth, who became the wife of William Booth, and Anne, who was "Austin" Washington's bride. The second marriage of William Aylett was to Elizabeth Eskridge, daughter of George Eskridge of Sandy Point. Her two daughters were a second Anne, born 1738, whose husband was Richard Henry Lee, and Mary, subsequently Mrs. Thomas Ludwell Lee. Much confusion has been caused some genealogists by the fact that Col. William Aylett was the son of an earlier William, and had two daughters named Anne. See 4 *V* 474; 5 *ibid.,* 355–56. The date of the marriage of Anne Aylett to Augustine ("Austin") Washington is not known, but it was between June, 1742, when "Austin" returned to Virginia, and Mch. 29, 1744, when Colonel Aylett in his will mentioned Augustine as his son-in-law. See 10 *Westmoreland Wills,* 51.

[26] Eaton, *op. cit.,* 20, and Eubank, *op. cit.,* 38, reported the tradition that while George was at the Pope's Creek plantation he attended the school Henry Williams conducted near Mattox Creek at the present Laurel Grove. No direct evidence of this has been found. In view of Mary Washington's subsequent unwillingness to permit George go to sea (vide *infra,* 193 ff), it scarcely is probable that she would have consented to have him at a distance from her and attending school in Westmoreland when Rev. James Marye's school at Fredericksburg was accessible by a ferry from her own farm. Had George been in residence at Henry Williams's school, the yearly expense would have been 1000 pounds of tobacco for board and 200 pounds for instruction. (9 *W* (1) p. 241.)

was almost as if someone had lifted a wide curtain and had disclosed a new world.[27]

West of the fall line, near which George had his home, the settlements fringed toward the frontier of the Blue Ridge and the Valley of the Shenandoah. Democracy was real where life was raw. In Tidewater, the flat country East of the fall line, there were no less than eight strata of society. The uppermost and the lowliest, the great proprietors and the Negro slaves, were supposed to be of immutable station. The others were small farmers, merchants, sailors, frontier folk, servants and convicts. Each of these constituted a distinct class at a given time, but individuals and families often shifted materially in station during a single generation. Titles hedged the ranks of the notables. Members of the Council of State were termed both "Colonel" and "Esquire." Large planters who did not bear arms almost always were given the courtesy title of "Gentlemen." So were Church Wardens, Vestrymen, Sheriffs and Trustees of towns.[28] The full honors of a man of station were those of Vestryman, Justice and Burgess. Such an individual normally looked to England and especially to London and sought to live by the social standards of the mother country.[29] "Like one of the patriarchs," a Virginia planter wrote in 1726: "I have my flocks and herds; my bond men and bond women. Thus, my Lord, we are very happy in our Canaan if we could but forget the fleshpots and onions of Egypt." [30]

The magnitude of the holdings of the Northern Neck planters has been described. Their social peers of the James were their rivals in acreage. Benjamin Harrison, fourth of that name, owned at least twenty-three tracts of land, eight of which were described as plantations.[31] Two years before George Washington was born, a grant to William Byrd of 3000 acres in Brunswick County and one of 10,000 acres in Spotsylvania to Francis Conway had been casual entries in the

[27] In the following survey of "Virginia During the Youth of Washington" (p. 79 to 186), the aim is to describe conditions that existed in 1740–50. As numerous phases of life in the Colony remained substantially unchanged for the half century that preceded the outbreak of the Revolution, some latitude of dates is allowed in the citation of source material. Where there is reason to doubt whether conditions prior to 1740 or subsequent to 1750 were different from those within that decade, the tenses of the verbs or brief footnotes call attention to the possibility of anacronism. For convenient reference to this somewhat detailed study of Virginia life at the middle of the eighteenth century, a topical outline is given in Appendix I–8.

[28] The title appears to have been no more accurately used than was "Honorable" when applied to the public men of the late nineteenth century in the United States.

[29] Jones, *Virginia*, 32.

[30] William Byrd to Charles Earl of Orrery, July 5, 1726; 32 *V* 27.

[31] 3 *V* 124 ff.

Land Office.[32] Alexander Spotswood's holdings, though not on the James, had been 85,000 acres.[33] His son John, to pay the father's legacies, sold a trifle of 9000 acres, which subsequently were repurchased.[34]

Men of this level of society were fortunate and were not unmindful of it. A stranger might say that "all annoyances and inconveniences of the country may fairly be summed up under these three heads, thunder, heat and troublesome vermin." [35] Virginians would have to admit these were nuisances, but they proudly, gratefully and sometimes boastfully returned thanks for almost everything else in the Colony. Many a rich planter was doing more than making a pious profession when he repeated in his will substantially what George's own great-grandfather had said of "goods, chattels and debts . . . it hath pleased God far above my deserts to bestow upon me . . ." [36]

Sometimes these favored colonials were ostentatious. Sir John Randolph specified in his will that his widow should have, among other things, "my coach, chariot and chaise, with everything that belongs to them, and my coach horses, riding horses, mares, and colts . . ." [37] William Beverley, who died when George Washington was twenty-three, disposed of a large landed estate [38] and expressed a desire that "My Executors will buy for each of themselves a pair of good horses fit for coach or chair and charge my estate with their cost." [39] Similarly, Charles Carter of Cleve was to provide, a few years later, that his "coach or chariot [should] be kept with six horses, coachman and postilion, at the expense of the estate" for the use of his daughters and their chaperone.[40] Nor was the bestowal of favor limited to Virginia. John Grymes of Brandon,[41] dying in 1748, provided in his will that his executors purchase and present to Horace Walpole "a diamond ring of fifty guineas value as an acknowledgment of the many obligations" Grymes felt for Walpole's "long continuance of . . . favor and pro-

---

[32] 36 V 350. Conway, it will be remembered, was grandfather of President James Madison.
[33] See the sketch of him in *DAB*.
[34] *Spotsylvania Wills*, B, 389.
[35] F. L. Michel, 1702; quoted in 24 V 39.
[36] Ford, *The Washington Family*, 75 ff.
[37] Will probated Apr. 28, 1737; 36 V 378. Punctuation has been added.
[38] The two properties, among many, of which he mentioned the acreage in his will, amounted to more than 16,000 acres.
[39] 22 V 300.
[40] Will of Sept. 10, 1762; 31 V 64.
[41] This property was not one of the familiar Brandons of James River but was in Middlesex and had been purchased from the heirs of Maj. Gen. Robert Smith. Nothing now remains of the large brick mansion formerly on the site (27 V 404).

tection . . ." [42] Cash bequests and other transactions covered by this will amounted to £3730.

The wealth of such men assured Virginians, as a visitor phrased it, "the reputation of living nobly." [43] One of their own historians wrote of "the families" as if all of them flourished opulently on great plantations. [44] In reality, the owners of expansive estates dominated completely the political life of the Colony in 1750 and gave its society a certain glamour, but these men were, had been, and remained numerically a minority. The majority of the white population was composed of farmers whose holdings of land were small in comparison with those of the great planters. Racially, in background and in native intelligence, no line could be drawn between the owners of the larger and the lesser properties. This likewise was true of their appearance. Above the level of the ignorant and the vicious, the colonials were, according to a contemporary, "for the generality comely handsome persons of good features and fine complexions . . . of good manners and address . . . an idiot or deformed native being almost a miracle." [45] As for the women, the subtlest compliment paid to their health and height was that of the second William Byrd. "We are all well on this side the globe," he wrote his brother-in-law, "and because Maypoles are not the fashion here, our daughters grow enough to serve in their stead." [46]

Economically, the gradation was downward from great estates to self-dependent farms and then to small holdings. Almost 40 per cent of the 5066 known farms in the older Tidewater counties of the Colony, outside the Northern Neck, contained 200 acres or less in 1704. Farms of 100 acres or less represented 13 per cent of the total. [47] The mean of all farms at that time was about 250 acres. Those agricultural properties with an acreage between 1000 and 5000 numbered only 448. Again with the exception of the Northern Neck, Tidewater plantations of more than 5000 acres are believed to have numbered eighteen. Later acquisitions swelled the holdings of the rich planters who speculated in western lands, but these additions did not affect greatly the size of

[42] 27 V 408.
[43] See François Jean Marquis de Chastellux, *Voyage dans l'Amerique* (cited hereafter as *Chastellux*), v. 2, p. 135.
[44] Robert Beverley, *History of Virginia* (reprint, Richmond, 1855, with an introduction by Charles Campbell, cited hereafter as *Beverley*), p. 45.
[45] Jones, *Virginia*, 43.
[46] Letter of Apr. 5, 1740 to Major Otway; 37 V 101.
[47] As calculated, 676 of 5066; VHS photostats of quit rent rolls.

farms East of the fall line. Where change occurred there between 1704 and 1750, it involved a substantial reduction in the mean.[48]

Mere ownership of an unstocked farm of 200 to 300 acres meant little in terms of economic assets. According to Governor Dinwiddie, there were about 1,000,000 acres of land in Virginia either unpatented or occupied without patent.[49] "We are still a nation of woods," an acting Governor wrote in 1751.[50] The abundance of land made it cheap. In 1726, fifty acres at the head of Lynnhaven River, Princess Anne County, were transferred for £12 current money [51] and probably were considered dear at that.[52] "Well-timbered" land on Great Guinea Creek in Goochland County had been offered for sale in 1736 at £10 per 100 acres.[53] That was the year and Goochland the County of William Randolph's familiar transfer to Peter Jefferson of 200 acres of land "for and in consideration of Henry Wetherburn's biggest bowl of arrack punch." [54]

Leases, of course, were proportionately cheap and, in the eastern part of the Colony, were made with scant expectation of any increase in value. John Mercer advertised in 1752 his willingness to lease "near 30,000 acres of extraordinarily good fresh land in Fairfax and Prince William . . . for three lives of twenty-one years." [55] In Washington's native Westmoreland, Thomas Clayton leased a farm of 150 acres for

---

[48] The lack of full quit rent rolls makes specific statement impossible. Princess Anne is one of the few Counties for which rolls of 1704 and of a later date, 1775, exist. In the seventy-one years covered by these two rolls, farms with an acreage of 100 or less underwent startling change: In 1704, the number was seventeen; in 1775, it was 207. This was probably an extreme case. The Virginia State Library has photostats of other quit rent rolls as follows: Culpeper Co., 1764; Fairfax Co., 1761; King George Co., 1769; Lancaster Co., two parishes, 1750; Prince William Co., 1754; Richmond Co., two parishes, 1746, and consolidated roll, 1765; Westmoreland Co., 1740. The figures for Princess Anne, 1775, appear in *Lower Norfolk Antiquary*, v. 3, p. 1, 69, 100, 152. Lunenburg returns for 1764 will be found in L. C. Bell, *Sunlight on the Southside*, Chap. II, IV.

[49] This was one basis of the imposition by the Governor of a fee of one pistole for sealing a patent. For references to the development of the controversy over this "pistole case," or "pistole fee," see *infra*, p. 171. A good summary of the land system of Virginia will be found in Dinwiddie to the Lords of Trade, June 16, 1753, P.R.O.: C.O. 5, 1327, p. 671–72, quoted in 4 *Gipson*, 262 n.

[50] Lewis Burwell to the Lords of Trade, Aug. 21, 1751; 3 *Gooch MSS*, 1066; P.R.O.: C.O. 5, 1327.

[51] "Current money," which will be quoted throughout this chapter unless otherwise indicated, roughly included any medium of generally accepted exchange within Virginia, other than sterling exchange on England. According to the varying rate of exchange, £12 of this "current money" would have been £8 to £10 sterling. The deed for the 50 acres, mentioned in the text, was from John Thorowgood to Katherine Creedle and is recorded in 4 *Princess Anne Wills and Deeds*, pt. 1, p. 60. Princess Anne leases continued for a long period to run according to "willing free and voluntary livery of seisin by tyrf and twig."

[52] Joseph Ball thought land in this area was too high.

[53] *Va. Gazette*, Sept. 10, 1736, advertisement of Daniel Stoner.

[54] 2 *Goochland Deeds*, 1734–46, p. 222.

[55] *Va. Gazette*, Mch. 5, 1752, terms of lease not specified.

as little as 600 to 800 lbs. of tobacco annually though he had to promise to build two small structures and to plant 200 trees.[56]

Because low prices prevailed for land, a small farmer could not sell advantageously any part of his farm to buy implements, utensils or house furnishings. As a result, he acquired these things slowly from the proceeds of the tobacco he grew or from the increase of his slaves or stock. If he owned any land, he usually had a horse, but the stables and pigpens of farms differed amazingly. In a typical inventory of personal property to the value of £58, a small farmer of Richmond County included a horse, a mare, a colt, a yoke of oxen, six cows, a bull and a number of calves, two hogs and twenty-one geese.[57] A farmer in Brunswick had fifteen head of cattle but only one horse.[58] In Westmoreland, a farmer, who apparently had "seen better days," left an estate of £17 only, and had as livestock "a young steer, one cow and two yearlings." [59] A frontierman with whom George was to have financial dealings owned at death "1 Bandy-legged grey horse, 1 pyed cow and calf, 1 Brindled Bull, 1 pied 2 yr. old heifer, 3 calves." [60] Sometimes, in these inventories, there was close calculation. For example, after the death of one citizen of Princess Anne, whose estate was put at £4, 6s, the executor solemnly listed "two shoats and a half," which must have meant that the dead man in some way had acquired a half interest in a litter of five pigs.[61] Many persons had as little as this or even less. If nine successive inventories of Princess Anne County are typical of what the average small farmer or laborer accumulated, he came to the end of his days with scarcely more than £16 of personal property.[62]

In spite of adverse circumstance and the competition of slave labor in the raising of tobacco,[63] many small farmers advanced themselves. So did numerous merchants and factors, who constituted the third class. Several of the merchant families of one generation were great proprietors in the next. A few of the sailors, the small fourth class, slowly lifted their economic level, but these were men of "rare parts." Most

[56] *Westmoreland Records,* Liber S, 1747–53, p. 67–68, lease of Oct. 30, 1749. It was rare that a lessor took as much care as in this case to provide for the upkeep of the property.
[57] Inventory of J. Hightower, Aug. 3, 1726; 5 *Richmond Co. Wills,* 16.
[58] Hardin inventory of Oct. 5, 1732; *Brunswick Deeds and Wills,* 1732–40, p. 147.
[59] Inventory of George Muse, Oct. 2, 1723, *Westmoreland Records,* 1723–46, p. 1. Another excellent example of the property of a small farmer is the report of the Sheriff of King George on an attachment against Humphrey Sawyers, Nov. 6, 1736 (2 *King George Deeds,* 88).
[60] This was the inventory, 2 *Frederick Wills,* 206, of James McCracken, mentioned *infra,* p. 244, n. 138.
[61] Inventory of John Day, June 2, 1725, in 4 *Princess Anne Deeds and Wills,* pt. 1, p. 17.
[62] See note 168 and *supra,* n. 51, on "current money."
[63] See *infra,* p. 88.

of the seafarers lived in England. If the men and women of the fifth class, that of the frontier folk, survived hardship, isolation and Indians, they usually accumulated a hut, some livestock and a few clearings in the far-sweeping forests. Some of the pioneers, patenting extensively, sold many small tracts to later settlers and grew rich.

George Washington probably was not aware of it at the time he began to visit at the homes of Lawrence and "Austin," but economically and sometimes socially, the class of largest progress in Virginia, from the sixteen-sixties to the seventeen-fifties inclusive, was that of the indentured servants. These were to be distinguished, on the one hand, from workmen and farmers who had saved or borrowed sufficient money to pay the expense of travel to Virginia, where they had taken out their "headrights." [64] On the other hand, the indentured servant should not be confused, though actually he often was, with the indentured convict. A still different subclass had been that of the artisan who had come to the Colony under specific contract for a particular service, on the conclusion of which he may have returned to the United Kingdom. [65]

Rises and declines there had been at intervals in the number of servants who signed an indenture by which they agreed to migrate to the Colony and to work a number of years in payment of the cost of passage. In general, the immigration of white servants fell during the first quarter of the eighteenth century, because Negro slave labor was believed to be more profitable, [66] but cargoes of indentured servants arrived not infrequently during the years of George Washington's youth. In the *Virginia Gazette* of June 13, 1751, a "choice parcel of indented servants" was advertised "on sale at York." The next spring the *Burwell* brought "tradesmen, farmers, seamstresses, stay-makers, mantua makers, etc." [67] At that very time, preparation was being made to simplify the law and to protect the rights of indentured servants. [68] Law or no law, the importing shipmaster could "sell" the indenture

[64] See *supra*, p. 1, for headrights.

[65] Jones, *Virginia*, 54. Interesting specification for a gardener and a smith—"two honest, sober young fellows"—will be found in John Carter, of Corotoman, to R. Cary, Aug. 11, 1735, *Carter-Plummer MSS*, 52. For a description of these MSS, see the Bibliography.

[66] The standard work is J. C. Ballagh, *White Servitude in the Colony of Virginia*. In his familiar book, Dr. Ballagh dated the decline of white servitude from 1726. In reviewing the monograph in 3 *V* 437, Dr. Philip Alexander Bruce expressed the opinion that immigrating white servants were fewer after c. 1700. For the conflict between the indentured servant, who became a small proprietor, and the Negro, who remained in bondage and begat children who were slaves, see T. J. Wertenbaker, *The Planters of Colonial Virginia*, 147 ff. A general view, with many references to Virginia, is A. E. Smith, *Colonists in Bondage*.

[67] *Va. Gazette*, May 8, 1752.   [68] 6 *H* 256 ff; Act of 1753.

for all it would bring; [69] and if he could find no purchaser along the Virginia rivers, he could bargain with "soul drivers" who would "buy a parcel of servants and drive them through the country" till the indentures could be turned into cash at a profit.[70]

The majority of indentured servants, escaping this fate, procured masters whose kindness or severity differed in almost every instance. Servants who were over nineteen at the time of indenture could not be made to serve longer than four years, if they fulfilled the terms of their agreement. Boys or girls indentured when under eighteen were released when twenty-four.[71] It probably was because most of them were young that these servants as a class, were known commercially as "kids." [72] No "kid's" indenture could be changed without his consent in open court, but sometimes a servant could covenant to make a specified number of bricks or shoes or to do other specified labor in a given time and, by diligent performance, could reduce his term of service.[73] Occasionally, too, a servant who had a trade might agree to teach it to persons designated by his master and, in return, might have his indenture shortened.[74] Those who had trades were, in fact, the most fortunate of servants. While indentured, they usually were well treated; when free, they found their services in demand at decent wages. A rare servant of some education might become the schoolteacher of the neighborhood and might be invited, at intervals, to eat with the family or might be allowed to entertain guests at the "great house." [75]

The most notorious failings of servants were, first, their proneness to leave their masters, and next, the sexual promiscuity of some of them. A runaway might be advertised as "a great rogue" or as "very dissolute,"

---

[69] Little information exists on prices paid. In the inventory of Thomas Youell, 1696 (2 *Westmoreland Deeds and Wills*, 59), two Irish women were valued at 3500 pounds of tobacco, almost three times the price of two mulatto children who belonged to the same estate.

[70] Diary of John Harrower, May 16, 1774, 6 *A. H. R.*, 77. Harrower, an indentured servant-teacher, will be quoted often in these notes. He kept a journal which probably is the most extensive and certainly the most intelligent and interesting that has survived from the pen of an indentured servant. It presents some similarities and many contrasts to the diary of Philip Fithian, an educated tutor from New Jersey, mentioned *infra*, p. 132.

[71] 6 *H* 356.

[72] Jones, *Virginia*, 53.

[73] See, as typical, two contracts between Isham Randolph and indentured servants, 1736, in 5 *W* (1) p. 109–10.

[74] E.g., John Bayly, joiner, who on Sept. 30, 1740, agreed with his employer, Mrs. Ann Harrison, to teach one or more of her sons his trade (*Westmoreland Records, 1723–46*, p. 240). For an example of an indentured worker's successful legal contest of his master's interpretation of his length of service, see the case of Richard Mynatt vs. Philip Ludwell Lee, July 31, 1754; *Westmoreland Orders, 1752–55*, p. 186a.

[75] Cf. Harrower, 6 *A. H. R.*, 106–07. Harrower was permitted by his employer to instruct other children and even adults and to retain the fees. See *infra*, p. 128.

but, if recovered, he usually was whipped and forgiven.[76] Against those servants who cohabited with Negroes, and against servant women who had bastard children, the law was stern. Another year of servitude or the payment of 1000 pounds of tobacco was the price of bearing an illegitimate child by a free white man. If the father was a Negro or mulatto, the punishment was the added year of servitude and the payment of £15 current money on the expiration of the woman's term. If she did not have the money, she was sold for five years. The parish received the fine or the proceeds of the sale of service.[77]

Difficult as the service of the average indentured servant sometimes proved, it usually was slightly better under a good master than that of the convict, the seventh class of colonial society. Some of these convicts of the seventeenth century had been political prisoners rather than criminals, defeated Scotch and Irish soldiers of the civil wars, or Cromwellian veterans after 1660. Others had been Monmouth's followers.[78] Of these men, in George Washington's youth, little more than tradition remained.

The convict servants who worked on the plantations in his boyhood were men and women who had been convicted of lesser felonies in England and had been sent to the Colonies under an act of 1717.[79] It was not unusual, in George's earlier years, for a shipload of these convicts to arrive in the Rappahannock or in the Potomac.[80] Some convict ships cast anchor as late as 1763 [81] and offered their live cargo to all who had cash or good credit. Their coming was most unwelcome, not only because many of the convicts were criminals but also because, as the planters complained, they often "spoil[ed] servants that were before very good," though some of the convicts proved "indifferent good." [82]

---

[76] See *infra*, p. 177. The quotation is from an advertisement by Richard and George Lee of Westmoreland in *Va. Gazette*, Sept. 27, 1749. For an advertisement to locate a female servant who had been "sold" three times and perhaps had inherited something after her disappearance, see William Fairfax's notice in *ibid.*, May 23, 1755. Among many advertisements for runaways, see one for a servant of John Champe in *Va. Gazette*, Apr. 8, 1775, and one for a servant of John Custis's, who "went away with irons on his legs." *Va. Gazette*, May 9, 1745. Washington's steward later was to complain that it scarcely was worth while to "iron" runaways because Negro blacksmiths in Williamsburg soon would file off the fetters.

[77] Sec. XIII, Act of 1753; 6 *H* 360–61. For earlier laws, see Ballagh, *White Servitude*, 72–73 n.　　　　　　　　　　　　　　　[78] Ballagh, *op. cit.*, 35–37.

[79] Ballagh, *op. cit.*, 37. The General Assembly in 1722 had passed an act that included provision "for the better government of convicts imported," but this had been repealed by proclamation, Jan. 18, 1723. See 2 *L. J.*, 673; 4 *H* 106. An anonymous paper in Holles's hand, n.m., n.d., 1751, among the Newcastle Papers (Br. Mus. Add. MS 33053, v. 18, folio 45) summarizes an argument whether hard labor in England might not be a better deterrent of crime than transportation was.

[80] *Va. Gazette*, July 15, 1737.　　　　　　[81] 2 *G. W.*, 409.

[82] Jones, *Virginia*, 53.

The Northern Neck had been a special dumping ground for convicts whom the Virginians undertook to segregate or to employ in the Royal Army.[83] In the revision, 1748, of the law for jury trial in criminal cases, the Burgesses and Council permitted the jury in the hearing of a convict to be chosen from bystanding freeholders. "Most of the felonies and other capital offences," the law explained carefully, were "perpetrated . . . by persons who have been convicted of felony, or other crimes in Great Britain or Ireland." It could be of "no benefit to such persons, who are commonly servants and little known in the neighborhood where they live, to have a jury of the vicinage." [84] During the period of his sentence, the convict, moreover, could not be a witness in court except against another convict.[85]

Slaves, who constituted the eighth class of society in Virginia, were increasing far more rapidly than were convicts or indentured white servants. This shift from free to slave labor had reached such proportions by about 1723 that 1000 to 1600 Negroes were imported annually.[86] Small planters, who purchased one or two slaves, represented a steady market.[87] Although the judgment of the Burgesses had been expressed in at least nine acts to restrict the slave trade before 1750, Virginians' demand for labor and the pressure of London merchants combined to strengthen the slave-trade policy of the British government.[88] In Washington's twenty-first year, the arrival of vessels with cargoes of "fine healthy slaves" [89] or of "fine slaves" [90] or of "choice, healthy slaves" [91] was to be advertised to an extent that would indicate the importation of considerably more than 4000 per annum.[92] The danger of uprisings by these Negroes had been discussed at intervals. Some alarms over

[83] *Landmarks*, 159. The colonials in 1738 had provided that none of these convicts could serve in the county militia, even as a substitute for a person exempted from personal attendance on musters (5 H 16–17).

[84] 5 H 545, with the punctuation slightly modified.

[85] *Ibid.*, 546–47.

[86] Ballagh, *History of Slavery in Virginia* (cited hereafter as *Ballagh's Slavery*), p. 13. No figures of the slave population for the whole of Virginia are in existence prior to those of the census of 1782–83.

[87] Wertenbaker, *Planters of Colonial Virginia*, 153. As late as 1782, in Westmoreland County, 116 farmers owned one or two slaves each. A total of 183 planters owned four or less (10 V 229). In Richmond County, 1783, each of 345 owners had a maximum of ten slaves. The total number of slave owners was 505 and of slaves, 4581 (4 V 298–99).

[88] See a note by W. G. Stanard in 16 V 86–87, with references to *H*.

[89] Ship *Boyne*, advertised in *Va. Gazette*, June 25, 1752.

[90] *Molly* in *ibid.*, July 3, 1752.

[91] *Anne*, galley, in *ibid.*, July 10, 1752.

[92] *Ibid.*, June 25–Oct. 27, 1752, listed vessels which, on the assumed basis of 200 slaves per ship, show 2193 slaves imported in four months. If this were the monthly average for the entire year, it would mean the entry of almost 6000 slaves in 1752, but it is thought that the trade declined in winter.

threatened violence had been sounded.[93] The prevailing opinion appears to have been that of the second William Byrd, who had written in 1735 that the Negroes were "not so numerous or so enterprising as to give us any apprehension or uneasiness." [94]

The economy of their employment was debated. Free white men, raising tobacco, sometimes may have thought that slave labor kept the price of the staple low, but William Byrd insisted that the slaves worked less than did the poor of other countries.[95] Robert Carter had said that the Negroes' "clothes come to more than they make." [96] At a slightly later date, the mistress of a Virginia plantation was to assert that if the Negroes were sold, the proceeds invested and the farmlands left fallow, the interest would be a greater income without the risk of losing the slaves or the crops.[97]

Treatment varied as much as opinion did. "Some masters," Governor Gooch had written in 1731, "use their Negroes no better than their cattle and I can see no help for it, tho' for the greater number the masters here are kinder than those the labourers in England serve." [98] Laws against the ill-usage of Negroes were more notable for penalties imposed on the blacks than for the mercy shown them; [99] but when a recognized legal right was asserted in court, it was examined fairly and fully.[100] In daily life on most farms, a master's own sense of the value of his Negroes was supposed to be a guarantee that he would not abuse his authority.[101] This was not vain logic. In a spirit of humanity or of economy or of both, Col. Richard Corbin wrote his manager in 1759: "The care of the Negroes is the first thing to be recommended that you give me timely notice of their wants that they may be provided with all necessities[.] The Breeding wenches most particularly, you must instruct the overseers to be kind and indulgent to, and not to force them when with child upon any service or hardship that will be injurious to

93 32 V 322; 36 ibid., 345; Ballagh's Slavery, 79.
94 9 V 235.
95 Ibid. Caution has to be shown in statements on this subject for the reason that most of the discussion involves a large element of theory on the basis of little factual evidence.
96 Letter of July 18, 1723, to Micajah Perry, Carter Transcripts, VHS.
97 Fithian, 123.
98 May 28, 1731; 1 Gooch MSS, 237.
99 Compare the mild reference in 2 L.J., 811 with the acts in 4 H 126 and 6 H 104 ff, p. 356 ff.
100 Cf. the case of Daniel vs. Gilbert Metcalfe on the charge that Daniel was kept as a slave beyond the age at which the will of his master had provided that he be set free (10 Richmond Co. Orders).
101 Cf. the act of 1668 or 1669 in 2 H 270: "it cannot be presumed that prepensed malice (which alone make murther ffelony) should induce any man to destroy his owne estate."

them . . ." [102] This was more a practical than a benevolent philosophy. For nearly half a century, the slave had been real estate at law, and had been passed with the land.[103] Legislative repeal of this in 1748 [104] was frustrated at the instance of Governor Gooch who regarded the old statutory provision as a convenience in the transfer of estates. The attempt to change the law was fired, he thought, by the amending impulse of a new General Assembly.[105]

Runaway slaves were sought as stolen cattle were. When, for example, one Tom Baker, alias Charles, was advertised as a fugitive, he was declared in the advertisement to be "a Virginian and speaks sensible." [106] Mrs. Margaret Arbuckle's slaves, held only a month before they ran away, were said to be "from Gambia and to understand no English." [107] Negroes who lurked in swamps or elsewhere, living on what they pilfered from farms, could be ordered by proclamation to return to their owners. When the slaves did not come home after this notice, they were outlawed and could be slain by anyone, in any manner, "without accusation, or impeachment of any crime for the same." [108] If the master killed a slave while punishing him for running away, no penalty was imposed unless malice could be proved. By court order, a persistent runaway could be dismembered, in a manner "not touching life." Where death resulted, there was no punishment.[109] Extremes of law were shaped to prevent cross breeding of the races [110] and to protect the owner in his use of his property.

The issue of his slaves was the principal source of increase in the wealth of the average planter. Some of the largest proprietors did not hesitate for a moment to engage in one part or another of the slave trade. John Carter, son of Robert of Corotoman, had a cargo of Negroes on his hands in 1737. He sold 145 of them at an average of about £15 a head, but he wrote his agent complainingly that most of

102 Letter of Jan. 1, 1759; 30 *V* 80. For similar instructions by George Washington's half-uncle, see *infra*, p. 191.

103 3 *H* 333; 4 *ibid.*, 226.   104 5 *H* 432; 2 *L.J.*, 1040, 1043, 1046.

105 Letter to the Lords of Trade, May 7, 1750; 3 *Gooch MSS*, 997; repeal noted Oct. 31, 1751, 5 *H* 432.

106 *Va. Gazette*, Apr. 3, 1746.

107 *Ibid.*, Oct. 17, 1745. Other advertisements for runaway slaves will be found in almost every issue. Of special interest are notices by Augustine Washington, June 9, 1738, Philip Lightfoot, Oct. 6, 1738, and Archibald Cary, Nov. 14, 1751.

108 Act of October, 1748; 6 *H* 110–11.

109 *Ibid.*, 111. The legal status of slaves, with special reference to the seventeenth and early eighteenth century, is described in *Ballagh's Slavery*, 75 ff.

110 See *supra*, p. 86, and *Ballagh's Slavery*, 56 ff. Moravian missionaries in 1753 found in the upper Valley a Negro smith who had as his wife a Scotch woman from Pennsylvania (Mereness, *Travels in the American Colonies*, cited hereafter as *Mereness*, p. 339).

the cargo consisted of children, for whom there was little demand. The sale, he went on, had not paid the insurance. In disposing of Negroes left in the cargo, he feared he might have to deal with "those wholesale chaps." [111] Subsequently, "Peter Randolph and Comp" advertised the arrival in James River of "200 choice healthy Gambia Negroes," [112] but it is not certain the head of this firm was Peter Randolph of Chatsworth, Clerk of the House of Burgesses, Councillor and member of the early Committee of Correspondence.[113]

The Indians scarcely were numerous enough to be regarded as a separate class. By 1740–50, war and disease had killed most of those East of the Blue Ridge. Others had migrated westward or southwestward. A few remained on the Eastern Shore but resided peacefully among the whites; South of James River, the Nottoway and Nansemond tribes did not count more than fifty fighting men. The Pamunkey Indians, on the river of that name, were reduced to approximately ten families that lived on tribal lands and eked a meagre subsistence by hunting and fishing.[114] In Orange County, when George Washington was ten years of age, some Sapony Indians had been accused of hog stealing and of burning woods. Instead of being pursued by an armed force, they were brought into court, where their plight stirred the pity of some of the planters. Bond was supplied. The redmen quit the County. To that peaceful and prosaic state had come the relations of conquered and of victor. It was different beyond the mountains.[115]

The houses of these eight classes of Virginia society exhibited the emergence of the wealthy and the lag of the poor in a Colony now almost 150 years old. Habitations, like their residents, were, so to say, in their second or third generation. The settlers' first homes had been succeeded by stouter buildings. Some of these—notably William Byrd's Westover and Thomas Lee's first home in Westmoreland—had been burned.[116] Newer and still finer structures were rising. Most of the

---

[111] John Carter to Foster Cunliffe, Sept. 25, 1737 (two letters); *Carter-Plummer MSS*, 162. As late as November, Carter still had some of these Negro children unsold.

[112] *Va. Gazette*, Sept. 12, 1751.

[113] Swem, in his *Index*, gave warning that the several Peter Randolphs could not be distinguished in every instance.

[114] *Burnaby*, 42; Governor Gooch's report in 3 *V* 120.

[115] Cf. Dr. A. G. Grinnan in 3 *V* 189–90.

[116] Westover sustained heavy loss Jan. 7, 1749 (*Va. Gazette*, J. Randolph notes, 20 *W* (1) p. 17). Colonel Thomas Lee's house on the Potomac was set afire by servants Jan. 29, 1729 (*Md. Gazette*, Feb. 4, 1729; Gooch to the Lords of Trade, Mch. 26, 1729, 1 *Gooch MSS*, 96). The fire at Colonel Richard Corbin's Laneville, mentioned *infra*, did not occur until Mch. 15, 1758 (*Corbin MS Letter Book*, VHS, 5). References to lightning rods appear in entries of 1759 (*Burnaby*, 10). For the manner in which fires sometimes were caused by coals from fireplaces, see *Fithian*, 80.

"great houses" erected after 1710 were of brick [117] without portico [118] and contained large but not numerous rooms. [119] The favored design was a rectangular building, two storeys high, with a central hall from front to rear. On either side were two rooms. The same arrangement usually was made on the second floor. One chamber was that of the master and mistress. Another usually was described as "the boys' ". A third was "the girls' ". In the fourth, guests or parents might be accommodated. Sometimes the rooms were known by the color of the paint.[120] If a dwelling of this size and type was outgrown, wings were added,[121] but not to the satisfaction of the aesthetically minded. A young Virginian who was running about such a house, and was answering to the name Tom Jefferson, lived to condemn in sharp terms these habitations. "It is impossible," he said, "to devise things more ugly, uncomfortable and happily more perishable"; but he never succeeded in weaning the people of his State from them.[122] Opposite the angles of some of the more imposing of these residences, four smaller brick houses were constructed. If four were too many or too expensive, there might be two outbuildings at the same angle to the front or rear of the main structure. Often these corner buildings served to set off the "great house." Behind it were wooden sheds, barns and work-

[117] Jones, in his *Virginia*, 36, said about 1720: "The Gentlemen's Seats are of late built of brick."

[118] The order of Apr. 4, 1748, in the *Stratton Major Parish Vestry Book*, 74, provided an interesting exception.

[119] The houses were essentially compact. Maycox, Prince George County, offered for lease in 1751, was 62 × 48 feet (*Va. Gazette*, Nov. 7, 1751). Colonel Corbin proposed to replace Laneville with a building 52 × 20 feet (*Corbin MS Letter Book*, VHS, 22). An interesting order for the sash and hardware of this new house will be found in *ibid.*, 14. Pecatone was 40 × 70 feet (see Ethel Armes, *Stratford Hall*, 202). George Eskridge's home, Sandy Point, seems to have had seven or eight rooms only. His and similar references to a "hall" must be understood to refer, in the eighteenth-century use of the word, to a large room, usually central, and not to a passageway. Often the "hall" served as a dining-room. (See Eskridge's inventory, Jan. 27, 1736, in *Westmoreland Records and Inventories*, 1723–46, p. 159.) A similar document concerning Henry Ashton listed only six rooms besides the kitchen (*ibid.*, p. 110). The appraisers of the estate of the second Richard Lee mentioned ten rooms, with kitchen, etc., in addition (5 *Westmoreland Deeds and Wills*, 479). Rawleigh Travers's inventory contained references to seven family rooms (*Stafford Deeds*, O, p. 77). These inventories must be used with caution because the contents of rooms sometimes included articles placed there, after the testator's death, for safe-keeping or for auction. Henry Fitzhugh's inventory of 1743, for example, stated that his "study" contained a siphon, an egg slicer, stone jugs, a coffee mill, four great pipes, a funnel and a gimlet (*ibid.*, 9).

[120] See the inventory of Col. John Tayloe, 5 *Richmond Co. Wills*, 1725–53, p. 547. This was the practice at Stratford, also, where there were blue, green, red and white rooms (4 *Westmoreland Records*, p. 77). In 1701, Ralph Wormeley wrote of the "nursery" and the "old nursery" (2 *W* (1) p. 170), but this was unusual.

[121] The floor-plans in Edith Tunis Sale's *Interiors of Virginia Houses of Colonial Times* include many interesting examples.

[122] *Notes on Virginia*, Jefferson's *Works*, Mem. ed., v. 2, p. 211. See also his remark in P. L. Ford, ed., *Writings of Thomas Jefferson*, v. 3, p. 257.

shops so numerous that a stranger might think, from a distance, he was approaching a village.[123] Such places always were few.

The fullest description of one of these establishments is of Nomini Hall, the home of Robert Carter on Nomini Creek near the Potomac: [124]

"Mr. Carter now possesses 60,000 acres of land and about 600 Negroes, but his estate is much divided, and lies in almost every county in this Colony. He has lands in the neighbourhood of Williamsburg, and an elegant and Spacious house in that City. He owns a great part of the well known ironworks near Baltimore in Maryland, and he has one or more considerable Farms not far from Annapolis. He has some large tracts of land far to the West, at a place call'd 'Bull Run,' and the 'Great Meadows' among the mountains. He owns lands near Dumfries on the Potowmac and large tracts in this and the neighbouring Counties. Out of these lands, which are situated so remote from each other in various parts of these two large provinces, Virginia and Maryland, Mr. Carter has chosen for the place of his habitation a high spot of ground in Westmoreland County at the head of the navigation of the river Nomini, where he has erected a large elegant house, at a vast expence, which commonly goes by the name of Nomini Hall. This house is built with brick but the bricks have been covered with strong lime mortar; so that the building is now perfectly white. It is seventy-six feet long from East to West, and forty-four wide from North to South, two stories high, the Pitch of the lower story seventeen feet and the upper story twelve.

"It has five stacks of chimneys, though two of these serve only for ornament. There is a beautiful jutt, on the South side, eighteen feet long and eight feet deep from the wall which is supported by three tall pillars. On the south side, or front, in the upper story are four windows each having twenty-four lights of glass. In the lower story are two windows each having sixteen Lights. At the East end, the upper story has three windows each with eighteen Lights, and below two Windows, both with eighteen Lights and a Door with nine.

"The north side I think is most beautiful of all. In the upper story is a row of seven windows with eighteen Lights a piece, and below six windows, with the like number of lights, besides a large portico in the

---

123 The will of "King" Carter, *loc. cit.,* mentioned about thirty-eight rooms, storerooms, lofts or outbuildings.

124 This description dates from 1774, but it is believed to be applicable, with minor changes only, to conditions approximately twenty years earlier.

middle, at the sides of which are two windows each with eighteen Lights. At the West end are no Windows. The Number of Lights in all is five hundred and forty nine. There are four Rooms on a Floor, disposed of in the following manner. Below is a dining-room where we usually sit; the second is a dining-room for the children; the third is Mr. Carter's study; and the fourth is a ball room thirty Feet long. Above stairs, one room is for Mr and Mrs Carter; the second for the young Ladies, and the other two for occasional company. As this house is large and stands on a high piece of land it may be seen a considerable distance. I have seen it at the distance of six Miles. At equal distances from each corner of this building stand four other considerable houses, which I shall next a little describe. First, at the northeast corner and at 100 yards distance stands the schoolhouse; at the northwest corner and at the same Distance stands the stable. At the southwest corner and at the same distance, stands the coach-house; and lastly, at the southeast corner and at an equal distance stands the work-house. These four houses are the corner of a square of which the great house is the center. First the school-house is forty five feet long, from east to west & twenty-seven from north to south. It has five well-finished, convenient rooms, three below stairs and two above. It is built with brick a story and a half high with dormant windows. In each room is a fire. In the large room below Stairs we keep our school; the other two rooms below, which are smaller, are allowed to Mr. Randolph the clerk. The room above the school-room Ben and I live in and the other room above stairs belongs to Harry and Bob. Five of us live in this house with great neatness and convenience. Each one has a bed to himself and we are called by the bell to the great house to breakfast etc. The wash house is built in the same form and is of the same size of the school house. From the front yard of the great house, to the wash house is a curious terrace covered finely with green turf and about five foot high with a slope of eight feet, which appears exceeding well to persons coming to the front of the House. This terrace is produced along the front of the house and ends by the kitchen; but before the front doors is a broad flight of steps of the same height and slope of the terrace.

"The stable and coach house are of the same Length & Breadth as the school-and wash-house, only they are higher pitched to be convenient for holding hay and fodder.

"Due East of the great house are two rows of tall, flourishing, beautiful poplars, beginning on a Line drawn from the school to the wash house. These rows are something wider than the house and are about 300 yards long, at the eastermost end of which is the great road leading through Westmoreland to Richmond. These rows of poplars form an extremely pleasant avenue and at the road, through them, the house appears most romantic, at the same time that it does truly elegant. The area of the triangle made by the wash house, stable and school house is perfectly level and designed for a bowling Green, laid out in rectangular walks which are paved with brick and covered over with burnt oyster shells. In the other triangle, made by the wash house, stable and coach house is the kitchen, a well-built house, as large as the school house, bake house, dairy, store house and several other small houses, all which stand due West and at a small distance from the great house and form a handsome street. These buildings stand about a quarter of a mile from a fork of the river Nomini, one branch of which runs East of us, on which are two mills. One of them belongs to Mr. Turberville, the other to Mr. Washington, both within a mile. Another branch of the river runs on the West of us, on which and at a small distance above the House stands Mr. Carter's merchant mill . . . To go to the mill from the house we descend I imagine above an 100 Feet. The dam is so broad that two carriages may pass conveniently on it and the pond from twelve to eighteen foot water . . ." [125]

These were more elaborate approaches than most estates, even of the first order, possessed. Flower gardens had not been numerous in Virginia at the beginning of the eighteenth century [126] and they were being developed slowly afterward [127] but they were not as exceptional as some thought.[128] A few planters devoted themselves especially to their flora. "I have a pretty little garden," John Custis had written from Williamsburg, in 1725, "in which I take more satisfaction than in anything in

[125] *Fithian,* 106 ff. Further contemporary material on Virginia houses will be found in Jones, *Virginia,* 32; the inventory of Robert Carter of Corotoman, VHS; 15 *W* (1), p. 261; *Va. Gazette,* Nov. 7, 1751, Feb. 13, 1752.

[126] *Beverley,* 261.

[127] Misapprehension on this point existed even as late as Chastellux's tour in the seventeen-eighties. See 2 *Chastellux,* 9.

[128] It sometimes is difficult to tell whether a garden mentioned in an advertisement is a flower or a "kitchen" garden. For example, John Henry Roimbough's property in Hampton almost certainly included a flower garden (*Va. Gazette,* Aug. 14, 1752), but the garden of Colonel Jenings's Williamsburg house, used as the Bristol Store, may have been for vegetables and herbs (*ibid.,* Sept. 3, 1736). An interesting summary of a contract for laying out a garden c. 1757 will be found in George Braxton's Letter Book, printed in Frederick Horner, *History of the Blair, Banister and Braxton Families* (cited hereafter as *Blair, Banister & Braxton*), p. 147–48. For certain of the early flower gardens, see Edith Tunis Sale, ed., *Historic Gardens of Virginia.* Needless to say, some of the plots devoted to flowers lay next to the ground where vegetables were raised. The inventory of Henry Lee, 1747, included a "tin engine to water garden" (*Westmoreland Inventories,* 1746–52, p. 62).

this world and have a collection of tolerable good flowers and greens from England; but have had great losses in their coming in, partly by the carelessness and ignorance of the master of the ships that brought them and sometimes by the ships coming in to[o] late." [129] The long voyage often ruined plants and even seed. "Any roots that are bulbous will come safe," Custis maintained, "if the ships come in early." Aside from these, in a normal passage to the Colony, the only plants to survive were those that "neither ignorance nor carelessness," in Custis's words, "[could] destroy." [130]

Indigenous plants and some of those long-seated in Virginia often beautified homes that were not comparable in splendor to the mansions of the great planters or even to the better houses in John Custis's Williamsburg. The small residences of parish clergy, for example, often were well arranged and well adorned. St. Paul's parish, Hanover County, proposed to erect a brick "glebe house," or rectory, thirty-four by twenty-eight feet.[131] St John's, Henrico, planned for its clergyman a residence forty-eight by twenty feet, with two outside chimneys and a cellar twenty by twenty.[132] A kitchen twenty-four by sixteen, in a parson's house, apparently was not considered unusual.[133] Household facilities sometimes were provided in these small residences. The rectory of Truro parish, Fairfax County, was of about 1200 square feet, brick, one storey high, with cellars below, and with "convenient rooms and closets as the land will allow." [134]

Small houses often were very small. Slave quarters and frontier huts

[129] John Custis to Robert Cary, 1725, n.d.; *Custis Letter Book*, No. 29. Custis's detailed instructions for the shipment of trees, plants, etc., from England, 1717, n.d., appear in *ibid.*, No. 4. For a description of these MS letters, see the Bibliography.

[130] *Ibid.*, and same to same, n.d., No. 44. Custis's numerous letters mention the importation at one time or another of the following shrubs and flowers: Arabian jessamine, arbutus, carnations, chrysanthemums, flowering honeysuckle, globe thistle, hollyhocks, India pinks, iris, Jersey lily, Jerusalem cowslips, laburnum, laurel, Monday rose, monthly rose, passion flower, Persian lilacs, phileria, polyanthus, ranunculus, scarlet honeysuckle, striped lily, tuberoses, tulips, and yellow jessamine. The trees mentioned by Custis and apparently imported by him include: fringe tree, holly (gilded, gold, silver and striped), larch, Siberian cedar, sorrel, stone pine, strawberry and yew. Custis referred also to peach-colored, yellow and white dogwood, but it is difficult to say, from his letters, whether these were imported or were indigenous. The same lover of nature tried his hand at the importation of these fruit and nut trees: almond, cassena, date, Italian acorn, Katherine peach, mulberry, nectarine, nutmeg, nutmeg peach, pistachio, plum and wild cherry. Dr. E. G. Swem has pointed out that some of the plants, shrubs and trees mentioned by Custis were native to Virginia. See Swem, "Brothers of the Spade," *Proc. Am. Ant. Soc.*, 1948.

[131] *Vestry Book*, 157.

[132] *Vestry Book*, 84. Nothing is said in either minute of a second floor. Vestry books have been found to be a useful source of contemporary information regarding houses of a type and a size that have survived in few instances only.

[133] *Vestry Book of St. John's, Henrico*, 19.

[134] *Va. Gazette*, Aug. 14, 1752.

A SUIT OVER WASHINGTON'S BIRTHPLACE

The records of Westmoreland County, Virginia, supply almost all the information that has been brought to light concerning the house in which George Washington was born.

Augustine Washington, George's father, contracted ten years before the boy's birth for the building of the residence. It is possible that the original agreement, if written, provided that the timber should come from Washington's woods and that some of the work should be done by his own servants; but the sum to be paid the builder, David Jones, was 5000 pounds of tobacco which, at the price then prevailing, was worth £41. Assuming a purchasing power ten times that of money in the middle of the twentieth century, the payment to

Jones was to have been not more than $2000. The house must, therefore, have been a simple place.

After the death of Jones, the residence still being incomplete, Augustine Washington had to bring suit against Jones's estate for money advanced and also for a settlement of the account for the Round Hill Church, which Jones also had been building under Washington's supervision.

To facilitate study of this interesting balance-sheet, which Augustine recorded in court, Apr. 7, 1726, the various items are printed in Appendix I-6, p. 535. The original is in Westmoreland County *Records and Inventories*, 1723-46, photostats of which are in the Virginia State Library.

Washington From April 1722 } The State of Andrew Jones 1728 Contra
Genl Estate viz — 1723 } Dr.

1722 } viz			
Recd. for sundry money & goods	33 .. 9 d	By building the roundhouse	£600 08 40
To do. that year as in £6 for sundry goods		By the Church	
from 1723 } £ for sundry in money & goods		By your Rent twice (paid)	3 ..
1724	24 16 .	C by my house for finish	5000
from 1724 } £ for sundry in money & goods	35 8 6 .	By sundry	.. 14
1725	9 18 15	By 2 Feather bed	.. 8
To ditto in Tobacco			
To ditto in Tobacco	18 8 2	By Table	.. 1 6
To the not finishing hanging house	3 00 .	By 2 Man to 2 forces	2 10
To the Rents and interest		By do ... do do do	..
allowed to pay Mard. do	5 00 .		230 2 .
Rect from Janry 15 as 1 to do		By making up balance	15 200 49 15 6
account over & above £33	18 3		
	13 90 15 67 : 16 2 4		15 200 49 17 6

March the 30th. 1726
This account was ... as follows
upon each one ... Washington
due Orders to E. Rose do

Received £8 00 00 Jan 8 1726

Pr sundry £ 6
27 0 15 7 : 18 : 8
13 90 1 6 16 2

GEORGE WASHINGTON'S HALF–BROTHER LAWRENCE

Lawrence Washington, George's elder half-brother and wholly devoted counsellor, was named after his grandfather Lawrence, who received that name from Rev. Lawrence Washington, M.A., Fellow of Brasenose College, Oxford, and later a country rector ousted by the Puritans for alleged drunkenness. The tie with the English parson had been forgotten in George's youth, or, if known to his elders, made no impression on the younger boy.

Lawrence, the elder brother, fourteen years George's senior, and not great-great-grandfather Lawrence, was the link of the family at Ferry Farm, Rappahannock River, with the great world. Lawrence had gone to school in England, had shared in the siege of Cartagena, and had married Anne ("Nancy") Fairfax, daughter of Col. William Fairfax and a cousin of the Proprietor himself. Besides, Lawrence was Adjutant of the Colony of Virginia, was an adventurer in the Ohio Company and was a member of the House of Burgesses.

He was everything an admiring boy wanted to be. Best of all, he had an affectionate interest in George, whose abilities he may have sensed. Lawrence is sketched on p. 76. This portrait of him, attributed to John Wollaston, is now at Mount Vernon and is reproduced here by permission of the Mount Vernon Ladies Association of the Union.

were no longer than the stems of trees that could be cut close at hand and then raised readily. Joseph Ball, George's half-uncle, probably set the absolute minimum of size in directing that for a Negress whom he was sending back to Virginia from England, a cabin seven by eight feet be erected.[135] When Robert Armistead leased part of the land of Eaton's Free School in Elizabeth City County, he covenanted to build two tobacco houses thirty by twenty feet, but the corresponding dwellings were to be twenty-six by sixteen, or the equivalent.[136] Buildings used as stores generally were of slight dimensions and in some instances were not more than sixteen by sixteen feet.[137] Taverns, styled ordinaries,[138] varied much. One offered for rent in the thriving town of Port Royal on the Rappahannock in 1751 was forty-six by twenty-eight feet.[139]

Around the ordinaries, stores and small homes were clustered sheds and storerooms. Precisely as outhouses made a great mansion appear to dominate a village, so the lesser houses were as a hen with chickens. A well-ordered plantation of moderate size could be described as one that had "a good dwelling house with brick chimneys and a brick cellar, all convenient outhouses and a good apple orchard besides a variety of other fruit trees such as peaches, damosels, cherries, etc." [140] A property of one acre, located where the owners hoped a town would be established, thus was advertised: "a dwelling house 26 ft. sq., commodious and neatly finished off, with a cellar the same dimensions, of a brick wall 7 ft. deep; a kitchen 24 ft. long and 18 wide; a store house 24 feet sq. in which is a counting-room 12 ft. by 16 ft. with a subdivision in the back part 24 ft. by 8; a garden 144 ft. sq. brick chimneys to the whole and weatherboarded with plank, with all conveniences and outhouses, the whole paled in after the best manner . . ." [141]

Of the interior of Virginia residences, a later traveler, the Marquis de Chastellux, was to say that the chief magnificence was in furniture, linen and plate,[142] but, had he looked more widely, he scarcely would

---

[135] Letter of Feb. 19, 1754, to Joseph Chinn, *Ball Letter Book.*

[136] The lease provided that these were to be well framed of good white oak or poplar timber (24 *W* (1) p. 36).

[137] For example, one in Cumberland County was advertised by Joseph Wyatt in the *Va. Gazette,* Jan. 30, 1752.

[138] See *infra,* p. 155.

[139] *Va. Gazette,* Aug. 1, 1751.

[140] Advertisement of John and William Goldsmith, *Va. Gazette,* Nov. 17, 1752. "Damosel" for "damson" does not appear in the *Oxford Dictionary* or in B. W. Green, *Virginia Word-Book.*

[141] Advertisement of John Pagan for sale of his property at Cameron, on Great Hunting Creek, Fairfax County; *Va. Gazette,* Apr. 18, 1751.

[142] 2 *Chastellux,* 150.

have generalized. A rich planter like John Carter, son of "King" Carter, ordered numerous articles duplicated for two great houses, Corotoman and Shirley, because pewter and linen were lost in moving from one home to the other; [143] but many men of station had modest personal effects. A Williamsburg lady once advertised the theft of nine tablecloths, two large diaper towels "with sundry other towels and napkins." [144] Another lady of the same town owned twenty-nine tablecloths. Charles Carter of Cleve had two dozen at the time of his death.[145] These were the exceptions. Linen was not always abundant, even in the largest establishments.[146]

Chastellux was entirely correct in what he said of furniture. Virginians of 1750 loved it, bought it, cherished and used it till they wore it out. They delighted, too, in importing what they considered new or fashionable, escritoires,[147] Japanned chests and tea tables,[148] tapestry,[149] and even "a pack of cards representing the bubbles of the South Sea in 1720," a treasure so much esteemed that when it was missing from a dead man's estate an advertisement for its recovery was published.[150] There were "lazy chairs" and dressing tables with twilights, physic presses,[151] French chests,[152] French walnut bureaux,[153] cane couches,[154] and writing desks. [155] Mirrors were to be found in all except the poorest homes.[156]

Clocks were less numerous, apparently, than watches. All were expensive. An old pendulum clock was worth £15.[157] For a watch to be given an adored daughter, a rich planter did not hesitate to spend

---

143 John Carter to Micajah Perry, Sept. 3, 1738; *Carter-Plummer MSS,* 197.

144 *Va. Gazette,* June 13, 1745.

145 26 *V* 176; for Carter, see 6 *King George Deeds,* 229.

146 It is remarkable how seldom towels are mentioned in the inventories of the mid-eighteenth century, though articles of no greater value often were listed.

147 E.g., William Byrd first, June 10, 1689, to Perry and Lane (26 *V* 26). The spelling was scrutoire, screetore or, in the inventory of Nathaniel Harrison's estate (31 *V* 364), screw tore.

148 Spotswood inventory in 1 *Orange Wills,* 181.

149 1 *V* 121, 1683.

150 Estate of Col. Thomas Bray, Nance Neck, Charles City County, *Va. Gazette,* Aug. 29, 1751.

151 All these in the inventory of Nathaniel Harrison, *loc. cit.*

152 Inventory of Moore Fauntleroy's estate, one of the most interesting that has survived (5 *Richmond Co. Wills,* 356).

153 26 *V* 176.

154 21 *V* 407.

155 Inventory of Mrs. Frances Spencer, May 31, 1727, *Westmoreland Records,* 1723–46, p. 66.

156 John Vivion's will (*Middlesex Wills,* 1698–1713, p. 169) mentioned "the great and the middling looking-glass" in 1705; William Hunter, printer, had two large glasses with sconces (7 *W* (1) p. 12). Daniel McCarty owned six looking glasses at the time of his death (*Fairfax Wills,* A, 1, p. 25).

157 Inventory of Col. John Tabb (17 *V* 322), but this was in 1762, a time of depreciated currency.

£40.[158] Loss or theft of such an instrument was a serious matter.[159] Tom Jefferson's lament was deep when, on a visit to a friendly plantation, he put his watch on the very spot where rain from a leak in the roof fell squarely. "It's my opinion," he wrote, "the devil came and bored a hole over it on purpose." [160]

Jefferson might well have assumed that if the rain leaked anywhere into the room, it would have fallen on a bed, because broad resting places occupied a most considerable part of the floor space of the homes of 1750. Bedsteads, in fact, were the furniture most carefully appraised and listed in every inventory. They were of wood and sometimes were ostentatious. Governor Spotswood boasted a "red water standing China bed," [161] from which eminence there was descent for the poor to the humility of canvas-covered couches.[162] Provision of a bed and bedstead for each son or daughter often took years and sometimes involved much planning. It had been in 1711 that George's mother had received under her father's will "all [the] feathers that are in the kitchen loft to be put into a bed for her," [163] but it was not until about 1720 that she had, by her mother's bequest, a bedstead of her own.[164] Poor families, owning few chickens or shooting few wild ducks, might never be the owners of a feather bed and might be forced to sleep on beds of chaff or flock. If a feather bed was acquired, it was something to be used for life and to become the chief treasure of a little estate.[165]

Three bedsteads in a room were not unusual.[166] William Byrd the first unabashedly had his bed in his parlor and he complained more than once that he slept without sheets, though not in his own home.[167]

---

[158] *Corbin MS Letter Book*, 46.

[159] Cf. offer of reward of three pistoles for watch stolen from Samuel Galt's shop in Williamsburg (*Va. Gazette*, Nov. 17, 1752). Samuel Rockwell at that time was operating a repair shop in Hampton and was selling clocks at the Raleigh Tavern in Williamsburg (*Va. Gazette*, Oct. 27, 1752).

[160] Letter of Dec. 25, 1762, to John Page, in *Jefferson Himself*, 9.

[161] 1 *Orange Wills*, 181.   [162] 5 *Richmond Co. Wills*, 356.

[163] 10 R. *Lancaster Wills*, 88. See *supra*, p. 43.

[164] See Mary Hewes's will in 8 *V* 284.

[165] E.g., Jane Coleman's inventory, Nov. 21, 1723 (*Westmoreland Records*, 1723–46, p. 1).

[166] Cf. 2 *Chastellux*, 150. It sometimes is difficult to distinguish in an inventory between a bed and a bedstead, unless the nature of the "bed," feathers or flock, is given. In the inventory of Col. John Tayloe, Nov. 2, 1747, before the building of Mount Airy, there is mention of beds and bedsteads of several types (5 *Richmond Co. Wills*, 547), but in Thomas Plummer's inventory (*ibid.*, 581), two years later, nine beds and one cot are mentioned in four rooms. There is no reference to standing bedsteads, only to "hide" and "cord." Often bedrooms and even parlors were overcrowded. An amusing jumble in the parlor of Walter Brodhurst, as early as 1661, is described in his inventory (*Westmoreland Deeds and Wills*, 1661–62, p. 48).

[167] Sheets, like towels, do not appear to have been abundant, but John Grymes of Middlesex boasted twenty-six pair (27 *V* 410). Nathaniel Pope had fifteen pair in 1719 (6 *Westmoreland Deeds*, 600). Charles Carter of Cleve in 1764 possessed twenty-three pair (6 *King George Deeds*, 229).

Thomas Lee had eleven beds and kept one of them in the library, to say nothing of two couches in the hall.[168] Henry Lee had thirteen beds,[169] the curtains of which, if fashionable, were of great variety. A few families boasted "musketo curtains." [170] Trundle beds were in general use.[171]

Chairs were abundant and of many sorts. Those most esteemed were of Russian leather or "turkey work." Damask was rare. In bedrooms or dining rooms, chairs usually had flag or reed bottoms. Arm chairs were not exceptional, but cushions were. Large families required many seats. Daniel McCarty had forty-two arm chairs.[172] Thomas Beale of Richmond County died with no less than thirty-seven chairs for his issue.[173] Willoughby Newton had a full dozen from the skilled hands of Spence Monroe.[174] A "groaning" chair was Andrew Monroe's proud possession.[175] The hall of Moore Fauntleroy's home in Richmond County contained thirteen chairs—as well as a large oval table, a desk, an escritoire, a tea table and a "gamon table." [176] In most residences, the numerous chests were of pine or walnut. Cherry, too, was a popular wood, as was oak.[177] Mahogany was being more frequently employed for chests by 1750, but still was somewhat unusual.[178] Rugs were not in general use, though a few rich planters had fine floor covering and also rugs for out-of-door ease taking.[179]

On the walls of about half of the dwellings were some pictures; other walls had only white-wash or the paint, bright or soft, that the taste of the owner suggested. William Byrd the second had been a patron of Charles Bridges; [180] William Dunlop, a merchant of Dumfries, had as his hobby, in George Washington's childhood, the collection of portraits of British political leaders and of men of letters.[181] John McAdam

---

[168] 4 *Westmoreland Records*, 77 a.

[169] *Westmoreland Records and Inventories*, 1746–52, p. 62.

[170] Ludlow inventory of 1767 in 21 *V* 406. This inventory lists four types of bed curtains. Henry Ashton's inventory of 1758 also mentioned mosquito curtains (4 *Westmoreland Records*, 66).

[171] *Westmoreland Records and Inventories*, 1723–46, p. 36, show three in the inventory of Spence Monroe. Robert Osborn's estate (*Fairfax Wills*, A, 1, p. 51), included a "truckle" bed.

[172] *Fairfax Wills*, A, 1, p. 25.   [173] 5 *Richmond Co. Wills*, 195.

[174] This was in 1766. See 14 *Westmoreland Deeds and Wills*, 461.

[175] 5 *Westmoreland Deeds and Wills*, 293.

[176] 5 *Richmond Co. Wills*, 356. For backgammon boards, see *infra*, p. 124.

[177] Zephaniah Wade, 1746, had a "cherry and maple painted table" (*Fairfax Wills*, A, 1, p. 172).

[178] Cf. John Michelson's advertisement in *Va. Gazette*, Sep. 5, 1751.

[179] Cf. John Carter's order from Edward Tucker, n.d., *Carter-Plummer MSS*, 146.

[180] Letter of Dec. 30, 1735 to Col. Alexander Spotswood, 36 *V* 211. See also Alexander W. Weddell, *Portraiture in the Virginia Historical Society*, 139.

[181] 15 *W* (1) p. 278–79.

of Northumberland probably was beginning his collection of prints and pamphlets on the preceding two centuries of European history.[182] Charles Stagg, of the Williamsburg theatre, owned twenty-five prints and maps when he died in 1736.[183] William Hunter, the printer, boasted a "sea piece" in a gilt frame, nineteen prints, a landscape, the "Ruins of Rome" in a frame fitly gilded, and a number of other pictures.[184] Perhaps the largest collection had been that of Alexander Spotswood. He had twenty small and forty-two large mezzotints.[185] William Fitzhugh owned five portraits by Hesselius.[186] In the home of George Johnston of Fairfax County were two paintings without frames, six Hogarth prints and thirty-six mezzotints.[187] The "specialty" of John Colville of the same County was "painted collections of flowers." Of these he had twenty, to say nothing of thirty-eight blank or unpainted "collections." He enjoyed in addition thirteen prints.[188] Philip Ludwell Lee's particular treasure in 1776 was to be a series of seventeen prints of some of Rubens's paintings.[189] Apparently, the "thirty-eight pictures" owned by Col. Thomas Jones of Williamsburg were diversified.[190] To some of these collections, Joseph Ball the second occasionally made additions. He was a connoisseur of prints and he delighted to describe in his letters the excellences of those he sent his Virginia friends.[191]

Poor homes had no pictures, no decorative furniture. For chairs, the struggling farmer used three-legged stools of his own making. If a family of the humblest station possessed a table, it probably was one of hewn planks set on trestles. There were no closets, no chests in such homes. Extra clothing was hung on pegs. A widow's portion might consist of a bed and its covering, a chest and a box, a candlestick and a few odds and ends.[192] She might be the envy of still poorer neighbors if she received from her husband's estate a feather bed and furnishings, a leather chair, a looking glass, a smoothing-iron and heater,

[182] 4 W (1) p. 156.
[183] 3 W (1) p. 251.
[184] 7 W (1) p. 12–14.
[185] See his inventory (1 Orange Wills, 181).
[186] 3 W (1) p. 141.   [187] Fairfax Wills, C, 1, p. 1.
[188] Fairfax Wills, ibid., 125; ibid., B, 1, p. 135.
[189] At least this is the most probable interpretation of the language of the inventory: "a set of Reubens, 17 pieces" (Westmoreland Records, 1776–90, p. 173).
[190] 26 V 176.
[191] Frequent references occur in his Letter Book.
[192] Cf. the settlement of Margaret Farrow, 45 V 180. While this is dated 1691, a generation before Washington's birth, it undoubtedly was typical of the estate of many persons in 1750.

a white cedar pail, a small spinning wheel, a table and some cut-lery.[193]

The particular will that included these bequests required the widow to pass on to her daughter "one pretty large iron pot," a possession typi-cal of those without which even the humblest could not subsist. Cook-ing utensils somehow were procured from England. Imported frying pans, iron kettles, pot hooks,[194] gridirons, spits—these and like articles were to be seen by every hearth. If one of these utensils was broken, the parts usually were saved in hope they might be sold as old metal.[195] The tableware of the poor, though meagre, was cherished. Crockery, in general, was brought "from home," but a small quantity was received from New England or Pennsylvania. A little was made in Virginia.[196] Knives, forks and spoons were of pewter and even of wood. In the great houses, the cutlery was of steel and silver and the tableware of china. Silver was increased from one generation to another until, in some families, there was superabundance of it. When the third, ex-travagant William Byrd was to become insolvent in 1769, he was to possess seven dozen knives and forks and was to owe £662 for plate.[197] The Washingtons and the Balls were not extravagant in their purchase of silver or of anything else. A great day there was to be in the winter of 1749–50 when Lawrence Washington was to bring home to his young half-sister Betty a present from her half-uncle Joseph Ball in England— a chest of tea, six spoons, a strainer and tongs of silver, and a box full of sugar "ready broke," as Ball wrote the girl, "so that as soon as you get your chest you may sit down and drink a dish of tea." [198]

Others of her class were as fortunate as Betty Washington, but every family suffered excessive loss of china through carelessness in the kitchens. At death, Mrs. Frances Spencer, who had lived on an ample scale, had twelve glasses only and not more than eighty-eight pieces of earthenware of every sort.[199] In some homes, no dishes or plates sur-

---

193 Will of John McCloud, Apr. 3, 1724, 4 *Princess Anne Deeds and Wills,* 9.
194 Cf. *Brunswick Deeds and Wills,* 1732–40, p. 147.
195 *Ibid.*
196 See *infra,* p. 196.
197 9 *V* 82. A description of some of the old silver of Virginia will be found in an article by E. M. Davis in 49 *V* 105 ff. For that part of the silver of Richard Lee the second that was "marked with a squirrel," from the family crest, see 5 *Westmoreland Deeds and Wills,* 479. William Fitzhugh's silver is described briefly in 2 *V* 140, 269, 277, 377. That of Henry Ashton is mentioned in 7 *W* (1) p. 177, and that of Willoughby Newton, 1776, in 14 *Westmoreland Deeds and Wills,* 461. A list of the silver stolen from Thomas Lee's home at the time of the fire (see *supra,* n. 90), appears in 34 *V* 104.
198 *Ball Letter Book,* Nov. 2, 1749.
199 *Westmoreland Records and Inventories,* 1723–46, p. 66.

vived long unless they were made of pewter.[200] Nor could any outlast
the voyage to Virginia unless packed with care and handled with more
tenderness than sailors and dock-men usually displayed. Wrote William
Byrd indignantly: "Your convict ship arrived safe with the goods, if
one may call that safe where everything is damaged and broke to pieces.
I never saw anything so demolished as every parcel that belonged to
me was . . . Everything that would break of mine was shattered to
pieces, and what would not break, was damaged . . . My Glasses were
all shattered . . . not one piece of glass as big as my nail to be found
in the straw." [201]

Over the china that escaped rough usage, on the tables of young
Washington's friends, shone the light of candles. Well-to-do homes
used bees' wax, but during the first quarter of the century, myrtleberry
wax had been harvested and put in widespread use. Tallow still provided the candles for plain homes and for kitchens.[202] The poor burned
pine knots in winter and sat without light in summer.

In almost every item of lighting, furniture and equipment, George's
own home at Ferry Farm was typical of the second order of Virginia
houses: it was far below the level of luxury that prevailed on the greatest estates, but it was adequate. The hall, which had a bedroom in rear
of it, was painted and was not adorned with pictures. A mirror hung
on one wall. Most of the eleven leather-bottomed chairs probably were
arranged around the larger of two tables. The arm chair doubtless was
that in which Augustine Washington had rested near a fireplace supplied with screen and fire-irons. This hall served, also, as dining room.
Its china, modest in value, was ample in quantity. The linen was in

---

[200] Cf. the inventory of George Mason of Aquia, Sept. 9, 1730 (*Stafford Wills*, 1729–48, p.
16). This inventory is exceptionally detailed in its references to household utensils, but in it
scarcely any china and little plain earthenware are mentioned. Another extensive inventory,
that of Mrs. Anne Lee McCarty (*Westmoreland Records and Inventories*, 1723–46, p. 123),
showed only five syllabub and five drinking glasses. Nothing is known of the fate of George
Lee's tortoise shell plates, mentioned in his inventory of Feb. 5, 1762 (4 *Westmoreland Records*,
160). A housewife doubtless would be apt to write "recently purchased" opposite the entry
concerning 138 pieces of queen's ware china and the thirteen "dissolved jelly glasses" in the
inventory, 1776, of Philip Ludwell Lee (*ibid.*, 173).
[201] Letter of July 10, 1741, no addressee; 37 *V* 110. See a somewhat similar note by
Colonel Gordon, Mch. 12, 1760 in 11 *W* (1) p. 197. Perhaps the carelessness of servants was
one explanation of occasional instances where even slave-owning families apparently preferred
"light housekeeping" with a chafing dish and few utensils. Cf. the inventory of John Miner's
estate, 1753; *Fairfax Records*, B, 36.
[202] An interesting list of different sorts of candles appears in the most informative inventory on the subject, that of Capt. Robert Kingman, but the relative use of wax and myrtleberry
may have changed somewhat by 1750. Kingman had seventy lbs. of myrtleberry wax, 229 lbs.
of tallow candles, and thirty-one lbs. of wax candles (4 *Princess Anne Deeds and Wills*, 41).

keeping with the china. Glasses were few, because of breakage. There was no plate, but the silver spoons numbered twenty-six.

The room intended for a parlor had been made to serve as a chamber in which were three beds. Into its closet was put a variety of unused or discarded articles—"lumber" the family styled the whole. Four other bedrooms contained a total of eight beds, two of which were old.

Mrs. Washington's chamber was directly in rear of the hall.[203] Its two windows had hangings; both its beds were furnished; a chest of drawers stood on one side of the room. A dressing glass, four rush-bottomed chairs, a trunk and a tea table made for comfort. Heat was supplied in winter from a separate fireplace.

The dairy was well equipped and was used, also, for washing clothes. Ironing was done in the kitchen. Numerous old tubs, which Mrs. Washington would not throw away, were kept in the storehouse. There, too, were the reserve pots and pans and all the cloth for making garments for the Negroes. To George's eyes, doubtless, none of these things was comparable in interest to a tripod and certain boxes that Augustine Washington himself had put carefully away in their appointed place. These were the surveying instruments which, with the rifle and the axe, were the symbol of the extending frontier.[204]

The food of Ferry Farm and of every plantation was supplied almost entirely from its own acres. To some visitors, the consumption of bread and meat seemed incredible.[205] A large family, servants included, disposed daily of fifty pounds of fine flour and of a like weight of "seconds" at the master's house alone.[206] On a plantation with approximately 250 slaves,[207] the consumption of food and drink in a year was estimated by one owner at 27,000 pounds of pork, twenty beeves, four hogsheads of rum, 150 gallons of brandy, 550 bushels of wheat and an unreckoned quantity of corn, which was the principal food of the

[203] There is a possibility that this was used as a guest room, but the description of the contents most certainly fits occupancy by a woman. As it never was customary for the daughter of a family to have a chamber below stairs, the assumption is measurably safe that this was the mistress' room.

[204] This description of the contents of the buildings of Ferry Farm is based on the detailed listing in *King George Inventories*, 1721–44, p. 285–91.

[205] For the excellence of food in homes of abundance, see *Beverley*, 237, 254.

[206] *Fithian*, 261.

[207] Unfortunately, the exact number of slaves on the Nomini estate in 1774 has not been established. Carter told Fithian that he owned about 600 altogether; (*Fithian*, 106), but these were scattered over numerous farms. According to the census of 1782, Carter had 278 slaves in Westmoreland, where Nomini Hall was located (10 *V* 230).

"field-hands," the slaves who tilled the soil.[208] Corn, indeed, was becoming the second staple of the Colony and was in another generation
to warrant the statement that in Northern Virginia tobacco paid the
. taxes and provided the luxuries, but that "everything lives on corn." [209]
Meat was cheap. Beef had been a penny a pound in 1740.[210] For those
who had the time or the servants to seek it, game still was abundant
in most sections of Tidewater. Breakfast, prefaced in most homes by
brief thanks to God,[211] was as early as dawn on small farms or as late
as 8:30 or 9:00 in the homes of the leisured.[212] For the meal there might
be both risen bread and some form of Indian cornbread on the table,[213]
with coffee, tea or chocolate. The main dish usually was a hash or
fricassee of whatever meat dish the family had eaten the day before.[214]
Dinner generally was served in the middle of the day, at any desired
hour between noon and 3 p.m.,[215] and was a serious affair. If salad
greens or other suitable vegetables were at hand, they were boiled with
bacon or shoulder. In the event there were no greens, the smoked meat
was served cold, but was more or less of a side dish. The main foundation was hot meat, game, or chicken, or more than one of these.[216] Fish
was consumed widely. Oysters, abundant in Tidewater,[217] were not
universally liked.[218] Supper usually was a light meal and might be
omitted altogether if dinner had been late and heavy.[219] For Sunday
dinner, to which numerous guests would be invited while the family
was at church, there might be greens, fish, roast pig, puddings, cheese,
and drinkables presently to be mentioned.[220] Such a meal made guests
from afar gape with amazement and then eat with approving zest.

208 *Fithian*, 100.
209 John David Schoepf, *Travels in the Confederation*, tr. Morrison (cited hereafter as
Schoepf) v. 2, p. 36.
210 William Byrd to "Mr. Southwell," May n.d., 1740, in 37 *V* 104. The low cost of
meat probably was one reason why board in 1724 was £15 per annum in Williamsburg (26
V 178).
211 Fithian (*op. cit.*, 56) wrote in 1773 that the grace always expressed "by the people
here," was in these words: "God bless us in what we are about to receive." After dinner, the
language was: "God make us thankful for His mercies."
212 *Ibid.*, 41, 46.
213 John Harrower to his wife, June 24, Dec. 6, 1774 in 6 *A. H. R.*, 83, 88.
214 "Observations," *London Magazine*, July 1746 (cited hereafter as *Observations*), in 15 *W*
(1) p. 146. For the author, Edward Kimber, see 54 *V* 344.
215 The secret diary of William Byrd shows that he dined consistently at noon. The hour
at Nomini Hall was 2:30 to 3:00 (*Fithian*, 21, 24, 46).
216 Harrower to his wife, 6 *A. H. R.*, 84. For hams and pork in general, see *infra*, p. 144.
217 See Michel's narrative of 1702 in 24 *V* 35.
218 Fithian, in his *Journal*, Dec. 19, 1773, p. 46, thought a supper of oysters an event of
sufficient interest to justify an entry.
219 Harrower, 6 *A. H. R.*, 89.
220 This was the menu at Nomini Hall, Apr. 3, 1774 (*Fithian*, p. 120).

Their chief criticism was of the bread: Virginians ate too much of it "hot and new"; [221] the cornbread "baked on the fire"—the revered cornpone of natives—some visitors scarcely could stomach.[222]

Small farmers probably ate corn in one or another form of bread at least twice a day. Wheat bread they had not more frequently than once daily, if that often. They consumed little beef. Smoked pork—hams, shoulders or sides—were their regular meat. Game was a luxury for the poor of Tidewater, though they often spent in hunting more time than they should.[223] West of Tidewater, food changed quickly toward the frontier. Wheat flour and even corn meal depended on mills. Opulent diet, as represented by the cherished hot breads of eastern Virginia, stopped at the farthest milldam.[224] When George Washington was eleven, Moravian missionaries found in Amelia County, not more than sixty miles from the magnificence of William Byrd's Westover, a family that had neither bread nor flour. The missionaries were fed on roasted potatoes.[225] Elsewhere if there was corn on the frontier and no mill, the best that could be done with it was to follow the Indian practice—to burn a crude mortar in the stump of a tree and to crack the corn with a log for a pestle. Hominy then could be made.[226]

The jug, too, seldom got farther westward than the mill. Wrote a surveyor near the frontier: "All we drink here is water and sometimes rum, but that is very dear and very little money to buy it." [227] Conditions were far different in those parts of Virginia long settled and accessible from the sea. Drink there was varied, was abundant and was enjoyed without abashment. When Ambrose Baxter had died in 1719, his coffin had cost 200 lbs. of tobacco, but three gallons of rum "and other funeral expenses" added 320 lbs. to the bill.[228] Young George Washington was to see the time when the drink bill of a party of men engaged in boiling salt from seawater equalled 90 percent the cost of feeding them.[229] John Harrower, indentured servant and school teacher, suspended his lessons daily at noon to give the children some recreation

221 Jones, *Virginia*, 52.   222 Michel, 24 *V* 114.
223 See *infra*, p. 119.
224 Even in the older settlements, the permit of a court to build a mill by damming a stream was a valuable asset. See George Turberville's application, Feb. 25, 1731 for extension of his permit to erect a grist mill on Nomini River (sic). *Westmoreland Orders*, 1721-31, p. 355.
225 Diary of Leonhard Schnell and Robert Hussey, Nov. 29, 1743, in 11 *V* 380.
226 Jones, *Virginia*, 53.
227 George Hume to James Hume, c. 1723, in 20 *V* 401.
228 *Westmoreland Records and Inventories*, 1723-46, p. 7.
229 This was in 1776; 17 *V* 377.

before dinner, and he had his master's standing permission then to enjoy "as much good rum toddy" as he chose to down. After that, he spread his legs under the table for a meal at which he quaffed "good strong beer." Perhaps it was not illogical for him to add, "[I] seldom eat any supper." [230] In other homes, there was "a good hearty cup to precede bed." [231]

Most planters prepared on their farms at least a part of their alcoholic beverages. They made persimmon beer or,[232] occasionally, persimmon brandy [233] and they produced an acceptable malted liquor with molasses, though they confessed a preference for the Bristol product [234] or for ale, which they imported largely. A hogshead of ale, in bottles, which John Carter ordered at least once,[235] may have been an unusual item on an invoice because it was in so many small, corked vessels, but the volume was not exceptional. From their apples, many farmers ground and fermented excellent cider, which, it was alleged, they often drank up before it matured fully.[236] The distilled liquors most generally produced at home were apple or peach brandy.[237] These did not compete in popularity with West Indian rum, which was much preferred to the cheaper New England product. Fluctuations in the price of this drink were watched anxiously.[238] Prudent men who loved their rum were careful to keep a stock on hand. An usher of the grammar school of William and Mary, for example, died in 1741 and left an estate of £124 only, but he had among his assets twenty gallons of rum.[239]

Along with these twenty gallons of rum, the usher had four dozen

[230] John Harrower to his wife, Dec. 6, 1774; 6 A. H. R., 89. Some superlatively bad verse, evidently written while Harrower had a remorseful "hangover," will be found in ibid., 105.
[231] Observations in 15 W (1) p. 146.
[232] Jones, Virginia, 52.
[233] Fithian, 72. For a Culpeper petition that the Crown permit all persons to retail without license liquors of their own making and distilling, see 2 L. J., 1062.
[234] Jones, loc. cit.
[235] John Carter to Edward Tucker, n.d., Carter-Plummer MSS, 146.
[236] Jones, op. cit., 41. A favorite imported cider was "Hughes's." (Va. Gazette, Mch. 12, 1752.) "Cyder Royall" is mentioned occasionally.
[237] From the frequent mention of stills in private inventories it would appear that fruit brandy was produced more generally than has been assumed. Joseph Ball the second was one of those who restricted to an absolute minimum the distillation of peach brandy, because the peaches were "for the hogs and they must have them." (Letter of Mch. 20, 1743–44 to Joseph Chinn, op. cit.) Subsequently Ball directed Chinn to sell all brandy except "a little for necessary use" and to be careful, for the future, to distill according to the best methods (Letter of Apr. 5, 1748, op. cit).
[238] The highest quoted by Colonel Gordon in his diary, 6 s. per gallon, was for Feb. 2, 1759, during the inflation caused by the French and Indian wars. See 11 W (1) p. 100. Current retail prices best are gauged by advertisements in the Va. Gazette and by the court records that show what charges the ordinaries might make. See infra, p. 156.
[239] 1 W (2) p. 56–57. Bottles were preserved with much care. The inventory of Townsend Dade, 1735 (Stafford Wills, 1729–48, p. 175) listed one gross and seven dozen.

bottles and half a pipe of a beverage especially liked in Virginia.[240] This was Madeira wine, brought chiefly by vessels that carried to the "wine islands" staves, wheat and other products of Virginia.[241] The "wine was available in hogsheads, pipes or quarters.[242] On occasion, a group of wealthy planters would charter a ship, load it with wheat, corn and planking, and dispatch the vessel to Madeira to exchange its cargo for wine. In doing this, it sometimes was necessary to put Madeira merchants strictly on notice, because they might send an inferior product.[243] Of European wines, hock and claret were the favorites,[244] but numerous ordinaries had prices set by the court for some wines which they may not usually have kept in their cellars— Canary, sherry,[245] "French white wine" [246] and perhaps others. Prices were high. In 1752, claret was selling in Williamsburg at 40 shillings a dozen.[247]

In serving these wines, there was no etiquette which prescribed or forbade certain wines for certain foods. At one notable dinner, the beverages were "porter beer," cider, rum and brandy toddy.[248] At another dinner, the offerings were "several sorts of wine," lemon punch, toddy, cider and porter.[249]

Dress for such dinners was elaborate. On most occasions, in fact, Virginians wore "the best of clothes according to their station; nay, sometimes too good for their circumstances." [250] In this, as in almost all else, London was the model for the wealthy.[251] The wives and daughters of the great planters were forever sending to England orders that must have been in complexity and particularity the despair of the merchants.[252] These feminine orders were costly to the planters, too, and

240 Jones, *Virginia*, 52.   241 See *infra*, p. 144.
242 Cf. advertisement of ship *Friendship* in *Va. Gazette*, Feb. 27, 1752. For the supply Robert Stobo carried with him on a military expedition in 1754, see *infra*, p. 382.
243 See John and Charles Carter to Captain of brigantine, Nov. 10, 1733, *Carter-Plummer MSS*, 22. Washington learned later that the wine merchants seldom parted with their best product for anything but coin of the realm or London exchange.
244 Cf. John Carter to Robert Cary, Aug. 1, 1734; *Carter-Plummer MSS*, 30.
245 Middlesex Co., March, 1770; 12 V 188.
246 10 *Richmond Co. Orders*, 1732–39, p. 268.   247 *Va. Gazette*, Mch. 12, 1752.
248 Men and women were present (*Fithian*, 120).
249 *Ibid.*, 76. Further references to drinking habits will be found in the section of this chapter that relates to ordinaries, *infra*, p. 156.
250 Jones, *Virginia*, 43.   251 *Ibid.*, 32.
252 Some of the most detailed of these will be found in the letters of Richard Corbin to English merchants, 1758–59; *Corbin MS Letter Book*, 16, 25 ff, 28, 70. Others worth consulting by anyone interested in the fashionable Virginia dress of 1725–30 are the orders of William Beverley (3 W (1) p. 225), of Mrs. Dawson (6 W (1) p. 124), of Mrs. Jones (26 V 163, 177) and of Col. John Lewis of Warner Hall for his step-daughter, Elizabeth Carter (*Conway's Barons*, 121). The inventory of Benjamin Berryman, 1749 (*Fairfax Wills*, A, 1, p. 274), showed a surprising diversity of fabrics on hand for ladies' dresses.

not always of the expected quality, though occasionally the spouse of a London merchant would shop with discriminating taste for the wife of a good Virginia customer.[253] To judge from the description given a few years later by a young Princetonian who was serving as a tutor in a rich Virginia family, the appearance of the women justified the outlay. Miss Jenny Washington chose "a chinz gown with an elegant blue stamp"; [254] Miss Lee had her hair "knotted up very high, and in it, neatly woven, a riband with a sprig of green jasmine." [255] Almost every lady wore a red cloak when she rode, and she wrapped a "white handkerchief over [her] head and face." [256] In contrast this was the garb of a "lusty" servant woman, aged 30, who absconded: "She had on an old striped India cotton gown, the forebreadth of which she had taken out and put in a breadth of something else. She also had on two old quilted petticoats, a drugget westcoat without sleeves, lined with brown linen and bound with bombays, a shift and apron of Prince's linen." [257] Sometimes the runaways picked with much discrimination from their mistresses' wardrobes. Servant Sarah Benfield, "about 60 years old, of a dark complexion, with bad teeth and black hair which [curled] down her back behind," departed in "a pair of fine pink colored worsted stockings and leather shoes, an old dark brown quilted petticoat, a checked apron, a striped Mancaster bed gown and a black beaver hat." [258] Anne Barret, 24, carried off "new pumps with red heels, red cloak, and several head dresses and ruffles, aprons, &c." Her companion in running away, John Osborn, 25, stole "a suit of fine broad-cloth, shirts, stocks, boots, gray cut bob wig and fine hat." [259]

Men's dress was elaborate on high occasions. Fortunately, for persons not of exalted social station, dress did not have to be formal except on the King's birthday and then only in Williamsburg where every Englishman—of office or of station or of both—was supposed then to put on "handsome, full-dress silk clothes" and to call on the Governor.[260] At other times the individual could dress much as he pleased. Fashions did not change rapidly. A male might "wear the same coat three

---

253 Cf. *infra*, p. 165 and bill of "Mrs. Cary," Jan. 17, 1757 (*Custis Papers* VHS). One order of clothes for the womenfolk of Richard Corbin was £112 (*Corbin MS Letter Book*, Aug. 22, 1758, p. 25).

254 *Fithian*, 163.   255 *Ibid.*, 279.

256 *Ibid.*, 38.

257 *Va. Gazette*, Jan. 27, 1738. It is not thought that the dress of servant women changed materially in the next ten or twelve years.

258 *Va. Gazette*, Dec. 8, 1752.

259 *Ibid.*, Mch. 12, 1752. These runaways also stole two horses and saddles.

260 Stephen Hawtrey to his brother, Edward Hawtrey, Mch. 26, 1765; 16 V 210.

years." [261] Men shaved almost universally and much esteemed their collections of razors.[262] Perukes were seldom worn. Most men used light caps under their hats.[263] Some enjoyed two such caps.[264] As serviceable a wardrobe as a thieving runaway could take from a well stocked master was thus described: "an old blue broadcloth coat and jacket, a dark, colored coat with a cape; a felt hat; a pair of new britches; 2 pairs of woolen stockings, one dark, one white; two caps, one linen, the other yarn; two pairs of trousers, one linen, one oznaburg; two shirts, one checked, one oznaburg." [265] There were innumerable buttons on clothes of the better sort, mother of pearl, silver plated, double gilt.[266]

The material of clothing ranged, according to wealth, taste and season, from linen and silk to woolens of many kinds. For slaves and for the humbler whites, oznaburg, a coarse linen, was in general use as an outer garment in summer.[267] The price of this linen was not high. Nor were coarse woolens expensive.[268] Clothes of fashion, on the other hand, were so costly that sometimes proud men of station would not go visiting because they could not buy fitting apparel.[269] Shoes and stockings, regardless of price, were commercially a vexation. All except the crude shoes for slaves' winter wear, and many even of these, were bought in England. Measurements were vague; sizes were not standardized, though sometimes mentioned. Frequently a considerable part of a shipment of footgear for a plantation would prove too small.[270] In spite of disappointments and misfits, orders for numerous women's shoes of every smart fashion crowded the planters' inventories.[271] The

261 *Ibid.* Three years seem a moderate limit. Inventories of the less well-to-do classes often included threadbare clothes, bluntly described in one instance (7 *V* 363) as "old sorry clothes worth little."

262 Cf. in *Va. Gazette,* Mch. 20, 1752, an advertisement for two cases of stolen razors, "four in the set, with tortoise shell handles."

263 15 *W* (1) p. 158.

264 Cf. advertisement for runaway William Griffin, aged about 19: he "had on when he went away, a coarse hat much worn, an old silk cap full of holes, and a white ditto . . ." (*Va. Gazette,* Jan. 30, 1752).

265 *Va. Gazette,* Oct. 24, 1745.

266 John Harrower purchased some of all three sorts (6 *A. H. R.,* 92, 96).

267 Cf. Robert Carter to Thomas Colemore, July 24, 1723 (*Carter Transcripts,* VHS). The cloth was correctly spelled osnaburg, after the early seat of its manufacture, Osnabrück, Germany.

268 John Carter in 1732 had ordered £20 of "woolens and linens as cheap as may be that I may pay my father's legacy to the poor of the parish." (John Carter to M. Perry, Aug. 8, 1732—*Carter-Plummer MSS.*)

269 Cf. Mrs. Elizabeth Beverley to [first name unknown] Bland, her brother. c. 1745: "I am very sorry we should be deprived of your company for want of clothes and I wish it were in my power to give you some" (23 *V* 361).

270 Robert Carter's correspondence fairly groaned with complaints on this score.

271 See, as typical, those mentioned *supra,* p. 107, n. 252.

case was much the same with stockings. These always were needed and always were an article of ready barter.[272] The persons most to be envied, in the hot Virginia weather at the end of July, were the boys who went barefooted and wore only shirt and breeches.[273]

These lads fought their mock wars not with the Indian tomahawk only but also with wooden swords, made in crude imitation of those their fathers no doubt wore on ceremonial days. The dress sword was the main appurtenance of the gentleman's attire when, for example, he called at the Governor's Palace on His Majesty's aforementioned natal day. A Virginian of station was content to have one such sword [274] or to borrow one; a landed lord as careful in such matters as was "King" Carter might own several swords and might protest he had "never a belt that's fit to wear." [275] Jewelry was frequently but not generally used. Women often wore rings but they seldom had necklaces.[276] Men had gold shirt studs, carried seals [277] or snuff boxes,[278] or wore wedding [279] or mourning rings.[280]

These mourning rings were accepted as evidence not only of affection for the dead but also of recognition of the continuous presence of death even in a Colony so thinly peopled. That "fell Sergeant" was "strict in his arrest." Sickness and the nearness of death were a conspicuous part of life. Longevity already was somewhat greater than in the seventeenth century,[281] and was destined to increase perceptibly between 1750 and 1800; but illness was frequent at all ages, and fatal to many. Some of the sickness was heartbreaking. Wrote William Beverley in 1742, "My dear son John . . . departed this life at Col.

[272] John Harrower, for example, traded a pair of old worsted stockings for twenty-two feet of gum plank, ten inches wide, with which to make himself a chest (6 *A. H. R.*, 82).

[273] *Fithian*, 197.

[274] Cf. the inventory of Travers Downman, May 27, 1728; 5 *Richmond Co. Wills*, 99. The sword was appraised at £4. It had a silver hilt and a belt.

[275] Robert Carter to M. Perry, July 18, 1723; *Carter Transcripts*, VHS.

[276] One valued at £80 was an issue in a suit, probably between friends, brought by Daniel McCarty, attorney for Frances Spencer, against Peter Hack (10 *V* 321), but this was exceptional.

[277] Inventory of Henry Ashton, *Westmoreland Records and Inventories*, 1723–46, p. 110; *Va. Gazette*, Aug. 19–26, 1737, May 29, 1752.

[278] *Ibid.*, Sept. 1, 1738, for a description of one in the form of a coffin.

[279] Will of Joseph Copeland, Isle of Wight County, Feb. 25, 1726, bequest to his daughter Elizabeth of "two Negroes and a gold ring, the poesie being: As God decreed, we agreed." (7 *W* (1) p. 307.)

[280] In *Va. Gazette*, Oct. 29, 1736, is a detailed description of the ring given under the will of a prominent colonial.

[281] Prof. James C. Southall remarked in his genealogy of the Cocke family that he had not found the record of a single octogenarian in the seventeenth century (3 *V* 291). Apparently there is an interesting field of research in the gradual extension of the life-span in the Southern Colonies during the eighteenth century. The contrast between the age of decedents in, say, 1675, as compared with 1775 is startling and does not seem to be explained by anything that has been published concerning the prevalence of communicable disease.

Byrd's (where I had placed him at school) and that inhuman lady who kept my dearest boy, tho' very sick all along [alone?] in a cold room without fire or anybody to lie with him to keep him covered, though it was very cold, and to my extreme grief I got there two nights before he died, having with him only that old fool of a doctor we saw at Col. Bland's, who had no medicine, and before I could get a doctor it was too late . . . the sweetest boy that e'er was born . . ." [282] Even when illness was not serious, the ordeal of treatment was severe—boluses, emetics, purging powders and the like.[283] "I may suppose," wrote Thomas Jones, "I am to wade through rivers of water gruel and chicken broth, strengthened with molasses, with no other support than the yolks of four poached eggs once a day without bread or salt." [284]

Physicians were of every degree of competence and of quackery. Many of the practitioners were "discarded surgeons of ships," [285] apothecaries "or such"—to quote the act of 1736—"as have only served apprenticeships in those trades." [286] A few physicians were graduates of British universities and, in more than one instance, men of professional attainment. Perhaps the highest name in George Washington's boyhood was that of John Mitchell who had practiced in Urbanna and had kept an apothecary's shop there,[287] In 1745 he foreswore medicine for botany and the next year returned to England where he had a career of much scientific distinction.[288] If young Washington heard anything of Dr. Mitchell, it could have been praise only. Dr. John Tennent had been mentioned already.[289] His advocacy of the virtues of senega, or snake root, was carried so far that he and his supporters attributed to that herb healing qualities only one state short of the miraculous.[290]

Lack of physicians compelled many families to rely on home treatment.[291] In practicing on their slaves and servants, the planter or his

282 To John Fairchild, Mch. 7, 1742; 3 W (1) p. 231.

283 See as typical the bill of 1747 in the *Jones Papers*, 26 V 75. Cf. John Custis to unnamed correspondents, 1717, n.d.: "It is unknown the many mischiefs bad medicine do; the apothecaries think anything good enough for Virginia, whereas those medicines sent beyond seas ought to be the best [that] can be had; for my part I had rather pay a shilling for good medicine than 2 d. for an indifferent one" (*Custis Letter Book*, No. 5).

284 Thomas Jones to Mrs. Pratt, Oct. 14, 1725, 26 V 79.

285 William Byrd to Sir Hans Sloane, Apr. 20, 1706, LC trans. quoted in 1 W (2) p. 186.

286 4 H 509. This act probably expired in November, 1738. See Sec. IV, p. 510. Cf. Blanton, 400.   287 *Va. Gazette*, Nov. 21, 1745.

288 See *Blanton*, 137, and the numerous references there cited.

289 *Supra*, p. 62.

290 *Va. Gazette*, June 3, July 8, Dec. 9, 1737; 2 *L. J.*, 882; 3 W (2) p. 211; 5 *ibid.*, 107. This strange case is well summarized in *Blanton*, 119 ff.

291 Cf. 2 *Chastellux*, p. 129; 11 W (1), p. 202.

wife consulted such works as *Every Man His Own Physician,* a book which was third only to the Bible and to the Prayer Book in the estimation of the colonials. Many familiar, standard drugs were recommended in this volume [292] and were offered for sale by apothecaries or physicians,[293] but great faith was placed in secret treatments. Pagan, a Negro slave belonging to Mrs. Frances Littlepage of New Kent, had been credited in 1729 with so "many extraordinary cures" that upon disclosure of his secrets he was liberated at public expense by the payment of £50 to his owner. A residuum of prudence led the Council of the Colony to stipulate that Pagan should remain under the direction of the government until he made known his mysterious method of expelling poison and of achieving other marvels.[294] Later, Mary Johnson was to have £100 if three leading men of the Colony, duly designated, would certify to the efficacy of her medicine in curing cancer.[295]

Other rewards there were, and testimonials not a few. Tar water was alleged to prevent smallpox and to cure fever and consumption.[296] The second William Byrd, scorning physicians, thought ginseng close to a cure-all, ipecac a remedy for fever and for dysentery, and fern root an antidote for snake bite.[297] Governor Gooch in 1729 had gone to great pains to get the components of an herb medicine which an old Negro had concocted. Remarkable cures, said Gooch, had been effected by this medicine in Virginia, but difference in climate might make it of no avail in England, though he submitted it to London physicians.[298] Occasionally, this faith in mysterious methods and secret cures led families of distinction to subject themselves to quacks, even to Negro wonder workers. Suits for malpractice sometimes resulted.[299] More interesting and more readily avowed, were the experiences of white settlers with the frontier medicinal springs, the virtues of which the Indians doubtless had extolled. The Washingtons were becoming familiar with the most famous of these springs. Lewis Burwell, Presi-

---

[292] *Md. Gazette,* Aug. 2, 1734; *Va. Gazette,* Sept. 9, 1737, June 23, 1738. For a bibliographical description, see *Blanton,* 127 ff.

[293] *Va. Gazette,* Aug. 28, 1746, May 22, Aug. 14, 1752.

[294] 4 *E. J.,* 199.

[295] 2 *L. J.,* 1014; Dec. 6, 1747. Other rewards for alleged remedies are described in *Blanton,* 214–15. An advertisement of Richard Bryan's cure for dry gripes appeared in *Va. Gazette,* Mch. 27, 1752.

[296] Not to mention lesser ills; *Va. Gazette,* May 2, 1745.   [297] *Blanton,* 181 ff.

[298] June 29, 1729; 1 *Gooch MSS,* 116. For other testimonials, tributes to herb remedies, etc., see William Byrd in letters to Sir Hans Sloane, Sept. 10, 1708 to Apr. 10, 1741, LC trans. quoted in 1 *W* (2) p. 187. See *Va. Gazette,* Mch. 10, June 9, 1738, Mch. 20, 1752.

[299] See Colonel Gordon's diary, Mch. 23, 1760, in 11 *W* (1) p. 197; 10 *Richmond Co. Orders,* 81.

dent of the Colony, went to one of the primitive spas in 1751 and reported himself much benefitted.[300]

Burwell survived the journey not more than a year and a half.[301] In his burial, his family doubtless followed the prevailing usage of leaving a man to rest on his own ground. It was said of the Virginians that even those of modest means desired elaborate funerals and formal sermons by the minister.[302] If the clergyman insisted on delivering the sermon at church, the family, as a rule, had the actual interment at home, either in the garden or in the family graveyard.[303] Some there were, of course, who preferred to be buried in a churchyard or even in a church. Sir John Randolph, Speaker of the House of Burgesses, had the honor of sepulchre in the chapel of the College of William and Mary, where Rev. Thomas Dawson pronounced a eulogy in Latin.[304]

Some Virginians disliked funerals, at which crowds of half-strangers ate a vast deal of food and consumed all the rum that was offered them. Often a limit of expenses for entertainment at funerals was set in a will. Charles Carter of Cleve specified the mourning his friends should wear and he forbade black for the servants. The reason, he was to state in his will, was a determination "to put a stop to the ridiculous custom of involving families by pompous funerals and mourning which serve only to enrich men who watch for these occasions to impoverish their neighbors." [305] Even if they were victimized, most of Carter's friends wanted elaborate mourning. In a tragedy later to be described, a young man put himself and his manservant in black on receipt of the news of his sister's death; the girl's stepfather for months sealed his letters with black; [306] and, as he did not have time to procure the first or "deep" mourning of his wife and himself from London, he took pains to send for fashionable "second mourning" almost before he donned the sable.[307] Families were not to be cheated of ceremonious

[300] *Va. Gazette*, June 27, 1751. For a succession of later references to these springs, see *Blanton*, 9, and the article by Carl Bridenbaugh cited *infra*, p. 242, n. 126.

[301] His death was subsequent to Oct. 12, 1752, and may have occurred early in 1753.

[302] Jones, *Virginia*, 68.

[303] *Ibid.*, 67; *Fithian*, 56.

[304] *Va. Gazette*, Mch. 4, 1737. For reference to Randolph's monument and his career, see *ibid.*, Apr. 13, 1739.

[305] Will of Sept. 10, 1762, in 31 *V* 46. Thomas Lee, 1749, stated in his will: "Having observed much indecent mirth at funerals, I desire that last piece of human vanity be omitted and that attended only by some friends and relations that are near, my body may be silently interred with only the church ceremony and that a funeral sermon for instruction to the living be preached at the parish church near Stratford on any other day." (11 *Westmoreland Deeds and Wills*, 311.)

[306] 3 *G. W.*, 244.

[307] 3 *G. W.*, 141.

funerals. If season or circumstance necessitated a burial before kinsmen and cherished friends could be assembled, the funeral sermon might be deferred for days.

Monuments from England were expensive; epitaphs were elaborate; eulogies in the *Virginia Gazette* occasionally were in verse and, in the case of the famous toast Evelyn Byrd, ran to an acrostic.[308] Hannah Ludwell, wife of Thomas Lee, had the unusual distinction of a crude threnody in the *Gentleman's Magazine*.[309] Washington's cousin, Betty Washington, was eulogized in print simply as "a young gentlewoman of great merit and beauty . . . very much lamented." [310]

The interment of the poor accorded with their "short and simple annals" of which a young English poet was writing in 1750. For Thomas Franklin of Richmond County, coffin plank cost fifty pounds of tobacco and the making of the box a like amount.[311] To lay away Mary Fitzgerald of Princess Anne,[312] her estate was charged with £1, 1s 4d. The graves of the humble seldom were marked. When George Hume's uncle died at Germanna, then near the frontier, George accounted it greatly to Governor Spotswood's honor that pales were put around the burial place.[313]

Marriage and birth, like death, were a part of daily conversation and of correspondence. Before some girls were 16, they found mates.[314] The ceremony almost always occurred at the bride's home and, if the families were prominent, was an occasion of much entertainment.[315] If either husband or wife died, the survivor was expected to remarry as quickly as John Washington and his granddaughter Mildred and others of the family did. A second loss of a wife was no barrier to a third marriage. Four successive unions were not regarded, apparently, as representing either excess of ill fortune or of good. Six marriages were not unknown.[316] The issue often was in proportion. Although deaths among infants reduced the average family of the Colony to

---

[308] *Va. Gazette*, Dec. 2, 1737.
[309] Reprinted in 34 *V* 106.
[310] *Va. Gazette*, Feb. 18, 1737.
[311] This was in 1722. (*Richmond Co. Account Book*, p. 2.)
[312] Aug. 3, 1726; 4 *Princess Anne Deeds and Wills*, 66.
[313] Letter of June 20, 1723; 20 *V* 398.
[314] Mrs. Anne Muse, for example, provided in her will, admitted to probate Jan. 14, 1725, that her daughters were to have guardians until they were sixteen years of age, unless they married before that time (8 *Westmoreland Wills*, 58).
[315] Cf. as typical the account of Anne Gordon's marriage to Richard Chichester, given in Colonel Gordon's diary, June 9, 1759; 11 *W* (1) p. 104. After 1768, notices of marriages, sometimes with brief references to the charms of the bride, appear frequently in the *Va. Gazette*. See the issues of Mch. 16 and Nov. 2, 1769.
[316] Observations of James C. Southall, in 3 *V* 291.

approximately five persons,[317] the number of children sired by some of the colonial leaders was astounding. Fifteen were begotten by each of five men of conspicuous station—William Byrd the third, Lewis Burwell, Warner Washington, a cousin of George's, Mann Page and Thomas Marshall. The third Robert Carter had seventeen, John Page had twenty. Charles Carter of Shirley was the father of no less than twenty-three.

The aspect of married life most conspicuous in the court records and in the newspapers was that of wives who eloped or separated from their husbands and contracted debts in the men's names.[318] Financial dealings occasionally led to name calling that provoked judicial hearings or to bargains at the bar that neither should meddle in the other's affairs. Specifically in the case of John and Frances Custis, one provision of their reconciliation agreement read in this wise:

2nd. That Frances shall henceforth for bear to call him the sd John any vile names or give him any ill language, neither shall he give her any but to live lovingly together and to behave themselves to each other as a good husband & good wife ought to doe. And that she shall not intermeddle with his affairs but that all business belonging to the husband's management shall be solely transacted by him, neither shall he intermeddle in her domestique affairs but that all business properly belonging to the management of the wife shall be solely transacted by her.[319]

A Virginian of station left his "beloved wife" a life interest in his entire property but added: "In case of my wife marrying, embezzling or squandering any part of my estate, it shall be directly taken out of her hands to be taken care of for the use of my six children." [320] Debt and extravagance often clouded married life; parsimony sometimes did; [321] but if love had on occasion a pecuniary cast, it usually was wholesome and warm among the Virginians. There was earnestness in George Turberville's epitaph for his wife, Lettice Fitzhugh, who died in her twenty-fifth year after only five years of marriage: "She was beautiful but not vain; witty but not talkative; her religion was pure, fervent,

317 S. H. Sutherland, *Population Distribution in Colonial America*, cited hereafter as *Sutherland*, p. viii.
318 See *Va. Gazette*, Dec. 5, 1745, July 24, 1746, Sept. 4, 1746, Aug. 24, Dec. 5, 1751, Feb. 27, 1752, Dec. 11, 1766, Apr. 18, 1769. For a remarkable case in which husband and wife set forth their respective complaints in the same issue, see *ibid.*, Dec. 10, 1765.
319 June, 1714; *Northampton Record*, quoted in 4 *V* 64 ff.
320 Will of Daniel Gaines, 1757; 5 *W* (1) p. 91.
321 See the pathetic letter of Mrs. Elizabeth Beverley to her brother, Captain Bland, July 5, 1745, in 23 *V* 362.

cheerful and of the Church of England; her virtue steadfast, easy, natural; her mind that mixture of nobleness and gentleness as made her lovely in the eyes of all people." [322]

Affection did not express itself in epitaphs only. Husbands sometimes specified in their wills that they be entombed as near their wives as possible. Thomas Lee directed, for example, "that I be buried between my late dearest wife and my honored mother and that the bricks on the side next my wife may be moved and my coffin placed as near hers as possible without moving it or disturbing the remains of my mother." [323] Occasionally avowals less beautiful were made in wills. One colonial of station provided before his death for a woman "who came into this country in my ship and lived with me several years." He gave her land "in consideration of her services," and bequeathed 1000 acres to her daughter, whom he acknowledged as his own. [324]

Love letters anticipated much that wills fulfilled. Typical in their ardor but almost unique in their combination of courtship and report of bodily ills were the letters of Col. Thomas Jones to the widow, Betty Pratt. He won her in spite of his narration of his symptons and sickness, but after their marriage she herself had much of unhealth and she repeatedly was absent, in Philadelphia and even in London, for medical treatment. Thomas Jones's letters were full of his protestations of love and of the most intimate details of the children's maladies. He began Oct. 22, 1736: "My Dearest Life[:] I have not heard anything from you since your letter by Mr. Booker, which I have read over about twenty times since I received it not only with regard as a truly kind and tender husband, but with the pleasure of a passionate lover that flatters himself with the hopes some time or other of being possessed with his Mistress's Charms. I am always very sensible of the very great affection I have for you but never so much as to your absence. If there is any true happiness it is with one like you, where it is mutual, but as my portion is not so sublime in this World, I must be content with having that in my possession I most desire and is dearer to me than my own life." He did her the courtesy of dropping to the next line for a new paragraph, but he made his transition with no waste of words: "Tom has taken three Purges since you went . . ." [325]

---

[322] 7 *W* (1) p. 95.
[323] 11 *Westmoreland Co. Deeds and Wills,* 311. The will of George Lee, 1761, contained a like request to be buried "as near my wife [Anne Fairfax, formerly Mrs. Lawrence Washington] as possible" (14 *ibid.,* 91).
[324] *Fairfax Wills,* B, 1, p. 97.   [325] 26 *V* 284.

Parents' concern over the health of their children was only one phase of their ideal of the family. This was well represented in the obituary of the merchant Thomas Nelson of Yorktown: "As he lived just, so was he blessed not only with the increase of his wealth but in the comfort of his children whom he lived to see . . . all happily married, settled and enjoying the greatest honours and preferments." [326]—an ideal not easily achieved.

The youthful Virginians were full of fire. Sisters sometimes had long memories of brothers' shortcomings—that Bob had been "flogged often by their Pappa; often by masters in the college; that he had stolen rum and had got drunk and that he used to run away." [327] Sisters, too, might quarrel so violently over a brush that one might take off her shoe, throw it at her sister and, with feminine misaim, break a window pane.[328] When a girl had temper, she could voice it in her diary as surely as in rebuke of the offender. Wrote Sally Cary Fairfax, then 12 years old, concerning a servant who had killed a cat for scratching him: "A vile wretch of new negrows, if he was mind I would cut him to pieces, a son of a gun, a nice negrow, he should be kilt himself by rites." [329]

Of like temper, perhaps less violently expressed, there was abundance; but along with it there was much beauty and some pathos in the relations of mothers and daughters and of fathers and sons. Occasionally, a father had to protect his boy against some designing woman. Thomas Baber of Caroline County advertised that his seventeen-year-old son was "supposed to be in company with Winefred Bailey, an ill-disposed wench whom I understand he intends to marry." All clergymen were put on notice not to perform the ceremony till the boy became of age.[330] A youth, in turn, occasionally might seek to protect his father, as in the letter John Spotswood, son of former Governor Alexander Spotswood, wrote the *Virginia Gazette:* "I have learnt my book so far as to be able to read plain English where printed in your papers and finding in one of them my papa's name mentioned often by a scolding man called Edwin Conway, I asked my papa whether he did not design to answer him. But he replied: 'No, my child, this is a better contest for you that are a school boy, for it will not become me to answer every fool in his

---

[326] *Va. Gazette,* Oct. 10, 1745.   [327] *Fithian,* 66.
[328] *Ibid.,* 85.
[329] Entry of Jan. 3, 1772; 11 *V* 213; W. M. Cary, *Sally Cary* (cited hereafter as *Sally Cary*), p. 59. This diarist was not the Sally Cary who married G. W. Fairfax.
[330] *Va. Gazette,* July 24, 1746.

folly as the lesson you learned the other day of the lion and the ass may teach you.' This hint being given me, I copied out the said lesson and now send you the same for my answer to Mr. Conway's hint from, Sir, your humble servant, John Spotswood." [331]

This lightness of touch was unusual. Far more frequently the spirit of relations between father and children was as serious as that of Gawin Corbin's will. He specified that his daughter was not to marry until she was 21 years of age and then only with her guardian's consent. For violating either condition, she would lose the property. "This I desire," Corbin explained, "that a prudent choice may be made of a man of sense and family that she may live happily in the married state." [332] Where physical affliction occurred—it rarely did—anxious fathers were perplexed over the arrangements they should make. George Turberville had an epileptic daughter, Elizabeth, of whom he wrote in his will: ". . . her condition is such the more estate she has the readier she will be liable to ruin and destruction . . . I desire that Elizabeth Turberville live in my dwelling house and have the room called hers, as used in my lifetime, and to her I give the use of my negro woman Moll, who always takes care of her, and looks after her, to continue to do the same, and I beg and desire my dear wife Martha Turberville and my executors, to take all the care they can of my said poor unhappy daughter Elizabeth, that she doth not suffer for the want of necessaries of life suitable to her circumstances, and the same I give and allow out of my estate during her life providing the rents and profits of her own lands should prove insufficient." [333]

If there was sorrow in the Virginia of Washington's youth, there was sport as well, sport that provided the rich with most of their amusement, and the poor with much of their subsistence. The master hunted for the fun of it, the servant for the meat of it. A botanist in 1739 listed carefully the game of Virginia: "Deer in great plenty, bears, buffaloes, wolves, foxes, panthers, wild cats, elks, hares . . . squirrels, 3 or 4 sorts, raccoons, opossums, beavers, otters, musk rats, pole cats, minks and there has been two porcupines killed here, but they are very scarce." He went on: "Then for fowls, wild turkey's very numerous, partridges, wild geese, swans, brants, cormorants, teal, duck and mallard, black ducks

[331] *Va. Gazette*, June 10, 1737. His age at the time is not known precisely, but as he was the eldest child of parents married in 1724, and as his sister Dorothea was born in 1727, he probably was in his twelfth or thirteenth year.
[332] 13 *Westmoreland Deeds and Wills*, 265.
[333] Will of Oct. 6, 1740; 9 *Westmoreland Deeds and Wills*, 200.

and another sort we call summer ducks, plover 2 or 3 sorts, soris (a delicious eating bird in shape and way of living like y'r water rails), heath fowls (called here improperly pheasants) 2 sorts, wild pidgeons in prodigious great flocks, fieldfares, woodcocks (but what is very strange they come here only in summer), snipes, herons, bitterns, eagles, larks 2 sorts, one of w'ch are here all the year round, are as big as quails, the other are seen only in winter and are much like your lark." [334]

From this abundance of game, the hungry man shot what he chanced to find. If he had his choice of hunting, the average Virginian would seek the deer because that swift-footed creature of swamp and forest presented only a momentary, fleeting target that called for instant aim and sure fire. [335] Next in general preference and incontestably first in many counties was fox hunting. After that was what Washington from boyhood called "ducking," a trial of marksmanship against water fowl. In the mountains and elsewhere along the frontier, bear hunting came first because of the warmth of the skin and the bulk and toothsomeness of the meat. [336]

After hunting, horse racing was a favorite but, for many years, a restricted sport. In 1674 the Court of York County had fined James Bullocke, a tailor, for racing his mare against a horse of Mathew Slader. The reason, deliberately set forth, was that it was "contrary to law for a labourer to make a race, being a sport only for gentlemen." [337]

Even gentlemen then raced merely the native horse, which seldom was taller than 13½ hands. [338] After prosperity fattened the colonial purse, during the seventeen-thirties, some of the rich breeders began the importation of superior British stallions [339] whose fleet sons and daughters gave Virginia fine stock. Racing became a popular fad and then a colonial institution. Many planters had their own tracks, [340] on which, by subscription, races were held at advertised dates. April and August apparently were the favorite months for meets. Purses were as high as £90 [341] before the colonial currency began to depreciate, but

334 John Clayton to Samuel Durrent, Mch. 21, 1739, 7 *V* 173-74.
335 *Ibid.*   336 *Ibid.*
337 Quoted by W. G. Stanard in his "Racing in Colonial Virginia," 2 *V* 293 ff.
338 Jones, *Virginia,* 49. Cf. 2 *L. J.,* 803 for a proposed regulation of horse breeding. A discussion of the reason for the lack of height of these early colonial horses will be found in Fairfax Harrison, *The Equine F. F. Vs.,* 40 n. Robert Carter's reference to Virginia horses as "runts" will be found in his letter of July 18, 1723 to M. Perry—*Carter Transcripts,* VHS.
339 Fairfax Harrison listed them, *op. cit.* A typical order for such a horse will be found in George Braxton to Thomas R. Rootes, Sept. 21, 1761, *Blair, Banister and Braxton,* 146.
340 Those of Northumberland had numbered three, at least, prior to 1705. See the unhappy episode of Thomas Pinkard, who issued a challenge and did not redeem it (10 *V* 320).
341 *Va. Gazette,* Aug. 8, 1751.

the average was about thirty pistoles.[342] The superlative stake of the era of good money was the 500 pistoles the wanton spendthrift William Byrd the third bet that his chestnut horse Tryall could outdistance any contender. When the race was held, Dec. 5, 1752, Tryall was beaten by the renowned mare Selima, owned by Col. Benjamin Tasker of Maryland.[343]

Weight and distance of this famous match are not recorded. Usually the weight was about 130 lbs.; sometimes it was as low as 120 [344] and on occasion as high as 150.[345] Distances varied. The favorite race was of four heats of a mile each, with half an hour's rest between heats.[346] One such race of "four mile heats" was to be run in April, 1760, and was to be the subject of endless talk: The first heat was won easily by Mr. Edloe's Silvertail; the second was awarded to Colonel Randolph's Fortunatus but was warmly disputed; the third went to Mr. Hardiman's sorrel Pilot; the fourth could not be decided between Pilot and Fortunatus; this necessitating a fifth heat between the two, Fortunatus won by five feet. "Never," reported the *Virginia Gazette*, "was finer sport shown." [347]

If the races were held on "court day," they drew larger crowds of men who drank deeply and gambled heavily on the horses. This soon shocked a new Governor, Robert Dinwiddie, who, in a message to Council and Burgesses, invoked action against "gaming, swearing and immoderate drinking, particularly at county courts." The Governor said he was informed that gaming had become "pretty general" and was

[342] Slightly over $100, modern currency. Cf. 2 V 300–301. In *Va. Gazette*, Jan. 11, 1739/40, was advertised a race meet on the second day of which horses "not exceeding 13 hands" were to run. For another typical race at thirty pistoles, see *ibid.*, Aug. 14, 1746. The purse at Dudley's Ferry, King and Queen County, October, 1751, was advertised as "about 32 pistoles" (*ibid.*, Sept. 12, 1751. Cf. *ibid.*, Apr. 3, 1752).

[343] For these horses, see Fairfax Harrison, *op. cit.*, 51–52. After the depreciation, races for 100 guineas were not unusual. Cf. Harrower, 6 *A. H. R.*, 86. Fithian attended a race at Warsaw where Col. John Tayloe's Yorick ran against Dr. William Flood's Gift for £500, "besides innumerable small bets." This was Nov. 25, 1773 (*Fithian*, 32).

[344] Dudley's Ferry, October, 1751, *Va. Gazette*. Sept. 12, 1751.

[345] Same track, April, 1752. *Va. Gazette*, Apr. 3, 1752. For the 50-pistole race at the June fair of Fredericksburg, 1751, the weight was 140.

[346] *Va. Gazette*, Apr. 11, 1751; Mch. 27, Aug. 7, 1752. As will appear in its proper place, George Washington was one of the managers of a race at Alexandria, May 28, 1761, when the distance was "three times round the ground (being near three miles) the best in three heats" (*Md. Gazette*, Apr. 23, 1761). In a somewhat similar race in Richmond County, the first mile of the second heat was run in what was considered excellent, one minute and fifty seconds. (*Va. Gazette*, Aug. 4, 1768).

[347] John Randolph's abstract of the *Va. Gazette* of Apr. 11, 1760, cited in 16 V 207. For contemporary races at Leedstown and Annapolis, see *Md. Gazette*, Aug. 2, 1749, Sept. 4, 1751. The Marylanders had the practice of listing in their advertisements the names of the judges. In the races advertised Aug. 9, 1749, "all disputes [were] to be determined by the Mayor and Aldermen present."

practiced among the lowest class of our people; I mean tradesmen and inferior planters." [348] So much of a lure were horse racing and gambling that in 1752 the College of William and Mary forbade any student to keep a race horse in Williamsburg or nearby, or to be "concerned in any way in making races or in backing and abetting those that do." [349]

The young collegians likewise were denied by these regulations even so much as a glimpse of cock fighting which was, after hunting and horse racing, the favored Virginia sport, though some did not dignify it by that name. Gentlemen of different Counties selected their finest birds and formed mains of twenty to thirty. These fought for as much as five guineas a battle and fifty guineas for the odd match or the winning main.[350] Usually, the meet was at an ordinary, where, in later years, owners and spectators were so numerous that they spread their blankets on the floor and spent the night there in order to renew the battles in the morning; [351] but on special occasions the gentlemen might watch the fights all day and, in the evening, tender their indulgent ladies a ball.[352] Interest in cock fighting was destined to increase for a generation, until boys teased their tutors into permitting them to attend bouts,[353] and Negroes staged fights in the stable yards.[354]

The craze did not develop without protest. In 1752 an anonymous writer maintained in the *Virginia Gazette* that as man's property right in animals was derived from God, it was a matter of conscience whether man did or did not kill animals for food, but that it certainly was not his right to deprive an innocent animal of life for his own pleasure.[355] Reasons of a different sort were to prompt Robert Page to express in his will a desire that neither of his sons should ever be allowed to go to horse races or to cock fights, because these affairs were "only consuming of time." [356]

In this will Robert Page was to link "other public diversions" with horse racing and cock fighting, but such amusements were few in

---

348 See R. A. Brock, ed., *The Official Records of Robert Dinwiddie* . . . (cited hereafter as *Din.*), v. 1, p. 30, with the punctuation conformed to modern usage.
349 Regulations of Aug. 14, 1752; 2 *W* (1) p. 55. For other parts of these regulations, see *infra*, p. 134.
350 *Va. Gazette*, Feb. 27, 1752, May 24, 1770; 20 *W* (1) p. 16; 10 *V* 325.
351 2 *Chastellux*, 24. For George's presence at one main, on his return from Barbados, see *infra*, p. 257.
352 As, for example, after the match of Apr. 4, 1767, at Sussex Court House "between the Brunswick and Sussex Gentlemen" (10 *V* 325).
353 *Fithian*, 160.
354 *Ibid.*, 128.   355 Issue of Jan. 2, 1752.
356 Will of Aug. 15, 1765 (34 *V* 275-76).

number. Boat races sometimes were held along the rivers.[357] Young George Washington found delight in billiards, which could be played at some ordinaries.[358] On rare occasions, the people of a County would assemble out of doors for trials of speed on foot, for the inevitable horse races, for cudgeling, for fiddling and for ballad singing—"the best singer to have the prize, and all of them to have sufficient liquor to clear their wind pipes." [359] Fairs were held semiannually in Williamsburg, Fredericksburg, Alexandria and other towns.[360] These apart, the "public diversions" offensive to Mr. Page were chiefly in Williamsburg. There, balls and assemblies were held, especially during sessions of the General Assembly, by professional hostesses and by ordinary keepers who provided lights, music, liquors and collation usually at half a pistole [361] or at five shillings a person.[362] Once, at least, there was the added inducement of a "likely young negro fellow" [363] and once of "a likely young negro woman and her child . . . to be raffled for." [364] Besides affairs of this sort, which were duplicated sometimes in Norfolk,[365] there were occasional lectures [366] and exhibits.[367] On the King's birthday, the flag was flown at the capitol, the cannon at the palace were "thrice discharged," the annual calls of college professors and ranking citizens were made on the Governor; in the evening the palace, the college and some of the private homes were illuminated.[368] Victories [369] and public holidays [370] were celebrated gaily. Even observance of the death of members of the royal families took on an air

---

[357] *Fithian,* 198. Earlier references are scanty. Joseph Ball second was interested in having a house built for his boat which, in his absence, nobody was to use (Letter of Mch. 20, 1743/44 to Joseph Chinn—*Ball Letter Book*).

[358] See an interesting description of a billiard table offered for sale in the *Va. Gazette*, Jan. 16, 1746.

[359] *Va. Gazette*, Oct. 7, 1737. The announcement of this celebration of St. Andrew's Day and the subsequent report of the success of the occasion (*ibid.*, Dec. 2, 1737), would indicate that it was exceptional.

[360] 6 *H* 269, 286, 300; 7 *ibid.*, 652; 2 *Gooch MSS*, 542, letter of Feb. 22, 1739 to the Lords of Trade; 2 *L. J.*, 1063; *Va. Gazette*, Nov. 30, 1739. In his diary, John Harrower started to write an account of the Fredericksburg fair of 1774, but as the poor man that day had his horse, saddle and bridle stolen, he had no heart to describe the festivities in detail (6 *A. H. R.*, 87).

[361] E.g., *Va. Gazette*, Oct. 14, 1737.

[362] *Ibid.*, Apr. 13, 1739. For other announcements of balls and assemblies in Williamsburg, see *ibid.*, Feb. 18, 1737; Apr. 11, Oct. 24, 1751; Feb. 27, Mch. 5, 1752.

[363] *Va. Gazette*, Mch. 17, Apr. 13, 1738.

[364] *Ibid.*, Apr. 1, 1738.

[365] *Va. Gazette*, Mch. 7, 1751.   [366] Cf. *ibid.*, Jan. 8, 1767.

[367] *Ibid.*, Oct. 17, 1755.

[368] *Va. Gazette*, Nov. 2, 1739; Oct. 31, 1745; Nov. 17, 1752.

[369] As, for example, of Culloden, *Va. Gazette*, Jan 9, July 24, Aug. 21, 1746. Included were accounts of the exercises in Norfolk and in Hanover County.

[370] For a list of colonial legal holidays compiled by C. E. Gilliam, see 23 *W* (2) p. 517.

of display: the Governor and "several gentry" appeared in deep mourning, flags were at half mast, minute guns were fired.[371]

Official mourning was not permitted to interfere with an amusement particularly enjoyed by Williamsburgers and envied by all the other colonials—the theatre of the capital. This had been established in 1716 by Charles Stagg and William Livingston, husband of Susannah, already introduced in Fredericksburg, but the undertaking had been of doubtful financial success.[372] When the company could not supply sufficient entertainment, the "young men of the college" offered drama and not in light vein only. Boldly in 1736 they presented the tragedy of "Cato." [373] It probably was not the young gentlemen's amateur competition, nor yet the indifference of the audience, but the paucity of players and of rewards that closed the theatre about 1741–42 and led to the acquisition of the building by the town as its Court House.[374] In 1751 a new theatre was constructed, not without strain,[375] and was opened that autumn with a performance of "Richard III" and "a grand tragic dance composed by M. Demeter called the Royal Captive after the Turkish manner." [376] That year and the next, the Hallam players appeared in Williamsburg and probably in other towns,[377] though, for reasons unknown, they temporarily were denied the privilege of performing in the summer of 1752.[378]

The construction of the playhouse was far from good.[379] Apparently the stage was low and the spectators' floor was level. In later years, the Williamsburg paper was to report, perhaps with fictitious flourishes, a colloquy between a masculine patron and a lady in front of him who refused to take off her hat. "I am so short, Madame," he said, "that I can see nothing unless you will be so obliging." To this the lady replied

---

371 *Va. Gazette*, Mch. 24, 1738. Cf. *ibid.*, Feb. 24, 1738.

372 Its history is traced in L. G. Tyler, *Williamsburg, the Colonial Capital* (cited hereafter as Tyler, *Williamsburg*), 226.

373 *Va. Gazette*, Sept. 10, 1736; Thomas Jones to his wife in Caroline, Sept. 17, 1736; 26 *V* 180.

374 The indenture of Dec. 4, 1745 stated that the playhouse had not been "used for several years" and was "going to decay." See the document in 24 *W* (1) p. 29. See also *Va. Gazette*, Dec. 12, 1745.

375 *Va. Gazette*, Oct. 24, 1751.   376 *Ibid.*, Sept. 26, 1751.

377 The players advertised that they would make their bow in Norfolk (*ibid.*, Nov. 14, 1751), in Petersburg (*ibid.*, Dec. 19, 27, 1751), and at Hobbs' Hole and Fredericksburg (*ibid.*, Apr. 30, 1752).

378 Council minute of June 13, 1752 in 5 *E. J.*, 404. It was the opinion of Fairfax Harrison, who found this minute of Council, that refusal to permit the theatre to open at the time was due to concern over the prospect of war with France (*ibid*). The players were again before the public in September, 1752 (*Va. Gazette*, Aug. 21, 1752).

379 *Va. Gazette*, Aug. 21, 1752.

tartly: "Then, Sir, you should not have come here until you were
taller."[380]

By those, tall or short, who were not privileged to enjoy the delights
of the theatre and the festivities of the little capital of the Colony,
indoor winter amusements of a lesser sort had to be devised. In districts
where numbers of rich planters lived, there were itinerant dancing
schools[381] and occasional balls which might continue several successive
nights.[382] More frequently there were evenings of cards or of backgammon and of informal dancing to a fiddler's tune,[383] with abundance
of mirthful, bibulous song.[384] Some families had a genuine interest in
music,[385] and occasionally a delight in the African instruments the
Negroes still knew how to make.[386] Most of these diversions were
innocent enough, but some of the rich colonials had the Englishman's
traditional love of gambling on cards as well as on horse races and
cock fights. More than one estate was ruined by its owner's lack of skill
or luck at cards. In 1774, the son of a distinguished family was to come
home from Williamsburg in utter misery and with the confession that
he had lost at least £500 by gambling during the session of the House
of Burgesses.[387]

Small provision was made for the amusement of women. Some of
them were taught music; most of the well-to-do knew how to dance.
They rode horses, they visited, and they interested themselves, willingly
or perforce, in the stock on the plantation.[388] Many women had special
pets,[389] though they did not always find happiness in them. One lady

[380] *Va. Gazette*, Mch. 10, 1768.

[381] *Fithian*, 27, 42, 43, 88. For advertisements of dancing and fencing teachers in Williamsburg, see *Ludwell Papers*, VHS. Mch. 28, 1716, and *Va. Gazette*, Mch. 20, 1752 supplement.
In the accounts of Henry Fitzhugh's estate, Mch. 19, 1740, there is an item: "Cash paid Dearing
the dancing master, £8 12s 3d" (*Stafford Records*, O, p. 124). Visits of itinerant dancing
masters at Mount Vernon are mentioned in J. C. Fitzpatrick, ed., *The Diaries of George Washington 1748-1799* (cited hereafter as *Diaries*) v. 1, p. 377, and in S. M. Hamilton, ed., *Letters to
Washington* [1752-1775] (cited hereafter as *Hamilton*) v. 4, p. 31.

[382] *Fithian*, 63.

[383] Harrower's diary, Oct. 12, 1775, 6 *A. H. R.*, 103. For backgammon boards, see the
inventory of Henry Fitzhugh (*Stafford Deeds*, O, p. 5) and the inventory of George Eskridge
(*Westmoreland Records and Inventories*, 1723-46, p. 159).

[384] *Fithian*, 76.

[385] *Ibid.*, 39, 68, 167. The advertisement of a violin teacher, who wished, at specified fees,
to organize classes in and adjacent to Williamsburg, appeared in *Va. Gazette*, June 12, 1752.
Violins are mentioned frequently in the inventories of planters, e.g., Nathaniel Pope (6 *Westmoreland Deeds*, 600) and Rawleigh Travers third (*Stafford Deeds* O, p. 76). Henry Fitzhugh
had a German flute (*ibid.*, 5). In 1776, the inventory of Philip Ludwell Lee included a bassoon
and a spinet (*Westmoreland Records*, 1776-90, p. 173).

[386] Harrower's diary, Mch. 25, 1775, with particular reference to a barrafou; 6 *A. H. R.*, 93.

[387] 12 *Journ. So. His.*, 356-57.

[388] See Mrs. Robert Carter's observation to Fithian (*op. cit.*, 42), that to live in the country
and to take no interest in animals, poultry etc. "would be a manner of life too tedious to endure."

[389] See advertisement of a leopard for sale, *Va. Gazette*, Feb. 20, 1752.

was to write ruefully "We caught a great many red and mocking birds but by one accident or other we lost them all." [390] The women lived, usually, for their household duties, their families, their friends, their clothes, their religion and their celebrations. All the music, all the laughter, all the preparations led up to Christmas—holiday for the servants, festivity for the masters, and for the children freedom from school.[391]

Christmas might be, also, for the studious, a season for communion with literature. Virginians, it had been said, were more inclined to "read men by business and conversation than by books." [392] Most colonial families had begun with Bible and Prayer Book to which they added schoolbooks,[393] almanacs,[394] guides to home medicine,[395] works on the care of horses,[396] and volumes on business law. Poorer persons, if they possessed any non-religious book, may have acquired the original or some imitation of the *American Instructor,* which contained mathematical tables, writing lessons, guides for carpentry, instructions for dyeing, a description of the American Colonies, directions for health and medical treatment, "with instructions for marking on linen and how to pickle and preserve." [397] To these and similar volumes, William Parks, printer extraordinary in Williamsburg, added numerous books of his own manufacture on law, religion, history, and diversified subjects.[398]

[390] 21 *V* 90.

[391] Fithian, *op. cit.,* 45, 53, gave the most beautiful picture now extant of Christmas on a great plantation. There is, unfortunately, no corresponding account of the manner in which the average Virginian spent the Christmas season.

[392] Jones, *Virginia,* 44. Cf. Chastellux in the seventeen-eighties: The Virginians are "ignorant of the comfort of reading and writing" (*op. cit.,* v. 2, p. 150).

[393] Cf. Jones, *Virginia,* 44; 26 *V* 175.

[394] See *Va. Gazette,* Oct. 22, 1736.

[395] To judge from the manner in which it was advertised, the most popular such work, as noted supra, p. 112, was *Every Man His Own Doctor.*

[396] *The Gentleman's Pocket Farrier* was published in Williamsburg. See *Va. Gazette,* July 7, 1738.

[397] The versatile author of this inclusive collection of lore and wisdom was "George Fisher, Accountant." See *Va. Gazette,* Sept. 19, 1751.

[398] For Parks's first petition, 1726, to print the laws of Virginia, see 32 *V* 2. His compensation is described in 2 *L. J.,* 879, 899, 1054, 1055. Other references to Parks and to books and pamphlets printed by him will be found in *Va. Gazette,* Oct. 22, 1736, Apr. 7, July 7, 1738, Mch. 21, 1744/45, Aug. 8, Oct. 24, 1751, Jan. 17, Feb. 27, Mch. 20, Apr. 10, 1752. There are approximately 101 Parks imprints, but as no copies of five of these are known to be in existence, it is not certain they were issued. In particular, there is doubt whether *The Virginia Miscellany of 1731* appeared. Not included in the estimate of 101 titles is Charles Peale's projected *Essay toward Rendering the Rudiments of the Latin Tongue More Ease,* because there is no evidence this advanced beyond the subscription-lists mentioned in *Va. Gazette,* July 21, 1738. Titles known to have been issued by William Hunter, who was Parks's successor, were at least forty-seven in the years 1750–59 inclusive. Copies of all forty-seven are extant. In addition, Hunter may have published some books and pamphlets that have disappeared. Lest these figures for Parks's and Hunter's press leave the impression that the two produced literary

Successive printers conducted, also, a bookstore where, in 1751, about 200 titles were in stock; [399] but to judge from the works advertised, most of the customers must have been clergymen or pious church wardens.[400] Apparently, the clerical purchasers would have approved Commissary James Blair's recommendations of 1738 that in the expenditure of a legacy of £50 for books, it was better to "let the classics alone at this time and to lay out the £50 in more useful works of divinity." [401]

By no means all the affluent laity were of that mind. They had not become subscribers in any large number to the magazines then popular in England,[402] but most of the planters who bought books at all purchased something besides sermons. Taste varied extraordinarily. Some planters cared nothing for literature, had few books and often threw those into a neglected store room; other planters were enthusiasts.[403] As early as 1701, Ralph Wormeley had an excellent list of good books,[404] but a quarter of a century later, in John Chilton's estate of £1700, there were listed only "two small old Bibles and eighteen other books, mostly old." [405] Such contrasts persisted into the mid-century, though, naturally, as the Colony grew in age, it grew also in the accumulation of books. The largest known collection was that of William Byrd the second. He probably had 3000 books or more,[406] and he employed a librarian, who also served as tutor at Westover.[407] Other men with fewer books had some of the classics of their

---

works in considerable number, this classification may be permitted: Parks's publications included sixty-nine state papers, eight manuals and handbooks, two volumes of poetry, eleven religious works and nine almanacs. Hunter issued thirty-two state papers, four religious works, ten almanacs and a certain weekly journal, of which more is to be said.

[399] *Va. Gazette*, May 24, 1751.

[400] The table of contents of James Hervey's *Meditations and Contemplations*, a religious work of much popularity and most extravagant style, was printed *in extenso* in the *Va. Gazette* of July 30, 1752. For other advertisements of current books, see *ibid.*, Apr. 22, 1737, Oct. 24, 1745, May 30, 1751.

[401] James Blair to the Bishop of London, July 17, 1738; 20 *W* (2) p. 131.

[402] References to magazines are more numerous after 1765, though *The Gentleman's Magazine* was then thirty-four years old. See *Va. Gazette* (Rind's), May 26, 1768; *Fithian*, 93, 246.

[403] On this score, some Virginia historical writers have been singularly sensitive, as if the absence of books from inventories of estates was a reflection on the Colony and not merely a reflection of an individual's taste (cf. 7 *V* 299 ff and 10 *ibid.*, 389. See, also, infra, p. 152).

[404] 36 *V* 283.

[405] *Westmoreland Records and Inventories*, 1723–46, p. 44. The same record credited George Eskridge Jr. with an old Bible and four other books. Henry Moryson had eleven old books; John Pope had one only. The first reference to books observed in the records of Spotsylvania County is in the inventory of Elizabeth Warren, who had two books (*Wills*, B, 1749–59, p. 74).

[406] When the books were sold in 1778 they numbered 3625 (4 *W* (1) p. 156; 9 *V* 82, 12 *ibid.*, 205; 16 *T* 100 ff), but that total doubtless included the volumes bought by the third William Byrd.

[407] See the librarian, William Proctor, to his brother. July n.d., 1739; 10 *V* 300.

times. In the modest estate of Thomas Macredie of Spotsylvania was a *Don Quixote* in four volumes.[408] Daniel McCarty owned Cowley's works.[409] Robert Beverley possessed most of the Latin writers with the apparent exception of Livy.[410] When John Carter ordered a "Tully" in 1734, he admonished his agent to send the best edition procurable.[411] Among the treasures of the merchant William Dunlop, of Dumfries, were eighty-two works in French.[412] Dabney Carr had *Tristram Shandy* over which to chuckle.[413] Two decades later, when Wilson Cary came to draw up his will, he was to provide that his executors send to England and procure lettered and calf-bound sets of the *Spectator,* of *Pamela,* of *Clarissa* and of *Sir Charles Grandison* for Sarah Cary.[414] A contemporary of Cary's, Councillor Robert Carter, had at that time what even a candidate for the Presbyterian ministry described in some discouragement as "vast numbers of book on divinity." [415] Carter was careless with his treasures, but some Virginians, or their executors, took pains to look for the lost sheep and even to advertise for them.[416]

The medium through which the disturbed owners made known their loss was itself an organ of nascent colonial literature, a diversion as well as a depository of information. Established Aug. 6, 1736, by William Parks,[417] the *Virginia Gazette* was more or less of a court paper, with the usual reprint of news from European capitals,[418] but almost from the first it reported Virginia occurrences and published poems, essays and a bit of humor.[419] In time, the *Gazette* invented a fictitious character,

---

[408] *Spotsylvania Wills,* B, 1749–59, p. 170.
[409] *Westmoreland Records and Inventories,* 1723–46, p. 28.
[410] *Spotsylvania Wills,* A, 1722–49, p. 245.
[411] As will appear in Vol. III, Washington was equally careful in ordering books for "Jacky" Custis.
[412] 15 *W* (1) p. 275–79.   [413] 2 *V* 225–26.
[414] 10 *V* 190. Sarah was his granddaughter. For other interesting collections of books see Daniel Parke Custis's lot (17 *V* 404 ff); John Herbert's (1 *Chesterfield Wills,* 379, 18 *V* 181 ff); will of Sir John Randolph (36 *V* 376); Richard Hickman's law collection (34 *V* 216–19); description of Charles Brown's works on natural science, etc. (*Va. Gazette,* June 16, 1738); and George Turberville's inventory (*Westmoreland Records and Inventories,* 1723–46, p. 274). Joseph Ball's most treasured items are listed in his *Letter Book.* The collection of the second Richard Lee (2 *W* (1) p. 247) contained at the time of his death 248 volumes. Contrary to the subsequent belief in the family that he studied Hebrew, he had no book in that language. If any of his Bibles were printed in Hebrew, there is no indication of that fact in the inventory. An extended discussion of the literary tastes and books of colonial Virginians will be found in *Wright,* 117 ff.
[415] *Fithian,* 35.
[416] *Va. Gazette,* Apr. 24, 1752; *ibid.,* Mch. 24, 1774, quoted in 10 *V* 103.
[417] See his opening statement of that date.
[418] Particularly to be observed are the issues of September, 1737.
[419] Typical issues were those of Nov. 5, 1736, July 22, 1737, Jan. 6, April 7, 1938, Oct. 12, 1750, Feb. 26, Mch. 12, 1767, Mch. 16, 1769.

Tom Bell, who traveled far and played many pranks;[420] and it had an anonymous correspondent, Tom Truthteller, who sometimes was blunt in justifying his name.[421]

Prior to the establishment of this weekly publication, there had been some opposition to newspapers. In 1726, the testy John Custis had written his London merchant to protest against a charge of 3 s. for news sent him by John Clark. Said Custis: "I never have had any newspapers in my life nor ever desire any. I do not regard who has lost a spaniel bitch, who has died of the small pox and such stuff as Gazetts are stuffed with, and if Clark has charged you with any such thing on my account he is a rascal."[422] Time had changed this view. Although the *Virginia Gazette* contained in each issue an undue number of advertisements of standing stud horses and runaway Negroes, it was an accepted institution, nothing less.

Doubtless many young Virginians learned their letters from the *Gazette* and with its help prepared for one or another of the three types of school offered beginners. In several localities, men like Benjamin Syms, Dr. Thomas Eaton,[423] Hugh Campbell, William Horton,[424] John Farneffold,[425] Mrs. Mary Whaley,[426] John Yeates [427] and others [428] had made bequests for schools. While two and possibly more of these outposts of instruction remained in being as late as 1750, there was general regret that so few parts of the Colony had public parish schools.[429] For the well-to-do, this deficiency was made good by small private schools where a tutor, if procurable, shepherded the children of one family or of a small neighborhood.[430] In some of the

[420] Note especially Oct. 24, 1745 and July 24 and Aug. 14, 1752.
[421] Following the death of William Parks in 1750, the *Gazette* passed in January, 1751, to William Hunter who edited it until the summer of 1761 (see issues of Jan. 24 and Dec. 27, 1751). In the edition of Aug. 27, 1766, a new proprietor, Alexander Purdie, explained that the cost of paper and of everything else used in the printing business compelled him to raise the price of the publication to all subscribers. By that time, William Rind, at the instance of Thomas Jefferson, had set up a rival *Virginia Gazette* in Williamsburg. For a few years after 1775 the town had three *Gazettes* published by different printers.
[422] To M. Perry, 1726, n.m., n.d., *Custis Letter Book*, No. 38.
[423] 20 W (2) p. 3.
[424] Tyler, *Williamsburg*, 127.
[425] *Northumberland Records*, 1706–20, p. 234, a most interesting foundation.
[426] 4 (W) 1, p. 1–14.
[427] 5 W (2) p. 30.
[428] Cf. *Beverley*, 224, and *Wright*, 101 ff.
[429] 6 W (1) p. 82; Commissary James Blair to the Bishop of London, 1724, in 6 W (1) p. 79; Governor Gooch to his brother, June 28, 1729 (*Col. Williamsburg MSS*).
[430] Fithian, so often quoted in this chapter, taught only the children of Councillor Robert Carter: John Harrower, as noted, *supra*, p. 85, n. was permitted, for his own financial benefit, to instruct a few adults and some young students in addition to the Daingerfields (6 *A. H. R.*, 96, 97, 106). In Colonel Gordon's diary, 11 W (1) p. 99, 100, 101, 196, are several glimpses of a neighborhood school of thirteen children.

schools, Latin was taught,[431] and not always for the reason which prompted Bob Carter to brave the conjugations—the assurance that he could not have either of the Tayloe girls as his wife unless he knew that language.[432] Bob's older brother Ben was not so well-disposed toward the classics. When called upon to construe some Greek, he swore and wished he might kick Homer who, he had been told, had invented Greek.[433]

Although it was exceptional to teach Greek in family or neighborhood schools, instruction there in other subjects was sometimes excellent, often good and seldom bad. Of such intellectual training as was available, fathers usually wished their sons to make the most; but some parents were realistic concerning the unwillingness of young men to learn. Isaac Allerton, for example, provided in his will that his children were to be brought up to read and write, and were to be taught arithmetic, grammar and Latin. Should any of the boys be of "promising genius" he should be placed in the charge of someone by whose guidance he might gain. Any of the sons who lacked capacity was to be bound, at the age of 15, to any "mechanick trade" he might choose.[434]

Where it was not possible to put a boy or girl in a neighborhood school, because of poverty or distance, an effort usually was made by court or parish church to acquaint him or her with the rudiments. If the parents were illiterate or unreliable, their children sometimes were taken from them and were apprenticed. A general condition of apprenticeship or "binding out" was that the child be taught to read and write.[435] Orphans who had no property were given this third and poorest form of schooling. A fatherless child with an estate would be sent to school and would have the cost met, if need be, from the *corpus*.[436]

The greatest difficulty encountered in maintaining schools of any type was that of finding what advertisers were seeking constantly, "a sober person of good morals capable of teaching children." [437] From the

---

431 Perry, *Papers relating to the History of the Church in Virginia* (cited hereafter as *Va. Church Papers*),295; Daniel Hornby's will (*Richmond Co. Wills*, 1725-53, p. 593).

432 *Fithian*, 103.

433 *Ibid.*, 72. Ben was then about 18. A typographical mistake in 6 *V* 88 makes it appear that he was born in 1750 but the year actually was 1756.

434 Will of Nov. 27, 1739 (9 *Westmoreland Deeds and Wills*, 29-30).

435 See *infra*, p. 146. For a typical instance of taking children from unworthy parents, see *Charles City Orders*, March and June terms, 1737.

436 *Warwick Orders*, 1748-62, p. 163, 215; cases of Thomas Martin's children and of Elizabeth Jones, Mch. 1, 1753.

437 *Va. Gazette*, Mch 21, 1751. For similar advertisements, often in substantially the same language, see *ibid.*, Feb. 9, 1739, June 27, 1751, Mch. 5, 1752, Nov. 7, 1755 (in 25 *V* 20). See also Colonel Corbin's requirements, in his *MS Letter Book*, 73.

insistent repetition of the virtuous adjective "sober," it would appear
that good teachers were not always sober or sober teachers uniformly
good. In the early days of the Colony, tutors acted sometimes as clerks,
also. For example, Nathaniel Pope, George Washington's great-great-
grandfather, seeking a teacher, was given in 1652 the name of a man
who, he was assured, "can write a very good hand, sifer, and is able to
keep your accounts." [438] Such men rarely were available. "Often," an
observer reported in 1746, "a clever servant or convict that can read
and write and is of no handicraft business is indented to some
planter." [439] A better, though a scarce source of supply, was that of
young candidates for holy orders, who needed money for their education. [440] Of such honorable, temperate and competent men, an over-
large percentage were Scots, admired for their excellencies but shunned,
somewhat, because of their dialect. Their pupils acquired this and,
said one Virginian, never could "wear [it] off." [441]

The Scottish teachers might have replied that the Virginia planters
did not pay enough to deserve good speech. For a year's service, a
Scotsman usually received his "diet," shelter and £20,[442] though at a
later time a good Princetonian contracted at £35 sterling and received
£40.[443] A favored and successful teacher, taking boys into his own
home and lodging and feeding them for a year, might hope for £25
per student. For the instruction of individual small children, in a school
supported principally by one planter, the allowance was about £1
per annum.[444] Compensation, in fact, was so poor that when a teacher
from England started to open a school in Williamsburg, he took pains
to advertise that "Mrs. Walker, [his wife] likewise teaches young
ladies all kinds of needle work, makes capuchines, shades, hats, bonnets
and will endeavor to give satisfaction to those who will honor her with

[438] N. Hayward, London, to Nathaniel Pope, Nov. 25, 1652; 9 V 332.

[439] Observations, 16 (W) 1 p. 157.

[440] Fithian was in this category; so was the school master at the nearby plantation of the
Fauntleroys (Fithian, 33).

[441] William Beverley to M. Perry, July 2, 1741, 19 W (1) p. 145. Cf. Fithian, 125. Fithian
noted, op. cit., 234, that Lancelot Lee in 1773 swore that if a sister of his married a Scotchman,
he would never speak to her again, and that if he had a daughter and she married such a man,
he would shoot her dead at once.

[442] Beverley, loc. cit.

[443] 3 Hamilton, 360; Fithian, 7, 8, 262.

[444] 4 W (1) 3, 201. In a Westmoreland inventory, the estate of Capt. Daniel McCarty is
charged £9 for boarding John Pope one year (2 Westmoreland Records, 7). The report of
George Mason's guardian shows that in 1736-39 the boy was charged 1000 pounds of tobacco
for schooling (9 W (1) 241. Cf supra, p. 78, n. 26). In the Vestry Book of Charles Parish,
York County, appears the inventory of Jane Culley, teacher, in 1721. Unfortunately, this interesting document does not show the duration of the teaching covered by the different items,
the largest of which was £ 1, 10 s on account of Thomas Curtis.

their custom." [445] One dancing master discreetly withheld his list of fees when advertising.[446] An instructor in Williamsburg, on the other hand, was specific in stating that "a true method of singing psalms" would be inculcated for one pistole and an entrance fee of one dollar.[447]

Not all the grievances of teachers were over small pay. In some instances, chilly rooms and lack of candles added to the loneliness of a life which was in a family but scarcely of it. The teacher and librarian at the second William Byrd's Westover complained on both these scores and elicited this half-jesting, half-serious answer from the master: "If such [a candle] as you have . . . would burn an hour and a half, that is full long enough to read by candle light—which is not good for the eyes and after that meditation and devotions might fill up the rest of the winter evening." [448]

The day was occupied with lessons. "From one hour by sun in the morning until one hour by sun at night," a benefactor of a somewhat later date sternly provided that the children instructed from his bequest should have the teacher in attendance.[449] While this was the extreme, young Maria Carter complainingly summarized the normal routine when she wrote her cousin of the same name, Mch. 25, 1756: ". . . I am awakened out of a sound sleep with some croaking voice, either Patty's or Milly's, or some other of our domestics with Miss Polly, Miss Polly, 'tis time to rise, Mr. Price [450] is downstairs, and though I hear them I lie quite snug till my Grandmother uses her voice, then up I get, huddle on my cloaths and down to book, then to breakfast, then to school again, and maybe I have an hour to myself before dinner, then the same story over again till twilight, and then a small portion of time before I go to rest, and so you must expect nothing from me but that I am, dear cousin, most affectionately yours." [451]

Instruction in the seventeenth century had been difficult because of lack of books as well as of teachers,[452] but before 1750, school books had become abundant and comparatively inexpensive.[453] Quite often

445 *Va. Gazette*, Nov. 17, 1752.   446 *Ibid.*, Nov. 8, 1737.
447 *Ibid.*, Nov. 3, 1752.
448 William Byrd the second to William Proctor, Nov. 18, 1740; 37 *V* 108–09.
449 Nathan Yancey, 1789; quoted in 17 *V* 323.
450 Evidently the teacher.
451 Maria Carter of Sabine Hall to Maria Carter of Cleve, Mch. 25, 1756, 15 *V* 432–33. The routine of study at Nomini Hall in 1773–74 was substantially that of Sabine Hall (see *Fithian*, 41, 157). Harrower's school hours are mentioned in 6 *A. H. R.*, 106–7.
452 Of Hugh Jones's *Accidence to the English Tongue*, 1724, said to have been the first English grammar written in the Colonies and printed in England, the only known surviving copy is in the British Museum (19 *W* (2) p. 272).
453 See 6 *A. H. R.*, 78; 26 *V* 175.

the Bible was the "reader." [454] If a boy of humble station could spell out Holy Writ, write an intelligible letter and do simple problems in arithmetic, that was as much as usually was allowed him. The instruction of his sister was apt to be that which Mrs. Ann Beckham set forth in a last will: "My daughter's education is to be this: to learn to read, write and cipher and the use of her needle." [455] Where larger opportunity was offered, children frequently progressed fast. In 1774, an indentured servant-teacher taught a deaf-and-dumb lad of 14 how to read and write; [456] earlier, William Byrd the second introduced his son to astronomy at home. [457] The advance of a family school in one year at Nomini Hall, without any long summer vacation, was to do high credit to Philip Fithian. [458] In 1732, Betty Pratt, aged 10, had penned her eight-year-old brother in England a letter that compared the schooling of the old country with that of the new, and she demonstrated by her own words that the colonials were not altogether backward. She wrote: "I find you have got the start on me in learning very much, for you write better already that [sic] I expect to do as long as I live, and you are got as far as the Rule of three in Arithmetick, but I can't cast up a sum in addition cleverly, but I am striving to do better every day. I can perform a great many dances and am now learning the Sibell, but I cannot speak a word of French." [459]

By the time Betty had acquired the "polite language" and had seen more of English periodicals, she might have read in the *London Magazine* that Virginia girls "under such good mothers have twice the sense and discretion of the boys," [460] but the girls' training began and ended in the home.

A number of Virginia youths went to the English public schools, to the universities or to the Inns of Court. Edinburgh was the most favored university, Oxford was second, and Cambridge third. Of the schools, Wakefield in Yorkshire attracted the largest number of boys from the Old Dominion. Eton came next. For the training of lawyers, the Virginians preferred Middle to Inner Temple. The list at no time was long. For the decade 1740–50, few students went to England. In

[454] Harrower carried Bathurst Daingerfield through a reading of the entire Bible before teaching him to write (6 *A. H. R.,* 106).

[455] Dated Oct. 22, 1736; *Richmond Co. Wills,* 1752–53, p. 294.

[456] 6 *A. H. R.,* 82.

[457] William Byrd to Sir Charles Wager, Apr. 12, 1741, 37 *V* 109.

[458] See his journal, 25, 29, 33, 34, 37, 46, 83, 168. The last of these items covers a summary of the advancement of several of the Carter children in a year.

[459] Betty Pratt to Keith William Pratt, Aug. 10, 1732, 26 *V* 288.

[460] *Observations* in 15 *W* (1) p. 158.

the next ten years, the names of nineteen students known to be Virginian appear on the rolls of institutions of learning in the United Kingdom.[461]

The boys who did not go to English universities or to the Inns of Court in London could attend the College of William and Mary. This institution of the colonial capital was slightly more than half a century old in 1750 [462] and had experienced many financial difficulties.[463] In spite of these, it received some bequests,[464] improved its buildings,[465] and contrived to proffer annually to the Governor the two Latin poems required as quit rent.[466] Expenses at the college were not high, even for students who brought their servants with them.[467] "The young fellows," according to a contemporary, "are not much burdened with study, nor are their manners vastly polite . . . One thing [the Virginians] are very faulty in, with regard to their children, which is that when young they suffer them to prowl among the young Negroes which insensibly causes them to imbibe their manners and broken speech." [468] The professors were credited with "great knowledge and discretion" in 1746, "tho' yet [the college] cannot vie with those excellent universities of the Massachusetts . . ." This statement might well have served as the basis of a financial appeal for the college by Rev. William Stith, former rector of Henrico Parish and a historian of solid critical powers, who in 1752 became President.[469] On his demise in 1755, Rev. Thomas Dawson was made President.

The duties of the head of the college were not light. Masters sometimes were negligent and dames indulgent. Once, at least, a housekeeper had to be reminded "that plums, currants, etc. [were] to be used only at the common table or for the sick" and that she was to "have no boys at breakfast with [her] or to invite particular ones to tea as it

---

461 See the list, admittedly incomplete, in 21 V 196–99. Edinburgh from 1690 to 1780 attracted eighteen Virginians and probably more. The Oxford list, which is the only one believed to be accurate, includes thirteen names for the ninety years. Twenty-seven Virginians have been identified as resident at the Inns of Court during the same period. Tradition probably has exaggerated greatly the number of Virginians "educated in England."

462 Established 1693.

463 William Dawson to the Bishop of London, Nov. 22, 1734; Governor Gooch to the General Assembly, Feb. 20, 1745, 7 W (1) p. 124–25; 8 W (2) p. 239; Governor Dinwiddie to Lord Fairfax, May 6, 1752, 1 Din., 19. For the revenue law in support of the college, see 6 H 91.

464 For example J. Blair to the Bishop of London, May 28, 1743, 20 W (2) p. 135, and 8 W (1) p. 128.

465 Rev. Wm. Dawson to the Bishop of London, Aug. 11, 1732, 9 W (1) p. 220.

466 Md. Gazette, June 17, 1729.

467 See Wilson Cary's account and those of others in 1 W (2) p. 27–41.

468 Observations, in 15 W (1) p. 158.

469 Va. Gazette, Aug. 14, 1752.

cause[d] disturbances." [470] This might have been cited as evidence to justify a charge previously made that "the youth of these more indulgent settlements partake pretty much more in softness and ease than their neighbors more to northward." [471] If this was a true bill, it was in the face of rules which forbade to students all billiards, betting, and visits to an ordinary except on call from family or friend. A young academician could not even go to the millpond of the college without permission. [472]

Closely related to the college and to the social and intellectual life of the Colony was the established church. Its service and its sacrifice were not stern. On the contrary, by 5 P.M. Saturday on a plantation, "every face [looked] festive and cheerful." All made ready for what was to many "a day of pleasure and amusement." [473] Along the creeks and rivers would be found, any fair Sunday in summer, those who fished and sported, as well as those bound for the House of God. [474] Many went on horseback, so many, in fact, "that their churches looked like the outskirts of a country horse fair." [475] Business was transacted and views exchanged by the men until the clerk came to summon them to service. [476] If the sermon was brief—as was both fashionable and popular [477]—the male worshippers had more time to loiter after the benediction. [478]

Those clergy of the established church who ministered regularly to parishes were from sixty to seventy in number. Each of them was supplied with a glebe of 200 or 300 acres and a house. [479] Some received livestock. [480] The annual salary was 16,000 lbs. of tobacco [481] with an allowance of 20 shillings for every wedding by license and a like sum

[470] 3 *W* (1) p. 263.
[471] *Observations* in 15 *W* (1) p. 157. For charges of gay living on the part of some members of the faculty in 1774, see *Fithian*, 86.
[472] Regulations of Aug. 14, 1752; 2 *W* (1) p. 55. Reference already has been made, p. 121, to the fact that students could not keep race horses or attend cock fights.
[473] *Fithian*, 181.   [474] *Ibid.*, 252.
[475] *Observations*, in 15 *W* (1) p. 153.   [476] *Fithian*, 38.
[477] *Ibid.*, 55, 84.   [478] *Ibid.*, 38.
[479] See *supra*, p. 95. If quit rent was required for the glebe farm, the parish paid it. Cf. *St. George* (Spotsylvania) *Vestry Book*, Oct. 14, 1745. In earlier mention of the birthplace of Washington, *supra*, p. 36, reference was made to the fact that in the admirable specifications for a glebe house on Truro parish land (*Vestry Book*, 12) for a building to be 24 x 24 x 10, it was termed a "mansion house," precisely as George Washington referred to his birthplace as a "mansion."
[480] *Burnaby*, 24; Jones, *Virginia*, 71.
[481] Occasionally this was exceeded. The rector of Truro, for example, got 16,729 lbs. in 1737 (Slaughter, *History of Truro Parish*, 15). A Maryland parish is known to have paid 30,000 lbs. (Cf. *Archives of Maryland, Correspondence of Governor Horatio Sharpe*, cited hereafter as *Sharpe*, v. 1, p. 15.) It may be that a study of the compensation paid clergymen in different English Colonies in America would prove illuminating.

for every funeral sermon.[482] Stiff penalties were imposed on clergymen who refused to perform these services at the stipulated fees.[483]

While the living was not accounted poor, it did not appeal to a sufficient number of desirable clergymen. All those who served parishes had to be persons sent over by the Bishop of London or else had to be colonials who went to England, met with the approval of the Bishop and took holy orders there.[484] Some who received the episcopal blessing did not enjoy the parish's favor. The correspondence of Governor and of Commissary [485] contained many sad stories of clergymen who failed.[486] Impostors were not unknown.[487] In at least one instance a parish had to enter formal protest against its rector for refusing to exercise his office "in not christening of bastard children" and for his resistance to the singing of the new version of the Psalms.[488] The notoriety attending such cases exaggerated their number and evil significance. Quiet, God-fearing clergymen always were in the majority, but they did not appear in court and had no mention in the letters of officials. Nor did the frailties of the flock receive as much attention as the shortcomings of the shepherd. A minister of St. Peter's Church, New Kent, had reported to the Bishop of London, a generation previously, that his parishioners were "supinely ignorant of the very principles of religion and very debauched in morals." He cited instances of those who in illness or on their deathbeds could not repeat the Lord's Prayer. Then, after mentioning marriage with a brother's widow, he called the name of "another, a very important man [who] has a child by his own sister." One parishioner "keeps another man's wife as his concubine although he has been several years married to her sister." [489]

Whether they denounced the sinful or absolved the penitent, clergy were regarded as indispensable. Ministration had to be provided, in

---

482 Jones, *Virginia*, 72; *St. John's, Henrico, Vestry Book,* July 18, 1736, p. 34.
483 See 6 H 84.
484 Cf. Governor Gooch to the Bishop of London [?], June 29, 1729, concerning two tutors and a school teacher who were going to England to present themselves to the Bishop (1 *Gooch MSS,* 134).
485 For the functions of this Virginia representative of the Bishop of London, see *infra,* p. 180.
486 Governor Gooch to the Bishop of London, May 26, 1728, 1 *Gooch MSS,* 32; same to same, June 29, 1728, *ibid.,* 134–36. See also James Blair to "Mr. Forbes," June 20, 1723, *Va. Church Papers,* 251; same to Bishop of London, Feb. 20, 1724, *ibid.,* 250; same to same, July 17, 1738, 20 *W* (2) p. 131.
487 Cf. warning against James Trapp, "elderly, ill-looking and shuffles a little" (*Va. Gazette,* June 12, 1752).
488 This was in 1743; see 16 *V* 27.
489 John Lang to the Bishop of London, Feb. 7, 1726—*Letters of Clergy to the Bishop of London,* LC.

particular and regardless of the difficulties involved, to a church that had no regular priest, because the distance to the next church usually was too great for the faithful to attend.[490] Special services of this character were a matter of bargaining.[491] Occasional sermons came as high as 500 pounds of tobacco.[492] Even when agreement was reached easily at a fair price, there was no assurance of the quality of the sermon or of the dignity of the service. Conditions must have been humiliating and lax in some parishes to warrant the effort vainly made in 1748 to pass legislation for the "decent and uniform celebration of Divine Service."[493]

Provision of a permanent rector was the duty of the vestry, who within twelve months after the occurrence of a vacancy could accept or reject any available man among those approved by the Bishop of London.[494] For this and for its other responsibilities, the vestry was assumed to be qualified because the body was supposed to consist of the twelve most "substantial and intelligent men" of the parish."[495] The position of vestrymen was one of prestige and of training in government. Otherwise, even the most leisured planters scarcely could have taken the time required to discharge the twelve major duties that were entrusted to the vestry even when the parish had a priest. The vestry had: (1) to lay the levy for the support of the church and to make necessary exemptions;[496] (2) to "procession the parish," as required, for the verification of boundaries;[497] (3) to build and maintain roads to the church;[498] (4) to operate necessary ferries on the usual way of travel to the church;[499] (5) to enforce attendance on services;[500] (6) to collect debts due the parish, even though this involved the servitude of

[490] Cf. 1 *Gooch MSS*, 21, and Governor Gooch to the Bishop of London [?], June 29, 1729; cf. *ibid.*, 134.
[491] 6 *H* 88.
[492] See *Vestry Book of St. John's, Henrico*, Nov. 24, 1735; p. 17. Cf. a bargain in 1741 for seventeen sermons, four of them in French, to the members of King William Parish, 13 *V* 187. As noted, Truro Parish once arranged with Rev. Lawrence De Butts to preach three times a month for one year, at a compensation of 8000 pounds of tobacco.
[493] Neither the content of the bill nor the reason for the rejection of the measure appears in the records. (2 *L. J.*, 1022, 1028; *Journ. H. B.*, 1742–49, p. 280, 330, 336, 366, 393, 395.)
[494] Act of 1748, 6 *H* 90.
[495] For instances where the vestry was not acceptable, see 5 *H* 274, 381; 7 *H* 301. See also *Va. Church Papers*, 244.
[496] Cf. 6 *H* 88; *Bristol Parish Vestry Book*, 61, 73; *Stratton Major Parish Vestry Book*, 66. In *Va. Gazette*, June 20, 1751, appears notice of the sale, by the vestry, of 30,000 pounds of tobacco, which doubtless represented the levy.
[497] *Stratton Major Parish Vestry Book*, 8. For the statute, see 5 *H* 426.
[498] 2 *H* 103; *St. Paul's, Hanover, Vestry Book*, 103, 157.
[499] *Bristol Parish Vestry Book*, 57; *St. John's, Henrico, Vestry Book*, 7.
[500] Cf. presentments in Prince George County, 1738; 4 *V* 279. See the act in 5 *H* 226, for pleading attendance at some other church than that of one's own parish.

the debtor; [501] (7) to build churches; [502] (8) to provide the furnishings; [503] (9) to supervise the cleaning, maintenance and repair of the edifice; [504] (10) to seat the members and to settle controversies over the delicate question of precedence; [505] (11) to direct poor relief and the care of orphans; [506] and (12) to supervise the glebe. [507]

[501] See a case of 1738 in 4 *V* 278.

[502] See *Elizabeth City Orders*, 1723–29, p. 227, entry of Jan. 17, 1727 for burning brick for a church. In Michel's journal, 1701–02 (24 *V* 21), reference is made to the small number of brick churches in the Colony. For other informative details on building churches see, as typical, *Bristol Parish Vestry Book*, 72, with some specifications of Oct. 11, 1734; *St. John's, Henrico, Vestry Book*, 43, 61, 71; *Va. Gazette*, Feb. 28, June 6, 1751. The specifications of St. George's, Fredericksburg, are in Slaughter, *History of St. George's Parish*, 14. Truro, according to the contract of 1733, was to be 40 x 22 x 13 and was to cost 33,500 pounds of tobacco (Slaughter, *History of Truro Parish*, 6). Bishop Meade noted in 1838 (*op. cit.*, v. 2, p. 148), that Yeocomico Church, built in 1706, had required little repair and that it was not believed a single new shingle had been put on the roof.

[503] *St. Paul's, Hanover, Vestry Book*, 97; *St. John's, Henrico, Vestry Book*, 12, 73; *Truro Parish Vestry Book*, 16, where the prospective rector was allowed a commission of 50 per cent for procuring books and ornaments for the church. See *St. George* (Spotsylvania), *Vestry Book*, Oct. 2, 1733, for arrangements to procure pulpit cloths and cushions. *Vide* also an order from John Carter to M. Perry, Sept. 20, 1733, for certain articles, desired in Christ Church, according to an enclosed pattern—*Carter-Plummer MSS.* For reference to stolen church furnishings see 27 *W* (1) p. 28–33; *Va. Gazette*, June 26, 1746; May 15, 1752. In 1 *Gooch MSS*, 135, 2 *L. J.*, 1088 and 6 *H* 231 is mentioned an organ for the Williamsburg Church. An organ for Petsworth parish was provided in 1735. See 8 *W* (1) p. 130.

[504] *St. John's, Henrico, Vestry Book*, 7, 8, 50, 60, 82. In *ibid.*, p. 15, Mch. 2, 1732, ffield (sic) Jefferson was allowed 100 lbs. of tobacco for setting up a horseblock. For other repair orders, see *Stratton Major Parish Vestry Book*, 11; *St. Paul's, Hanover, Vestry Book*, 187. In *St. George* (Spotsylvania), *Vestry Book*, Oct. 3, 1743, are instructions to the sexton to sweep the parish church and chapel every week and to wash the floors four times a year. See *ibid.*, Aug. 29, 1754, for instructions to the wardens to procure sundials and to provide or repair horseblocks or steps.

[505] In the most interesting of examples, that of St. Paul's, Hanover, the wardens and, in their absence, the vestry were to "place the people in the church as they shall think fit" (*Vestry Book*, 195). This probably echoed some controversy that arose after the vestry in 1744 ordered a gallery built (*ibid.*, 180) and then prescribed (*ibid.*, 187) that it be for the use of "the gentlemen justices and vestrymen and their families." At Stratton Major Parish, the vestry in 1734–35 made definite provision for the seating of specific persons in the church (*Vestry Book*, 16, 20). In Bristol Parish, 1732, Richard Booker undertook to erect a chapel at a low figure and, in return, received permission to build a pew "for his family's conveniency" on one side of the communion table. He covenanted to leave sufficient room for the communicants to kneel between his pew and the table (*Vestry Book*, 66). In 1740, three of the notables of Truro Parish asked permission to construct at their own cost a gallery at the west end of the church for the exclusive use of their families. The interesting fact was that one of the petitioners was rector, though he here appears as "Charles Green, Doctor of Physick" (Slaughter, *History of Truro Parish*, 16).

[506] For poor relief in general see Jones, *Virginia*, 54; *Bristol Parish Vestry Book*, 67, 75, 80; *Stratton Major Parish Vestry Book*, 15, 21, 28, 30, 82. By an act of 1755 (6 *H* 475–78), the vestry of each parish was required to rent or purchase a tract of land for the maintenance and employment of the poor. Each resident of the farm was required to wear "in an open manner" a badge on which was cut in blue or red or green cloth the name of the parish. In *St. Paul's, Hanover, Vestry Book*, 144, Oct. 18, 1735, notice was given John Dimmock to keep his father and mother from becoming chargeable to the parish or else they would "be sent back from whence they came." The vestry of Stratton Major Parish in 1732 had a house twelve by sixteen feet built for Alice Daniel, who for years was supported by the parish (*Vestry Book*, 11). Instances of provision for medical care will be found in *St. John's, Henrico, Vestry Book*, 7, 8; *St. George* (Spotsylvania), *Vestry Book*, Oct. 3, 1743, Nov. 5, 1750; Slaughter, *History of Truro Parish*, 15, and *St. Paul's, Hanover, Vestry Book*, 145. The care of idiots also was a part of poor relief (St. John's, *supra*, 42, 68 ff). For the binding out and apprenticing of children,

In the discharge of these extensive duties the vestry had full legal authority, except where the rights of the clergy were involved. Then the vestry could advise but could not order. Rev. James Marye, for example, was in the habit of baptizing the white and the Negro children together. To this the vestry objected in 1751, but they could do no more than direct the wardens to "desire" the minister to baptize the races separately.[508] Where the authority of the rector was not involved, the vestry had the support of a considerable body of statute law for the protection of public morals. In the yard of a church, stocks might be erected for the punishment of "licentious and disorderly persons" who disturbed the worship.[509] A man could be fined 5 shillings for each oath he swore, though the act was mercifully mindful of the frailty of temper in this particular: It provided that judgment could not be given against an individual for more than four oaths at one time.[510] Anti-gambling laws, which generally were strict,[511] were especially so in penalties on proprietors of ordinaries who permitted gaming.[512] Credit sales of liquor were discouraged.[513] As noted already, bearing a bastard cost a servant woman an additional year of work for her master. The father had to give security that the child would not become a public charge.

All that law and custom could do to aid the established church was being done in Virginia, but dissent was increasing. Under an act of 1730,[514] exemption from parish levies had been allowed the Germans who originally had come to Virginia to mine and smelt iron in Governor Spotswood's "colony," but against other dissenters, heavy penalties were or could be invoked. In the year of George's birth, Thomas Moseley and John Shelton were committed to jail on information by a church warden that they had baptized a child. They were required to give bond for good behavior or to go to jail for thirty-one

---

see *Bristol Parish Vestry Book*, 11; *St. Paul's Hanover, Vestry Book*, 1; Slaughter, *History of Truro Parish*, 16; *Westmoreland Orders*, 1731–39, p. 48.

[507] For glebe maintenance, see *Stratton Major Parish Vestry Book*, 5, 7. The second of these references contains interesting specifications of a barn. Specifications of a garden and fence will be found in *St. Paul's, Hanover, Vestry Book*, 193, 195. Cf. *ibid.*, 199 for glebe quit rents, and *ibid.*, 155 and 5 H 597 for the sale of glebes. For the lease of a glebe to the highest bidder, see *Stratton Major Parish Vestry Book*, 67.

[508] *St. George* (Spotsylvania), *Vestry Book*, Aug. 29, 1751.

[509] *St. Peter's Vestry Book*, 240.

[510] 5 H 225–26. Cf. 3 *ibid.*, 72, 138.

[511] 5 *ibid.*, 229.

[512] *Ibid.*, 103; 6 *ibid.*, 76.

[513] Act of 1748, 6 H 74. For amendment of 1762, see 7 H 595.

[514] 6 H 360–61.

days and to receive thirty-one lashes on the bare back.[515] Such severity inspired new dissent. Quakers by 1738 had become sufficiently numerous to petition for exemption similar to that allowed the Germans.[516] The next year, George Whitefield made his first appearance in Virginia and greatly moved his audiences.[517] There were subsequent fulminations against the Catholics in 1745 [518] and in 1746–47 against New Light, Moravian and Methodist itinerants.[519] The effect was the same: dissenters multiplied.[520] Some of the clergy still would not learn the obvious lesson. Complaints were made that the Presbyterians in general and Samuel Davies in particular were exceeding the toleration allowed them under the act of 1689; [521] but occasional voices were lifted in their behalf. "Philo Virginia," a frequent correspondent of the *Virginia Gazette,* wrote of the Presbyterian frontiersmen: [522] "Though they are dissenters, they have enough religion as renders them good subjects and to entitle them to **an** extensive toleration. Laborious, they strengthen the colony in its weakest parts and furnish us with the necessities which our eternal piddling about the sovereign weed, tobacco, hinders us from providing in sufficient plenty. As they provide their own clergy they should not be asked to pay the parish levy . . . In Virginia they would be most useful in settling the frontier as they alone have fortitude enough to encounter the numberless discouragements that must attend an infant plantation in a distant part of the continent." [523]

That sharp reference to "piddling about the sovereign weed, tobacco" was a reminder that the staple farming in the Colony of Virginia tended to fix its castes and classes, supplied the means for its social and

[515] For the status of the Germans in 1737, see the report of Pastor John Casper Stover, reprinted in 14 *V* 147. The case of Moseley and Shelton is set forth in *St. George* (Spotsylvania), *Vestry Book,* Aug. 1, 1722.

[516] See the petition in *Va. Gazette,* Nov. 15, 1738. The notorious lampoon on "making a Quaker" appeared in *ibid.,* Nov. 17, 1738.

[517] See *Va. Gazette,* Dec. 21, 1739. For later impressions, see *ibid.,* Oct. 24, 1745.

[518] See Governor Gooch's proclamation in *Va. Gazette,* Apr. 24, 1745.

[519] Proclamation of Feb. 3, 1746, 3 *Gooch MSS,* 843; text of 1747 in 11 *V* 228.

[520] A list of tithables of Fairfax County, 1749, contains some interesting comments by Rev. Charles Green on the "Papists," Presbyterians and Anabaptists of the parishes in the County. Dr. Green remarked that when he had Goose Creek in his care, "I never had one communicant, though several times prepared to administer the sacrament." (*MS,* LC.)

[521] *Va. Gazette,* Oct. 31, 1745; Governor Gooch to the Lords of Trade, May 11, Sept. 1, 1750, 3 *Gooch MSS,* 1022; William Dawson to the Bishop of London, July 27, 1750, 20 *W* (2) p. 222. For Davies, for the bitter battle over Rev. John Roane, and for other aspects of dissent at this period, see H. R. McIlwaine, *The Struggle of Protestant Dissenters for Religious Toleration in Virginia,* 46 ff.

[522] Issue of Mch. 5, 1752.

[523] For Presbyterian activities in Virginia in 1759–63, see Colonel Gordon's diary in 11 *W* (1) p. 102, 105, 198, 199; 12 *ibid.,* 3. An interesting monograph could be written on the changing attitude of Virginians toward religious liberty, as set forth in their letters, etc., from 1730 to the outbreak of the Revolution. Two informative items appear in *Fithian,* 82, 96.

intellectual activities, and supported, by the annual 16,000 pounds of tobacco, the spiritual ministration of the established church in each parish. The curse of this sort of agriculture in the older parts of Virginia was that farmers ate up their own fields. Land was abundant —as late as 1759 one estimate was that "not a tenth" of it had been cultivated [524]—but on the average plantation, the ground was worked until its fertility failed. Then new acres would be cleared. The old would be left to fare as they would, to wash away or to grow up in bushes.[525] Always the excuse was that in the "back country" was "as fine and rich a land as any in the world." [526] While these western regions were being opened and the eastern were being wasted, the older plantations had to cope with drought or excessive rainfall and with occasional invasions by caterpillars,[527] cankerworms [528] and squirrels and crows.[529] Crop failure was not infrequent [530] even as respected so vital a supply as apples for cider [531]—victim of late frost and sudden changes of weather.[532] To all the hazards of climate and pests there often was added on larger plantations the widespread and continuing difficulty of procuring honest and competent overseers.[533]

Whether directed by overseer or owner, on great estate or on small, the growing of tobacco was the first and sometimes almost the exclusive farming activity. George might be King but tobacco was master. From the time the plant beds were burned in February until the crop

[524] *Burnaby,* 19.
[525] Fithian in his journal, 118, gave an excellent description of agricultural malpractice which was as bad in 1750 as when he wrote in 1774. Fences are seldom mentioned, but see *ibid.,* 98. The standard work on this general subject is A. O. Craven, *Soil Exhaustion as a Factor in the Agricultural History of Virginia and Maryland, 1606–1860.*
[526] Lord Adam Gordon, quoted in *Mereness,* 404. This was written in 1765 but entirely applicable in 1750.
[527] Governor Gooch to the Lords of Trade, June 8, 1728, 1 *Gooch MSS,* 37; Council journal of Apr. 1, 1729, 4 *E. J.,* 196.
[528] *Va. Gazette,* May 18, 1738.
[529] In 1728, n.d., Governor Gooch wrote the Lords of Trade that every tithable on the Eastern Shore had been required, under heavy penalty, to kill six squirrels and six crows annually for three years (1 *Gooch MSS,* 56). A somewhat similar act of 1734 will be found in 4 *H* 446. Governor Gooch's letters are among the best sources on the agriculture of colonial Virginia.
[530] Governor Gooch to the Lords of Trade, 1728, n.d. 1 *Gooch MSS,* 53; John Carter to Robert Carter, Aug. 13, 1733, *Carter-Plummer MSS,* 12. For the dire drought of 1737, see John Custis to Peter Collinson, *Custis MS Letter Book,* No. 112; *Va. Gazette,* Aug. 19, 1737, 3 *W* (1) p. 228.
[531] *Va. Gazette,* Sept. 3, 1736.
[532] Cf. *Burnaby,* 9 n. for the freezing of the Potomac, Dec. 19, 1759, in a single night that followed a mild and temperate day.
[533] Carter brothers to William Dawkins, Aug. 10, 1736, *Carter-Plummer MSS,* 4; Harrower's diary in 6 *A. H. R.,* 93, 96, 97; Anburey, *Travel through the Interior Parts of America* (cited hereafter as *Anburey*), v. 2, p. 191. A good example of a contract between a planter and a "steward" or general manager of a number of plantations, Nov. 4, 1755, will be found in the *Custis Papers,* VHS. The parties were D. P. Custis and Joseph Valentine.

was put aboard ship perhaps a year later, Virginia labored over tobacco. It had been so ever since the infancy of the Colony. Until 1730, the price and quality of crops shipped overseas were subjects of deception and dispute. Sailors were suspected of stealing the leaf en route and of running it illegally ashore.[534] Merchants insisted that much of the tobacco was shipped wet, or was mixed, or was nothing but trash; planters maintained that good tobacco was depreciated by merchants who got more for it than they reported.[535] The chief reason for low prices and consequent argument and economic distress was the rapid rise in the number of slaves after 1700. This had led to a corresponding increase in the crop at a time when war narrowed markets.[536]

Out of this confusion came in 1730 the passage by the General Assembly of "An Act for Amending the Staple of Tobacco, and for preventing Frauds in his Majesty's Customs." [537] As revised in 1748,[538] this law provided that all tobacco for export had to be brought to warehouses established and maintained by the Colony, and there had to be viewed by two official, bonded inspectors.[539] They examined, weighed and stamped the hogsheads and gave the owner notes that were current money in that and the adjacent Counties.[540] The product then could be shipped on account of the owner or of the person to whom the notes had been transferred.[541] Mouldy leaf was burnt by the inspectors; mixed tobacco, good and bad, could be sorted by the owner within a month after it had been refused the stamp.[542] This system restored the market for Virginia tobacco and, according to Governor Gooch, brought prosperity to Virginia. As early as 1732 he wrote: "Had it not been for the law the country had this year been ruined, and though by inspection, the quantity will be lessened, yet what is sent home will pay the King's duty if the officials are careful, and will bring the proprietors more money than if the whole had been exported; besides enabling them to purchase such manufactures as they really need, from Great Britain,

[534] Governor Spotswood to the Council of Trade, Mch. 6, 1711; 1 *Spotswood Letters*, 57.

[535] See complaints of Edward Athawes, merchant, to John and Charles Carter, Jan. 12, 1735, June 8, 1736; 23 *V* 162, 164.

[536] Governor Spotswood to the Commissioners of Trade, Aug. 18, 1710; to the Council of Trade, Mch. 6, 1711; to the same, Mch. 20, 1711; 1 *Spotswood Letters*, 12, 56, 72.

[537] 4 *H* 247 ff. Short-lived earlier acts of 1723 and 1729, mentioned by title only in *ibid.*, 134 and 197, were printed in 20 *V* 167–78. See also in 4 *H* 241 the act of 1730 for the same purpose.

[538] 6 *H* 154.

[539] For their appointment see *ibid.*, 159.

[540] *Ibid*, 163.

[541] *Ibid.*, 190.

[542] *Ibid.*, 166–67.

and what for want of a price for their tobacco they have for sometime gone without insomuch that the Negroes go naked all the winter, have not proper food to work with and their quarters, for want of nails, are tumbling down." [543]

The Governor was overoptimistic. Although his law undoubtedly helped the tobacco trade, the staple had its bad years as well as its good. "Tobacco," wrote Joseph Ball in 1749, "is not much better than dung in London," [544] but in Virginia, season after season, tobacco continued to reach the warehouses on scores of boats. [545] Other farmers' crops were packed in hogheads for transportation by road. Spikes were driven into either end of the hogshead to serve as an axle tree. Between shafts made of a split sapling, a horse was harnessed or an ox yoked. Then the hogshead was rolled to the warehouse. [546] During a normal year, about 1750, the total tobacco shipped from Virginia was approximately 50,000 hogheads that weighed about 850 pounds each. Close to 40 per cent of this was from the rapidly developing "upper District of James River." [547] How this was handled by the merchant vessels that came annually to Virginia is a part of the story of commerce. [548]

By 1755 or 1760, wheat was beginning to receive attention where the yield of tobacco was declining; [549] as noted already, corn provided food for the slaves and feed for the stock. It was grown in every part of Virginia but in 1750 scarcely found a market except in barter. [550] Of other agricultural products and of fruits, the Virginians thought they had abundance and, on occasion, they were disinclined to encourage

[543] Governor Gooch to the Lords of Trade, May 27, 1732; 2 *Gooch MSS*, 285.

[544] Letter of Mch. 21, 1749 to Joseph Chinn, *Ball Letter Book*.

[545] For the inspectors and a list of the original sixty-five warehouses, see 4 *E. J.*, 284–85, and 4 *H* 266. See, for the use of boats, 6 *H* 157.

[546] See a detailed description by R. A. Brock in *Tenth Census of the United States*, v. 3, Agriculture, 219, with a reference to Samuel Mordecai, "Tobacco," in *Transactions of the Virginia Agricultural Society*, v. 1, 1853, p. 57. Prior to the act of 1730, warehouses often were styled "rolling houses" because they were at the end of "rolling roads." The approval of the County Court was necessary to establish or to discontinue a "rolling house." See *Spotsylvania Orders*, 1724–30, p. 317. Cf. also 1 *Spotswood Letters*, 78, and *Eaton*, 4.

[547] These estimates are based, in large part, on Governor Gooch's reports to the Lords of Trade, 3 *Gooch MSS*, 971 ff. See also Brock, *loc. cit.*, *Burnaby*, 21, and 1 *V* 97 ff. For difficulties over North Carolina tobacco, see Spangenberg's diary, Sept. 25, 1752, in the *Records of the Moravians*, v. 1, p. 38. The Carolinians thought the Virginia warehouse inspectors unjust to them.   [548] See *infra*, p. 146.

[549] Washington's part in this is described in Vol. III of this work, but, as respects dates, a general caveat has to be entered. The trend toward wheat production was strong by 1765–75 (See 15 *V* 350, 437; 43, *ibid.*, 102; Harrower's diary, 6 *A. H. R.*, 81, 82, 87, 96, 97 and an important letter of his to his brother-in-law, Mch. 28, 1775). At mid-century, the crop appears to have been chiefly for plantation use. Michel in his journal (24 *V* 32), gave a picture of Virginia wheat harvest that would have been as accurate in 1801 as when he wrote a century earlier.

[550] Cf. Harrower's diary, Apr. 24, 1775, for an account of corn planting (6 *A. H. R.*, 94).

experiments with semi-tropical products.[551] Peaches prospered and fed both hog and still; cherries of several varieties throve; apples, to repeat, were valued primarily for their cider.[552] Experiments in wine-making, in olive-growing and in the production of hemp were not rewarded with profit.[553] Always, among diligent farmers, there was interest in good seed [554] and in improved vegetable gardens.[555]

Stock raising supplemented the product of these gardens but did not add greatly to the income of farmers. In Tidewater, cattle received little attention. As Counties at the head of navigation developed, settlers in some of them found grazing profitable.[556] On many of the large eastern plantations, sheep were raised, for meat and for fleece.[557] To the westward, wolves were so numerous that few farmers could spare the time to protect their sheep, which consequently had little market.[558] Bounties for killing wolves sometimes consumed a third and more of the county levy, and led to much fraud, but the enemy of the sheep-herder continued to lurk on the edge of advancing settlement.[559] Hogs also fared ill on the frontier. In Eastern Virginia, though swine were small [560] and sometimes were regarded when wild, as little more than "vermin," [561] they were esteemed for the flavor of their meat. To protect the reputation of Virginia pork and beef, the General Assembly in 1742 provided for the inspection, weighing and stamping of all meat for export, whether it was of native origin or was imported for trans-

[551] Cf. William Mayo to "a gentleman in the Barbadoes," Aug. 27, 1731: "I thank you for the yams, eddoes &c sent with your letter of Mar 27th last, such things will not come to such perfection in this climate as to be worth the pains of planting and the great plenty of other good things that we have make them the less wanted" (4 R 85).

[552] Ibid.; Fithian, 121; Harrower's diary 6 A. H. R., 80. For cider, see supra, p. 106.

[553] For the beginning of these enterprises, see Jones, Virginia, 60; William Byrd II to "Mr. Collenson," [Peter Collinson?] July 18, 1736, V 354; and same to Sir Jacob Ackworth, 1728, n.d., 36 V 39. William Fitzhugh's experiments with olives are mentioned in 1 V 271.

[554] Va. Gazette, Jan. 6, 1738; Thomas Jones to his wife, Sept. 30, 1728, 26 V 173; John Parke Custis to Colonel Baylor, Aug. 15, 1752, in 21 V 92.

[555] Va. Gazette of Sept. 3, 1736, mentioned Edmund Jenings's garden in Williamsburg. See also Jones, Virginia, 26, 11 W (1) p. 200, Va. Gazette, Aug. 12, 1737. This last reference is to a cucumber "a yard in length and near 14 inches around the thickest part," grown in the garden of Daniel Parke Custis of New Kent County.

[556] Robert Carter to M. Perry, July 18, 1723. The price of a "fat young cow at killing time" was put at 35s cash. A steer of 7 years was worth 50s (Carter Transcripts, VHS). See 18 V 188 for a Chesterfield inventory of live stock in 1760. Cattle then were 25s; sheep 5s; hogs 7s; shoats 5s; horses £4 to £20. These figures probably showed the effect of the depreciation of currency.

[557] Cf. Harrower's diary, 6 A. H. R., 80.

[558] In 7 V 109, is a statement that an inventory of 1746–47 valued twelve sheep at 83 cents each.

[559] Jones, Virginia, 51; 3 V 189; 4 V 278; 2 L. J., 810. The Spotsylvania records show that about 50 per cent of the county levy in early years went for bounties.

[560] Harrower noted, Dec. 14, 1774, that the hogs slaughtered at Colonel Daingerfield's averaged about 150 pounds each (6 A. H. R., 92).

[561] Robert Carter to M. Perry, July 18, 1723, Carter Transcripts, VHS.

shipment.[562] The principal market for Virginia meat in 1750 was the West Indies.[563] England continued to be the outlet for what remained of the colonial fur trade. In the seventeen-thirties, some beaver skins were included in almost all outgoing cargoes and probably were, pound for pound, the most valuable product of the Old Dominion,[564] but by the middle of the century these had become scarcer. Most of the trade was in deer skin, which still was abundant,[565] though the protection of the animal in the breeding season had become a matter of concern.[566]

In addition, the Virginians built up their plantation industries to include the weaving of coarse cloth,[567] tanning,[568] distilling,[569] shoe-making,[570] blacksmithery, and milling;[571] but they felt they were neglecting larger industries,[572] and some of the leaders succeeded at length in developing a considerable commerce in timber, staves and ships' stores.[573]

[562] 2 L. J., 922; 5 H 164 ff.

[563] 3 Gooch MSS, 977. Surprisingly little appears in contemporary accounts regarding the sale or export of Virginia hams, which subsequently attained renown. The recipe of William Byrd first for cooking ham is printed in 15 V 85. In the Journal of Nicholas Cresswell (New York, 1924) under date of Apr. 13, 1777, p. 199, precisely the "cure" of hams used in the twentieth century on the best farms is described.

[564] Cf. Va. Gazette, July 29, 1737, memorial relating to tobacco trade.

[565] In the exports of 1771–72 were included 134,000 lbs. of raw and 21,000 lbs. of dressed deer skins (Sutherland, 308).

[566] Governor Gooch to the Lords of Trade, Nov. 20, 1734, 2 Gooch MSS, 368; 2 L. J., 872, 878; 5 H 61. In 1752, the General Assembly rejected a bill to limit the number of dogs that might be kept by overseers, servants and slaves in the Counties of the Northern Neck (2 L. J., 1065).

[567] Burnaby, 21; Gooch in Cal. Treasury Books and Papers, 1729–30, No. 666; 6 A. H. R., 103, 105, 107.   [568] 11 W (1) p. 105.

[569] Ibid., 102.   [570] Ibid., 110.

[571] One of the fullest accounts of these industries will be found in Governor Fauquier to the Board of Trade, Dec. 17, 1766; 21 W (1) p. 169.

[572] Va. Gazette, May 9, 1751, with particular reference to whaling.

[573] See Governor Gooch's report in 3 Gooch MSS, 977. His figures on the volume of exports are vague. The first inclusive and detailed report of imports and exports is that of 1771–72 published in Sutherland, 276 ff. This showed exports to England and Scotland: pitch, 24 bbls.; tar, 16,100 bbls.; turpentine, 1890 bbls.; black walnut, 28 tons; oak board and plank, 63,800 feet; pine board and plank, 69,000 feet; hoops, 13,000; handspikes, 1700; lock stocks, 20,600; staves, 2,038,000; shingles, 25,000. To Ireland were sent: oak board and plank, 5100 feet; pine boards and plank, 5000 feet; staves 6500; oak timber, 36 tons. To Southern Europe and the "Wine Islands" (i.e. the Madeira and Canary Islands) were exported: shingles, 34,000; staves, 225,000. These figures probably represent a considerable expansion of trade after 1750, but in the absence of accurate totals for the mid-century, all assumptions are dangerous. Little concerning the protection of timber appears in the records. See John Custis to Philip Ludwell, Apr. 18, 1717, concerning Governor Spotswood's slashing of timber (46 V 244–45). In Westmoreland Records, Liber S, 1747–53, p. 68, is a lease to Thomas Clayton who agreed, among other things, not to use any timber growing on the place. Henry Ashton in 1716 sued George Turberville for entering his premises and cutting down thirty trees, but the outcome of the action is not known (Westmoreland Orders, 1705–21, p. 290). Augustine Washington, leasing 250 acres to Richard Fry, shipwright, Nov. 25, 1730, stipulated that the lessee was to make no use of the timber, otherwise than for building and repairs, without Washington's consent (8 Westmoreland Deeds, p. 152). A partial description of some Virginia lawn trees will be found in Lancelot Lee to Thomas Lee, May 21, 1745, Mag. of Society of Lees of Virginia, v. 1, p. 98, Oct. 1923.

Next to tar and timber, the industry most assiduously nourished in Virginia had been that of iron mining and smelting, to which Augustine Washington, John Tayloe, Governor Alexander Spotswood and others had devoted themselves.[574] By 1750, most of the furnaces had failed; survivors were moderately prosperous in a small way. The annual export of pig-iron probably did not exceed, if indeed it reached, 4000 tons.[575] Development was being hampered by the fact that most of the known iron deposits were in the domain of Lord Fairfax, who demanded a royalty of one-third of the ore brought to the surface.[576] Other promising adventures in iron came to nought.[577] Only two furnaces, to repeat, were in operation in 1750–60.[578] This was a humiliation to Virginians who were compelled to purchase even agricultural hoes in England.[579]

Other industries had much the same fate. William Parks, printer of the *Virginia Gazette* and of numerous books, constructed near Williamsburg a paper mill with the counsel and assistance of Benjamin Franklin and had it in operation in 1744.[580] The opportunity seemed large,

[574] For their activities, see *Landmarks*, 425 ff. See also, *May*, 23 ff. Cf. an assayer's advertisement in *Va. Gazette*, June 9, 1738. The advertiser, Dr. Samuel Tschiffely, a Swiss physician of some distinction, is mentioned in *Blanton*, 38, 86, 204, 337. Absenteeism, drunkenness, trespass and falsification of accounts by some of Spotswood's iron-workers may be traced through the court records of Spotsylvania County. For Spotswood's proposals to lease the works in 1729, see Lester J. Cappon, *Iron Works at Tuball*. The general failure of the industry is sketched in *Landmarks*, 427 ff.

[575] This was the figure given in 1749 by Governor Gooch, whose statistics were not always reliable. See 3 *V* 123. By 1771, the export of pig-iron had fallen to 1732 tons. That of bar-iron was only 144 tons (*Sutherland*, 276 ff).

[576] *Burnaby* 46–47. Cf. George Hume to James Hume, Feb. 11, 1748: "Lord Fairfax has almost got all our back lands from the King . . ." (20 *V* 403).

[577] *Landmarks*, 427–29.

[578] See Governor Gooch's full report of 1749 in 3 *Gooch MSS*, 971–84. No record has been found of the successful establishment of any other furnace before 1760. It is believed that Germanna was one of the two furnaces reported by Gooch and that "England's Furnace" at Accokeek was the other. John Ballendine's furnace two miles above Colchester was in operation sometime before Burnaby visited it in October, 1759. See *Landmarks*, 427–28 and H. Whiteley, "History of the Principio Company," in 11 *Penn. Mag.*, 63 ff.

[579] Joseph Ball's *Letter Book* contains numerous references to "hows," axes and nails he was sending to Virginia from England. See, also, Richard Corbin to Charles Gore, June 15, 1758, *Corbin MS Letter Book*, 16. Cf. Edward Athawes to J. and C. Carter, Dec. 31, 1736: "The Ironmonger is much concerned as well as myself to find the Hoes sent last year were not so good as they ought to be and assures me those now sent are the best sort and charged to 2s per doz. cheaper than usual to make amends" (23 *V* 165). Ephraim Goosley of Yorktown advertised in 1751 that he "made and sold . . . all sorts of axes and hoes at the low price of 40 per cent more than they cost in London" (*Va. Gazette*, Oct. 31, 1751). Another of his advertisements will be found in *ibid.*, June 13, 1751. The importance of hoes on the average farm may be gathered from the fact that Lawrence Washington's partial inventory of 1752 (*Fairfax Wills*, B, 1, p. 114), showed twenty-nine weeding hoes and, apparently, seventy-one tilling hoes. Daniel Parke Custis, as late as 1755–57, complained often of the poor design of English hoes; MS, *Gratz Coll., Penn. His. Soc.*

[580] See Rutherfoord Goodwin: *The William Parks Paper Mill at Williamsburg*, 12 ff. Cf. *Virginia Gazette*, May 19, 1745; 14 *T* 185.

because paper was very high in Virginia,[581] but to judge from Parks's will, the enterprise had not become successful by time of his death in 1750.[582] Some paper made there was used as late as 1763.[583]

Kindred attempts to establish a whaling industry,[584] to manufacture nut-oil,[585] and to make potash[586] had no better fortune. Nor did indigo thrive.[587] "Merchant milling" depended, unhappily, on the importation of suitable millstones,[588] but in a few instances produced "superfine" flour. Planters who grew large crops of wheat and operated their own establishments occasionally were successful with bakeries for ships' biscuit.[589]

The chief obstacle to the development of all these industries was the lack of skilled labor. Every trade appeared to need more workers than the Colony possessed. As early as 1736, efforts had been made to draw laborers from Virginia to Georgia.[590] While this actually cost Virginia few men, there was an instability, a coming-and-going of artisans that hampered old industries and frustrated new.[591] In spite of this, apprenticeship was long and poorly remunerated. An intelligent boy of 14, Edmund Pendleton, had been "bound out" in 1734/35 to a court clerk for a term of six years and six months. All that was promised him was sufficient meat and drink and apparel fitting for an apprentice.[592] Another youth contracted in 1752 for six years' labor, during which he was to be taught to read and write. On the expiration of his service he was to receive "£5 current money or the value thereof in clothes or tools."[593]

---

[581] Ten quires for the use of a church in 1733 cost 12s 6d. See 14 V 139. For surveyor's paper, see *infra*, p. 238, n. 106.

[582] See his will in 2 W (2) p. 92–96, 202–09.

[583] R. Goodwin, *op. cit.*, 19.

[584] See *supra*, n. 572.

[585] *Ibid.*, Oct. 24, 1745.   [586] 3 L. J., 1164.

[587] See three letters of George Braxton, Mch. 13, Dec. 19, 1756, Sept. 7, 1757, in *Blair, Banister and Braxton*, 141, 142, 145.

[588] Cf. John Carter to R. Cary, Nov. 29, 1737, *Carter-Plummer MSS*, 178.

[589] Cf. Will of Charles Carter of Cleve in 31 V 45–61. In the *Va. Gazette* of May 8, 1752, Francis Willis advertised that purchasers of his "bisket" could pay in rum, sugar or molasses. Benjamin Harrison's biscuit sold in 1739 at 10s per cwt (*Va. Gazette*, June 8, 1739; 11 V 105). Councillor Robert Carter's bake house could use 100 lbs. of flour at each heating of either of his two ovens. See various references to this enterprise in *Fithian*, 85, 91, 99, 249, 250. Washington's experience in the baking and sale of biscuit is sketched *infra*, Vol. III.

[590] *Va. Gazette*, Sept. 3, 1736.

[591] For typical advertisements for labor, see these issues of *Va. Gazette*: Sept. 5, 1751, for "good overseers"; Aug. 29, 1751, for a bricklayer at £4 per month; Oct. 11, 1751, for a tailor at 10s a week with "diet, washing and lodging"; Oct. 24, 1751, for another tailor at 12s 6d a week and "his board"; Jan. 24, 1752, for "a young man who understands merchants accounts"; Mch. 5, 1752, for joiners in Norfolk, men who had survived the small pox; Feb. 27, 1752, for a York River oysterman.

[592] *Caroline Orders*, 1732–40, p. 282.   [593] *Spotsylvania Wills*, B, 101.

Beyond the narrow range of these undermanned and often unprosperous industries, there was little except shop-keeping and the conveyance of men and goods. Most of the stores were kept by Scotsmen,[594] some of whom operated on their own account and some as factors for merchants in the United Kingdom.[595] Often the merchant's wife helped in the shop.[596] Stocks were not large. Virginians of the interior had scant cash with which to buy the little that the stores offered. Williamsburg and Yorktown and Norfolk, with tailors and wigmakers and tinkers and men of other trades, sometimes but not always represented the exception to the general scarcity of goods and services.[597]

As a reason for this scarcity, communication was a factor equal to the lack of skilled labor. Heavy products could not be moved easily beyond the rivers and the deep creeks. Although transportation was an industry of magnitude that demanded the work of many hands, it was adequate only on streams where sailing vessels could be navigated. Creeks that were kept clear of debris and of falling trees were used by lighter craft.[598] For short distances, a boat with four oarsmen could proceed as fast as a man could ride down the road that paralleled the bank of the stream.[599]

Near their homes and across their own property, farmers had overnumerous roads, lanes, paths and trails. Beyond these, after 1632, the lawmakers of the Colony had sought again and again to extend and to maintain roads.[600] In 1748, a year of extensive revision, the older road laws had been simplified and consolidated to this effect: The court of each County was to provide roads toward Williamsburg, to the Court House, to all parish churches, and to all public mills and ferries. Every

[594] *Fithian*, 39.

[595] Jones, *Virginia*, 55. Although the two clauses of the sentence in the text bridge fifty years, there is no evidence that the nature of this trade changed greatly between 1724 and 1754.

[596] Cf. the advertisement of a newly-arrived merchant, the death of whose wife led to the abandonment of his plan to open a store in Williamsburg (*Va. Gazette,* Jan. 2, 1752).

[597] The following advertisements of Williamsburg merchants in specified issues of the *Va. Gazette* may be found of interest: Breeches maker and glover, Sept. 14, 1739; hatmaking (which Governor Fauquier praised in 1766, 21 *W* (1) p. 170), Sept. 14, 1739; wigmaking, May 2, 1751, and many times afterward; watches and clocks and the repair of timepieces, Apr. 7, 1738, and almost continuously thereafter; upholsterer, Nov. 21, 1745.

[598] A list compiled in 1702 ff of the navigable rivers and creeks of Eastern Virginia will be found in 1 *V* 362–63. Legislation to improve navigation was slight. An act of 1752 to clear the Appomattox and the Pamunkey appears in 2 *L. J.,* 1070, and 6 *H* 291.

[599] *Fithian*, 40. Cf. *ibid.,* 189. Few references to small craft are to be found in wills and inventories. Nathaniel Harrison had a flat, a pinnace, a canoe, a sea sloop and "a boat" (31 *V* 361–79).

[600] The principal acts from 1632 to 1738 inclusive, all of them highly interesting, will be found in 1 *H* 199; 2 *H* 103, 261; 3 *H* 85, 392; 4 *H* 53, 229, 297; 5 *H* 31. A summary of the seventeenth-century laws was published in 10 *V* 53 ff.

person was forbidden to obstruct any of these roads and, if he did so by felling a tree, he had to remove it within forty-eight hours. The court was required, further, to divide the County into precincts and to assign to each of these a supervisor and the tithables residing in the precinct. Every tithable had to work on the road when ordered to do so, unless he was exempt or had two or more male slaves over 16 years of age to labor in his stead.[601] Provision was made on the same principle for the construction and maintenance of bridges.[602] Owners of mill dams, all of which might be used as bridges, had to see that these dams were twelve feet wide and were fenced.[603]

This was the governing road law of George Washington's young manhood, but its enforcement was not easy or adequate. Because a supervisor's neighbors were loath to send their sons or slaves to repair the roads, he often was reluctant to order out the tithables.[604] In general, the roads followed the watersheds and, in avoiding deep or miry streams, usually made a circuit around their head.[605] A chronic inconvenience was the insistence of landowners on putting fences and gates across roads that passed through cultivated fields.[606] Disregard of the law for the removal of felled trees was chronic.[607] Every County Court in the newly settled parts of the Colony was plagued and besieged to open new roads to the West and to change the course of existing roads to suit the convenience of planters.[608]

Traditions were numerous concerning the origin of many of the roads. Some of them were supposed to be, and a few probably were, old Indian trails; [609] but by 1700, paths had become so numerous through

---

601 6 H 64–66.

602 *Ibid.*, 66.

603 *Ibid.*, 67–68. The law provided, similarly, for the marking of crossroads (Cf. Michel in 24 V 115), and for hearings on new routes, on changes in the roads and on proposals for roads that linked two Counties.

604 See 7 H 577 for an amendatory act of 1762. This authorized a Justice on his own view of a road, bridge or mill dam to issue his warrant against the negligent supervisor or the owner of a mill dam out of repair.

605 Jones, *Virginia*, 35, 51.

606 Fithian counted seventy-nine such gates between Annapolis and Port Tobacco. See P. A. Bruce, *Economic History of Virginia in the Seventeenth Century*, v 1, p. 585. In 1734, the Westmoreland Court authorized Landon Carter to erect gates across a public road, provided they were so made that "all travelers with burdens or otherwise and all wheel carriages [could] pass commodiously" (*Westmoreland Orders*, 1731–39, p. 149).

607 In 1734, even so prominent a planter as Willoughby Newton was presented to the grand jury for this offence (10 *Richmond Co. Orders*, 1732–39, p. 18).

608 Cf. 2 L. J., 1015, 1016, *Westmoreland Orders*, 1721–31, p. 255., *ibid.*, 1731–39, p. 54, 64, 131. The *Spotsylvania Order Books* for 1724–30 and 1730–38 contain many examples of the petitions and orders, common in Washington's boyhood, for the extension of highways.

609 For the various theories and some of the evidence, see *Eaton*, 3; Groome, *Fauquier during the Proprietorship*, 192–93; *Landmarks*, 445 ff, 50 V 64.

the woods that a traveler would have been bewildered to know which were the trails of the aborigines and which were tracks to habitations.[610] Recent as was the settlement of Washington's neighborhood between the Occoquan and the new town of Belhaven, that district in 1750 was close to four of the seven main roads of the Colony. That fact stimulated pride and promised profit. In seeking to dispose of a lot on Great Hunting Creek an advertiser proclaimed that the neighborhood was "in the centre of four very public roads leading up and down the country." [611]

One of these roads ran from Alexandria southward past the head of Little Hunting Creek to Colchester on the Occoquan and thence, still southward, to Falmouth and to Fredericksburg. In wet weather this was a route notoriously bad because part of it was through a long, stubborn swamp that was impassable even if rain-swollen rivers were not. To escape this road, travelers sometimes crossed the Potomac at Belhaven, rode through Maryland, down the left bank of the river, and then recrossed that stream and rode over the Northern Neck to Fredericksburg. From that promising town, the road turned to the Southeast. At Massaponax, it divided.[612] The northern branch paralleled roughly the course of the Rappahannock, passed Port Royal and went on to Hobbs Hole or Tappahannock. There the road left the river, turned South-Southwest and struck the Mattapony at Walkerton. South of the Mattapony, this road reached King William Court and united again with the fork from which it had separated on the Massaponax. This southern branch traversed uninteresting country and touched few places of importance on the stretch of twenty-five miles. From King William, another track ran to New Castle on the Pamunkey, but the main road cut southeastward. At a point about twelve miles Southeast of King William Court House, it again divided. One branch led to Delaware or West Point, at the head of York River. The other fork crossed the Pamunkey at Gooch's Ferry and proceeded on the watershed between the York and the Chickahominy to Williamsburg and on to Hampton by way of Yorktown. It was, therefore, entirely permissible for a Virginian of 1750 to boast, when the sun shone, that the Colony had a continuous road, with the necessary ferries, from Hampton, via Yorktown, Williamsburg, King William Court House,

---

[610] Cf. Michel, in 24 *V* 115.
[611] John Pagan in *Va. Gazette*, Apr. 18, 1751.
[612] For this reason, the road is counted as two of the seven here described.

Walkerton, Hobbs Hole, Port Royal, Fredericksburg, Falmouth, Dumfries and Colchester to Belhaven.[613]

From Belhaven two westward roads crossed the Blue Ridge to Frederick Town or Winchester.[614] To Winchester, also, by 1750 had been opened a trail—it scarcely could be styled a road—from Fredericksburg.[615] West and Northwest of Winchester another trail struggled to the upper Potomac opposite the mouth of Wills Creek at the fort and storehouse that later were Cumberland, Maryland.

Past Winchester from the South ran what the mapmakers specifically, if somewhat imaginatively, termed the "Great Road from the Yadkin River thro Virginia to Philadelphia distant 435 miles." South of Staunton, otherwise Augusta Court House, this obstructed track was a mockery, a snare and a provocation to oaths and dismay, but North of the Court House it was easily distinguishable.[616]

The only other long roads on the most useful map of Washington's youth were two that led toward North Carolina from the James River, opposite Williamsburg. One began at Swann's Point and coursed almost due southward to Edenton, North Carolina.[617] The other route was from the James at Tyler's Creek Southeast to Suffolk and thence southwestward to the Chowan and the Roanoke.[618]

Besides these "wagon roads" there were scores that a man on horseback might follow for miles through the woods. In accordance with laws ill-enforced, other and shorter roads led uncertainly to parish churches. Rolling roads to the warehouses had to be kept in decent order. The seven roads here described, to repeat, were all that two of the most capable of colonial engineers thought it worth while to trace on their map. Young Washington was fortunate to live close to three of these roads and not far from a fourth.[619]

[613] This (1948) is U.S. Route 17 from Hampton to Yorktown, Va., Route 238 to Williamsburg, and Va. 165 to Va. 33. Thence there is a present gap, beyond which a succession of minor roads leads to U.S. 360 and thence, Northwest of Tappahannock, to U.S. 17. From Fredericksburg to Alexandria the route is on or close to U.S. 1.

[614] The roads followed approximately the line of U.S. Route 7, via Leesburg and Berryville, and Va. Route 50 via Fairfax, Aldie, Middleburg and Upperville.

[615] See *infra,* p. 208 for Washington's travel over this trail in 1748. The route does not appear to have corresponded to any of the present main highways. It probably was East of Va. 17, and it crossed the Blue Ridge at Ashby's Gap. A somewhat vague description, as of 1754, will be found in 4 *W. Va. His. Mag.,* 110.

[616] This corresponds roughly to the present U.S. Route 220 from Greensboro to Roanoke. Beyond Roanoke, northward, the road is U.S. Route 11. From Lexington to the Potomac this was the "Valley Pike" of a long era in the Shenandoah Valley.

[617] There is no corresponding direct route at this time (1948).

[618] This is, roughly, Va. 10 and 32 to Suffolk, and then substantially the route of the Atlantic Coast Line Railroad toward Tarboro, North Carolina.

[619] That is, the road from Fredericksburg to Winchester.

Every traveler, of course, found the inconvenience of ferries added to the discomforts of the road. Ferriage was a price the Virginians had to pay for living in a well-watered country. From 1641 onward, the Assembly had legislated on this subject,[620] until, in 1748, the Burgesses and Council had simplified and consolidated the enactments.[621] Forty-three public ferries were established on James River and its tributaries, twenty on the York, twenty on the Rappahannock, fifteen on the Potomac, two on the Nottoway, and one on the Eastern Shore.[622] Permissible charges for the passage of a man and his horse were provided by statute at each crossing. The minimum at any ferry was tuppence, the maximum 7s 6d, except from the Eastern Shore to the Peninsula or to Norfolk. For this, the charge was 15 or 20s, according to the number of passengers.[623] Operators of all ferries were subject to punishment for charging more than the statute allowed. Other persons were heavily fined if, for a fee, they transported anyone across a stream where a ferry was provided. Men who handled the regular ferry boats were exempt from the county levy, from muster, and from work on the highways. If the County Court felt that an ordinary was required at a ferry, the man who provided this convenience was relieved of certain fees.[624] All regulation of the type of boat and of the number of hands to be employed on a ferry was at the discretion of the same tribunal.[625]

Some of these ferries were hazardous; [626] some were so essential and unprosperous or were so generally used that the County availed itself of the authority granted it by the General Assembly and operated them with men who received an agreed annual compensation.[627] Among ferries on the same river or on routes to Williamsburg, there was rivalry over the saving of distance or the speed of service.[628] William

620 The following are the known acts prior to 1748; 1 H 269, 348, 411; 2 H 310; 3 H 469, 474; 4 H 45, 93, 112, 179, 362, 438, 531; 5 H 66, 104, 189, 249, 252, 364.

621 Effective June 10, 1751; 6 H 13–23.

622 This last, in 1755, was made a monopoly (6 H 496).

623 *Ibid.*, 19.

624 *Ibid* 23.   625 *Ibid.*, 21.

626 Jones, *Virginia*, 51. For Washington's own experience with such a ferry across the Potomac, see the petition of George Augustine Washington, Oct. 10, 1790, in 9 T 39–40.

627 This practice dated from the late seventeenth century. Cf. 45 V 369 and *infra*, p. 206 for the Occoquan Ferry long operated by the Masons. See also F6 *Lancaster Orders*, 16, Nov. 14, 1716, for an agreement to keep a ferry which remained in the hands of the Carter family until 1745 or after. Spotswood's proposal for service at Germanna Ferry will be found in *Spotsylvania Orders*, 1724–30, p. 44. The annual pay for keeping these ferries ranged from 1400 to 4000 lbs. of tobacco.

628 Cf. John Waller's advertisement of Graves's, formerly Willis's Ferry, over York River near West Point, *Va. Gazette*, Mch. 23, 1739. For the Potomac Ferry of William Clifton, Fairfax Co., with a useful table of distances from Annapolis to Williamsburg, consult *Md. Gazette*, Aug. 6, 1746. In *ibid.*, Nov. 15, 1749, Benjamin Fendall advertised his ferry across the Potomac, opposite the estate of Captain Hooe, for whom see *infra*, p. 226.

Thornton, for example, wished to assure patrons of his Chapahoosic Ferry that if they made "a smoak on the other side of the river, the boat [would] be immediately sent over." [629] Other ferrymen were equal in profession if not in performance, but travelers complained less of the delay than of the cost of ferriage. It was the heaviest expense of a journey. [630]

These ferry charges until 1720 had been exclusively in terms of man and horse—so much for the rider, so much for the animal. After 1720, prices covered vehicles of two wheels or of four, with teams of as many as six horses. [631] Amendment of the law reflected a rise in the number of vehicles, which, by 1750, included perhaps as many as fifty coaches. [632] These were expensive. One was known to have cost 200 guineas and another £250. Still another was to call for bills of exchange to a total of £315. [633] Proud planters were slow to buy second-hand coaches or chariots, [634] though some were not careful in the least to match their teams. [635] Lighter vehicles were less costly and more generally used, but never, in the eighteenth century, did they supersede the riding horse. As late as 1782, there were to be in the whole of Westmoreland only 136 wheels. [636] The favorite vehicle was a "riding chair" of two wheels for one or more persons. Almost equal in popularity was a chaise, normally of four wheels but often little more than a chair de luxe. [637] The fashionable might draw other distinctions: a coach was

[629] *Va. Gazette*, Apr. 11, 1751; cf. 13 *W* (1) p. 158.   [630] Cf. *Fithian*, 22–24, 146.
[631] See 4 *H* 93–94 and the subsequent measures listed in n. 620 *supra*.
[632] This, like the collection of private libraries in Virginia, has seemed to some writers to involve a matter of pride. They have been at pains to prove that the Colony had many pleasure vehicles. For a reasonable estimate, here accepted, see a note by W. G. Stanard in 24 *V* 110. Other references will be found in Jones, *Virginia*, 32, 49, and in *Observations*, 15 *W* (1) p. 223. A description of Governor Spotswood's chariot is given in *Va. Gazette*, Oct. 19, 1739. Specifications of 1768 for Hannah Lee Corbin's coach are printed in Ethel Armes's *Stratford Hall* p. 120. Bequests of coaches, chariots, etc., are frequent, as, e.g., Moore Fauntleroy, 1739, in *Richmond Co. Wills*, 1725–53, p. 347; William Randolph, 1742, in 4 *Goochland Deeds*, 100; Benjamin Harrison, 1743, in 3 *V* 125; Richard Kennon, 1761, in 14 *W* (1) p. 133. Williamsburg by 1739 had a sufficient number of coaches, etc., supplementing those of neighboring planters, to justify a coach-maker's establishment (*Va. Gazette*, Mch. 30, 1739). A decade later, it was published that the President and the Council "went all in coaches" to wait on the Governor (*Va. Gazette*, July 13, 1749, quoted in 20 *W* (1) p. 16).
[633] This was in 1768 (2 *G. W.*, 489–90 n.), when prices were higher.
[634] Francis Jerdone to William Hamilton, Sept. 20, 1753; 8 *W* (1) p. 40. See an advertisement in *Va. Gazette*, June 18, 1752 of a "chariot, harness and four horses," which probably had belonged to Thomas Lee. In 1774 Councillor Carter imported a "plain carriage" that cost £120 sterling (*Fithian*, 248).
[635] See *Observations*, 15 *W* (1) p. 232.
[636] 10 *V* 235. Of the other Counties for which the personal returns of 1782–83 survive in VSL, Chesterfield had the largest number of wheels, 180. Princess Anne was next with 160. Then came Fairfax with 140. Spotsylvania, Prince George and Westmoreland each had 136.
[637] For some details of these vehicles, see *Va. Gazette*, July 18, 1751; *ibid.*, Oct. 27, 1774; 13 *V* 313; 26 *ibid.*, 152–53. See also will of John Moore of King George Co. in 52 *ibid.*, 65, and

a large, closed four-wheeled carriage with two seats that faced each other, and other seats outside. A chariot was four-wheeled but not so heavy. It had the driver in front and it contained a back seat only. A Berlin was a four-wheeled covered carriage with a seat behind, protected by a hood.[638] On the Virginia frontier, all this meant nothing. No wheeled vehicle of any sort is known to have been used in the Shenandoah Valley prior to 1749.[639]

Travel time by private conveyance varied with the season, the grade and the equipage. A later visitor was to be told that Virginians drove six horses, covered eight to nine miles an hour, and frequently went sixty miles to dinner,[640] but such statements were made in jest. A ride of fifteen miles for a visit was not remarkable, though probably longer than most families traveled in a coach for social calls.[641] A clergyman, touring Virginia in May and June, 1759, covered from eighteen to fifty miles daily on horseback.[642] Mounted Moravian missionaries equalled this maximum ride in a wild part of the Colony.[643] Other missionaries, traveling on foot, made thirty miles on each of two successive days, though on one of these days they had to cross streams about thirty times.[644]

During the winter, a messenger might fight twelve days to conquer the mud between Winchester and Williamsburg.[645] In a well-settled country of sandy roads, a stage wagon of twelve passengers went regularly in summer from Hampton to Williamsburg, via Yorktown, in one day. The distance was approximately thirty-two miles.[646] On almost every important route, in spite of time and weather, Virginians traveled widely and, year by year, less slowly. Governor Spotswood

---

John Custis to Captain Friend, n.d. [1736?], *Custis Letter Book*, No. 104. Frequent mention of the use of a chair will be found in Colonel Gordon's diary, 11 *W* (1) p. 99, 103, 107, 111; 12 *ibid.*, 6. See *infra*, Chap. VII, p. 262 for the specifications of William Fauntleroy for a chair, a "whip with [his] name on it" and, if not too expensive, the decoration of the chair with his coat of arms. In England, according to Ralph Straus, *Carriages and Coaches*, 140–41, 148, a chaise and a chair were essentially the same vehicle and became later the gig. A chaise might be built with shafts for one horse, but might be drawn on occasion by three animals, one on either side of the horse in the shafts.

[638] These are the definitions in the *Oxford Dictionary*. Straus, *op. cit.*, 119, 141, gave the structural pecularities of two perches and leather braces.

[639] 7 *V* 109–10.

[640] Lord Gordon, 1765, in *Mereness*, 405.

[641] Fithian, *op. cit.*, 24, recorded a ride of fifteen miles for a call.

[642] *Burnaby*, 51, 61.

[643] 12 *V* 75–76.

[644] 11 *V* 125.

[645] 1 *Din.*, 82, but the calculation assumes the letter was answered the day it was received. It may not have been.

[646] 16 *V* 207. The fare was 12s.

had estimated that in five years and one month, 1711–16, he had covered 3626 miles over roads and through the wilderness.[647]

The post did not emulate the Governor who had much to do with its development. Carriage of letters was slow and uncertain. A law of 1657–58 had required the forwarding of public dispatches, properly superscribed, from one plantation to the next by the proprietor and at his own cost,[648] but in 1692–93, the Colony hopefully had accepted the colonial post office monopoly given Thomas Neale by William and Mary in 1691. This came to nothing, so far as Virginia was concerned, though Neale's deputy, Governor Andrew Hamilton of New Jersey, organized by 1697 a post from New England as far South as New Castle, Delaware. Hamilton himself was against the inclusion of Virginia and Maryland in the service because he did not believe 100 letters a year would be exchanged between those two Colonies and those to the North.[649]

Although Neale's monopoly was acquired by the government from his heirs in 1707, the General Post Office in London did nothing to expedite mail to Virginia. "We have," John Custis complained in 1718, "a damd confounded pretended post-office here which keeps letters as long as they see fit; it is a general grievance to the country, but am not sure of its being redrest." [650] It remained for Governor Alexander Spotswood, Deputy Postmaster General after 1732, to arrange a post that was carried southward to Virginia, but neither he nor his successors could be sure of maintaining a schedule. In the winter of 1736–37 no post arrived from the North for six weeks or more.[651] As late as 1749 it was stated that the post South of Philadelphia might be irregular because the carrier would not start until he had a sufficient number of letters to guarantee his wages.[652] Extension southward from Williamsburg began in 1738, when Spotswood employed William Parks, Virginia printer, to operate a stage once a month to Edenton, North Carolina.[653] Later the line was carried to Charleston, South Carolina,[654] but it was difficult in the seventeen-fifties to procure men

---

[647] 3 W (2) p. 40–45.
[648] 1 H 436 and renewed, with amendment, in 1661/62, 2 H 108–09.
[649] See William Smith, *The History of the Post Office in British North America, 1639–1870*, p. 8–9, 14, 22.
[650] Letter, n.m., n.d., to unnamed correspondent; *Custis Letter Book*, No. 10.
[651] *Va. Gazette*, Jan. 28, 1737.
[652] Douglas, *Historical and Political Summary*, quoted in William Smith, *op. cit.*, p. 25.
[653] *Va. Gazette*, Apr. 21, 1738.
[654] *Va. Gazette*, June 15, 1739.

for the post office.[655] In at least one instance, a postrider was bitten fatally by a rattlesnake.[656]

Where fact was not conveyed, falsehood ran ahead. So easily was rumor spread that Virginia Burgesses in the time of the Commonwealth had passed a law for the punishment of those who circulated false reports.[657] Eighty years later, the colonials still were so hungry for reports from the outer world that they broke open private letters and intercepted newspapers.[658] Men with correspondents in England often were suspicious, in John Custis's words, that their letters were "peep'd into." [659]

Much news and at least as much rumor were spread by postriders and travelers who stopped at "ordinaries." These establishments, usually styled taverns in other Colonies,[660] had been subject to regulation by the Assembly after 1639-40 and had been licensed subsequent to 1644.[661] They had been few and unprosperous then, because most planters were glad to welcome and to entertain a guest for the sake of the information he brought.[662] A tradition persisted to 1800 of one sociable planter who was so hungry to see new faces that he would send a servant to the ordinary with a note in which he informed any gentleman staying there for the night that if accommodations were not agreeable, the servant was under instructions to escort the guest to the nearby home. As most of the travelers accepted and thereby deprived the ordinary-keeper of his profit, the hospitable planter secretly compensated the proprietor.[663] In contrast, more intimate visitors at private homes sometimes were suspected of resembling Will Wimple in the duration of their sojourn.[664] A sponge of this sort could not remain

655 *Va. Gazette*, Apr. 30, 1752.

656 *Md. Gazette*, July 19, 1752.

657 March 1657/58; 1 H 434-35.

658 *Va. Gazette*, Jan. 28, Mch. 31, 1737; 2 *G. W.*, 181; 1 *Hamilton*, 323. Overseas correspondence is discussed *infra*, p. 166-67, with Commerce.

659 Letter of 1718, n.m., n.d., cited in n. 650 *supra*.

660 Cf. *Fithian*, 232. "Ordinary" was the proper name for nearly all of them as they served only regular, or "ordinary," meals at fixed hours.

661 1 H 229, 287. Subsequent regulatory acts are given in 1 *ibid.*, 300, 411, 471, 522; 2 *ibid.*, 19, 131, 234, 269, 361, 393; 3 *ibid.*, 45, 395; 4 *ibid.*, 109, 428. The controlling law in the seventeen-fifties was the statue of 1748, for which see 6 H 71. To be consulted, also, is the anti-gambling act of 1740, in 5 H 103. An interesting explanation of the measure of 1734, forbidding certain credits by ordinaries, will be found in a letter of Governor Gooch to the Lords of Trade, Nov. 20, 1734, 2 *Gooch MSS*, 369.

662 *Beverley*, 254; Jones, *Virginia*, 49.

663 John Bernard, *Retrospections of America*, quoted in *Landmarks*, 486, as part of a most interesting account of ordinaries in old Prince William.

664 Cf. *Fithian*, 78. Washington was doomed to have a number of guests who sat at his table almost as often as they ate at their own board.

long at an ordinary, because prices were high [665] and food consisted usually of little more than bacon and corn bread.[666]

A few establishments were known for toothsome, savory viands and were well furnished, besides; [667] but, good or bad, ordinaries were licensed annually by the County Court [668] and might be kept near a ferry, adjoining a race course [669] in a man's own home [670] or at any point regarded as suitable.[671] While the court could punish for the operation of a disorderly house [672] or for violation of the anti-gambling act,[673] the chief routine function of this class of justice was to fix in each County the charges at ordinaries for food, drink, lodging and pasturage. A diligent court, if it so elected, might prescribe one price for a feather bed with clean sheets and another price for a flock bed with clean sheets.[674] Silence concerning the condition of sheets at ordinaries in other Counties represents a judicial mystery not easily resolved.[675] The ideal was set forth near the frontier by a court's demand of a bond of 10,000 pounds of tobacco that the keeper of an ordinary should "constantly provide in his said ordinary good, wholesome and cleanly lodging and diet for travelers and stablage for horses," [676] but this was an ideal seldom attained.

Against the wickedness, as well as against the dirtiness of these places,[677] complaint often was made; but the worst enemies of the ordinary-keeper were lack of patronage and excess of competition. Changes of proprietors or lessees were frequent.[678] Even when ordi-

---

665 Cf. *Landmarks*, 513, n. 149.   666 2 *Anburey*, 198.

667 *Eaton*, 2–3, 1 *Hoppin*, 180–82. For an inventory of the furnishings of a tavern, see also, 2 *Chastellux*, 24; for conditions in the seventeen-eighties, *vide* 23 *W* (2) p. 8–26. Hostelries at Yorktown are mentioned in 2 *Schoepf*, 30. The last of these writers affirmed that the best ordinaries, as a rule, were those most plastered with hand bills and notices. A note on Henry Witherburn—the name is spelled in at least three ways—will be found in 4 *T* 30.

668 6 *H* 71–72.   669 *Spotsylvania Orders*, 1738–49, p. 51.

670 31 *V* 349. See, also, 1 *Chesterfield Orders*, 4, 5.

671 6 *H* 72.

672 10 *Richmond Co. Orders*, 1732–39, p. 13.

673 5 *H* 103. See *Va. Gazette*, Jan. 28, 1739, for the activities of an employee who appears to have discharged the duties of official "bouncer" for the ordinary near Gloucester Court House.

674 See *Spotsylvania Orders*, 1730–38, p. 24, Mch. 3, 1731.

675 For typical orders fixing prices, see *Westmoreland Orders*, 1731–39, p. 16, Mch. 29, 1732; 10 *Richmond Co. Orders*, 1732–39, p. 268, Mch. 4, 1735; 6 *Princess Anne Minutes*, 7, Apr. 3, 1745; *Albemarle Orders*, Mch. 27, 1747; Middlesex prices of March, 1770, in 12 *V* 188. Prices of wine, in particular, were high.

676 Albemarle County, July 25, 1745; *Papers Albemarle Co. His. Soc.*, v. 5, p. 21.

677 See a vigorous protest by a clergyman against the opening of a new ordinary; *Va. Gazette*, Apr. 11, 1751.

678 The following are a few only of the many advertisements of ordinaries for lease or sale: Caroline Court House (*Va. Gazette*, Oct. 17, 24, 1745); Fredericksburg (*ibid.*, May 2, 1751); vicinity of Fredericksburg (*ibid.*, Mch. 7, 1751); Williamsburg (*ibid.*, Aug. 24, 1751); King William Court House (*ibid.*, Nov. 17, 1752); vicinity of Claiborne's Ferry (*ibid.*, Apr. 3, 1752); Swan Tavern, Yorktown (*ibid.*, Aug. 15, 1751).

naries were advertised, their virtues scarcely could have impressed. Of his tavern on the Ridge Road in Caroline County, the best that George Keeling could say to readers was that it was on a route "some miles the nearest way from several of the northern counties to Williamsburg." [679] William Dunn, in presenting his Crown Tavern opposite the Printing Office in the capital, was content to deny the allegation of "some ill-disposed persons" that he had "not given sufficient entertainment." [680] The business, take it as one would, nowhere was romantic in Virginia.

Most of the travelers, lingering as briefly as they might at an ordinary, were on their way to one or another of the towns of the Colony. There should have been forty-four towns, a visitor was told in 1759, but he was to discover that half of these did not include more than five houses each. To his British eyes the remaining half appeared "little better than inconsiderable villages." The reason, he learned, was the lack of reason for the existence of towns. Farm land was cheap; almost any man could make his living by agriculture. Most plantations were so close to a river that tobacco could be shipped directly overseas. It need not be brought to a large settlement.[681] So little use was there for towns, in fact, that eight only in 1750 may have deserved the name. Even to some of these a critical visitor might have applied the British word "village."

The pride of the Colony was its capital, Williamsburg. So designated after the burning of Jamestown in 1698, Williamsburg was the seat of the Governor and the meeting place of the General Assembly, of the Council, and of the General Court. Rivaling any of these in dignity was the College of William and Mary, chartered by the Crown in 1693. When first chosen, the site of Williamsburg was proclaimed "healthy and agreeable to the constitutions of the inhabitants of this his majesty's colony and dominion, having the natural advantage of a serene and temperate air, dry and champaign land, and plentifully stored with wholesome springs, and the conveniency of two navigable and pleasant creeks, that run out of James and York rivers . . ." [682] While there may not have been experiential unanimity, so to say, in this tribute, the town took on the dignity of a city by royal letters patent of July 28, 1722,[683] and, indeed, had received earlier that year what came to be,

[679] *Ibid.,* Sept. 5, 1751.
[680] *Ibid.,* Mch. 12, 1752.
[681] *Burnaby,* 20. Jones, in his *Virginia,* 35, had given much the same explanation.
[682] 3 H 419.   [683] 4 H 138.

in time, the evidence of emergence in Virginia to civic importance. That is to say, in May, 1722, it had at the hands of the General Assembly the boon of an act to prevent swine from "going at large" within the corporate limits.[684] Its hogs confined, the city had grown steadily if not swiftly. By 1759, Williamsburg consisted of about 200 houses, ten or twelve of which were rated as the permanent residences of gentlemen's families. The principal, though often very dusty, street was proclaimed "one of the most spacious in America"; the appearance of the town was handsome; its population was about 1000.[685] A few years later, 1765, another visitor was to report that Williamsburg "resemble[d] a good English country town and that its people were well-bred, polite and civil to strangers." [686]

Most of the other important towns of the Colony were close to Williamsburg. Across the narrow Peninsula between the York and the James, distant by road about twelve miles, was Yorktown, which had been established in 1691. Its rise had been due to the depth of the York at that point and to the proximity of Chesapeake Bay. Many vessels made it their destination. Merchants built large stores there. No town in all Virginia had a fairer site or an appearance more picturesque. Above the masts and yards of the ships in the sparkling river, houses were perched along the hill-mounting road, as if they merely were resting in their climb. On the flat and cheerful cliff were the homes of the merchants, the Court House and the better ordinaries.

Farther down the Peninsula, almost at its tip, on the sheltered shores of a creek that might as readily have been called a bay, was the town of Hampton. This was next to Jamestown in age among the Virginia outposts and, after the abandonment of Jamestown, it was to be the oldest English settlement of continuous existence in America.[687] Formal incorporation dated from 1705, when the General Assembly fashioned on paper a long list of ports and towns.[688] Hampton was more fortunate than some of the others: in spite of pirates, storms and pestilence, it prospered as a port and haven. As early as 1716, it had 100 houses

[684] 4 H 116.
[685] *Burnaby*, 6.
[686] Lord Gordon in *Mereness*, 403. The literature on Williamsburg is ample and accessible. See in particular the standard work already cited, L. G. Tyler, *Colonial Williamsburg*. The guide to Williamsburg, issued by the Williamsburg Restoration, and styled *A Brief and True Report for the Traveller concerning Williamsburg in Virginia*, contains an accurate general description of the town in addition to a full account of the buildings and grounds restored in fine taste and with scientific regard for accuracy. Because of the comprehensive research made on Williamsburg, it has not been thought necessary to include any long description here.
[687] L. G. Tyler, *Hampton*, 6.   [688] 3 H 415.

and enjoyed the largest business in Virginia. If there was a British fleet in the Chesapeake, or if a convoy was assembling, it lay at Hampton.[689] The population of the town in the middle of the eighteenth century was said to be 3000,[690] a total unhappily swollen in 1755 by more than 1100 Acadians whom the English troops had removed from Nova Scotia. These subjects of France were permitted to land and to remain for the winter and then they were required to depart.[691]

Below Hampton, at the very end of the Peninsula, was the fort of Old Point Comfort, which was considered strong, with its twenty-two guns, until a hurricane in 1749 destroyed it.[692] Across beautiful Hampton Roads, and a few miles up the tolerant and hospitable river that bore the name of Queen Elizabeth, the town of Norfolk was thriving in the seventeen-fifties. As William Byrd had said, the place had the "ayr of a town" [693] and consisted of something more than a cluster of ordinaries. It enjoyed a brisk trade with the West Indies from which it imported more of throat-searing rum than was good for the Colony.[694] At Norfolk, too, the produce of North Carolina was finding an outlet. Residents were principally merchants, ship's carpenters, artisans and seamen [695] who together had been numerous enough in 1736 to be constituted a borough. They had then a Mayor and eight Aldermen and, as Recorder, no less a person than Sir John Randolph,[696] but they took pains that the franchise should be exercised by those only who owned fifty acres or more of land or had served five years at a trade in the town.[697]

Although Norfolk had endured a bad West Indian plague of some sort in 1744,[698] it had not been shaken in its activity, its self-confidence or its humor. On the June day of 1755 set aside for the election of a Mayor, sundry burghers mockingly seized upon a Negro slave named Will, proclaimed him Mayor, seated him and drank his health—how often they did not confess. The lawful executive was outraged; the Aldermen were shocked. Before them, two days later, the offenders were summoned. Remorse having done its work, the celebrating gentle-

---

689 Journal of John Fontaine in Fontaine, *Memoirs of a Huguenot Family*, 262.
690 Tyler, *Hampton*, 36. The figure seems high.   691 2 *Din.*, 268, 347, 396, 444.
692 Tyler, *Hampton*, 36; Governor Gooch in 3 *V* 119–20.
693 William Byrd, "History of the Dividing Line," in *Writings*, ed. Bassett, 28.
694 *Ibid.*
695 *Ibid.*, 29.
696 2 *L. J.*, 857; *Va. Gazette*, Nov. 19, 1736.
697 For the complete charter, see 3 *Lower Norfolk Antiquary*, 87 ff. The text in 4 *H* 541 is incomplete.
698 *Norfolk Council Orders*, 1736–98, p. 12.

men apologized. His Honor and the Aldermen were appeased.[699] It was a trivial but a typical incident. Norfolk always had shifting tides of fortune but a constant delight in life.

Williamsburg, Yorktown, and Norfolk were within a circle of twenty-five miles from Hampton. The Colony's next town of rising dignity was Richmond, more than fifty miles up the James from Williamsburg and at the falls of the river. This had been the site of the public warehouse of Shoccoe's and had been on the land of William Byrd the second, by whose order the town was laid out in 1737.[700] Five years later, Richmond was incorporated as a town [701] and in 1751 was chosen as the site for the Court House of Henrico County.[702] The population at the middle of the century probably did not exceed 250 or perhaps 300; [703] but the location was promising: Westward, with Richmond as the natural market on the nearest navigable stream, were hundreds of thousands of acres of good tobacco land.

About fifty-five miles North of Richmond, at the falls of the Rappahannock, the town of young George Washington's frequent observation was rising in three tiers from the river bank to a high wooded ridge. North of Fredericksburg and of Falmouth, which already have been described, the nearest settlement of size was the seat of several active Scotch merchants, the new town of Dumfries on an arm of the broad Potomac. Although it was not chartered until 1749,[704] Dumfries was drawing settlers. Twice within twelve years the area of the town was enlarged. Because the tobacco trade was thriving,[705] everything else was incidental or was taken for granted. Men built more rapidly than permanently. Dumfries was to be challenged in 1753 by a new town, Colchester, eight miles North of it, and on the Occoquan, an affluent of the Potomac. Colchester had been the site of an iron foundry which, it will be remembered, had enjoyed a brief period of prosperity and then had perished.[706] It was not destined to rise again.

Still farther up the Potomac and directly on that stream, thirteen

699 1 *Lower Norfolk Antiquary*, 6.
700 *Va. Gazette*, Apr. 29, 1737; William Byrd to Lord Egmont, July, n.d., 1736; 36 *V* 217.
701 2 *L. J.*, 926; 5 *H* 191.
702 *Va. Gazette*, Jan. 17, 1751, in 12 *W* (1) p. 73.
703 This figure is scarcely more than a guess, because records are meagre. For the early years of the town, see W. A. Christian, *Richmond, Her Past and Present*, 8 ff.
704 The title only of the incorporating act was given in 6 *H* 214, but Fairfax Harrison printed the full text in *Landmarks*, 670 ff. For George Washington's familiarity with Dumfries before 1749 see Chapter V.
705 In *Landmarks*, 395, the references are cited.
706 *Barnaby*, 46; *Landmarks*, 425. For the incorporation of Colchester, see 6 *H* 396.

miles Northeast of Colchester by air, another new town, Alexandria or Belhaven, was in the very pangs of birth.[707] Beyond Alexandria, the new road of adventure led the frontiersmen to the small settlement of Frederick Town, or Winchester. Southwestward from this raw place of residence, there was not even a village in the fertile Shenandoah Valley for a distance of eighty-five miles. Then, it will be remembered,[708] the traveler came to Augusta Court House or Staunton, a place of some twenty roofs.[709]

East of the Blue Ridge were eight other settlements that might become towns or even cities. Delaware, or West Point, was on the peninsula formed where the Pamunkey and the Mattapony joined waters as the good-tempered York; up the Pamunkey were Hanovertown, which boasted several stores, and Newcastle, which had bustled in 1744 but had failed to develop.[710] On the Rappahannock were the respected village of Urbanna and the town of Hobbs Hole or Tappahannock, an early settlement and a thriving tobacco port.[711] Next upstream was Leedstown. This had been incorporated in 1742,[712] and was possessed later of an ordinary that had an excellent name.[713] Between Leedstown and Fredericksburg was Port Royal, which was established as a town in 1744.[714] On Appomattox at the fall line, at the site of early Fort Henry, William Byrd had planned a town in 1733 and had named it Petersburg.[715] It was rising slowly but it was a place of promise.

For these towns, new and old, promising or prostrate, the House of Burgesses and Council prescribed few conditions. Taxes were to be paid, militia musters held and the law enforced. Beyond this, legislation for towns was on a narrow arc. Residents were forbidden to permit their hogs, horses or cattle to roam at large.[716] Nor were wooden chimneys allowed on houses.[717] In at least one instance the selling of

---

[707] For the details, see *infra*, p. 232.   [708] See *supra*, p. 150.

[709] 12 *V* 146.

[710] 2 *L. J.*, 957, 974, 1013, 1037. Both Newcastle and Hanovertown were in the minds of those Burgesses who sought, after the burning of the capitol at Williamsburg in 1746, to have the seat of government established at a town "more convenient to the inhabitants of this colony." (2 *L. J.*, 1011, 1078; Blair's diary, Feb. 20, 1751, in 8 *W* (1) p. 3.)

[711] For the singular antecedents of its incorporation, see 5 *H* 304.

[712] 5 *H* 193.

[713] 9 *T* 69.

[714] 5 *H* 287. Cf. notice of the sale of the remaining lots, *Va. Gazette*, June 27, 1745.

[715] "Journey to the Land of Eden," in *Writings*, ed. Bassett, 292.

[716] Governor Gooch to the Lords of Trade, July 30, 1728. Almost every town had a separate act of Assembly on this subject (*Gooch MSS*, 56. Cf. *supra*, p. 158 for the Williamsburg act).

[717] See, as typical, 2 *L. J.*, 799, 920, 948.

strong liquor in small quantities was forbidden all except regular merchants.[718] These measures compassed the "Shall" and "Shall not" of colonial law. The remainder was for the choice of free men.

Few of the towns enjoyed large trade in anything other than tobacco. Life was dull and easy for the merchants there in comparison with that of the men who went beyond the frontier and traded with the Indians. Even the sailors had a life of far greater variety than a dweller in a quiet town could hope to enjoy. A fleet of about 120 vessels came annually to Virginia, many of them in ballast,[719] in order to move the tobacco crop, which, it will be remembered, usually consisted of approximately 50,000 hogsheads.[720] When competition for large cargoes was brisk,[721] there often was haste in loading; [722] but usually ascent of the sluggish tidal rivers was slow. A month might be consumed in getting up James River from Hampton to Bermuda Hundred.[723] Long, idle "lay days" might be spent at anchor before a cargo was to be had or, if promised, loaded.[724] In wartime, moreover, ships had to wait until a strong convoy was assembled. No less than sixty-seven ships, mounting 359 guns, had ridden off Hampton in 1705.[725] Yorktown was the favorite port of entry for many years,[726] but, after the development of the upper valley of the James as a tobacco-growing area, Yorktown declined in exports.[727] From no part of Virginia were there large shipments to any other markets than to those of the United Kingdom.[728] As noted already, pork and staves, grain and lumber went in moderate quantities to the West Indies and to the "wine islands." Vessels seeking cargoes of tobacco often would solicit business on the Potomac after loading in part on the Rappahannock. Trade from one river to another occupied perhaps sixty small craft.[729] Shipbuilding was on a limited

718 This was Yorktown, 1736. See 2 L. J. 854; 4 H 543.

719 1 Din., 385. Of fifteen vessels mentioned in the Va. Gazette as arriving at Yorktown between Mch. 28 and June 24, 1745, six were in ballast. Ships sometimes brought Liverpool salt as ballast (15 V 24).

720 Gooch reports in 3 V 117-18. See, also, supra, p. 142.

721 See Va. Gazette, Aug. 14, 1752; Richard Adams to Thomas Adams, Aug. 12, Oct. 19, 1771, 5 V 135, 137; 11 W (1) p. 106.

722 11 W (1) p. 196.

723 Thomas Adams to Perkins, Buchanan and Brown, April n.d., 1770, 23 V 54-55.

724 For the act of 1732, authorizing masters to use their own sloops and boats in carrying tobacco from the public warehouses to their vessels, see 2 L. J., 791 and 4 H 309.

725 9 V 257. Cf. the notice of the prospective departure in September, 1758 of a convoy from York River, Md. Gazette, June 29, 1758.

726 Va. Gazette, June 22, Dec. 25, 1739; Oct. 31, 1745; Mch. 12, 1752.

727 See Va. Gazette, Jan. 2, 1745, and supra, p. 142, for the extent of the crop in the valley of James River.

728 Cf. Gooch's report in 3 V 117-18.

729 Gooch in 3 V 123.

scale.[730] So was the sale of vessels, most of which were laid down, manned and owned in England.[731] Planters who operated vessels or chartered ships for the movement of their tobacco had, of course, to concern themselves with masters and maintenance, as well as with insurance, and often to their vexation and loss.[732]

Other planters might have protested that their troubles were no less than those of their ship-owning neighbors, because they had to deal with the traditional adversary of Virginians, the English and Scotch merchants. To those traders, nearly all the tobacco was consigned; they acted as bankers and as purchasing agents for their customers in the Colony.[733] Meeting at the Virginia Coffee House in St. Michael's Alley,[734] the London merchants discussed interests that were reciprocal and sometimes were considered common to them and to their customers. One planter went so far as to say, "I know there is something that may not improperly be called a commercial friendship because I feel it glowing in my own heart which takes its rise from a long correspondence and is established by a punctual and steady integrity on both sides."[735] This sentiment was exceptional. Distrust of the merchants was widespread and customary. So bad had been the relations between Virginia producer and London merchant in the seventeentwenties that Governor Gooch, in reviewing his own services to the Colony, rated among the foremost what he believed he had done to put mercantile relations on friendly terms.[736]

Merchants did not share the prevailing belief that "prodigious" numbers of Virginia planters were "immensely rich."[737] Traders knew, on the contrary, that the planter often lived beyond his means, but still

---

[730] For one of the comparatively few known instances of construction for sale, without advance order, see *Va. Gazette*, Apr. 17, 1752. Needless to say, virtually all small craft were built in Virginia.

[731] Notices of sale are found in *ibid.*, June 27, 1745, Feb. 27, 1752. For offer of a wharf, see *ibid.*, May 22, 1752. Shipchandlery, fires on ships, and the employment of masters are mentioned in *ibid.*, Feb. 27, 1738, July 24, 1746, Apr. 30, 1752.

[732] The fullest files, prior to the Revolution, are the letters of Robert Carter, ed. Wright, those of his sons, in the *Carter-Plummer MSS*, those of Col. James Gordon in 11 and 12 *W* (1), those of the first and second William Byrd, and those of Blair, Banister and Braxton. Shorter and later but highly informative records of Thomas Adams and of Roger Atkinson survive. They appear in 23 *V* 52 ff and in 15 *ibid.*, 345 ff. Still later are most of the interesting papers in Frances Norton Mason, ed., *John Norton and Sons.*

[733] Cf., as illustrative, John Carter and his brothers to William Dawkins, Aug. nd., 1732; *Carter-Plummer MSS.*

[734] On the site of the later George and Vulture, familiar to all readers of the *Pickwick Papers*; 26 *V* 82–83, 27 *ibid.*, 374–75.

[735] Richard Corbin to Colonel Hunter, June 13, 1758, *Corbin MS Letter Book,* 12.

[736] Address of Aug. 6, 1736; *Journ. H. B.,* 1727–40, p. 242.

[737] *Observations* in 15 *W* (1) p. 146.

they competed one with another in making advances to Virginians whose accounts were desired. One Londoner, for example, wrote in candor to the sons of Robert Carter: "The benefit I receive from my commission in transacting the business of the estate I owe to your friendship and hope to preserve by a punctual discharge of my duty and at the same time I shall readily contribute to the convenience of all concerned by advancing money as far as my abilities go or your occasions require." [738] Such practices justified the indictment William Byrd drew in one of his letters to a merchant: ". . . you are all rivals in the trade and are as jealous of one another as you would be for a mistress. You are fearful others should be beforehand with you and so run away with the consignments." [739]

Although in this respect the righteous and conservative merchant had to suffer for the unrighteous tempter, the first result of competitive credit in London was overbuying by Virginians. This practice was epitomized in three sentences from a letter of a planter to his London merchant: "I have shipped you two hogsheads of extraordinarily fine tobacco. If it should so happen that I have sent for more things than the tobacco is sufficient to pay for, you have other effects in your hands. I desire then that you would omit sending the saddle, bridle and books, but if possible omit nothing." [740] The merchant usually "omitted nothing," with the result that the rich planters eagerly imported everything from conch shells [741] to coffee, and from millstones to millinery. Orders of tobacco growers and of merchants resident in Virginia amounted by 1750 to more than £150,000 per annum. [742] In theory, the planter paid no freight on these imports, but he was more or less under obligation to export his tobacco on the vessels that brought over, with the shipmaster's compliments, his goods from England. [743] Often, it will be remembered, this service of courtesy was disservice, because fragile goods were shattered by rough handling [744] or were put ashore at some other landing than the owner's. [745]

[738] Edward Athawes to John and Charles Carter, Apr. 16, 1739, 23 V 171.

[739] William Byrd the second to unnamed correspondent, Aug. 20, 1733, 9 V 115. See also his letter, n.d., to Captain Porford, *ibid.*, 128, and William Byrd to John Custis, July 29, 1723, 36 V 37.

[740] George Braxton the second to Samuel Lyde, Aug. 24, 1755, in *Blair, Banister and Braxton*, 140.

[741] William Mayo to "a gentleman in the Barbadoes," Aug. 27, 1731, 4 R 86.

[742] Gooch gave the figure £150,000 in 1750; 3 *Gooch MSS*, 977. Imports probably increased slightly in the next five years.

[743] Jones, *Virginia*, 34–35.

[744] See *supra* p. 102.

[745] Cf. *Va. Gazette*, June 18, July 24, Aug. 14, 1752.

Still the planters bought, lavishly and recklessly. Diligent, skillful merchants often grew rich. Although the greater part of the imports were of farm implements, sugar, molasses, rum, salt and Negro slaves,[746] luxury goods in large quantity were brought through the Virginia Capes—cloth of many kinds,[747] ladies' garments,[748] toys.[749] Of food delicacies there were olives, capers, anchovies,[750] lemons, figs,[751] citron, nutmegs, caraway,[752] olive oil, raisins and sweetmeats.[753] Jewelry and kid gloves were offered, as were toilet articles and drugs,[754] and sometimes the mixed treasures of a prize ship.[755] As noted in connection with house-furnishings, most of the crockery, glassware and kitchen utensils were English.[756] A limited volume of pottery was being sent down the coast from New England [757] as were a few hats [758] and some furniture. [759] Glass from Philadelphia also had a market.[760] Rope, cordage and most other articles of ship chandlery came from England or from East India.[761]

In purchasing these goods at Yorktown or at Williamsburg, the planter could pick and reject, though stocks were small and prices nearly double those "at home"; but if he bought directly in England, through his merchant, he often felt that he had no recourse should goods prove inferior. The frequency with which clothing and manufactured articles had the appearance of being designed to cheat the planters was irritating and created in many minds the feeling that the merchants considered anything good enough for the colonials. Not all of the Virginians were as crotchety or as hard to please as John Custis, but some of his experiences were typical. "You sent me a hd. of . . . Beer as it is called," he wrote his merchant, ". . . such trash as was never before brewed; I offered it to my Negroes and not one would drink it; the worst molasses rum that ever was brewed was a cordial to it." [762] Again Custis wrote: "[Starke of Glasgow has] sent thirteen pieces of plaid: there is but two or three that looks anything like new. The rest have

---

[746] *Sutherland*, 276 ff.

[747] Excellent lists will be found in *Va. Gazette* advertisements of June 27, 1745 and Mch. 12, 1752. For the standard cloth measure of the period, see 51 *V* 53.

[748] See *Va. Gazette*, June 13, Oct. 31, 1745; Mch. 20, July 24, 1746; July 24, 1752.

[749] *Ibid.*, June 27, 1751.   [750] *Ibid.*, July 24, 1746.

[751] *Ibid.*, Apr. 18, 1751.   [752] *Ibid.*, May 24, 1751.

[753] *Ibid.*, Feb. 27, 1752.   [754] *Ibid.*, July 25, 1751 and Apr. 17, 1752.

[755] *Ibid.*, June 26, 1746.   [756] *Ibid.*, May 22, 1746.

[757] *Ibid.*, Jan. 16, 1746. See *supra*, p. 101.   [758] *Ibid.*

[759] *Ibid.*, May 18, 1739. For misgivings of William Byrd the second, in 1739, regarding the increase of New England shipping in Virginia waters, see 36 *V* 359–60.

[760] *Va. Gazette*, Mch. 21, 1751.

[761] Cf. *Va. Gazette*, Aug. 21, 1746.

[762] John Custis to Robert Cary, 1719 [1729?], n.m., n.d., *Custis Letter Book,* No. 55.

been old shop keepers I am certain, for many years, being sullied and eaten by the moth and worm as full of holes as they can well be; there might be some slight room to allege they were thus eaten on ship board after they came from Mr. Clark; but this mask is quite taken off by endeavoring if possible to hide that by darning up abundance of the holes, so that they are full of holes and darns patched together, which makes it very manifest it is a piece of villany somewhere." [763] Over and over, his complaint was the same. [764] Other planters had like grievances, [765] which no doubt they charged against England, as surely as against the offending tradesman or agent. Sometimes, a customer successfully warned his representative to serve notice on a tailor or an ironmonger that quality was required. John Carter, for instance, wrote his representatives in London: ". . . if you all desire I should have any dealings with Cartony, he must be told that I have not lost my taste by living the great part of my time in this country." [766] Occasionally, merchants were enjoined not to let it be known that invoices were for export. [767] Even then, the most vigilant and exacting Virginia planter could not tell what he would get or when he would receive it. Caveat emptor was outdone. Purchase was lottery.

The time required to transport goods across the Atlantic varied much. In 1750, William Beverley and his family went from Virginia to Liverpool in six weeks. [768] The western voyage was made now and again with like speed. [769] In 1766, a vessel was to sweep from the Virginia Capes to Dover in twenty-nine days. [770] The average time from a Channel port to Hampton Roads, or vice versa, was approximately nine weeks, [771] though as long as five months might be required. [772] For a letter to pass from England to an addressee in Virginia, two months and a half appear to have been regarded as a reasonable time. [773] The lapse of three months between dispatch and receipt called for no comment. [774] Carriage of letters usually was through the courtesy of some shipmaster

[763] John Custis to unnamed correspondent, May 5, 1729; *Custis Letter Book*, No. 133.

[764] See *ibid.*, Nos. 20, 41 and 89.

[765] Cf. Colonel Gordon in 11 *W* (1) p. 106.

[766] John Carter to R. Cary, July 14, 1734, *Carter-Plummer MSS*, 144.

[767] Cf. Washington's order for a spinet, Oct. 12, 1761; 2 *G. W.*, 370.

[768] 36 *V* 161–69.

[769] *Va. Gazette*, Dec. 19, 1745.

[770] 16 *V* 206.

[771] Cf. passages noted in *Va. Gazette*, Feb. 24, 1737, May 2, 1745 (Glasgow), Sept. 9, 1745; *Burnaby*, 1, 5.

[772] 24 *V* 1. A passage of less than forty-eight hours from New York to James River was reported in *Va. Gazette*, Aug. 12, 1737.

[773] Cf. Harrower's diary, May 21, 1775, 6 *A. H. R.*, 96.

[774] Cf. John Carter to M. Perry, Sept. 5, 1738; *Carter-Plummer MSS*, 197.

and often in violation of the post laws of England.[775] If personal passage to or from England was desired, the charge was entirely a matter of individual bargaining. In 1701–02, it was possible to cross for £5 or £6 if the passenger provided his own food and bedding.[776] By 1760, a man who ate the officers' fare, had wine served him twice a day, and slept in a berth with ship's bedding, might expect to pay from £20 to £30.[777]

All prices, all profits, all economic advances were affected by four shortcomings of the monetary system. These were the lack of adequate British specie, the substitution of inferior Spanish coin, the extent of counterfeiting and clipping and, fourth, excessive fluctuation in exchange. As early as 1724, the shortage of coin had made the English shilling worth 14 pence in Virginia.[778] The same condition forced the Colony to the awkward arrangement by which "tobacco notes"—in reality certificates of inspection—became a medium of exchange at the average rate of tuppence a pound of tobacco, colonial money.[779] "This," said a Virginia resident in 1723, "is the worst place for [coin] I could have pitched, for there is so little in the country that I believe a great many of them does not know it if they saw it only." He added: "They make a parcel of tobacco which they make to buy themselves clothes, and that is all they seek after here . . ."[780] It was much the same thirty or forty years later. If money appeared in Virginia, it soon went to England.[781] "What a damned situation our country is in," roared John Mercer: "No money to be had but at horse racing and gaming tables and that not sufficient to open the eyes of the people who frequent those places."[782]

The Spanish coin used to supplement the British had the disadvantage of being baser metal by 15 per cent,[783] but it lent itself readily to being "clipped" and passed as British gold. "Clipping" was not always or even generally a process to circulate the coin at less than its proper

[775] William Smith, op. cit., 23–24. Cf. John Custis to unnamed correspondent, 1718, n.d.: "I desire you to put all my letters in a small box, directed to me, and give them to the Captain's charge and then I may be in some hopes of having them safe and not peep'd into." (Custis Letter Book, No. 10.)

[776] Michel's journal, 24 V 1.

[777] 16 V 210.

[778] Jones, Virginia, 45.

[779] For variations in the price of tobacco see 51 V 43, and Brock, as cited supra, n. 546.

[780] George Hume to Ninian Hume, June 20, 1723; 20 V 399.

[781] Lord Gordon in Mereness, 405. See also W. L. Royall, "Virginia's Colonial Money" in 1 Va. Law Journal, 447, and W. Z. Ripley, The Financial History of Virginia, 1609–1776, p. 109.

[782] Letter of May 31, 1754, to D. P. Custis; Custis Papers, VHS.

[783] Jones, Virginia, 45.

weight in gold. The coin was "clipped," or cut into small pieces, in order to get gold to serve as small change. This process had been prohibited by law in Virginia in 1727, but it had not been stopped.[784] Even those householders who handled little coin had to keep scales for weighing gold.[785] The counterfeiter of gold and of paper currency was active. When caught and convicted, he was hanged.[786]

As a result of malpractices and of a seasonal, indeed a permanent adverse balance of trade, Virginia always had to pay a premium for sterling. This varied from year to year and often from month to month. So far as is known, prior to about 1755, it never was less than 5⅝ per cent,[787] and usually it was 25 to 30 per cent.[788] At that, Virginia "currency of the country"—a combination of mixed coin and tobacco certificates—commanded a premium over Maryland and Pennsylvania currency.[789] The prevailing interest rate "between man and man" was 5 per cent. The "constant rate" for a period of many years [790] was 6 per cent, but that rate, the value of "currency of the country" and the rate of exchange were changed in many ways when Virginia in 1755 was compelled to do what all the other Colonies previously had done—issue paper money. The reason and the result are a story yet to be told.[791]

Even before that calamity befell the Colony, careless credit, overbuying, bad money and adverse exchange had put many of the planters in debt.[792] With more of realism than of rhetoric, a man of the upcountry wrote in 1753, "The goods always were most extravagantly dear but now therefore got the parties so much in debt to the merchants

[784] 4 H 220. Gooch explained the practice in a report of July 30, 1728, to the Lords of Trade (1 Gooch MSS, 51).

[785] Such scales appear in many inventories.

[786] Va. Gazette, Aug. 11, 1738, May 9, 1751.

[787] Apr. 15, 1730; 4 E. J., 212.

[788] In W. Z. Ripley, op. cit., 139, the statement is made that a "premium of about 25 per cent for London exchange was maintained with remarkable constancy," but variations sometimes were marked. (Cf. 5 E. J., 177, 214, 305, where the recorded range was 25 @ 33½ per cent.)

[789] Cf. 2 G. W., 238; Spotsylvania Orders, 1738–49, p. 14; Orange Orders, 1746–47, p. 60. An excellent summary of the "state of the exchange," dated probably in 1754, will be found in Stanley Pargellis, Military Affairs in North America 1748–1765 (cited hereafter as Pargellis), p. 41–43. In P.R.O. (P.C. George II, f. 129, June 21, 1757) is a protest of London merchants against debt payment by Virginians in paper currency instead of in sterling. The allegation was that this currency would destroy their trade with Virginia.

[790] Cf. Robert Carter to M. Perry, July 4, 1723; Carter Transcripts, VHS.

[791] The first of several such acts was that of May, 1755, for which see 6 H 467. In 1749 the General Assembly passed a measure for the relief of insolvent debtors and thereby started a famous controversy over exchange (4 Osgood, 232–33); but as this was a more acute issue in 1762–64, it is treated in Vol. III.

[792] See Fithian's observations to Rev. Enoch Green at a later stage of the fast-changing Virginia economy, Dec. 1, 1773; Journal, 35.

[that] they might [not] be able to pay this money in years if ever yet." [793] Suits were instituted and judgments entered. The second William Byrd at one time owed Micajah Perry more than £2000 and had to assign to the merchant the property of Mrs. Byrd as security.[794] After Virginia currency depreciated, settlement of so large a debt as James Mill's £10,500 [795] or of the £5,561 due by the third William Byrd [796] was ruinous. Scarcely more successful was to be the effort of Virginia planters to collect from merchants who failed.[797] Beyond doubt, debt was one and perhaps the principal reason the General Assembly frequently was asked to terminate entails of landed property. At first, in legal terminology, the entail was not "docked," but was transferred from one tract to another.[798] From 1738, entails were docked and the proceeds of sale were used to settle estates [799] or to purchase slaves.[800] Adverse economy even at that date was beginning to challenge both the hereditary descent of lands and the landed caste based on that descent.

The agrarian economy of Virginia was decaying in 1750 and, in hard reality, though not by public admission, had little prospect of recovery. Agricultural producers who could not control the price of their tobacco were forced to pay normally £7 and occasionally as much as £16 a ton freight,[801] plus 2s per hogshead export duty.[802] Then, with inferior currency, they had to purchase in England, from the proceeds of their tobacco, almost everything they could not grow, weave or fabricate on their own acres. Nothing of quality was manufactured in Virginia for general sale. Conditions had not greatly changed after

793 George Hume to his sister, Feb. 23, 1753; 20 V 409.

794 See his letters in 9 V 115, 248, 250.

795 October, 1760; 12 V 3.

796 This was due Joseph Farrall and William Jones, merchants of Bristol, and was secured, in part, by a mortgage on the Westover plate and on 159 slaves (9 V 81). Byrd had other large debts.

797 See the letter of the Virginia Committee of Correspondence to Edward Montague, Apr. 30, 1761; 11 V 18 ff. This was a sore subject as early as 1727. See Governor Gooch to the Lords of Trade, Feb. 2, 1727; 1 Gooch MSS, 16.

798 See, for example, the cases of Francis Yeates (4 H 28), of William Manley (4 H 36), of George Weedon (4 H 377), and of Carter heirs (4 H 454). The basic law on docking entails was that of 1705, in 3 H 320.

799 Cases of Ralph Wormeley (5 H 85–89), of George Eskridge (5 H 392), and of Rebecca Clinch (6 H 297–99).

800 Case of Thomas Todd of Gloucester County (5 H 395); February, 1745.

801 Cf. William Byrd in 9 V 115. The rate varied according to the season and the number of ships. The Custis Papers show a rate of £8 a ton in April, 1744, and £16 a ton in November, 1748. Occasionally, to hasten his sailing, a master of a ship would offer the remaining space in his hold at a lower price per ton than he had allowed those planters who earlier had agreed to use his vessel. See 2 G. W., 435.

802 3 H 490–91. The antecedents of this act dated from 1657–58. Duty on tobacco entering England was paid by the importer.

that time of economic mockery, about 1691, when the first William
Byrd, a large exporter of leaf, repeatedly directed his London agent to
send him a box of smoking tobacco.[803] Virginians of 1750 accepted their
economic disadvantage as a matter of course. They were born to it;
they blindly believed they would overcome it as the Colony developed;
they regarded compliance as part of their duty to a King, among whose
"most zealous" subjects they counted themselves.[804]

The King's representative, the titular spokesman of the colonists in
approaching the throne, was the Governor. From Sept. 6, 1737, till his
death, Dec. 23, 1754, the Earl of Albemarle held this office. His successor through the remainder of the decade was the Earl of Loudoun.
Neither of these men ever came to Virginia, though Loudoun was in
the Northern Colonies in 1756–57 as British commander-in-chief. The
active head of government in Virginia was another royal appointee, the
Lieutenant Governor, who held office during the King's pleasure and
occasionally sought the counsel of the Governor. Between the two
officials, for the Governor's benefit, there always was some private
financial arrangement, which the Lieutenant Governor, within limits,
was able to afford, because he received a salary of £2000 and perquisites
of at least £400 per annum.[805] In addition, the Governor had in
Williamsburg the use of a handsome house, which on occasion somewhat pretentiously was styled "the Palace." [806]

Lieutenant Governor Sir William Gooch, always called Governor
Gooch, died June 20, 1749. In his stead, three Virginians acted briefly
as Governor until the arrival Nov. 20, 1751, of Robert Dinwiddie, the
new appointee.[807] Dinwiddie was then about 58 years of age and had
been an active civil servant in the British West Indies for more than
two decades. In Barbados he had displayed both judgment and tact in

---

[803] 28 V 22.

[804] See the address of Council and Burgesses, Mch. 3, 1745, on the occasion of the Jacobite
rising under the "young Pretender." (2 L. J., 966). Much the same sentiments were voiced in
the addresses of Feb. 29, 1752 and Apr. 15, 1757 to Governor Dinwiddie (2 ibid., 1060 and 2
ibid., 1160).

[805] P. S. Flippin, The Royal Government in Virginia, 1624–1775 (cited hereafter as Flippin)
p. 66–77. From Dr. Flippin's study, which was based on the primary sources, the greater part of
this sketch of the administration of Virginia is drawn, though use has been made of the Governors' reports to the Lords of Trade on the government of the Colony and the state of its trade.
One of the best of these reports is in 1 Din., 380 ff. On this particular question of the perquisites of the office, Governor Gooch wrote his brother, Jan. 7, 1730, that his had been reduced and would be diminished still more because of the low state of trade (Gooch MSS,
Colonial Williamsburg, Inc.).

[806] Flippin, 80, with quotation from Jones, Virginia. For detailed reference to "the Palace,"
see Williamsburg guide mentioned supra, p. 158, n. 686.

[807] Koontz's Dinwiddie, 95 ff. He had been appointed July 4, 1751.

dealing with frauds, but soon after he came to Virginia he precipitated a costly quarrel with the Burgesses and some of the land speculators.

Dinwiddie found that men of influence made it their practice to procure "orders" from the Council for the issuance of land patents which they did not take out formally under seal. In this way they avoided paying the fee for the patent and also escaped the quit rent on the land; but they prevented or at least confused the grant to others of lands for which they had "orders." In an attempt to stop this practice, Dinwiddie demanded that the patent be issued when the "orders" were approved and that the authorized fee of one pistole [808] be paid him for each patent he signed and thereby validated for the seal of the Colony. The controversy grew violent and, for a time, deprived Dinwiddie of influence he might have exerted over the wealthy landed class, but it illustrated both the extent of land speculation [809] and the nature of the powers the Governor could exercise.[810]

Those powers were as real as they were numerous. The Governor could convene, prorogue and dissolve the General Assembly. He could veto any of its bills or direct that a clause be inserted to suspend the operation of a new law till the "King's pleasure" was known.[811] The Governor likewise could pardon all crimes except treason and wilful murder and could remit fines and forfeitures not in excess of £10.[812] It was the Governor's prerogative to commission the Justices of the County Courts, to appoint numerous officials, to license all lawyers and teachers, and to regulate all salaries and fees, though in this last respect his authority and that of the General Assembly were concurrent. With the assent of the Council, the Governor made the land grants and authorized the Secretary to issue the patents. Through the hands of the Governor passed all addresses, petitions and reports to the ministry in England. As a judicial officer, he sat on the General Court [813] and he had the right, which he usually delegated, to act as judge of piracy.

808 In modern currency, $3.60.

809 See *infra*, p. 188.

810 *Flippin*, 129–30; *Koontz's Dinwiddie*, 201 ff; Koontz, *Virginia Frontier, 1754–63*, p. 36–37. T. J. Wertenbaker's article on Dinwiddie in *DAB; Journ. H.B.*, 1752–58, p. xvi–xvii.

811 In theory, no bill could become law until it had been sent to England and had been given the King's assent (1 *Din.*, 383). In practice the assent of the Crown was taken for granted except for legislation of a doubtful wisdom or unusual nature. The Governor insisted more frequently after about 1750, that new or debatable measures include a clause that suspended them until they had been reviewed by the King. (*Flippin*, 200–01.)

812 Even as respects treason and murder and fines and forfeitures above £10, the Governor could suspend execution till the King's pleasure was known.

813 See *infra*, p. 180.

He was Commander-in-Chief and Vice-Admiral and appointed all militia officers except those of the lowest rank, but he was without authority to declare war. In his hands was the seal of the Colony and the care of the church. He could recommend Virginians who wished to take orders and he submitted to vestries the names of clergymen sent over by the Bishop of London.[814]

Formidable as was the authority of the Governor as the direct representative of the King, he had to please the colonials, and he could not become too often or too deeply involved in quarrels with the General Assembly. "Our government," William Byrd the second had written in 1735, "is so happily constituted that a Governor must first outwit us before he can oppress us, and if he ever squeeze money out of us he must first take care to deserve it." [815]

Closest to the Governor was the Council of twelve members, who were "of the principal gentlemen of the Colony." Vacancies were filled by the King's nomination under sign manual, but the Governor, as a rule, either recommended names or explained why he did not.[816] No term of office was specified. Usually it was for life. Suspension by the Governor was possible, though not easy. Compensation was from an annual fund of £600, later £1200, which was divided among the members according to the number of meetings they attended.[817] The functions of the Council were advisory, judicial and legislative,[818] but, in time, certain administrative duties had been taken over by the Council from the Governor. In theory, this arrangement had been for his convenience. As practiced, the aim of some members of the Council was to restrain the absolutist bent of Governors who, in turn, believed the real purpose of the Council was to increase its own power.[819] The senior Councillor held a position of much prestige and acted as Governor during a vacancy, unless other arrangement was ordered by the King. In general, the Council was more conservative than was the House of Burgesses. A majority of the Council and not

814 This summary of the powers of the Governor is based on *Flippin*, 86–96, and on Gooch's explanation in 3 *V* 114 ff. For the order of precedence at the colonial "court," see 16 *V* 87. This was established in 1760 but apparently was not used until the governership of Lord Dunmore.

815 William Byrd to Mr. Beckford, Dec. 6, 1735; 36 *V* 122.

816 Cf. Governor Gooch to the Lords of Trade, Oct. 5, 1732, Jan. 24, 1744, 2 *Gooch MSS*, 318; 3 *ibid*. 775. Dinwiddie's language concerning the Council was that members were "appointed by mandamus from His Majesty" (1 *Din*., 385).

817 For tax exemption and other privileges lost before 1750, see *Flippin* 157–59.

818 3 *V* 116. For its advisory function in ecclesiastical matters, see *infra*, p. 180.

819 Cf. Spotswood, quoted in *Flippin*, 165.

infrequently all the members could be counted upon to support the Governor.

As a judicial body the Council had duties elsewhere described.[820] Its legislative function was that of the upper house of the General Assembly. In this particular, the authority of the Council in the enactment of laws was concurrent with that of the lower house,[821] though money bills had to originate among the Burgesses. After about 1725, the Governor no longer sat with the Council when it was acting as a part of the General Assembly.[822]

The House of Burgesses was the popularly-elected branch of the General Assembly, the lawmaking body of the Colony. As late as 1705, the legislators had imposed a fine of 200 pounds of tobacco on every male adult freeholder who did not appear and vote in his County for its Burgesses; [823] but by 1736, members complained that "to create and multiply votes" there had been "divers frauds by making leases of small and inconsiderable parcels of land, upon feigned considerations, and by sub-dividing lots of ground in towns." [824] Freeholders consequently had been defined in that year as male persons who (1) had at least 100 acres of unsettled land, or (2) possessed twenty-five acres with a house and plantation or (3) leased such a property to tenants for a term of years [825] or (4) owned a house and lot or house and part of a lot in a town. Where a house and town lot, or part of a lot, were owned by several persons, one vote only could be cast on account of it.[826] Free Negroes, mulattoes and Indians had no franchise.

As of 1755, the House of Burgesses consisted of two members for each County, one for the College of William and Mary, and one each for Jamestown, Williamsburg and Norfolk, a total of 104.[827] The vigor of the canvass for these seats depended on the constituency and on the number of aspirants. Where three or more candidates offered themselves, there frequently was such a scene as at the viva-voce election Col. James Gordon witnessed at Lancaster Court House in 1761: The gentlemen who wished to be Burgesses "treated the people very freely —those are now taken by the hand and treated that are passed by at

---

820 See *infra*, p. 180.   821 See Gooch in 3 *V* 115.
822 For all of this in more detail, see *Flippin*, 155–80, 206.
823 3 *H* 238.   824 4 *H* 475.
825 *Ibid.*
826 *Ibid.*, 476. For details of these changes of franchise, see E. I. Miller, *The Legislature of the Province of Virginia*, 61, 63.
827 Governor Dinwiddie in 1 *Din.*, 383. The moderate compensation of the Burgesses is described in *Flippin*, 195–96.

other times." [828] Candidates or their representatives usually sat on a platform to which each elector came to make known his choice. If the voter declared for a particular candidate, that gentleman was expected to step forward and thank the citizen.

The successful "treaters" and their easily chosen fellows normally met every two years but they assembled more frequently if special occasion required. They elected their own Speaker, who was exceedingly well paid. The office consequently was sought eagerly and was held tenaciously. When a new Speaker was to be chosen, the contest was bitter. "Unless I vote for him to be Speaker," wrote William Beverley of Col. Edwin Conway, "I suppose he will do me all the prejudice he can." Beverley added manfully, "I assure you I cannot vote for him." [829] The Clerk, after the sixteen-eighties,[830] was named by the Governor.

Served by these officers and by their own committees, the Burgesses had broad rights of legislation, in the exercise of which the Council was free to concur or to dissent. Almost any law, it must be repeated, might be made inoperative by the Governor's order or by his insistence on the "suspension clause" until the King's pleasure was known. If a bill were approved, it could not be repealed except by the Burgesses with the assent of the Crown.[831] This was one of the most cherished rights of the Colony.[832] Other powers, if not formal rights, the Burgesses were acquiring by attaching conditions to appropriations. The legislators had devised, moreover, what they considered an effective control of the purse-strings: Their own appointee, the Treasurer of the Colony, they elected regularly as Speaker of the House [833] in the belief that close touch with the Burgesses and the fear of losing the remunerative speakership would make him circumspect as Treasurer.

The revenues at the disposal of the General Assembly were not large. Except in time of special emergency, there was no general levy for the support of the colonial government. Three class taxes were imposed permanently: First and most productive was the tax of 2s per hogshead of tobacco exported, subject to a discount of 10 per cent if paid in bills

[828] Entry of Feb. 20, 1761; 11 W (1) p. 218.
[829] 3 W (1) p. 227.
[830] See Appendix I-1.
[831] *Flippin*, 199.
[832] See the letter of the Committee of Correspondence to Edward Montague, the London agent of the Colony, Apr. 30, 1761, 11 V 19.
[833] *Flippin*, 210–13. When Francis Fauquier came to Virginia as Governor, he was directed to look into this double tenure of office. In a letter of June 28, 1758, to the Lords of Trade, Fauquier explained how the practice had developed and why, in the circumstances then existing, he had not thought it prudent to demand separation of the offices (P.R.O., C.O. 5, 1329, f. 175).

of exchange; second was the port duty of 15*d* a ton on all ships trading in Virginia waters; third, and of small consequence, was a levy of 6*d* per capita on all passengers brought to Virginia by ship. In addition, some revenue was derived from fines and forfeitures and, in years of active land speculation, a considerable sum from the charge of 5*s* per 100 acres for the grant of lands by the Crown. Together, these sources yielded the Colony, as of 1750, about £6500 annually, though there was variation from year to year. Regular charges were computed at £4345, of which £3200 represented the salaries of Governor and Council. Every other colonial expense, including that of the House of Burgesses, was covered in peacetime from the remaining £1100.[834] If supplementary revenue had to be raised, the precedent was for voting a general poll tax of specific amount, collectable by the Sheriff of each County.[835] That same official, the Sheriff, visited the farms and plantations and called on the owners to pay the county levy, which in normal years provided the money for all the modest activities of government outside the narrow range of what was done by Governor and General Assembly. This county levy was primarily the concern of men who belonged, in a titular sense at least, to the judiciary of Virginia.

Judicial functions of the colonial government were wide and were divided among courts of five types. The court of first instance, the so-called County Court, was the one that fixed the rate of local taxation and, by that and a score of other activities, gave the largest number of citizens an acquaintance with law and justice. As a court for each County, the Governor named eight or more Justices of the Peace, four of whom constituted a quorum.[836] These Justices usually were the more conspicuous men of the County and were almost a caste. Two members of a court of Spotsylvania, for example, declined to serve because three of the men named to the tribunal by the Governor had not been suggested by the Justices already sitting. Five other Justices declined because they said they believed that William Lynn, the same Doctor Lynn who kept the apothecary shop,[837] had "begged himself into the commission, not being recommended by the court, which [they

---

[834] All these figures may be slightly too high for 1745–50, as they are those for 1754 or 1755, reported by Dinwiddie to the Lords of Trade, Jan. n.d., 1755; 1 *Din.*, 389. Explanation of the meagreness of colonial revenue will be found in 1 *Din.*, 353.

[835] This was the principal device of the period of the French and Indian war.

[836] The clearest, most succinct statement of the judicial system, as of 1755, is that in 1 *Din.*, 383–84. As respects County Courts, the governing act in the seventeen-fifties was that of 1748 (5 *H* 489). Interesting specifications of Nov. 5, 1673, for building a court house 35 by 30 feet will be found in *Westmoreland Deeds and Patents*, 1665–77, p. 165.

[837] See *supra*, p. 62.

took] to be slighting the court." [838] In 1752, a clergyman's commission as Justice of Stafford County was cancelled on the ground "that every clergyman has enough to do to discharge his duty as a minister, without engaging himself in civil affairs." [839]

Justices individually could issue warrants and, when they sat together, had general jurisdiction except in criminal offences involving life or limb. Even in these cases, if the accused were a slave, the Governor could vest the Justices with the powers of a Court of Oyer and Terminer.[840] Appeal was allowed from all criminal convictions and in all civil causes where the amount in controversy was more than £5. When boundaries or titles were concerned, appeal was of right.[841]

The second William Byrd had boasted that Virginians lived with unbarred doors because there were no cities to shelter thieves or pawnbrokers to receive their wares; [842] but actually the Counties had to provide court houses, jails, permanent [843] or temporary,[844] stocks, pillories, whipping posts and ducking stools.[845] The chief offence before the average County Court was stealing, which increased after the coming of the convicts.[846] Theft ranged from deerskins to post office tills.[847] Horse stealing was so notorious and so easy that a special reward of £10 was offered for the arrest of any culprit,[848] but this did not suffice to break up the practice.[849] More serious still was arson. In the winter of 1728–29,[850] the house of Thomas Lee in Westmoreland County was robbed, set afire and burned by convict servants in revenge on the

838 1 C 237.

839 Council Journal, Nov. 2, 1752; P.R.O., C.O. 5; 1429, f. 183.

840 If the slave were executed, the General Assembly usually paid the owner for him (3 V 116).

841 3 V 115; 1 Din., 383. Hustings Courts, with jurisdiction in all civil causes of less than £20, were provided in Williamsburg and in Norfolk (3 V 115).

842 9 V 235. See Jones, Virginia, 30, for reference to the fact that imprisonment for debt was "very rare."

843 Spotsylvania Wills, A, 1722–49, p. 67; Va. Gazette, Mch. 19, 1751.

844 Spotsylvania Orders, 1730–38, p. 131.

845 Ibid., 1749–55, p. 98; Stafford Records, 1664–93, p. 211, Feb. 11, 1692; 46 V 20.

846 Cf. Va. Gazette, Sept. 9, 1737. See also Governor Gooch's recommendation to the Lords of Trade, July 18, 1732, for an increase in the salary of the Attorney General, to compensate that official for extra trouble "occasioned chiefly by imported convicts whose morals are not changed by a change of air" (2 Gooch MSS, 300).

847 Va. Gazette, Dec. 15, 1738, June 27, 1745, Jan. 7, 1768; Spotsylvania Orders, 1750–55, p. 98. In January, 1737–38, Ann Bush was given twenty lashes and was required to post bond of £20 on conviction of stealing a pot of butter (2 King George Orders, 137).

848 With £50 to the family of any man who was killed in apprehending a horse-thief—Governor Gooch to the Lords of Trade, Oct. 25, 1744 (3 Gooch MSS, 812).

849 Cf. Va. Gazette, May 9, June 27, 1745; Apr. 18, 1751; Harrower's diary in 6 A. H. R., 94.

850 To be precise, Jan. 29, 1729. See supra, p. 90.

Colonel, who as a Justice had issued a warrant against one of their number.[851] Similar acts of arson were to follow, though the number never was large.[852] Murder, the disappearance of servants,[853] the bearing of bastard children,[854] insolence to the court,[855] vagrancy,[856] tendering seconds of tobacco,[857] swearing profanely,[858] cursing the King,[859] singing "scandalous and approbrious songs, reflecting on the King," [860] non-attendance at church,[861] drunkenness [862] and gambling [863]—all these were heard by the County Court and sometimes, if the offence was not felonious, were decided as much by what a man was as by what he had done. Where an individual of station was involved,

[851] *Md. Gazette*, Mch. 4, 1729; Governor Gooch to the Lords of Trade, Mch. 26, 1729, Jan. 9, 1730; 1 *Gooch MSS*, 96, 149. This was the fire at "the first Stratford" which inspired the tradition that Stratford was rebuilt by the Crown. Actually, as the quoted letters show, Gooch sought and the home government allowed Lee £300 because the house and contents were lost by Lee in the discharge of his duty as a justice. Col. Richard Corbin subsequently undertook, without success, to procure similar compensation because his residence was destroyed by fire during his absence on public business. See *supra*, p. 90, n. 116, and Richard Corbin to James Buchanan, Apr. 26, 1758; *Corbin MS Letter Book*, 5.

[852] Cf. 1 *Gooch MSS*, 265, 269; 2 *ibid.*, 298. In *Va. Gazette*, Mch. 17, 1738, was a report of a prison fire that presumably was started by an inmate who perished in the flames.

[853] Cf. an interesting case in Spotsylvania, June 1, 1725, in which a runaway was brought into court by his master, who freely forgave him but asked that the man receive as many lashes as the court saw fit. The Justices ordered twenty "on the bare back, well laid on" (*Orders 1724–30*, p. 48). Quite similar was the case of a convict runaway woman servant of Willoughby Newton's, July 26, 1732 (*Westmoreland Orders, 1731–39*, p. 31). Running away sometimes was encouraged by the careless issuance of passes, for which reason, forging a pass was accounted a serious offence. See 2 *King George Orders*, 2, 137, and *Md. Gazette*, Aug. 31, 1748. For the disappearance of one of Lawrence Washington's servants with two horses and various personal effects, see *infra*, p. 265, n. 33.

[854] 10 *Richmond Co. Orders*, 1734–39, p. 13, 70.

[855] The most notorious case was that of John Mercer of Prince William, attorney at law (4 *E. J.*, 318, 348, 432, 443).

[856] *Spotsylvania Orders*, 1738–49, p. 288.

[857] Repeated cases will be found in 10 *Richmond Co. Orders*, 1732–39.

[858] *Westmoreland Records and Inventories*, 1723–46, p. 94; *Spotsylvania Orders*, 1724–30, p. 339; 10 *Richmond Co. Orders*, 1732–39, p. 221. This last was the imposition of a fine of 20s or 200 lbs. of tobacco on "Hon. John Tayloe, Esq., of Lunenburg Parish," who had been summoned "for swearing four oaths." He did not appear in answer to the summons. Fithian (*Journal*, 39) remarked that some gentlemen swore "bitterly" but that the practice seemed to be "generally disapproved."

[859] *Spotsylvania Orders*, 1730–38, p. 176. The punishment was costs and five lashes at the common whipping post.

[860] *York Records* of July 19, 1725, quoted in 2 *T* 159. The penalty: 20s and costs, on a plea of guilty.

[861] Here again the justices of Westmoreland and of Richmond County struck high. In Westmoreland, George Eskridge was tried by jury for being absent from church for two months, and was acquitted (*Westmoreland Orders*, 1705–21, p. 124). One of their victims in Richmond County was Edward Barradall, for whom see 10 *Richmond Co. Orders*, 1734–39, p. 12. For the case of a man accused simultaneously of being drunk and of non-attendance at church, see *Westmoreland Orders*, 1731–39, p. 11, Feb. 23, 1732.

[862] The Westmoreland Clerk did not fail, in reporting a summons to Burdett Ashton for drunkenness, to write "Gent." after the name (*Westmoreland Orders*, 1731–39, p. 56).

[863] Usually punished with a fine of 5s or 50 lbs. of tobacco. Gooch, July 30, 1728, had explained that the General Assembly had passed an act for preventing "excessive and deceitful gambling" because "many loose and idle persons were got into the vile way of thus spending their time." (Governor Gooch to the Lords of Trade, 1 *Gooch MSS*, 47.)

drunkenness, for example, though punished, was not regarded over-seriously. In 1733—to cite only one case—George's cousin Robert Washington, Gent., was fined 5s for being drunk. Three months later Robert was on the bench as a "Gentleman Justice." [864]

Punishment of serious offences was stern, sometimes cruel. For entering a storeroom with a false key and for stealing goods worth 2s 12d, a Westmoreland slave was condemned to death.[865] In 1688, George Washington's grandfather, Lawrence, had been one of a bench of Justices who had found a Negro, Sam, guilty of attempting several times to incite a slave rebellion. Sam was condemned to have a halter put about his neck, to be whipped "at a cart's tale from the prison round about the town and then to the gallows and from thence to the prison again." After that, he was to be conveyed to Westmoreland County where he was to be whipped at the next court. This done, he was to have a "strong iron collar affixed about his neck with four springs." That torture Sam was to endure until hanged.[866] A Negro slave woman, Eve, accused in 1745 of poisoning her master, was found guilty and was burned alive.[867] In Nansemond, nine years previously, another slave woman had been burned for murder.[868] Sometimes Negroes were hanged and quartered.[869] Mass hangings occasionally were held. On one occasion in Williamsburg, two of seven executed malefactors were an overseer and a white accessory who had been convicted of whipping a slave to death.[870] Women criminals did not escape the noose.[871] There was firm belief, too, that the Almighty did not wait on the law of man: the vengeance of a God mocked by a sinner was attested and believed.[872]

If the criminal functions of the County Court sometimes were involved in such superstitions as this, the administrative duties of the Court were not lacking in practical realism. Some of those duties as

---

[864] Westmoreland Orders, 1731–39, p. 72 and 74.

[865] Westmoreland Orders, 1721–31, p. 367, with the language of the death-sentence included.

[866] Order of May 30, 1688; Westmoreland Orders, 1675/76–1688/89, p. 644.

[867] 3 V 308 ff.

[868] Va. Gazette, Feb. 18, 1737. See 4 V 341 for a partial list of like punishments in other Colonies.

[869] Cf. 1 V 330, 356, 358.

[870] Va. Gazette, Nov. 16, 1739. See ibid., Nov. 24, 1738, for a careful description of a hanging during which the rope broke.

[871] Ibid., May 5, 1738, case of Elizabeth Blair.

[872] See ibid., Mch. 17, 1766, for the case of a man who wished that "his flesh might rot and his eyes never shut, if he did not win the next game of cards." When he was going to bed, "mortification" began. He died in a day or two, his flesh "quite rotten." The Gazette added: "Nor could his eyes be shut notwithstanding all the efforts of his friends to close them."

they related to highways have been described already.[873] Other responsibilities were numerous. The Court was required by law to call on the vestry of a parish to "procession" its confines in order to determine boundaries and to prevent unlawful hunting and "ranging" on private property.[874] Warrants of the County were issued by the Court and, on its order, were paid. Near the frontier, it will be remembered,[875] a considerable percentage of a County's revenue went for bounties on wolves' heads. Prevention of fraud concerning these bounties called for vigilance on the part of the Justices. Theirs, also, was the duty of recording cattle marks,[876] and of appointing inspectors of flour, packed meat, tar, pitch or turpentine for export.[877] Each Court in a County adjoining a navigable stream had, after 1751, to name one or more persons to oversee the unpacking and delivery of cargo and ballast.[878] On the Court, also, rested the duty of ordering periodical inspection of weights.[879] Annually, too, in some Counties, a particular term of court was prescribed for the presentation of the accounts of minor orphans,[880] who, if needy, might be bound out by the Justices,[881] though the care of these children was primarily the concern of the parish vestries.[882] The same rule applied to poor relief,[883] which was not managed always with adequate mercy.[884] One measure of relief was for the Court to exempt the aged and feeble from payment of the county levy.[885]

Varied and exacting as were the duties of the County Court, they were well discharged. From its decisions, appeals were not frequent. When

---

[873] See *supra*, p. 147. For a court order to the road Supervisor to keep signposts in position at crossroads and ferries, see *Spotsylvania Orders*, 1738–49, p. 334.

[874] The basic act, as amended, was that of 1710; 3 *H* 531. Normally, land three times "processioned" in the prescribed manner was considered to have its boundaries unalterably fixed. For processioning as late as 1735–36 in Richmond County, see its *Orders*, v. 10, p. 280, 363.

[875] See *supra*, p. 143.

[876] In Spotsylvania, for example, it was duly set down that the mark of Rev. James Marye's cattle was a swallow-tail fork in the right ear and a crop in the left ear (*Orders*, 1749–50, p. 116).

[877] *Spotsylvania Orders*, 1749–55, p. 232.

[878] *King George Orders*, 1751–67, p. 21. Each Court had to provide, also, for its record books, which came from England (cf. *Westmoreland Orders*, 1721–31, p. 286), and for employing a man to serve water to the Court and to keep the Court House clean (cf. *ibid.*, 46).

[879] *Fairfax Orders*, 1749–54, p. 46.

[880] See *Va. Gazette*, Mch. 14, 1751; *Stafford Wills*, 1729–48, p. 303 ff.

[881] 10 *Richmond Co. Orders*, 27, 28; *Spotsylvania Orders*, 1738–49, p. 398.

[882] See *supra*, p. 137.

[883] For typical allowances for the care of indigent sick and for the burial expenses of such persons, see *Westmoreland Orders*, 1731–39, p. 10.

[884] Cf. William Beverley to John Fairchild, Aug. 28, 1738: "We have had very scarce times in this river, several poor people having lived on herbs growing in the fields without bread or meat" (3 *W* (1) p. 228). This condition doubtless was due to the drought mentioned *supra*, p. 140, n. 530.

[885] See as typical, 10 *Richmond Co. Orders*, p. 79. For the duties of the Sheriff as executive officer of the court, see *infra*, p. 183.

taken, all were to the General Court, which consisted of the Governor and Council, any five of whom constituted a quorum. This tribunal had original jurisdiction in chancery cases and in all civil cases over £10, unless the issues arose in towns that had Hustings Courts. As already stated, the General Court heard all appeals from County Courts in cases of land titles or boundaries and in others where the amount at issue exceeded £5. Before the General Court at the regular term, all criminal cases affecting free persons were heard if the punishment was life or dismemberment. From the General Court, appeal lay to the Crown in cases of £300 or more.[886]

The General Court was convened in April and in October.[887] Between terms, in June and in December, were held courts of a third type, those of Oyer and Terminer, on which sat members to hear serious criminal cases that had developed after the General Court had risen.[888] No juries were authorized in civil cases, but they were provided for all felony trials except when the accused person was a slave. Then the Justices of a County Court, acting as a Court of Oyer and Terminer, were deemed sufficiently numerous to be the equivalent of a jury.[889]

Besides these three Courts, there were two others in Virginia. One of these was an Admiralty Court, rarely convened, under a judge commissioned by the British High Court of Admiralty.[890] The other was the Court of the Commissary of the Bishop of London. In matters ecclesiastical the Council, as stated,[891] had advisory jurisdiction in "the punishment of the immoralities of the clergy," but the Commissary's Court proceeded "by monition, suspension or deprivation," with appeal to the delegates appointed for such purpose in England.[892] Over this Court for fifty-four years prior to his death in 1743 had presided Rev. James Blair, who also was President of William and Mary after 1693. He was active in many things and more often was damned than praised. Governors Andros and Nicholson had ugly verbal wars with him; Governor Gooch privately had denounced him as a "very vile old fellow."[893]

886 1 *Din.*, 383–84.   887 *Ibid.*, 383.
888 *Ibid.*, 384.   889 3 H 269.
890 *Ibid.*   891 *Supra*, p. 172.
892 The language is Governor Dinwiddie's, *op. cit.*, 381. Brydon, as cited in the next note, described in detail the functions of the Commissary and quoted Cross, *Anglican Episcopate in America*, on the authority the Bishop of London exercised over the church in the Colonies.
893 Governor Gooch to his brother, June 9, 1728 (*Gooch MSS*, Colonial Williamsburg, Inc). The fullest study of Blair is that of G. MacLaren Brydon, *James Blair, Commissary*. This was published originally in the *Historical Magazine of the Protestant Episcopal Church*, June, 1945 and subsequently appeared in Dr. Brydon's comprehensive *Virginia's Mother Church*.

Some were to apply that adjective "vile" to the greater part of the royal government of Virginia within less than fifty years after Gooch wrote; but in the seventeen-fifties there still was pride in all three branches of His Majesty's rule, legislative, executive and judicial. Under one or another of those branches were the following officers, with some of whom young Washington gradually became acquainted.[894]

1. The Secretary of the Colony held the oldest office in Virginia and had duties broadly analogous to those of the Lord Chancellor "at home." Although named by the Crown, the Secretary was, as a rule, a person previously recommended by the Governor. The position included a seat in Council and had much prestige. All important records were in the custody of Mr. Secretary; he operated the Land Office and, on order of the Governor, issued all land patents, all writs and all passes. His patronage was considerable, because he named the Court Clerks; his compensation was so large that the office was much desired.[895] Robert Carter had paid £1500 to have his son John named Secretary in 1722.[896] When John Carter's death seemed imminent in 1741, William Beverley was willing to give £2000 for the succession.[897]

2. The Attorney General had been a crown appointee for some years after the office was created in 1643, but subsequently the Governor chose and could suspend his chief legal counsellor.[898] Prosecution in crown cases before the General Court and the Courts of Oyer and Terminer was in the hands of the Attorney General. He prepared most of the legal papers of the Colony and advised the General Assembly as well as Governor and Council. Although his duties increased after the convict servants spread crime in the Colony,[899] his compensation never was high, presumably because he was supposed to share the general prosperity of members of the bar. Their profession was said to have "an easy time" in the Colony. If a lawyer was "clever," practice was regarded as a "sure step to an estate." [900]

3. The colonial Treasurer doubtless would have disputed any order of precedence that placed him below the Attorney General. As custodian

---

[894] Here, again, it is proper to call attention to the fact that the writer has done little original research on the administration of Virginia and has relied on *Flippin*.

[895] *Flippin*, 223–29.

[896] Robert Carter to M. Perry, July 4, 1723; *Carter Transcripts*, VHS.

[897] William Beverley to Christopher Smyth, Mch. 10, 1741, 3 *W* (1) p. 229. Carter did not die until 1743.

[898] Apparently, in the seventeen-sixties the Crown again exercised the prerogative of naming the Attorney General (*Flippin*, 321).

[899] See *supra*, p. 86.

[900] *Observations*, 15 *W* (1) p. 147.

and disburser of revenues that amounted to about £6500 per annum,[901] he was the appointee and virtually the agent of the General Assembly. He could say proudly in 1750, that from 1699 onward, the successive Treasurers had been also the Speakers of the House of Burgesses.[902]

4. The Auditor was a royal appointee whom the Governor, for cause, could suspend, or, in case of death, temporarily could replace. It was the duty of the Auditor to examine all accounts, to lay them before the Governor and Council and then, duly attesting them, to forward them through the Auditor General to the Lords of the Treasury. An annual duty was that of directing the sale of quit rent tobacco.[903]

5. Originally the office of Receiver General had been that of Auditor, but in 1705, the posts had been divided. The Receiver General then had become a royal appointee, to whom were paid the quit rents, the export duties and all funds not placed, under law, in the hands of the Treasurer.[904]

6. Six Collectors were appointed by the Commissioners of Customs and were under the supervision of the Surveyor General of Customs for the Southern District of America. They consequently were independent, in large measure, of the Virginia executive and of the General Assembly, but the Governor administered to them the oath of office and could remove them for fraud. On them rested the duty of collecting the export tax of 2s per hogshead on tobacco. Various imposts, also, passed through their tills. The office was profitable and not exacting in the attention it required. Lest it become a sinecure, provision had been made that the Collectors could not be Councillors or "persons much concerned in trade."[905]

7. Naval Officers, named under the great seal of Britain, had districts corresponding to those of the Collectors. It was the obligation of these officers to record the ships that entered and cleared, to authorize the loading of merchantmen, to seize vessels trading unlawfully, and to take charge of prizes, pirates and runaway servants.[906] The post was profitable;[907] its duties were not onerous. Councillors were forbidden to hold the position of Naval Officer, but they could give their ap-

---

[901] See *supra*, p. 175; 1 *Din.*, 389. Revenue had been approximately £5000 in the seventeen-forties (Gooch in 3 *V* 122).

[902] See *supra*, p. 174. The offices were separated again on the death of John Robinson in 1766 (*Flippin*, 275–77).

[903] *Flippin*, 266–67.   [904] *Flippin*, 269, 271.

[905] Quoted in *Flippin*, 249.

[906] *Ibid.*, 255–56. Additional Comptrollers of Customs subsequently were appointed (*ibid.*, 261).

[907] *Ibid.*, 254.

proval to the temporary appointment of sons or kinsmen of their colleagues.[908]

8. The Surveyor General was an appointee of the King or of the Governor until 1693. After that year, the Visitors of the College of William and Mary discharged the functions of the office and appointed as many Surveyors as the Governor and Council thought "necessary and convenient." [909] A qualified Surveyor could work anywhere in Virginia, but usually one such official was designated for each County, with authority to appoint deputies for whom he was responsible. Over all these men the General Assembly held a rein, because it fixed their fees. Their discharge of their duties, moreover, was under the general direction of the Governor and his official advisers.[910] Compensation for each survey rose steadily through the years but the total reward for a year's labor of course varied according to the activity in the patenting or transfer of land in a given County.[911]

9. The Sheriff of each County was appointed by the Governor and Council on recommendation of the Court of the County. Besides collecting the levy [912] he acted as the administrative officer, executed the orders of the Court, made the arrests, held the elections, and discharged a diversity of minor duties. The office, compensated by fees, had ceased by 1750 to yield the high profit it had before 1700, and in the main, it no longer attracted men of the first rank in the community.[913] Working with the Sheriff were the law-enforcement officers, the Constables, who were appointed by the County Courts.[914]

10. The Coroner held inquests on persons who came to a violent end and he administered their estates. In the absence or disability of the Sheriff, the Coroner could be designated to act for him.[915]

What might be termed the diplomatic service of the Colony was under the Solicitor of Virginia Affairs. He was the Colony's agent

908 Cf. 4 E. J., 210, session of Nov. 1, 1729, when Robert Carter resigned. His son Charles was named in his place. 35 V 270.

909 The college did not begin to exercise its function until after May 8, 1695, when the death of Alexander Culpeper, the last Surveyor General, was reported to the Governor and Council. See 1 L.J., 327. Strictly speaking, the controlling body was the "Board of Governors and visitors," who succeeded the original Trustees.

910 Flippin, 218-19. Acts concerning the office of Surveyor, which probably deserves closer study, are 3 H 3299 ff, 4 H 511 and 6 H 33 ff.

911 For the fees collectable during the seventeen-fifties, see 5 H 340. A list of County Surveyors in 1757 appears in 50 V 368-69.

912 See supra, p. 179.

913 Flippin, 315-16. For example, "Benjamin Berryman, Gent.," Sheriff of King George, thought so little of his office that he did not attend a particular term of court in 1737, a dereliction that brought a fine of 30s. (See 2 King George Orders, p. 112.)

914 Flippin, 318-19, 360.   915 Ibid., 320-21.

in London and might hold the same position for other Colonies, also. His combined funds were ample, his status was accredited. In emergencies and with increasing frequency after the middle of the century, the General Assembly would vote money and would send to England a special agent. This was done in 1754 during the controversy over the "pistole fee." [916]

Officers of the militia were numerous, so numerous in fact, that a stranger, it was said, might think himself in a "retreat of heroes." [917] Each rural unit of government had its County Lieutenant, its Colonel, its Lieutenant Colonel and one or two Majors, as well as a number of Captains determined by the size of the militia mustered in that jurisdiction. All white males, other than convicts, between the ages of 21 and 60, belonged to the militia.[918] Of these defenders of the Colony, George Washington soon was to know more and to think less. Their numerical strength was disputed. In 1749, Governor Gooch estimated the total at 176 Companies of infantry, numbering about 8800, and 100 Troops of cavalry, or 5000 mounted men. The aggregate thus was 13,800.[919] Governor Dinwiddie reported in a similar document six years later: "Our militia may now amount to 27,000 men from 21 to 60 years of age." [920]

This difference of close to 100 per cent in estimates of 1749 and 1755 was due to the lack of any census of Virginia. The only general enumeration was of the "tithables," those persons who paid a per capita tax. Had the system of counting "tithables" been the same for both races, it would have been possible to determine the percentage of the population within the age limits of the levy and, on that basis, to compute readily the number of souls in the Colony. The difficulty was that tithables were white males above the age of sixteen and Negro males and females of sixteen years and more. White women, in short, were not tithable. A rough rule had been to reckon the white females over sixteen and the white and Negro children under sixteen as treble the number of white tithables.[921] Even this crude rule was not applied accurately. In 1730, Governor Gooch incorrectly figured the total population as 114,000.[922] A heavy mortality from "a malignant fever and pleurisy," he said, had been offset by the large importation

916 *Ibid.*, 186–88.   917 *Observations*, 15 *W* (1) p. 147.
918 See *infra*, n. 924. The basic militia laws will be found in 6 *H* 112, 421, 530. Earlier laws were summarized in 10 *V* 146. See, also, 4 *H* 197; 5 *H* 16, 24, 81. For a general review, see *Beverley*, 217.
919 3 *V* 119.   920 1 *Din.*, 387.
921 Governor Gooch to the Lords of Trade, July 23, 1730; *Gooch MSS*, 189.
922 *Ibid.*

of Negro slaves and white servants, by early marriage, and by the "prolific temperament of the women, black and white ..."[923] Gooch's estimate for 1742 was 134,000, which included 16,000 militia;[924] for 1743, it was 132,000;[925] the next year Gooch set down 140,000,[926] a total he kept for 1747.[927] In 1749 he reckoned the population at 135,000.[928] The acting Governor, Thomas Lee, used the same figure for 1750.[929]

Such wide variations discredited the estimates. Robert Dinwiddie, the next Governor, was an experienced public servant with some statistical knowledge. He concluded promptly that the population was larger than his predecessor had thought, and he probably made inquiry to determine whether it was a fact that white females over sixteen and the children of both races under that age were three times the number of white tithables. In the end, four, instead of three, seemed to Dinwiddie the correct multiplier. On that basis, in 1756, he computed that Virginia had 173,316 whites and 120,156 Negroes, a total of 293,742.[930]

No test of these figures could be made for a generation. When a census finally was taken in 1790, it was to show the white males over sixteen years of age to be 48.9 per cent of all Caucasian males; the tithables of that race were to constitute 25 per cent of all whites and 14.8 per cent of the entire population. If the percentages were the same in 1756, the population in that year was 292,700, a total within about 700 of Dinwiddie's estimate. His figure consequently may be accepted as substantially correct. In the middle seventeen-fifties, the population of Virginia probably was between 290,000 and 300,000.[931]

[923] 3 *Ibid.*, 706.
[924] See Evarts B. Greene and Virginia D. Harrington, *American Population before the Federal Census of 1790* (cited hereafter as *G. and H.*), p. 140.
[925] *Ibid.*   [926] *Ibid.*
[927] 3 *Gooch MSS*, 901.   [928] *G. and H.*, 140.
[929] *Ibid.*
[930] 2 *Din.*, 345. In *G. and H.*, 145 n., the opinion is expressed that Gooch was more nearly correct than Dinwiddie in the multiplier employed. A list of the tithables in nineteen Counties of Virginia, 1755 (P.R.O., C.O. 5, 1328, f. 443) shows a total of 43,329 white and 60,078 black tithables. The number of white tithables exceeded the Negro tithables greatly in August (2273 to 40) and in Frederick (2173 to 340), somewhat moderately (1312 to 921) in Fairfax, and slightly (1221 to 1217) in Culpeper. Elsewhere in the listed Counties Negro tithables outnumbered the white. These Counties were Charles City, Dinwiddie, Essex, Gloucester, Henrico, James City, King George, Lancaster, Middlesex, New Kent, Northumberland, Prince William, Richmond, Stafford and Westmoreland. The greatest excess of Negro tithables was in Gloucester—3728 to 1137.
[931] In *Burnaby*, 21, the tithables of 1759 were stated to be 105,000, of whom 40,000 were white. According to the formula of the census of 1790, this would mean a total of 270,000, a figure Dinwiddie accepted (see *G. and H.*, 141). If the ratio of white and black tithables was the same in 1773 as in 1759, the inhabitants immediately prior to the Revolution numbered 391,000. In a *Century of Population*, Table I, p. 9, quoted in Sara K. Gilliam, *Virginia's People*, 82, the following United States census estimates for the population of Virginia were given: 1730, 153,000; 1740, 200,000; 1750, 275,000; 1760, 346,000; 1770, 450,000.

The magnitude of the domain inhabited by these Virginians was their pride, the basis of much of their hope and speculation. Tidewater was well settled, the Piedmont was being occupied, the realm beyond the mountains lured and excited.[932] In 1744–45, precisely when George was beginning to understand something of the life around him, [933] two events widened the frontier of Virginia for all settlers. After the signing of the Treaty of Albany in 1722, it may be repeated, there had been doubt whether the Five Nations had relinquished title as far westward as the crest of the Blue Ridge or the higher saddle of the Alleghenies. The preamble of the Virginia ratification of the preliminary treaty had mentioned only the "great ridge of mountains." [934] The "greater" ridge was that West of the Shenandoah, but the term "ridge" was used primarily for what previously had been called the "Blew Mountains," East of the rich Valley of the Shenandoah. The colonials, of course, interpreted the treaty to cover everything as far westward as the crest of the Allegheny Mountains; the Indians were not willing to allow this extended claim otherwise than for solid gifts.

Patient maneuvering finally brought together at Lancaster, Pennsylvania, the representatives of the Five Nations [935] and the emissaries of Virginia and of Maryland. From June 22 until July 4, 1744, the negotiations continued. Final agreement, stoutly compensated by gifts from the white men, gave the colonials the land they sought and more than they had hoped to get. The Shenandoah Valley was not to be entered by Indians. Settlers could open in peace its fat lands and those beyond it, lands which stretched endlessly West of the farthest boundary to which Lord Fairfax laid claim.

Announcement of this treaty was news to whet the appetite of every land-hungry Virginian, but the extent to which princely patents could be issued through the King's office in Williamsburg depended, in part, on the outcome of the contest over the boundary between Virginia and her sister Colonies. The argument with North Carolina could wait

[932] An excellent brief summary of the state of settlement about 1750 appears in Hayes Baker-Crothers, *Virginia and the French and Indian War*, 22–23. Conditions in a frontier County just organizing its government are set forth admirably in *Papers of the Albemarle Co. His. Soc.*, v. 5. These include the *Order Book* of the Albemarle County Court for 1744/45.

[933] As the survey of Virginia in 1750 ends at this point, it may not be amiss to call attention again to the outline of this sketch, Appendix I–8. If any reader has occasion to consult this review of conditions in Virginia, he perhaps may save time by consulting the outline instead of the Index in Vol. II.

[934] See *supra*, p. 13.

[935] Strictly speaking the treaty was with the Six Nations, but no Mohawks were present.

because most of the disputed lands were far from navigable streams. With Maryland, the issue was narrow. A doubt of a singular nature existed concerning the line between Virginia and Pennsylvania. West of the boundary of Maryland, the contention of the authorities of the Old Dominion was that "Virginia resumes its ancient breadth and has no other limits . . . than what its first royal charter assigned it, and that is to the South Sea, including the island of California." [936] Part of this domain manifestly was taken from Virginia by the charter given William Penn in 1681, but subsequently there was dispute whether the western boundary of Pennsylvania, which was to be five degrees West of the Delaware River, conformed to the windings of that stream or was a straight line drawn directly North and South at a distance of five degrees from some fixed point on the Delaware. [937] This rendered doubtful a district that was small in area but valuable for its streams even though the wealth of its minerals was not realized.

Controversy over the boundary of Lord Fairfax's proprietary was on a vast scale. If his contention were denied by the Privy Council, [938] then almost the whole of the new country acquired from the Five Nations would be royal domain; but if Fairfax prevailed, all the finest land close to the Potomac and as far West as the South Branch of that river would be his, to patent or to withhold, to sell to all comers or to parcel to his family and among his friends.

The case was a close one. The Governor and Council maintained that the Northern Neck extended from the forks of the Rappahannock, above Fredericksburg, to the junction of the Shenandoah and the Potomac. With this western limit, the estimated area between the Rappahannock and the Potomac was 1,470,000 acres. By assuming the northern fork of the Rappahannock to be the base of the western line, acceptance of the same northern limit, where the Shenandoah entered the Potomac, would make the proprietary consist of 2,053,000 acres, as nearly as the Governor could compute. If Fairfax's contention were upheld in full, his boundary would run from the headwaters of the Rapidan, which is the southern fork of the Rappahannock, all the way to the "head springs" of the Potomac, far in the mountains West of the Alleghenies. The proprietary then would include approximately

936 Dinwiddie to the Lords of Trade, Jan. n.d., 1755; 1 *Din.*, 381.

937 The case is summarized admirably in S. J. and E. H. Buck, *The Planting of Civilization in Western Pennsylvania* (cited hereafter as *Buck*), p. 159 ff, with bibliographical references, 512–13.

938 For the details of the controversy that led to this appeal, see Appendix I-1.

5,282,000 acres, or as much land as that on which quit rents were paid the Crown in the remainder of the Colony.[939]

An order in Council for the determination of the boundaries had been issued in November, 1733; the report of Fairfax's surveyors and that of boundary commissioners named by the Colony had been completed in August, 1737. Thereafter, year on year, the peer had attended the meetings of the Commissioners for Trade and Plantations, and had sought to get favorable action on his plea for the widest boundaries of the Northern Neck. Finally, in the winter of 1744–45, he received permission to appear before the Privy Council and to offer a compromise to this effect: If his contention regarding boundaries was allowed and quit rents for lands within those limits were paid him in the future, he would confirm all royal patents issued in the disputed area, would waive all accumulated quit rents on his own account there, and would pay to the Crown all arrearages he collected of rents due under the King's patents.

Sometime in the early summer of 1745 word reached Belvoir that on the 11th of April the Privy Council had taken final action in the case of Fairfax vs Virginia. The Proprietor's compromise was accepted; his title was recognized in toto. Instead of the 1,470,000 acres the Colony was willing to admit were Fairfax's, he was vindicated in maintaining that he had more than three and a half times as much.[940]

George was then thirteen years old and, though he was precocious in all that related to business, he still was too young to understand the full meaning of Fairfax's victory and of the new and vast speculative movement that began as soon as the colonials knew where the Proprietor would set his stakes. Around young George whenever he was at Mount Vernon, the talk was of patents, of surveys, of trails, of settlements and of the profits that might be made by organizing land enterprises beyond the farthest bounds of Fairfax's grant. John Robinson quickly procured 100,000 western acres from the Governor. James Patton sought a like domain "on three branches of Missippi River"; John Blair and his associates reserved 100,000 acres "to the westward of the line of Lord Fairfax, on the waters of Potomac and Youghyaughye"; Thomas Bassett and others solicited a modest 50,000 acres but they wanted it "in the forke of Mississippi river and to run up and down

939 All the details, as summarized here, are set forth in Appendix I–1.
940 P.R.O., C.O., 5, 1326, p. 293–304, LC trans. See Appendix I–2, Part 2.

both said forks and down said river." [941] Much of all this was dream, much was speculation, though a few bold men under John Howard and John Peter Salley already had penetrated from Virginia to the Mississippi and had descended it.[942] On behalf of the Loyal Land Company, Thomas Walker was to set out in 1750 to find where the richest meadows and the widest river bottoms lay in a region soon to be called Kentucky. There was admiration for the explorers, but there was envy of the speculators where their plans were known. Rivalry was stirred among different patentees; ugliness showed itself; but Fairfax's following, which included the Washingtons, had both content and ambition. Under the decision of the Privy Council, lands taken out by them within the western reaches of the proprietary would have secure title. Beyond those lands was the great, open, unclaimed Valley of the Ohio—with the promise of a fortune for young men of enterprise and courage.

[941] 5 *V* 175-76. See the comment of Dinwiddie, June 16, 1753, quoted in 4 *Gipson*, 262 n.

[942] See Fairfax Harrison, "Virginians on the Ohio and Mississippi, 1742," 30 *V* 203 ff. Cf. also 31 *V* 172-73.

CHAPTER V

George Touches the Frontier
(1746–April, 1748)

George appeared to have in 1746 small prospect of any part in exploring the domain the decision of the Privy Council awarded Lord Fairfax. In fact, Lawrence did not believe it was to George's best interest to become in time another of the young speculators who were looking to the Shenandoah Valley and beyond. Aboard Vernon's flagship in the Cartagena expedition, Lawrence had seen something of the better side of life at sea, and he could think of no finer career for his tall young brother than one that began as Vernon's had, in the capacity of a "volunteer per order," Royal Navy. If that were impossible for a colonial, George might start on a Virginia merchant vessel and, in time, might become mate, captain or owner even. George was not averse to this, but he was dependent on his mother's will, whim and judgment. As his guardian, she could approve or she could veto. Short of running off, there was no way of starting a sailor's life otherwise than with the acquiescence of a lady who seemed to have little of the Balls' ancestral interest in shipping and the sea.

In this she was of one mind with her half-brother, Joseph Ball, who then resided in England but was the head of her line of the house of Ball and, in Mary Washington's eyes, a man of wisdom. Joseph's career had not been exciting but his personality was both interesting and provoking. Born Mch. 11, 1689,[1] he led the normal life of a well-to-do planter's son until, in February, 1708, he received by deed of gift from his father a property that yielded sufficient income to support him "at home." He migrated, established himself temporarily in London and there, Dec. 3, 1709, he married Frances Ravenscroft of West Ham parish, Essex.[2] After four and a half years subsequent and prob-

---

[1] *Hayden,* 76.
[2] *Ibid.*

ably intermittent residence at Gray's Inn he was called to the bar.[3] He must have engaged in other scholarly pursuits, also, because he accumulated Latin, French and Greek books in considerable number. The contents and not merely the bindings of these volumes were, apparently, of interest to him.[4] Some, perhaps all, of his collection, he brought back with him to Virginia. He was in the Colony in 1722 and probably bought additional land;[5] but the attractions of life in England proved stronger than the associations of the Northern Neck. During 1730–38, he resided in England for approximately eighteen months, and after another six years in Virginia, he left permanently in the winter of 1743–44.[6] Before his final departure he named as his manager in Virginia his nephew Joseph Chinn, a son of his unhappy sister Esther.[7] This young man either possessed vast patience or else suffered grievous necessity. Nothing less would have kept him at his new task in the face of the endless instruction, the carping complaint and the shackling restrictions imposed by the absentee proprietor.

Joseph Ball had amazing memory of detail. He remembered even the old garments he had packed away in Virginia and when he was occasionally in the mood of philanthropy he would direct Chinn to look in a specified chest for a particular garment and to give it to a designated individual.[8] Ball's conceptions of economical management were positive and inflexible. He wanted the fullest possible return from the Negroes' labor, but he insisted that care be taken to save them from illness that cost him their service. Chinn was ordered to see that wood was made accessible to them. "A good fire," said he, "is the life of a Negro." Again, "let not the overseer abuse my people, nor let them abuse their overseer." Care of pregnant slaves and of their issue was enjoined in clear understanding of the pride of motherhood. "Let the breeding wenches have baby clothes, for which you may tear up old sheets or any other old linen, that you can find in my house . . . and let them have good midwives and what is necessary." The slaves must

[3] Foster, *Men-of-Bench-and-Bar*. Ball was called to the bar Feb. 10, 1725. He became a bencher Jan. 31, 1743.
[4] See his letters of Mch. 20, 1743/44, July 17, 1745, and Aug. 5, 1755, to Joseph Chinn; *Ball Letter Book*. Ball's relationship to Chinn is explained in the next paragraph of the text.
[5] In a letter of Mch. 20, 1743/44 to Joseph Chinn, *op. cit.*, he spoke of quit rents on 1800 acres in Lancaster and on 400 acres at Little Falls in King George County.
[6] He arrived in England during the autumn of 1743. The sojourn of 1736–38 cannot be fixed positively as respects months. It may have covered only 1737 and part of 1738, or some part of 1736 and the whole of 1737. Joseph himself was not specific in his only known reference to the subject. (See Joseph Ball to Rev. John Underhill, Jan. 28, 1744; *Ball Letter Book*.)
[7] For the marital misadventures of Esther Ball Chinn, see Appendix I–5.
[8] See his letter of June 30, 1749, *op. cit.*

have meat, also, especially when they were sick. At "hog-killing time," every adult working Negro was to receive sixty pounds of pork. The children were to have thirty pounds each.[9] Negroes who "go after the creatures or work in the wet," he told his manager, must be furnished with two pairs of shoes. Garments for the slaves must not be "cut too scanty nor bobtailed."

The management of slaves called for greater diligence, Ball thought, than those who supervised them were apt to show. Overseers, he reasoned, might tend their own stock and neglect his, wherefore he limited the number of animals they might keep. In ordering his manager to discharge one of the men in charge of a farm, Ball was emphatic: "You can't well get a worse. You must, if it be possible, get a fellow that will stay at home and work." Chinn must see to it, also, that a certain new fence was strong, "for if you don't," Ball wrote, "I know the overseers are such a parcel of slubboring sons of bitches that it wont be worth a farthing when it is done."[10]

His suspicions were not limited to overseers. Doctors had an equal measure of his distrust and scorn. They generally did "more harm than good" in treating the slaves, he wrote,[11] but he had complete confidence in his own system of medication which he required his manager to apply.[12] Part of it was unwise by modern standards—as, for example, his employment of bleeding—but some of his regulations were soundly and shrewdly directed to the end he emphasized, namely, a low death rate among his young Negroes: They must have sufficient covering, "drams" when sick and, he repeated, good fires.[13]

If Ball became involved in controversy, he was apt to be short, sharp and sometimes snarling: The fences of the Chinns must not be joined to his otherwise than as they were when he left Virginia. "It will be attended with inconvenience to me; and it must not be done." In another instance, he concluded that it was worth £40 a year to look after the English business of his cousin, Mrs. Ellen Chichester. If she would not pay that much, he would have nothing to do with her affairs.[14] Similarly, Joseph Chinn was directed to inform Major Ball that no

9 Joseph Ball to Joseph Chinn, Feb. 18, 1743/44, *op. cit.* This letter is a full statement of the methods Chinn was to follow on Ball's plantations, and it is to be commended to anyone interested in colonial farm direction in the South.
10 Letters of Feb. 18, 1743/44 and July 17, 1745, *op. cit.*
11 To Joseph Chinn, Feb. 18, 1743/44, *op. cit.*
12 To the same, July 18, 1745, June 27, 1749, *op. cit.*
13 Joseph Ball to Joseph Chinn, June 27, 1749, *op. cit.*
14 Joseph Ball to Mrs. Ellen Chichester, May 18, 1744, Apr. 26, 1745, *op. cit.*

land would be sold him "upon any terms" for a mill site at the Little Falls.[15]

Mary Ball Washington had some of her half-brother's characteristics. She was as positive as he was and more acquisitive. In her dealings with servants, she was strict. They must follow a definite round of work. Her bidding must be their law. A thousand trifles were her daily care to the neglect of larger interests. In his will, for example, her husband had provided that she should have the use of the Bridges Creek quarter for five years while she was developing a quarter on her Deep Run tract.[16] The end of the five years was approaching, but nothing substantial had been done on the upper Rappahannock. Hers, too, was to be the management of her sons' property during their minority; she was handling it as her own but not with wisdom. In the Virginia vernacular, she was a "poor manager"; the farm already may have begun to "run down." Perhaps, also, Mary Washington was in the first stages of what later became a fixed state of mind—that her family and her kinsfolk should help her because she did not have enough to meet her needs.[17] A little later, when her complaints frequently drew money from the purse of her son, it somehow was spent to no purpose and was forgotten as a gift. Mistress of much or of little, mistress she was resolved to be, and in nothing more certainly than in deciding what should be done by her first-born, her pride and her weakness. She would hold him fast, safe from the temptations of a sailor's life and from the dangers of the frontier. Lawrence might counsel and plan, but she would decide: George was her son, not Lawrence's.[18] This must have been plain to her elder stepson. He realized that any dealings with her and any effort by him to persuade her to permit George to go to sea had to be conducted with high caution and superlative diplomacy.

So, on a sultry Monday, the 8th of September, 1746, George went

[15] Letter of May 2, 1745, *op. cit.*
[16] See *supra*, p. 74.
[17] Cf. 26 *G. W.*, 43-44.
[18] Of Washington's letters to his mother, six only survive. Four of these were written in 1755. There is not one between October, 1757, and February, 1787. Washington seldom referred to her in his letters to other members of the family and then usually at long intervals with combined resignation and impatience, when her affairs were in some confusion or fancied distress. What is said of her in the text consequently is based, first, on the implications of his letters to or about her, and, second, on the evidence his ledgers and cashbooks afford of his repeated gifts to her. In some instances, as will appear later, he thought it proper to jot down the name of the person in whose presence he handed her money. Although there never can be a biography of her, it is plain that she was not the Spartan matron tradition has made of her.

across the ferry from the farm to Fredericksburg and there met Col. William Fairfax, who was preparing, with William Beverley and Lunsford Lomax, to mark the newly established boundaries of the proprietary. Colonel Fairfax had come directly from Belvoir. He brought news of Nancy and of Mount Vernon and, more particularly, he put into George's hands two letters from Lawrence. One was addressed to George himself, the other was to Lawrence's stepmother. Fairfax explained that Lawrence wished George to read and to ponder the letter meant for him, but not to mention to his mother that he had received it; the letter to Mrs. Washington from Lawrence simply was to be delivered by George when circumstances seemed auspicious.

On opening the folded sheet from his brother, George probably found it to be a statement by Lawrence of the advantages of a life at sea. With this was coupled a private admonition for George to hold steadily to his purpose and not to let his mother know that Lawrence was urging him to do so. In addressing his stepmother, Lawrence doubtless was deferential but probably did no more than mention the benefits that might come to George from service on the deck of a good ship.[19] George understood the diplomacy of this approach. He promised then, or at some other time in his conversation with Fairfax, to be steady and to follow the advice of Lawrence, who, he said, was his best friend.[20]

Either from George or from an acquaintance in Fredericksburg, Colonel Fairfax learned that Doctor Spencer was visiting often at Ferry Farm and was exercising some influence over Mrs. Washington, who was then not older than thirty-seven and consequently not beyond all thought of remarriage. The Doctor was urged to use his influence to persuade the widow to look more favorably on the plan for George

[19] The two documents on this aspect of the plan to send George to sea are William Fairfax to Lawrence Washington, Sept. 9, 1746, and Robert Jackson—who witnessed Augustine's will—to Lawrence Washington, Sept. 18, 1746. These letters in the L. W. Smith Collection, *Havemeyer Papers,* were printed for the first time in *Conway's Barons,* 236 ff. Colonel Fairfax said only of the papers entrusted to him by Lawrence: "I gave [George] his mother's letter to deliver with caution and not show his." This may indicate that George's letter from Lawrence had been sent previously, but if that had been the case, the warning not to show the letter would have been conveyed more readily in the letter itself. As for the contents of the two letters, the conclusions of the text are inferential, but one can imagine no other reason for Lawrence's caution in dealing with Mrs. Washington other than his conviction that she would object to the proposal if she believed her stepson was presuming to tell her what to do with her son.

[20] This is the first remark that may be attributed to Washington on the basis of documentary evidence. Fairfax's exact words were: "George has been with us and says he will be steady and thankfully follow your advice as his best friend." L. W. Smith Collection, *Havemeyer Papers.* Both Conway in his *Barons* and Rupert Hughes (*George Washington,* cited hereafter as *Hughes*), v. 1, p. 33–34, interpreted Washington's remark to indicate that he had been in some sort of a scrape, but no evidence of this exists.

to go to sea.[21] By Doctor Spencer's representation or by some other device, Mrs. Washington was half-converted, but within a few days she was back to her original state of mind. As a friend of the family wrote about a week after the delivery of Lawrence's letter, "she offers several trifling objections such as fond and unthinking mothers naturally suggest and I find that one word against [George's] going has more weight than ten for it." [22]

There, for the time, the matter rested, though it continued to be discussed in family letters and eventually in one from some of the kinsfolk to Joseph Ball, Mary's half-brother in England. Mary had plans of her own and one in particular, that to a certain extent involved Joseph Ball. In spite of previous negligence, she had to look forward to 1753 when George would be of age and by the terms of the will of his father, would come into possession of Ferry Farm. Not far down the Rappahannock was the property that Mary's father had divided between her and Joseph. If the brother would permit her to cut timber and to collect stone from his part of the property, she could assure herself a home there when she should leave Ferry Farm. Joseph deserved his name among his brethren; he was the wealthy member of the Ball family. There was no reason, Mary thought, why he should not give her the timber and the stone for foundations and chimneys. He could afford, indeed, to make a handsome present to his niece Betty, Mary's daughter. To solicit both these gifts, the building materials and something for the girl, Mary wrote her brother on the 13th of December, 1746, and entrusted the letter to James Dun, who was starting for England.[23]

If George was not to go to sea until his mother had made up her mind, he had abundant, nearer activities. After he was thirteen or fourteen, he grew so fast that he seemed to pass in a single year from boyhood to young manhood. Strong of frame and of muscle, he still was studying mathematics, with or without an instructor, and he was learning to write a swift, clear "hand" that made copying less tedious than it would have been for most boys. Among young Virginians of his class there was circulating, perhaps in manuscript, an abbreviated

[21] William Fairfax to Lawrence Washington, Sept. 9, 1746, *loc. cit.* Doctor Spencer probably was the man who gave a "Course of Experimental Philosophy" in Williamsburg. See *Va. Gazette,* Jan. 19, 1745/46. Spencer appears also in T. B. Cohen, *Benjamin Franklin's Experiments,* 49–54, in 2 Bigelow's *Franklin,* 171–72, and in *Blanton,* 324.

[22] Robert Jackson to Lawrence Washington, Sept. 18, 1746, L. W. Smith Coll., *Havemeyer Papers.*

[23] See Joseph Ball to Mary Washington, May 19, 1747, *Ball Letter Book.*

version of Francis Hawkins's *Youth's Behaviour*.[24] George read this and, to keep it before him, transcribed the rules with boyish lack of discrimination. He did not attempt to discard those that manifestly were intended for urban English or Continental life, rather than for the Colonies. Hawkins, for example, had written that in France, "for so much as the place near the wall is ordinarily more high, more sure, for easier walking, and cleaner, commonly one giveth it to the more worthy, namely, where there are but two." [25] This echoed the remark of an English woman, mother of a famous son, who had maintained that in London "there were two sets of people, those who gave the wall and those who took it, the peaceable and the quarrelsome." [26] To George, in a Colony with few towns and no cities of any size, "giving the wall" could have meant little; "giving the path" would have been explicit and in accordance with the practice of civil persons. George drew no distinctions: as the text was, so was it copied. At the end he transcribed: "Labour to keep alive in your Breast that Little Spark of Cetial fire Called Conscience" and then he wrote "Finis" with many flourishes. He did so well with his copying that he scarcely deserved a black mark for writing "Cetial" instead of "Celestial." Besides, the "Ce" came at the end of the line anyway. He was to apply the maxim though he marred the word.[27] Of religion, there was at Ferry Farm an acceptance of belief in God and a compliance with the ritual of the church, but no special zeal or active faith. Such religious instruction as George received in youth was of a sort to turn his mind toward conduct rather than toward creed. He was beginning on his own account to reason that there were certain principles of honesty and fairplay by which a man ought to live.

In his small world he tried to practice those principles, but already he was looking beyond Ferry Farm and the Rappahannock. Everywhere the talk was of surveys—of the boundary stones that were being set, of the tracts that were being opened in the region West of the Blue Ridge, and of the greater designs Lawrence and some of his friends

24 Based principally on *Bienséance de la Conversation entre les Hommes*, prepared in 1595. See Charles Moore, cited in the next note, and M. D. Conway's *George Washington's Rules of Civility Traced to their Sources and Restored*, 1891.

25 Charles Moore, ed. *George Washington's Rules of Civility and Decent Behaviour*, 7. This edition is in every way superior to those that preceded it, and it proves the fallacy of Toner's contention, in his edition of 1888, p. 8, that the rules "were compiled by George Washington himself when a school-boy" of thirteen.

26 Boswell's *Johnson*, ed. George Birkbeck Hill, v. 1, p. 128. Mrs. Johnson's remark to Samuel dated from 1737 but related to her own earlier life in London.

27 Charles Moore, *op. cit.*

were formulating for a company to develop the Ohio country that was accessible under the new Treaty of Lancaster. Whatever career the sea might hold later, the land was full of interest and of promise. Already George was developing an ambition to share in the profits his seniors were predicting. He wanted to be like Colonel Fairfax and Lawrence —and not to be merely the owner of a farm of moderate size.

The means of advancement were at hand. In the storehouse at home were the surveyor's instruments that had belonged to George's father.[28] Across the river in Fredericksburg and elsewhere in the neighborhood lived men who knew how to use the surveyor's compass.[29] Every County had its Surveyor; some of these men had deputies. From one or more of these officials, George quickly learned in 1746-47 the elements of surveying [30] and began to run lines at Ferry Farm or on the plantations of his kinsmen. The work entranced him. He could not do enough of it. By Aug. 18, 1747, and perhaps before that date, when fifteen years and six months old, he had attained to the required standard of accuracy on simple assignments. Within a few weeks he was deft and soon proficient on surveys that were not unduly complicated.[31] Probably as some friendly Surveyor's deputy, he was com-

[28] See *supra*, p. 103.

[29] Apparently this simple instrument, with a Jacob's staff, was George's principal equipment, except, of course, for his pole and chain. All the surveys of young Washington are in terms of degrees, and never in minutes as well. This fact of itself suggests the surveyor's compass, because that instrument was accurate enough for degrees, but not for minutes. Of the books he used in learning the surveyor's art, nothing definite is known. The most popular English works of the time were: William Leybourn, *The Compleat Surveyor*, 5th ed., 1722; John Norden, *The Surveyor's Dialogue*, 4th ed., 1733; and the older book, John Love, *Geodæsia*, London, 1688, which was designed especially for those laying out "new lands in His Majesty's Plantations in America."

[30] There is a possibility that George Byrne was Washington's instructor in drafting and in surveying. The *Fairfax Papers* in the Huntington Library make it plain that Byrne was surveying in Prince William County for the Proprietor as early as March, 1741. Other references show Byrne was there, in Stafford and in King George as late as 1752. Nowhere in his extant records is George Washington mentioned, though Washington's lettering and design resembled Byrne's. The earlier tradition that George Hume was the instructor of Washington cannot be discarded altogether, but Hume's letters in 38 *V* 201 ff suggest that he may have been ill and in residence at the Forks of the Rappahannock while Washington was learning to survey land opposite Fredericksburg. In general, also, when Hume was able to work at that period, he was engaged nearer the mountains. Examination in the Library of Congress of some of the MS notes of Hume's surveys shows that initials taken for "G. W.," and consequently assumed to represent Washington's work, are in reality "S.W." and are meant to mark a point of the compass.

[31] None of the interesting early surveys in the *George Washington Atlas*, e.g. plates 3, 5 and 8, bears a specific date; but in the *Miscellaneous Accounts* of Washington in LC (cited hereafter as *Misc. Accts. G.W.*) are references to several. Among others is this note: "[1747] Aug. 18. Then surveyed the following piece of land at one station in the school house Oldfield bounded as per field book." This is believed to be the first "dated survey" of Washington's extant. In 1 Sawyer's *Washington*, 76, are reproduced some early examples of George's boyish signature as they appear on the title page of a volume that once belonged to Samuel Bowman, mariner, for whose last testament of June 18, 1742, see *Stafford Wills*, 1729-48, p. 337.

pensated, though perhaps at less than the regular fee. One batch of his surveys at the beginning of October brought the boy £2, 3s.[32] This was in cash, not in tobacco notes. The law specified the fees in terms of tobacco[33] but George got cash when he could. It was welcome coin to a boy who already had money-making as one of his ambitions. Surveying not only had interest and yielded a profit but it also offered excellent training. A good Surveyor had to be accurate and thorough: as George wanted to excel in surveying and in everything else he undertook, he painstakingly gave neatness and finish to surveys he made with the fullest care he knew how to display.[34]

Young Washington was in the first excitement of this entrancing work and of his first acquisition of earned money when his mother received a somewhat strange reply to the letter she had written her brother Joseph in December, 1746, concerning the use of timber from his woods for the construction of her proposed new house on her land downstream from Ferry Farm. Joseph, who then was fifty-eight years of age, was as confident as ever of the soundness of his own judgment and of the wisdom of his business methods. He began with little ado:

Stratford by Bow 19th May 1747

Sister

I recd yrs of the 13th of December last by Mr. James Dun, and am Glad to hear of your and children's and Sister Pearson's and Cousin Daniel's Health, though I don't know whether you mean Mr. Daniel or his wife, and I wonder you don't mention Rawleigh Travers. I suppose he is dead, though I never heard of it.

I think you are in the Right to leave the House where you are, and to go upon your own Land; but as for Timber, I have scarce enough for my own Plantations; so can spare you none of that; but as for stone, you may take what you please to build you a House.

When Peace comes (which I hope will be within a year) I will send Cousin Betty a small token to Remember me by.

I understand you are advised, and have some thought of sending your son George to sea. I think he had better be put aprentice to a tinker; for a

---

[32] *Misc. Accts. G.W.,* supra. These surveys, which represent the first known earnings of George Washington, were for Richard Rose, Francis Jett, Mrs. Elizabeth Washington and Richard Barnes.

[33] 5 H 340. The basic fee for a new survey and plat of not more than 1000 acres was 500 pounds of tobacco, which at 12s 6d per 100 pounds was £3, 2s 6d. The price varied much from year to year. In 1745, standard tobacco brought 14s per cwt. In 1756, the top price was 18s. Between the two years it fell as low as 8 to 10s.

[34] For these statements no specific source can be cited, but the supporting, inferential evidence is strong and clear in every surviving record of George's youth.

common sailor before the mast has by no means the common liberty of the Subject; for they will press him from a ship where he has 50 shillings a month and make him take three and twenty; and cut him and staple him and use him like a Negro, or rather, like a dog. And as for any considerable preferment in the Navy, it is not to be expected, there are always too many grasping for it here, who have interest and he has none. And if he should get to be master of a Virginia ship (which will be very difficult to do) a planter that has three or four hundred acres of land and three or four slaves, if he be industrious, may live more comfortably, and leave his family in better Bread, than such a master of a ship can. And if the planter can get ever so little beforehand, let him begin to chinch, that is, buy goods for tobacco and sell them again for tobacco (I never knew three men miss while they went on so) but he must not pretend to buy for money and sell for tobacco. I never knew any of them but what lost more than they got: neither must he send his Tobacco to England to be sold here, and goods sent him; if he does, he will soon get in the merchant's debt, and never get out again. He must not be hasty to be rich; but must go on gently and with patience as things will naturally go. This method, without aiming at being a fine gentleman before his time, will carry a man more comfortably and surely through the world, than going to sea, unless it be a great chance indeed. I pray God help you and yours. My wife and daughter join with me in love and respects to you and yours and the rest of our relations.

Your Loving Brother
J. B.[35]

When you write again
direct to me at Stratford
by Bow nigh London

To Mrs. Mary Washington
nigh the falls, Rappa River
Virg^a

This eulogy on the profits of chinching [36] did not interest the younger Washingtons, but arguments against a mariner's life for George probably were decisive with Joseph's half-sister. Nothing more was said in advocacy of such a career at a time when to Mrs. Washington's refusal were added George's profitable employment and a further event that might open many opportunities: Lord Fairfax—the Proprietor him-

[35] *Ball Letter Book.* Incomplete versions of this letter will be found in *Hayden,* 77, in 1 *Hughes,* 35, and in various other lives of Washington.

[36] This use of "chinch" as a verb seems to have escaped both the editors of the *Oxford Dictionary* and the no-less-diligent Dr. B. W. Green.

self!—had arrived in Virginia during the summer of 1747 [37] and had established himself at Colonel Fairfax's home, Belvoir, close to Mount Vernon.

This had occurred while George was at Ferry Farm or was surveying and visiting in Chotank among his young cousins, who incidentally were beginning to borrow bits of the money he was earning.[38] Pleasant as was the companionship of his kin, George of course was anxious to meet the Proprietor, whom he never had seen unless it was during the time of Fairfax's first visit, when the boy was too young to remember the appearance of His Lordship. One circumstance after another delayed George now in ascertaining for himself how a peer of the realm looked and acted. It probably was not until February, 1748,[39] that George journeyed to Mount Vernon and soon afterward went down to the next plantation to pay his respects to the great landlord.

The ride to Belvoir was an easy one, even in winter; the house itself, though almost new, was familiar to George. It was of brick construction, sixty by thirty-six feet, two stories over a full basement. On the entrance floor were a large central passageway and four rooms; above stairs were five chambers. Already some of the outbuildings had been erected; the place was taking on the usual appearance of a small village.[40]

The Proprietor had of course been described in advance to George. Consequently the boy could not have been surprised greatly by the oddities then and subsequently disclosed. Thomas, Lord Fairfax, was fifty-four years of age in 1748 and was not conspicuous either for good looks or for ugliness. Doubtless in the eyes of the youthful visitor, who was of the age and temperament to admire dress, the strangest charac-

---

[37] 34 *V* 37, with citation of the *Md. Gazette* of Nov. 11, 1747. The exact date of Fairfax's landing is not known. His provision for Robert Fairfax, his brother and heir presumptive, is explained in 34 *V* 46.

[38] Cf. his *Misc. Accts.*, July 29, Aug. 18, Aug. 24, Sept. 10, 1747 (*Account Book* A, 1). This last item covers the first of uncounted small loans to kinsmen, in this instance, 2*s* 10½*d* to "Mr. Lawrence Washington of Stafford."

[39] George was in the Chotank district on Jan. 11, 1748 (George Washington's *Cash Accounts*, LC, unpaged) and, as his survey of Lawrence's turnip field shows (*Washington Atlas*, Plate 3), he was at Mount Vernon by Feb. 27, 1748.

[40] See *supra*, p. 92. The best description of Belvoir is the advertisement of sale, *Va. Gazette*, Aug. 25, 1774. Dimensions given in the text are from the account in Snowden's *Historic Landmarks*, 94, of his visit to the ruins. There were five brick outbuildings, which included offices, stables and coach house, but as the dates of the erection of these houses are not known, it is not permissible to include them in any sketch of the estate as it was in 1748. For the same reason, no use has been made of the Belvoir inventory of 1774 (*Conway's Barons*, 218) or of the list of Fairfax's books, *post* 1781.

teristic of the owner of the Northern Neck was a disdain of fine apparel. Fairfax would buy of the best and the newest and never would wear what he purchased. Year by year his unused wardrobe increased, while he went about in the plainest garments.[41] One of his favorite complaints was that at the time of the marriage of his younger brother Robert, he had been compelled for an entire month to wear clothing appropriate to the exchange of ceremonial visits.[42] The reason for his neglect of dress probably was one of deeper characteristics, a fixed and ineradicable indolence from which nothing except the threat of financial loss could shake him. Another peculiarity was Fairfax's dislike of the company of women. Even among men, as his Virginia kinspeople were to find, he occasionally was silent and sullen; in the presence of ladies he almost always was reserved and embarrassed. This, it was whispered, was because he had been jilted in young manhood after an engagement had been made and all the clothing and equipage for a fashionable wedding had been ordered.[43]

If these were peculiarities discernible to the intelligent young Washington and to all neighbors and guests, there was about Fairfax nothing that barbed antagonisms. His intellect was far from brilliant, but he was sufficiently wise to employ competent counsel when he needed judgment, knowledge or experience to supplement his own. If some accounted him dull, none accused him of being vicious. In many things cautious and often suspicious, he was not ungenerous. His greatest satisfaction, perhaps his one lively interest, was in hunting. He never was to have—and never undertook to have—an influence on George comparable to that exerted by Colonel Fairfax or by Lawrence. Although time was to mellow His Lordship, and long residence in a remote region was to make him almost a legendary figure, he would in 1748 have been a commonplace citizen of the Northern Neck, an uninspiring guest, had it not been for his title and his possession of a vast domain.[44] Colonel Fairfax, on the other hand, had accumulated rich experience in his fifty-seven years of life. He had served in the

---

[41] Cf. Johnson in his preface to the *Fairfax Correspondence*, cxxix, "although costly suits were sent out to him every year from London, he never put them on, preferring that rougher costume which better corresponded with his out-of-door habits." The inventory of Fairfax's clothing, prepared after his death and printed in 8 *V* 11 ff, is one of the longest in Virginia records.

[42] Johnson, in *Fairfax Correspondence*, cxxviii.

[43] See *infra*, Appendix I-1.

[44] The fourth appendix to Burnaby's *Travels*, (ed. 1795) with the traditional view of Fairfax, was written after 1791 and was colored by the sentiment of those who did not know Lord Fairfax till he was an old man, the patriarch of the Shenandoah.

Navy at the beginning of his career, and later he had carried a sword in Spain. When he and Lawrence talked of battles and sieges and of the good opinion that an officer's gallant service won, they probably made a soldier's life appear attractive to George. Such a career could not be excelled even by that of the successful speculator who could pick the rich land in the Indian country.

Then, too, among the Fairfaxes were young women who had grace and good manners and wore fine clothes as if born to them. One of Colonel Fairfax's daughters, Sarah—two or three years younger than Lawrence's wife Nancy [45]—had married the rich merchant and shipmaster John Carlyle of Alexandria. The resplendent young man of the circle was Colonel Fairfax's oldest son, George William, born in the Bahamas but well-schooled and well-polished in England. He was twenty-three in 1748, seven years older than George, and already a Justice of the County and a newly-elected member of the House of Burgesses. With these acquisitions would be coupled a great fortune in land. What finer model could there be, or one more certain to arouse emulation in the heart of George Washington? [46]

Chance now offered George in the spring of 1748 an opportunity of being in the company of this polished young gentleman in circumstances that would permit George to be useful at the same time that he was having a fascinating experience. A surveying party was about to start for the remote South Branch of the Potomac. James Genn, a veteran Surveyor, was to be in charge; the Proprietor was to be represented by George William Fairfax—"Mr. Fairfax" as George deferentially styled him. Chainmen and other helpers were to be recruited on the frontier. If George cared to do so, he could go with the party. In the work, he would find training and a measure of just such adventure as the heart of every red-blooded boy coveted. Somewhat surprisingly, permission

45 Sarah was born in 1728 and died Jan. 22, 1761. See 18 *W* (1) p. 210.

46 For Fairfax, see *Landmarks*, 507. Not one specific reference can be cited to justify the statements in the two preceding paragraphs concerning the influence of the Fairfax circle in arousing George's ambition and in creating an interest in a military life. All persons best qualified to give testimony on the subject died while Washington still was young, or else they left the country. The conclusions in the text are reached by elimination but are not believed to be less valid on that account. If George's subsequently-confessed devotion to arms had an origin outside his own thought, it could have been aroused by no other known persons than Colonel Fairfax and Lawrence Washington. At Ferry Farm Mrs. Washington was opposed inflexibly to anything that would expose her oldest son to danger. She demonstrated this in two known instances. The extent to which Washington's social ambitions were stirred by his visits to the Potomac is similarly undetermined on the basis of surviving evidence but, here again, all the probabilities are on one side. From the plain, though adequate living of Ferry Farm, Washington emerged in young manhood with refined tastes. He had no large opportunity of developing them except in the society of the Potomac.

was given by George's mother; he probably was told that he might be allowed to do some of the surveying.[47]

The 11th of March, 1748, was fixed as the date for leaving Mount Vernon and Belvoir. An important date it was in George's life, because it both marked his farthest journey from home and brought his first personal contact with the new frontier about which there was constant talk among the elders. George was not unequipped for the enterprise. Although he had just observed his sixteenth birthday, he was physically his father's son and, in strength, almost a man. He was systematic, he had achieved his ambition of learning to write swiftly and clearly, and he could perform readily enough the simple mathematical problems of surveying. His mind found interest chiefly in matters of business, concerning which he was mature beyond his age, though he had little imagination except for planning how he could advance himself. On nearly all aspects of farm life, he had the information and the attitude of the plantation owner. For good land he was developing already a critical and appraising eye. He knew crops; he loved trees and could identify with ease all those of the forests around his home; he rode admirably; he made on adults an excellent impression of vitality, courtesy and integrity at the same time that he won the good will of the young.

Along with these excellencies he had the softness of the young gentleman who would ride horseback by the hour but always would come back to a comfortable house and a good bed. Although he was far from rich, he was accustomed to an ease quite different from the life of the frontier. Instead of wearing a hunting shirt and telling time "by sun," he carried a watch [48] and enjoyed some of the clothes of fashion.[49]

Thus apparelled, George and "Mr. Fairfax" [50] set out. As they rode toward the Occoquan, they traversed a country and passed a number of homes typical of the society that had developed on the Potomac above Chotank during the previous half century.[51] Not far from Bel-

[47] No documentary basis has been established for the familiar tradition that Lord Fairfax employed George as one of the surveyors of the South Branch. As the last days of the survey will show, George's behavior was not that of a young man under contract.

[48] See the note in his *Journal of 1748*, ed. Toner, 70.

[49] Cf., *ibid.*, 162, his "Memorandum to have my Coat made by the following Directions."

[50] George's journal of 1748 contains no reference to his companion otherwise than as "Mr. Fairfax" or "George Fairfax, Esq."

[51] It will be understood that this brief sketch of a part of the youthful Washington's environment is not designed to be inclusive. A few only of what are believed to be typical estates, large and small, are mentioned. Residents of the first of the "Washington neighborhoods"

voir, they were within sight of some of the land of Rev. Charles Green, minister of Truro parish. Much had happened to Doctor Green after George's father had proposed the physician as a possible candidate for holy orders.[52] The rector had patented numerous tracts along the Potomac and now, with more than 9000 acres in his name, probably was becoming "land-poor." [53] He had a dwelling on his own property but he was not content with it. Four years subsequent to the time young Washington and George William Fairfax passed his lane, Doctor Green was to demand that a residence be built for him on the glebe land "according to law" and that it be a brick structure.[54] The parson's peculiarities were familiar, but so were his virtues. He was respected as a man of "sound learning" who, in a pinch, would physic a parishioner.

Farther southward, on their right, the two Georges may have caught a glimpse of Cedar Grove. It was beautifully situated on Pohick Creek [55] and it had both romance and tragedy. Dennis McCarty, second son of Daniel McCarty of Longwood,[56] had wooed Sarah Ball but had to deal with a rival who, when defeated, was alleged to have made some slurring reference to the lovely Sarah. The story came to Dennis's ears. He forthwith reckoned the day when he was apt to find his fiancée's traducer at the Lancaster Court, and, waiting impatiently, he at length rode down and confronted the swain who had permitted disappointment to poison the tongue. Faced with the choice of a flogging or a retraction, the young man apologized. Thereupon the gallant Dennis invited him to the wedding. That, at least, was the way the story ran.[57] George perhaps had heard it. He almost certainly knew of the later tragedy—how Dennis McCarty had died in 1743, how two ministers had preached funeral sermons, and how, when Dennis's accounts were examined, the debts were so heavy that many of the

---

were named in connection with George's infancy, *supra*, p. 49. Fredericksburg was portrayed on p. 60. This sketch covers the region from Little Hunting Creek to Quantico. The "Chotankers" are described *infra*, p. 224. Treatment of the neighborhood from Mount Vernon to Alexandria is reserved for Vol. III, which covers the period of George Washington's personal tenancy of the estate. This division may prove less tedious than a portrayal in a single chapter of all the "neighborhoods" would be.

52 See *supra*, p. 54.

53 His twelve patents for 9036 acres between Oct. 23, 1739, and Oct. 29, 1742, appear in L. O. *Records*, N. N., E, 134, 145, 164, 226, 268, 299, 350, 475, 499, 500, 501, 515.

54 See the vestry's advertisement for proposals, *Va. Gazette*, Aug. 14, 1752.

55 1 Rowland, *Life of George Mason* (cited hereafter as *Rowland's Mason*), p. 111.

56 Longwood, it will be remembered, was in Westmoreland, near George's birthplace. See *supra*, p. 49.

57 *McCarty Family*, 40. The marriage bond of Dennis McCarty and Sarah Ball appears in *Lancaster County Marriages*, Sept. 22, 1724.

Negroes had to be sold.[58] That part of the life history of Dennis Mc-
Carty was to be repeated grimly and often in George's day and not infrequently in his neighborhood.

Beyond Cedar Grove was an estate with a different history. In 1694,
George Mason the first had patented 1150 acres along Accokeek Creek,
the stream on which Augustine Washington later had operated his iron-
mine.[59] The district had developed so slowly for a number of years that
as late as 1722, Governor Spotswood had named the Mason house at
Pohick as the place where the Indians, in accordance with a treaty,
were to deliver runaway slaves.[60] When the second George Mason died
in 1730, his personal property was essentially that of a pioneer—pewter
dishes, powder horn, shot bottle, saddles [61]—but his son, George Mason
III, by that time was achieving distinction. He received the freedom
of Glasgow for his assistance in developing the French tobacco trade
of that city; he enjoyed other honors and, apparently, had a fine career
ahead of him in 1735. That year, in an attempt to cross the Potomac
during a storm, he lost his life. His widow, Ann Thomson,[62] was left
with three children, and, as he died intestate, she did not have even the
comfort of knowing that she was using the estate as he would have
disposed of it.[63] At the time George Washington and young Fairfax
rode by the Mason plantation, the widow was economizing hard in
order to save money with which to purchase lands for her younger
children.[64]

Past a site that later was to be Bradley, the home of George's friend
Lee Massey, the two companions rode.[65] Then they came close to
Belmont Bay, where Catesby Cocke, son of a former Secretary of the
Colony, had the headquarters of his land speculation. Cocke, who was

[58] His will, probated Apr. 21, 1743, is in *Fairfax Wills*, A, 1, p. 13; the estate account,
showing debts of 62,965 pounds of tobacco, will be found in *Fairfax Records*, B, 32.

[59] *L. O. Records, N.N.*, 2, p. 33.

[60] 1 *Rowland's Mason*, 36.

[61] *Stafford Wills*, 1729-48, p. 6. There is a possibility that this is the inventory of the
first George Mason, but if so, he was, for the times, an old man.

[62] She was a daughter of Stevens Thomson, a lawyer of distinction.

[63] 1 *Rowland's Mason*, 51; Helen Hill, *George Mason* (cited hereafter as *Hill's Mason*),
p. 6-8.

[64] It is pleasing to note that she succeeded. According to Miss Rowland (1 *op. cit.*, 51),
Mrs. Mason ultimately purchased for her younger children 10,000 acres of land in Loudoun
County. Subsequent development of this tract gave the younger children better estates than
their older brother inherited. The episode illustrates both the ambition of the dominant class
to perpetuate itself and the opportunities of achieving that ambition West of the early settlements. See *supra*, Chapter I.

[65] 1 *Mason's Rowland*, 110. The interesting accounts of young Lee Massey for 1745 appear
in *Stafford Deeds*, O, 185. Lee paid £1 for schooling and £8 for a year's board, and indulged
himself in a pair of leather breeches that cost £1, 1s 6d.

forty-six at the time of George's journey, had heard years previously of a vacancy in the clerkship of Stafford and had moved to the upper Potomac to procure the office. Thereafter, as he learned where the fat lands lay, he had patented them assiduously until, doubtless, he lost account of how many tracts he owned at a given time. First and last, it would appear, he held sixty-seven to a total of almost 30,000 acres.[66]

If the boys had reached the lovely Occoquan at Woodbridge, they could have used the ferry operated ancestrally, so to say, by the Masons; and if the young riders had crossed the river higher up, they probably would have been on the land of Peter Wagener, one of the most interesting men in that part of the Colony. Peter's father of the same name had been for a term of years a minister in Virginia. Somewhat sharply, Governor Gooch had observed that the senior Wagener was better remembered as a bad painter than as a minister. About 1707 the parson carried his canvases and his books back to England, but his son Peter returned to the Colony in 1738 at the age of twenty-one. Soon the younger Wagener married a daughter of Councillor John Robinson [67] and set out to make his fortune by the favored process of holding office and patenting land. In the one, if not in both, he had something more than the average good luck of intelligent planters. He became Clerk of Prince William, though he resided in what subsequently was a part of Fairfax County. At the time Fairfax was established, Catesby Cocke was named Clerk, which office in due time he passed to his son-in-law, John Graham. As it chanced, Graham then had his home in Prince William. An exchange of positions between him and Wagener seemed in order. With the consent of obliging Justices, it was arranged: Wagener soon could sign himself Clerk of Fairfax; Wagener affixed his seal where he had his flocks and herds—in Prince William. Such were the conveniences and amenities of office-holding.[68] The limits of Peter Wagener's influence were not those of Clerk and of planter, or even these plus the post of vestryman to which he was later elected;

[66] To be exact, according to a check of the *L.O. Records*, 29,349 acres. Some patents may have been overlooked. In the words of Fairfax Harrison (*Landmarks*, 266), Cocke and George Eskridge were "ubiquitous land speculators." Twelve years after George rode by Belmont Bay, he was to write in his diary: "I was informed that Col. Cocke was disgusted at my house, and left because he see an old Negroe there resembling his own image." (1 *Diaries*, 112). For this short title see the bibliographical note, 84, p. 210, *infra*.

[67] Confusion regarding her has arisen because she was the daughter of one John Robinson, Councillor, and the sister of another John Robinson, Speaker and Treasurer. See *Landmarks*, 433, 16 V 217, 33 V 56 n, 39, and Slaughter, *History of Truro Parish*, 110.

[68] Slaughter, in *History of Truro Parish*, 110; *Landmarks*, 394.

he was a physician as well, and before many years was to prove himself the Romulus of a new if somewhat unprosperous town.[69]

South of the Occoquan, where George had traveled often, though he did not now enter, was the estate of Leesylvania which looked toward the Potomac and also toward the smooth waters of Neabsco Creek. The frequent transfers of Leesylvania were an epitome of what short lives and changing interests could do to confuse land titles. The patent dated from 1658, but the property had passed from Corbins to Lees, from Lees to Wrights, to Graysons and, seven years before George's journey, back to the Lees again. In their hands it was to remain for two generations and part of a third. There, eight years after Washington's first journey to the Valley, was born a handsome boy who was christened Henry Lee but was called Harry.[70]

Across Neabsco and between that stream and Powell's Creek was Rippon Lodge, the home of Richard Blackburn, who, like Wagener of the Occoquan, was a native of the British Isles. Mrs. Blackburn was the widow of Henry Ashton of Westmoreland, and had been born Mary Watts, reputedly a kinswoman of a dissenting clergyman, Isaac Watts, whose hymns and philosophical works, notably *The Improvement of the Mind,* were creating talk among the learned and the pious. Blackburn was as industrious in business as his wife's cousin was in hymnology. An architect and builder, a planter and Burgess, Richard Blackburn was prospering. George and George William subsequently were to have pleasant relations with the versatile gentleman, who was one of the closest friends of Col. William Fairfax.[71]

Farther to the South was the pleasant course of Powell's Creek and, beyond it, the placid Quantico. On that stream another tide than that of the Potomac was rising. Scotch merchants were coming there, were establishing themselves to buy the tobacco of the region, and were talking even of a charter for a new town there. Valentine Peyton had blocked the project and had maintained that if any town was to be built in Prince William, it must be on Occoquan, where his interests lay. Thereupon, the merchants on the Quantico and those who sought to build a town at Belhaven had made common cause. In these plans

[69] Colchester, for which see *supra,* p. 160 and *Landmarks,* 387. Peter Wagener's inventory of Sept. 19, 1774, to a total of £1215 will be found in *Fairfax Records,* C, 249. It is a disappointing list of personal effects to have belonged to so interesting a man.

[70] The line of descent is traced in *Lee of Virginia,* 291 ff. Ownership of the property is outlined in *Prince William Guide,* 84.

[71] 4 *W* (1) p. 266; *Prince William Guide,* 84.

for the town that subsequently was to become Dumfries,[72] one guiding hand was that of Benjamin Grayson, Scotch-born and Glasgow-bred, who had all the avidity of John Mercer or Catesby Cocke in land speculation and a fair measure of success. A possession of Grayson's that was to prove of greater importance to the Colony than all his lands was a twelve-year-old son, William, a lad of most uncommon promise.[73] William's mother had been born Susanah Monroe, of the family that had lived near George's birthplace on Pope's Creek.[74]

Of these and other friends, George had no occasion to speak to his companion. Instead of riding past plantations that were taking on something of the appearance of established estates, they turned to the Northwest, at the Occoquan, and traveled through a country which, in part, was one stage only in development from the primal wilderness.[75] Farms were few and trails were dim. Twenty miles the young men had to journey in woodland and new ground, by way of the recently established second Court House of Prince William County;[76] and forty miles they had covered for the day when, at last, they drew rein at the ordinary of George Neville, located about two-thirds of the way to Ashby's Bent on the trail from Fredericksburg.[77]

Neville was not a host of the traditional type to come arunning at a call from the village Falstaff. Already a landowner of station, Neville was a speculator and planter who kept the best of such society as existed at so great a distance from Williamsburg. He had both the disposition and the ability to contend with the crudities of life near the frontier

[72] See *supra*, p. 160.

[73] It is not absolutely certain that William Grayson was born in 1736, though that seems the most probable year.

[74] She was an aunt of James Monroe, fifth President.

[75] As Fairfax Harrison pointed out in *Landmarks*, 471, the natural route for the two men to take would be that directly to Vestal's Gap; but for reasons not plain, they decided to go via Neville's Ordinary. The surmise of Mr. Harrison was that George William Fairfax may have chosen this route because, as a newly-elected Burgess from Frederick, he may have wished to see what improvements had been made and might be made to the trail from Fredericksburg to the Valley. If Neville's Ordinary was the objective, then the best route of travel by road would have been southward to Quantico and then westward to the trail from Fredericksburg to Ashby's Gâp. It is plain that this was not the way the two followed, because Washington stated specifically that the day's journey was forty miles. This is the distance of no convenient route except that southward to the Occoquan, then up that river and on, Northwest, to the ordinary.

[76] On the basis of researches made by George C. Round, and reported in the *Manassas* (Va.) *Journal* of May 19, 1911, Fairfax Harrison in *Landmarks*, 316, accepted the view that the second Court House was on the farm known as Ashmore, North and East of the village of Orlando. That village is in the present County of Prince William and is on Route 508, two and a half miles South of Brentsville. "In 1748, this second Court House," Harrison wrote, "stood in the forks of the Dumfries road and so was accessible not only from tidewater but from all parts of the inhabited back country."

[77] According to Green's *Word-Book*, bent "in the old land surveys," was a mountain pass or, as other Virginians of that generation called it, a gap.

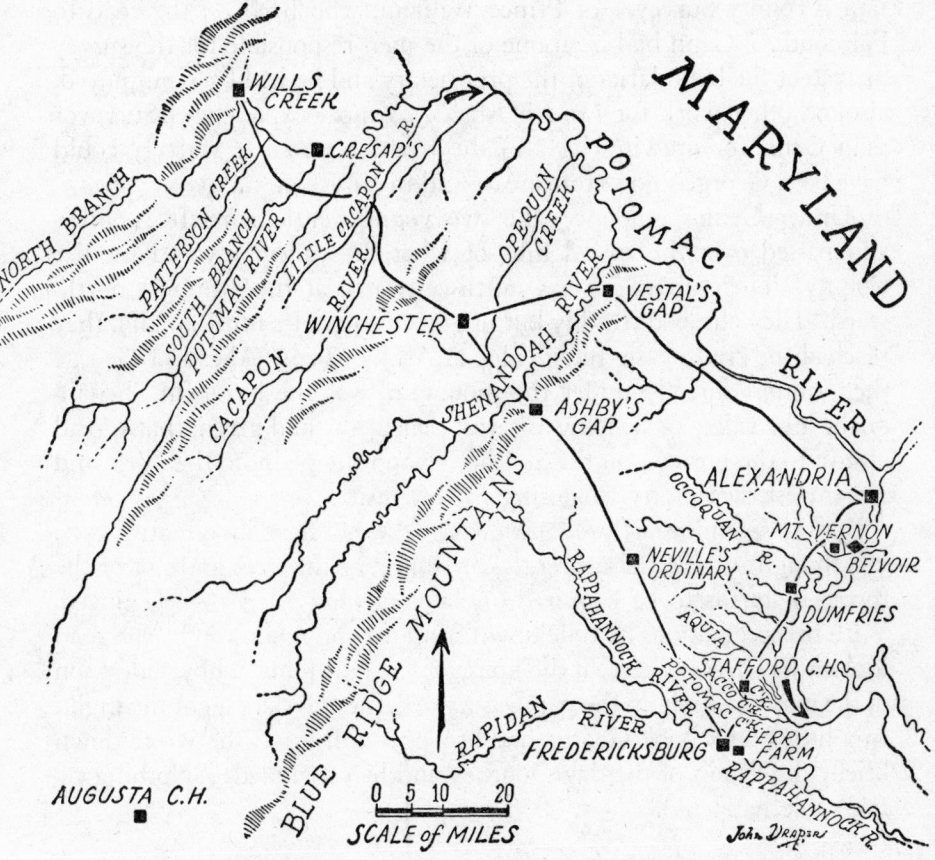

EARLY ROUTES TO WINCHESTER AND WILLS CREEK

When Washington and George William Fairfax made their journey to the Shenandoah Valley in 1748, the "road" from Fredericksburg by way of Neville's Ordinary and Ashby's Gap was a mere trail. Beyond Winchester the route to Wills Creek was changed frequently as early roads were washed out or "short cuts" were discovered. The line drawn Northwest of Winchester is, consequently, no more than an approximation of the paths and river banks along which Washington traveled prior to 1755.

and to shape them to the semblance, even to the substance, of civilization.[78] The ordinary, if then under license,[79] was operated as much for the convenience of travelers as for the profit of the host. It was a place of sufficient comfort to satisfy the young gentlemen from Fairfax, who were accustomed to good beds and to clean sheets.

The next morning, Mch. 12, 1748, up rode James Genn, the commis-

[78] Cf. *Landmarks*, 471, 491, Toner's ed. of *Washington's Journal of 1748*, p. 19. The site was near the present village of Auburn; the building itself stood until 1927. Neville's Ordinary sometimes has been confused with West's, for which see *infra*, p. 223.

[79] The first recorded license to Neville in the present Fauquier County bears date of 1759.

sioned county Surveyor of Prince William, who lived on the road to Falmouth.[80] Genn had been one of the men responsible for the survey in 1746 of the boundaries of the proprietary and he had been employed, also, on other work for Lord Fairfax.[81] A more experienced Surveyor than Genn for drawing lines in the frontier woods it scarcely could have been George's good fortune to find in Virginia.

Under Genn's guidance, the two young gentlemen left Neville's and passed over the round hills of what subsequently was Fauquier County. Their direction was northwestward, at times almost northward. They climbed steadily but not on steep grades until, finally, they reached the crest of the Blue Ridge at Ashby's Bent. Ahead of George then, almost directly under the mountain, was the beautiful Shenandoah,[82] the valley of which was a vast plain, gray and green, that spread almost to the horizon on the South. Beyond the plain, to the West and Northwest, were lofty, enclosing mountains.[83]

For the splendor of this scene, George did not have imaginative eyes. His thought was of the nearer, lesser things, of the trees and not of the forest, of farms to be acquired and not of landscapes to be enjoyed. With his companions he rode down from the mountain top by the road to Ashby's Ferry. There, at the house of Captain John Ashby, eldest son of the man after whom the gap was named, the travelers spent the night. In a little blank book George had brought with him,[84] he wrote down briefly the details of the day's journey and he concluded: "Nothing remarkable happen'd." [85]

[80] Near the present Catletts, *Landmarks*, 507.

[81] Toner ed., *op. cit.*, 21; *Landmarks*, 507.

[82] Then usually spelled Shenando.

[83] The best description of approximately the same period is that of Rev. Andrew Burnaby, who crossed in the same direction as George, from East to West, at the end of May, 1760. He found the mountain "completely covered with chamædaphnes" (leather-leaf).

[84] For events from Mch. 11, to Apr. 13, 1748, the prime source is the first of Washington's journals, which he styled "A Journal of my Journey over the Mountains began Fryday the 11th of March 1747/8." The MS of this is in the Library of Congress. In a letter of May 7, 1946, Dr. St. George L. Sioussat described the journal as originally a parchment-bound volume of forty-two leaves, eighty-four pages, 6" x 3¾", with the watermark Pro Patria. The journal covers twenty-five pages. Part of the book was used "in reverse" for a variety of survey notes, copies of letters and miscellaneous memoranda. Dr. Sioussat called attention to the fact that Jared Sparks's account of the discovery of the journal appears in H. B. Adams, *Life and Writings of Jared Sparks*, v. 2, p. 39–40. Cf. *ibid.*, 48, 237. Dr. J. M. Toner's edition of this journal (1892) is the fullest and is cited several times in this chapter for certain of the editor's notes and for items omitted by others; but as the inclusive edition of the *Diaries of George Washington*, edited by John C. Fitzpatrick (4 vols., 1925) is used throughout the present work, reference to the journal, under the short title *Diaries*, is to Fitzpatrick's edition. To avoid confusion, it may be noted again that Fitzpatrick's *Writings of Washington* are cited throughout this work as *G.W.*

[85] 1 *Diaries* 4. Apparently some of the entries in this diary were written at night and some the next morning.

Many things "remarkable" had "happened" previously in that region of rolling green field and abounding wild life,[86] and most of these developments had occurred during George's own lifetime by way of the trail that ran close to the farms on which he had played in childhood. The successive western thrusts of settlement had followed the Potomac and Rappahannock and had not spread far from the immediate valleys of those rivers. When Thomas Lee had staked off as his own the Virginia shore of the Potomac opposite the Great Falls, he had been dreaming of a future city and not of a succession of large plantations. After him came Robert Carter, new dreams and new ventures.

Then, in the year of Carter's death and George's birth, another speculator, William Beverley, saw opportunity of patenting a vast tract of valley land, which he hoped to resell to Pennsylvania farmers. They would be willing, Beverley heard, to pay £6 or £7 per 100 acres. This was a price exceedingly profitable to a Virginia patentee but it was less than already was demanded for good land in Pennsylvania.[87] Beverley and several associates procured in 1734 a grant of some 15,000 acres in the "little fork of the Rappahannock, East of the mountains." In September 1736, Beverley and two other public men of influence promised to pay quit rents on 118,000 acres beyond the mountains,[88] but by that year the Governor had allotted land in the same region to settlers from New York, New Jersey, Pennsylvania, Germany and Switzerland.[89] For some time, also, controversy over the Treaty of Albany and over the boundary of the Fairfax proprietary resulted in various suspensions of land grants in the Valley. Settlers temporarily were as reluctant to buy as Fairfax was to release acreage. One of the early patentees, Jacob Stover, found so much difficulty in inducing families to come to his tract that he was alleged to have given human names to all his domestic animals and to have represented them as "heads of families" within the terms of his grant.[90]

---

[86] For a brief description of its fauna, see Kegley, *Virginia Frontier*, 34.

[87] 1 *C* 217.

[88] 13 *V* 360. For the grant of 1734, see 13 *L.O. Records*, 316–17, and 15 *ibid.*, 395. The patent of 1736 is in 18 *ibid.*, 154. Beverley is said to have acquired subsequently the rights of his partners.

[89] The most succinct and accurate account of this settlement is that of Charles E. Kemper in 30 *V* 172 ff. For correction of unfortunate typographical errors in that article, see *ibid.*, 291–92.

[90] Kercheval, *History of the Valley of Virginia* (cited hereafter as *Kercheval*) p. 49. The much-disputed grants to Jacob Stover were as follows: Dec. 15, 1733, 5000 acres as headrights in Spotsylvania, beyond the mountains (15 *L.O. Records*, 127); Dec. 15, 1733, 5000 acres similarly as headrights in the same region (*ibid.*, 129); Dec. 13, 1738, four grants to a total of 2370 acres (18 *ibid.*, 145, 146, 147, 148).

With an eye to procuring the land for himself, William Beverley protested in 1733 the title of farms sold to settlers by Stover, who failed in his enterprise.[91] Lord Fairfax, in turn, denied the validity of a grant Jost Hite had acquired from Isaac and John van Meter, who had received it from Governor Gooch.[92] In spite of all this, in the face of the continuing threat of Indians raids, and in defiance of occasional floods and bad seasons, the settlement had progressed. By 1734, Jost Hite was said to have established fifty-four families in the Valley.[93] Four years later, 1738, Frederick County was established in the wide section that drains into the Potomac West of the Blue Ridge. In 1742, an effort was made to organize militia.[94] By November, 1743, the County Court was measuring out frontier justice [95] to aggrieved persons who were pleased to bring their complaints before their peers of a grand jury. A miller was presented for exacting unlawful toll; an informer alleged that Jonathan Curtis had plowed on Sunday, whereupon Curtis brought his assailant into court on the charge of swearing two oaths and of getting drunk besides.[96] Business had developed as justice had established itself. A peddler was licensed in 1744; an ordinary was opened the same year; [97] the first road was laid off; [98] iron works were promised; [99] a settlement called Frederick Town was beginning to approach the dignity of a village, even if it did not yet justify the word "town." These developments had deepened the interest of land speculators who resided in the older parts of the Colony. George William Fairfax had begun to dabble in Shenandoah lands; so had Lawrence Washington.[100]

Lawrence's younger brother, George, having a first view of the Valley, perceived quickly why the country was exciting gamblers and attracting settlers. About four miles South of Ashby's Ferry, beyond the left or western bank of the Shenandoah was the tract of some

[91] 1 C 219.

[92] See infra, p. 220 and Kercheval, 154. A singularly fanciful interpretation of the subsequent Fairfax-Hite suit will be found in Conway's Barons, 223.

[93] 30 V 175. For the location of their property, South of the present city of Winchester, see Kercheval, 49.

[94] 1 C 235, one of the most remarkable examples of strange misspelling to be found in the Virginia archives; 5 H 78; Norris, History of the Lower Shenandoah Valley (cited hereafter as Norris), p. 70.

[95] Norris, 19.

[96] Ibid., 75.

[97] Ibid., 73, 76.

[98] Ibid., 73.

[99] Ibid., 81. The frequent citation of Norris indicates the richness of the details he gave of life on the Virginia frontier.

[100] Ibid., 81.

thousands of acres that Lord Fairfax had established as a "quarter" the previous year.[101] This land, which became known as Greenway Court, George William Fairfax and George Washington set out to examine on Sunday, the 13th of March. The country fascinated the boy. He saw sugar trees of the sort about which he perhaps had heard his elders speak when they mentioned the McCartys,[102] and he crossed fields the fertility of which did not escape him. Although the view of the Valley from Ashby's Gap had occupied him, apparently, for a few minutes only, he devoted hours to examining the trees and the soil of Fairfax's new "quarter." After he got back to Captain Ashby's he wrote in his journal, with the enthusiasm of a planter and land speculator: "We went through most beautiful groves of sugar trees and spent the best part of the day in admiring the trees and the richness of the land." [103] It was a domain of promise and of profit. George could see that even before the "Jacob's staff" was set.

The first surveying of the expedition was not to be at Greenway Court but about twenty miles northward, down the Shenandoah, on tracts known as Cates Marsh and Long Marsh. For men working there, the vicinity of Frederick Town, subsequently Winchester, was better suited as headquarters than was Ashby's Ferry. On Monday morning, March 14, the baggage of the surveying party was sent to the house of Jost Hite near Frederick Town; Genn, Fairfax and George proceeded on their own mounts along the river bank where early settlers had cleared some of the finest land and had planted it in grain, in hemp and in tobacco. George observed and admired. The ground, he told himself, was like that of Greenway Court, exceeding rich and fertile.[104]

For the greater part of a ride of sixteen miles, the surveyors found the scene repeated and then, before nightfall, they reached the home

---

[101] It is to be regretted that this vagueness has to be employed in describing Greenway Court, so named after the manor purchased in Kent, England, by Sir Thomas Culpeper the elder. The area of Fairfax's Leeds Manor is known—149,387 acres (*L. O. Records,* N.N., E., 34)—but that manor ended on the east bank of the Shenandoah. The Great Falls Manor contained 72,588 acres (*ibid.,* p. 38). By these standards, Greenway Court might have been vast. On May 21, 1752 (*ibid.,* Book H, 179), Fairfax transferred to his nephew, Thomas Bryan Martin, 188 acres of unclaimed land on the Opequon and 8840 acres adjoining. The Proprietor directed that all this be called the Manor of Greenway Court, but this does not mean, necessarily, that the tract given Martin constituted the whole of Greenway Court. Cf. 34 V 37–38.

[102] See *supra,* p. 50.

[103] 1 *Diaries,* 4. In this and in all subsequent quotations, "ye" has been written "the" and the capitalization and punctuation employed by Washington have been conformed to modern usage, except where the language and form of Washington's sentences leave any doubt of the meaning he sought to convey. In all such instances, the quotation is verbatim. The reasons for this editorial treatment are given in the Introduction.

[104] See his entry of March 14 in his journal, 1 *Diaries,* 5.

of Isaac Pennington, where they lodged. By the 15th, Genn probably
had finished recruiting his chainmen and other assistants and had prepared to run a line around part of Cates and Long Marshes. The party
set out eagerly but soon encountered a rain, which increased so much
in severity that the surveyors had to seek shelter. They waited and
chafed and, when the sun finally came out again about 1 o'clock, they
decided to resume their work. Much ground was covered before darkness sent the entire party back to Pennington's.

Their host had made a point, the previous night, of giving the
surveyors his best beds; but now after supper, perhaps because the
company was larger, Pennington had to place all or most of his guests
in one main chamber, next which there was a vacant closet or storeroom.[105]

George, being inexperienced, did not make an examination of the
beds in this closet. His weariness led him to disrobe as if he were at
home,[106] and then to seek rest. He was horrified, when he went to
the sleeping quarters, to find that his "bed" was matted straw with
nothing over it except one threadbare blanket. Not to embarrass his
host or to show how little he had expected such a pallet, George lay
down. He soon discovered that blanket and bed were an independent
establishment of vermin so numerous that they seemed to weigh as
much as the blanket itself.

The person who had brought light into the room lingered unduly,
George thought, and to his great discomfort. When the light at last
was carried out, George jumped up, felt his way back into the main
room, put on his clothes and lay down, fully clad, on the floor with the
other members of the party.[107] A most uncomfortable night it was.
He would not have slept at all, he told himself, had he not been so
weary. The only thing worse than sleeping on the floor would have

[105] Washington's failure to write down any complaint about his bed on the night of March
14 makes it fairly certain that he had one, but the reason he was not assigned a like place
on the evening of the 15th is conjectural. The explanation given in the text seems justified by
the fact that in a survey of the next day, two chainmen, a marker and a pilot are mentioned
(1 *Diaries*, 5 n). These men increased the party to seven. In an allotment of beds, George
would not have ranked higher than third, if that high. He probably was the youngest member
of the party but was rated a "gentleman." No information concerning the sleeping space is
available. Part of the room may have been cut off for that purpose, or a lean-to may have
adjoined.

[106] His own words were that he "strip[p]ed very orderly."

[107] In his detailed account of this episode (1 *Diaries*, 5), George made no mention of any
laughter and jesting by his companions. Perhaps, as a "young gentleman" he was spared, but
in such matters, the ways of the frontier were rough and rude. A practical joke on a stranger
was a source of pride and loud guffawing and was described endlessly. It was a poor prank
indeed that was not talked about for weeks and remembered for years.

been lying on that wretched straw! He resolved that when he could not sleep decently indoors, he would spend the night in the open air before a fire [108] or in the tent that had been provided.

In this resolution and with such rest as he had won, George observed next day a survey of certain lands that his friend George William Fairfax had patented in the two "marshes" where the party was working. It was a commonplace survey and it may have made no impression on Washington; but like many a similar incident that was to come under George's eye, it was wholly typical of what the enterprising young men of the Colony were doing: they were moving ahead of actual settlement and were buying up some of the best of the lands. When George could, he would, too. That was so natural a way of making money that he probably never became conscious of reaching any formal decision to share in current land speculation. It was of course the thing to do.

The surveys on Cates Marsh and on Long Marsh were completed by 1 o'clock, Wednesday, the 16th of March. Next ahead of the party, then, was the task of reaching by the easiest practicable route the upper waters of the South Branch of the Potomac, where a large and almost inaccessible tract was to be divided into small parcels. Had the ride been directly from Frederick Town across the mountains to the designated part of South Branch, the distance would not have been more than forty miles; but that would have involved a battle with roadless mountains, through muddy bottoms and across unbridged, swollen streams. A longer, roundabout journey was so much easier on men and on mounts that it was selected; but before a beginning was made, the travellers resolved to enjoy a last touch of the fringe of civilization at Frederick Town. Thither the whole party rode on the afternoon of the 16th and there, happily, they received the luggage that had been sent to Jost Hite's.

After relentless chase of the vermin accumulated at Pennington's, the surveyors had a saunter through a village which, though beautifully situated, had not acquired either the size or the architectural interest to wear out the muscles and to excite the eyes of the newcomers. Back, then, went the visitors to their lodgings, where they had left orders for food and drink. These were not stinted. Wine and rum punch were provided in plenty, and a dinner the fastidious young gentlemen pronounced good. They were comfortable in stomach and in spirit

[108] 1 *Diaries,* 5.

when they sought sleep. George's bed was of feathers; his sheets were clean. This homelike luxury he set down in his journal as "a very agreeable regale." [109]

The start for the South Branch of the Potomac was delayed by rain the morning of the 17th, but by 10 o'clock, George and his companions got on the road [110] and, at the day's end, reached the residence of Andrew Campbell, about 25 miles from the town. "Nothing remarkable this day or night," George entered in his journal, and then, remembering his unhappy hours at Pennington's, he added, "but that we had a tolerable good bed [to] lay on." [111]

As the trails ran, the ride the next day to the Potomac was thirty-five miles and was disappointing besides. Opposite Thomas Barwick's farm, which was on the Potomac Northwest of the mouth of the Shenandoah, [112] the water was six feet above normal and was rising. As Surveyor Genn planned to cross the river and to proceed along a trail on the Maryland side, he was balked. Residents said the stream was carrying down the melted snows from the Allegheny Mountains. It would not be fordable for several days, a situation that was irritating but not unusual. That same year, a Moravian missionary, Matthias Gottschalk, was to warn the mother church at Bethlehem, Pennsylvania, concerning travel along the streams of the Potomac Valley. Said he: "The summer is the best time to visit these people, for the river is then low and can easily be forded . . . Spring and fall are not so suitable." [113]

Whether ignorant of this in advance of the expedition or disdainful of flood waters, the surveyors had to go back to Frederick Town and wait, or stay impatiently where they were, or find some occupation of their time till the flooded Potomac fell. Their decision was to visit the Warm Springs about twenty-five miles upstream from Barwick's. [114] It was large labor to small end. The place made little impression on George, who found much more of interest in the prospect of camping for the night in the tent the party carried with it. This experience, too,

109 1 *Diaries,* 6.
110 Little is known concerning the course of the early trails in Frederick. For later roads, see *Norris,* 89, and Thomas K. Cartmell, *Shenandoah Pioneers,* 50–52.
111 1 *Diaries,* 6.
112 That is to say, Northwest of the present Harpers Ferry. To judge from the distances gives in George's journal, Barwick's was not far from Falling Waters.
113 11 *V* 227.
114 These later were called Berkeley Springs and are in the present Morgan County, West Virginia. See *supra,* p. 113 and *infra,* p. 242.

was a disappointment. George had to write again that "nothing remarkable happen'd." [115]

By the afternoon of the third day on the Potomac, Sunday, March
20, the surveyors reasoned they could swim their horses across the
Potomac, could return to the Virginia side and, the next day, could
carry their belongings to the Maryland shore in a canoe. It was a bit
reckless, perhaps, but it was successful.[116] Monday, the 21st of March,
found the surveyors again on their horses and plodding westward
along the Potomac trail in Maryland. In continuous rain, the riders
pushed their mounts forward over what George pronounced the "worst
road ever trod by man or beast." [117] A contemporary was more specific.
"The road," said Brother Gottschalk, "is a single narrow path, frequently hardly recognizable, partly because traveling is not very
frequent there, and partly because the path is blocked with trees and
overgrown with grass and weeds." [118] With or without a guide, the
surveyors escaped accident, avoided the cowpaths that led from the
trail [119] and came at last to the well-stocked trading post and the size-
able residence—half home, half fort—of Thomas Cresap,[120] a renowned frontiersman whom George was to know better in days that
lay ahead.

There was shelter at Cresap's and a measure of comfort that kept
George from putting any complaint in his journal about his bed for
the night.[121] The boy, in fact, was beginning to adapt himself to life
on the frontier. He may have been worn and he certainly was vexed
at the end of the long ride to Cresap's, but after that first admission
of weariness the night he fought vermin at Pennington's, he had not
written a line about tired legs or sleeplessness. His trouble at Cresap's
was the one that had plagued him and his companions from the third
day of their arrival beyond the Blue Ridge: the rain kept pouring
down.

All day Tuesday it fell; Wednesday morning it still mocked the

---

[115] 1 *Diaries*, 6.

[116] The horses were placed for the night on the land of Charles Polk, who lived in the
vicinity of the later Williamsport, and kept what Brother Gottschalk called "a very disorderly
house" (12 *V* 65, 79n).

[117] 1 *Diaries*, 7.

[118] 12 *V* 79.

[119] *Ibid.*

[120] 1 *Diaries*, 7.

[121] Kenneth P. Bailey, *Thomas Cresap, Maryland Frontiersman*, 65; Winthrop Sargent, *The
History of an Expedition against Fort DuQuesne*, cited hereafter as *Sargent*, p. 372-73.

young gentlemen from Fairfax. After noon, the downfall ended and the skies cleared; but the Potomac still was too high and the road too wet for Genn to think of riding farther up the river bank to the point where he intended to recross to the Virginia side. There was the prospect of continued boredom when, to the surprise of all and to the particular delight of George, thirty Indians appeared from nowhere. They were a war party, they told their friend Cresap, but they were somewhat chagrined to own that their expedition had been unprofitable. One scalp was all they had to show for their hardships and their journey.

George probably never before had seen so many savages together and he certainly had never encountered a war party that had a contingent of young braves. He watched them with charmed eyes. Presently, from the store of liquor the surveyors carried with them, a friendly offering was tendered the redmen. It raised their spirits and stirred them to make preparations for a dance. Some of them borrowed one of Cresap's pots and half filled it with water. Then they stretched a deer skin over it to make a drum. Another savage brought out a dry gourd to which was attached a part of a horse's tail. In this gourd were shot enough to yield a rattle. Other natives, all the while, were clearing a piece of ground and were fetching wood. Damp as was the day, they soon had a roaring fire around which they seated themselves in a circle. One of their leaders then launched into a speech unintelligible in every grunt but manifestly done in the best manner of sylvan eloquence. George gathered from gestures and responses that the orator was describing to his tribesmen how they should perform the dance.

As to all speeches, even the longest and dullest, there was an end at last. No sooner had the speaker emitted his liberating grunt than a lithe savage jumped into the circle as if he still were dazed with sleep. Whether that was part of the ceremony or a pantomime of the somnolent effect of the speech, George could not determine. The comedy of it was entrancing. Other Indians joined the first performer; the drummer and the man with the rattle began their accompaniment of the dance. George watched closely and later he wrote carefully in his journal a brief account of the whole occurrence.[122] It would be something to tell the household at Mount Vernon and the friends in

---

[122] 1 *Diaries*, 7.

Chotank, and, of course, if it was to be described at all, it must be recorded accurately. That already was part of George's code.

So interested was George in the redskins that he spent the whole of Thursday, March 24, with them. He may have stayed so long and may have received so many impressions that he did not attempt to commit them to paper. The next day, Friday the 25th, the current of the river West of the mouth of the South Branch did not seem to be swift enough to endanger a horse that undertook to swim to the Virginia shore. The men, it appeared, could get across in a canoe. Accordingly the party left Cresap's and rode upstream to a point opposite Patterson Creek, which empties into the Potomac seven miles above the mouth of the South Branch. Everything went well there. The crossing was made without incident. On the south bank, the animals were saddled and reloaded; the caravan proceeded up Patterson Creek. This was a march to save a march, because the leaders reasoned that if they ascended the creek and then cut eastward, they would make better time than if they had proceeded up the bank of the South Branch. To reach Patterson Creek, via Maryland, had been Genn's aim from the first.[123] Nightfall found him and his party at the farm of Abram Johnston, fifteen miles up the creek. Camp was made there, but the prospect of sleeping out of doors under canvas no longer excited George. He had been vindicated in his decision to choose the open air every time there was danger of a second such night as the one at Pennington's.[124]

Another ride up Patterson Creek on the 26th brought the surveyors to the settlement of Solomon Hedges. That worthy was one of the Justices of the Peace for Frederick County and was *in propria persona* a symbol of the westward extension of His Majesty's rule, but, as it chanced, Hedges was not equipped on the frontier for the elaborate entertainment of guests. He could provide food and a table on which to eat it; for shelter, the gentlemen would have to use their tent or, if they preferred, sleep under the stars and their blankets. This did not seem altogether a bad arrangement. Camp was prepared; Squire Hedges's servants cooked the meal and put it on platters. When George answered the summons and took his place at table, he was astonished to observe that the board was without a cloth and that no table-knives

[123] See *supra*, p. 215.
[124] I *Diaries*, 5, 7–8.

were provided. He did not know that this was customary on the
frontier and he counted it fortunate that every member of the party had
an individual jackknife.[125]

The 27th was the Sabbath. Religious service was held and no work
was done, but no compunctions prevented a day's journey. Guided
and escorted by the respected Justice Hedges, the men left the creek,
turned East and reached the long-sought middle stretches of the South
Branch of the Potomac at the cabins of Henry van Meter.[126] Of this
man's remarkable father, Isaac, and of his uncle John, apparently
George had heard little. Had young Washington known their history,
he might have been as interested in them as he had been in the Indians
at Cresap's. John van Meter, Indian trader of New York, had come
South with a war party of savages about 1725 and barely had escaped
with his life when they were defeated in battle on the upper
Potomac; [127] but what he had seen of the richness of the land prompted
him to advise his sons to migrate there. Two of these younger men,
Isaac and John, took his counsel to the extent, at least, of making an
early visit to the Colony. On their representation of a purpose to bring
settlers to the western frontier, they received from Governor Gooch
and the Council in 1730 grants of 40,000 acres,[128] which they soon transferred to Jost Hite. In 1736 or 1737, Isaac and perhaps John moved
from New Jersey and, in 1744, settled on the South Branch. There
John died in 1745, but Isaac lived on with a patriarchal family. Henry
van Meter was one of Isaac's sons and consequently was of the third
generation of van Meters on the Virginia frontier.[129]

At Henry van Meter's, the surveyors were about thirty miles from
the district where, as a preliminary, they were to undertake some
surveys for James Rutledge. The business of Monday, March 28, was
that of going up the South Branch to Rutledge's property. On the
29th, eighteen days after the start from Belvoir, the first tract of
Rutledge's was surveyed. Then, on the 30th, the principal subdivision
was taken in hand near the Stump settlement. The next day, for the
first time on the expedition, George himself ran the lines of one of
these surveys.[130]

125 1 *Diaries*, 8.   126 *Ibid.*
127 *Kercheval*, 46.   128 13 *V* 115 ff.
129 *W. Va. Hist. Mag.*, v. 2, no. 2, p. 10 ff; v. 3, p. 69; v. 4, p. 227–28. Some conflict of
evidence exists regarding the movement of certain of the van Meters to New Jersey, and the
date of the coming of the second John van Meter to Virginia is in doubt; but the earlier confusion of the first with the second John van Meter has been removed by the studies here cited.
130 1 *Diaries*, 9.

Interesting experiences crowded the next week. George found the wild turkeys of the region a difficult target for his rifle; he had the excitement of a fire in the straw where he and his companions were asleep; the tent was blown down twice; on the 3rd some of the German settlers came to visit the camp. By Monday, April 4, word had passed along the frontier of the strange performances of the surveyors. Work was suspended, farms were deserted. In George's own words, the party was followed through the woods "by a great company of people, men, women and children." Young Washington observed them with amazement. Never among white men had he seen such strange beings. Their lack of acquaintance with English seemed to him positively perverse. Said he: "I really think they seemed to be as ignorant a set of people as the Indians. They would never speak English but, when spoken to, they speak all Dutch." [131]

Almost daily after that, George had much the same company of voluntary observers who trooped through the woods and made endless, unintelligible comment on the work of the surveyors. George's own duties were not extensive or difficult. Most of the time he merely made the field notes of lines and boundaries, and in this he found his work much simplified by his knowledge of the forest trees around him. Often a patent would mention as a boundary a "large hickory and a red oak" [132] or "two red buds and a black walnut" [133] or "two locusts" [134] or almost any other species of the abounding forest. George knew them all, apparently, and had no difficulty in identifying the markers.

George William Fairfax on the 4th of April left the party temporarily, perhaps to arrange for new supplies. As his own funds did not quite suffice for his mission, whatever its nature, he borrowed five shillings from his young companion. George duly jotted down the loan, and he put it into his account book after he returned home, though he made a mistake of one day in recording the date. [135] At the moment, there on the frontier, the absence of Fairfax deprived George of most of the fun of the expedition. Apparently, Genn and his assistants were not companionable. Nor was the weather of a sort to comfort young Washington. The air was so heavy on the evening of the 5th of April that all hands had to leave the smoke-filled tent; on the 6th the party

---

[131] 1 *Diaries*, 9–10.
[132] Washington's *MS Journal*, entry of Mch. 15, 1748, partly omitted from 1 *Diaries*, 5.
[133] Ibid., *MS Journal*, April 4.
[134] Ibid., *MS Journal*, April 6.
[135] *MS Account Book*, A, 3.

WASHINGTON'S NEXT-DOOR NEIGHBOR

George William Fairfax was the most favored young man of the neighborhood when George Washington began his long and frequent visits to his one-time home Epsewasson, which his brother Lawrence had named Mount Vernon.

Fairfax was the son of the owner of Belvoir, the nearest large estate on the Potomac River, and after 1748 was the husband of Sally Cary, whom Washington found altogether the most attractive young woman he had met.

Before that marriage, when George William Fairfax went to the Shenandoah Valley to see how surveyors worked in the field, George Washington accompanied him. At that time, George William, who was by seven years the older of the two, appeared in Washington's journal as "Mr. Fairfax"—an impressive person, already a member of the County Court and of the House of Burgesses.

Relations were reversed at the end of another decade: Washington was by far the more conspicuous then. It made no difference in relations which had become close, neighborly, and confidential. The picture of Fairfax on the opposite page was painted by an unidentified artist after he returned permanently to England in 1773. It shows a gentleman who might have ended abruptly the career of Washington had he not been satisfied that his young neighbor's regard for his wife did not even approach the scandalous.

To: Mr Washington

Whereas Thomas Byrne, Son of Geor[ge]
of St William County

Hath informed That There are About Four
hundred... Acres of Waste & ungranted Land in
Augusta County joyning on Miller including part of a Mead[ow]
Lying on the upper side of sd Miller & belonging to [the] Manner[?]
And Desiring A Warrant To Survey the same
in Order to Obtain A Deed being Ready to pay the
Composition and Office Charges ————

These Are Therefore To Empower you The said
Washington To Survey The said Waste Land
for The said   Provided this be the fir[st]
Warrant hath issued for the Same And you
are to Make True Just & accurate Survey
Thereof Describing The courses & Distances
Wd Pole also The Buttings & boundings
Of The Several Persons Land Adioyning &
Where you cannot Joyn on any Known Lin[e]
You Are To Make the Breadth of The Tract To
Bear at least the proportion of one third [part]
Of the Lengthe as the Law of Virginia Direc[ts]
You are Also To insert the Name of the
Pilot & Chain Carriers Made use of & Empl[oyed]
A Plat Of which said Survey with this
Warrant you are to Give into This Office
Any Time Before the twenty fifth Day of
March ——— Next Ensuing Given
under my hand & Seal of the Proprie[tors]
Office this Eighte Day Dec in The twenty 3[d]
Year of His Majesty King George the
Second Reign ——

EARLY INSTRUCTIONS TO SURVEYOR WASHINGTON

Young Mr. Washington, not yet eighteen years of age, appears to have been ready when Thomas Byrne procured from William Fairfax, the Proprietor's agent, a warrant for the survey of about 400 acres of land in Augusta County, Virginia. George, in fact, may have prepared in advance a manuscript "form" that could be filled in quickly when presented at the Proprietor's Land Office. The whole of the document, decorative eagle included, appears to be in Washington's youthful handwriting. Some of the spelling—"whareas" and "King George the Second Rain"—is neither better nor worse than that of many contemporaries.

The year of the warrant, 1749, was one of much activity in the extension of settlement in the Shenandoah Valley which the Six Nations had agreed in the Treaty of Lancaster, July, 1744, they would not enter. Young Washington that year had become a commissioned County Surveyor, with Culpeper County as his special charge, though he could survey anywhere he was employed in Virginia.

This early example of a warrant for a survey is after an original in the Huntington Library, San Marino, Calif., and is reproduced by permission.

finished its work at Stump's and started back to Henry van Meter's, only to be caught in so violent a rain that refuge had to be taken under a straw shed.[136] Perhaps even then the Virginians were fortunate. That same day, toiling over the crest of the Blue Ridge, a Moravian missionary encountered a snowstorm.[137] Along the South Branch, the rain continued until about 1 P.M. on the 7th.

A little later, George heard the good news that Fairfax had returned and was at Peter Casey's,[138] two miles away. Off went Washington, boylike, to see his friend, and with Fairfax he spent the rest of the day. He even walked with George William to van Meter's and back again to Casey's in order not to lose an hour of pleasant company. The two spent the night at Casey's—"the first night I had slept in a house," George proudly wrote in his journal, "since I came to the Branch." [139] He doubtless felt he was getting to be a pioneer, and the next day he added to that credit. In a wild region on the evening of the 8th, the surveyors pitched camp and lighted a fire. Then each man took out such food as he had, and proceeded to cook it. "Our spits," George recorded, "was forked sticks, our plates was a large chip; as for dishes, we had none."

Although the young gentlemen would do their own cooking where they must, they at least wanted something to cook, and they did not relish what they had the next day, to wit, an empty stomach. Their store of provisions was exhausted; the man who was to bring a new supply did not appear. Nothing was to be had otherwise than by foraging among widely scattered farms. While an all-day quest for food was being made, George and Fairfax remained at the camp, under the canvas, and none too happy. Their adventure was becoming unpleasant; novelty and excitement were giving place to hunger and discomfort. They would be more comfortable at home. George previously in his journal had made no mention of impending departure, but now he and Fairfax suddenly decided they had had enough of the wilderness or else their designated time was up. In any event, they ate some of the food that reached the camp between 4 and 5 P.M. and then they said goodbye and headed for the lower Potomac.

They lost no time on the road. The first evening they went to John

---

136 1 *Diaries*, 10.
137 Brother Gottschalk's journal, 12 *V* 70.
138 George spelled the name Cassey and may have done so correctly, though "Cassey" appears five times only in *Swem*.
139 1 *Diaries*, 11.

Collins's for an early start the next day; on the 10th the two rode boldly over the hills and mountains that Genn had avoided, and, when they reached a settlement on the Cacapon, they estimated they had covered forty miles. Hard riding on the 11th brought them to Frederick Town by noon. There they had the satisfaction of dining in something of their normal comfort, and then, again well-lined, they rode on to Jost Hite's and spent the night.

Fate, haste or negligence—all three of them being footpads—denied George and Fairfax the completion of a sure and direct journey according to the best art of the woodman. The two riders intended to make for Williams's gap and then to proceed along the road to Belhaven. In some manner they lost direction and got as far South as Ashby's Gap before they discovered their mistake. Doubling back to Williams's was a tedious vexation. Once again on the right trail, they crossed the Blue Ridge and went on to William West's Ordinary at the head of Bull Run Mountain.[140] The sole reward of the humiliating and exasperating day was a good look at "a rattled snake, the first," George noted, "that we had seen in all our journey." [141]

When that journey ended the next day, April 13, for Fairfax at Belvoir and for George at Mount Vernon,[142] their expedition to the Valley could not be described as an adventure of frontier hardship unflinchingly borne, but it could be written down as compassing the most useful thirty-three consecutive days that George ever had spent. Doubtless he had acquired more of profitable knowledge in like time spent in his first surveying lessons, but he had learned gradually the elements of the surveyor's art. All the milder, less arduous experiences of the frontier had been crowded one upon another. Some days had been wet and tedious and some nights long and smoky, but George had learned that he could run a line in the wilderness. He had camped out; though neither with skill nor to his satisfaction, he had cooked his food over the flames, and he had slept by a fire in the open; he had been among Indians, and he had learned as much about their ways as he could in two days. Even if there had been an element of farce in the return ride, he had seen with his own eyes the fine western lands. He had felt the frontier.

[140] Near the present Aldie (1 *Diaries*, 11–12 and n). For the persistent confusion of West's and Neville's Ordinaries, see *Landmarks*, 494, 637, and *supra*, p. 209, n. 78.
[141] 1 *Diaries*, 12.
[142] *Ibid.*

CHAPTER VI

GEORGE'S PART IN NEW SPECULATION
(April, 1748–February, 1752)

THE STORY OF George's half-amusing, half-instructive experiences
beyond the mountains was one, of course, that all his kinsmen wished
to hear. After telling it at Mount Vernon to Lawrence and Nancy, the
young gentleman who had been to the frontier had to repeat his
narrative at Ferry Farm, probably at Pope's Creek and, in June, among
the pleasant families of Chotank whom he was now of an age to
appreciate.

The name Chotank or Jotank was that of a Washington plantation,
of a creek and of a long stretch of quiet country along the south shore
of the Potomac East and West of the creek. So friendly were most of
the residents of this part of King George County that they never drew
a rigid boundary of their neighborhood. Agriculturally it was rolling
tobacco country with a stiff, rich soil;[1] spiritually, its life centered
around St. Paul's Church.[2] Family history was the only history made
or written in Chotank.[3]

Chotank plantation had come into Washington hands through the
distaff line. The immigrant Lawrence, brother of George's great-
grandfather, had married as his second wife the widow Joyce Fleming,
by whom he had a son, John. Of this John, a letter survives that summarized his career: "My mother married another man after my father
died, who spent all, so that I had not the value of 20s of my father's
estate, I being the youngest and therefore the weakest, which generally
comes off short." He continued: "But I thank God my fortune has
been pretty good since as I have got a good and kind and loving

---

[1] 2 Smyth, *Tour in U.S.*, 177. For later descriptions see 1 *Southern Literary Messenger*, 43,
Landmarks, 108, and *De Bow's Review*, v. 1, n.s., pt. 4, p. 496.
[2] Originally the church of Chotank Parish, formed in 1680 and also called the lower part
of Potomac Parish (Brydon, *Parish Lines*, 32; 2 *Meade*, 187). The church still (1948) stands.
Its parish register is extant, but its vestry book is lost.
[3] *De Bow's Review*, loc. cit.; cf. *Va. Gazette*, Oct. 7, 1737.

wife." [4] She was Mary Townsend whose father, Robert, gave her the Chotank plantation as a wedding present. Included in the tract was a fine house site, on a high bank, that commanded a superb view up and down the Potomac.[5] On the death of John and Mary Townsend Washington, the Chotank estate passed to their son John Washington, known as the second John of Chotank. He married Dade Massey's daughter Mary, who, as Mary Washington, often has been confused with George's mother.[6] The son and heir of John second of Chotank and of Mary Massey Washington was Lawrence,[7] who was four years older than George and a steadfast friend for life.

Not far from the Washingtons of Chotank lived their cousins of Hylton. Their descent was from John Washington, son of John the immigrant and of Anne Pope, George's great-grandmother. John of the second generation purchased the Hylton tract from Francis Dade II, and settled there with his wife, who was born Anne Wickliffe. The youngest son of this union, Henry Washington, married Mary Bailey and acquired Hylton from his eldest brother, Lawrence. By the will of Henry Washington, his second son, John, inherited Hylton. A third son, Bailey, one of George's friends, received land on Aquia Creek. John Washington, born in 1730, was later to marry his cousin Catherine Washington, by whom he was to have twelve children. The Chotank neighborhood, in a word, was, and increasingly was to be, the home of George's cousins. By marriage, moreover, the Chotank Washingtons were connected with many of the prominent families of that part of the Northern Neck.

The great name of the district around the Washington plantations was that of William Fitzhugh. He, it will be recalled,[8] had been a pioneer in the establishment of large, up-river plantations, and had served as representative of the proprietary at a time when he and his fellow agent, George Brent, had been "their own best customers." [9] On the Northern Neck there was a tradition that, with the exception of a few intervening tracts, Fitzhugh at one time had owned land that

---

[4] John Washington to Mary Gibson, July 22, 1699; 1 *Hoppin*, 133. The name of Joyce Fleming sometimes is printed wrongly as Jane. It appears unmistakably as Joyce in 1 *Old Rappahannock Wills*, 219, Sept. 27, 1675, and in 6 *Rappahannock Deeds*, 7, July [?], 1677.

[5] *Eubank*, 18.

[6] See, for example, Mary Massey Washington's advertisement of a lost horse, *Va. Gazette*, May 9, 1745. This advertisement has been attributed to Mary Ball Washington.

[7] The last testament of the second John Washington of Chotank is in *Stafford Wills*, 1729–48, p. 329.

[8] See *supra*, p. 8 and *infra*, Appendix I–1.

[9] *Ibid.*

stretched from the Potomac to the Rappahannock.[10] By the period of George's visits to Chotank, William Fitzhugh had long been dead. Bedford, immediately downstream from Chotank Plantation, had the original centre of the Fitzhugh domain. Marmion and Eagle's Nest had been carved out of it.

Beyond Bedford, toward a familiar point on the Potomac, was Albion, the estate of the Townsends and later of the Dades, through a daughter of the Townsend stock.[11] The direct Virginia ancestor of the Townsends was Richard, who was in York County in 1629 and served in Council in 1643-45. His son Robert patented the land later called Albion. It was Robert's daughter Mary who married John Washington, son of the immigrant, Lawrence.

At the point of the Potomac, downstream from Albion, was Barnsfield, the home of the Hooes, a family resident in Virginia from 1621.[13] The second generation had moved to Westmoreland. In 1715-18, descendants patented 2900 acres and established the estate on which they and their issue were living at the time George made the rounds of Chotank.[14] Wealth did not come to all the Hooes, but a stable family life was theirs on the land and in the church.[15] The most prosperous and influential of the family in Washington's day was John Hooe, who married Anne, daughter of Col. Robert Alexander.[16]

In the opposite direction, upstream from Chotank plantation was, first, Cedar Grove, residence of the Rev. David Stuart. He had come to Virginia in 1715 after the defeat of the Old Pretender, had married Jane Gibbons, daughter of Sir John Gibbons, Governor of Barbados, and, from 1731, had been rector of St. Paul's. His daughter Sarah was a girl at the time George most frequently rode down to Chotank.[17] Close to Cedar Grove was Eagle's Nest, South of which, on a high hill overlooking the Potomac valley, was Litchfield, where the Dade family lived. They were the descendants of a man of mystery. In 1658-62,

[10] *Eubank,* 16.

[11] 2 *W* (1) p 88.

[12] *Eubank,* 27; 1 *H* 138, 239; 10 *W* (2) p. 67; 1 *L.O. Records,* 705; 3 *ibid.,* 159. For a grant to "Mrs. Frances Townsend, widow," see 2 *L.O. Records,* 285, entry of Feb. 7, 1650.

[13] R. A. Lancaster, *Virginia Homes,* 348; 4 *V* 427. The name is pronounced like that of the implement, the hoe.

[14] *Prince William Guide,* 26. In *Stafford Deeds,* O, 14, is the inventory of Rice Hooe, who bore the name of the founder of the family, Rhys Hooe. This document covers an estate of £519.

[15] Lancaster stated, *loc. cit.,* that seven generations of Hooes were born at Barnsfield. If he was informed correctly, this was a most unusual record.

[16] See 12 *V* 319. Nathaniel Washington married Sarah Hooe, Dec. 12, 1767 (*St. Paul's Register,* of that date).

[17] She later married Thomas Fitzhugh of Boscobel (7 *V* 426).

"Major John Smith" patented Northern Neck lands, which subsequently were claimed by the descendants of Francis Dade. These heirs convinced the court that John Smith and Francis Dade were the same individual. Why Dade called himself Smith, nobody could say.[18] His son, the second Francis Dade, married into the Townsends; the second Francis's sister-in-law became the wife of John Washington.[19]

Across the Northern Neck from Chotank, but never regarded as a part of that neighborhood, was the Rappahannock estate of Cleve, which "King" Carter had provided for his son Charles. The house, built about 1729, was the centre of much activity in farming. Charles Carter was Burgess for many terms and did some other duty as a public servant.[20] His prime distinction was that of a careful planter who knew how to grow large crops without exhausting his land.[21] Charles Carter was accustomed to speak proudly of his property, which was in tail male,[22] as "my manor of Cleve," and he was rich enough to live in a style that was in keeping with his pompous phrase.[23]

Like his father, whom he emulated assiduously, Charles Carter believed in a "manor church" and contributed generously to building an edifice, for which his neighbor, Col. John Champe of Lamb's Creek plantation, gave a site as well as cash. Champe, who was a Burgess and a holder of many county offices,[24] supplied, also, the party of the first part in a wedding of importance that linked Cleve and Lamb's Creek plantation: his son married Anne Carter, Charles's daughter.[25]

Among these kindly and sociable families of Chotank, George spent some enjoyable days in June, 1748, and then he paid a visit to the Turner

[18] The dates of course suggest that he was a royalist who for some reason feared the wrath of the Cromwell regime if he were identified. See *Hayden*, 731; 20 *V* 326.

[19] The most interesting of the Dade wills that now survive probably is that of Langhorne Dade, Oct. 9, 1752 (*Stafford Deeds*, O, 242, 310). Townsend Dade's brief will of June 10, 1735 is in *Stafford Wills*, 1729–48, p. 172; inventory, *ibid.*, 175.

[20] In 2 *King George Orders*, 140, he is mentioned, Feb. 3, 1737–38, as surveyor of highway from the Falls to Horseshoe Run. According to *ibid.*, 1751–67, p. 64, he and Charles Champe were named, June 4, 1752, to draw the dividing line between Stafford and King George Counties. Charles Carter served also as one of Lord Fairfax's commissioners for marking the western boundary of the Northern Neck proprietary.

[21] His will of Sept. 12, 1762, printed in 31 *V* 39–69, refers, p. 64, to his "new system of Virginia husbandry, or the little farm improved . . ."

[22] 31 *V* 67.

[23] *Ibid.* He was thrice married—to Mary Walker, then to Anne Byrd and, finally, to Lucy Taliaferro. His inventory, Aug. 2, 1764 (6 *King George Deeds*, 229), listed 138 Negroes and total property, in King George and Stafford, of £2848. Approximately £2069 of this covered holdings in King George.

[24] For example, Sheriff in 1731 (37 *V* 125); Highway Surveyor in 1737 (2 *King George Orders*, 108); Coroner in 1742 (16 *V* 20); long-time Justice of the Peace.

[25] *Eubank*. Subsequently, John Champe's daughter Jane became the first wife of George's brother Samuel (*ibid.*, and George Fitzhugh in 1 *DeBow's Review*, n.s., 616).

plantation, on the north bank of the Rappahannock, opposite Port
Royal. There George displayed to his friend and his father's contemporary, Thomas Turner, Clerk of the Court, what he recently had
learned of the art of billiards. As the Clerk was a bit skeptical of
George's skill, friendly bets cost the senior 1s 3d. The cash was not
forthcoming immediately but that was no concern to George. He had
opened a rough account book and in it, along with others, he wrote
down Turner's debt.[26]

Perhaps from the Rappahannock, another journey of the summer
carried George on his first known visit to Yorktown, where he did some
shopping for his mother.[27] There was more ready cash in the family
that summer because the active executors of Augustine Washington's
estate—Lawrence Washington and Nathaniel Chapman—had exercised
authority given in a codicil of Augustine's will and for £110 sterling
had sold on George's account about 165 acres of the Ferry Farm to
Anthony Strother. Ultimately the purchase price would be added to
the young man's estate. For the time, it would be in the hands of his
mother as his guardian.[28]

George did not linger on his narrowed acres. In August there was a
ride to the falls of the Potomac with Lawrence,[29] whose continuing interest in western lands was evidenced by the purchase during 1748
of more than 1300 acres in the Shenandoah Valley.[30] As will appear
later, Lawrence shared, also, in far bolder dreams. Nearer and less
alluring but promising a profit was a plan in which Lawrence,
"Austin" and others were engaged, to move the colonial capital from
Williamsburg to a more convenient, healthier site in the region where
the Washingtons and their friends were large landowners. The plan
was an old one but it had a new argument behind it that year: Williamsburg was suffering from an epidemic of dysentery so serious that a
postponement of the meeting of the House of Burgesses was advocated.[31]

This proposal to change the seat of colonial government interested
George as a young man of business but it did not excite him. He was

[26] Entry of June 4, *Account Book* A, 5.
[27] Entry of July 15, 1748, *ibid.* He may have been on a visit to his cousins in Gloucester
County.
[28] 3 *King George Deeds*, 276.
[29] Entries of Aug. 15, 17, 1748, *ibid.*, 7.
[30] *Norris*, 81.
[31] Augustine ("Austin") Washington to Lawrence Washington, Aug. 28, 1748—L. W.,
Smith Coll., *Havemeyer Papers*. See, in contrast, Tyler's *Williamsburg*, 209.

making occasional surveys [32] and he was reading the *Spectator* and a little of English history,[33] but, above all, he was enjoying life. Besides billiards, which could not be played in many private homes, George had learned whist and loo by the autumn of 1748, and he did not object to playing for stakes that were worth winning. In September at Wallace's plantation, he beat his friend John Lewis at loo for a total of 9s 8d,[34] and at Nominy, the home of his brother's sister-in-law, he took his brother "Austin" into camp for 7s 6d.[35] Lawrence apparently was the only one of the circle who consistently had George's measure at loo.[36]

George was enjoying other social pleasures, too. His clothes and his appearance became increasingly his concern. At sixteen, he was shaving, and when he went on a visit to Fairfax in 1748, he did not fail to write down his razor at the head of the list of the articles he was to carry with him. Nine shirts, six linen waistcoats, a cloth waistcoat, six bands,[37] four neck-cloths and seven caps were the wardrobe he thought he would need while absent from home.[38] Another new acquirement was dancing. Later in the year, probably, George attended a school [39] where that art was taught, but whether ill or well, his expense account did not show.

In the acquisition of social graces, George's model and mentor continued to be Lawrence, who was acquainted with the best usages as well as with the best families of the Colony. Sickness now was interfering with Lawrence's service to the public. From the time Fairfax had separate representation in 1744, George's older half-brother had been a Burgess and a member of the important committee on Propositions and Grievances.[40] He had served, also, on numerous special committees.[41] Apparently without hesitation or fear of consequences,

---

[32] Perhaps at Alexandria, though he probably did not work there until 1749.

[33] Notes in the *MS Journal of 1748*; entries subsequent, apparently, to August 17.

[34] Entry of Sept. 22, 1748, *Account Book* A 7.

[35] *Ibid.*, 8.

[36] On Feb. 14, 1748/49, Lawrence won 5s from him (*ibid.*, 7). George's account book and miscellaneous cash accounts show him to have been at Wallace's, Sept. 22, at Woodward's Oct. 4, at Nominy plantation, Oct. 22, at Pope's Creek, Oct. 26, at "Col. Carter's" and at "the Frenchman's" Nov. 7, 1748.

[37] These were collars or supports for stocks.

[38] Memorandum in *Journal of 1748*.

[39] As George neither sang nor played an instrument, dancing instruction seems the only easy explanation of this curious entry in his account with his mother: "[1748], Sept. 10 to cash pd. per Musick Master for my Enterence, 3 s., 9 d." (*Account Book* A, 5).

[40] *Journ. H. B.*, 1742–49, p. 78, 157, 258. The first of these references includes a statement of the functions of the committee, on which Lawrence's grandfather and greatgrandfather had served.

[41] *Ibid.*, 93, 95, 146, 189, 284, 303, 308.

Lawrence sponsored bills in which his parochial and sometimes his selfish interest might have been alleged, as, for example, when he sought to dissolve the vestry of Truro Parish,[42] or to prevent the building of a new church for Overwharton Parish,[43] or to confirm certain disputed titles in the forks of the Rappahannock.[44] Lawrence could have replied that these bills were of more concern to the County than to him in any personal manner. His fellow Burgesses certainly did not disparage his measures. Seniority and influence were rising when, in December, 1748, he had to ask leave of absence because of ill-health.[45] He returned to Mount Vernon, where George remained with him for part of the cold season.[46]

If this was a time of solicitude on account of Lawrence, it was a time of pleasurable excitement, also, because of a shining event at Belvoir. George William had wooed and won Sarah Cary, daughter of Col. Wilson Cary of Ceelys, an excellent estate on James River, and about three miles from Hampton.[47] The marriage had been solemnized on the 17th of December;[48] the proud young Fairfax had brought his bride immediately to his father's house and had introduced neighbors who, of course, were eager to see her. As George observed her that winter of 1748–49, Sarah Cary—Sally to all her friends—was an altogether charming and somewhat tantalizing person. She was eighteen, not two years older than George, and she had much grace,[49] with a high forehead, a long face, a sharp chin and a general appearance of intelligence and amiability.[50] At a later time, Washington was to write of her "mirth, good humor, ease of mind and—what else?" as if he knew he could not catch her essential, elusive personality in the stiff net of his awkward words.[51] He may not have fallen consciously in love with her, but he probably regarded her, from the first, as the most fascinating girl he knew. As she was destined to have no children, she was to retain her youthful figure and to increase in charm with the years. Belvoir, indeed the whole sweep of that part of the Potomac, was the brighter for her presence. Having met her, it doubtless was difficult for George to go

[42] *Ibid.*, 133, 136, 374; 5 H 274.
[43] *Journ. H. B.*, 1742–49, p. 109, 199, 203.   [44] *Ibid.*, 320.
[45] *Ibid.*, 323. The entry in the journal does not give ill-health as the reason, but that undoubtedly was the condition that prompted his request for leave.
[46] He was there the second half of February when, on two occasions, he beat his sister-in-law for 5s at whist (*Misc. Accts.*, Washington Papers, LC).
[47] *Sally Cary*, 16.
[48] *Ibid.*, 22.   [49] *Ibid.*, 3 n.
[50] A reproduction of her portrait appears between p. 235 and p. 236.
[51] 2 *G. W.*, 288.

back to Ferry Farm for a brief period, or even to find full pleasure in visits elsewhere.[52]

The spring of 1749 found Lawrence plagued with so stubborn a cough that he talked of leaving Virginia.[53] Pluckily, as became a veteran,[54] he took up his duties when the House of Burgesses was convened, but in May, 1749, he had again to be excused from attendance.[55] The distress created by this ominous illness of the oldest son of the family was deepened by loss of one after another of Nancy's children by Lawrence. Her baby Jane, born Sept. 27, 1744, had died when four months old. Fairfax, who was born Aug. 22, 1747, did not live more than two months.[56] On Sept. 28, 1748, Nancy had been delivered of another girl baby, christened Mildred, but she, too, was sickly and succumbed in 1749.[57] Three times the mother had seen the body of her only child carried to the grave.[58] There was, also, the unhappy prospect that if Lawrence yielded to his malady, which looked more and more like consumption, he would have no heir of the body. Augustine had provided that in this event, the land and mill left to Lawrence should pass to George unless "Austin" desired the Hunting Creek property. Should "Austin" wish to own Hunting Creek, if Lawrence died without issue, then, it will be recalled, Augustine had stipulated that his second son must transfer the Maddox-Pope Creek estate to George.[59]

Lawrence's illness and loss of his children were much the saddest but not the only concerns of the family in 1749. After her brother Joseph Ball had declined to permit her to cut timber from his adjoining tract, Mary Washington had abandoned her plan for building a house on her lower farm.[60] That had not been her only alternative, because, in making provision for her future, Augustine Washington had thought it would be well for her, after his death, to employ her slaves on the Deep Run property.[61] He accordingly had stipulated that while a quarter

---

[52] Apparently, George was at "Austin's" plantation on Feb. 5, 1749, and on January 27 he was at Port Royal (entry of that date, *Account Book* A, 7).   [53] 1 *G. W.*, 13.

[54] He still was trying to get his half pay for service in the Cartagena expedition. See William Fitzhugh to Lawrence Washington, May 15, Sept. 9, 1747 (L. W. Smith Coll., *Havemeyer Papers*).

[55] *Journ. H. B.*, 1742–49, p. 387. This time leave formally is entered "for the recovery of his health."

[56] For a letter of sympathy from William Fairfax to Lawrence, Oct. 2, 1747, on the death of this child, see L. W. Smith Coll., *Havemeyer Papers*.

[57] 32 *G. W.*, 28. The exact date of Mildred's death is not known.

[58] This assumes the correctness of Washington's statement, 32 *G. W.*, 28, that Mildred died in 1749, and not, as some authorities have stated, in 1751.

[59] See *supra*, p. 74 and Ford, *The Washington Family*, 94 ff.   [60] See *supra*, p. 195.

[61] Deep Run flows into the Rappahannock from the left bank, above "the forks" where the Rapidan joins the Rappahannock.

was being built there, she should have the right to grow crops for five years on the Bridges Creek plantation, which was bequeathed to "Austin." The five years now were ended, but Mrs. Washington still had done nothing to establish a quarter on Deep Run. She simply "stayed on" at Ferry Farm as if the property were her own and was not to pass to George when he became 21. Besides there was a threat that a ferry might be authorized across the Rappahannock at her lower tract—in George's indignant words, "right through the very heart and best of the land." [62]

George explained all this to Lawrence in May, 1749, at a time when the younger brother was busy as a surveyor and was planning still larger things in that profession. The long-desired town at Belhaven, on the Potomac, above Hunting Creek, was about to become a reality. A warehouse had been erected there in 1732; factors had opened stores; ambitious rivals who advocated a different site [63] had been beaten at last. In May, 1749, the General Assembly had named trustees and had authorized the establishment of the town on sixty acres of land that belonged to Philip and John Alexander and to Hugh West. [64] All three of the Fairfaxes—the Proprietor, Colonel Fairfax and George William—were among the trustees. [65] Much to the regret of some of its residents, the new community was stripped of the name Belhaven, which Scotch merchants had given it in admiration for John Hamilton, second Baron Belhaven, a vehement adversary of the union of England and Scotland. [66] By the Virginia legislative act of 1748, the place was to be "called by the name of Alexandria," in honor of the owners of the great part of the tract, descendants of John Alexander, who had surveyed for Nicholas Spencer and John Washington the land that later became Mount Vernon. [67]

Regardless of differences over the name, the trustees were resolved to establish the town at once. On May 27, a short time after the law

[62] George Washington to Lawrence Washington, May 5, 1749 (1 *G. W.*, 13–14). This is the earliest of George's surviving letters to which a definite date may be assigned.

[63] Mrs. Powell, *The History of Old Alexandria* (cited hereafter as *Mrs. Powell*), p. 25; *Landmarks*, 405.

[64] *Journ. H. B.*, 1742–49, p. 265, 355, 405; 6 *H.* 214. See *supra*, p. 161.

[65] Lawrence was added to the list of trustees Mch. 28, 1750 (see *Proceedings of Trustees*, 4).

[66] *Landmarks*, 406, 414. Belhaven's speech of Nov. 2, 1706, long was famous among Scots.

[67] See *supra*, p. 21. For the Alexander genealogy, which does not seem germane to this narrative, see Culbertson, *The Hunter Family of Virginia; Hayden*, 192; 2 *W* (1) p. 89. In *Landmarks*, 415–16, is a note on the circumstances that led to the selection of the name Alexandria. An unsuccessful effort was to be made in 1752 to call the place Belhaven again (*Landmarks*, 414, with a reference to *Journ. H. B.*, 1752–58, p. 34).

went into effect, the *Maryland Gazette* announced that the lots in Alexandria would be sold to the highest bidders on the 13th of July. To have all the parcels laid off by that time, the regular Surveyor, John West, Jr., most advantageously used young Mr. Washington as an assistant.[68] George worked fast. By approximately the 17th of July,[69] he had finished his part of the survey and had drawn a plan of the town. Twenty-five of the lots changed owners by public vendue on the 18th of July at prices that ranged from eight to fifty-six and a half pistoles.[70] Other sales soon were added to this number.[71] The purchasers loyally included almost all the leading men of that part of the Northern Neck. Lawrence, "Austin," George William Fairfax, and his younger brother William Henry were among them. George did not buy, though he probably had made money enough from his surveying to have purchased a lot if he had so desired. He was looking in a different direction and was seeking, also, to procure appointment as Surveyor in the newly created County of Culpeper.

Although Lawrence doubtless was doing his utmost to assist George in getting this office, he was in bad condition physically. His cough defied local doctors and home treatment. In growing concern, Lawrence determined to consult physicians in London and while there to advance a colonial business enterprise that was exciting him and some of his neighbors.[72] At first, Lawrence planned to sail with Governor Gooch who was "going home" in retirement because of failing health; but as there was a chance that His Honor's [73] departure might be delayed, Lawrence and a friend [74] booked passage on the ship of the good-natured Captain Kelly. With toasts for a pleasant voyage and with prayers for a sure and swift recovery, Lawrence was bidden farewell shortly before the vendue at Alexandria.[75]

[68] *Mrs. Powell,* 33.

[69] In a letter to Lawrence Washington, July 17, 1749, William Fairfax said: "What relates to the sales of the lots in our new town will be communicated, together with a plan by your brother George" (L. W. Smith Coll., *Havemeyer Papers*). A drawing believed to be another, undated copy of this plan appears in the *George Washington Atlas,* Plate 19.

[70] *Proceedings of Trustees of Alexandria,* 1.   [71] *Ibid.,* 1–3.

[72] It nowhere is stated that Lawrence went to England for consultation rather than for rest and cure, but the brevity of his absence from Virginia makes it virtually certain that this was the case. When he subsequently went away for treatment, he was out of Virginia for a much longer period.

[73] At this period, the Governor usually was styled "His Honor," and not "His Excellency."

[74] He is mentioned only as "Mr. Carter" and cannot be identified among Lawrence's many contemporaries of that name.

[75] William Fairfax to Lawrence Washington, July 17, 1749 (L. W. Smith Coll., *Havemeyer Papers*). There is a minor conflict of dates here. In the *Proceedings of the Board of Trustees* of Alexandria, Lawrence is recorded as present the day after Fairfax addressed him as if he already were on his way to England. See *infra,* p. 239, n. 109.

This was the grief of the summer of 1749. The gratification was the success of George in his application for the surveyorship of Culpeper. On the last day of July,[76] he completed the long ride to the temporary quarters of the Court [77] and presented his commission from the President and Masters [78] of the College of William and Mary, who alone could commission County Surveyors.[79] As this document was in proper order, George was directed to swear allegiance to the person and government of the King. Then, under oath, he disclaimed all allegiance to the issue of James II, or anyone professing descent from James.[80] Next George took the "test oath" of non-belief in transubstantiation, and finally the special oath of Surveyor, "that he [would] truly and faithfully to the best of his knowledge and power, discharge and execute his trust, office and employment." [81] Being sufficiently sworn, George proceeded immediately to exercise his new authority. He surveyed 400 acres in Culpeper for Richard Barnes of Richmond County [82] on July 22 and received promptly his fee of £2, 3s.[83] Soon, too, George was copying for customers deeds already recorded.[84]

Of other work in the proprietary, there was little during the summer. The principal reason was controversy regarding the title of Jost Hite to certain lands he had acquired in the Shenandoah Valley and then had resold in part.[85] "Orders" for the land had been issued by Governor Gooch during the period he and the Council declined to recognize the right of Lord Fairfax to any territory beyond a line drawn from the forks of the Rappahannock to the mouth of the Shenandoah. Subsequently, it will be remembered, as a means of getting royal approval of the extended bounds of the proprietary, Fairfax had promised to accept and to validate all grants and patents made by the Crown in

---

76 The entry in the court record, cited in the next note, is O. S., July 20.

77 The act of March 23, 1748 creating the County is given by title only in *H*. A full text from the British records will be found in 27 *V* 377. This act did not specify where the court was to be held.

78 The text in Howe's *Historical Collections of Virginia* (cited hereafter as Howe, *Hist. Coll.*), p. 237, reads "Master."

79 See *supra*, p. 183.

80 This was the so-called "abjuration oath."

81 Act of October, 1748 (6 *H* 33). This law required a surveyor to post bond with two "sufficient sureties" in the sum of £500 current money. Absence of any reference to this in the Culpeper entry, as cited by Howe, probably means that neither the Court nor the Surveyor knew of this new statutory provision.

82 His will was probated in Richmond County, Nov. 2, 1761 (6 *Richmond Co. Wills*, 212).

83 *Account Book* A, 14. This is the survey of which two plats, in somewhat differing form, are used as frontispiece and as tailpiece of the *George Washington Atlas*. It is probable that George made numerous other surveys, but as nearly all the records of Culpeper County prior to 1775 have been destroyed, it is impossible to ascertain the extent of George's work in the County.

84 *Account Book* A, 16.   85 See *supra*, p. 212.

the region between the new and the old lines. Legislation to effect this was adopted at the session of the General Assembly that opened in October, 1748.[86]

Upon the passage of this act, Hite and his fellow landholders called on Fairfax to issue them patents because, they argued, the "orders" for land, given them by the Governor and Council, were grants within the meaning of the new law. Fairfax refused the patents. The statute, his attorney contended, specifically applied to "all grants and patents whatsoever, under the seal of the Colony." Hite's "order" had never passed under that seal. Not unnaturally, Hite regarded this as a fraud. He retained counsel, inquired whether an injunction might not be procured, and even talked of appealing in England for disallowance of the act that referred to patents "under the seal of the Colony." [87] Because of Hite's threat, Lord Fairfax closed the Land Books of Frederick County to most applicants in 1749.[88] This action temporarily denied George any surveying of new tracts in Frederick, where business otherwise would have been brisk. He scarcely could have undertaken to ride over the mountains, even had the land office been open, because of an attack of malaria, which, said he, "I have had to extremity." [89] Had he been able to go, he might not have been happy. Lord Fairfax had been in a strange, uncommunicative mood at the time of Lawrence's departure [90] and early in the autumn had left Belvoir, without announcement, for the Valley. He would not have been a pleasant companion there.[91]

With the return of Lawrence, a short time prior to the 7th of November,[92] interest shifted temporarily. As a young student of the art of making money, George now had a new lesson. Although Lawrence had not improved in health and had not even learned the nature of

[86] 6 H 198–99.

[87] William Fairfax to Lawrence Washington, July 17, 1749 (L. W. Smith Coll., *Havemeyer Papers;* 13 V 354–55, with citation of *Virginia Revised Code* of 1819, v. 2, p 344–47). In 1786, the case finally was decided in Hite's favor (Hite *vs.* Fairfax, 4 C 42).

[88] L. W. Smith Coll., *Havemeyer Papers,* but the books themselves show that they were not completely closed, as has been supposed. From June 11, 1749, to the end of the year, eight grants were made in Frederick to a total of slightly over 5600 acres. Of these 3023 were assigned George William Fairfax (*L. O. Records, N.N.,G.*).

[89] George Washington to Mrs. Lawrence Washington (1 *G. W.,* 18, undated but evidently of September or October, 1749).

[90] L. W. Smith Coll., *Havemeyer Papers.*

[91] G. W. to Lord Fairfax, 1 *G. W.,* 18. Although without date, this manifestly was written in the early autumn of 1749.

[92] G. W. to Mrs. Lawrence Washington, n.d., (1 *G. W.,* 18); Lawrence Washington to unnamed correspondent, Nov. 7, 1749 (L. W. Smith Coll., *Havemeyer Papers*). Cf. T. Stafford to Lawrence Washington, Nov. 13, 1749 (*Ibid*).

SALLY CARY FAIRFAX, TANTALIZING BUT PRUDENT

George William Fairfax's marriage in December 1748 to Sally Cary of Ceelys on the lower James was a great event at Mount Vernon as well as at Belvoir. Anne Fairfax, the young wife of Lawrence Washington, George's elder half-brother, was sister of the groom but had no nearer sister of her own than Sarah, who had married John Carlyle and was living up the river where the new town of Alexandria soon was to rise—too distant for frequent conversation.

Sally Cary meant new companionship to Anne Washington. To George her coming soon was to afford him the companionship of a good-humored, fine-spirited girl, two years his senior, who could relieve his tongue of some of its awkwardness in the presence of womankind.

As the years passed, Washington found Sally always more interesting; and when he quickly acquired distinction she undoubtedly had pride as well as interest in him, but always this was salted with prudence: There survives not one echo of the gossip that would have been audible all along the Potomac had there been anything amiss in their relations.

The tantalizing portrait of her on the opposite page is from a photograph of a lost original, and is reproduced by courtesy of Mrs. Seymour St. John, Wallingford, Conn.

Nov.r 24th 1750 / Survey'd for myself
the Land at the Head of the Marsh wch I
bought of Capt.n Rutherford and after
granted by Lord Fairfax Beg at 2 white Oaks
Corner to Chas. Washingtons Patent Line
and run thence No 10 Et 60 poles to a wh
Oak on a Limestone Ledge in very ho
Ground thence No 65 Wt 340 poles two
angular white Oaks on flat Ground th
No 20 Wt 222 poles to a white Oak co
knowl No 53 Et 272 poles to 2 hic
Saplins in Majr Lawe Washingtons
line near a spring pole thence po th
his Line No 13 Et 20 poles to 3 hic
Saplins in a hollow th No 27 Et 160
poles to a Large red Oak & hicky on
and one Corner th So 27 Et 20 poles to a
stooping & forked white Oak th So 63
57 poles to another white Oak th th
No 65 Et 44 poles to the Beg Con ͭ
Chas. Washington & Benj Rutherford wr
Saml Washington

GEORGE WASHINGTON'S FIRST LAND GRANT

The acquisition of good land under the easy terms of the Fairfax Proprietary was so natural a way of "getting on in the world" that young George Washington probably looked forward from boyhood to the time when he would have made money enough to take out patents.

Whether or not he planned it so, the records do not show; but he picked the vocation of all others that would give him a knowledge of where the best "ungranted" lands were located in the lower Shenandoah Valley.

As a Surveyor, too, he could demand cash or tobacco certificates at the time he completed the survey and made the plat. Surveying, in fact, was one of the few "cash businesses" in Virginia.

George saved a considerable part of what he earned, though he spent somewhat freely for clothing, for mounts and for horse-furnishings. By November, 1750, he had funds with which to buy an excellent tract in a fertile part of Frederick County.

On the facing page are reproduced the field notes of the survey he made of his "land at the head of the marsh." The original of these notes is among the Washington Papers in the Library of Congress.

his malady, he displayed the energy of renewed interest in a project
that had been shaping itself ever since the completion of the Treaty
of Lancaster [93] had inspired James Patton, John Robinson and others
to procure grants for the development of the domain beyond the Allegheny Mountains. Thomas Lee, Lawrence Washington, several more
Northern Neck landowners, and some of their speculating friends in
lower Tidewater planned an even bolder project for an "Ohio Company." With the help of the Duke of Bedford [94] and of John Hanbury,
a wealthy London merchant, the company received a grant of 200,000
acres from King George on Feb. 23, 1749.[95] If the terms attached to
that grant were executed, an additional 300,000 acres were to be allotted.[96]

With this land at their disposal, Lawrence and his associates were
convinced they could attract settlers and secure the frontier against the
possibility of occupation by French who might come down from
Canada. More immediately, Lawrence reasoned that a fort and an
Indian trading post in the western country could be supplied from the
upper Potomac far more readily and regularly than would be possible
for the French from the St. Lawrence River and the Lakes.[97] Thus
a larger part of the fur trade might be captured. The Indians, getting
the goods they wanted, might be more firmly the friends of England.
Nor could Lawrence overlook the further fact that if the upper Potomac became the base for this new trade, land owners in that region
might profit handsomely.

The immediate task, therefore, was to establish the trading post and
to see that "Indian goods" for it were brought over promptly from
England and were forwarded in ample quantity. All advice to the
stockholders of the company from frontiersmen indicated that the
junction of the Allegheny and Monongahela would be the ideal site for

[93] See *supra*, p. 186.
[94] See T. P. Abernethy, *Western Lands and the American Revolution* (cited hereafter as
Abernethy, *Western Lands*), p. 7.
[95] The actual grant was made July 12, 1749, by Governor Gooch. The original members of
the Ohio Company are listed, as of July 7, 1749, in *Council Journal*, P.R.O., C.O. 5, 1423.
Thomas Nelson, Thomas Cresap, William Nimmo and John Carlyle withdrew from the company
at one or another of the early stages of its organization.
[96] Kenneth P. Bailey published in 1939 an adequate account of this undertaking, under the
title, *The Ohio Company of Virginia and the Westward Movement, 1748–1792* (cited hereafter
as *Bailey, Ohio Co.*). Reference here consequently is brief. Essential documents, used by Bailey,
appear also in 3 *Gooch MSS*, 915, 917, 948, 959, 1011. Perhaps the frankest brief account of the
purposes of the enterprise is that of Lawrence Washington, Nov. 7, 1749, cited *supra*, n. 92.
[97] *Ibid.*

the post.[98] Until it could be established, a warehouse was to be maintained on Wills Creek,[99] forty-five miles Northwest of Frederick Town.

The prospect of opening this enlarged traffic had appeared to be bright early in 1749, but it had been clouded somewhat by the time of Lawrence's return from England. "Those very Indians that had encouraged [the company] at first," wrote Thomas Lee in disgust, "had been persuaded that our design was to ruin, not to trade with them; and such a spirit of jealousy is raised among them that without a treaty and presents we shall not be able to do anything with them." [100] In addition, on the very day that the Governor and Council had confirmed the grant to the Ohio Company, they had allotted 800,000 acres to a somewhat similar enterprise, that of the Loyal Company, which had the support of Speaker John Robinson and his friends. The lines of the two companies, though vaguely drawn, were far enough apart to avoid direct conflict, but new rivalry was stirred. Neither company was willing to trust the other or to withhold a blow that could be delivered secretly.[101]

These matters were vexing to Lawrence and were particularly exciting to George because he now was about to return to the frontier. As a qualified County Surveyor, he could work anywhere he was engaged, and he accepted gladly an invitation from Fairfax to meet the Proprietor in Frederick at the November term of court.[102] The ground was to be similar, in general, to that he had seen in 1748, but there was a most material difference: On this new expedition he was to be responsible for surveys instead of being merely an observer and a volunteer assistant.

Work began on the 2nd of November, 1749.[103] A few evenings, George was close enough to Frederick Town to go to the ordinary and sleep in a bed. The other nights he spent by a fire on straw or bearskin.

[98] *Ibid.* For the commercial aspect of the undertaking, see Wroth, in 9 *Md. His. Mag.*, 24–25. The larger bearings are discussed in 4 *Osgood*, 286 ff.

[99] *Bailey, Ohio Co.*, 74. Flowing from the North, Wills Creek enters the North Branch of the Potomac at the present Cumberland, Maryland. This mischoice of a site perhaps was prompted by a desire to locate the trading post West of Cresap's establishment and as close to the mountains as possible. Military considerations that later made the position burdensome apparently were not regarded if, indeed, they could have been appreciated at the time.

[100] Thomas Lee to unnamed correspondent, Oct. 18, 1749; 3 *Gooch MSS*, 1011.

[101] Abernethy, *Western Lands*, 7 ff.

[102] G. W. to Lord Fairfax, not dated but of late September or early October, 1749 (1 *G. W.* 18).

[103] G. W.'s *Field Book*, 1749, p. 7; 733 *Papers of G. W.*, LC, 30–41.

Not once, while sleeping out, could he enjoy the relief of taking off his garments. Around him, to use his own words, were "man, wife and children, like a parcel of dogs or cats, and happy's he that gets the berth nearest the fire."[104] The dwellers in the Valley he disliked as acutely as on his previous visit. "A parcel of barbarians . . . an uncouth set of people," he termed them.[105] So disgusted was he with the settlers that he said of his life among them, "There's nothing would make it pass off tolerably but a good reward." He confided with pride: "A doubloon is my constant gain every day that the weather will permit my going out, and sometime six pistoles."[106] This was fine compensation for a young man not yet eighteen but it could not be earned for long. The weather was too cold even for a strong Surveyor who was willing to sleep in his clothes—"like a Negro," as George put it. His last surveys for the season were made on the 11th of November.

When George came back to Mount Vernon with his new earnings, he was more and more frequently called upon to make small loans and to pay minor accounts for his brothers and, less frequently, for cousins and friends. Lawrence and "Austin" seem often to have lacked small coins; George always had them and readily lent them. To be certain they were charged against borrowers, he decided that he should open a ledger, after the manner of good men of business, and should no longer content himself with such a rough record—half ledger, half cash-book—as he had been keeping since his sixteenth year. He did not know a great deal about bookkeeping and he had much liability of error and confusion, but about the 9th of December, 1749, he wrote in the clean, new volume that he had that day paid "Austin's" account with Humphrey Wallace in the sum of £1, 13s. Two days later, the elder brother settled with a pair of leather breeches valued at £1, 15s.[107] Times there were when "Austin" advanced and George repaid;[108] but, in the main, George was the creditor of the family as respected petty cash. This manifestly was a distinction not devoid of a certain element

---

104 Letter to "Richard," n.d., but manifestly written about Nov. 8, 1749 (1 G. W., 17).

105 Ibid.

106 Ibid. The doubloon varied in value from 33 to 36s sterling or roughly 36 to 40s Virginia currency. A pistole was half a doubloon. Consequently, six pistoles would be 108 to 120s or £5, 8s to £6 Virginia currency. From this compensation, George had to deduct his expenses and the pay of his helpers. If the wages he paid were substantially the same as those allowed by William Ball to his aides in surveying and mapping the watercourses of Lancaster and Northumberland in 1737 (1 C 224, 18 W (2) p. 406), the pay of an assistant was about 2s 6d per day. Paper in 1737 cost Ball slightly under 7s a gross.

107 George Washington's Ledger A (cited hereafter as Ledger A), folio 2.

108 Ibid., entries of June 29 and July 8, 1749.

of risk, as well as of bother. It was flattering to be in one's eighteenth year the banker of the family: it might prove expensive.

At Mount Vernon, at Belvoir, everywhere, George continued to hear discussion of business ventures and of speculative enterprises. Contact with Lawrence and with the Fairfaxes was itself a business education for the younger Washington. Although the health of Lawrence was no better, he discharged patiently his duties as one of the trustees of the new town of Alexandria,[109] he engaged in additional land transactions,[110] and he sought to hasten the dispatch of goods to the frontier for the Ohio Company. Its affairs were not developing as rapidly or as favorably as the Virginia promoters had hoped. The suspicions on the part of the redmen [111] were unrelieved. In addition to the threat presented vaguely by the French, moving from Lake Erie southward, there was nearer rivalry by Pennsylvanians who showed every intention of competing for the fur trade and vigorously asserted title to part of the territory given the Ohio Company.[112] During the months when these were pressing business concerns, talk between the two brothers at Mount Vernon must often have been of the western country.

George went to Fredericksburg in January, 1749/50, and of course spent some time with his mother at Ferry Farm.[113] Conditions there had not changed greatly. Death had taken none of the family, though Catherine Washington Lewis, wife of Fielding Lewis, was near the end of her brief years.[114] Mrs. Mary Washington, George's mother, continued busy with many small things and was charged with three young sons as well as with Betty, who was now sixteen and a half years old and, of course, would soon be marrying. Apropos of matrimony, if Doctor Spencer ever had been seriously inclined to make his addresses to the mistress of Ferry Farm he had ceased to visit her. George heard all this and doubtless observed closely the state of property that was, in theory, to be his when he was 21, but his heart was not at Ferry Farm. Mount Vernon and its activities had come to mean far more to him than the home place on the Rappahannock.

109 He is recorded as present at six meetings between Feb. 27, 1750 and Aug. 3, 1751, though perhaps on occasion and in the instance cited *supra*, p. 233, the record may have credited busy trustees with good intentions rather than with actual attendance (*Proceedings of Trustees* of Alexandria).
110 *Birch Cat.* 663, items 8, 50, 196.   111 See *supra*, p. 237.
112 Thomas Lee to unnamed correspondent, Oct. 18, 1749 (3 *Gooch MSS*, 1011); George Mason to Lawrence Washington, May 27, 1750 (L. W. Smith Coll., *Havemeyer Papers*).
113 He was in Fredericksburg on Jan. 11, 1749/50, according to *Ledger A*, and he may have been at Ferry Farm for the Christmas holidays, but positive proof of this is not available.
114 She died Feb. 19, 1750 (Sorley, *Lewis of Warner Hall*, 136).

From "the Fredericksburg neighborhood," George went back to the Potomac early in the year and probably spent at Lawrence's home his eighteenth birthday. He now had to be regarded as a serious young man of business. Pleasure had its place; making a fortune came first. Pistoles and doubloons were to be sought in strict accordance with the code of honorable conduct that George was developing steadily, but within the limits that character and honesty imposed, gold was to be pursued and caught. Settlers were increasing rapidly on the lower stretches of the Shenandoah; there was work enough there for George, highly profitable work that would reconcile him to sojourning among the "barbarians." He rode over the mountains to the Valley, made on Mch. 30, 1750, his first survey of the spring and continued to use his compass and Jacob's staff, with scant interruption, until the 28th of April. Most of his lines were drawn close to Lost River, where the tracts were not large or the ground confusing. The charge for the average survey and warrant was about £3.[115] As George surveyed forty-seven tracts, his gross compensation must have been close to £140, which few men of his time in Virginia would have regarded as poor pay for approximately one month's work.[116] Before George had gone to the Valley, he had bought himself a handsome set of pole-chair harness at the stiff price of £10, 15s.[117] On his return, he had money for the full enjoyment of his equipage, and he likewise had the consciousness that when he came upon a particularly good piece of unpatented land, he could afford to pay the quit rents on it.

Much had happened on the well-settled part of the Northern Neck while George was in the Valley; still more was about to occur. Catherine Washington Lewis had died on the 19th of February [118] and had left a son, John, who was about three years of age. Her husband, Fielding Lewis, turned at once to George's sister Betty. The siege was brief, surrender was unconditional. On May 7, 1750, Betty was married to him. That event was pleasant, if somewhat precipitate; but at Mount Vernon and at Belvoir, there were troubles. Sally Fairfax, Nancy's sister [119] and the wife of John Carlyle, was pregnant and had symptoms that suggested cancer of the breast. Col. William Fairfax himself had gone to England.

[115] E.g., William Miller's, John Wetlon's, and Walter Wilton's tracts (*Ledger A*, folios 18, 20).
[116] For a list of the surveys, see *Book of Surveys*, ed. Toner, 103-31, and 733 *Papers of G. W.*, LC.
[117] *Ledger A*, folio 7.   [118] Sorley, *Lewis of Warner Hall*, 136.
[119] Sally was a child of Col. William Fairfax's second marriage and consequently was full sister of George William Fairfax.

He was distressed, as were Lawrence and Nancy, at the continued, strange coolness Lord Fairfax was displaying to his kinspeople. None of them could understand why the Proprietor talked of moving permanently to the Shenandoah Valley, or why he was developing what appeared to be positive dislike of those who wished nothing better than to please him. Colonel Fairfax summarized the whole baffling affair in a letter written after his arrival in England: "I hope G[eorge William] F[airfax] will not do anything to offend so as to make a pretext for the intended removal . . . Then if it should happen we might with better reflection intend to make the best of it." [120] Apparently it did not occur to any of the family that the Proprietor had become suspicious of Colonel Fairfax, precisely as he had of his earlier agent, "King" Carter, because he thought his cousin had patented too much land for himself, for his children and for his wife's relative, Gedney Clarke. The grants and purchases of the Fairfaxes and their connections were, in reality, far less than those of the Carters but they certainly passed 57,000 acres.[121]

Most of these clouds were swept from the sky of the Mount Vernon-Belvoir neighborhood in the spring and summer of 1750. Betty's venture in matrimony was manifestly a happy one; Sally Fairfax Carlyle improved in health; [122] George made some remunerative surveys in Culpeper and had a round of visits that extended from Yorktown to Pope's Creek.[123] The continuing distress of the Washington-Fairfax circle was Lawrence's physical condition. Warm weather brought him no relief. Another "change of climate" seemed desirable. As the springs of Berkeley, which George had visited in 1748, were gaining in reputation, it was thought that a visit there might invigorate Lawrence. With him George gladly agreed to go as companion and, if need be, as nurse.

By July 25, 1750, the two brothers were en route to the primitive resort.[124] With a great bend of the Potomac lying to the North, the

120 William Fairfax to Lawrence Washington, Oct. 12, 1750 (L. W. Smith Coll., *Havemeyer Papers;* cf. same to same, July 6, 1750, *ibid*).

121 In *Landmarks,* 263, 272, 340, 342, Fairfax Harrison gave references to 53,000 acres owned by this branch of the Fairfaxes. In addition, *supra,* p. 76, Nancy is known to have had 4000 acres. Harrison insisted (*Landmarks,* 272) that the difference between William Fairfax and Carter was that Fairfax "bought his lands."

122 William Fairfax to Lawrence Washington, Oct. 12, 1750 (L. W. Smith Coll., *Havemeyer Papers*).

123 G. W.'s *Cash Accounts,* LC; *Ledger A.* Established dates are: Culpeper, May 26; Yorktown, June 19–20; Pope's Creek, June 24–July 6; Mount Vernon, July 8.

124 The date is fixed by George's loan of 14s 8d to Lawrence, "going to Warm Springs" (*Ledger A,* folio 4).

approaches to the baths were interesting, but the immediate surround-
ings were commonplace or worse. The springs, George subsequently
reported, "are situated very badly on the east side of a steep mountain,
and inclosed by hills on all sides, so that the afternoon's sun [125] is hid
by 4 o'clock and the fogs hang over us until 9 or 10 which occasion
great damps, and the mornings and evenings to be cool." [126] The water
was devoid of medicinal taste and, having a temperature of $72°$ to $74°$,
was insipid but was assumed to possess curative qualities. It was considered even more beneficial as a bath than when used internally.[127]
While the benefit to Lawrence was transitory if perceptible at all, the
sight of much good land in the region of the Shenandoah revived his
speculative impulse. Either on the basis of patents already issued to
him, or else in the knowledge that his father-in-law would approve
grants for any unoccupied land he desired, Lawrence had George survey three tracts. In addition, George found two customers who desired
his services, with the result that the journey yielded credit entries.[128]

George's departure from the Shenandoah Valley was not earlier
than the afternoon of Aug. 26, 1750, but he lost no time in getting
home and in picking up a few honest pounds. On the 28th, he made
a survey in Fairfax for Capt. George Johnston.[129] After that, work
alternated with play. Late in September or early in October there was
an excursion to Yorktown, where George William Fairfax borrowed

[125] He was writing on Aug. 26, 1761.
[126] Letter to Charles Green (2 G. W., 365). This is the earliest description of the springs
found in the present research. Quotation from this and other accounts of 1769 ff will be found
in Carl Bridenbaugh's article in 3 W (3) p. 160 ff. The Baroness de Riedesel was at the springs
in the summer of 1779 in attendance of her husband, an invalided prisoner of war. She gave a
few hints of life, food and visitors at "Frederick-spring," as she styled the place. A traditional
account of conditions at the resort at a later, unspecified date is printed in J. J. Moorman. *The
Virginia Springs* (1859), p. 308–09: "Rude log huts, board and canvas tents, and even covered
wagons, served as lodging-rooms, while every party brought its own substantial provisions of
flour, meat, and bacon, depending for lighter articles of diet on the 'Hill Folk,' or the success of
their own foragers. A large hollow scooped in the sand, surrounded by a screen of pine brush,
was the only bathing-house; and this was used alternately by ladies and gentlemen. The time
set apart for the ladies was announced by a blast on a long tin horn, at which signal all of the
opposite sex retired to a prescribed distance . . ."
[127] Moorman, *op. cit.*, 315–16.
[128] One of these surveys was for Richard Stevenson and William Davis; the other was for
Edward Musgrave. The list of surveys (733 *Papers of G. W.*, LC) does not specifically state that
the surveys for Lawrence were in the Shenandoah Valley, but the first of the three entries was
made the day after the one for Stevenson and Davis, which is marked "Shenandoah R."
Lawrence's other surveys followed immediately. As the mouth of the Shenandoah is about thirty-
two miles by air from Berkeley Springs, one has to take into account the possibility that Lawrence
and George had left the springs and had come back to Hite's or to Frederick Town before George
began on August 16 the surveys on the Shenandoah, but of this there is no evidence one way or
the other. If the brothers were back in a district close to the river as early as August 16, their
stay at the springs was for less than three weeks.
[129] *Ibid.*

1s 3d that George did not fail to charge against him.[130] As it chanced, the amount was precisely that of George William's part of a bottle of rum, which the two clubbed at Mitchell's in the same town.[131] From Yorktown, George must have proceeded almost directly back to Frederick and must have started surveying as soon as he arrived there.[132] From October 11 to October 24, he ran the lines of approximately sixteen tracts, one of which was "Austin's." Six belonged to Lawrence.[133]

Then, on the 25th, George had a new and delightful experience. He had saved much the greater part of his earnings as a surveyor while cherishing ambition to buy good land when he found a tract that particularly appealed to him in price and quality. The time now came. On the 16th of October he had the high satisfaction of asking transfer of patent for a tract of 453 acres, known as Dutch George's, which he bought of Captain Rutherford—the first spread of friendly Shenandoah land to become his.[134] This was not all: on the 25th of October, he submitted to record a deed from Lord Fairfax for 550 acres of land in Frederick.[135] Part if not the whole of these first lands purchased by George on his own account were located on the north side of the south fork of Bullskin Creek, between the lands of George Johnston and Robert Worthington.[136]

Back George went to his surveys. Now that he was buying land, cold and adverse weather were less of a deterrent to surveying. When early November rains kept him from the fields and forest, he simply waited for a fair day. Not until the 26th of November did Washington make for Lord Fairfax what probably was his last survey West of the

---

[130] Entry of Oct. 7, 1750; *Account Book* A 3.

[131] *Ibid.*, George frequently used in his ledger the term "your club of a bottle of wine" or rum, and in so employing the word was adhering to good usage of the seventeenth and eighteenth centuries. Pepys wrote "club" in the same sense. For Mitchell's ferry and ordinary, see *Ledger* A, folio 8, entry of Mch. 20, 1752, and 23 *W* (2) p. 11, 21, 25.

[132] *L. O. Records, N. N.,* G, 434. The short lapse of time between the entry at Yorktown and the date of this survey shaped the reference in the text to "late September or early October." It is entirely probable in this instance and in numerous others that the ledger entry was made from memory and may not give the precise date.

[133] *L. O. Records, N. N.,* G, 437–73. For his report of Oct. 23, 1750 on Captain Pennington's land in Frederick, see 52 *V* 31.

[134] *L. O. Records, N. N.,* G, 465; 14 *L. O. Records,* 465. The exact location of "Dutch George's" has not been ascertained. It lay between tracts of Robert Worthington and Lawrence Washington. George's own survey of this property was made Nov. 24, 1750 (see his *Survey Book,* LC).

[135] *Birch Cat.* 663, item 82; *L. O. Records, N. N.,* G, 466. The patent was dated Oct. 25, 1750.

[136] *Ibid.* Bullskin Creek flows into the Shenandoah from the West about four miles South of Charles Town, in what is now Jefferson County, W. Va. Robert Worthington had patented 3000 acres in 1730 near the later village of Charles Town and close to Harewood (*W. Va. Guide Book,* 310). George Johnston was a prominent planter for whom George made numerous surveys,

mountains that season.[137] This done, George rode back over the Blue
Ridge, but he was not quite through with his investments for the year.
On Bullskin Creek, West of Vestal's Gap, were 456 acres of James Mc-
Cracken's that would make a most desirable purchase. As soon as
George was at Mount Vernon and could arrange the details, he paid
McCracken £45, took a deed, and promised to tender the balance of
£77 within a few months.[138] George duly met this second payment to
McCracken and could list the farm as his unencumbered own. Sur-
veying was profitable! Besides a handsome income, it had yielded him
1459 acres of good land, part of which he soon leased to a tenant.[139]

George found the household at Mount Vernon busy with a different
balance-sheet. While he had been absent in the Valley, his sister-in-law
Nancy had given birth on Nov. 7, 1750, to her fourth child, another
girl. The new baby was welcomed the more eagerly because she was
the only one in the immediate family, and she was named Sarah, in
honor of her grandmother Fairfax. If Lawrence was disappointed that
the child was a girl, no record survives. Nancy was young and strong
enough to bear him other children, but the condition of the health of
Lawrence raised more acutely than ever the question whether he would
live to look into the face of a boy who would bear his name and inherit
his property. George must be, in a sense, son as well as younger brother.

Lawrence's work that winter of 1750–51 was not a sort to improve his
physical condition. In November, 1750, Thomas Lee, president of the
Ohio Company, came to the end of his remarkable career.[140] His
death in any circumstances would have been a loss to the enterprise; but
occurring when it did, it was certain to hamper difficult negotiations
then under way for the sale of 50,000 acres to German settlers. These
men were disposed to buy, but they were unwilling to pay taxes, as all
Virginians did, for the support of the Church of England. Purchase of
the tract, with consequent prosperity for the Ohio Company and a
measure of protection of the frontier, depended on procuring at the
hands of the General Assembly an act to exempt the settlers from parish-
levies. Passage of such a law would have called for all the skill and

---

[137] *Survey Book,* LC.

[138] Entries of Dec. 4, 1750, and Mch. 16, 1751; *Ledger A,* folio 5. The circumstances suggest
the possibility that the seller came to Mount Vernon with George to complete the transaction.
McCracken may have decided at this date to transfer his energies from farming to distilling.
When he died in 1756, his principal possession was a still with cap and worm (2 *Frederick
Deeds,* 206).

[139] This tenant was John Garner (*Ledger A,* folio 10).

[140] A photograph (VHS) of the inscription on his monument leaves in doubt whether the
date is the 4th or the 14th.

experience of Thomas Lee. Even he might not have succeeded unless all the circumstances had been favorable. Now that he was dead, this parliamentary task and the direction of much of the other business of the company devolved on Lawrence Washington.

"I am well assured," Lawrence wrote soon after he assumed sponsorship of this measure of freedom of religion, "we shall never obtain it by a law here." He explained: "This Colony was greatly settled in the latter part of Charles the First's time and during the usurpation by the zealous churchmen; and that spirit which was then brought in, has ever since continued, so that except a few Quakers we have no Dissenters.[141] But what has been the consequence? We have increased by slow degrees except Negroes and convicts whilst our neighboring Colonies whose natural advantages are greatly inferior to ours have become populous." [142] In this belief, Lawrence appealed to the company's English partner, the London merchant John Hanbury, and to Robert Dinwiddie, who then was in the United Kingdom and on July 20, 1751, was to be appointed Lieutenant Governor of Virginia.[143] Unfortunately, Parliament was preoccupied and John Hanbury was sick.[144]

Harassment over the affairs of the Ohio Company and a further decline in health had forced Lawrence to return again to the Warm Springs even before he wrote his brief discourse on the economic benefits of allowing freedom of religion. George preceded or escorted him. While Lawrence "took the cure" and told German settlers about the riches of the Ohio country,[145] George undertook the usual round of surveys in Frederick.[146] By March 26, Lawrence was ready to leave; [147] but George still had before him the mild adventure of surveying in a

---

141 In this assertion, needless to say, Lawrence was mistaken. Presbyterians were numerous in Virginia; Baptists were arriving from the North.

142 Lawrence Washington to John Hanbury, n.d., but probably written in April, 1751, after Lawrence's second visit to the Warm Springs, mentioned *infra*. See Jared Sparks, ed., *Writings of Washington*—old but indispensable—v. 2, p. 481. Sparks's free editing of Washington correspondence is so notorious that this general critique has to be applied: Unless papers appearing in *Sparks* are printed correctly elsewhere, or are verifiable from the MS, their literal accuracy never can be taken for granted. The meaning seldom is changed perceptibly.

143 Again the reminder may be in order that the titular Lieutenant Governor was active Governor. See *supra*, p. 170.

144 Robert Dinwiddie to Lawrence Washington, Mch. 20, 1751; L. W. Smith Coll., *Havemeyer Papers*.

145 2 *Sparks*, 481.

146 Washington's *Survey Papers*, LC, and *L. O. Records* show surveys from Mch. 1 to May, 1751. The only fixed date of Lawrence's visit is the one covered by the next note.

147 George's ledger entry of March 26 (*Ledger A*, folio 4) shows that he lent Lawrence 2s 6d that date. Two days later, Lawrence was present as a member of the Fairfax County Court (*Fairfax Orders*, 1749–54, p. 135).

new County. Augusta had been formed from the western part of Orange in 1738 [148] and had been required in 1744 to pay its part of the cost of establishing and marking a line between it and Frederick, its northern neighbor.[149] Now that the boundary was fixed, George passed over it and, on June 1, 1751, officially ran his first lines in Northern Augusta. He worked there till the 6th [150] and then he turned homeward again.

Back at Mount Vernon, there was other business to transact—always business now for the young surveyor and trader in lands. Lawrence was sharing in plans for a lottery at Belhaven to raise funds for a church and a market.[151] George concerned himself with the three Fredericksburg lots, left him by his father, on which stood a tavern that had been operated by Doncastle & Black. As this property now was vacant,[152] George had to decide what to do with it. Fredericksburg was crowded at the time; extension of its streets was in prospect; [153] a good price might be had, perhaps, if the lots were sold at auction during the June fair. With the approval of the executors, George advertised two of the lots and offered eight months' credit to the purchaser on proper security. At the time, he found no takers.[154]

The season of the fair and of the proposed sale was that of high grass and of obscuring foliage, the season least favorable for surveys and, as always, the one most appropriate for holidays and excursions. George was not so engrossed in making money that he would deny himself pleasure when no profitable work was at hand. He doubtless went that summer to Chotank and he also spent some time at Ferry Farm, where he had a misadventure. One hot day he walked to a quiet spot on the Fredericksburg side of the river, took off his clothes, and went "washing." [155] When he came out, he found that his clothes had been

[148] 5 H 78.

[149] Ibid., 275.

[150] L. O. Records, N. N. G, 526–38. Washington, needless to say, may have surveyed some Augusta lands before the boundary was marked.

[151] The older name, and not the official "Alexandria," was used in advertisements of this lottery, which was a failure. See Va. Gazette, May 2, July 4, Nov. 7, 1751.

[152] It is not known whether the tenants had left the tavern or whether George had terminated their lease.

[153] Va. Gazette, May 22, 1752; Birch Cat., 663; items 175, 188.

[154] Va. Gazette, Apr. 18, 25, 1751. Two of these lots, Nos. 33 and 34, were sold for £280 current money, Apr. 2, 1753, to Andrew Cochrane, et al., Glasgow merchants (Spotsylvania Deeds, 1751–61, p. 109). The third lot was sold in February, 1755, at £50 to Mrs. Frances Thornton for the benefit of her son John (Spotsylvania Deeds, E, 231; Washington's Ledger A, folio 32).

[155] In rural Virginia, to the end of the nineteenth century, "washing" was used in the current sense of "swimming" or "bathing."

robbed.[156] He complained to the Sheriff or to a Constable, and doubt-less thanked Heaven, as a modest man, that the thieves had not carried off his garments. As suspects, two women servants of Fredericksburg, Ann Carrol and Mary McDaniel, were arrested and locked in jail. George did not linger on the Rappahannock until the women were tried.[157] In August he went with Lawrence on his first recorded journey to Annapolis—a somewhat expensive journey, to judge from George's loan en route of £3, 18s to Lawrence.[158]

Travel was more and more difficult now for Lawrence. The same depressing cough racked him. Although he remained courageous, it did not appear wise—not to say safe—to subject him to another winter in Virginia. A few months in a balmy climate might stay his malady and perhaps restore his health. Whither he should go for this experiment was decided largely because of association. Barbados Island, thirteen degrees North of the Equator, had a reputation as a haven for persons with diseases of the lungs. Winter there was dry and neither too hot nor too cold. Besides, the island was accessible directly from the Potomac by ship. More particularly, Barbados was the home of Gedney Clarke, a merchant of distinction, member of the insular council and a connection of William Fairfax by the Colonel's third marriage.[159] Clarke owned land in Virginia and would help in making arrangements for Lawrence. In short, every circumstance favored Barbados,[160] but manifestly Lawrence could not take Nancy with him. She could not leave her baby; to carry a ten-month-old infant to the tropics would be murderous. If Lawrence was to have companionship, which was almost essential, the arrangement made for the journeys to

---

156 Unfortunately for a good story, the court record makes it reasonably plain that his clothes were not carried off. The culprits were "charged with robing the cloathes of Mr. George Washington." At that period, "rob" had lost the middle English meaning of "steal" and had come to imply "plunder." It is possible, of course, that the Clerk of Spotsylvania used the word "rob" in the earlier sense; but, as stated in the text, the conviction was for petty larceny, not for grand larceny. Virginia at that time had no state law of her own defining petty and grand larceny, and consequently adhered to the common law which drew the line between the two at 12d, provided the theft was not from the person. Had George's clothes been carried off, the conviction certainly would have been of grand larceny.

157 When they were heard, Dec. 3, 1751, Ann turned King's witness and testified against Mary, who was found guilty of petty larceny and was given fifteen lashes on her bare back at the whipping post (*Spotsylvania Orders, 1749–55*, p. 141).

158 Entry of August n.d., *Ledger A*, folio 4.

159 1 *Diaries*, 22, n. 3. There has been difference among the authorities whether Clarke was the brother-in-law or the stepson of Col. William Fairfax, but the genealogy in 34 *N. E. Hist. and Gen. Reg.*, 37, shows Clarke to have been a brother of Mrs. Deborah Clarke Fairfax. The brothers John and Gedney Clarke cannot always be distinguished.

160 For the possibility that Lawrence's choice was influenced by a reading of Griffith Hughes's *Natural History of Barbadoes*, see *infra*, p. 255.

the springs must be repeated; George must accompany his half-brother. "Austin" was too busy; the other boys were too young.

In a measure, of course, the voyage would be a pleasant and perhaps a fascinating experience for a young man who once had thought he would be a sailor. Financially, long absence from Virginia would be serious for George. It would involve the loss of the autumn season of surveying and, perhaps, the sacrifice of the chance of finding some new bargains in frontier lands. No hint of any balancing of loss against gain or of cost against duty appears in anything George is known to have said then or afterward. Family obligation came first; Lawrence needed his company. That was enough. Everything else could wait.

The vessel left the Potomac Sept. 28, 1751,[161] and by October 4 she had gone far to the Southeast of the Virginia Capes and was standing eastward in the latitude of the Bermudas. George was interested in the tacks and the runs before the wind, because these were much like the lines he made in platting his surveys. He either took out a blank book he had brought with him or else he made one from sheets of paper he procured on the vessel; and, day by day, he diligently ruled the spaces in the form of a log, and made careful, regular entries. It was almost intuitive to set down the progress he was making, whether to Barbados or to the status of landed proprietor.[162]

Besides keeping his log, George determined to learn the ropes and rigging, the spars and the sails, concerning which he knew little. As always, he applied himself diligently to a new subject, and by October 16[163] he could employ the regular logging abbreviations in describing changes of sail. Hourly, he scanned the horizon and determined the type and course of ships that were sighted, a task not difficult for a young man who, on the Potomac, had seen vessels of almost every cut and rig. He jotted down in his log a few words about each merchantman that passed, and, when weather and seas were favorable, he fished. Apparently he did no reading and probably had taken no books with him.

Frequent rains led the sailors to swear, after the manner of their calling, that they never had seen such weather before. The sole excitement came when a sloop that had been within sight for two days

---

161 1 *Diaries*, 16 n. Her name is not given.

162 The position of the ship every day on the outward voyage is shown on the inside cover-page of the *George Washington Atlas* from fragmentary entries printed in Toner's edition, 1892, of the *Daily Journal of Major* [sic] *George Washington in 1751–52*. Fitzpatrick's text of the diary begins, without explanation, on October 4, as if there were no previous entries.

163 1 *Diaries*, 18.

hoisted a signal. Whether it was one of distress, the officers on George's ship could not tell. Even had the sloop been asking help, the wind was so contrary that no relief could have been afforded. Nothing more was seen of the vessel.[164]

Daily, after that, as October drew to its close, the weather improved. On the 30th George could write: "This morning arose with agreeably [sic] assurances of a certain and steady trade wind which after near five weeks buffeting and being tossed by a fickle and merciless ocean was glad'ening knews . . ."[165] The second dawn afterward, at 4 o'clock, George was awakened by a sudden cry, "Land, land." He and Lawrence sprang out of their bunks and ran to the deck, half fearful the vessel was heading for a reef. Instead, they found to their delighted surprise that the southwestern tip of the island of Barbados was about three leagues off to the eastward. According to the officers' faulty reckoning, the ship should at the time have been almost 150 leagues from a landfall and should have been approaching the eastern side of the island. "Had we been [distant] but three or four leagues more," George wrote, "we should have been out of sight of the island, run down the latitude and probably not have discovered [the] error in time to have gain'd land for three weeks or more."[166]

Beating inshore and entering shallow Carlisle Bay on the southwestern coast was slow work but was completed on the 3rd. Lawrence and George went ashore to a tavern in Bridgetown, the principal settlement on the island, and they soon met Major Clarke.[167] Through the kindness of this gentleman, who insisted that the Virginians lodge temporarily at his house, arrangements were made for an examination of Lawrence the next day by Dr. William Hilary, a physician of much experience in treating diseases of the lungs.

George must have waited in affectionate anxiety as Doctor Hilary talked with Lawrence on the 4th, and he must have felt joyful relief when he heard the physician's conclusion: Lawrence's disease was not so deeply seated that it could not be cured. Of this, Hilary gave confident assurance. His encouragement led the two young men to start off late that same afternoon in quest of lodgings, which the doctor

---

164 1 *Diaries*, 19–21.   165 *Ibid.*, 21.

166 *Ibid.*, 21. A satisfactory map of Barbados at this period is that of Emanuel Bowen. LC has a copy.

167 It is impossible to say whether this was John or Gedney Clarke. Further, as the page covering the entries for November 3 and part of November 4 is missing from the diary, a complete narrative of George's first hours on the island cannot be written, but some fragmentary references are mentioned *infra*, n. 182.

urged them to take outside the town.[168] As there were no inns or
taverns in the rural parts of the island, inquiry had to be made at private
homes. No suitable quarters in a residence were found that evening;
but if this was a disappointment to Lawrence, the ride was exciting to
his younger brother. George was almost overwhelmed by the beauty
of the tropical landscape.[169] It was the first time he ever had seen any
other foliage than the reserved greens of his own Virginia. He scarcely
could believe that vegetation could be so lush or fruits so rich.

Letter writing on the 6th and much hospitality on the 7th were followed the next day by conclusion of a bargain for board and lodging
at the house of Captain Crofton, commander of Fort James. The price
was outrageously high—£15 a month exclusive of liquors and washing
—but to George the site was almost ideal. It was close to the water and
not more than a mile from the town.[170] "The prospect," George wrote,
"is extensive by land and pleasant by sea, as we command the prospect
of Carlisle [171] Bay and all the shipping in such manner that none can
go in or out without being open to our view." [172]

The delights of the view were equalled by the cordiality of the residents of the island. Except for the Governor, Henry Grenville, who
kept himself aloof from nearly all society on the island, each of the
dignitaries seemed anxious to entertain the Virginians. Lawrence soon
discovered that he had to do his visiting in the evening or, as he explained, "by the first dawn of the day, for by the time the sun is half
an hour high, it is as hot as any time of the day." [173] George did not
find this temperature so complete a barrier to free movement. He
purchased on the 9th a barrel of limes that Fielding Lewis had asked
him to buy and forward, and he commanded his memory to remind him
to charge Fielding the 15s he laid out.[174] Many other fruits George saw
and admired at homes to which he received invitations while Lawrence
was forced to remain indoors. One of George's visits was to Fort
James, which he viewed as critically as if he had been a military engineer. "It's pretty strongly fortified," he wrote in his diary, "and
mounts about 36 guns within the fortifications, but [has] two fascine

---

[168] 1 *Diaries*, 22.   [169] *Ibid.*

[170] The home where Washington is said to have resided, in the southeastern part of the
present town, is preserved, though somewhat altered—*Letter of Vice Consul Samuel H. Young,*
Jan. 24, 1947.

[171] He spelled it Carlyle.   [172] 1 *Diaries*, 23.

[173] 2 *Sparks*, 422. The letter quoted in the text is said by Sparks to have been addressed,
n.d., by Lawrence to "Lord Fairfax," but the tone indicates it was written to Col. William
Fairfax.

[174] *Ledger A*, folio 8.

batteries mg.[175] 51." No officer was to know from George's manner that this probably was the first fort the visitor ever had seen.[176]

On the evening of the 15th George had another experience that was unusual, if not new.[177] A hospitable gentleman of Bridgetown gave him a ticket to the playhouse, where "George Barnwell, a Tragedy"[178] was to be presented. George may not have been so informed, but this was one of the most popular English dramas of half a century. Written by George Lillo and first presented at Drury Lane, June 22, 1731, it had won the praise of Alexander Pope and had drawn the tears of twenty audiences before the summer was out. Thereafter it had been a part of the company's repertoire and had been played, in particular, at Christmas and at Easter, because the theme was laudatory of London merchants and was thought to be good for the morals of their apprentices.

Young Washington took his seat in the playhouse and listened to the prologue, which announced:

"A London 'Prentice ruin'd is our theme,
Drawn from the fam'd old song that bears his name."

The scene was in London and in a village outside the city; the time was that of the Spanish Armada. A rich merchant's beautiful daughter, doomed to marry a courtier, was in love with one of her father's apprentices. With the ancestral craft of her sex, she doubtless would have found a way of making him love her, and, having done that, she would have won her father's consent—but for the unfortunate fact that the apprentice fell into the hands of a bourgeois Lady Macbeth. She seduced him, turned him into a thief and a murderer and, at last, betrayed him. Doomed and in his prison, he received a visit from his master's daughter who confessed her love and then agonized as he was led out to execution. His final message was:

If any youth, like you, in future times
Shall mourn my fate, tho' he abhors my crimes;

175 That is, mounting pieces that fired balls of fifty-one pounds.
176 1 *Diaries*, 25. George wrote only that he visited "the fort," but the proximity of Fort James makes identification almost certain. Had any other fort been inspected, he doubtless would have named it.
177 There is no previous mention in the records of a visit by George to a "playhouse," but as those records are far from complete, the possibility of attendance at a Williamsburg theatre cannot be eliminated. See n. 198 *infra*.
178 The original title was "The London Merchant, or the History of George Barnwell" (*DNB*, article, George Lillo).

Or tender maid, like you, my tale shall hear,
And to my sorrows give a pitying tear;
To each such melting eye and throbbing heart,
Would gracious Heaven this benefit impart,
Never to know my guilt, nor feel my pain,
Then must you own, you ought not to complain
Since you nor weep, nor shall I die in vain.[179]

George listened and looked and, if he wept, he did not admit it on paper. Instead he wrote: "The character of Barnwell and several others was said to be well perform'd. There was music a Dapted and regularly conducted by Mr.   ." [180] Apparently George was not quite sure about "adapted"; but if that was what more experienced persons said, it went into his journal and into his vocabulary.

The next day George and Lawrence received a morning visitor; that evening George dined with Major Clarke. On the morning of November 17, the younger Washington felt a curious rigor and then had a high fever. Before evening he was seized with a violent headache and with pains in his back and loins. The next day the debilitating symptoms were the same. Doctor Lanahan, who was called in early, may not have alarmed George with a diagnosis then or on the third day, which brought no abatement of headache or of pain. By the 20th, red spots were discernible on the young man's forehead and among the roots of his hair. In a few hours, these spots became thickly set papules. Then, of course, no doubt was left: George had the smallpox. The development of the papules, which changed to vesicles by the 22nd, was a relief, because George's temperature dropped. For a short time only was he less uncomfortable; on the 25th or 26th there was a return of the fever.[181]

It was the worst of fortune that George should have been stricken on

---

[179] One cannot be sure the version given at Bridgetown included the absurd epilogue by Colley Cibber. In this, the afflicted maiden appeared in front of the curtain and began in words befitting a Virginia widow of George's own day:

Since fate has robb'd me of the hapless youth
For whom my heart had hoarded up its truth;
By all the laws of love and honour, now,
I'm free again to choose—and one of you.

She thereupon teased her audience through some twenty stupid lines and at last made her bid:

. . . my heart to this conclusion draws;
I yield it to the hand that's loudest in applause.

[180] *Diaries*, 25.

[181] These dates are not given in any surviving record but are used on the assumption that the malady followed the normal course of confluent smallpox.

his first visit to a beautiful tropical country that had entranced him. Apparently, he had contracted the disease before he and Lawrence moved to Captain Crofton's. Indeed, George may have had his contact with an active case on the day after he landed.[182] As for Lawrence, he was inconvenienced and distressed, of course, but he was immune.[183] Lanahan also must have had the disease previously, because he did not hesitate to attend George.[184] Kind oblivion has covered what Captain Crofton had to say about the embarrassing outcome of the profitable bargain for the entertainment of the Washingtons.

George was busy with his painful battle until about the 28th. Then the pustules that had developed from the vesicles quickly dried up. The "suppurative fever" diminished and then disappeared. George's entire body and particularly his face itched furiously. Soon the scabs began to fall off. Underneath were reddish brown spots. George knew that these would leave "pits" which he would carry with him through life, but he had won the fight that almost every man of his generation expected to have to wage. On Thursday, December 12, Washington was dismissed by his physician and was able to visit Bridgetown and to dine with the Clarkes. If they perhaps had exposed him unwittingly to the disease, they had atoned generously. Members of the family had called on him often and had supplied everything they could to ease his illness.[185]

The day he first went to town, George resumed his diary and in a single sentence of thirty-one words described his combat with the disease. All that he admitted on the sheet before him concerning his pain and fever was that he "was strongly attacked." [186] The one unimaginative adverb "strongly" must cover everything he suffered. Moreover, after he wrote briefly that evening a few words about his visit to the Clarkes, he put his malady behind him and, without losing even half a line for a new paragraph, went on to describe the sensational

[182] The period of incubation probably is from ten days to a fortnight, or in George's case, between November 3 and 10. According to Jared Sparks's version of the journal, the missing entry for November 4 was in the manuscript when he edited it. This entry records that Major Clarke invited Lawrence and George to breakfast and to dine with him on the 4th. "We went," Sparks has George say, "—myself with some reluctance, as the smallpox was in the family" (2 *Sparks*, 424, quoted in Toner, *op. cit.*, 40).
[183] No positive record of Lawrence's illness from smallpox has been found, but the circumstances and the quoted language of George's diary leave no doubt that the elder brother did not fear exposure.
[184] 1 *Diaries*, 25.   [185] 1 *Diaries*, 25.
[186] "17th. Was strongly attacked with the small Pox: sent for Dr. Lanahan whose attendance was very constant till my recovery, and going out which was not 'till Thursday the 12th of December." (1 *Diaries*, 25.)

trial of Colonel Chaunack. The Colonel must have been a retired or militia officer, and, according to island gossip, was "a man of opulent fortune and infamous character." A maid servant having complained that the Colonel had raped her, he was indicted, was tried, and, as George had it, was acquitted on the testimony of a single individual who was believed to have been suborned.[187]

Doubtless this trial was a subject of argument at a succession of dinners that George and Lawrence attended every day, except one, between the 13th and the 20th. In private, discussion between the two brothers concerned their own plans. Lawrence was discouraged. He had no dependence on George for nursing and he gave no indication of sudden or swift decline, but he had not gained in health and he greatly missed Nancy and their little girl. The sameness of the climate and of the view from Captain Crofton's house depressed him. No diversion was offered other than dancing, which was supposed to bring on yellow fever. His sensitiveness to the heat of the island almost imprisoned him at his quarters and made him yearn for a change of season. "Our bodies," he said, "are too much relaxed and require a winter to brace them up." Although not quite prepared to call his visit a failure, he was close to a decision that if he did not improve soon, he would go to the Bermudas. If that did not help, he would return home and try once more the dry air of Frederick County.[188]

All this would involve more months away from Mount Vernon. During that time, George could be of small assistance to his brother, though the best season for surveying in Frederick might pass when the trees leafed in the summer of 1752. George might as well return to Virginia—and on Captain John Saunders's vessel *Industry* which was then in Carlisle Bay and soon was to sail for Virginia. This was agreed. On the 19th of December, 1751, George purchased the clothing and other articles he would need on the long voyage. Two days later he said farewell to Lawrence and the friends he had made on the island. By noon, the *Industry* was out of Carlisle Bay.[189]

George did not resume the detailed log he had kept while outward bound, but he made frequent entries in journal form and, in particular, wrote a description, about 750 words in length, of the island he had left. As was to be expected of a young man of business, the essay was concerned primarily with the economy of Barbados. Its fruits much

187 1 *Diaries*, 25–26.
188 Letter to Fairfax cited in 2 *Sparks*, 423.   189 1 *Diaries*, 26–27.

interested George, especially its pineapples, but as he knew these were described in Rev. Griffith Hughes's *Natural History of the Barbadoes*, which he had read,[190] he did not elaborate.

The growing of sugar cane was interesting, also, to George. He had questioned islanders concerning costs and the relationship between the price of rum and the profit on sugar. Their figures baffled him: "How wonderful that such people should be in debt! and not be able to indulge themselves in all the luxuries as well as necessaries of life. Yet so it happens. Estates are often alienated for debt." The interest rate, he had found, was 8 per cent, which he considered a "cancer" to a property bought entirely on credit, "but," he went on, "how persons coming to estates of two, three and four hundred acres (which are the largest) can want is most wonderful to me." George remarked the absence from the island of those "who," as he put it, "may be called middling people." There were "either very rich or very poor for, by a law of the island, every gentleman is obliged to keep a white person for ten acres, capable of acting in the militia, and consequently persons so kept can't but [be] very poor."

The young Virginia planter, brother of a Cartagena veteran, did not overlook the defenders of Barbados: "They are well disciplined and appointed to their several stations so that upon an alarm every man is at his post in less than two hours. They have large intrenchments cast up wherever it's possible for an enemy to land and may not (as nature has greatly assisted) improperly be said to be one entire fortification."[191]

All this information Washington stored in his mind. For the rest, the homeward voyage interested him little. On the 23rd, the combination of a brisk trade wind and a heavy swell was too much for George. He was "very sick"—the first and only admission in his journal that he did not have the full equipment of a good sailor[192]—but Christmas Day found him restored. With the ship's captain he ate heartily of a long-fattened goose, of beef and of other viands, and drank to the health of absent friends.[193]

Year's End and New Year's Day, 1751/52, brought an unpleasant storm. After that came varying weather, more often boisterous than

---

190 His one reference to this book, published in 1750, gives no indication whether he first saw it on the island, or had read it before he left Virginia. The list of Virginia subscribers included both Lord Fairfax and Col. William Fairfax. Consequently, there may have been one or perhaps two copies of the volume at Belvoir. The possibility is obvious that interest aroused by this book may have been a minor consideration in leading Lawrence to go to Barbados. See *supra*, p. 247.   191 1 *Diaries*, 28–29.
192 1 *Diaries*, 29.   193 *Ibid*.

mild, but nothing else of interest or excitement until the 10th. Then, in going through his chest, George discovered that he had been robbed of sixteen pistoles. He set down the fact in his journal and added not one word of complaint or suspicion. Much as he disliked to lose the equivalent of £10 and more, he unconsciously was developing the character to accept without complaint what he could not prevent or cure.[194] The case was different with matters, particularly money matters, he could control.

On the 16th, *Industry* spoke the sloop *Glasgow,* bound from St. Kitts for Norfolk. The next day Captain Saunders was hailed by the master of a bilander [195] sailing from St. Kitts to Philadelphia. The two officers agreed to keep together, if they could, but lost sight of each other in a storm on the 18th and 19th of January. Nothing then relieved the tedium of the voyage until the 23rd. That day the good weather led the mate to leave the cabin where, in the language of George's journal, "since the third or fourth day after leaving Barbados, [the officer had] been cooped up with a fashionable disease contracted there." To George, the enticement of the unhappy gentleman to the deck suggested "a snail enlivened by the genial heat of the sun." [196]

On the thirty-sixth day out of Carlisle Bay, land birds were seen. Sedge and marsh weed floated with the waves. Soundings showed only twenty-two fathoms of water. The next day the Virginia capes were sighted; by 11 P.M. that 27th of January, the vessel was off the mouth of the York River. After landing on the 28th,[197] George hired a horse and rode over to Williamsburg to call on the Governor and to present letters entrusted to him.[198] Governor Dinwiddie had gone to Green Spring, six miles off, but as he was expected back later in the day, George spent the intervening hours in "the great metropolis," as he half-jestingly termed the town. When the Governor returned in the evening he received George cordially, invited him to stay and dine, and inquired thoughtfully concerning the health of Lawrence. It was George's first chat with a man he was to know much better at a later

---

[194] 1 *Diaries,* 32.

[195] A bilander was a small coastal vessel of the general design of a Dutch hoy, which usually was sloop-rigged. On a bilander, no two sides of its quadrilateral sail were parallel; that is to say, the sail was trapezoidal.   [196] 1 *Diaries,* 34–35.

[197] The date is torn from the MS of the journal but the arrangement of the entries makes it reasonably certain.

[198] This visit of Jan. 28, 1751/52 is the first recorded appearance of George in Williamsburg, but he may have been there in July, 1748, and in October, 1751, and he probably went to the city at an undetermined date to get his commission as Surveyor.

time, though Dinwiddie was in no sense a stranger to Virginia. He had been Surveyor General of the Southern Colonies for some years before he had been made Governor.[199]

From Williamsburg, George returned on the 29th to Yorktown. There he found Col. John Lewis,[200] who had come to town, along with the gentry of that region, to witness a great main of cocks. To battle those fowls that triumphantly had challenged the dawn on Queen's Creek, gentlemen of Gloucester had brought from their estates a hundred that had won barnyard renown. The affair, moreover, was not to be one in which the owners of the cocks merely were to observe in critical detachment the fine points of attack and counterstroke. Five pistoles were staked on each battle and 100 on the odd bout. If the gamble did not sharpen spurs, it indubitably sharpened interest. George was not averse to watching and to betting; but this time the main was too long for him or, more probably, for the Colonel. The two left together in Lewis's chariot and rode to that gentleman's home.[201] Thence, in conveyances loaned him by planters, George went to Hobb's Hole, later Tappahannock, and on to Layton's Ferry. It probably was on the 5th or 6th of February, 1752, that he reached Mount Vernon and reported to Nancy on Lawrence's condition and plans,[202] and on his own experiences.

Besides giving him some acquaintaince with the loose tropical economy of the island, George's visit to Barbados had shown him something of the markets offered Virginia in the British West Indies. More personally, he had demonstrated on the island what he probably had no reason to doubt—that he could go into new society and, when he accepted an invitation, could so conduct himself that he received new invitations from guests he met. That was not the sole gain from the voyage or the only item to be written on the ledger. Money had been lost because time had been. Others had made the surveys that

199 As noted *supra*, p. 170, Dinwiddie had been appointed July 4, 1751 in succession to Sir William Gooch, who died in December, 1751. The arrival of Dinwiddie at Yorktown had been on Nov. 20, 1751. Apparently the death of Gooch was not known in America until some months after its occurrence (see *Md. Gazette*, Mch. 12, 1752; *Va. Gazette*, Feb. 27, 1752).

200 Fitzpatrick (1 *Diaries*, 36) suggested that this might be Robert Lewis, but that gentleman was residing then in Albemarle. All the circumstances indicate that George's companion was John Lewis, father of Fielding Lewis, George's new brother-in-law.

201 For the special characteristics of a chariot, see Chapter IV, *supra*, 153. Cockfights are described in the same chapter, p. 121.

202 The dates are torn from the final pages of George's journal. Only fragments are left of the entries (1 *Diaries*, 36). Manifestly the dates "March 4," etc., in *ibid.* n. 3, should be February.

would have been assigned George. The worst feature of the stay on the island proved to be the best: That pain, that burning fever, that ugly eruption of smallpox had left George immune. He could go now to frontier, to camp, or to barrack without fear. The ancestral foe could not strike him down.

CHAPTER VII

THE ADJUTANT MAKES A DECISION
(February, 1752–October, 1753)

THE SIX MONTHS that followed George's return from Barbados in February, 1752, were crowded with incident. After rest and visits to kinspeople, he went to Frederick County in March and undertook new surveys that occupied the greater part of his time until nearly the 1st of May.[1] In gross receipts, the work was as profitable as ever, but it was subject, at least in theory, to a deduction not previously made. Under the charter of 1693, which gave the College of William and Mary exclusive authority in Virginia to commission County Surveyors,[2] the institution received one-sixth of the fees those officers collected. Lord Fairfax and his surveyors apparently had ignored this provision of the college charter, which had the effect of law. Indeed, Fairfax had employed surveyors for his domain precisely as he hired men for other work, and apparently he had not troubled himself to ascertain whether they had qualified before the college.[3] At the instance of the President,[4] Governor Dinwiddie tactfully admonished Lord Fairfax in May, 1752, to have the surveyors procure commissions and pay the college the stipulated one-sixth of their receipts.[5] The first of these two requirements did not trouble George, because he already had a Surveyor's commission, but compliance with the demand for the college's share of his fees would reduce his gross income by 16-2/3 per cent.[6] In spite of this, George's thrift and diligence yielded money enough in 1752 for him to increase his holdings of land on Bullskin

---

1 See Ledger A, folios 5 and 6; Survey Papers of G. W., LC., Mch. 19, 1752; 674 Papers of G. W., 11, LC. Ledger A shows that after May 1, George was in Fredericksburg.

2 See supra, Chapter IV.

3 Fairfax had been treated with great courtesy by the colonial government and had been given an honor unique. By action of the Council, Oct. 13, 1749, he had been empowered to act as a Justice of the Peace in all the Counties of the Northern Neck (5 E. J., 301). For his qualification, Nov. 17, 1749, as Justice and County Lieutenant of Frederick, see Norris, 86.

4 William Dawson, who died July 24, 1752.

5 Dinwiddie to Lord Fairfax, May 6, 1752; 1 Din., 19–21.

6 Nothing whatever concerning this demand or Washington's compliance with it has been found. Records of William and Mary show no payments by him.

Creek, Both he and Lawrence had regarded that part of Frederick County as particularly desirable; both had bought extensively there. Now, from George Johnston, on Mch. 16, 1752, George acquired 552 acres at a price of slightly over 4s an acre. From his savings, George was able to pay the £115 within less than a month after he received the deeds.[7]

On his return from Frederick County, following this transaction, George was stricken with pleurisy which, as he subsequently wrote, reduced him "very low" and left him much weakened.[8] This embarrassed and doubtless irritated him because, at that particular and appropriate season, he was engaged in what he considered a most important negotiation. George was in love. That, of course, was no new experience for a young man in his twenty-first year. From the time he had romped in school at Fredericksburg, he had possessed a normal boy's interest in the opposite sex, but he was not glib of speech and he had a certain self-deprecatory attitude in dealing with girls. From early youth he had been confident in all his work and all his pleasure, so long as men were involved; with girls, he must have been self-conscious. Occasionally he wrote vague, sighing poetry to them, or about them. When Frances Alexander had attracted him, approximately at the time of his first journey beyond the mountains in 1748, he ardently but laboriously had begun this acrostic in her honor:

> From your bright sparkling Eyes, I was undone;
> Rays, you have more transparent than the sun,
> A midst its glory in the rising Day,
> None can you equal in your bright array;
> Constant in your calm and unspotted Mind;
> Equal to all, but will to none Prove kind,
> So Knowing, seldom one so Young, you'l Find
> Ah! woe's me, that I should love and conceal,
> Long have I wish'd, but never dare reveal,
> Even though severly Loves Pains I feel;
> Xerxes that great, was't free from Cupid's Dart,
> And all the greatest Heroes, felt the smart.[9]

[7] *Ledger A,* folio 5. George paid £105 16s 3d on order to Thomas McCradie. The balance was covered by various small items of service rendered Johnston. Bullskin Creek flows into the Shenandoah from the West, at a point four miles South of Charlestown.

[8] G. W. to William Fauntleroy, May 20, 1752 (1 *G. W.,* 22). This attack of pleurisy raises a question: Did George contract tuberculosis from Lawrence and subsequently shake it off? G. W. P. Custis wrote, *op. cit.,* 527–28, that Washington late in life was noticeably flat-chested.

[9] 1 *G. W.,* 19.

There he had stopped. Although he had contrived to get awkwardly over the hurdle of the "x" in "Alexa," he did not finish the "nder."

Perhaps discouraged but not deterred, he had tried his hand at another:

> Oh Ye Gods why should my Poor Resistless Heart
> Stand to oppose thy might and Power
> At Last surrender to cupid's feather'd Dart
> And now lays Bleeding every Hour
> For her that's Pityless of my grief and Woes
> And will not one me Pity take
> Ile sleep amongst my most Inveterate Foes
> And with gladness never with [sic] to Wake
> In deluding sleepings let my Eyelids close
> That in an enraptured Dream I may
> In a soft lulling sleep and gentle repose
> Possess those joys denied by Day.[10]

If he intended this to be a sonnet, he had balked at the final couplet, and he had not employed any of the punctuation he usually introduced with a generous if uncritical hand. As he left the lines in his journal, there no doubt they remained. More personal relations had not been lacking, though they had not been taken too seriously. He had sighed over a "Low Land Beauty" when he still was too young to marry,[11] and he had found attraction in an unidentified "Sally" when he was a little older.[12] The girl with whom he was most frequently thrown at Belvoir and at Mount Vernon was Mary Cary, younger sister of the tantalizing Sally Cary, whom George's friend, George William Fairfax, had married. Washington's family connection with Sally was somewhat tenuous—that of the brother of her husband's sister's husband. With Mary, not even a Virginia genealogist could have found kinship for George; but the girl was at hand and, in George's word, was "very agreeable." [13] He might have fallen in love with her had he not been, at first, in a tangle of affection for other girls.

Now, in the spring of 1752, he turned seriously in another direction. At Naylor's Hole in Richmond County, diagonally across the Rappahannock and upstream from Hobbs's Hole, lived William Fauntleroy,

---

[10] *Ibid.*

[11] G. W. to "Friend Robin [Washington?]" n.d., but probably c. 1748–49 (1 *G. W.*, 16).

[12] G. W. to "Sally" n.d., but, from the style, perhaps two years later than the letter to "Friend Robin" (1 *G. W.*, 16).

[13] G. W. to "Friend Robin" and to "Sally," *loc. cit.*

fourth of that name in Virginia. He was thirty-nine years of age in 1752, was son of the third William Fauntleroy and of Apphia Bushrod,[14] and was Justice and Burgess of the County. His interests were more in ships and in trade than in crops and plantations.[15] Like many of his peers he operated a ferry and collected tithes for the parish.[16] In a word, Fauntleroy was of the established, dominant class, though not of the wealthiest or most eminent. He was proud of his station and anxious to maintain it. When only 28, he had ordered "a handsome chair to go with two horses abreast and a whip to have my name on it." If his coat of arms on the chair did not cost too much, Fauntleroy wanted that, too.[17] By his first wife, Elizabeth, he had a daughter of the same name. Familiarly "Betsy," this girl was in her sixteenth year [18] when she dazzled the eyes of George. As befitted a young gentleman who had examined critically the fortifications of Barbados, he undertook the siege of Betsy's heart by formal approaches. Repulsed in his first attack, he had to wait until he had recovered from the pleurisy. Then, as his convalescence was ending, he wrote her in May, 1752, and, on the 20th, forwarded the letter under cover of one to her father. It read:

Sir: I should have been down long before this, but my business in Frederick detained me somewhat longer than I expected, and immediately on my return from thence I was taken with a violent pleurise, which has reduced me very low; but purpose, as soon as I recover my strength, to wait on Miss Betsy, in hopes of a revocation of the former cruel sentence, and see if I can meet with any alteration in my favor. I have enclosed a letter to her, which should be much obliged to you for the delivery of it. It [sic] have nothing to add but my best respects to your good lady and family.[19]

Diplomacy and persistence alike were unrewarded. Betsy's answer again was in the negative, so strongly negative, in fact, that George abandoned the siege. Her name never again appeared in any of his correspondence that survived the years.[20]

14 P. A. Bruce in 1 V 224 mistakenly named Apphia Bushrod as the wife of William Fauntleroy IV.

15 Juliet Fauntleroy, Colonel Moore Fauntleroy, his Ancestors and Descendants, 527. The fourth William Fauntleroy may have lost part of his lands before his death in 1793, but at that time he held 1360 acres only.

16 Ibid.   17 32 V 129.

18 Born, July 26, 1736.

19 1 G. W., 22, original in 674 Papers of G. W., 12, LC.

20 She married, first, Bowler Cocke of the Bremo estate on James River, in Henrico—not to be confused with the Bremo in Fluvanna—and after his death, she became the wife of his

If George felt any real grief over his rejection by Betsy, he now had a deeper, absorbing concern over his elder half-brother. Lawrence had lingered in Barbados approximately three months after George's departure. Then, as previously planned, Lawrence went to Bermuda. His letters from that island in April indicated that he had moved too early in the year. The chill of the spring had renewed the worst of his symptoms. After a time he showed some improvement but, as he wrote, he was "like a criminal condemned, though not without hopes of reprieve." He was denied by his doctor all meat and strong liquor and was required to ride as much as he could endure. Lawrence explained: "These are the only terms on which I am to hope for life. My doctor is an excellent guide for me to follow, who by a perseverance in a milk diet has restored his constitution from a most desperate state. These are hard terms, but what he adds are worse yet, that winter in Virginia will not only render it of no service but will most certainly destroy me . . . As my endeavor to overcome this cruel disorder has already cost me much money and fatigue, I should unwillingly give over the pursuit while any just foundation for hope remains. Six weeks will determine me what to resolve on." He speculated on the possibility that he might remain in Bermuda a year. If he did so, he said, he would like George to bring out Nancy and the baby to see him, but he left the decision to her and her friends.[21]

Lawrence's next letter [22] was grimmer in tone. He wrote: "The unhappy state of health which I labor under makes me uncertain as to my return. If I grow worse I shall hurry home to my grave; if better, I shall be induced to stay here longer to complete a cure." [23] While this uncertainty remained, Nancy Washington kept close to Mount Vernon and to Belvoir. George went to Ferry Farm and then with his younger brother Samuel made a round of visits, though doubtless always on call if any news of Lawrence arrived.[24]

cousin Thomas Adams, who resided in Henrico and later on Cow Pastures, Augusta County, and subsequently was a member of the Continental Congress (Fauntleroy, *op. cit.*, 527). The identification of Betsy as the "Low Land Beauty" of Washington's earlier love affair may be rejected with reasonable certainty because of her age. All the internal evidence suggests that the letters which mention the "Low Land Beauty" were written in 1748 or, at latest, in 1749. Betsy then was twelve or thirteen. That would not have been too early an age for the courtship of a well-developed girl in the early days of the Colony. By 1750, conditions were different. A boy of sixteen or seventeen then would have been interested in girls nearer his own age.

21 Lawrence Washington to "a friend," April, n.d., 1752; 2 *Sparks,* 423.

22 That is to say, the next that has been preserved.

23 Addressee not named, 1752, n.d., quoted in 2 *Sparks,* 423.

24 *Ledger A,* folio 7, covering Samuel's account, shows they were at Andrew Drummond's May 23 and 31 and "at the play-house" June 2, 1752, but no details are given.

Instead of another letter, Lawrence himself came. Sometime prior
to June 16 he landed from Bermuda—with his death sentence written
on his face. He knew that his end was at hand and he proceeded
courageously, if hurriedly, to put his affairs in such order as was possible
after so long an absence. "In consideration of love and affection," he
transferred to George his share in the reversion under his father's will
of the three lots in Fredericksburg, and he had his mother and his
younger half-brothers witness the paper.[25] On the 20th of June, he
hastily completed and signed his will in the presence of William
Waite, John North and Andrew Warren; and on the 26th of July,
1752, at the age of 34 or 35, he breathed his painful last,[26] to the overwhelming distress of the younger brother, who looked on him as more
than a brother. George had the sombre duty of arranging for the
funeral and for the construction of a burial vault.[27] His, too, was
much of the early work in the execution of Lawrence's will, which
proved to be complicated and vaguely drawn.

The master of Mount Vernon bequeathed his wife a life interest in
that property and in his lands on Bullskin Creek, together with half his
slaves; and he provided that all his estate, exclusive of specific bequests,
should descend to his infant daughter, Sarah. Were Sarah to die without issue, part of her estate was to go to her mother, if alive, and part
of her lands were to be divided equally among Lawrence's brother
and half brother. "Austin," in this contingency, was to have specified
land and the iron furnace stock, subject to the payment to Mrs.
Lawrence Washington of one-third of the profits from the stock.
George was to share equally in the real estate that was to go to
Lawrence's brothers in the event of Sarah's childless death. Further,
if Sarah died without issue, George was to have Mount Vernon and
all of Lawrence's other real estate in Fairfax County when Nancy's
life ended.[28] At least, this was the interpretation the Washington

25 June 16, 1752; *Birch Cat.* 663; item 188. This probably is the "indenture of release"
mentioned, July 7, 1752, in *Spotsylvania Orders*, 1750-55, p. 181. Another copy exists in
L. O. Records, N. N., E, 49. The fact that this paper was witnessed by Mary, Samuel, John
and Charles Washington suggests the possibility that Lawrence had landed on the Rappahannock
and had gone to Ferry Farm. This actually may have been the case, but the inclusion of
William Fairfax and Martha Posey among the witnesses may invalidate that view. As Martha
Posey was a member of the family that lived below Mount Vernon, the reasonable assumption
is that Lawrence signed that paper at Mount Vernon while Mary and the younger sons were
there to attend his terminal illness.
26 Presumably George was present but of this there is no positive evidence. George Mason's
note of July 29, 1752 (1 *Hamilton*, 1), expressing regret at the inability of its writer to attend
Lawrence's funeral, is supposed to have been addressed to George.
27 Some of the funeral expenses are listed in *Fairfax Wills*, B 1, p. 113.
28 Ford, *The Washington Family*, 107; to be found, also, in 14 *Ford*, 423.

brothers put on the will. Executors named by Lawrence were Col. William Fairfax, George Fairfax, Nathaniel Chapman, John Carlyle and "Austin" and George Washington.[29]

Seven times in his will Lawrence mentioned his debts and the arrangements he wished these executors to make in payment of these obligations. The reason for this emphasis soon developed. Lawrence's affairs, to use George's words, were in "utmost confusion." [30] The tobacco grown on all Lawrence's farms did not average twenty-four hogsheads a year; [31] the abandonment of the Principio iron furnace was in prospect; [32] like nearly all his neighbors, Lawrence probably had maintained a style of living not justified by his income; [33] in addition, he had been compelled to sustain heavy expenses in Barbados and in Bermuda. There were no very large debts, but of small accounts, some of them representing charges that continued after Lawrence's death, there were many.[34] As George was the book-keeper of the family, it fell to his lot to assist John Carlyle, the active executor, in disentangling and verifying the accounts; but it was Carlyle, not George who had to go to Williamsburg in connection with three law suits. Carlyle similarly made a journey to Frederick to examine the plantation and to sell some of the property of the estate.[35]

The settlement of Lawrence's affairs was as slow as it was complicated. Appraisers were not appointed by the court of Fairfax County till September 26.[36] It was December 23 when the inventory was completed and was copied by the young surveyor.[37] A sale of personal

29 Lawrence's will provided that each of his executors, among others, be given a mourning ring. One of these, said to have been George's, was listed in *Birch Cat.* 663; item 261.

30 G. W. to Robert Orme, Apr. 2, 1755, 1 *G. W.*, 111.

31 According to the estate accounts of 1752–55, the crop varied from nine hogsheads in 1752 to thirty-one in 1753 and in 1754 (*Fairfax Wills*, B, 1, p. 120–23). There is no evidence that these figures reflected any curtailment of acreage after the death of Lawrence.

32 11 *Penn. Mag.*, 194.

33 Little direct evidence on this point survives, but all of it indicates an expensive standard and an elaborate *ménage*. Indirect evidence of a minor sort is afforded by the advertisement Lawrence inserted in the *Md. Gazette*, Aug. 31, 1748, for his runaway servant Robert Millby who stole a stallion, a "fine large bright roan mare" and colt, a "long-bodied close riding coat," a "new soldiers' musket," a pair of sheets and three hunting saddles, one of which was new and had "a large green cloth housing bound round with scalloped leather."

34 The accounts for 1752 probably are the most informative that remain. They will be found in *Fairfax Wills*, B, 1, p. 177 ff.

35 *Ibid.*, 120. The language of part of Carlyle's entry, charging the estate £60, reads: "To my expense and riding charges attending 3 Law suits at Wmsb'g and going to F'k Co" etc. From the wording, it is impossible to say whether this legal business involved three separate journeys, or whether all the suits were heard on one visit to the capital. Normally, the only term of the General Court held in 1752 after the date of Lawrence's death would have been in October. See *supra*, p. 180.

36 *Fairfax Orders*, 1749–54, p. 239.

37 *Birch Cat.* 663; item 169.

effects was held that same month,[38] when George, one of numerous purchasers, bought live-stock to the value of £33.[39] Final balancing of his accounts with the estate of his brother was to be delayed there-after for more than three years.[40]

Lawrence's death involved the transfer of his varied duties as a trustee of Alexandria, as a stockholder in the Ohio Company and as Adjutant of the Colony. This last office either had been vacated before Lawrence's death or else had been held with the understanding that Lawrence would resign when a successor was chosen. George had sought actively from the spring of 1752 to get the place. He had never seen a day's service as a soldier, or had any contacts with troops except briefly in Barbados; but his interest in military affairs, which had been given an edge by Lawrence's service in the Cartagena expedition,[41] had been sharpened, doubtless, by Lawrence's activities as Adjutant of the colonial militia. To seek to succeed his brother was, for George, a natural ambition.

By mid-spring, 1752, or approximately at that season,[42] it was under-stood that the Adjutancy would be divided among three men, to each of whom would be assigned a district. Further, George knew that if Col. William Fitzhugh would accept it, that gentleman could have direction of the district in which the Northern Neck was to be in-cluded. Fitzhugh, who was eleven years older than George, had been an officer in the Cartagena campaign and had been on half-pay. He had won the hand of Martha Lee, daughter of Richard Lee and widow of George Turberville, and after her death, Fitzhugh married on Jan. 7, 1752,[43] Anne Frisby, who was then the relict of John Rousby, of Calvert County, Maryland. As his second wife had large property in Maryland, Fitzhugh had gone to that Colony and was residing there in May, 1752.

George had been anxious to know whether this change of abode meant that Fitzhugh would forego the office of Adjutant of the Northern Neck. Accordingly, a short time before Lawrence's return from Bermuda, George probably had ridden to Williamsburg, had seen the Governor about the succession to the position, and then had

38 "To James Hamilton for crying the sale, £4, 1s," December, 1752 Fairfax Wills, B 1, p. 117.
39 For payment of this account, see Vol. II, p. 5 and Ledger A, folio 4.
40 Ibid. As much of this work for Lawrence's estate had to be done at Mount Vernon, there scarcely seems foundation for the statement that George regretfully took formal leave of the place in the summer of 1752 (cf. 1 Stephenson and Dunn, 66–67).
41 See supra, p. 70 ff.　　42 See infra, n. 49.　　43 30 V 20.

gone to Maryland [44] to consult Fitzhugh. The Colonel said that he would accept on conditions, but that he did not think these would be approved by the Governor and Council. Apparently Fitzhugh stipulated that he would discharge the greater part of his duties from the Maryland shore, though, when circumstance admitted, he would erect a house in Virginia and would reside there "sometimes." Fitzhugh obligingly gave George a letter in which he told the Governor of the terms he would have to impose if he took the office. George went back to Ferry Farm, wrote the Governor of his visit, enclosed Fitzhugh's letter and said, all in a breath: "If I could have the honor of obtaining that [Northern Neck adjutancy] in case Colonel Fitzhugh does not, or either of the other two; should take the greatest pleasure in punctually obeying from time to time your Honor's commands, and by a strict observance of my duty, render myself worthy of your trust reposed in me; I am sensible my best endeavors will not be wanting, and doubt not, but [by?] a constant application to fit myself for the office, could I presume your Honor had not in view a more deserving person." [45]

George had pending, in a short time, another application of a different sort. On Sept. 1, 1752, a new lodge of Masons held its first meeting in Fredericksburg and soon attracted members. Under Daniel Campbell as Master, a class of five were initiated, Nov. 4, 1752, in a hall over the market at the corner of Caroline Street and Market Alley. George, one of this number, paid his initiation fee of £2, 3s as an Entered Apprentice. [46]

44 See Washington to [Governor Dinwiddie?] June 10, 1752: "Being impatient to know Col. Fitzhugh's result; I went to Maryland, as I returned home . . ." (G. A. Ball's *Washington Letters*, 5). A critique of this letter will be found below. George's accounts with Fielding Lewis (*Ledger A*, folio 8) show that a considerable sum was paid by Lewis to Mitchell of Yorktown, Mch. 12, 1752, but this does not necessarily mean that George was with Lewis at the time. The contrary was more probable.

45 Washington to [Governor Dinwiddie?], June 10, 1752, *loc. cit.* It is probable the letter terminated: "I flatter myself I should meet with the approbation of the gentlemen of the Council." As printed in Ball's *Washington Letters* this paper is a strange combination of two unrelated documents with an "N.B." equally strange. The first paragraph of the letter undoubtedly is authentic, though the date may not be; the second paragraph is part of a letter from Washington to Governor Dinwiddie, June 10, 1754, two years later to the day. This second letter is printed in 1 *G. W.*, 75. It is followed in the Ball text by: "N.B. This occurred when Braddock arrived in Virginia." If this was added by Washington to the original letter of 1754, it represents a strange lapsus on his part because the events described in the second paragraph predated by more than eight months the arrival of General Braddock in Hampton Roads. The final sentence of the letter is the one quoted at the beginning of this note: "I flatter myself," etc. It is altogether possible that the letter, as printed in Ball's book, was put together by some person who observed the date "June 10" and did not note the difference in years. On the other hand, the date "June 10, 1752" may be erroneous though the events fit that year.

46 Eggleston, *Masonic Life of Washington*, 110 ff; J. H. Tatsch, *Freemasonry in the Thirteen Colonies*. Washington passed fellow craft March 3, 1753. He was raised to Master Mason, Aug. 4, 1753.

Two days afterward, Nov. 6, 1752, the situation created by the death of Adjutant Lawrence Washington was reviewed by the Council of Virginia.[47] There was accord between Governor and Council on "the great advantage of an Adjutant to this country, in instructing the officers and soldiers in the use and exercise of their arms, in bringing the militia to a more regular discipline, and fitting it for service, besides polishing and improving the meaner people." Governor and Council agreed, moreover, that one man could not discharge all the duties of the office. Virginia consequently was divided, not as George had expected, into three districts, but into four—each of which was to have an Adjutant. For the frontier, Thomas Bentley was chosen; the "Middle Neck" between the Rappahannock and the York was assigned to George Muse; the Northern Neck was made the district of William Fitzhugh. To George was alloted the Southern district, the most re- mote and the least interesting. It extended from Princess Anne County to the western fringe of settlement, and it covered the entire region between James River and the North Carolina boundary.[48]

It was, of course, a distinction for George to be named Adjutant before he was twenty-one, and to be allowed pay of £100 per annum. The young man was gratified but not satisfied. He still wanted the district of the Northern Neck. On Feb. 1, 1753, he presented his com- mission to the Court of Spotsylvania and took the various oaths[49] as Adjutant of the Counties of James River;[50] but, meantime, he sought and procured the influence of the powerful William Nelson for the vacancy that might occur if Fitzhugh found himself unable to serve.[51]

When George took the oaths as Adjutant, he became officially Major Washington. He might have regarded the title as a present on his "coming of age," because, a few days later, he observed his twenty-first birthday. How well he had advanced during the ten years that had passed after his father's death! The younger son of a second marriage, he had received as his inheritance ten slaves, the small Ferry Farm, three Fredericksburg lots and half of the Deep Run tract.[52] He now

---

[47] As of Sept. 2, 1752, the Gregorian calendar was adopted by Great Britain. Subsequent dates are all "N.S.," new style.　　　　　[48] 5 E. J., 413.

[49] Spotsylvania Orders, 1750–55, p. 284. His commission bore date of Dec. 13, 1752. In Ledger A, folio 45, the opening entry on Washington's account with "The Colony of Virginia" reads as follows: "1752, Oct. 25, To my salary as Adjutant the last ½ year £50"; but all the circumstances indicate that this was a slip of the pen. The year should have been 1753, not 1752.

[50] The oaths were those taken when he became Surveyor, except, of course, that the special oath of Surveyor was not included.

[51] See William Nelson to Washington, 1 Hamilton, 1.

[52] See supra, Chapter IV.

had a remunerative profession as County Surveyor and from his own earnings he had bought ample clothing and good equipage. In the rich Shenandoah Valley he held 2000 acres of excellent land, which would increase steadily in value as settlement became dense. If he counted his moiety of the Deep Run tract and what remained of Ferry Farm, he already was the owner of 4291 acres of unencumbered land and thus, as respected acreage, he was in the class of the larger proprietors.[53] With the advantage of immunity to smallpox, he could travel freely. Although he had suffered from pleurisy and from malaria, he was strong and was able, without complaint or great discomfort, to sleep out of doors, in his clothing and on the ground. The softness of 1748 was gone, but without the loss of his love of good apparel and of comfortable living. Fixed in his methodical habits, he kept his accounts carefully, though not in a manner to give him full information. If his English grammar and composition still were poor, he was progressing in these, too. Socially, he was capable of entering the best of colonial society without embarrassment. He could not sing or play any instrument, and he probably felt a certain awkwardness in the presence of young women, but he could dance and he had proficiency in cards and billiards. While not particularly accurate as a marksman, he squared accounts by the superlative excellence of his horsemanship. Now, with the thoroughness that marked all his acquisition of new knowledge and his every performance of his daily work, he—Major George Washington—was to learn the duties of District Adjutant of Virginia.

They were not onerous duties at the outset. Governor Dinwiddie and the Council had decided that general musters of the militia should be held in September, 1753, and they reasoned rightly that the first work of the District Adjutants should be to exercise the county officers so as to qualify those men, in turn, to drill the separate Companies when assembled.[54] In George's instance, this meant that he had to instruct himself in order that he might train the county officers. Study must in consequence have occupied much of his spare time during the spring and summer of 1753. Available books on tactics were hard, complicated reading for any man who did not have opportunity of drilling and exercising soldiers. George was denied this advantage. As far as

53 Specifically: 100 acres at Ferry Farm; 2180 acres, being one-half of Augustine's holdings of 4360 acres, on Deep Run; 453 acres of Dutch George's 550 acres patented Oct. 20, 1750; 456 acres purchased from James McCracken, and 552 acres acquired from George Johnston, Mch. 16, 1752.   54 1 Din., 41.

surviving records show, he did not visit in 1753 any of the Counties under his care.[55]

George's interest shifted as his duties changed. His few letters of later boyhood contained not one line on public affairs and not a single reference to the duty a Virginian owed King and Crown. All his relations with the frontier had been those of Surveyor, of land-purchaser, or of a friend of the Proprietor's family. Such activities of the Ohio Company as had come under his observation had been designed to capture the fur trade and to promote the sale of the stock-holders' lands. Now, as Major Washington, Adjutant of the Southern District, George began to learn more about the political aspect of dealings on the frontier, and, in particular, about the advance of the French.

The treaty of Aix-la-Chapelle, Oct. 18, 1748, had ended the war of the Austrian Succession; but, so far as England and France were involved, the settlement merely provided for restitution of the territory each had taken from the other. Like wrestlers well matched, the two ancestral adversaries broke off their struggle in order to get a new hold when an opening was offered. A current phrase in Paris—"bête comme la paix" expressed the feeling on both sides of the Channel.[56] No boundary was drawn on the watershed of the Ohio, which both countries claimed.[57] The French thought the English planned to separate Louisiana from Canada and to conquer the two Colonies separately;[58] the British suspected that the French intended to cut them off from the back country and to pin them to the Atlantic coast.[59] In the foreground was the prospect of winning or losing the fur trade. Until the English traders went West of the Allegheny mountains, the French had charged almost anything they had chosen for goods. Nine beaver skins had been demanded for a blanket, four for a trade shirt, three for a pound of powder. "With the French," said one Chief, "a man must hunt a year to clothe himself." [60]

In full appreciation of what the loss of the fur trade would mean, the French had become aggressive. During the first days of the Ohio Company the protection of the frontier had been little more than an

[55] It is possible, of course, that he discharged his duties without leaving any record in the courts of the Counties. Those tribunals, it should be added, scarcely would have had made any entry concerning the musters the Adjutant held.   [56] Beer, *British Colonial Policy,* 10.

[57] Leduc, *Murder of Jumonville,* 32, with a reference to Arch. Pub. du Canada, Min. des Aff. Etrang., Cor. politique, Angleterre, v. 438, folios 20–25, 755. See, also, Horace Walpole's *Memoirs,* v. 1, p. 341–42.

[58] Paris, Aff. Etrang., Mém. et Docs. Amérique, 24.

[59] Walpole, *loc. cit.*

[60] Paris, Arch. Nat., Min. des Col., C-11-A 95, 397, May 22, 1750.

argument to facilitate large grants to Virginia land speculators; now it was different: A bogey had become a reality. In 1749, the Marquis de la Galissonière, French Governor of Canada, had sent the Chevalier Céloron de Bienville to the Ohio Valley to reassert the claim of France to that region. Céloron had visited numerous Indian tribes and had penetrated to Logstown.[61] There he had warned the Indians against the English. Said Céloron in the name of Galissonière: "The English intend to rob you of your country; and that they may succeed, they begin by corrupting your minds. As they mean to seize the Ohio which belongs to me, I send to warn them to retire." [62] Céloron had made good his pledge to the extent that wherever he had encountered English traders, he had ordered them, under penalty, to quit French territory. This done and French sovereignty asserted on tablets ceremoniously buried, Céloron had returned to Canada.

When word of Céloron's expedition reached the English Colonies to the eastward, it convinced both Pennsylvanians and Virginians that they should strengthen their ties with the Six Nations [63] and, in particular, that they should confirm the treaty which had been made at Lancaster in 1744 but never had been ratified acceptably. Forts must be built, moreover, to resist the French if they should return. The Pennsylvanians had undertaken to do this in 1751 and had found the Indians friendly, but the Assembly of Pennsylvania had not been willing to vote the money for forts which would command the frontier.

It was shortly after this failure that Governor Dinwiddie had arrived in Virginia and had become interested, financially and politically, in the Ohio Company and in the settlements it proposed to establish in the region claimed by the French.[64] Soon he commissioned Joshua Fry, Lunsford Lomax and James Patton to do three things—to deliver a present to the Six Nations at Logstown on the 15th of May, 1752, to procure the desired ratification of the Treaty of Lancaster,[65] and, in general, to renew friendly relations and to procure new concessions. Fry and his companions reached Logstown without difficulty, but they had to spend many days in coaxing the Indians into a new agreement. Finally, on June 13, 1752, they won full confirmation of the Treaty

[61] Close to the site of Ambridge, Pennsylvania, which is on the right bank of the Ohio, eighteen miles Northwest of Pittsburgh.
[62] Quoted in the familiar account of this expedition in Francis Parkman, *Montcalm and Wolfe*, v. 1, p. 50. The French view is given in Moreau, *Mémoire*, 16.
[63] Board of Trade to Duke of Bedford, Jan. 10, 1750/51; P.R.O., C.O. 5, 1344.
[64] Cf. Abernethy, *Western Lands*, 8.
[65] The preliminaries are described in 1 *Din.*, 6 ff.

of Lancaster. Permission was given the English to build two strong trading posts on the Ohio and to establish settlements South of that river.[66]

This success of English colonial diplomacy was offset that same month of June, 1752, when Charles Langlade, a French trader, mustered 250 Ottawas and Ojibwas and badly defeated the Indian Chief, Old Britain, oddly styled the Demoiselle, a known friend of England.[67] In this fight of Pickawillany on the Miami,[68] the Demoiselle was slain and the power of France was raised in the estimation of the savages. After that, nothing was heard of new French activity in the disputed region until the winter of 1752–53. Word then reached Governor Dinwiddie that the Twigtwee or Miami Indians had gone over to the "other side" and that fifteen or sixteen French had come to Logstown and were establishing themselves there. Dinwiddie was alarmed: ". . . it is to be feared they will take possession of the river Ohio, oppress our trade and take our traders prisoners, &c. We would fain hope these people are only French traders, and they have no other view but trade. I hope there is no great army of French among the lakes." [69]

His hope was vain. A force of 1500 French troops landed in the spring of 1753 on the southern shore of lake Erie and built forts and some stretches of road. These soldiers of King Louis spread their dominion swiftly and without resistance, only to find disease a worse foe than the Indians or the negligent English colonists. By autumn, most of the survivors were sent back to Montreal.[70] The number of those who remained at Forts Presqu'isle and Le Boeuf [71] was not known to the Virginians, nor was Governor Dinwiddie aware of the manner in which Indians who previously had been friends of the English had been overawed by the strength and boldness of the French. This much was plain: These men from Canada were in territory claimed by England, and if they pushed southward, they would reach the Ohio and would close to English traders and settlers the rich lands that speculators had been eyeing even since the Treaty of Lancaster had been signed.[72]

[66] See *Buck* 65–66. The commission, journal, etc., of the Virginia plenipotentiaries are printed in 13 *V* 143.

[67] A visit to Old Britain's town is recorded under date of Feb. 24, 1750, in Darlington's edition of *Gist's Journal*, p. 50. For this work see *infra*, 276, 278.

[68] Parkman, *Montcalm and Wolfe*, v. 1, p. 89.

[69] Dinwiddie to Captains Cresap and Trent, Feb. 10, 1753; 1 *Din.*, 22.

[70] Parkman, *op. cit.*, v. 1, p. 93, 136.

[71] Actually 300.

[72] Parkman, *op. cit.*, v. 1, p. 135–36.

The young Adjutant of the Southern District read in the *Virginia Gazette* of some of these events, and doubtless he learned from Colonel Fairfax that the situation on the Ohio had been described in dispatches to the home government. Perhaps, too, it was Fairfax who told him that the Governor had resolved to send a warning to the French commander to leave the country of the British King. George reflected, saw an opportunity, determined to seize it—and set out for Williamsburg. He would volunteer to carry the message to the Ohio.[73]

[73] The language of the journal of the meeting of council, Oct. 27, 1753, makes it plain that Washington volunteered to make the journey and did not, as Adjutant, receive an order to do so. See 5 E. J., 444.

CHAPTER VIII

A MISSION UNCOVERS A PENDING ADVANCE
(November, 1753–January, 1754)

WHEN GEORGE reached Williamsburg at the end of October,[1] 1753, to tender his services to Governor Dinwiddie, he found the taverns crowded with Burgesses. The General Assembly had been called to meet November 1, in circumstances that had aroused even more than the usual curiosity of colonials notoriously eager for news. On the 21st of October a sloop of war [2] had brought special dispatches to the Governor, who promptly had sent letters under the King's seal, North and South, to the executives of the other Colonies.[3] The proclamation for an early session of the Virginia lawmakers had then been issued.

George soon learned part of the reason for this activity. At the "palace," he was ushered into the presence of the Governor, whom he had met on his return from Barbados.[4] Dinwiddie, 60 years of age, bulky and benevolent in appearance, with blue-gray eyes,[5] was now concerned and aroused and probably was impressed by the importance of the steps he was about to take. The previous 16th of June he had written the home government concerning the need of building forts to prevent the French from occupying the Ohio country [6] which he claimed as a part of His Majesty's Colony of Virginia.[7] Although Dinwiddie was averse to reprisals for individual acts in violation of the treaty existing between Britain and France,[8] he was ready to resist

---

[1] It was approximately October 26. See 5 *E. J.*, 444.

[2] The date, etc., are given in Dinwiddie to Gov. Horatio Sharpe, Aug. 23, 1753 (1 *Sharpe*, 9).

[3] *Journ. H.B.*, 1752–55, p. 104. For Dinwiddie's instructions to dispatch these letters, see Holderness to Dinwiddie, Aug. 28, 1753; P.R.O., C.O. 5:1344, p. 141–45.

[4] See *supra*, p. 256.   [5] See illustration between p. 281 and p. 282.

[6] See the acknowledgment in Holderness to Dinwiddie, Aug. 28, 1753, P.R.O.; C.O. 5:1344, p. 152, and also Halifax to Bedford [?], Aug. 12, 1753, *ibid.*, 131.

[7] For the basic laws, etc., of the controversy over the boundaries of Virginia, see 1 *H* 59–60, 88, 99–100. The view prevailing in 1750 is given in Thomas Lee to the Board of Trade, Sept. 29, 1750 (45 *Shelburne Papers*, 169–185); Joshua Fry to Lewis Burwell, May 8, 1751 (P.R.O., C.O. 5:1327, p. 363–81); Dinwiddie to Lords of Trade, Jan. n.d., 1755 (*Sparks Transcripts*, VSL, 27). Cf. 4 *Gipson*, 234–36, 239.

[8] 1 *Din.*, 17.

invasion by strengthening the English alliance with the Indians and, if need be, by taking the field against the French.[9]

Dispatches of August 28 had brought him instructions that accorded with his judgment. In fact, His Gracious Majesty himself had honored the Governor with a statement of his royal will, over his own signature. Encouraging promises of military equipment had been made.[10] As a first, prudential step, Dinwiddie had been instructed to warn the French of their encroachment and formally to call on them to leave British territory.[11] The Governor had made an indirect effort the previous summer to have Governor Clinton of New York inquire why the French were sending troops into English territory.[12] Later the Virginia executive had employed William Trent and William Russell to locate

[9] *Ibid.*, 39–40, an extract from his message of Nov. 1, 1753, to the General Assembly, for which see *Journ. H.B.*, 1752–55, p. 104.

[10] P.R.O., C.O. 5:211, p. 1, 43.

[11] It is not known to what extent Dinwiddie acquainted Washington with the text of his instructions. The Governor had, of course, to give some information, but he may have been restrained in what he said. He did not communicate to the Burgesses until November 8 (*Journ. H.B.*, 1752–55, p. 107, 112), the substance of his orders from England. These were contained in instructions from George II, supplemented by further directions from the Earl of Holderness, Aug. 28, 1753. Dinwiddie was told that his proposal for building forts on the Ohio was approved, that his request for ordnance to arm them was granted, and that he should "use [his] utmost endeavour to erect the said forts, as soon as the nature of the service will permit." The instructions continued: ". . . And lest you should meet with any unexpected difficulties or obstructions in carrying the said works on, our further will and pleasure is that you shall forthwith cause the whole or such part of our militia in Virginia now under your Government, to be drawn forth and armed, as you may judge necessary for our service, and in case any of the Indians not in alliance with us or dependent upon our crown, or any Europeans under pretence of alliance with the said Indians, or under any other pretext whatever, should presume to molest or interrupt you in the execution of these our orders, you are first to represent our undoubted right to such parts of the River Ohio as are within the limits of our province of Virginia or any other province or provinces in America, and to require the peaceable departure of any such Europeans or Indians offering to molest or hinder you from carrying on the forts you are hereby authorized and empowered to erect, but if notwithstanding such peaceable representations they should still persist in endeavouring to obstruct the execution of these our orders, our will and pleasure is that you should repel force by force and whereas we have received information of a number of Europeans not our subjects, being assembled in a hostile manner, upon the River Ohio, intending by force of arms to erect certain forts within our territory on the said river, contrary to our peace and to the dignity of our Crown, we do hereby strictly enjoin you to make diligent enquiry into the truth of this information and if you shall find that any number of persons whether Indians or Europeans shall presume to erect any fort within the limits of our province of Virginia you are first to require of them peaceably to depart and not persist in such unlawful proceedings and if notwithstanding your admonition, they do still endeavor to carry on such unlawful and unjustifiable designs, we do strictly charge and command you to drive them out by force of arms, in the execution of which all our officers civil and military within the limits of your government are to be aiding and assisting to the utmost of their abilities. [Sig.] George R." (P.R.O., C.O. 5, 1344, unpgd.) It has been assumed erroneously that Dinwiddie's instructions were identical with those contained in the circular letter to all the Governors, which was the document Dinwiddie had been required, on arrival of the sloop of war, to forward to them. Copies of that circular will be found in 1 *Sharpe*, 3–4, and also as cited by Gipson, *op. cit.*, v. 4, p. 290 n., in 6 *N.Y. Col. Docs.*, 794–95 and 5 *Penn. Col. Records*, 689–90.

[12] The sources are cited in 4 *Gipson*, 294–95. Included is Dinwiddie to Gov. James Glen of South Carolina, May 23, 1753; *Journ. H.B.*, 1752–55, p. 517.

the French outposts and to warn the commanders they were encroaching on King George's lands; but neither of these envoys had proceeded farther than Logstown.[13]

Governor and council accepted promptly George's offer to carry the message.[14] Orders were drafted. Without delay he was to proceed to Logstown and there was to call on friendly Indian Sachems for a guard to attend him as far as he thought proper en route to the French commanding officer. When he reached the French station, Washington was to present a letter, which Dinwiddie handed him,[15] and he was to demand a reply, for which he was to wait not more than a week. This answer having been given, Major Washington was to request a proper French escort on his way back to the Virginia settlements. In addition, George was of course to procure all the information he could of the numerical strength, armament, defences, communications and plans of the intruders.[16]

Besides his written instructions, George received more detailed verbal orders: He was to proceed first to Wills Creek and there was to deliver to Christopher Gist a written request from the Governor and Council that Gist act as Washington's guide on the mission.[17] The Virginia messenger, moreover, was to inquire of the French why they had made prisoners of British subjects trading with the Indians, and why they had driven John Frazier from the house where he had lived for twelve years.[18] Finally, speed was enjoined. As soon as George received his answer, he was to "return immediately back."[19]

This mission was assigned young Washington at the very time of the year when the sparkling autumn weather of Western Virginia was turning to the rains and the bleakness of November. George knew well

---

13 Dinwiddie to Lords of Trade, Nov. 17, 1753; P.R.O., C.O. 5:1328, p. 13. See the more detailed sources listed in Abernethy, 9.

14 Dinwiddie's mention of Washington's official position will be found in Dinwiddie to the French commander, Oct. 31, 1753, quoted *infra*, p. 309. In Dinwiddie to Sharpe, Nov. 24, 1753 (1 *Sharpe*, 10), George was described as "a person of distinction," with the inference that the mission was of an importance that called for such an individual. Not all of the Governor's references to Washington were in this tone. Writing to the Lords of Trade, Nov. 17, 1753, Dinwiddie merely said he had dispatched "one of the militia adjutants" (*Sparks Transcripts*, VSL). The report in the *Gentleman's Mag.*, v. 24, p. 190, April 1754, stated that a "messenger was sent." No name was given. For all details, see 5 *E. J.*, 444–45.

15 Along with a passport, a commission and written instructions, the texts of which are in 2 *Sparks*, 428–29.

16 *Ibid.*, 428. Reference to the time limit of one week is in Washington's commission, *ibid.*, 429.

17 See *Christopher Gist's Journals*, ed. by William M. Darlington (cited hereafter as *Darlington*), p. 80.

18 Dinwiddie to the Lords of Trade, Jan. 29, 1754; *Sparks Transcripts*, VSL. In 2 *Sparks*, 431, part of this letter is printed with no indication of the sentences omitted.

19 Washington's commission, *loc. cit.*

enough how unpleasant that month could be out-of-doors in Frederick, and usually, at that season, he had ended his surveys and had ridden home. Now he was told to go into a wilder and a colder country than any in which he had worked; but he was being honored by the assignment, and, in addition, he had such an opportunity as no young Virginian had enjoyed in his generation of winning reputation and of acquiring a name. Besides, it was a duty becoming to an Adjutant of the Colony.

Off George went that same day to Fredericksburg, and as he rode he planned part of his expedition. Besides Christopher Gist as guide, he would need several men to look after the horses and baggage and to pitch a tent, the walls of which, as he had learned on his surveys, afforded the best shelter in the wilderness.

Unless Gist knew the Indian tongues, it would be necessary, also, to procure an interpreter. Further, as the negotiations with the French commander probably would be conducted in that officer's language, with which George was unacquainted, someone must make the journey who could translate French and could converse in it. George believed he could procure such a man. To the vicinity of Fredericksburg in 1752 had come a young Hollander, Jacob van Braam by name, who affirmed that he had been a Lieutenant in the Dutch Army. Van Braam was able-bodied and, though his English was meagre, he was said to have a knowledge of the French language. In fact, he had advertised in 1752 as a teacher of French in Annapolis. If van Braam now was at his temporary abode, two miles from Fredericksburg, he would be the very man George wanted, and, by reason of his service on the Continent, would be familiar with the usages of His Christian Majesty's Army.[20]

On reaching Fredericksburg, November 1,[21] George found van

[20] A memoir of van Braam's, P.R.O., C.O. 5: 16, p. 43, cited in 30 V 394-95, includes a statement that he sailed to Virginia in 1752. His advertisement as a teacher appears in *Md. Gazette,* July 30, 1752. At his trial in 1756 (for which see *Rapport de l'Archiviste de la Prov. de Québec,* 1922-23, p. 309) van Braam testified that he was 27 at the time of his immigration. This disposes of the tradition, mentioned in Charles Campbell's *History of Virginia,* p. 461. and subsequently reprinted many times, that van Braam had served under Lawrence Washington in the Cartegena Expedition. No evidence has been found to support the further tradition that van Braam taught George Washington swordsmanship. In his *MS Diary,* Aug. 22, 1754, Landon Carter spoke of van Braam as a "juggling servant"; but at his trial van Braam described himself as "gentleman." His handwriting was that of an educated man.

[21] If Washington followed the route recommended in the *Virginia Almanac* for 1756, he went from Williamsburg to Chiswell's Ordinary, 16 miles; to Claiborne's Ferry, 12 miles; to King William C. H., 12 miles; to Todd's Warehouse, 12 miles; to Taylor's Ordinary, 20 miles; to Caroline C. H., 10 miles; and to Fredericksburg, 21 miles; total, 103 miles. Subsequently, Washington learned certain "short cuts" and, on occasion, went out of his way to visit friends. See A. P. Gray, "Washington's Burgess Route," 46 V 299 ff and the map in Vol. III.

Braam, who agreed to accompany him to the Ohio; and as the
young Dutchman had no encumbrance, the two set out promptly for
Alexandria. There Washington purchased part of the supplies and
equipment he thought he would require. From Alexandria, the road
of the emissary and the interpreter was the familiar one via Vestal's
Gap to Winchester, where the young Major bought horses and baggage,
probably including a tent; and thence he started with van Braam for
Wills Creek,[22] which he reached on the 14th of November.[23] From
Wills Creek, which soon was to be styled Fort Cumberland, George
saw the "new storehouse" on the Virginia side of the river, a strong
two-storey building of timber and logs, ample not only for the goods
of the Ohio Company but also for its agents' quarters.[24] Nearer at
hand, on the Maryland shore, was the cabin of Christopher Gist.

Most fortunately, Gist himself was there and not at his "new settlement," which was about seventy miles distant and beyond the headwaters of Red Stone Creek. When George delivered the letter in which
Governor and Council asked Gist to accompany the Major to the
Ohio, the frontiersman consented.[25] While Gist made ready, George
hired four men as hostlers and orderlies, or in the young Virginian's
unceremonious words, as "servitors." One of these men, the Indian
trader Barnaby Currin, was to prove himself capable of bearing some
of the responsibility of the wilderness.[26] Another, John MacQuire, also
had traded with the Indians; still another, Henry Steward, had some
knowledge of the frontier.

When, therefore, the party set out on the 15th of November, it con-

[22] 1 *Ford*, 11. This edition, rather than *Diaries*, is recommended for the mission of 1753-54,
because it contains in the footnotes many pertinent quotations from Gist's journal. More detailed study of the mission requires the use of the notes in *Darlington*. If Washington followed
in 1753 the road laid out on Evans's map in 1754 he went from Winchester slightly West of
North to Enoch's, which is depicted on the east side of the Cacapon, about ten miles from the
Potomac, in the vicinity of the present village of Largent. There George turned West to Cox's,
where the Little Cacapon flows into the Potomac. At that point George crossed the Potomac
and went on to Cresap's. The route on Dalrymple's revision of the map of Jefferson and Fry (for
which see *supra*, p. 150) ran almost West from Winchester across the mountain, down the east
bank of the Cacapon to a point opposite Edwards's, then westward to Patterson Creek, down
that stream to McCracken's and on to the Ohio Company storehouse across the Potomac from
Wills Creek. The *Virginia Almanac* for 1756 recommended Winchester to Lewis's, 21 miles;
to South Branch Ferry, 22 miles; and to Cresap's, 9 miles. From Cresap's to Wills Creek, the
distance was 16 miles (1 *Ford*, 11).   [23] *Darlington*, 80.

[24] *Darlington*, 137; W. H. Lowdermilk, *History of Cumberland, Maryland* (cited hereafter
as *Lowdermilk*), p. 30.

[25] Gist said (*Darlington*, 80) that the letter was from "The Council in Virginia," but on a
matter of so much importance the Governor doubtless would have written in his own name
and perhaps in the Council's also.

[26] Gist mentioned him in his journal of 1750-51 as a trader for the Ohio Company
(*Darlington*, 35, and note *ibid.*, 100).

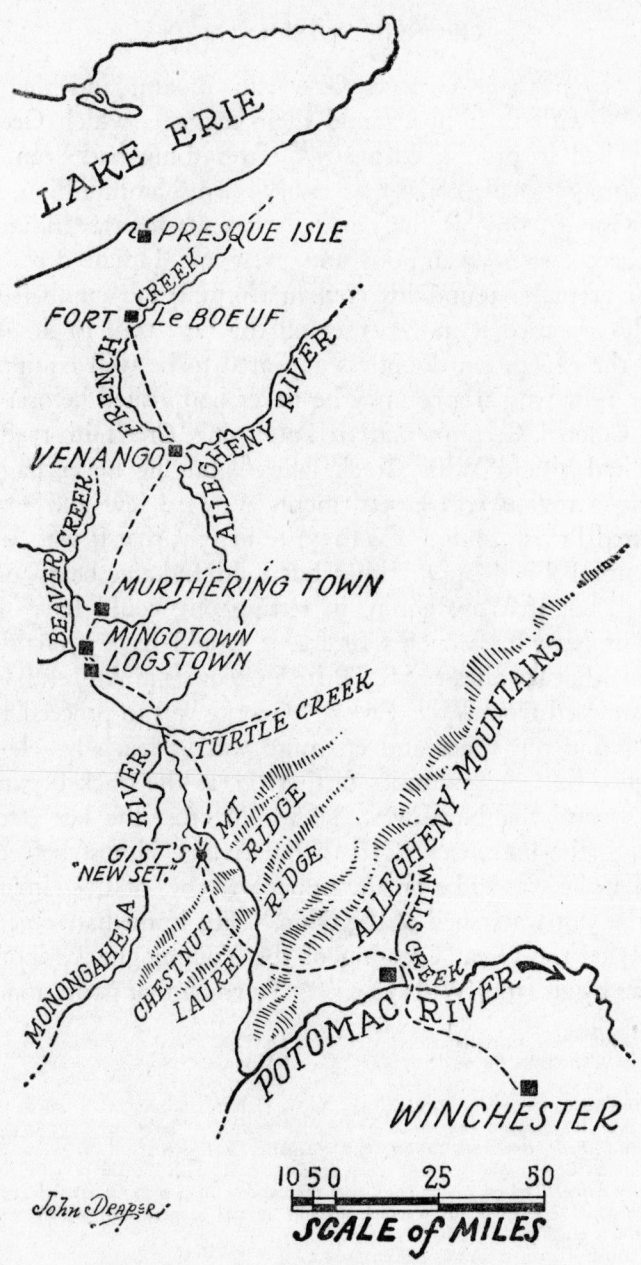

LAKE ERIE

PRESQUE ISLE

FORT Le BOEUF

FRENCH CREEK

VENANGO

ALLEGHENY RIVER

BEAVER CREEK

MURTHERING TOWN

MINGOTOWN
LOGSTOWN

TURTLE CREEK

MT RIDGE

RIDGE

MONONGAHELA RIVER

GIST'S
"NEW SET."

CHESTNUT RIDGE

LAUREL RIDGE

ALLEGHENY MOUNTAINS

STILWI CREEK

POTOMAC RIVER

WINCHESTER

John Draper

10 5 0   25   50
SCALE of MILES

HOW WASHINGTON RODE TO FORT LE BOEUF IN 1753

Washington's own map, as submitted to Governor Dinwiddie on the young Adjutant's return
to "the settlements" in January, 1754, is reproduced between p. 281 and p. 282. If that map is
correctly orientated, it shows that Washington did not make many serious mistakes in estimating
distances and in getting his compass bearings.

sisted of seven men—George, Gist, van Braam, and the four attendants [27]—with their horses and their baggage, which George subsequently had to pronounce heavy.[28] Everything had been included
that Washington had thought necessary—arms, ammunition, compass,
tent, provisions, corn for the horses,[29] presents for the Indians, medicines, tobacco, some wampum and even an "Indian dress" for the
Major in event he found his civilian clothing too cumbersome. To
those who watched it move away on the new trail to the Youghiogheny,[30] the expedition doubtless appeared to be well equipped.

George now was in a country he never had visited before. He had
been to Colonel Cresap's and to Patterson's Creek in 1748 and he
perhaps had visited Wills Creek later;[31] but he never had entered
previously a region where settlements were so few and so isolated.
A disgusted British soldier was to write in 1755 that it was "a desolate
country uninhabited by anything but wild Indians, bears and rattle-
snakes";[32] but if Washington, in setting out, could have sensed its
mystery or have foreseen his future, it would have been a thrilling
symbol of what lay ahead of the British Colonies in America. Climbing
steadily upward from Wills Creek,[33] George was to proceed westward
for about fourteen miles and en route was to reach an elevation of
almost 3000 feet. A few miles farther on, as the track began to turn
slightly toward the Northwest, he would cross the last stream that
flowed into the Potomac. Beyond that rivulet, almost before he was
aware of it, he was to be on the upper stretches of Casselman's River
and on the vast watershed of the Ohio.[34] His immediate objective was
a ford styled the Great Crossing of the Youghiogheny, about thirty-
four miles by air from Wills Creek.[35] To reach that point, many ridges

[27] It is possible that an Indian interpreter, John Davison, joined the party at Wills Creek but
it is much more probable he was employed later at Logstown. See *infra*, p. 290.

[28] 1 *Ford*, 35.   [29] 1 *G. W.*, 92.

[30] For this road, see Bailey, *Cresap*, 94; A. B. Hulbert, *Washington's Road*, 95 ff; C. H.
Ambler, *George Washington and the West* (cited hereafter as *Ambler*), 33; 4 *Gipson*, 247–48;
R. G. Thwaites, *Early American Travel* (cited hereafter as *Thwaites*), v. 1, p. 21; and *Buck* 3,
231–32. Thomas Cresap was said to have opened the road with the aid of a Delaware Indian,
Nemacolin by name. The Ohio Company bore the expense of clearing what was supposed to be
a thirty-foot road, serviceable for wagons; actually it was a mere trail which seems to have
been overgrown quickly.

[31] No record of such a visit has been found.

[32] William Johnston's letter in 11 *Penn. Mag.*, 93.

[33] To repeat, later Fort Cumberland and now Cumberland, Md., about 115 miles Northwest
of Washington, D. C., and ten miles South of the Pennsylvania boundary.

[34] Casselman's River joins the Youghiogheny at Confluence, Penn.; the Youghiogheny flows
into the Monongahela at McKeesport.

[35] The "Great Crossing" is now Somerfield, Penn., directly East of the river-boundary between Somerset and Fayette Counties.

had to be crossed; West of the river and frowning upon it, was the long mountain ridge, on an axis somewhat East of North, known as Laurel Hill.

The very name made guides and traders groan; but once the pioneer was on the Youghiogheny, he followed a route shaped by a river system of exceeding interest. Thirty miles West of the Great Crossing of the Youghiogheny was the Monongahela. These two rivers, flowing generally northward,[36] represented a small inverted "v." About forty-eight miles NNW of the Great Crossing,[37] the sides of the inverted "v" came to the angle. Thence the Monongahela swept on a long arc, counter-clockwise, toward the Northwest. Ten miles beyond its junction with the Youghiogheny, the Monongahela became part of what appeared on traders' crude sketches as a greater capital "V" of rivers, set firmly on the meridian. Actually, the right or eastern stream of this mighty "V" was the Allegheny River, which came down from the North and then turned to the Southwest. After it received the waters of the Monongahela, it became the Ohio and swept northwestward for a short distance as the left side of the "V." Then the Ohio bent its banks southwestward again on its long adventure to find the Mississippi, the "Father of Waters." The place where the inverted small "v" of the Youghiogheny-Monongahela met the upright capital "V" of the Allegheny-Ohio was at that time nameless; but it was the point of all points most to be desired in the contest between France and Britain for the domination of the Ohio Valley.[38] Beyond the junction of the Monongahela and the Allegheny, about thirteen miles downstream on the right bank of the Ohio was George's second objective, the Indian village of Logstown.[39] North of that settlement, in seeking the French commander, George would have to rely on Indian guides and on such information as could be supplied by John Frazier, the English trader who had been driven by the French from a place known as Venango, vaguely understood to lie on French Creek.[40]

On the first day's march, it appeared that George might have to grope his way toward the French outpost. He and his companions had

---

[36] The course of the Monongahela, though meandering, holds for a long stretch between 79° 50′ and 80°; the Youghiogheny fights its way northwestward.

[37] I.e., to repeat, at the present McKeesport.

[38] First the "Fort on the Ohio," then Fort DuQuesne, and then Fort Pitt before it became Pittsburgh.

[39] The present Ambridge, Allegheny County.

[40] Now Franklin, Venango County.

WASHINGTON'S MAP OF HIS FIRST MISSION

By 1754, young Washington found himself well-qualified for some of the new opportunities that circumstance and the necessities of the British cause in America brought. He had use for everything he had learned.

When, for instance, Washington returned to Williamsburg with the document reproduced between pages 343 and 344, Governor Dinwiddie was so much alarmed by his messenger's report that he told George to write out immediately all that had been ascertained concerning the plans of the French to advance to the Ohio from their forts immediately South of Lake Erie. Washington had kept a loose sort of a journal while on his mission and he copied this with the utmost speed in his swift, clear handwriting.

Then his experience in drawing plats as a Surveyor made it possible for him to put together his field notes and compass readings and to prepare the map on the opposite page. It is not greatly at variance with similar records completed later on the basis of detailed study of the ground. Even today, with no other paper than this, a traveler who used a compass probably could journey from Cumberland, Maryland, to the site of Fort Le Boeuf, about twelve miles South of Erie, Pennsylvania.

The illustration is reproduced from the *George Washington Atlas,* after the original in the British Museum.

A Scale of Miles

Part of Lake Erie

The French are now coming from their Forts on Lake Erie & on the Creek, to Venango to build another Fort — And from thence they design to the Forks of Monongahela and to the Logs Town, and so to continue down the River building at the most convenient places in order to prevent our settlements &c.

NB. A little below Shanapins Town in the Fork is the place where we are going immediatly to Build a Fort as it commands the Ohio and Monongahele.

Venango

River

Gt. River Creek

Kuskuskee Town

Murdering Town

The Logs Town

Ohio

Mr. Frazier

Turtle Creek

Queen Aliquippa

Monongahela

Aligany

Mountains

Potomack River

ROBERT DINWIDDIE, WASHINGTON'S "COMMANDER"

Three men influenced materially and in varying degree the youthful career of George Washington. These three were his half-brother Lawrence, his neighbor Col. William Fairfax, and his first commander-in-Chief, Robert Dinwiddie, Lieutenant Governor of Virginia, whose portrait is reproduced on the opposite page, after the original in the National Portrait Gallery, London.

When George undertook his first military mission in the autumn of 1753, Governor Dinwiddie had been at the head of the royal government in Virginia for little more than twenty-three months. He was sixty years of age, a veteran of the British colonial service and an inflexible supporter of the royal authority wherever and howsoever asserted.

Dinwiddie had no military training and in Virginia could take counsel of none who had made arms their profession. The Colony had no garrison, not even any retired Captains or Majors of the British regular establishment. As Dinwiddie possessed his full measure of determination, he made mistakes which Washington, his inexperienced senior field officer, did not know how to prevent or to correct.

The relations of the two men involved several misunderstandings and ultimate estrangement, but Dinwiddie has a place of honor in American history as the man who gave Washington his first opportunity.

covered eight miles only and had camped at George's Creek when a
messenger came stumbling along with letters to Gist from one of his
sons.[41] The papers conveyed bad news: The young man had fallen
sick while on his way home from the Cherokee country, and was at
the mouth of the Conegocheague,[42] where he needed the medical
attention his father could give him.

The elder Gist sought the counsel of Washington and of the others:
Should he remain with them or hasten to his son? To this, George's
answer was, of course, that Gist should continue with the party. He
was on public business of large importance; he could not turn back.
George did not have to press the argument. Gist complied. The
frontiersman took a medicine from the baggage, prepared it, wrote a
letter to his son and told the messenger to carry the paper and the
package to the younger Gist.

It was a small incident but it was typical of many Washington was
to observe on the journey. Christopher Gist, a Marylander, was then
in his middle forties,[43] and had been a frontiersman and fur trader on
the Yadkin before coming to Wills Creek. There he had performed a
variety of services for the Ohio Company. In 1750–51 he had been sent
by the company to the valley of the Ohio to explore the rivers and to
locate the good lands.[44] From November, 1751, through March, 1752,
he had examined a wide stretch of country to ascertain the best route
for a road from Wills Creek to the Monongahela and then he had
resumed the work of the previous year.[45] At Logstown, in May, 1752,
he had represented the Ohio Company under commission from
Governor Dinwiddie.[46] Later he had been appointed with Thomas
Cresap and William Trent to contract for the building of a fort on the
hill "below Shurtees Creek" on the Ohio.[47] Gist, in a word, was one
of the most active of those who at different periods were fur traders,
explorers, engineers and Indian diplomatists.

His character became his varied roles. Adversity never seemed to
depress him. If he had to write in his journal of sickness or of delay

[41] For the three sons, Nathaniel, Richard and Thomas, see 1 *Hamilton,* 4 n. and *Western Penn. Hist. Mag.,* v. 15, p. 191–218.

[42] So Gist, in *Darlington,* 80, spelled the name. His reference was to the Conococheague, which enters the Potomac about six miles Southwest of the present Hagerstown, Md.

[43] His parents, Richard and Zipporah Gist, were married in 1705 and had three sons.

[44] See his instructions in *Darlington,* 31–32.   [45] His instructions are in *ibid.,* 67–68.

[46] *Ibid.,* 232 ff, and his MS expense account, Apr. 8, 1754; *Col. Papers,* VSL.

[47] *Darlington,* 236. Shurties Creek is correctly Chartier's Creek, which enters the Ohio directly West of Brunot Island, about two and three-quarter miles downstream from the junction of the Monongahela and the Allegheny.

on account of weather, he always added an optimistic antithesis: He was sick, but he recovered; he had been kept in camp by rain, but he had killed a bear. Although not healthy, he had vast endurance. Solitary as his daily life was, he had been known to leave an Indian town and to sleep in the forest, rather than keep the company of those he denounced as "reprobate traders." [48] No frontiersman understood the Indians better or had greater patience in dealing with them. Gist was a good shot, a fine hunter who seldom went hungry if there was any game in the woods, and he had a quick eye for good land. Few could excel him in making himself comfortable in the wilderness, as, for example, when he drove a panther from its lair under an over-hanging rock and slept cheerfully there a January night in 1752. [49]

Gist was a man of some education [50] and of religious principles, reared in the Church of England; but he was accustomed to view stoically the ways of savages he knew he could not reform. In the Wyandot town at the Muskingum, [51] Christmas Day, 1750, Gist held what probably was the first Protestant religious service in the region destined to become the State of Ohio. [52] The next day he had to stand passively by while the natives loosed a captive Indian woman whose fate he thus described: ". . . The persons appointed for the purpose pursued her and struck her on the ear, on the right side of her head, which beat her flat on her face on the ground; they then stuck her several times through the back to the heart, scalped her, and threw the scalp in the air, and another cut off her head." [53] The Indians who were capable of this were devoted to Gist, whom they named Annosanah. This, they said, "was a name of a good man that had formerly lived among them." [54]

Washington was to find Gist capable of handling both compass and canoe, a man altogether conscientious in the performance of duty and, at the same time, not disposed to volunteer counsel on matters entrusted to his young companion. He would advise George when asked; otherwise he would leave the young Adjutant to make decisions unless the circumstances involved an element of danger with which Washington was unacquainted. More than any other man, Gist was to be George's teacher in the art of the frontiersman who had to deal with the un-

[48] See his journal entries of Nov. 25–26, 1750; *Darlington*, 34–35.
[49] *Darlington*, 72.
[50] His autograph letters are beautifully written.
[51] For the use of this term see *Darlington*, 106.   [52] *Darlington*, 38, 113.
[53] *Darlington*, 39. She was buried that evening by the same Barney Currin who accompanied George on the mission of 1753–54.
[54] *Ibid.*, 38.

certain savages. George scarcely could have had a better instructor: he had now to demonstrate how apt a pupil he would be.[55]

The opening days of George's apprenticeship were novel and interesting enough, but they were not exacting. He, Gist, van Braam and the others climbed upward, descended to the narrow valleys, mounted again to the top of the passes, and crossed the stony streams. Part of the woodland was open; elsewhere the trail was challenged by the greedy laurel thicket;[56] but the horses still were strong and were fed on the corn brought in their packs. As there were no wheeled vehicles, the journey was as rapid as the difficult country permitted. The Great Crossing of the Youghiogheny was passed where the water flowed northward. George did not follow the stream as it continued in that direction for about six and a half miles and then, turning westward, broke through Laurel Hill at an elevation of about 1200 feet. Instead, Washington and his companions, continuing West and Northwest from the Great Crossing, reached Laurel Hill at a distance of approximately three miles.

Up its steep and forbidding eastern flank they climbed to a ridge of 2400 feet and then they passed down to a plateau approximately 1700 feet above sea level. This area, Gist told George, was known as the Great Meadows. At the moment the place was interesting only because the ground, though boggy in spots, was less wooded than the high ground that looked down on it.[57] West and Northwest of the Great Meadows loomed Chestnut Ridge, beyond which, on a straight line to the West, at a distance of twelve miles, were the upper waters of the Monongahela.[58] These distances may not have been known to Gist, and certainly they were beyond the range of George's study or experience. Nor did Gist have any information on the possibility of using canoes on that part of the Monongahela.

[55] Cf. Washington to John Robinson, May 30, 1757: "[Captain Gist] has had extensive dealings with the Indians, is in great esteem among them, well acquainted with their manners and customs, is indefatigable and patient, most excellent qualities indeed where Indians are concerned. And for his capacity, honesty and zeal, I dare venture to engage" (2 G. W., 43–44). Apparently, in December, 1754, Governor Sharpe had some concern regarding Gist's financial probity (1 Sharpe, 139).

[56] For a sound, conservative description of the Pennsylvania forests, see Buck, 6 ff. This is in gratifying contrast to what has been written in imitation of Parkman by persons who did not have that author's accurate knowledge of the country portrayed in his books.

[57] The name Laurel Hill was used loosely by travelers, traders and soldiers in the region. Confusion resulted. Dalrymple, on his revision of Jefferson and Fry's map, plainly marked both Laurel Hill and Chestnut Ridge in approximately their correct position, but many contemporaries spoke of Laurel Hill as West, not East, of Great Meadows and thereby mistook Chestnut Ridge for Laurel Hill.

[58] The distance from the Meadows to the top of Chestnut Ridge is about six miles. Consequently, the shortest air line from the Meadows to the Monongahela is approximately eighteen.

Of one thing he felt sure: it was easier to turn North from the Meadows on the way to the Ohio than to attempt to follow the dim and difficult trail over Chestnut Ridge and then to descend the Monongahela.[59] Northward the men accordingly moved through the mountains and, as they advanced, encountered their first snow. It was Sunday, November 18, with the snow ankle-deep, when they reached Gist's new settlement between the Youghiogheny and the Monongahela, a point George estimated to be seventy miles by road from Wills Creek.[60] He found Gist's settlement to consist of the trader's house, twenty by thirty feet,[61] and of some outbuildings. Only one family besides Gist's own had established itself there as yet.[62]

The next morning, November 19, George and his companions started North and crossed the Youghiogheny.[63] This march of about twenty miles brought them to Jacobs Cabins, an abandoned settlement that probably took its name from the Delaware Sachem, Captain Jacobs, whom George was later to meet on a red and hideous day.[64] As if in warning that Jacobs would not prove a pleasant companion, the first mishap of the expedition occurred at the cabins. During the night some of the horses contrived to break away and wandered off. They were not recovered and loaded again until 11 A.M. Then rain slowed down the advance, which now was toward the Northwest and parallel to the general course of the Youghiogheny. Weather did not daunt

[59] Had Gist so chosen, he could have gone Northwest from the Meadows and at a distance of twenty-five miles would have reached the mouth of Red Stone Creek on the Monongahela, for which see Bailey, *Cresap*, 95. This is substantially the route of the National Pike through Uniontown to Brownsville. From Red Stone Creek, Gist and Washington could have proceeded by canoe to the "forks of the Ohio" and thence to Logstown. The overland route, to be described in the text, covered approximately sixty-two miles, but, had the water route been followed, horses would not have been transported beyond Red Stone Creek unless batteaux had been built there. The route followed, therefore, was the more economical and probably the more expeditious.

[60] 1 Ford, 17. His estimate was substantially that given in the *Virginia Almanac* for 1756: Wills Creek to Little Meadows, twenty miles; to the great crossing of the Youghiogheny, twenty miles; to Great Meadows, twelve miles; to Gist's Plantation, twelve miles; total, sixty-four miles. George Croghan's estimate (2 *Penn. Arch.*, 134), was sixty-two miles.

[61] It was so described the next year by Villiers in his report, Paris, Aff. Etrang. Mém. et Docs. Amér. 10:1:97–109.

[62] Washington's map, *Darlington*, 80, showed three buildings at Gist's settlement. Lowdermilk's study (*op. cit.*, 40) led him to conclude that in 1753 Gist's house was merely the "nucleus of another settlement," though Hadden (*Expeditions*, 12) mistakenly stated that eleven families were settled there by Gist in 1753. For the fact that only one family had settled at Gist's, in addition to his own, see his petition in *Journ. H.B.*, 1752–58, p. 223.

[63] The contours suggest that the party rode up from the South, at some distance West of the left bank, to a point about a mile North of Connelsville. Then the riders went down the flats under the hill and crossed in the bend opposite the mouth of Galley Run. This was approximately the location of Stewart's Crossing.

[64] The *Handbook of the American Indian*, ed. F. W. Hodge (cited hereafter as *Hodge*), leaves the identification of the site and the association with Captain Jacobs in some doubt.

Gist. He killed a deer and that night could offer his drenched companions broiled venison.[65] The rain continuing all day on the 21st, venison doubtless was again in order.

On the 22nd, refreshed in spite of gloomy skies, the embassy set out again in the same direction and passed some miles to the East of the point where the Youghiogheny flowed into the Monongahela. Twelve miles from their starting point, the Englishmen reached the "deep and gentle" Monongahela [66] at the mouth of Turtle Creek, close to the settlement of John Frazier.[67] Fortunately this well-known trader was at his home, where he operated a store and repaired the rifles of frontiersmen and Indians.[68] Frazier always had pushed on. In 1741, he had gone to Venango, where French Creek joins the Allegheny, and there he had traded and had mended guns until driven out in 1753.[69] One of George's verbal instructions, it will be remembered, was to inquire of the French commandant why Frazier had been forced to leave Venango.[70]

The trader had much news to relate. For one thing, said Frazier, friendly natives headed by Half King and other Sachems recently had visited him and had left a string of wampum and a message for the Governor of Virginia to the effect that three nations of French Indians had taken up the hatchet against the English. Frazier passed the wampum to George along with the warning. Another item of information was that French troops had been advancing toward the Ohio from Lake Erie when mounted messengers—"expresses" they were styled— had arrived with news that the "General" of the French, Pierre Paul, Sieur de Marin, had died. After that, the greater part of the French had been withdrawn northward to winter quarters.[71]

In this intelligence, the good and the bad were mingled. George knew that Dinwiddie and the royal government depended, in large measure, on friendly Indians of the Six Nations for the defence of the Virginia frontier. Change of sympathy on the part of those natives would be a calamity; any war that weakened them was a danger to the

[65] *Darlington*, 80.
[66] Evans's *Analyses of the Map of the Middle Colonies* in L. H. Gipson, *Lewis Evans*, 171.
[67] 1 Ford, 12; *Darlington*, 80.
[68] *Lowdermilk*, 42. No record has been found in this study of any actual manufacture of arms by Frazier, but Mrs. Ruby Frazier Frey is satisfied that he made weapons and she bases the major plot of her novel, *Red Morning*, on that premise. Her research has been thorough.
[69] *Ibid.*, and article on Venango in 2 *Hodge*, 880.
[70] See *supra*, p. 276. Frazier's name appears in the records also as Frazer, Fraser and Freser.
[71] 1 *Ford*, 12.

settlements.[72] As for the French withdrawal, it might have large meaning for the future and might give England an advantage. At the moment, as concerned George, return of the French toward Lake Erie might add many miles to the wilderness trail he and his attendants would have to cover in order to deliver Dinwiddie's letter to the French commander.

Every such mile was harder to traverse now. The weather was colder, but not cold enough, as yet, to freeze the streams. Rain had swollen Turtle Creek and the nearby Monongahela. The same condition doubtless prevailed on the swift Allegheny, which joined the Monongahela at right angles about ten miles Northwest of Turtle Creek. Neither of the rivers could be crossed otherwise than by swimming the heavily laden horses. Frontiersmen were equal to the resulting task. Frazier cheerfully lent a canoe on which the baggage could be loaded. Barney Currin and Henry Steward, accustomed to handling this treacherous type of craft, could paddle down the Monongahela to the junction of the rivers and could leave the baggage on the right bank of the Allegheny. Horses and riders, traveling light, could go from Frazier's northwestward to the Allegheny. There the horses could be made to swim to the right bank,[73] where the baggage could be picked up.

On the 23rd of November, in weather not unfavorable, this plan was carried out. While Barney and Henry were coming down the Monongahela, George rode on and had perhaps the most stirring view of the entire journey: Emerging from the wooded hillocks, he reached the strategic objective of the rival English and French, the wind-swept, uninhabited point of land where the Allegheny, which was turbulently Gallic, received the slow, English waters of the powerful and silent Monongahela. There, or nearby, Governor Dinwiddie planned to erect the fort that was to keep the French from the Ohio and the Monongahela.

George previously had seen no forts except some of those on Barbados, but now he studied the ground carefully in order to ascertain, if he could, how the nearer stretches of the two rivers could be commanded by English guns. He reasoned that the French would advance down the Allegheny or southward parallel to that stream, and on that basis he reached conclusions which he jotted down in notes for the rough journal he was keeping. Later he elaborated his views to this

---

[72] Lords of Trade to Duke of Bedford, Jan. 10, 1750/51; P.R.O., C.O. 5:1344, f. 101–03.
[73] *Darlington*, 80; 1 *Ford*, 12.

effect: "The land in the forks . . . I think extremely well situated for a fort, as it has the absolute command of both rivers. The land at the point is twenty or twenty-five feet above the common surface of the water; and a considerable bottom of flat, well-timbered land all around it, very convenient for building. The rivers are each a quarter of a mile or more across and run here very near at right angles, Allegheny bearing northeast and Monongahela southeast. The former of these two is a very rapid and swift running water; the other deep and still, without any perceptible fall." [74]

About the time George finished the examination of this site, Currin and Steward arrived with the canoe and the baggage. They unloaded safely on the farther side of the Allegheny and then ferried over the other members of the party while the horses swam the chilly stream.[75] This crossing put the Englishmen on the right bank of the river, down which they could ride the next morning to their first objective—Logstown, where George hoped to meet Half King.

Camp was made on the shore. The night was uneventful but it opened an interesting and, to George, an eventful day. Nearby lived the Indian Chief Shingiss,[76] a friendly Delaware whom it seemed wise to invite to the council George had been instructed to hold with Half King at Logstown. Policy and politeness dictated a personal call on Shingiss and on a lesser Chief, Lowmolach. The Major went the more readily because he had been told, probably by Gist, that Shingiss resided where William Trent had contracted to build a fort for the Ohio Company.

Shingiss and Lowmolach both were at their village and, when acquainted with George's purpose, were entirely agreeable: They would go at once with the white men to Logstown. While the savages made ready, George examined the proposed location of the company fort. He was quick to see disadvantage in comparison with the strength and sweep of the high ground directly in the forks of the Allegheny and the Monongahela. "I think it greatly inferior," he said of Shingiss' site, "either for defence or advantages, especially the former." He explained: "For a fort at the forks would be equally well situated on the Ohio, and have the entire command of the Monongahela, which runs up to our settlements and is extremely well designed for water carriage, as it is of a deep, still nature. Besides, a fort at the forks might be

---

[74] 1 *Ford*, 13.   [75] 2 *Darlington*, 80–81,
[76] Often spelled Shingas,

built at much less expense than at the other place. Nature has well contrived this lower place for water defence; but the hill whereon it must
stand, being about a quarter of a mile in length, and then descending
gradually on the land side, will render it difficult and very expensive
to make a sufficient fortification there. The whole flat upon the hill
must be taken in, the side next the descent made extremely high, or
else the hill itself cut away: Otherwise, the enemy may raise batteries
within that distance without being exposed to a single shot from the
fort." [77] Self-taught military engineering this was, but sound. George
was learning on the frontier what he could not have acquired in any
town on the narrow coast where England's rule might be challenged.[78]

By the time George had finished this field lesson in soldierly science,
Shingiss and Lowmolach were ready to leave on the first march George
ever had made with Indians. Down the bank of the Ohio the savages
and the white men went until, between sunset and dusk, they came
to a rich bottom, half a mile wide, that stretched along the right bank
of the Ohio, as they afterward discovered, for a distance of about five
miles. Not far from the point where high ground came closer to the
river, they reached a little creek beyond which a steep ridge ran almost
North and South.[79] In the bottom were the huts and the long house
known as Logstown, scene of Indian conferences and the home of
Half King.

To Gist, the site was familiar, because he had been there in November, 1750, and again in June, 1752; [80] to George, arrival was the real
beginning of the serious part of a mission. To that date, George doubtless had enjoyed his "command" and he had felt the challenge of the
cold forest, but in other respects, the twenty-five days had been remarkably, perhaps disappointingly, free of adventure. Now, under his instructions, George was to find Half King and the other Sachems and
was to ask them to supply guards for the journey to the French post.[81]
George's call on Shingiss had been of small importance compared with
this visit to Half King. To deal with that chief of Chiefs, the most in-

[77] 1 Ford, 13–14.
[78] George Mercer's opinion of this site was contrary to Washington's. See the quotation in
4 Gipson, 293–94.
[79] Colonel Bouquet's description of "old Logstown" (quoted in Darlington, 99) states that
the ridge was low but steep. Actually the crest is 420 feet above the flat South of the creek
mouth. The town was eighteen miles downstream from Pittsburgh on the right bank of the
Ohio, and, according to Darlington, 95, was "immediately below the present town of Economy,"
which is directly North of Ambridge, Beaver County. For the various visits of French and
British to Logstown, see 1 Hodge, 773, and 1 Thwaites, 24, n. 17.
[80] Darlington, 34, 97.   [81] See supra, p. 276.

fluential ruler of the district, George needed an interpreter, because Gist, with all his accomplishments, had never learned the Indian tongues of that region. What Gist lacked, the well-known trader John Davison possessed. He had traveled far North of the Ohio and had learned to converse readily with the natives.[82] Attended by this experienced master of the Indian speech, George sought the Indian ruler.

Half King, as it chanced, was fifteen miles away, at his cabin on Little Beaver Creek, but George learned that Monakatoocha, a Chief second only to Half King, was in the village.[83] So Washington left some of the men to pitch the tent and, probably with Shingiss, Lowmolach, Gist and John Davison, he went to call ceremoniously on the Chief. Through Davison, who seemed to have no trouble in making himself understood, George explained to Monakatoocha that he was a messenger to the French commander and was directed by the Governor of Virginia to inform the Sachems. Then, with due formality, George presented the Chief a string of wampum and a twist of tobacco.[84] This done, he asked Monakatoocha to send for the Half King. When the Chief promised to dispatch a runner the next morning, George thanked him and invited him and the other great men of the tribe to visit the English tent. They accepted and tramped after him across the meadow to the spot where the canvas had been raised and the horses tethered. The Indians remained for an hour, but if George led the conversation or offered them any refreshment, he did not note the fact in his journal.[85] It was a satisfactory though not a brilliant interview. Gist wrote of it only this: ". . . We spoke to the chiefs this evening, and repaired to our camp." [86]

[82] For Davison's familiarity with the region, see Evans's *Analysis,* loc. cit., p. 10. It will be noted that the text avoids the direct statement that George employed Davison at Logstown. No mention of him is made in Washington's journal prior to November 24, at Logstown (1 *Ford,* 14). In a reference to Davison at Venango, December 7, Washington spoke of him as "the Indian interpreter whom I brought with me from Town" (*ibid.,* 28). If George had said, "from the town," there scarcely could have been doubt of his meaning, because Logstown usually was called, in that region, simply "the town." The doubt consequently remains, though the probability is strong that Davison's services were recruited at Logstown. When one remembers that as many as 300 English traders went into the Indian country every year, George ran little risk in not providing an interpreter until he reached the Indian settlements. He had, in fact, a far better chance of hiring there a man who knew the required speech than he had of finding such a person at Winchester, at Cresap's or at Wills Creek.

[83] The tribal connection of Monakatoocha is variously given. He and Half King have been confused. Some writers apparently have thought Monakatoocha another name for Half King.

[84] 1 *Ford,* 14.

[85] 1 *Ford,* 15. For the significance of the tobacco, see *infra,* n. 297.

[86] *Darlington,* 81.

The next day, November 25, was one of sensation. Into the town came a small group of men in travel-worn French uniform.[87] They doubtless were the first soldiers of that nationality George ever had seen, and they were of the most discreditable type that wore their country's coat—deserters. George of course wanted to know how they reached Logstown and, with van Braam as interpreter, he talked at length with them and with the man who had them in charge, a British fur trader named Brown. The French deserters said that they were part of a force of 100 who had been sent up the Mississippi, with eight canoes of provisions, to meet at Logstown a similar detachment from the garrisons on the south side of Lake Erie. They had been on Great Beaver Creek but had slipped away before the troops arrived from the North. It had been the deserters' understanding that their contingent was to go farther up the Ohio than Logstown.[88]

All this seemed to be dark confirmation of what had been suspected at Williamsburg. George doubtless guessed that the French had intended to advance to the forks and to build a fort there. Eagerly, therefore, he continued this first examination of deserters, an ugly type of indispensable military duty, with which he was in time to be better acquainted. How many men, he asked, did the French have on the Mississippi, and how many forts?

There were, said the deserters, four small forts between New Orleans and the Illinois.

"Isles Noires?" van Braam probably queried.

"Oui, Illinois," the French replied.

"Black Islands," van Braam translated.

George dutifully noted there were four small forts between New Orleans and the Black Islands. Neither he nor van Braam ever had heard previously of the Illinois Indians.[89] As the deserters continued to describe the country in which their government had forts and posts, George heard other Indian names in a French accent—Obaish, which the English were to spell Wabash, and Chawanon, or Shanoah, which later was to be rendered Shawanoe, Showanese and still later

[87] Washington wrote "four or ten Frenchmen," but he scarcely could have meant that. "Four or five" probably was what he intended to say.

[88] Search of the French military papers in the Canadian archives has failed to bring to light anything bearing on this expedition.

[89] 1 Ford, 15. The conversation is put in this form because it appears to be the simplest means of illustrating how the mistake occurred. It was seized upon later to demonstrate the incompetence of van Braam as an interpreter, but the error was a natural one. Although the Illinois had been known to French Jesuits from 1660, the English settlers and traders nowhere had come into contact with this powerful federation.

Shawnee.[90] Never had he received in so strange a manner a lesson in geography. It probably continued most of the day, until word came at 3 P.M. that Half King had arrived from Little Beaver Creek.

Etiquette required, of course, that the English visitor should make the first call. George accordingly went over to the Sachem's cabin and met Half King. This cherished friend of the English, whose tribal name was Tanachariston, was then about fifty-three but was in full vigor with his fiery eloquence at its top flame. He was an intelligent man, vain, brave, as candid as an Indian ever was, and possessed of an unusual knowledge of white men and their methods of fighting. Like most of the natives he loved strong drink and he delighted in attention and flattery, but within the limits of native cunning, he had staunchness and character. When his passion was stirred, the Half King would assert that the reason he hated the French was that they had killed, boiled and eaten his father.[91] More immediately and most personally, he had a bitter grudge because of the treatment he recently had received at the hands of the Sieur de Marin. Part of this experience was known along the river and had been reported to George.

As soon as greetings were exchanged through John Davison, the interpreter, George invited Half King to his tent and there, in private conference, asked the Chief to tell him about the routes and distances to the nearest French fort. George may have been coached in this procedure by Gist, or he may have been guided by his own sense of the proprieties. In any event, he found Half King more than willing to talk—anxious, in fact, to give all the information he could and to set forth his grievances with the full fury of outraged pride. All routes were quickly described. The better of them was impassable because of the swamps made by the overflow of streams.[92] It would be necessary to proceed via Venango. Five or six good days' journeys would be required.

This explained, Half King launched into an account of his visit to

---

90 Cf. 1 Ford, 16.

91 1 Hodge, 526–27. Few Indians of Western Pennsylvania were so often consulted as was Half King but none was more frequently confused with other chieftains. Buck (op. cit., 29) accepted the tradition that the headmen of the Iroquois in 1747 sent "two Oneida chiefs, Tanachariston and Scarouady to maintain their authority in the region [of Ohio]." It was explained: "Tanachariston, who was usually called the Half King by the English, looked after the Delawares, and Scarouady after the Shawnees." In 2 Hodge, 485, Scarouady is identified as Monacatuatha or Monakaduto whose name must be a variant of that of Monakatoocha, mentioned by Washington as second Chief at Logstown. He probably succeeded Tanachariston, on the death of that Sachem. See Beauchamp, Iroquois, 301.

92 George styled them "many large, mirey Savannahs" (1 Ford, 17).

the French fort.[93] He had been received by the Sieur de Marin with much sternness and had been asked very brusquely what he wanted. Half King had prepared in advance a speech for the occasion, and, as he told George of the episode, he insisted on repeating the substance of what he had announced to the French commandant. Then, or later, George did Half King the honor of writing down for the information of Governor Dinwiddie all the Indian said he had hurled at the master of the fort.

If Half King told the truth about his speech, it was a bold call on the French to leave the watershed of the Ohio. "For be it known to you, fathers," Half King quoted himself as affirming, "that this is our land, and not yours." He said he had continued: "If you had come in a peaceable manner, like our brothers the English, we should not be against your trading with us, as they do; but to come, fathers, and build houses upon our land and to take it by force, is what we cannot submit to." Half King then had indulged in a few flourishes and had concluded: "So, fathers, I desire you to withdraw, as I have done our brothers the English: For I will keep you at arm's length. I lay this down as a trial for both, to see which will have the greatest regard to it, and that side we will stand by and make equal shares [94] with us. Our brothers, the English, have heard this, and I am come now to tell it to you; for I am not afraid to discharge you off this land." [95] Half King manifestly thought this a good speech, and he went on to tell George that he had followed it by returning to the French commander a string of wampum, symbolic of one the French had given the Indians when the savages had made a previous, amicable visit.

Then the Chief gamely and with burning eyes repeated the defiant reply of the Sieur de Marin, a reply deliberately phrased to humiliate the redman. With few preliminaries, the Frenchman had demanded: "Where is my wampum that you took away, with the marks of towns in it? This wampum I do not know which you have discharged me off the land with. But you need not put yourself to the trouble of speaking, for I will not hear you."

Contemptuously the Frenchman then had told Half King: "I am not afraid of flies, or mosquitos, for Indians are such as those. I tell you, down that river I will go and will build upon it, according to my com-

---

93 The date of this visit is not recorded, but it probably was in the summer or early fall of 1753.
94 The original perhaps was *sharers*.   95 1 *Ford*, 17-18.

mand. If the river was blocked up, I have forces sufficient to burst it open and tread under my feet all that stand in opposition, together with their alliances; for my force is as the sand upon the seashore: Therefore here is your wampum; I fling it at you."

He doubtless had fitted his gesture to his word and then he had sounded this blast in the Indian's ears: "Child, you talk foolish; you say this land belongs to you, but there is not the black of my nails yours. I saw that land sooner than you did, before the Shanoahs and you were at war: Lead [96] was the man who went down and took possession of that river; It is my land, and I will have it, let who will stand-up for, or say against it."

Mockingly the Sieur de Marin had concluded: "I'll buy and sell with the English! [97] If people will be ruled by me, they may expect kindness, but not else!" [98]

This conversation had infuriated Half King; but, as repeated by him, it must have confused and alarmed and, at the same time, must have pleased George. He could not have understood, at the moment, the full meaning of what had been said about the wampum given and demanded back in place of that which Half King had returned. Along with his uncertainty regarding this, George had new evidence of the French determination to occupy the Ohio, though he could afford to be happy that de Marin had outraged Half King's pride. The French commander thereby had reduced almost to nothingness the possibility that his successor ever could wean the Chief from support of England.

In answer to questions, Half King now went on to inform George about other matters covered by the young emissary's instructions. At the fort, the Sachem reported, he had asked about the two English traders whom the French had seized. The commandant, said Half King, had made this answer: "Child, you think it a very great hardship that I made prisoner of those two people of Venango. Don't you concern yourself with it: we took and carried them to Canada, to get intelligence of what the English were doing in Virginia." [99]

That, too, was something for George to ponder: it was unqualified admission that the French had made prisoners of peaceful traders in the area of dispute. More than that, the French evidently were beginning to suspect that military preparations were under way in Virginia.

[96] Doubtless La Salle, an interesting example of the ease with which, by double translation, poorly written names were distorted.

[97] Here in the final text of his report, George inserted "(mockingly)."

[98] 1 *Ford*, 18.   [99] 1 *Ford*, 18–19.

Doubtless at George's request, Half King explained what he had seen of French defences in the country between Logstown and Lake Erie. There were two forts, said the Chief. One was on the lake; the other was fifteen miles inland on French Creek and near a small body of water. A wide wagon road connected the two places. The forts were alike, though the one on Lake Erie was the larger. From memory, Half King obligingly drew a sketch [100] of the ground plan of the stockades.

All this was creditable to Half King's candor and to his powers of observation. Now it was George's turn to answer Half King's questions. At the moment, the Sachem put two only—what had become of the Indians in Carolina jail; who was the white boy a party of French Indians were said to have carried toward the North from some English settlement? George probably could give a vague answer to the first question, but he knew nothing about the boy.[101]

The long interview now was ended. Half King left the tent with the understanding that he would assemble his great men the next morning to hear Washington's request for an escort. George, for his part, had no reason to be dissatisfied with anything he had done or said in this initial conference with the influential Half King; but he had an ordeal immediately ahead—a public speech, and to savages at that.

Next morning, at unrecorded expenditure of thought and preparation, George was steeled to the effort.[102] He went to the Long House, the first dark structure of its kind that he probably had entered.[103] There he greeted the assembled leaders and, with Davison again his interpreter, undertook to explain his mission. Almost certainly he had written out what he proceeded to say: "Brothers, I have called you together in council by order of your brother, the Governor of Virginia, to acquaint you that I am sent, with all possible dispatch, to visit and to deliver a letter to the French commandant, of very great importance

100 Perhaps he previously had drawn it and merely produced it now. Washington's language is not quite explicit (1 *Ford*, 19).

101 1 *Ford*, 19. The lad mentioned by Half King may have been the one Governor Dinwiddie had in mind when he told the Burgesses that "very lately a poor man on the South branch of the Potomac [was] robbed of his son" (1 *Din.*, 74).

102 Nowhere in Washington's report is there any indication of the extent to which Gist assisted him in anything besides the journey through an unfamiliar wilderness.

103 The use of the Long House for councils does not appear to have been reported frequently by white men, probably because most of the treaties were completed in summer and consequently out of doors. Among Virginia Indians, the Long House was used for ceremonials and probably as a place of general entertainment (*American Anthropologist*, n.s., v. 9, p. 60). Gookin's early references to the Long House of New England Indians (1 *Mass. Hist. Col.*, 150) would indicate these structures were devoted to communal living only. For the Iroquois' Long Houses, see *Chadwick*, 26; *Buck*, 31; Beauchamp, *Iroquois Trail*, 124.

to your brothers, the English, and I dare say to you, their friends and allies."

This was a formal opening, which was proper, but it was not a prudent beginning because it was certain to arouse among the natives a curiosity Washington would not be at liberty to satisfy. George proceeded: "I was desired, brothers, by your brother the Governor, to call upon you, the Sachems of the nations, to inform you of it, and to ask your advice and assistance to proceed the nearest and best road to the French. You see, brothers, I have gotten thus far on my journey."

Major Washington continued: "His Honour likewise desired me to apply to you for some of your young men, to conduct and provide provisions for us on our way, and be a safeguard against those French Indians who have taken up the hatchet against us. I have spoken this particularly to you, brothers, because his Honour our Governor treats you as good friends and allies, and holds you in great esteem. To confirm what I have said, I give you this string of wampum." [104]

This might pass muster, but besides leaving the nature of his errand a mystery—a defect that George recognized—the speech might alarm the savages in this particular: What Washington asked in the way of an escort might involve Half King's followers in a quarrel with French Indians or with the French themselves at a time when the English allies of the friendly tribes were far off. This danger probably had been increased by the clash between Half King and the Sieur de Marin. If the Indians furnished a large escort and went boldly northward, they might be marching straight into a wintry war.

In spite of this, Half King was altogether for compliance with the Englishmen's request. He was determined, in fact, to go back to the French fort and to repeat to the new commandant what he had told de Marin. More than that, Half King was resolved to collect all the treaty belts the French had given the tribes, and to return this wampum as notice that the Indians were, in Washington's subsequent words, "shaking off all dependence upon the French." [105] In words that Davison did

---

[104] 1 *Ford*, 19–20.

[105] 1 *Ford*, 23. This use of wampum as a sign of disavowal of dependence must have been peculiar to the region or else it was an original device of Half King's; but no positive statement is possible because, as Dr. H. B. Collins, Jr. of the Bureau of American Ethnology of the Smithsonian Institution has said verbally, there is little direct evidence on wampum from contemporary authorities. The Indians themselves left no records. Those agents who had dealings with the natives, where wampum was employed, usually were more concerned with results than with emblems. Sir William Johnson, the Indian agent, was the great colonial authority on wampum, the ceremonial use of which he developed (see W. M. Beauchamp, *Wampum and Shells*, cited hereafter as *Beauchamp*, 394), but Johnson's own papers fail to

not attempt to translate, Half King urged the other Sachems to approve this. After some discussion, they apparently acquiesced.

Thereupon Half King arose and, with only two preliminary sentences, made this promise: "We shall put heart in hand and speak to our fathers the French concerning the speech they made to me; and you may depend that we will endeavor to be your guard." Then Half King addressed himself more directly to the young Virginian: "Brother, as you have asked my advice, I hope you will be ruled by it and stay until I can provide a company to go with you." He explained: "The French speech belt is not here; I have to go for it to my hunting cabin. Likewise, the people whom I have ordered in, are not yet come, nor cannot until the third night from this: till which time, brother, I beg you to stay." The Chief added: "I intend to send a guard of Mingos, Shawnees and Delawares, that our brothers may see the love and loyalty we bear them." [106]

This assurance doubtless was given in slow and awkward translation, quite different from the comparatively smooth idiom into which Washington subsequently recast it. At the moment, George did not suspect

---

explain much of the symbolism he sponsored. White wampum indicated good will; if tobacco was attached, it was an invitation to peace (Thomas Forsyth in 2 *Blair*, 238). Sometimes plain white wampum, or white wampum with diagonal black lines, typical of Long House beams, signified peace (*Beauchamp*, 416). If an alliance was consummated, figures as numerous as the parties to the agreement would appear on the wampum (*ibid.*, 391, 394, and Weiser's journal in 1 *Thwaites*, 30). Dark wampum, black or deep purple, was for "state occasions" (*Beauchamp*, 394), a notice of death (*ibid.*, 437), or a warning of misconduct (Easton Conference, in *Indian Treaties*, 229). Black and white, according to the size of the belt, represented high honor (Croghan's journal in 1 *Thwaites*, 77), and likewise accredited a messenger (Weiser's journal in *ibid.*, 31). A black line on white wampum was a road of friendship (*ibid.*, 30). White wampum, painted red, with the figure of a tomahawk woven in one end, was a declaration of war (*Beauchamp*, 394). Black wampum, accompanied by an actual hatchet, was an invitation to declare war on a common foe (1 *Din.*, 429, 430). Other specialized uses are described in Forsyth's *Memoires*, in 2 *Blair*, 238, in Speck *Memoirs*, 6, and in Conference at Easton, *Indian Treaties*, 251–52. The old chiefs were the custodians of the wampum and were supposed to know what each belt or string signified (*Morgan*, 121); but sometimes the natives did not understand the meaning of the signs on some of their accumulated wampum (Conference at Easton, *Indian Treaties*, 251–52). By no means all the meaning of wampum in diplomatic exchange was conveyed by the color and the markings. To throw a wampum belt on the ground in a certain manner was to profess sincerity, but to throw it in another manner was a declaration of war (*Beauchamp*, 430). Contempt or hostility, but, it would appear, not war itself, was indicated by throwing wampum in the giver's face, or by kicking it away (*ibid.*, 431). Rejection of a message was indicated by throwing wampum into the fire, pulling it out, kicking it around and refusing to touch it (Post's journal in 1 *Thwaites*, 255. Cf 1 *Johnson Papers*, 277). To pick up a wampum belt laid down by an emissary was to accept a proposition (*Beauchamp*, 430). The return of wampum delivered by a messenger likewise indicated acceptance of a proposal (1 *Johnson Papers*, 287–88, *Voyages and Travels of an Indian Trader*, 46). For wampum in general, see 2 *Hodge*, 904 ff, with a fine bibliography; Gookin, 1 *Mass. Hist. Col.*, 152; Carver, *Travels* (ed. 1813), 362; Lafitau, *Moeurs des sauvages*, n.p.; 8 *Penn. Minutes*, 217; Woodward, *Wampum*, 22; Reichel, *Memorials*, n. to ch. 32; Heckewelder, *Indian Customs*, 109–10.

[106] 1 *Ford*, 20.

that any doubt or division lay behind Half King's request for delay. He thanked the Chiefs but, through inexperience in dealing with the natives, he undiplomatically added that his business with the French commandant required haste, and that he consequently could not wait three days. This remark of course heightened the curiosity of the Indians and at the same time visibly displeased Half King. He could not consent, the Chief replied, that the party should go forward without an escort because, if any accident occurred, it would be a reflection on him. Then Half King gave a hint of misgiving on the part of the other Sachems. "This is a matter of no small moment and must not be entered into without due consideration: For now I intend to deliver up the French speech belt and to make the Shawnees and the Delawares do the same."[107] To add dramatic force to this announcement, Half King turned to Shingiss and told him to bring his tribe's treaty belt to Logstown two nights later,[108] and to have two of his men ready to set out with the English the next morning thereafter.[109]

George saw now that if he insisted on immediate departure, he would offend Half King most dangerously. The Major therefore acquiesced, though with inward reluctance, and in an effort to create a more pleasant feeling, he produced the wampum he had received at Frazier's along with the announcement that three nations of French Indians had taken up the hatchet against the Indians. He would be glad, Washington said, if the Sachems would repeat to him the speech they wished to be delivered to Governor Dinwiddie. For reasons not plain to George, this request made the Indians reticent. They said only that they would postpone restatement of their message until they had held a full council with the Shawnee and Delaware Chiefs.[110] As this left nothing more to be said, George ended the council and returned to his own quarters. He probably had learned more of the Indian mind that day than he had acquired in the whole of his previous life, but he had been mystified as much as he had been enlightened.

The next day, November 27, passed almost without incident. Runners were sent off early to summon the Shawnee chiefs; two friendly Sachems gave the visitors some food;[111] Half King set out to get the speech belt from his cabin and did not return until the afternoon of

---

[107] 1 *Ford*, 21.
[108] This conference was on Monday, November 26. Shingiss was to report on the evening of the 28th.
[109] 1 *Ford*, 21.   [110] 1 *Ford*, 21.
[111] *Darlington*, 81.

Tuesday, November 28. Then, with Monakatoocha and two other leaders, he asked the question with which they fairly had been bursting for two days: What was the business on which Major Washington was visiting the French fort? George of course had anticipated the question but had not felt he had a right to disclose the reason for his journey. He consequently gave a general answer, which, he subsequently wrote, "allayed their curiosity a little."

If curiosity was lessened, concern was increased. Monakatoocha, in particular, had a long story he had picked up from an Indian who had been at Venango: The commander there, Captain Joincare, had called together all the natives living around the village and had explained how cold weather had kept the French from moving down the Allegheny that fall. They were coming in greater number the next spring, Joincare had said. He had warned the savages to stand aside and to have no part in what was about to happen. The French expected three years of war with the English, and believed that by the end of that time they could conquer. If both sides proved equally strong, then, Joincare was alleged to have said, the French and the English would join to cut off all the Indians and to divide the land. Although the French had lost their General and a few of their men, he boasted that they could get reinforcements and would become masters of the Ohio.[112]

George, of course, was at once too loyal and too skeptical to show any dismay over talk of the sort Monakatoocha passed on. The only effect of it on Washington probably was to increase still further his impatience to complete his mission so that he could carry back to Williamsburg an early warning of what was in prospect. George began to suspect, also, that some of the Sachems were afraid of becoming involved with the French by aiding the English messengers. He probably made no answer, for these reasons, to Monakatoocha's report.[113]

Half King's promise had been that the guard would be ready to start on the 29th of November, but early that morning he and Monakatoocha came to George's tent with a plea for one more day. The Shawnee chiefs, they explained, had not yet sent in their wampum, though this certainly would be done before nightfall. Moreover, Half King said, Shingiss had not collected his men and had been kept at home by the sickness of his wife; but this would not matter, the two

---

112 1 *Ford*, 22–23.
113 The general form of Washington's own report would indicate that if he had replied to Monakatoocha with anything more than a deprecatory smile or gesture, he would have summarized his answer.

visitors insisted, because the wampum that Shingiss' tribe had received from the French was at Venango in the keeping of Chief Kustaloga. The inference was that this treaty belt could be picked up on the way to the French fort. As for the wampum of the Shawnees, if it did not arrive by the time of departure the next day, it could be sent after the party.

The Major was satisfied from this report that Shingiss was afraid to share in the supply of a guard. As a novice in the significance of wampum, George was confused, perhaps, by the talk of treaty belts but he concluded that a formal return to the French of the wampum of the tribes would be, in effect, a termination of their agreements and a consequent reaffirmation of the English alliance of Half King and his tribes. This unexpected turn of the mission seemed to be immediately more important than another delay of twenty-four hours in getting to the French fort and back to Williamsburg. With careful restraint from all show of impatience,[114] George consented to remain another day at Logstown.[115]

Before the day was out, Half King and Monakatoocha again were at George's tent-flap. They reported that the Shawnees had not arrived, but that they had all else in readiness. The treaty belt which de Marin had demanded, the one with the marks of the towns on it, was to be returned to him by one of the old Chiefs, Jeskakake,[116] whose speeches already were prepared. Thereupon, without apology or warning that a deluge of eloquence was about to engulf the tent, Half King repeated what the senior was to say. Not content with this display of his oratory, Half King proceeded to tell the Englishmen how he proposed to warn the French once again to leave the Indians' lands. It was, George noted, with perhaps a touch of boredom, "near the same speech he had done before."[117]

This was not all. Half King showed George some wampum that Shingiss had sent for delivery to Kustaloga at Venango. This was in the nature of a warrant for Kustaloga to carry the tribe's treaty belt to the fort and to deliver it with the others. Finally, Half King brought out a very large string of black-and-white wampum. He explained that Jeskakake was to deliver to the French a third and final warning to

[114] Cf. Washington's report (1 *Ford*, 23): ". . . I believed an offence offered at this crisis might be attended with greater ill consequence than another day's delay."
[115] *Ibid.*
[116] He probably was one of the historians of the wampum mentioned *supra*, 297, n. 105.
[117] 1 *Ford*, 24.

quit the lands of the Six Nations. If the French remained disdainful, then this string of black and white shells was to be circulated among the Six Nations immediately. It would be, in effect, a notice of the decisive nature of the action Half King had taken and, perhaps in its symbolism, an appeal to all the tribes to do as he had done.[118]

George, of course, was encouraged by this evidence of Half King's resolution to end all accords with the French, but the next morning, November 30, brought evidence that the friendly Chief might not always be able to control the other Sachems. Instead of the large guard that George had been led to expect, four men only appeared with equipment for the trail—Half King, old Jeskakake, another senior Chief[119] known as White Thunder, and a young hunter who was to kill game for the party to eat.[120] Half King explained that after he had visited Washington the previous evening, he and the other Sachems had held a council at the Long House. Their conclusion had been against sending any large escort because, if they did so, the French might become suspicious and might treat them rudely. It would be better to send only the three "great men" with a single hunter.[121]

This naïveté might have prompted the young emissary to ask the Indians why they expected any other than a rude reception if they were, in effect, to notify the French of a rupture of friendly relations. George raised no such question. Debate might delay a departure for which he had been waiting with far more impatience than he had shown. Off he went with his companions and his Indian friends on the trail, nor did he tell anyone that he believed the failure of Half King to furnish a larger guard was because he could not prevail on the hunters to come to Logstown.[122]

Now the direction of the march changed. From a northwesterly route, Gist led the party a little East of North, toward the junction of French Creek and the Allegheny River. The first day's journey of approximately fifteen miles brought the party to a settlement which had the somewhat unattractive name of Murthering or Murdering Town. Located on a branch of Great Beaver Creek, it probably had been the scene of some forgotten crime; but to George it represented advance,

118 1 *Ford*, 23–24. This has to be stated with some reservation because the precise tribal meaning of this black-and-white belt has in part to be inferred.
119 *Darlington*, 81.
120 This Indian may have been Kiashuta, who later attained sufficient prominence to be mentioned in *Hodge*. See 1 *Diaries*, 423.
121 1 *Ford*, 24.
122 1 *Ford*, 24.

and, incidentally, food. Corn and dried meat were procured there and doubtless were devoured heartily after the contest with mud and chill.[123] An early start and a rapid pace on the 1st of December carried George and his party thirty miles, as they reckoned it, to the crossing of what they took to be Beaver Creek on the trail from the Kaskuskies to Venango.[124] Here, December seemed to say, "Not so fast, strangers." In the early morning of the 2nd, rain was falling. It continued to mock the restless young Major all day, but it brought one consolation. The Indians went out and stalked two bucks, which they easily killed. Savory cuts from these animals, broiled over the campfire, brightened a gloomy day and a dark night.[125] The next morning, December 3, the skies relented. Although the woods were cold and dripping, the little expedition covered about twenty-two miles and camped on what Gist thought was one of the head branches of Great Beaver Creek.[126]

Fifteen miles' riding on the 4th of December brought George to Venango, at the point where French Creek empties into the Allegheny River.[127] George knew that the village was in French hands, but his heart must have beaten a little faster when, over a log structure, he saw the fleur-de-lis flying. Doubtless his companions told him the building was the trading post and shop from which John Frazier had been driven earlier that year.[128] The house evidently had been constructed for defence as well as for trade. No fort had yet been erected.

George told the attendants to pitch the tent, and, with van Braam and Gist, but unattended by Indians, he went over to the building where the flag was flapping. At the entrance the trio were met by three French officers whose leader introduced himself as Capt. Philippe Thomas Joincare, Sieur de Chabert. Politely, he invited the visitors

---

[123] *Darlington,* 81. The stream undoubtedly was Connoquenessing Creek; the camp must have been in the vicinity of the present Zelienople, Butler County. For a general description of the country at approximately this period, see the "Journal of a Ride from Fort Pitt to Venango," 1760, perhaps by Capt. Thomas Hutchins, in 2 *Penn. Mag.,* 149 ff.

[124] *Darlington,* 81. Unless the party had to make numerous detours, George overestimated the distance. The day's journey must have ended on Slippery Rock Creek, not far from Branchton, Butler County.   [125] *Darlington,* 81.

[126] *Ibid.* If Gist was correct in his statement of his position, he was a considerable distance off his direct route for Venango. The only tributary of Great Beaver Creek that fits his description would be the upper stretch of Wolf Creek, near Henderson, Mercer County. He then would have been eight miles West of a straight line from Logstown to Venango. Except for the distances involved, Gist's account would indicate that he was on Sandy Creek, a tributary of the Allegheny, in the vicinity of Raymilton. There again he would have been West of a straight line to Venango.

[127] The site is that of the city of Franklin. Evans's map shows Venango on the west (right) bank of the creek.

[128] See *supra,* p. 286. If other traders posts were standing, no contemporaneous account of them has been found.

to enter. George, of course, had sufficient social experience not to be embarrassed in strange company, even when he had to speak through an interpreter; but he must have looked as intently as was courteous at a man of whom he already had heard often on his journey.

Captain Joincare—that was the name by which the Indian traders knew him—was the son of a Seneca squaw by a French officer, and he had been so reared that he could deal equally well with his mother's and with his father's people. In bearing he was, at forty-six years of age, not unlike any other company officer of His Christian Majesty's Regiments in Canada, but in influence he stood almost as high as the Governor or the commanding General. From the time of his father's death in 1740, Joincare had been the man to whom the French Indians of the region had looked for guidance. He operated the trading post and the portage at Niagara and made large profits from both. In the service of France, along with his rank as Captain, he had the title of Chief Interpreter for the Six Nations.[129] Having accompanied Céleron on the expedition of 1749, he knew the Ohio country and the characteristics of the savages who dwelt on its upper watershed. All in all, he was one of the ablest and most resourceful of the French spokesmen in Canada.[130] Another of the French officers who met the Englishmen at the entrance was Commissary La Force, a man who apparently made no impression on Washington at the moment. Later George was to discover that the Commissary was regarded by many as the shrewdest of all the French on the Ohio in dealing with the Indians.[131]

The reception these men gave Washington was flawless. In answer to Washington's inquiry concerning the French commander, to whom a communication was to be delivered, Joincare replied that he himself was in charge on the Ohio, but that there was a general officer at Fort Le Boeuf, up the creek and close to Lake Erie. Joincare's advice was that George carry his letter thither. Meantime, would Monsieur Washington and the other gentlemen sup with him and his comrades that evening? [132] George was not pleased at having to go forty or fifty miles farther up the creek but he of course accepted the invitation to eat with the distinguished Captain. In choosing Gist, van Braam and probably Davison as his companions at Joincare's table, Washington left the In-

---

129 *Darlington*, 81; 1 *Thwaites*, 54, n. 16.
130 Of many references to Joincare, perhaps the most informative are those in 1 *Thwaites*, 54, n. 16. Joincare on occasion has been confused with the Marquis de la Jonquière, Governor of Canada.
131 Leduc, *Murder of Jumonville*, 120.   132 1 *Ford*, 25.

dians behind deliberately. He was not sure the French commander would want them and, besides, as he knew something of the half-breed's influence over the natives, he did not want to expose his Indian escort to Joincare's wiles when he possibly could avoid doing so.[133]

Joincare set out for his guests the best that he had, and both offered and drank wine in great abundance. As he and the others talked to George, who kept sober and listened intently, their tongues and their Gallic pride alike were loosed. They had perceived clearly that a contest for the Ohio was brewing. It was their design to take possession of the river, they said, and, by God, it would be done. The English, to be sure, could raise two men to their one, but their rivals would start too late and move too slowly to stop them. The Ohio was France's, because it had been discovered by La Salle, a name George did not remember he ever had heard previously.[134] What France was undertaking, continued Joincare, was to prevent the settlement of English on the river or on any of its tributaries. Some English families, they had heard, already were moving out.[135]

When the host and the other two French officers had exhausted themselves on this theme, George began to inquire about their troops, their forts and the distances covered by their lines of supply. On some of these subjects, the Frenchmen talked without restraint, and gave George information he undertook to remember with accuracy.[136] Most politely, too, Joincare promised a French escort for the messenger on the ride to the headquarters of the commander at Fort Le Boeuf.

George's worst enemy of the wilderness, the cold and merciless December rain, reasserted its power on the 5th. It would have been too inclement to take the road up French Creek, with his new French escort, even if the Indians had not by that time become engaged in solemn council with their allies the Delawares, who lived in and near Venango. At the proper stage, Half King gave Chief Kustaloga, or one of that Sachem's warriors, the wampum from Shingiss and the order of that potentate to return to the French the speech belt with the marks of the four towns on it. The Delaware shook his head and cunningly found an excuse. "It is true," he said, "King Shingiss is a great man, but he has sent no speech, and," he added with finality, "I cannot pretend to make a speech for a King." It was in vain that his

[133] 1 *Ford*, 27.
[134] Washington wrote: "from a discovery made by one La Salle sixty years ago" (1 *Ford*, 25).
[135] 1 *Ford*, 25–26.
[136] *Ibid.*, 26.

guests urged him. He was sure of his ground—no speech, no return of wampum.[137] The inference was that if the speech belt was to be returned, Half King himself must take the risk: Kustaloga would not. A party of French Indians recently had gone northward with a captive boy and eight white men's scalps. It was a time for peaceable men to attend to their own affairs.[138]

Before long, [139] the Frenchman heard that a council had been held and that Half King was in it. With much politeness and perhaps with some sarcasm, Joincare asked why Washington had not brought the Chief to headquarters. George not unskillfully replied that he had doubted whether the presence of the Indians would be agreeable to Joincare because he had heard the Captain "say a good deal in dispraise of Indians in general." To this Joincare replied with an order to one of his men to go to the natives' camp and to invite the Chiefs to visit him forthwith.

When Half King, Jeskakake and White Thunder arrived, Joincare did not display a touch of the biting sternness that de Marin had exhibited toward Half King. On the contrary, Joincare acted as if these Indians were the closest of allies and the warmest of friends. How could they be so near, he inquired half reproachfully, and not come to see him? With that, he made them a few presents, offered them liquor and, when they had drunk it, bade them have more. Again and again he plied them with brandy until all three of the savages were too drunk to realize what they were doing. Not a word could Half King say, at the end, concerning the return of the belts. Nor did he voice one syllable of the warning he had sworn he would give the French to leave the land.

When George in disgust went back through the rain to his tent, he realized what previously he perhaps had sensed dimly—that he was engaged in a diplomatic battle with the French for the support of the Indians. He had come to deliver a message; he found himself called upon, with Gist's understanding aid, to save an alliance.

This challenging turn of events was even plainer the next day, December 6, the date set for a start up French Creek to the fort. Early in the morning, Half King was at the entrance to George's tent. He was completely sober, probably ashamed of himself, and once again

---

[137] *Darlington,* 82. From the particularity of Gist's account, he probably was present at this council.
[138] Cf. *infra,* p. 310, for the story told at Fort Le Boeuf concerning the boy and the scalps.
[139] The sequence of the day's events is in some doubt.

entirely resolute. It was his purpose, he said, to make his speech to
the commander of the French and to repeat his order that they quit
the Indians' country. Earnestly the Chief urged that they delay their
departure long enough for him to serve this notice on Joincare.

George's observation the previous day of that officer's skill in dealing
with Half King made him exceedingly anxious not to expose the Chief
again to the Captain's wiles and wine. Besides, time was slipping and
cold was advancing. The mission must be completed as soon as possible. So, when Half King argued that the party should linger at
Venango, George tried to dissuade him, and to have him withhold his
warning until they reached Fort Le Boeuf. Half King would not
yield: Joincare, he said, was to light a council fire at Venango; that
was to be the place where all business of this sort was transacted; Joincare had sole management of Indian affairs.

George most unwillingly consented: There was no escape. He had
to remain, listen, and take whatever risks might develop from Half
King's defiance of the French. All that Washington could do to
recover any of the lost time would be to send the horses upstream and
across the creek so that he could set out promptly when the council was
ended, "which," George said later, "I knew would make it near
night." [140]

He did not misjudge his orator. The council assembled about 10
o'clock, but the preliminaries must have been interminable. Finally
Half King began his speech. It was in substance the one he had delivered to the Sieur de Marin, but it produced no such effect on Joincare
as it had on the French commander at the fort. When Half King
reached his climax and returned the speech belt, with the marks of
the four towns on it—the one that Kustaloga had declined to deliver
to the French—Joincare refused to accept it. Displaying no anger, he
insisted that the belt should be presented at Le Boeuf. After that, and
with scarcely any concealment of his purpose, the Captain did everything he could to detain the Indians in the hope that he could win
them over.

Finally, late in the day, the council ended. Joincare returned to his
quarters; Washington went to his tent and, after a while, sent for the
Indians. They reported that they could not come at the time because
they had to see Chief Kustaloga again in order to find out more about
his reasons for not giving up the belt. Washington became suspicious

140 1 *Ford*, 27–28.

that this was a pretext for some undisclosed mischief and he directed John Davison, the interpreter, to go over to the Indians' camp with positive orders: In no circumstances was Davison to let himself be separated from them; he must remain and find out what was afoot.

It had been a disquieting day of a sort George had not been called on to endure previously. There he was, at the French outpost, with a handful of Englishmen, faced by the possibility of losing his native escort and, perhaps, even the alliance with the Indians. He was inexperienced in such matters; the French were full of wiles.

The next day, December 7, scarcely gave promise of being any better. Commissary La Force came to the Englishmen's quarters with three soldiers and reported himself ready to escort Monsieur Washington to the fort. George and his white companions were prepared to start but the Indians were not there. Washington waited and, at length, in desperation, sent Christopher Gist to bring them to the trail. It was nearly 11 o'clock when the guide came back. He had the three Chiefs and the young hunter with him, but he had to admit that prevailing upon them to forego the allurements of Venango had taxed his powers of persuasion.[141] In his own diary, Gist wrote later: "Joincare did everything he could to prevail on our Indians to stay behind us, and I took care to have them along with us." [142]

The advance now was somewhat West of North but it did not follow the course of French Creek. That stream, flowing southward, describes a long arc toward the West, and from Fort Le Boeuf to Venango has a course of almost fifty miles. The chord of this arc offered a route of about thirty-six miles. It could not be followed on a straight line but it was noticeably shorter than a ride directly up the bank of the creek. Even by the best trail known to La Force, the journey was difficult. Many of the branches flowing into the stream were so swollen that crossings had to be made on felled trees.[143] It was cold and dismal but not so bad that the Major failed to have an eye open for good land. There were, he later reported, "several extensive and very rich meadows, one of which I believe was nearly four miles in length and considerably wide in some places." [144] A military mission, in short, did not blind a young land-speculator.

After sunset on the 11th of December,[145] the end of the fourth day

141 *Ford*, 28.
142 *Darlington*, 82. There is a difference of one day in Gist's and Washington's journals at this point, but Washington's apparently is accurate.
143 *Darlington*, 82.   144 1 *Ford*, 29.   145 *Darlington*, 82.

on the trail, the party of sixteen—eight Englishmen, four Indians and four French [146]—reached the point on the creek opposite Fort Le Boeuf, which was on the western bank.[147] It was too late for Washington to see much in the twilight except, doubtless, the light of a few fires and, perhaps, the paler glint of a candle here and there. George accordingly halted and sent Jacob van Braam [148] across the stream to notify the commandant of his arrival. In a short time, several French officers came over in a canoe and invited the emissaries to the fort. Major Washington was agreeable, of course, and soon was received, as Gist put it, "with a great deal of complaisance." [149] Doubtless because of the hour, nothing official was undertaken that evening.

As early as he thought polite the next morning, December 12, George presented himself, with Gist and van Braam, at headquarters. The second in command received him and ushered him into the presence of the senior officer of the post, an elderly gentleman who had lost one eye [150] but, despite this disfigurement, had very much of the air of a soldier. He was the Sieur Legardeur de St. Pierre de Repentigny, Knight of St. Louis, briefly Legardeur de St. Pierre. It developed that he had been sent to the post after the death of de Marin and had been there only a week when the English mission arrived.[151]

A young gentleman of Virginia was not to be outdone in courtesy, of course, even by a Knight of St. Louis. Through van Braam, who seems to have interpreted readily, Washington begged leave to show his passport and commission [152] and then tendered the letter from Governor Dinwiddie. Politely but positively the commandant declined to receive it at that time. Would Monsieur Washington retain the communication and the other papers until the arrival from the next fort of Monsieur Repentigny, who had been sent for and was expected shortly? [153] The young emissary had to acquiesce and bowed himself out.

The delay gave George time to examine the fort casually. He found

146 This assumes that La Force and his men attended George all the way from Venango. Their arrival at Fort Le Boeuf is not mentioned, nor is there any indication in George's journal or in Gist's that the Frenchmen had turned back to Venango.

147 1 Ford, 29.   148 Darlington, 82.

149 Darlington, 83.   150 Sargent, 42.

151 1Ford, 29–30. Ford added in his note that Legardeur de St. Pierre "had just returned from an expedition toward the Rocky Mountains when he was sent to succeed the dying Marin."

152 Darlington, 83.

153 George understood the name to be Riparti, but it seems quite probable that it was de Repentigny, and that its bearer, otherwise unknown, was a kinsman of the commandant. Cf. 1 Ford, 19, n., with credit to Shea for the explanation.

it a stout frontier structure of four houses built as corner bastions with the space between them stockaded.[154] Before he was able to study the armament, he was informed that the officer from the other fort, Presque Isle, had arrived. Not long after 2 o'clock, George again went to headquarters with Gist and van Braam. After an introduction to Captain Repentigny, who knew a little English, George delivered the papers he had brought on the long journey from Williamsburg. St. Pierre took them and went into another room so that the Captain, without distraction, could turn the documents into French.[155]

A translation, in due course, was placed in Washington's hands, with the request that van Braam peruse and, if need be, correct it by the English original, which read as follows:

[Williamsburg, Va., Oct. 31, 1753]

Sir.

The lands upon the Ohio River in the western parts of the colony of Virginia are so notoriously known to be the property of the Crown of Great Britain that it is a matter of equal concern and surprise to me to hear that a body of French forces are erecting fortresses and making settlements upon that river within H.M.'s Dominions.

The many and repeated Complaints I have received of these acts of hostility, lay me under the necessity of sending in the name of the King my Master, the bearer hereof, George Washington Esq., one of the Adjutants-General of the Forces of this Dominion; to complain to you of the encroachments thus made, and of the injuries done to the subjects of Great Britain in open violation of the law of nations now existing between the two Crowns.

If these facts are true and you shall think fit to justify your proceedings I must desire you to acquaint me by whose authority and instructions you have lately marched from Canada, with an armed force and invaded the King of Great Britain's territories in the manner complained of, that according to the purport and resolution of your answer I may act agreeably to the commission I am honoured with from the King my Master.

However, Sir, in obedience to my instructions it becomes my duty to require your peaceful departure; and that you would forbear prosecuting a purpose so interruptive of the harmony and good understanding which His Majesty is desirous of cultivating with the most Christian King.

I persuade myself you will receive and entertain Major Washington with the candour and politeness natural to your Nation; and it will give me the greatest satisfaction if you return him with an answer suitable to my wishes

[154] Thomas Forbes's journal, 4 Md. His. Mag., 274. Cf. 4 Gipson, 273.
[155] 1 Ford, 30.

for a very long and lasting Peace between us. I have the Honour to subscribe myself . . .

Robert Dinwiddie [156]

When the translation of this was approved, Major Washington asked for an early answer; the commandant said he would call a council to consider the question; with due courtesy and formality the conference ended.[157] George retired to await St. Pierre's decision and, meantime, to get such information as he could of the fort and of the minor matters covered by his instructions. It was not difficult. He had abundant opportunity of examining the stockade, which consisted of piles driven into the ground so that their sharpened upper ends were twelve feet in the air. Eight six-pounders were mounted in each bastion. Several barracks stood within the enclosure; outside were stables, a smith's shop and other buildings. The Major did not himself examine the canoes along the creek, but he instructed the men with him to count those completed and those under construction.

As opportunity offered, the young Virginian talked informally with the commandant and the other officers, and most particularly he asked St. Pierre by what authority British subjects had been made prisoners of war. "He told me," George recorded subsequently, "that the country belonged to [the French]; that no Englishman had a right to trade upon those waters; and that he had orders to make every person prisoner who attempted it on the Ohio, or the waters of it." [158] George had his answer.

As for the question Washington had been instructed to ask about the English boy who had been carried North, before the arrival of the commandant, the visitors learned that Repentigny had questioned the youthful prisoner for several hours; but when George asked the Captain where the lad had been seized, the interpreter pretended to have forgotten. All he remembered was that the Indian captors had the scalps of two or three white men. George did not fail to note the discrepancy between this account and the one the Indians at Venango had given him. They had said that the northward-bound French savages had eight scalps. When George inquired about two Pennsylvania traders

---

[156] *Sparks Transcripts,* VSL.

[157] *Darlington,* 83.

[158] 1 *Ford,* 35. Strictly speaking, if St. Pierre still was acting under Du Quesne's instructions of the spring of 1752, the Allegheny River was to be guarded in order that English traders might be kept out of the region (Paris, Arch. Nat.: Col. C, 11, A 97:258); but, actually, the French spoke of the Allegheny as if it were the Ohio.

whom the French had taken, his hosts perceived that he knew enough about the facts to make evasion futile. They told him frankly, therefore, that the men had been sent to Canada but later had been returned to their homes.[159] All this exchange was with impeccable courtesy and in the most hospitable spirit. The French even offered to supply a canoe or two to facilitate George's return.[160]

Had the young Virginian undertaken that night and the next day to analyze the information he and his men had acquired at Fort Le Boeuf, he would have found two items important. First, there did not appear to be the least doubt in the mind of the commandant that the French had a valid title to the Ohio and could hold that river and its tributaries. Second, the intruders were preparing to extend their occupation the next spring. On this point, George's companions reported that they had counted along the creek at Fort Le Boeuf fifty birch canoes and 170 of pine. Many others were being blocked out. All these preparations convinced Washington that the French were making ready on a large scale for an early descent on the Ohio. If they were to be outstripped to that goal, Virginia must act quickly and in strength. Not one day must be lost in getting to Williamsburg the news of what the French were undertaking.

Equally apparent on the 14th was the French aim to detach the Indians from their British alliance. George did not know what information Commissary La Force had brought the commandant from Captain Joincare, but he did not see any indication that St. Pierre would be as austere and unfriendly to Half King as de Marin had been. On the contrary, the tactics employed to entice Half King at Venango were being used at Le Boeuf. The Chief was as anxious as ever to return the treaty belt, but, he said, the commandant would not give him an audience. It was manifest that St. Pierre, realizing George's impatience to return, was seeking to delay the Indians in the hope that George would leave without them. If that happened, the French knew precisely how to wean the natives from the English and to win them back with rum, presents and promises. That was a game the French always conducted with skill.

Perhaps it was a game in which all the odds were against George, but it was not a contest the young man would forfeit. He would play it out and would try to meet cunning and experience with determination and resourcefulness, the only cards he had in his hand. His aim

[159] 1 Ford, 32.   [160] Ibid., 31.

must be to procure an early answer, to depart with the Indians, after that, to get to Williamsburg as soon as possible. In this spirit he met St. Pierre's next proposal—that Monsieur Washington proceed to Quebec and present to the Governor of Canada the communication from His Excellency of Virginia.

George flatly declined: His orders were to deliver the letter to the commander on the frontier the French had occupied. He had no authority to go farther or to place the paper in the hands of anyone else. From this stand he did not permit himself to be shaken. He decided, further, that he would avail himself of the generous if somewhat incautious offer of the French to lend him a canoe or two. He would ask for two and, if he got them, he would have Barney Currin and two others take the horses, without packs, back to Venango at once. If the animals survived and if Currin found there was a good chance the rivers would freeze hard enough to bear the weight of the creatures and their loads, Barney would await George's arrival at Venango; but if the rivers did not freeze to that extent, Barney could push on with the horses to the forks of the Ohio and could stay there till George arrived. Meantime, George would do his utmost to spur Half King to press for the council St. Pierre was trying to avoid. Immediately after Half King made his speech and returned the treaty belt, young Washington intended to load the canoes, to put the white men in one and the Indians in the other, and to start down the creek. By this arrangement, if all went well, he could save at least a day and, what was of like importance, could remove the Indians from the wiles and enticements of St. Pierre.

Washington got the horses off without difficulty and then he urged Half King again to seek an interview with the commandant. Half King was willing enough and by some device he got St. Pierre to receive him late that evening, December 14, but this was done privately and with only one or two other officers—virtual defeat in itself because the Chief had wished the return of the treaty belt to be formal and public.

When Half King came with Davison to report to Washington, he had a lame tale to tell. He had undertaken to deliver back the wampum, he said, but St. Pierre had not been willing to accept it, even though de Marin previously had demanded it. St. Pierre, continued the Chief, had protested that he had great friendship for the Indians over whom Half King held sway. The French wished to trade with the tribes, the commandant had assured him, and, as proof of this, would send goods immediately to Logstown.

George had received a hint [161] that some of the French were going down the creek, and that an officer was accompanying them. Coupled with what St. Pierre previously had said about seizing all English traders on the Ohio, the commandant's talk of forwarding goods to Logstown made the young Virginian suspect that the Frenchman's intention was to send men southward to pick up English traders.

Whatever his plan, St. Pierre evidently did not intend to permit Washington to remain at Le Boeuf to see it executed. The commander was ready to speed the parting guest. That evening George received the formal written answer to Governor Dinwiddie's letter. Along with the paper was assurance that the two promised canoes would be at Monsieur Washington's disposal the next morning.

St. Pierre was as good as his word. Early on the 15th of December, there was much activity on the part of the French in seeing that the emissary be made comfortable for his voyage down the creek. Liquor and provisions were put aboard with the compliments of St. Pierre; but, at the same time, George observed that every blandishment was being offered the Indians to keep them from leaving with the Englishmen. Great consideration was shown Half King; there were hints of much pleasure for him and his companions if they remained. It was not cleverly done. The artifice was plain, but defeating it was another matter. George confessed afterward: "I can't say that ever in my life I suffered so much anxiety as I did in this affair: I saw that every stratagem which the most fruitful brain could invent, was practiced, to win Half King to their interest, and that leaving him here was giving them the opportunity they aimed at." [162]

In this critical affair, on which the continued support of the Six Nations might depend, the young Virginian instinctively relied on moral force. He went straight to Half King and, with all the strength of argument at his command, tried to prevail on the Chief to depart with him. For the first time in George's dealings with Half King, the Indian palpably evaded: The commandant, he said, would not let him go until the next day. George walked forthwith to St. Pierre and squarely faced the old soldier: Would the commandant complete his business with Half King and permit the natives to leave? Ill treatment was being accorded an emissary, because to delay the Indians was to hamper his own departure.

161 Probably from one or another of his men who had been among the canoes on the bank.
162 1 Ford, 33.

St. Pierre may have sworn under his breath at the impertinence of
a young Adjutant of militia, but the commandant suavely gave assurance that he was not detaining either Monsieur Washington or the
Indians. On the contrary, he would do all in his power to further the
return journey of the gentlemen. As for the Indians, he was ignorant
of the reason they lingered.

None of this satisfied George. He went back to his own quarters and
to his own counsels and probably called in Gist to find out what the
guide had ascertained. From him or from some other member of the
party, the troubled young leader of the little expedition learned the
truth: The Indians were waiting because the French had promised they
would receive the very next morning a present of guns and of the supplies they most loved. For the sake of a few rifles, the savages were
delaying a start of the rapid return journey, on which English control
of the Ohio might depend.

At the same time—such were the perversities of clock and calendar—
if the Indians were to stay, George quickly made up his mind that he
also would remain. Then, if the French redeemed their promise, the
savages would get the presents and still would go with the Virginians.
If the French delayed the gifts, then George could accuse them before
the Indians of breaking promises. It was a simple expedient, but it
might succeed. In addition, Washington determined once more to try
to wring a promise from Half King to start down the creek the following morning. He made the effort. Perhaps to his surprise, the Sachem
agreed. When Half King was committed, the Major quietly settled
down for another day at Fort Le Boeuf.

The next morning, December 16, St. Pierre and his lieutenants saw
that Washington had the advantage. Without further chicanery, the
presents duly were brought out and were given the Sachems with appropriate ceremony and fine words. Then the French played their last
card: Liquor was offered the redmen. Would they not fortify themselves for their cold passage? George knew, of course, that if the
savages took any of it, they soon would get drunk and neither would
nor could attempt that day the difficult work of steering their canoe
down the creek; so, once again, George appealed to the Indians. He
reminded Half King of the promise the Chief had made to leave that
day, and he argued vigorously for strict fulfilment of the Indian's
pledged word. The party must start, and at once! Half King and his
three companions looked at the jugs and listened to John Davison's

interpretation of George's earnest words, and then, to Washington's immense relief, they went about the final preparations for departure. Soon both canoes were ready. George gave the word. The paddles struck the water. They were off, all hands. George had won.

The Indians soon outdistanced the white men and disappeared around one of the bends of the creek. Not until the next day, Monday, December 17, did the Major see anything of them. Then, on the bank, he found their canoe and their camp but not the natives themselves. As everything indicated that the Indians had gone hunting, George decided to await their return. In due time they reappeared, with the meat of no less than three bears; but they had to report that one of their number had become separated from them. That night the party feasted and rested, but they did not have the pleasure of welcoming back the absentee.

When he did not appear the next morning, the other Indians ate, sat by the fire and showed no inclination to touch a paddle till their friend found his way to the camp.[163] George respected their consideration for the missing man, but besides the urgency of getting home, as fast as he could, he faced another new condition: for fourteen of the first fifteen days of the month, he had endured rain or snow,[164] but now the precipitation had ended. The creek was falling fast. If there was long delay at the Indians' camp, the stream soon might be too low to float canoes. It was necessary, then, to start at once and to trust the skillful Indian boatmen to overtake the whites after the strayed hunter had come to camp.

There followed three days of hard paddling down the creek, which began to freeze heavily. By the 21st, the ice was so thick at one turn that a channel could not be broken. The canoe[165] and its contents had to be carried a quarter of a mile overland to less heavily frozen water below the bend. While George and the others were completing this task, they were surprised to see four canoes come down the creek in the channel they had opened. One of these boats contained Half King, the missing hunter and the other Indians; three were crowded with French, overcrowded, in fact, because it developed that a French boat,

---

163 All the indirect evidence indicates that the absentee was White Thunder, who either had injured himself on the hunt or else did so while returning to camp.
164 1 Ford, 39.
165 Gist wrote (Darlington, 83) "our vessels," as if the white men had both boats, but Washington correctly reported "our canoe" (1 Ford, 34).

loaded with powder and shot, had been lost. The men from that canoe
had been taken aboard the others.[166]

George was not pleased, of course, to see that Half King and the
other Indians were again in the company of Frenchmen but he could
do nothing about it. Besides, the party was approaching Venango
where there already were French, whose wiles the Indians had to overcome. The one satisfaction of this chance meeting with the French
came the next day, December 22. As the canoes were negotiating a
difficult rocky shallow, another of the French boats overturned. The
Englishmen had the pleasure of observing, as they ran past, that the
brandy and the wine from the French canoe were bobbing protestingly
on the surface.[167]

Later that 22nd of December, George and his party reached Venango.
There they found their horses and the men who had brought the
animals down from Fort Le Boeuf. The creatures manifestly were in
poor condition, but Washington saw no prospect that they would be
stronger if they were held longer at the French outpost. He made ready
to start the next day and sent for Half King in order to learn whether
the Indians were going overland with the Englishmen or intended to
continue to Logstown by water. Half King explained that White
Thunder had been so badly injured he had to use the canoe for the
rest of the journey.

It was impossible for George to determine whether this was the fact
or merely was an excuse for remaining at Venango in the hope of getting liquor or presents from Captain Joincare. In either event, George
no longer had to depend on Half King and could not wait indefinitely
at Venango to protect the Chief against the cunning of Joincare. It
was enough to have pulled the savage from the better-baited trap at
Fort Le Boeuf. Going North, Joincare had seemed most dangerous;
coming back he was less to be feared by far than St. Pierre had been.
At that, George took pains to warn the Indians against the Captain.
Half King was reassuring in answer: Washington need not be concerned; the Chief knew the French too well to be deceived by them.
If possible, Half King would get the trader Joseph Campbell to meet
the Major at the forks of the Ohio and to deliver him a speech for Governor Dinwiddie. Further, if Washington desired it, Half King would
have the young hunter remain with the white men to get provision for

[166] 1 *Darlington*, 83.
[167] 2 *Darlington*, 84.

them.[168] The Chief made this offer cheerfully. He had not yet satisfied himself concerning George's abilities but he had a measure of affection for the tall Major and a certain belief in the future of the young white emissary. Half King already had given him an Indian name, Caunotaucarius, Towntaker.[169] What this new brother of the Six Nations needed, the tribes would endeavor to supply.

George thanked the Chief and bade him farewell. The next day, December 23, the white men set out from Venango for Murthering Town; but as they traveled, George became more and more fearful the hungry, enfeebled horses could not complete the journey. Five miles only were covered before the early twilight and the weariness of the animals forced Washington to call a halt. The next morning he put on a deerskin hunting jacket and directed that all members of the party, except the drivers, give up their riding horses and divide among the mounts part of the load the pack animals had been carrying.[170]

All that day, snow fell; the following day, Christmas, was spent in a weary tramp over an icy trail. "The horses grew less able to travel every day; the cold increased very fast; and the roads were becoming much worse by a deep snow, continually freezing"—such were George's subsequent memories of that struggle through the wilderness.[171] He knew, of course, that he had to expect colder weather on a return journey in December than on an advance in November; but he had no records to admonish him that the drop in the mean minimum temperature was nine degrees, and that December was apt to bring six inches of snow and might inflict nearly four feet, compared with a mean of less than two inches in November and a maximum of approximately fifteen. Had he known country and climate, he could not have expected more than six clear days in November or more than four in December. Every day save three, during the last month of the year, he might have had some rain or snow.[172]

By the morning of December 26, three of the men were so badly

---

[168] 1 *Ford*, 34–35.
[169] 29 *G. W.*, 37. This was the name by which the Indians had called George's great-grandfather.
[170] 1 *Ford*, 35; *Darlington*, 84.
[171] 1 *Ford*, 35.
[172] Snowfall figures are for the winters of 1900–01 to 1945–46 inclusive at the Pittsburgh Weather Bureau. The other statistics cover the years since 1874. For a discussion of the tradition that the winters were more severe in the colonial era, see *Buck*, 16–17. The conclusion of those writers is that dense forests would delay the thaw of accumulating snows, but that "temperature readings taken some distance above the tops of the trees" perhaps would not differ greatly in colonial times from those recorded now.

frost-bitten that they could do nothing.[173] They had to make themselves a temporary shelter and stay there till the weather moderated. If the other members of the party kept with the horses, a long, long time would be required to reach the fringe of the older English settlements. Something else had to be tried. George stood inflexibly to his resolution to get the answer of the French to Williamsburg without the loss of a day that could be saved. He reasoned that if he proceeded Southwest [174] to Murthering Town, quit the trail there, turned Southeast, crossed the Allegheny on the ice and made for John Frazier's, he then would be able to get fresh horses at the trader's and to hasten on to Wills Creek.[175]

When George proposed to Gist that they leave the horses and strike out on foot, the experienced frontiersman did all he could to dissuade the Virginian, because he knew Washington was unaccustomed to walking long distances in the woods. The Major was insistent: it must be done. His message could not be delayed. Gist at length acquiesced and assisted Washington in preparing a pack that could be carried in the least burdensome manner. Van Braam was put in charge of the horses and men, who were later to follow the trail to John Frazier's. Money and full directions were given the Dutchman. Then, with his singular regard for his apparel, George dressed for the journey. An unmistakable self-consciousness lingered when he wrote later: "I took my necessary papers, pulled off my clothes, and tied myself up in a match coat.[176] Then with gun in hand and pack at my back, I set out with Mr. Gist, fitted in the same manner." [177]

George had new reason to respect the judgment of Christopher Gist before the end of that 26th of December. Although the two men followed the easiest trail that led toward Murthering Town, the pace was exhausting, the cold, in George's own words, "scarcely supportable," [178] and the small streams so tightly frozen that it was difficult to get even drinking water.[179] The guide was correct: this was not the life for

173 George did not record this in his journal but he confided it to Col. William Fairfax in August, 1754 (1 G. W., 91).
174 Actually SW by S.
175 Although part of this plan is mentioned explicitly in Washington's journal (1 Ford, 38), the impression left by some narratives is that George set out from the vicinity of Great Beaver Creek to walk all the way to Wills Creek, a distance of approximately 120 miles on a straight line and of at least 150 as Washington and Gist would have been compelled to travel.
176 A "match coat" did not take its name, as often asserted, from the fact that it was made of "matched" skins. The original and correct term was "matcho," which probably is an Indian word but is of unknown meaning.
177 1 Ford, 36.   178 1 G. W., 91.   179 Darlington, 84.

a gentleman accustomed to traveling on horseback. In spite of chill and dragging legs, George kept on. Eighteen miles the companions tramped until, at length, they came to an empty Indian cabin that offered shelter for the night. "The Major," Gist observed, "was much fatigued," but at 2 o'clock on the morning of December 27, he was able to start again through woods half-lighted by the snow on the ground.[180]

When the two white men at length reached Murthering Town, they found among the natives coming out to see them one who spoke English and professed to know Gist, whom he called by his Indian name. The frontiersman thought he had observed this savage among those at Joincare's station, while the party had been en route to Fort Le Boeuf, but he was not sure. Washington apparently did not remember having seen the redman, who had several questions to ask concerning the route the two had followed and the reason they had come on foot. It seemed good fortune that this fellow had been encountered, because George now was more determined than ever to carry out his plan of leaving the trail and making for the nearest crossing of the Allegheny. The Indian might be able to show them the shortest route. On inquiry, he said he could, and would do so gladly.

With this new guide, Washington and Gist then set out. As the Indian carried George's pack easily, in addition to his own rifle, they made good speed for eight or ten miles. Then the Major had to admit that his feet were getting very sore and that he was weary. It would be well, he said, if they camped. On this, the Indian offered to carry George's gun as well as his pack, but George did not wish to part with his rifle or to give the strange Indian two. Refusal displeased the savage. He became churlish and insisted that the party press on because, he said, there were Ottawas in the woods. If the white men stopped and went to sleep, these Indians would attack and scalp them. What they should do, he explained, was to come to his cabin, where they would be safe.

Gist had become suspicious by this time, and had noticed that the man was proceeding too far to the Northeast to reach the nearest crossing of the Allegheny. For this reason, and because the Indian manifestly was in ill humor, Gist questioned him: How far was it to

[180] The account of Gist would suggest that the moon lighted the snow but, actually, the moon was new on the 24th and as late as the 28th was below the horizon at 8:29 P.M. (*John Nathan Hutchins' Almanac*, 1753).

the cabin? The distance a gun could be heard. Very well: Lead in that direction. The Indian went on and again veered too far from the lower crossing of the Allegheny.

George had not received either a glance or a whisper, as yet, from Gist to show that the frontiersman distrusted the Indian, but George himself was growing dubious. The redman continued to turn toward the left and North. How far were they now from the cabin? Two whoops, the Indian answered.[181] The white men said no more but tramped on. Soon two miles had been traversed after the savage had said they were close to his cabin. In the belief that the Indian was leading them astray, Washington told him that when they reached the next water, they would stop.

If the native guide made any reply over his shoulder, George did not remember it afterward. He noticed only the back of the savage less than fifteen paces ahead, and the wideness of a meadow, spotted here and there with trees. The three had gone a little way into this meadow when George saw the Indian wheel, lift his rifle and fire straight at them.

"Are you shot?" George cried to Gist.

"No," answered Gist, who had not seen the Indian fire.

As they looked, the man ran ahead a little way, got behind a big white oak and started to reload his rifle. Almost instantly the two white men were upon him. Gist would have killed him without a word, but Washington restrained his companion. The Indian stolidly continued to load his gun as if his previous shot had been an accident or a signal; but the moment he started to put in the ball, Gist and George seized him.[182]

Silently and alertly, then, with the Indian in front of them, the travelers crossed the meadow and went on downgrade to a little run. There George called a halt and directed the savage to make a fire. While the man collected sticks and got them aflame, George either stood by the guns or saw that Gist was within instant reach of the weapons.

Presently Gist whispered: "As you will not have him killed, we must get him away and then we must travel all night."

George agreed. Gist went about arranging things as if they were

---

[181] That is, twice the distance the whoop of a warrior could be heard.
[182] Gist said (*Darlington*, 85), "we took care of him" and told him to start on the way again.

to camp there, and at length turned to the Indian. "I suppose," said he, "you were lost and fired your gun."

The bewildered savage answered only that he knew the way to his cabin and that it was nearby.

"Well," Gist answered indulgently, "do you go home, and as we are much tired, we will follow your track in the morning; and here is a cake of bread for you, and you must give us meat in the morning."

The native had thought, of course, that he was going to be killed, and when he saw that he had a chance to get away alive, he was happy to depart without word, or loot, or scalps of white men. Gist followed him some distance and listened to be sure the Indian continued to put many yards between him and the camp fire. Not long after 9 o'clock, Gist came back and told George they must move to another site. Weary as Washington was, he picked up his pack and tramped about a mile. Then Gist stopped again and lighted a fire so they could see to set their compass. This done, they fixed their course and started for the Allegheny River.[183] Although George had thought early in the day that he could not go any farther, new strength came with danger. In the knowledge that his trail could be followed rapidly in the snow,[184] George was able to travel all night and, with occasional rest, all day of the 28th.

Toward night, with dismay, George and Gist came upon the tracks of Indians who evidently had been hunting. On the chance that these savages might return that way, the two white men separated but set a rendezvous and, after dark, met there. They now thought they had gone far enough to have escaped the most serious danger of surprise and, being exhausted, they went to sleep.[185] The next day, December 29, the two reached the shore of the Allegheny about two miles from Shannopin's Town.[186] One glance at the stream was enough to dishearten and almost to paralyze: Instead of the solid frozen sheet across which he had expected to walk easily, George saw only about fifty yards of ice adjoining each of the banks. In midstream was angry, open water, down which broken ice was driving.

There now was no friendly John Frazier close at hand and able to

---

[183] Darlington, 84–85; 1 Ford, 36.   [184] 1 Ford, 36.

[185] Darlington, 86. There is perhaps a conflict of one day here in the dates of the two diaries, but it is equally possible that Washington's separate references to "the next day" (1 Ford, 36) were intended to refer to the 28th and the 29th.

[186] I.e., within the corporate limits of the present Pittsburg, though the Indian town was about two miles from the confluence of the Allegheny and the Monongahela. Cf. 1 Thwaites, 24, n. 16, and Sipe, Fort Ligonier, 7.

supply a stout canoe, as on the northward journey. Frazier doubtless was at his trading-post on Turtle Creek, but he could not be reached across the stream. Nor could a canoe have lived in that ice. A raft offered the only means of traversing that turbulent and forbidding stream, a raft that had to be built of standing timber, for felling which the pack included only one hatchet! With that implement, George and Gist worked alternately in the biting cold. It would have been to servants at home a strange and shocking sight; gentlemen of the Northern Neck would have smiled to see their companion chopping furiously in the snow at the stubborn stem of a young tree. What had to be done, George would do: he must get the earliest possible news to Dinwiddie of the defiant plans of French advance to that very crossing!

An all-day job the two men had, but just after sundown the raft was complete. George and Gist shoved it across the ice to the open water, and, each with a long setting pole, got the rough platform into the stream. Out they pushed—and had instantly to battle with heavy blocks of ice that threw them now back, now downstream. Before they could push halfway across, they were in an ice jam that threatened to overwhelm the raft. It flashed over George, on the downstream side, that he might be able to stop the raft and let the ice run past. Quickly and with all his strength, he pushed his pole downward in about ten feet of water. Then he swung to it.

On the instant, the force of the current threw the raft against the pole with so much violence that the top of the pole was dashed forward —with George hanging to it. He fell into the water and might have lost his life had not one of those long arms of his reached a log of the raft. He gripped it, pulled himself up, and, in freezing garments, gave such help as he could to Gist in handling the raft. It was to no purpose. The two men could not push to either shore. At last, finding themselves near a little island in the river, they left the raft, waded through the water and got on the bit of ground. George was sheeted in ice; Gist had his fingers frost-bitten.[187] The island was of all resting-places the bleakest and the coldest; but the two men were still alive and had their packs, their guns, their hatchet . . . and the dispatch to Dinwiddie.

If George realized how deep the water was between the island and the left bank of the Allegheny, he made no later mention of it. Gist

---

[187] George said (1 *Ford*, 38) that "some of [Gist's] toes were frozen, also," but Gist (*Darlington*, 86) mentioned only his fingers.

either knew or suspected that the depth was past wading, but apparently he said nothing to George that night. It was enough to lie down and, in that frightful, penetrating dampness to keep from freezing. When dawn came they still could move their muscles and could focus their eyes on the left bank. Ordinarily, at the end of December, the always-fretful Allegheny would have looked intolerably forbidding, but that morning, to George and to Christopher Gist, daylight brought an entrancing sight: from the shore of the little island to the bank that was their goal, the river was frozen over solidly and stoutly enough to bear the weight of men with their packs. George and Gist crossed without any sort of trouble and, after a tramp of ten miles, entered the hospitable door of John Frazier's trading-post.[188]

Encamped at Frazier's was a war party of twenty braves, who recounted a tale of going southward as far as the head of the Great Kanawha. Washington recorded their experience: "[There] they found seven people killed and scalped (all but one woman with very light hair.) They turned about and ran back for fear the inhabitants should rise and take them as the authors of the murder. They reported that the bodies were lying about the house, and some of them much torn and eaten by hogs. By the marks which were left, they say they were French Indians of the Ottoway Nation, &c., who did it." [189] George did not forget that the Indians had failed to scalp the blonde woman they had killed; nor did he forget they belonged to the tribe whose warriors, according to the treacherous Indian guide, had been lurking in the woods through which he and Gist had tramped.

The remaining days of the mission were tedious but not dangerous. While horses were being procured at Frazier's store, George went to call on Queen Aliquippa, a nearby Indian ruler of Delaware Indians,[190] who had complained because he had not visited her on his way to Fort Le Boeuf. "I made her a present of a matchcoat and a bottle of rum, which latter was thought much the best present of the two"—that brief summary of George's was evidence enough that he felt his diplomatic duties now were behind him.[191]

At Gist's new settlement, which he reached Jan. 2, 1754, Washington

188 *Darlington*, 86; 1 *Ford*, 38.
189 1 *Ford*, 38. This evidently was the family of Robert Foyle or Foyles, massacred on the Monongahela, not on the Great Kanawha (2 *V* 399, and 1 *Din.*, 119). The place of the massacre appears on the Dalrymple edition of Jefferson & Fry's map. For some details of the later discovery of the bodies, see *Penn. Gazette*, Mch. 12, 1754.
190 See note in 1 *Diaries*, 66. Cf. Toner, ed., *Washington's Journal of 1754*, p. 99.
191 1 *Ford*, 39.

bought a horse and saddle, so that Frazier's might be sent back to him.[192] Then George started for Wills Creek. It was speed, speed, speed to arouse Virginia for the prompt occupation of the country the French were preparing to seize. As the young emissary hurried on, he met a pack train of seventeen horses with material and supplies for the fort William Trent was to build on the Ohio—a pleasant sight if it meant that other supplies and a sufficient armed force were to follow. Westward-bound settlers were passed the next day, January 7.[193] That same day [194] Wills Creek was reached; on the 11th George was at Belvoir. There he had a story to relate that paled the accounts he had brought home previously from the quiet frontier of Frederick County.

If, as a part of his narrative, he had described what had happened in his own training and education, he could have told the friendly Fair-faxes, without boast, that he had found himself capable physically of enduring the stern rigors of the intolerant forests. Even Gist had come back frost-bitten; George was unhurt in any member. Young Washington had learned how to protect himself in a winter outdoors and how to make his way through the woods. He had seen enough of Indians to realize, at the least, the importance of tact, of patience and of firmness in dealing with them. Joincare, La Force and St. Pierre had embodied the spirit and the resourcefulness of the French who ceaselessly were trying to alienate the unstable Indians from the British alliance. Wampum, ceremonial, councils, speeches to the Indians, the character of Half King and other leaders, the nature of the country leading to the Ohio—all this in varying measure had become a part of George's store of knowledge.

A single day at Belvoir scarcely sufficed for a recountal, but George did not feel he could linger when he had news for the Governor of the avowed purpose of the French to occupy the Ohio. Washington hurried to Williamsburg and, on Jan. 16, 1754, placed the letter from St. Pierre in the hand of the official who eagerly and anxiously had been awaiting his return.[195] Precisely one month had passed from the day George had left Fort Le Boeuf—season considered, a splendid achievement.

The paper itself, intact and untouched by water, read thus:

192 *Ibid.*
193 They may have been going to Gist's new settlement.
194 Gist, in *Darlington*, 87, gave the date as January 6.
195 Cf. Dinwiddie to Sharpe, Nov. 24, 1753; 1 *Sharpe*, 10.

Sir:

As I have the honour of commanding here in chief, Mr. Washington delivered me the letter which you wrote to the commandant of the French troops.

I should have been glad that you had given him orders, or that he had been inclined to proceed to Canada, to see our General; to whom it better belongs than to me to set forth the evidence and reality of the rights of the King, my Master, upon the Lands situated along the River Ohio, and to contest the pretensions of the King of Great Britain thereto.

I shall transmit your letter to the Marquis Du Quesne. His Answer will be a law to me; and if he shall order me to communicate it to you, Sir, you may be assured I shall not fail to dispatch it to you forthwith.

As to the summons you send me to retire, I do not think myself obliged to obey it. Whatever may be your instructions, I am here by virtue of the orders of my General; and I entreat you, Sir, not to doubt one moment, but that I am determined to conform myself to them with all the exactness and resolution which can be expected from the best of officers.

I do not know that in the progress of this campaign anything has passed which can be reputed as an act of hostility, or that is contrary to the treaties which subsist between the two Crowns; the Continuation whereof as much interests, and is as pleasing to us, as the English. Had you been pleased, Sir, to have descended to particularize the facts which occasioned your complaint, I should have had the honour of answering you in the fullest, and, I am persuaded, most satisfactory manner.

I made it my particular care to receive Mr. Washington, with a distinction suitable to your dignity, as well as his own quality and great merit. I flatter myself that he will do me this justice before you, Sir; and that he will signify to you in the manner I do myself, the profound respect with which I am

SIR,

Your most humble, and

most obedient Servant

Legardeur de St. Pierre.

From the Fort sur
   La Riviere au Beuf
the 15th of December 1753 [196]

This firm but noncommital answer and George's own description of conditions on the frontier so impressed Dinwiddie that he asked Washington to write a report that could be laid before the Council the next day. This required George to throw together hastily the entries he had

---

[196] Reproduced between p. 343 and p. 344. See also, 5 *E. J.*, 459.

made almost daily in his journal. The product was a narrative of 7000 words, loosely constructed and in some passages obscure; but it had interest and it contained much information at once accurate and apropos.

In one passage only did the young Adjutant perhaps color his report a little. When he came to describe the arrival at Murthering Town and the departure across country for the Allegheny, he wrote: "We fell in with a party of French Indians, who had lain in wait for us. One of them fired at Mr. Gist or me but fortunately missed." [197] Then he went on to describe the incidents of December 27.[198] George most assuredly did not intend to exaggerate or to misuse the words "fell in"; but neither did he understate the danger to which he and Gist had been exposed. The Indian who had pretended to guide them to the Allegheny had said there were Ottawas in the woods; George had heard the returning braves at Gist's new settlement say that men of that tribe had killed seven white persons on the Great Kanawha: he chose to believe they had "laid in wait" for him and for Gist.

In his own journal the more experienced Gist wrote nothing to indicate that he thought he and George "fell in" with Indians who actually "laid in wait" for them. While Gist expounded no theory, he hung the entries in his diary around the one Indian they saw. Apparently Gist believed this wretch was trying on his own account, and without the aid of others, to get the two white men where he could murder them and rob their bodies.

George ended his journal-report with a customary flourish: "I hope what has been said will be sufficient to make your Honour satisfied with my conduct; for that was my aim in undertaking, and [my] chief study throughout the prosecution of it." [199]

[197] 1 *Ford*, 36.
[198] See *supra*, p. 319 ff.
[199] *Ford*, 40.

CHAPTER IX

WASHINGTON UNHAPPILY LOSES HIS FIRST RACE
(January, 1754–April, 1754)

WHEN GEORGE had completed the revision of his journal and could move about Williamsburg he found himself and his mission the objects of much curiosity. He was applauded by the friends of the Governor and was accused secretly by the enemies of His Honor and by rival speculators of magnifying the danger in order to get help for the Ohio Company.[1] Washington's own immediate desire was to know what had happened in the colonial capital while he was on his mission to Fort Le Boeuf—and what would be done to anticipate the advance of the French to the Ohio.

The General Assembly, which was about to meet when he left on his mission, had remained in session until Dec. 19, 1753, and then had adjourned with scant praise by the Governor.[2] Much of its time had been given to debate over the right of the Governor to the fee of one pistole he had demanded for signing a land patent and thereby validating it for the seal of the Colony.[3] Although Dinwiddie had undertaken earnestly to procure a grant of funds for defence against the French, the Burgesses had not voted a shilling. Nor had they done anything to encourage better relations with the Indians. The only enactment that concerned military affairs was one for the extension of an expiring law on the use of militia to repel invasion.[4] Dinwiddie had hoped that before the Burgesses adjourned, Major Washington would return with a report that would stir them to action, but in this, too, he had met with disappointment.[5]

The Governor had been left in grim humor but resolute. Failure both

---

[1] 2 *G. W.*, 7, and *infra*, p. 332. Cf. the summary of Washington's mission and report in *Md. Gazette*, Feb. 7, 1754. See, also, *ibid.*, Feb. 14, 1754.
[2] The session began November 1. See *Journ. H.B.*, 1752–58, p. 103–17.
[3] See *supra*, p. 171.   [4] 6 *H* 350.
[5] Dinwiddie to Gov. Horatio Sharpe, Nov. 24, 1753, 1 *Sharpe*, 10. For Dinwiddie's review of the failures of the General Assembly, see his letter to the Board of Trade, Dec. 29, 1753; P.R.O., C.O. 5, 1328, n.p.

of the Winchester council with the Indians in September [6] and of the conference at Carlisle [7] had not destroyed his belief—as expressed in his words to Governor Sharpe of Maryland—that he should "endeavor to have a firm alliance concluded between the . . . Indians [and] the Crown of Great Britain." [8] To consummate this, Dinwiddie had set May, 1754, as the time and Winchester as the place for another council, to which all the friendly Indians of the country beyond the mountains had been invited.[9] Now the Governor saw in George's report a vindication of his fears, a sharp spur to his efforts, and a new, compelling argument for action by the Burgesses to meet the French advance. George believed the French certainly would paddle down the river in the spring of 1754 to build a fort at Logstown.[10] Dinwiddie felt sure that this was planned and he reasoned that the very boldness of the French design would make the Burgesses vote a supply of money.[11] "I hope," he wrote, "to bring them into a proper way of thinking when they meet . . ." [12]

Dinwiddie believed that in the larger contest, success hung on speed. Unless the English raised troops immediately and hastened their march to the Ohio, the French would get there first and would so strongly secure themselves that the might of England would be taxed to drive them away. As surely as with Washington on the way home, it was speed, speed, speed. Soon after George's return, the Governor changed the date for the meeting of the prorogued Assembly from April 18 to February 14. [13] In advance of the session of the lawmakers, he felt he should provide an adequate guard for the protection of the men whom he already had dispatched to build a fort at the junction of the Monongahela and the Allegheny. He estimated that 200 men would suffice temporarily for this purpose and he felt sure he had authority, the Council consenting, to call that number to duty without waiting for the permission of the Burgesses. By doing this, he could save weeks that might be invaluable in frustrating the French.

The enlistment of a Regiment of volunteers appeared to be the

---

[6] See 4 *Gipson*, 286–87.   [7] 4 *Gipson*, 286.
[8] Letter of Nov. 24, 1753, *supra*, n. 5.
[9] Dinwiddie to the Board of Trade, Nov. 17, 1753; P.R.O., C.O. 5, 1328, p. 13.
[10] Dinwiddie to Lord Fairfax, n.d. [c. Jan. 25], 1754; 1 *Din.*, 48–49; Dinwiddie to Governor Glen, n.d., 1754; 1 *Din.*, 61.
[11] The customary term was simply a "supply." As employed again and again in Dinwiddie's correspondence, the word had all the implications of a British "supply bill" or a modern American "appropriation bill."
[12] Dinwiddie to James Abercrombie, Feb. 9, 1754; 1 *Din.*, 72.
[13] *Journ. H.B.*, 1752–58, p. xviii. For the advice of Council on this, see 5 *E. J.*, 460.

simplest means of procuring an adequate guard, but when he searched the militia law, the Governor could find nothing that empowered him to pay troops raised in this manner. Consequently, Dinwiddie had to seek 200 from the Indian traders and from the frontier militia for immediate service, and he had to rely on the Burgesses, when they reconvened, to provide necessary funds for these men. He resolved to ask, also, that after the 200 were sent to the Ohio, an additional 400 be raised in the spring and dispatched there. While Virginia was undertaking to provide this force of 600, Dinwiddie would call on the Governors of the other Colonies to assist with men and supplies.

Accordingly, on Jan. 21, 1754, five days after his return, Major Washington, as Adjutant of the Northern Neck District, was authorized to enlist 100 of the militia of Augusta and Frederick Counties; the Indian trader, Capt. William Trent, was directed to raise a like force among men of his own calling, whose property and livelihood were most threatened.[14] The quota did not seem too high. Of the 300 English traders who went out yearly into the Indian country, a third assuredly might be expected to volunteer.[15] By the time these 200 men had reached the Ohio, the 400 to be requested of the General Assembly could be enlisted. If other Colonies then would send contingents, these combined forces, "with the conjunction of our friendly Indians," Dinwiddie explained, "I hope will make a good impression on the Ohio and be able to defeat the designs of the French."[16]

When George examined the instructions given him in accordance with this plan,[17] he found that fifty of his men were to be supplied from the militia of Frederick by Lord Fairfax, County Lieutenant. James Patton, County Lieutenant of Augusta, was to furnish a similar number. By February 20, these two detachments were to be in Alexandria, where George was to train and discipline them.[18] Many of the militiamen were expected to volunteer for service at the pay of fifteen pounds of tobacco *per diem,* authorized by existing law;[19] but if volunteers did not suffice, the required total was to be reached through a draft by lot.[20]

[14] These men were to be enlisted "in Augusta and in the exterior settlements of this Dominion" (Dinwiddie to William Trent, [Jan. n.d., 1754], 1 *Din.,* 55). The advice of Council (5 *E. J.,* 460) had been that Washington have general command and that Trent "raise what traders and other men he can to annoy the enemy," but Dinwiddie set 100 as the number Trent was to enlist and he said nothing of Washington's command over Trent.

[15] Giddens, "French and Indian War in Maryland," 30 *Md. His. Mag.,* 282. The figures are for 1748.

[16] Dinwiddie to William Fairfax, n.d. [January, 1754], in 1 *Din.,* 51–52.

[17] 1 *Din.,* 59.　　　　　　　　　　　[18] *Ibid.* For the date, see *ibid.,* 50.

[19] 6 *H* 116. Troopers received twenty pounds of tobacco daily.　　　　[20] 1 *Din.,* 49, 50.

Thus began the adventure of Virginia and of this son of hers in colonial defence that soon might be the bloody business of war. It was new to the people and vastly more complicated than Dinwiddie or young Washington or any of the others realized. Virginia had trained no officers, had kept no troops, had organized no wagon train, and had possessed few arms. There probably was not one man in Williamsburg, if indeed in all Virginia, who could say how long it would take 200 troops to march to the Monongahela, or how many wagons and horses would be required to transport over the mountains the food, the equipment and the ammunition needed to sustain even this small force. Novices were inviting war in a forbidding land.

When these inexperienced leaders came to details, the militia law seemed amply strong to provide men to repel invasion. Every free white man over twenty-one years of age was subject to call in person or through a substitute furnished at his own expense; and every such militiaman was required to supply specified arms and ammunition.[21] Few lawmakers assumed that all the planters and their sons had complied with the terms of this law; still fewer realized, perhaps, how feeble the organization of the militia actually was.

To speed the muster, George procured the Governor's permission to send Jacob van Braam to assist the County Lieutenant of Augusta.[22] In person, George hurried to Frederick to act with Lord Fairfax.[23] On arrival in a region where he had completed many surveys and possessed a wide acquaintance, George quickly uncovered in its worst form the condition that had troubled Dinwiddie in planning the defence of the frontier: the militia, as the Governor had phrased it, were in "very bad order."[24] In Frederick, a more nearly accurate word would have been "non-existent." Lord Fairfax apparently had no roll of the men liable to military duty; he possessed no facilities other than those of the tax-

---

[21] The basic militia act in 1754 was that of 1738, for which see 5 H 16 ff. This was amended in 1748 to provide for calling out the militia of one or more Counties where such a force would be adequate to cope with invasion or insurrection (6 H 112 ff). Under this law, the Governor could furnish arms from "his Majesty's magazine and other stores within this colony" for militia "not otherwise sufficiently provided" (p. 118). The amendatory law of November, 1753 has been mentioned already. A supplementary measure of February, 1754 (*ibid.*, 421), covered "patrollers" only, i.e., militiamen called to temporary duty to patrol and visit Negro quarters suspected of entertaining unlawful assemblies, etc. At the session of August, 1755, a more explicit act was to be passed. See 6 H 530 ff.

[22] 1 *Din.*, 51. The date and circumstances of van Braam's return from the frontier are not known.

[23] *Ibid.*, 49–50.

[24] Dinwiddie to Lords of Trade, Jan. 29, 1754, *Sparks Transcripts*, VSL, 7. This is the best concise summary of Dinwiddie's plans. A reading of Dinwiddie's several letters of Jan. 27, ff, 1754 (1 *Din.*, 48–71), will make plain the full details of the Governor's plans and difficulties.

lists for preparing a roster; he had raised absolutely none of the fifty men George was supposed to find ready for him to lead to Alexandria.[25] What was worse, there was virtual defiance of the proposed draft and little or no support of the County Lieutenant. Fairfax could accomplish nothing otherwise than by drafting and seizing fifty men. Either he had procrastinated or else, more probably, he had feared resistance if he made the attempt.[26]

George waited impatiently but helplessly until about the 11th of February and then, disillusioned, he started back to Williamsburg with a letter in which Lord Fairfax confessed to the Governor that the draft was a failure.[27] Verbally, Washington doubtless told Dinwiddie what he subsequently wrote formally: "You may, with almost equal success, attempt to raise the dead to life again, as the force of this County." [28] Like reports came from Augusta, though it had suffered during the previous summer from an Indian raid.[29]

Thus defeated in both recruiting districts, the angered Governor called together his Council. Dinwiddie was for invoking the penalties of the law against those who refused compliance with the militia act, and he insisted on vacating the commission of any officer in Frederick who had failed in performance of duty; [30] but when it came to drafting men for guard duty on the Ohio, he found his Councillors doubtful about a newly discovered restriction of law. In the act renewed the previous November for repelling invasion,[31] there was specific provision that the Governor could authorize officers in charge of men from several Counties to exercise command inside the County from which

[25] On a MS "Roll of the officers and soldiers who engaged in the service of the colony before the Battle of the Meadows the 3 day of July . . ." Washington gave the date of his command as Jan. 25, 1754 (1 *Papers of G. W.*, LC). In a letter to William Fairfax, Aug. 11, 1754, he spoke of the period of enlistment for the Virginia forces as "from the first of February to the first of May" (1 *G. W.*, 93). If he left Williamsburg immediately after being assigned to his special duty, he would have reached Winchester in approximately one week, that is, by Feb. 1, 1754.

[26] *Order Book* No. 5 of Frederick County shows Lord Fairfax on the bench as President at every meeting of the Court, except that of April 5, 1754, from November, 1753, to June, 1754. The Court commissioned various officers on order of the Governor (*ibid.*, 475) and swore in those who later produced their commissions (*Order Book* No. 6, p. 18, 33). No other references to the militia have been found in the *Order Books* prior to Sept. 3, 1754 (*ibid.*, 49), when ten individuals were fined 10s each, or were to suffer confinement for twenty days, because they refused to obey orders to guard French prisoners. This near-mutiny is the basis for the statement in the text that fear of resistance "more probably" explained Fairfax's failure to enforce the draft.

[27] Dinwiddie to Lord Fairfax, Feb. 23, 1754; 1 *Din.*, 82. This letter, acknowledging Fairfax's of Feb. 11, 1754, contains substantially all that is known of occurrences in Frederick during Washington's period of waiting for the militia.

[28] Washington to John Augustine Washington, May 28, 1755; 1 *G. W.*, 129.

[29] 1 *C* 249.   [30] 1 *Din.*, 82.

[31] *Supra*, p. 327.

any of their men came, precisely as the officers would discharge their duty in "any other Counties and places within this Dominion." [32] The probable intent of this was to assure the Governor and his lieutenants the right to command over the officers of a given County, who might maintain that their militia were exclusively theirs to direct so long as the men remained in their County. As drawn, the quoted language had unanticipated meaning. If officers could command "within this domain," that was a limitation as well as a permission: The militia could not be employed beyond the limits of the Colony. Were or were not the forks of the Ohio in Virginia? If they were not—most men admitted a doubt—the Governor had no power to send militiamen thither. Members of the Council and "other persons of weight," as Dinwiddie described them, advised against an attempt to march members of the militia to a district that might belong to Pennsylvania. [33] The expulsion of the French was subordinated to the interpretation of a law.

About the time George brought to Williamsburg the news from Frederick that subsequently raised this question of law, the General Assembly met. On the opening day, February 14, Dinwiddie delivered a message in which he summarized Major Washington's report of the mission to Fort Le Boeuf. His Honor [34] gave warning that 1500 French, with their Indian allies, were preparing to advance early in the spring, to rendezvous at Logstown, and to "build many more fortresses" on the Ohio. With a fervent description of the horrors of a frontier war, the Governor called on the Burgesses to vote a "proper supply." [35] The next day Dinwiddie transmitted Washington's journal and St. Pierre's answer to the message George had delivered at Fort Le Boeuf. [36]

With this information in hand, the Burgesses began in Committee of the Whole to review the Governor's appeal for funds. There was no enthusiasm for an expedition to the Ohio. Some officials insisted, as Washington later indignantly recorded, that the report was "a fiction and a scheme to promote the interest of a private company," the

---

[32] 6 H 115.

[33] Dinwiddie to Lord Holderness, Mch. 12, 1754; 1 *Din.*, 93. For the involved issue of the Pennsylvania boundary, see *supra*, Chapter IV.

[34] It may be permissible again to note that this and not "His Excellency" was used consistently by Washington at this period in formal references to the Governor.

[35] *Journ. H.B.*, 1752–58, p. 175–76. In this message he spoke of having ordered "some part of the militia" to the Ohio. This is the reason for stating that George's information "subsequently" raised the question of the Governor's authority to send the militia to the forks of the Ohio.

[36] *Ibid.*, 178.

Ohio Company, of course.[37] One Burgess went further and asserted that the disputed region belonged to the French.[38] Debate was precipitated; dissent was vigorous; in all likelihood some who wished to escape taxation convinced themselves that the alleged danger did not exist. Those who saw the threat had to open their colleagues' eyes to it. "With great application," Dinwiddie subsequently reported, "many arguments and everything I possibly could suggest, the [Burgesses] at last voted £10,000 for protecting our frontiers," [39] but they attached a proviso that fourteen leading men of the Colony or any nine of them, with the consent and approbation of the Governor, should decide how the money was to be spent.[40]

Dinwiddie was furious at this proviso, which he considered a gross infringement on his right to direct the application of all funds for the defence of the Colony. He was incensed, too, that the measure named to the committee four members of his Council of State, without their consent. The Burgesses, he protested, "clogged this bill with many things unconstitutional and derogatory to the prerogatives of the crown," [41] and were "very much in a republican way of thinking." [42] He would have preferred to dissolve them forthwith,[43] but as funds had to be available immediately if the designs of the French were to be frustrated, he reluctantly gave his assent to the bill [44] and the same day, February 23, prorogued the General Assembly.[45]

As soon as the £10,000 had been voted, Dinwiddie abandoned all attempt to employ militia to assist in building the fort on the Ohio. With the consent of the Council he undertook, instead, to raise six Companies of fifty men each and to dispatch these 300 new soldiers to the contested river.[46] To stimulate recruiting, Governor Dinwiddie decided, in advance of final legislative action, to proclaim that a fort was to be built at the mouth of the Monongahela and that, for the encouragement of volunteers to "erect and support" this defence against

37 Letter of [Jan. n.d.] 1757 to Lord Loudoun, 2 G. W., 7.

38 Dinwiddie to John Hanbury, Mch. 12, 1754; 1 Din., 102.

39 Same to same, ibid.

40 6 H 418. The statute was entitled "an act for the encouragement and protection of the settlers upon the waters of the Mississippi." For the various legislative stages, see Journ. H.B., 1752–58, p. 181, 182, 183, 185.

41 Dinwiddie to the Lords of Trade, May 10, 1754; 1 Din., 160–61.

42 Dinwiddie to Lord Halifax, Mch. 12, 1754; 1 Din., 100.

43 Ibid., 161.

44 Ibid., 93, 98, 161, and Journ. H.B., 1752–58, p. 185.

45 Journ. H.B., loc. cit.

46 Council Minutes, Feb. 23, 1754; 1 Hamilton, 28; Dinwiddie to [Lt.] Gov. James De Lancey, Feb. 23, 1754; 1 Din., 79.

French and Indians, 200,000 acres of land were set aside. Half of the acreage was to be adjacent to the fort; the other half was to be on or near the Ohio. Upon completion of the service of the volunteers, the land was to be divided among them, according to their respective merit, and was to be free of quit rents for fifteen years.[47] This bounty was in addition to the daily pay of 15 lbs. of tobacco allowed an infantry-man.[48]

To command these 300 volunteers, officers had now to be commissioned directly by the Governor—a fact that immensely interested George. He was in Williamsburg for at least a part of the brief legislative session[49] and he had the honor, if the somewhat frail financial reward, of £50 voted him by the General Assembly to "testify [its] approbation of his proceedings on his journey to the Ohio." [50] The Governor, moreover, put him on duty at the active pay of a militia Captain from the time he had arrived in Williamsburg after his mission to the French post.[51] All this was acceptable, though George considered the financial reward outrageously inadequate,[52] but if new military service was to be offered and new honors won, Washington must have a share in them!

His chance was not unfavorable. At first, it seemed probable that the Governor would name Col. William Fairfax to the general command of the new force,[53] in which event George could not ask for a better sponsor; but soon it was apparent that Fairfax's health would not permit his acceptance of field duty. With Fairfax out of consideration, there was, of course, no reason why George should not appeal to Dinwiddie directly when he had opportunity of talking with the busy Governor. George doubtless did, and, in addition, he solicited all the influence he could of friends close to Dinwiddie. Among others, George saw Richard Corbin at Green Spring, the Ludwell country house, and asked that long-time friend of the family about the appointments that would be made. Corbin as a member of the Council had information

---

[47] 5 E. J., 461–62, 499–500; *Penn. Gazette,* Mch. 12, 1754; Dinwiddie's explanation of the reasons for offering this bounty is given in a letter of Mch. 12, 1754, to Holderness, 1 *Din.,* 94–96.

[48] Troopers were to receive 20 lbs. (6 *H* 116). In current money, infantry pay was 8*d* daily.

[49] Writing to Lord Fairfax, Feb. 23, 1754, Dinwiddie acknowledged receipt of a letter of February 11, "per Major Washington" (1 *Din.,* 82).

[50] *Journ. H.B.,* 1752–58, p. 182, 183, 185.

[51] See the account-book entries quoted in 1 *Ford,* 44 n.

[52] 1 *G. W.,* 156.

[53] Dinwiddie to Maj. John Carlyle, Feb. 25, 1754; 1 *Din.,* 83. The note R. A. Brock appended to this letter manifestly rested on misconception.

which prompted him to hint that George might hope for a commission above that of Major.

This was good news! Ambitious as George had become, he told himself in all candor that he did not have the age or the experience to justify him in aspiring immediately to the general command of the expedition to the Ohio; but he believed that if he could get a commission as Lieutenant Colonel under a qualified senior, he would not fail.[54]

In all such matters, even when ambition was to be gratified and adventure enjoyed, George's impulse, as a thrifty, acquisitive young man, was to ascertain the financial responsibilities and compensations. So, when he had Dinwiddie's ear, he asked the Governor what pay a Lieutenant Colonel would receive in the new organization. The Governor answered it would be 15s a day.

George protested at once that this was too little, whereupon Dinwiddie assured him that provisions would be allowed the officers. This, the Governor went on, was the reason the pay of the Colony's officers was to be less than that of British regulars.[55] Speaker Robinson of the House of Burgesses thought the Virginia scale of pay too low, and he said so; but as Dinwiddie was in authority, George had to be content with the explanation given.[56] He put the Governor's assurance in the book of his memory and renewed his effort to procure a commission in the new military establishment. After he returned home, he wrote Richard Corbin and confessed frankly his ambition. Said he: ". . . if I could entertain hopes that you thought me worthy of the post of Lieutenant Colonel, and would favor me so far as to mention it at the appointment of officers, I could not but entertain a true sense of the kindness." [57]

While Dinwiddie considered and Corbin advised, George went about the task of recruiting for the new force. In doing this, he was allowed to act now at his rank of Major on active duty, with pay on that basis and not at the modest annual compensation of a District Adjutant.[58] His headquarters were in Alexandria,[59] where he had closer relations

54 Washington to Richard Corbin, n.d. [probably late February or early March], 1754; 1 *Ford*, 43–44.
55 Washington to Dinwiddie, May 29, 1754; 1 *Ford*, 77.
56 For Robinson's views, see 1 *Ford*, 18.
57 1 *Ford*, 44.
58 Cf. 1 *Ford*, 44 n.
59 The date of his opening headquarters in Alexandria is doubtful. Washington wrote Dinwiddie from the town on the 7th or 9th of March in terms which indicate he had been there long enough to get some understanding of his problems of recruitment (1 *Din.*, 92). Dinwiddie's

with John Carlyle. That gentleman, on January 26, had been appointed Commissary of Supply for the expedition to the Ohio.[60] As Carlyle had married Sarah Fairfax, a daughter of Col. William Fairfax and a sister of Mrs. Lawrence Washington, he belonged to the society in which George lived.[61] Thirty-four years of age and a native of Dumfriesshire, Major Carlyle was one of the incorporators of Alexandria, had been active in the affairs of the Ohio Company, and enjoyed high reputation as one of the most vigorous and probably the most successful of the Scotch merchants of the new town. His fine house, built on the foundations of the old fort, was the most conspicuous residence of Alexandria.[62] George had a good opinion of Carlyle and, after some experience with him, concluded that the Commissary was altogether capable and most painstaking.[63] At the time, there was nothing in Carlyle's record to indicate that he was a man too ready to accept promise as performance.

It was fortunate for George's spirits that he had the company and counsel of Carlyle because almost everything else proved to be adverse. The weather was excessively bad;[64] there was no enthusiasm for enlisting; those young men who were sufficiently interested to make inquiry wanted to know, first of all, what they would receive and whether they would be paid as regularly as British soldiers were. After approximately a week of hard persuasion, George enlisted about twenty-five individuals, most of whom he described as "loose, idle persons," devoid of shoes or shirts and of almost every garment. Once he enlisted them, George soon was able to arouse in them the new recruit's desire to look decent in a uniform, but, haplessly, there were no uniforms and no credit for buying any. "They are perpetually teasing me," George wrote the Governor, "to [provide them clothing and to deduct the cost from their pay], but I am not able to advance the money, provided there was no risk in it, which there certainly is, and too great for me to run, though it would be nothing to the country . . ."[65]

acknowledgment of Mch. 15, 1754 referred to letters from Washington dated March 3 and 7. In 5 E. J., 464, it is stated that these letters were from Belvoir. No large error will be made in accepting March 1 as the approximate date when George began recruiting in Alexandria.

[60] 1 Din., 54.

[61] See supra, p. 61. Sarah Fairfax, born in 1729, died Jan. 22, 1761 (Md. Gazette, Feb. 12, 1761). John Carlyle's second wife was Sybil West, daughter of John West the fourth.

[62] 18 W (1) p. 2.

[63] Washington to Dinwiddie, June 12, 1754; 1 Ford, 99.   [64] 1 Ford, 42.

[65] Washington to Dinwiddie, Mch. 7 or 9, 1754; 1 Ford, 42–43. Concerning the uncertainty of the date, see ibid., 41 n.

A few recruits who were enlisted elsewhere [66] drifted into Alexandria, but the upbuilding of the force to the stipulated strength of 300 was provokingly slow in itself and dangerously slow in the light of the news that came from William Trent on the Ohio. He was believed to have recruited and assembled a good part of the 100 men [67] he had been directed to raise among the traders in order to assist in building and guarding the English fort on the river, but he considered himself far too weak for the task assigned him. From the forks of the Monongahela, where Christopher Gist had joined him, Trent now repeated in a letter to Washington what friendly Indians had told him of great threats made by La Force, the French Commissary who had accompanied Washington from Venango to Fort Le Boeuf. Another savage reported that 400 French were expected on the Ohio. The natives, said Trent, were alarmed and restless. Christopher Gist wrote of still larger reported movements of French up the Ohio and down to that river from Lake Erie. Trent urged that Washington hasten to him. Gist took it for granted that this would be done.[68]

For George to read all this and to sense new danger on the Ohio must have made the slack recruiting of additional "loose, idle fellows" a test of patience and of faith. Dinwiddie, for his part, was cheerful, though overworked, and was fashioning great designs. He had reconciled himself to the legal barrier in the way of employing militia to protect the fort to be built on the Ohio, and he had concluded that 300 volunteers would be of more service than 800 militiamen anyway.[69] He was the less disturbed because he accepted the assurance that England was to have the aid of 1000 Cherokee and Catawba warriors.[70] Besides, the home government had notified him that an Independent Company of regulars from South Carolina and two Companies from New York would be sent to Virginia,[71] a prospect that Dinwiddie wished to keep secret for the time, because, he said, "new raised forces do not incline to mix with the regulars." [72]

---

[66] Cf. 1 Ford, 45.

[67] On Mch. 21, 1754, Dinwiddie's information was that Trent had recruited seventy men (1 Din., 120). Actually, it would appear, Trent never had more than approximately forty men. See infra, p. 351.

[68] A summary of Trent's letter of Feb. 19, 1754 and extracts from Gist's of Feb. 23, 1754, appear in Md. Gazette, Mch. 14, 1754.

[69] Dinwiddie to Lord Holderness, Mch. 17, 1754; 1 Din., 94 ff, ibid., 118, 122.

[70] Ibid., 94.

[71] Holderness to Dinwiddie, Jan. 18, 1754; P.R.O., C.O. 5:211, p. 25. The orders confused North and South Carolina, but did not mislead Dinwiddie.

[72] Dinwiddie to Sharpe, Mch. 1, 1754; 1 Din., 85.

Through correspondence, too, he was exhorting the Governors of the other Colonies to prevail on their lawmakers to supply funds and troops for the protection of the Ohio.[73] All these soldiers, he said, should be under his "general officers," [74] because "I think it would very much conduce to success that the command should be undivided." [75] Secretly, he was providing himself with a military uniform; [76] and if he was not already hoping to command the Virginia troops, he soon was to develop that ambition.[77] His acquaintance with the humdrum but indispensable details of supplying an army with food and equipment, and of the time required for that task, was somewhat less meagre than that of most of his associates, but it still was the knowledge of a theorist, not that of a leader who understood the hunger of frontiersmen and the slowness of transport in the wilderness. Alone with his comparative ignorance of supply, Dinwiddie had a continuing distrust of the men on whose vote of ample money his plans depended.[78] He was sure they would not acquiesce in any arrangement whereby each Colony would furnish a prescribed quota of men and money after a conference among the Governors. Such an agreement, said Dinwiddie, "would have no weight with my Assembly, as they are too headstrong to be under any direction but from their own opinions and arguments." [79]

These suspicions were outweighed by his confident determination to raise the 300 volunteers and to send them to the Ohio under the best officers he could select from an exceedingly short list of men with military experience, or even of extensive military reading. Virginia had few former officers among her citizens. She had engaged in no military operations after the Cartagena expedition; death had taken Sir William Gooch and Lawrence Washington, two of the seniors of the Virginia contingent in that campaign. William Fitzhugh was residing in Maryland still.[80] Of the District Adjutants, George Muse probably was the only one who had seen active service in the field.

Dinwiddie, sifting all he knew, soon chose Joshua Fry as the man best qualified to take the place intended for Col. William Fairfax; and as the Governor doubtless foresaw the expansion of the 300 into a

[73] See 1 *Din.*, 63 ff, 83 ff.
[74] 1 *Sharpe*, 33.   [75] 1 *Din.*, 67, 69.
[76] Dinwiddie to John Hanbury, Mch. 12, 1754; 1 *Din.*, 104.
[77] Dinwiddie to James Abercromby, Oct. 23, 1754; 1 *Din.*, 376.
[78] Dinwiddie to Lord Halifax, Mch. 12, 1754; 1 *Din.*, 100–01. Cf. *ibid.*, 103.
[79] Dinwiddie to Gov. James Glen of South Carolina, Apr. 15, 1754; 1 *Din.*, 128.
[80] See *supra*, p. 266.

Regiment, he decided to award a Colonel's commission to Fry, a former professor of mathematics at William and Mary, an engineer and cartographer who had gone in 1745 to the new County of Albemarle in the Piedmont. Fry had done no fighting but he knew men, won their respect easily, and displayed always a justice and serenity of spirit in dealing with them. He had served as County Lieutenant, had mastered the arts of the frontiersman, and had acted as one of the commissioners in the successful negotiations with the Indians at Logstown in 1752. Fry, in a word, had exceptional training and seemed more likely to succeed as head of the new forces than any other Virginia colonial.[81] Dinwiddie was not committed to retaining him in general command after the arrival of troops from other Colonies.

George Muse [82] was named Captain and soon was promoted Major [83] —an appointment that seemed wholly reasonable at the time [84] not only because of his rank in the militia organization but also because he had served in the Cartagena expedition.[85] Of the appointment of a third officer, Capt. Adam Stephen, who had acquired brief experience at sea, George probably heard also. The other commissions, as he ascertained gradually, went in most instances to ambitious young men who wished to learn something of the frontier. In selecting these officers, Dinwiddie had to disappoint more families than he gratified, but with the exception of a certain partiality for his fellow Scots, he chose with some independence of mind. John Augustine Washington was among those to whom the Governor refused a Lieutenant's commission, though willing, apparently, to make him an Ensign.[86] When the Governor had completed his roster he had to confess: "We are in much distress for proper officers, but have taken all possible care of choosing the best we have, but not so well acquainted with the arts of war as I could wish, but as our cause is just, I hope for the protection of Heaven." [87]

Of his place in the organization, George had received some assurance

[81] His age is not known precisely, but he probably was in his early fifties. For a sketch and bibliography, see *DAB*. According to Washington's list of officers (*supra*, p. 331), Fry's command began as of February 25.

[82] 30 *V* 272–73.   [83] 1 *G. W.*, 36.

[84] For confusion over the name, see 1 *V* 465, 2 *V* 102.

[85] See Toner's note in *Washington's Journal of 1754*, p. 105. Washington's subsequent opinion of him will be found in 2 *Ford*, 343. Irving's description of Muse in 1 *Washington*, 65, is entirely fictitious.

[86] Cf. 1 *Din.*, 111. This, incidentally, is one of many proofs of the non-existence of a Washington-Fairfax coalition that has been assumed, in spite of the lack of any supporting evidence, to have exercised large control over Dinwiddie. The influence of the Fairfaxes was strong, but young George Washington was, after the death of Lawrence, the only member of his family who was conspicuous in public affairs, and he was not influential until later.

[87] Dinwiddie to Gov. Horatio Sharpe, Mch. 1, 1754; 1 *Din.*, 86.

before he knew who were and were not to be his companions-in-arms. By the 20th of March, a messenger brought him a letter of instructions from the Governor and, probably, a note in which Richard Corbin said briefly: "I enclose your commission. God prosper you with it." [88] The commission was at the rank of Lieutenant Colonel, the second in command of the expedition. Behind the document was the Governor's faith in George's good sense, and his hope and expectation that the young man who had gone to Fort Le Boeuf would discharge the new mission with equal speed and vigor.[89]

The new Lieutenant Colonel was pleased. He was seeking the good opinion of the prominent people of the Colony—"honor," as he termed it—and he was willing, too, to serve his King and country.[90] George felt, also, that his constitution was "hardly enough," to quote in his own words, "to encounter and undergo the most severe trials." [91] He accepted the commission in this spirit, Mch. 20, 1754,[92] and he found in Dinwiddie's instructions much that was exciting and pleasant; but, almost from the first, one thing vexed him: In his interview with the Governor, it will be remembered, he had been told that the pay of a Lieutenant Colonel was to be 15s per day,[93] but now he was informed tersely in Dinwiddie's letter, "pay, 12s 6d per day without any trouble of commanding a Company." [94] This was 2s 6d less than the Governor had promised, and therefore even further than he previously had computed below the compensation an officer of like rank on the regular British establishment would receive. George made the revised calculation, took into account the current rate of exchange, and found that the difference was nearly 10s daily, or almost £15 a month. As for the assurance formerly given that the officers were to have provisions, George found the allowance was to be one soldier's ration a day—and no more. All this offended both Washington's pride and his sense of justice. He told himself that it was the work of a committee, not of

[88] Dinwiddie's letter is in 1 Din., 106–07; Washington's answer appears in 1 Ford, 44; Corbin's note is in ibid., 44 n. As Dinwiddie wrote that he was enclosing the commission in his letter, it seems probable that Corbin's lines was a sub-enclosure. Washington's journal stated that the commission was received Mch. 31, 1754, but this manifestly is an error in a document discussed infra, n. 112.

[89] Cf. Dinwiddie to Washington, May 25, 1754; 1 Din., 173.

[90] Cf. Washington to Dinwiddie, May 29, 1754; 1 Ford, 81.

[91] Ibid., 78.

[92] Washington to Dinwiddie, Mch. 20, 1754; 1 Din., 44.

[93] See supra, p. 335.

[94] Dinwiddie to Washington, Mch. 15, 1754; 1 Din., 107.

the Governor, to whom he felt he owed a debt of gratitude; [95] but the more George reflected on this discrimination against colonial officers, the more was he outraged. At length, he went to Colonel Fairfax at Belhaven, poured out his grievance and announced that he was going to resign the commission Dinwiddie had sent. George was sharp in his complaint and, to buttress his own position, told Fairfax that he was not alone in feeling that officers' pay was too low: Speaker Robinson had said as much.[96]

William Fairfax was both friendly and diplomatic. He showed plainly his interest in George's behalf and then he undertook to dissuade the young man from resigning. As Washington was not easy to move when convinced of the rightness of his position, Fairfax had to promise that he would communicate with Dinwiddie and would endeavor to have more money alloted the officers.[97]

After George agreed on this basis to withhold his resignation, he turned again to the gratifying part of his letter from Dinwiddie, a paragraph in which the Governor expressed surprise that the French were expected to move so early in the season to the Ohio. This, said Dinwiddie, "makes it necessary for you to march what soldiers you have immediately to the Ohio, and escort some wagons, with the necessary provisions." Colonel Fry was to follow with the other troops as soon as possible.[98]

There was an opportunity! While Colonel Fry gathered the last reluctant recruits, the Lieutenant Colonel was to command the vanguard on an advance to the river, and was to meet whatever adventure awaited the Virginians there. Washington's earlier instructions to proceed to the Ohio and to complete the fort there had hinted at some of the possibilities he might encounter. Dinwiddie had said: "You are to act on the defensive, but in case any attempts are made to obstruct the works or interrupt our settlements by any persons whatsoever you are to restrain all such offenders, and in case of resistance to make prisoners of or kill and destroy them. For the rest, you are to conduct

[95] 1 Ford, 76 ff. George may have been mistaken in blaming a committee, unless it was the committee of Burgesses named to supervise expenditures. Dinwiddie's announcement of the scale of pay antedated by more than a month the action of the Council, Apr. 27, 1754, in setting or at least approving the standard of compensation to which George objected. See 1 Hamilton, 28, and infra, p. 360 ff.

[96] 1 Ford, 78, and supra, p. 335.

[97] Ibid., 77–78.

[98] Dinwiddie to Washington, Mch. 15, 1754; 1 Din., 106.

yourself as the circumstances of the service shall require and to act as you shall find best for the furtherance of His Majesty's service and the good of his dominion." [99] That, surely, was warrant for doing whatever had to be done in order to assure British control of the river that flowed through rich meadows.

George pondered his problem and his resources: In person, he had enlisted approximately fifty men; other officers had sent in about twenty-five; for these seventy-five he was attempting to procure uniforms; [100] and with the assistance of Jacob van Braam, [101] he was trying to instill some discipline. It was a difficult thing to undertake, almost unaided, with men who, George admitted grimly, were self-willed and ungovernable. [102] More officers were needed, more wagons and more supplies, because the weather had made the roads so muddy that nothing could be sent ahead. [103] As for artillery, guns recently sent from England were so heavy for their calibre that Dinwiddie had shipped only ten of them to Alexandria. [104] It was almost certain that these cannon could not be moved overland until a warmer sun had dried the roads.

Young Lieutenant Colonel Washington put all these facts together and concluded there was one way only by which he could proceed quickly to the Ohio with his men: he could use wagons for the march to Wills Creek and, after arriving there, he could go forward in light marching order if a sufficient number of pack animals could be assembled at that base. Eagerly he and Maj. John Carlyle wrote Capt. William Trent to ask if that officer could collect the necessary horses. In due time assurance came from Trent that the pack beasts would be provided at the creek. [105]

The speed of preparation increased at Alexandria. As George tried

99 Dinwiddie to Washington [Jan. n.d., 1754]; 1 *Din.*, 59.

100 1 *Din.*, 106, 118.

101 In the MS memorial, cited in 30 *V* 394-95, van Braam asserted that he had been charged exclusively with the discipline of the force.

102 Washington to Dinwiddie, Mch. 20, 1754; 1 *Ford*, 45.

103 *Ibid.*

104 Dinwiddie to John Carlyle, Jan. 27, 1754; 1 *Din.*, 53; Dinwiddie to Governor Hamilton of Pennsylvania, Mch. 21, 1754; 1 *Ford*, 120. A list of ordnance for Virginia had been drawn up May 15, 1753 (P.R.O., C.O. 5, 1328, no p.), had been approved August 10, and had been mentioned in Dinwiddie's instructions of August 28 (P.R.O., C.O. 5, 1344, p. 152). At first the royal government had not intended to send any powder with this shipment, but finally did so and scolded Dinwiddie for failure to provide it in advance out of colonial revenue. (Holderness to Dinwiddie, Aug. 28, 1753; P.R.O., C.O. 5, 211, p. 43.) Beer explained (*British Colonial Policy*, 6) that during a time of peace in Europe the defence of each Colony against local enemies devolved on the Colony itself. Assistance was to be given by the home country in those cases only where the empire itself was put in jeopardy.

105 Washington to Dinwiddie, May 9, 1754; 1 *Ford*, 57-58.

to make soldiers of his homeless and destitute volunteers, Carlyle sought to procure supplies and equipment. Both officers communicated at intervals with Dinwiddie, who had learned by this time that some of the other Colonies were not disposed to give him the assistance he had hoped to get. North Carolina had voted a supply of £12,000 of paper money of her own issue, and was recruiting forces that were expected ultimately to reach 750; but Maryland had provided no help. Action by Pennsylvania, though hopefully expected, was not certain,[106] in spite of the fact that rumors of a war with France were sweeping Philadelphia.[107] Dinwiddie swallowed his disappointment, remained as zealous as ever, and with the passing of the winter became increasingly convinced that whatever was undertaken on the Ohio had to be launched quickly.[108]

George did his utmost to have it so. He decided to start with supplies sufficient only for the march to Winchester and then to get additional wagons and provisions there for the long journey to the Ohio. When his troops at Alexandria increased to 120, he organized them into two Companies, one temporarily under Jacob van Braam and the other under Peter Hog, who had reported for duty and had the Governor's commission as Captain. This officer—the name pronounced with a long "o" [109]—was a Scot, fifty-one years of age, and a resident of Augusta County where he had married Elizabeth Taylor only a few days before he left home to join the expedition.[110] It is entirely possible that Hog was in the Jacobite rising of 1745, the year of his migration to Virginia, but nothing was said of this.[111] In any event, he had interest in military affairs. Van Braam, it will be recalled, had said that he had been a Lieutenant in the Dutch Army before he came to the New World. With these two officers, five Subalterns, two Sergeants and six Corporals, all of them probably inexperienced, George continued to give his men such drill and to inculcate such discipline as they would take; but they still were raw recruits when, at the beginning of April, 1754, their Lieutenant Colonel issued marching orders.

On the morning of the 2nd, astride one of his good horses, George

---

[106] Dinwiddie to Sharpe, Mch. 25, 1754; 1 *Din.*, 127. The situation approximately one month later is described in *ibid.*, 134.

[107] Joseph Shippen to James Burd, Apr. 2, 1754; *Shippen Papers*, 31.

[108] Cf. Dinwiddie to Governor De Lancey of New York, Mch. 21, 1754; 1 *Din.*, 116–17.

[109] It subsequently became familiar and distinguished as Hoge.

[110] Waddell, *Annals of Augusta Country,* 63; 11 *Va. His. Col.*, 211; Toner, ed., *Washington's Journal of 1754*, p. 20 n.

[111] Unless Hog had previous military experience, it scarcely seems probable that he would have been commissioned at fifty-one years of age for frontier duty.

HISTORIC FRENCH ANSWER TO DINWIDDIE

All that twenty-one-year-old George Washington really knew about the mission on which he set out in November, 1753, was that he had to find a French commanding officer somewhere in the Ohio Country and had to deliver to that gentleman a letter in which the Governor of Virginia protested against occupation of British territory and demanded that the French evacuate it. There were various minor details that Washington had to regard. The essential was that he present the letter and wait no longer than a week for a reply.

It proved to be, first of all, a mission in Indian diplomacy, an art with which the young Adjutant of Virginia militia was wholly unacquainted. He doubtless had seen a few straggling redmen in the Shenandoah Valley, and once, at Cresap's, when he was sixteen, he had watched for two days the behavior of a returning war party of thirty braves.

This was the range of his experience when he found himself projected overnight into a quarrel that involved "speech belts" and "treaty belts" and Indian usages and alliances that might have puzzled even the oldest of the traders. Then, in a few days, Washington discovered

(*Continued on third page following*)

Comme j'ay l'honneur de commander icy en chef, Monsieur
Washington m'a remis la lettre que vous écrivez au commandant
des trouppes françoises.

J'aurois été charmé que vous luy eussiez donné ordre, ou qu'il eut
été disposé à se rendre en Canada, pour voir Monsieur notre
général au quel il appartient mieux qu'à moy de mettre au jour
l'évidence, et la réalité des droits du Roy mon maître sur les
terres situées le long de la belle Rivière, et de contester les
prétentions du Roy de la grande Bretagne a cet égard

Je vais adresser votre lettre a Monsieur le Marquis Duquesne
Sa réponse me servira de loy, et s'il m'ordonne de vous la
communiquer, Monsieur, je puis vous assurer que je ne négligeray
rien pour vous la faire tenir très promptement

Quand a la sommation que vous me faites de me retirer
je ne me crois pas dans l'obligation de m'y rendre, quelques
que puissent être vos instructions, je suis icy en vertu des
ordres de mon général, et je vous prie Monsieur de ne pas

douttés un instant que je suis dans la constante resolution
de m'y conformer avec toute l'exactitude, et la fermeté
que l'on peut attendre du meilleur officier.

J'ignore que dans le cours de cette campagne il se soit rien
passé qui puisse estre reputé pour acte d'hostilité, ny qui
soit contraire aux traités qui subsistent entre les deux
Couronnes, dont la Continuation nous interesse, et nous flatte
autant que Messieurs les Anglois: S'il vous eus été agreable
Monsieur d'en venir sur ce point a un detail particulier
des faits qui motivent votre plainte, j'aurois eu l'honneur,
de vous repondre de la façon la plus positive, et je suis
persuadé que vous auriés eu lieu d'estre satisfait

Je me suis fait un devoir particulier de Recevoir Monsieur
Washington avec la distinction qui convient a votre dignité,
a sa qualité, et a son grand merite; je puis me flatter
qu'il me rendra cette justice auprés de vous Monsieur
et qu'il vous fera connoistre ainsi que moy le respect
profond avec le quel je suis

Monsieur

du fort de la riviere au boeuf
le 15 Xbre 1753

Votre tres humble
et tres obeissant
Serviteur
Legardeur De St Pierre

that these Indian quarrels had larger meaning. They involved the support that might be given by the savages to one side or to the other in the event of war between Britain and France.

The delivery of the Governor's letter was almost swallowed up for a time in this backwoods diplomatic struggle. At Fort Le Boeuf, where he was treated with formal courtesy, Washington received from the French commander, Legardeur de St. Pierre, the letter that is reproduced on the two preceding pages. This answer, translated on page 325, was, in effect, an assertion of a French title to the Ohio country, which, said St. Pierre, he was occupying by order of his General.

Besides receiving this communication, Washington saw at Fort Le Boeuf so many evidences of French preparations to advance southward that he felt he should return to Williamsburg as rapidly as possible to warn Governor Dinwiddie. In hurrying through the snow of Pennsylvania and across the ice of the Allegheny River, Washington several times risked his life; but one month to the very day from the time he left Fort Le Boeuf, he placed in the hands of Governor Dinwiddie the French commander's letter. As it reposes now in the archives of Virginia it bears no mark of wear or water.

led his little column out of Alexandria and westward in the direction of the range the pioneers had called the "Blew Mountains." He had gone by that route frequently as Surveyor and civilian; the previous November he had ridden toward Vestal's Gap with a few companions on his mission to Fort Le Boeuf; but this was the first time he ever had commanded troops on the road. A long and a strange road it was to prove, the road of a career he coveted but had not planned.[112]

Along this rough way, two wagons followed the troops, two wagons only.[113] They carried the medical supplies, the tents, the food and the ammunition, and they symbolized a military want that was to be the curse of every campaign against the French on the Ohio, but at the moment they seemed adequate for the journey to Winchester, where additional vehicles [114] for the march to Wills Creek were to be obtained. From Wills Creek westward, George reasoned that the men could subsist on what the pack animals carried, until the road was cleared and the wagons were brought up. George and John Carlyle had agreed that this was a feasible plan of supply. Dinwiddie himself had believed there was abundance of food and of provender in the back country,[115] though he had directed specifically that the number of wagons be ample "to carry the stores and provisions out to the Ohio." [116] The Governor's orders has been, also, that any anticipated shortage of provisions for the expedition was to be covered in advance by requisition on Williamsburg and the older settlements.[117]

The first day's march was past Cameron's, the site of an abortive attempt to build a town to rival Alexandria.[118] Six miles from the starting point and four miles beyond Cameron's, the column rested at its first camp.[119] The next morning George directed his men [120] northwestward on the road that paralleled the Potomac.[121] Through a

112 At this point, the primary source becomes Washington's journal of 1754. For the history of this document, which exists as a French translation and as an English retranslation of a lost original, see Appendix I–9.
113 1 Ford, 47.
114 1 Din., 112.
115 Dinwiddie to Maj. John Carlyle, Jan. 27, 1754; 1 Din., 53.
116 Dinwiddie to Maj. John Carlyle, Feb. 25, 1754; 1 Din., 83. Cf. 84–85 ff, 108–09 ff.
117 Dinwiddie to Maj. John Carlyle, n.d. [probably early March, 1754]; 1 Din., 90.
118 Landmarks, 414–15. The name came to be applied somewhat loosely to an area of vague boundaries.
119 1 Diaries, 74. The name Cameron was in honor of Lord Fairfax, Baron Cameron. Washington's journal nowhere distinguished between camps and bivouacs, but at that season in Northern Virginia, troops were not apt to sleep in the open air if tentage was at hand.
120 The names of the participants appear in 1 V 278 ff.
121 Dalrymple's revision of Fry and Jefferson is an adequate map for the advance. Later maps, including plans of the forts, will be found in A. B. Hulbert, ed., The Crown Collection of American Maps, v. 1 and 2.

pleasant, budding country, the recruits continued their march on the 4th and the following days until, on the 6th, George halted them at the establishment of Edward Thompson, perched high, where later the village of Hillsboro was to stand.[122] Five days' advance had covered fifty-seven miles,[123] or, between sun and sun, slightly more than eleven miles a day, which was not a bad showing for green troops accompanied by two wagons. The next stage of the journey was to the crest of Vestal's Gap [124] and then down to the Shenandoah and across it by ferry.[125] Although the passage of these seventeen miles consumed two days, Washington scarcely could complain. Part of the upward grade was hard; progress necessarily was slow.

On the morning of April 9, George was in the familiar country of his earlier engineering surveys and on the road to Winchester. More than once while drawing lines in 1748 and later years he had looked forward to a day in the little town, because he could sup there at an endurable ordinary and could sleep between sheets. Now the road across the Valley held out the promise of two additions of force: one or more Companies of Fry's Regiment were to meet George there; wagons for the advance into the wilderness were to assemble, also, in the town. If both troops and vehicles were ready, then George could move quickly to Wills Creek and start thence without delay on the final leg of the journey to the forks of the Ohio, where the detachment under Capt. William Trent presumably was constructing the fort.

Half this hope was realized. When Washington reached Winchester [126] he found there the Company raised in that area by Capt. Adam Stephen.[127] This officer was a young Scot who had studied at Aberdeen, had pursued a medical course at Edinburgh and had served on a British hospital ship. If he had in youth the qualities he possessed later in life, he did not screen his lights or fail to put the highest valua-

---

[122] This date and camp site are fixed by an entry in Washington's recapitulation of his expenses. See Toner, ed., *Washington's Journal of 1754*, p. 180. As Washington made these entries from memory, after the loss of his papers at Fort Necessity, a margin of possible error concerning dates has to be allowed. For Edward Thompson's property and issue, see *Landmarks*, 481–82 and 512, n. 130. Hillsboro is six miles Northwest of Leesburg.

[123] According to the table of distances in Braddock's *Orderly Book*, quoted in *Landmarks*, 482.

[124] Styled Key's in Braddock's *Orderly Book*, loc. cit. For the identification, see *Landmarks*, 511.

[125] Expense account of Washington, Toner, *op. cit.*, 180.

[126] He probably arrived with his troops on the afternoon of April 10, but the date is determinable only by the fact that, as the roads then ran (*Landmarks*, 482), the distance from Vestal's Ferry to Winchester was twenty-three miles. As Washington crossed the ferry on the 8th, two marches of the same length as those made previously would have brought him to the town.

[127] 1 *G. W.*, 36; 1 *Diaries*, 74.

tion on what he had done at sea. He averred, in fact, that while he was aboard the hospital ship, he displayed a "coolness and presence of mind" that saved the vessel from capture by the French.[128] Subsequently, Doctor Stephen had left the navy, had declined a post in India and, "after wandering for a certain period," [129] had come to Virginia. He then returned to his profession and began the practice of medicine and surgery in Stafford, where he gained some reputation by successful operations.[130] In a short time, he moved to Frederick and established himself there.[131] Stephen then was a bachelor, and in that estate it was hoped by a lady in Scotland he would remain "till," as she wrote, "you think my Jeanie is fit for matrimony." [132] Among masculine admirers of Doctor Stephen was Col. William Fairfax, who had pressed him to accept a commission in the force being raised for the Ohio.[133] Governor Dinwiddie, too, already had formed a favorable impression of his fellow countryman Stephen, to whom he subscribed himself, even in official letters, "your friend"—a term His Honor seldom employed when writing.[134] In a word, at thirty years of age, or approximately that,[135] Stephen had overbundant self-confidence, substantial supporters, and at least some experience and skill in dealing with men.[136]

Washington's command was strengthened by Stephen and was raised to a total of 159 at a time when a firm hand was needed. The day George arrived in Winchester, he had satisfactory proof that four of his enlisted men had formed a scheme to desert, and would have succeeded

---

[128] Stephen's MS autobiographical sketch, in the Benjamin Rush papers, Lib. Co. of Philadelphia. Although framed in the third person, this paper is endorsed, "Col. Stevens' [sic] Life written by himself for B. Rush, 1775." This document was printed in 23 *Penn. Mag.*, 43–50, but it is cited hereafter from the original as *Stephen's "Life," Rush Papers.*

[129] *Ibid.*

[130] *Ibid.* The date of his arrival has not been ascertained, but he was established in Stafford at least as early as June 30, 1753, on which date he signed the indenture of Dudley Skinner, laborer, who covenanted to work for him one year (*Stephen Papers*, LC).

[131] In *Order Book* No. 5, Frederick County, 337, Mch. 7, 1754, is an entry concerning the extension of the term of an indentured servant of his for bearing an illegitimate child.

[132] Ann Miller, Edinburgh, to Adam Stephen, Feb. 22, 1753, *Stephen Papers*, LC. Mrs. Miller added of Jeanie: "[She] is improving in her education as much as can be expected."

[133] *Stephen's "Life," Rush Papers.*

[134] Cf. Dinwiddie to Stephen, Oct. 5, 1754, *Stephen Papers*, LC. It may be in order to add that as the sketch of Stephen in the *Rush Papers* came to light after the publication of Toner's edition of the journal of 1754, the references of Toner to the early career of Stephen (*op. cit.*, 27) have to be discarded.

[135] *Appleton's Cyclopoedia* gave the date of Stephen's birth as c. 1730, but he stated in the quoted MS memoir that he was in university with Dr. John Gregory, who was born in 1724. Besides, if Stephen remained at Edinburgh, as he stated, for four years after he left Aberdeen, he could not have been as young as twenty-four in 1754.

[136] See Toner, *op. cit.*, 28. Nothing in surviving records of 1754 shows that Stephen then was addicted to the drunkenness which subsequently put an end to his career as a soldier.

had not a soldier of stouter morals discovered their plan and exposed it. Washington at once paid a reward of £1, 4s—or six shillings per man— to the faithful soldier; but, of course, he was concerned to learn that this measure of disaffection existed in the ranks.[137]

Concerned or confident, George looked now for the transportation with which to carry to Wills Creek and on to the Ohio the supplies his men and horses must have if the expedition was to succeed. Washington knew that beyond the settlements on the South branch of the Potomac, thirty-two miles Northwest of Winchester on a straight line, no meat for men could be had otherwise than by hunting and no grain in large quantity could be procured by any device. After the grass began to spring, the animals could get some grazing, but the corn or oats they required for hard work the country did not provide. It was plain, precisely as George and John Carlyle had reasoned in advance, that everything had to be hauled in wagons to Wills Creek.

To his dismay, George now saw that virtually nothing had been done to assemble the needed vehicles. Dinwiddie had called Carlyle's attention to the impressment law and had said that it must be invoked if wagons could not be hired at reasonable rates,[138] but no official in Frederick had acted. George consequently had to ascertain, first of all, whether he could employ the statute about which the Governor had written to John Carlyle. It developed that authority to impress boats, wheeled vehicles and draft animals[139] was vested only in a County Lieutenant or in a field officer of the county militia. In addition, before any wagon or cart and team could be taken, "two good and lawful men" had to make an appraisal and had also to fix, in tobacco, a daily allowance for public use of the property. This procedure had to be followed in full by every officer. If he impressed without appraising and giving receipt, he could be sued by the aggrieved owner.[140]

This law manifestly placed in the hands of Lord Fairfax, as County Lieutenant, the power to impress wagons. If the militia of Frederick were reorganized as Dinwiddie had directed, its Colonel, Lieutenant Colonel or Major could act; but George held none of these offices in

[137] The sole evidence on Washington's first experience with desertion is the entry in his expense account: "April 10. To cash to B. Hamilton for discovering the plot of four soldiers to desert." (Toner, *op. cit.*, 180.) Hamilton was a private in Capt. Peter Hog's company (Toner, ed., *op. cit.*, 172), which fact suggests that the plan of the deserters may have been matured en route from Alexandria to the Shenandoah Valley.

[138] Dinwiddie to Maj. John Carlyle, Jan. 27, 1754; 1 *Din.* 53. Cf. *ibid.*, 54.

[139] See the act of 1748 "for making provision against invasions and insurrections," 6 *H* 112–18, notably sections V and VI, p. 114–15.

[140] *Ibid.*, sec. VI, p. 115.

Frederick, though the County was in his district as Adjutant. Doubtful as was his authority in these circumstances, George felt that he must act.[141] Otherwise his mission would fail. In the race to the Ohio the French would win. Diligently and doggedly, then, Colonel Washington went about the task of finding the wagons suitable for hauling supplies over the road through the wilderness. Where he discovered a stout vehicle, he impressed it and followed the procedure set forth in the law; but it was one thing to call for a valuation and another to get honest and willing appraisers. Even when two neighbors were willing to say what a friend's wagon and horses were worth, orders to deliver the vehicle and team were not easily enforced.

Forty wagons George impressed, fifty, sixty—and received at his camp not one in seven of them. He waited for the arrival of others that had been requisitioned, and when they did not arrive, he impressed still more. Days passed with an average of less than two wagons added to the park. Those that were placed at the disposal of the expedition had the poorest and oldest of the farmers' horses hitched to them. Subsequently George gave the Governor the precise figures: "Out of seventy-four wagons impressed at Winchester, we got but ten after waiting a week; and some of those so badly provided with teams that the soldiers were obliged to assist them up the hills, although it was known they had better teams at home. I doubt not that in some points I may have strained the law; but I hope, as my sole motive was to expedite the march, I shall be supported in it, should my authority be questioned, which at present I do not apprehend, unless some busybody intermeddles." [142]

When a week of fruitless impressment and argument had passed, George felt he no longer could wait, because all indications had been that the French would start early for the Ohio. The grumbling owners of Frederick wagons were left behind on or about the 18th of April.[143] Washington and his 159 men started westward across the mountain toward the South Branch of the Potomac. They now were beginning their seventeenth day on the road and they had behind them ninety-

---

141 There is no evidence, one way or the other, of participation by Lord Fairfax in the impressment.

142 Washington to Dinwiddie, Apr. 25, 1754; 1 *Ford*, 55, and wrongly dated April 15. Correctly dated in 1 *G. W.*, 40 ff.

143 This determination of date is based on the virtual certainty that Washington reached Winchester on the afternoon of April 10 and spent a week there, as stated in the quoted words of the preceding paragraph. Moreover, the infantry arrived at Pearsall's, about thirty-seven miles from Winchester, on the 20th. That advance would represent three days' march.

seven miles. This meant, in sum, that the delay of a week in Winchester, waiting for wagons, had cut their average daily march from eleven miles, the figure attained between Alexandria and Winchester, to less than six. Ahead were almost 200 miles to the junction of the Allegheny and the Monongahela.[144]

To make up for lost time, the movement of the three Companies and their twelve wagons must be expedited. The little column must press on to Wills Creek and there must organize immediately the proposed pack train to supplement or replace the wagons in the quickest possible march to the Monongahela. Time might be saved, also, if George rode ahead of the column to select camp sites and to survey crossings. Speed by those ignorant, leaden-footed soldiers and those dragging wagons might fix for the future the control of the great valley of the Mississippi by England or by France.

Toward that western country George rode over the North Mountain, which some of the natives called the Devil's Back Bone, and then he turned northward down the right bank of the Cacapon. He had crossed this river at Edwards' when he met a man who had ridden rapidly toward him with little equipage—an express.[145] This hurrying horseman brought from Captain Trent a number of letters that Washington unsealed and read eagerly. They were an appeal for reenforcement at the forks of the Ohio with all possible speed: eight hundred French troops were approaching, Trent wrote; he was expecting attack at any hour.[146]

Bad news—and worse prospect! If 800 French had been preparing to attack the English fort at the time the express had left there, how could the little British column arrive in time to save the place? George procured a messenger and sent him off promptly to convey Trent's dispatches to Colonel Fry, who presumably was in Alexandria.[147] Then George rode to Job Pearsall's on the South Branch to await there the

[144] Dalrymple computed the distance from Alexandria to the forks at 283 miles but he reckoned the distance between Alexandria and Winchester as eighty-six miles. Washington's route according to Braddock's *Orderly Book*, loc. cit., was eleven miles longer.

[145] Evidence that the meeting with the express was at Edwards' or nearby is to be found in Washington's entry in his expense account (Toner, *op. cit.*, 180): "To an express at Edwards, 7s 6d." As Washington did not pass Edwards' on any other occasion of proximate date, the identification is virtually certain. A first glance at the account might lead one to assume that the express was paid on April 10, but it is plain, on examination, that entries subsequent to the payment to Benjamin Hamilton are undated.

[146] 1 *Diaries*, 74.

[147] Dinwiddie, May, n.d., 1754, began a letter to Fry with the words: "You will allow me to be surprized, on receiving your letter dated at Alexandria on the 31st [sic] of April last, when I persuaded myself you must be near Wills's Creek" (1 *Din.*, 147).

arrival of the troops.[148] After they came on the 20th of April, he rode
down the South Branch, forded the Potomac and went once more to
Colonel Cresap's where, only a little more than six years before, he
first had witnessed an Indian dance.[149] On the way to Cresap's he heard
a report—unconfirmed but not improbable—that the unfinished fort at
the forks had been taken.

More trouble awaited George at Wills Creek.[150] When he inquired
for the pack animals that were to be used for a swift, light march
westward, he found that William Trent had failed completely to redeem
the promise to collect the horses. Not one was there. As far as George
could ascertain, none was on the road. The whole design of a rapid
advance had to be abandoned. Even a slow march with the wagons
had to be delayed because, if no pack animals were available, the twelve
wagons with the detachment would not suffice for a long journey to an
outpost where no supplies could be had from the countryside. The
only course open to George, now that Trent had failed him, was to
send back forty miles and impress or hire the few wagons owned by
pioneers on the South Branch of the Potomac.[151] Days inevitably would
be spent in doing this. Lack of transport might doom the expedition—
lack of transport due to lack of understanding of the time and effort
required to collect wagons from farmers!

Amid George's first grim reflections on this paralysis came the blackest news of all: The Ensign who had been in immediate command at
the mouth of the Monongahela rode up to Wills Creek on the 22nd and
reported that the fort had been captured. The French had won control
of the forks of the Ohio.[152] George had lost the race . . . almost before it had begun.

148 1 *Diaries*, 74.
149 See *supra*, p. 218.
150 He probably went up the left bank of the Potomac from Cresap's to Wills Creek on the
21st or 22nd to meet his troops who were advancing via the trail down Patterson Creek.
151 Washington to Dinwiddie, May 9, 1754; 1 *Ford*, 57–58.
152 1 *Diaries*, 75.

CHAPTER X

FIRST MILITARY SUCCESS
(April, 1754–May, 1754)

THE ENSIGN, Edward Ward, had a humiliating story to tell. He was
a Pennsylvanian and a brother-in-law of William Trent, for whom he
had been working when, in 1753, Trent had contracted to build a fort
for the Ohio Company. After the site for the fort had been shifted to
the mouth of the Monongahela, and Trent had been authorized by
Dinwiddie to enlist a Company of 100 men for the protection of the
artisans, Ward had been commissioned by Trent as Ensign. Washington's acquaintance John Frazier had been made Lieutenant. Ward
thereupon had been given direction of the forty-one men at the fort,
of whom only thirty-three were armed recruits. Trent had returned
to Wills Creek, ostensibly to get more provisions; Frazier had remained
all the while at his trading post and shop on Turtle Creek.[1]

On April 13, Ward had been shown a letter in which Washington's
previous interpreter, John Davison, had warned a trader, Robert Callender, that a large force of French would arrive at the forks by the 17th.
Ward on the 14th had sent a copy of Davison's letter to Captain Trent
at Wills Creek and had himself then hastened to Turtle Creek to consult Frazier. He found Frazier sure the report of the French was correct; "but," said he, "what can we do in the affair?" The most that
came out of the conference had been a decision to consult Half
King, who happened to be nearby with one of his Chiefs. Half King,
arriving promptly, had recommended that a stockade be built immediately at the forks. As this proposal seemed to be a sound one,
Ward had asked if Frazier would come down to the forks. The answer

---

[1] T. L. Rodgers in 4 *W. Va. His. Mag.*, 278 ff. There seems to have been some confusion
regarding the location of the fort that Trent first built. In *Penn. Gazette,* Apr. 4, 1754, is a
dispatch from Annapolis in which reference is made to letters Washington had received from
Trent and Gist. It is added that Trent had built a strong fort and a storehouse at the mouth of
Red Stone Creek, but no date is given. Later records indicate that the reference to the construction of a fort at that point was erroneous. Trent had erected storehouses but, apparently,
no fort.

admitted of no further argument: He had, said Frazier, a shilling to lose for every penny he had to gain by his commission at that time. Besides, he was engaged in a business transaction with his partner and could not finish it under six days. Frazier had not been violating the terms of his commission in saying this, because he had accepted his lieutenancy with the understanding that he would not reside at the fort, or visit it more frequently than once a week, or when he thought necessary.[2] He distinctly and prudentially had not thought it necessary to go there at the time of Ward's summons.

This indifference had angered Ward. If he could get no assistance from Frazier he would go back to the mouth of the river and erect a stockade with such help as he could muster there. He would hold that fort to the last extremity, Ward had vowed, rather than let it be recorded that the English had retreated before the French so much as arrived at the forks. The Indians no less than the French had been in Ward's mind when he spoke. He told himself that if he left the site, as his Captain and his Lieutenant already had, the savages thereafter would have no respect for the English.

Half King had approved what Ward had said and had agreed to go back with him to the forks. As soon as they had arrived, they had put all hands to work cutting timber and building a stockade. Half King himself laid the first log; the soldiers and the Indians had worked as never they had. In less than two days they had set all the uprights and, on the 17th, they were completing the last gate when, true to Davison's warning, the French had appeared. From Shannopin's Town a flotilla of canoes had been paddled almost to the fort. Soldiers who had come ashore had formed a line and had advanced to a point just out of range, where they had sounded a parley. Ward then had been told that he had an hour in which to surrender or face bombardment. At the suggestion of Half King, who doubtless took his lesson from what Joincare had said the previous winter, Ward had replied that he was not of a rank that gave him authority to answer such a demand. He asked permission to forward it to his superior officer. The French would have none of this: Ward must surrender instantly and, if he did so, he and his men could leave with all their arms, tools and belongings. Otherwise, the French would take the stockade and let the English take the consequences.

As the Ensign estimated that the French had about 1000 men in front

[2] Washington to Dinwiddie, June 12, 1754; 1 *G. W.*, 80.

of his forty-one, he had to accept these terms. On the morning of the 18th, he and Half King and all the Indians and whites had marched out. The savage Chief had been as defiant of the French as ever. When he passed them, he shouted that he had ordered the fort built and had laid the first log of it.

Ward related all this to Colonel Washington, and added that an Englishman who had attended the French commandant had given him an estimate of the strength of the expedition. The French were said to have 300 wooden canoes and sixty batteaux. Each of these boats carried four men. Eighteen cannon, including three nine-pounders, had been brought along.[3]

More tangible were two documents Ward handed George. One was the written summons the French commander had served on the Ensign. This paper asserted that the English schemes for occupying the Ohio were contrived by a Company "that has the interest of trade in mind more than to maintain the union and harmony existing between the Crowns of Great Britain and France." Ward was notified that, if he came by orders, he must withdraw under penalty of being driven off. If the purpose of the expedition at the forks was to trade, then he and his men would be seized and their property confiscated. Ward's other document, brought by two of Half King's young men, consisted of a speech by the Chief to be sent the Governors of Virginia and Pennsylvania, and another speech, intended for George. The address to the Governors was an exhortation "to have good courage and come as soon as possible; you will find us as ready to fight [the French] as you are yourselves." Half King concluded: "If you do not come to our assistance now, we are entirely undone, and I think we shall never meet together again. I speak with a heart full of grief." The Chief's message to George was an assurance of willingness to go in person, if need be, to the Governors.[4]

A grim budget of news this was—the forks of the Ohio lost, a French force estimated at more than 1000 men there to defy the 159 under Washington, the Indians clamoring for reinforcements, of whom only

[3] Ward's deposition of May 7, 1754, before the Governor and Council of Virginia, *Darlington*, 275 ff, after the original in P.R.O. There is every reason to believe this substantially the account given George by Ward. A summary of the deposition and of later news appeared in *Penn. Gazette*, May 9, 1754 and in the *Md. Gazette*, May 25, 1754. Dinwiddie's dispatch of May 16, 1754, to Holderness is in 165 *Newcastle Papers*, 221, P.R.O. In the Archives du Seminaire in Quebec is the MS report of a spy, de Simblin, who was sent in March, 1754, to ascertain what the British were doing at the forks of the Ohio. He heard various rumors that were circulating among the Indians but he discovered nothing of importance.
[4] 1 *Diaries*, 75; also conveniently in 1 *Ford*, 48.

a few weak Companies were within marching distance. Short of the defection of the Five Nations and the destruction of the little force at Wills Creek, the situation was about as bad as it could be, but it did not appall the young commander. He felt, instead, what he termed a "glowing zeal." [5] When he had learned all the Ensign had to tell, he called together his officers and discussed with them Ward's report and the new information concerning the strength of the French. The designs of the invaders, being set forth clearly in the summons, did not seem to George or to his companions to call for review. All the officers were agreed, too, that it would be foolish to march to the forks without reenforcement.

Beyond that, George's mind and his military inexperience would not yield to odds or circumstance. The Indians needed help and asked it in a spirit of loyalty that made George doubly anxious to extend it.[6] Besides, to withhold aid would be to lose the savages' support. Even with the insignificant force he had, George felt that he must advance as far as he could and must hold an advanced position from which the column, when reenforced, would proceed to the forks, recover the fort and drive the French away. That was the aim of the expedition and it was to be held inflexibly. What should be done, must be done.

When the young Virginian had reached this conclusion, his knowledge of the country shaped his action. He twice had covered all the cruel miles between Wills Creek and the forks of the Ohio and he remembered the strong points. The best station at which to hold his detachment until reenforcements arrived in sufficient number to justify an offensive was, he thought, a place he had not visited, the junction of Red Stone Creek with the Monongahela, thirty-seven miles above the forks. From the direction of George's approach, Red Stone Creek lay beyond the steep and formidable Chestnut Ridge, but it was the nearest place of importance on the Monongahela. From that point, it would be possible to send the artillery and the heavy supplies by water to the mouth of the river. At Red Stone Creek, moreover, storehouses already had been erected by the Ohio Company. These could be utilized to protect the ammunition and the men. In order to reach Red Stone Creek with the heavy guns and the wagons, it would be necessary to widen the trail into a road, but this could be done with the men

---

[5] Washington to Governor Sharpe, April 24, 1754; 1 G. W., 43–44.

[6] Cf. Washington to Governor Sharpe, April 27, 1754: ". . . Therefore I am persuaded you will take proper notice of the Indians' moving speech and [will] think their unshaken fidelity worthy of your consideration" (1 G. W., 43).

George had.[7] Meanwhile, of course, Dinwiddie and the Governors of Pennsylvania and Maryland must be informed of what had occurred in the hope they would send troops in large number and with least delay. His Honor of Virginia, in particular, must provide boats for navigating the Monongahela and must execute his favorite plan of bringing to the Ohio the Southern Indians who had offered their help.

After announcing his decision to his little council of war, George proceeded energetically to put it into execution. In doing this, he momentarily disregarded his own superior, Col. Joshua Fry. Notice of the danger on the Ohio had been sent Fry as soon as Washington had received Trent's first call for help.[8] After that, in the emergency, George acted on his own initiative. Critics were to say that he did this, and did it recklessly, because he was ambitious to have the credit of a bold achievement.[9] Whether or not there was any justification for this charge, George went still further in independent action and wrote directly to Governor Hamilton of Pennsylvania and to Governor Sharpe of Maryland in order to save the time that would be lost in communicating with them through Governor Dinwiddie. As promptly as practicable, Ward and one of the Indians were started for Williamsburg with Half King's speech and a letter from Washington to the Governor. To facilitate Ward's long ride, George hired one of his own horses, saddled and bridled, to the Ensign.[10]

With some difficulty Washington prevailed on the other young Indian, who had come with Ward from Half King, to return to the Chief and to carry a speech that George most carefully prepared. "This young man," Washington wrote, "will inform you where he found a small part of our army, making towards you, clearing the roads for a great number of our warriors, who are ready to follow us, with our great guns, our ammunition and provisions." George added a request that Half King or another designated Chief or both of them "should come as soon as possible to meet us on the road, and to assist us in council." This George signed with his own name and with the Indian title "Conoto carious" that had been given him the previous winter by Half King.[11]

[7] Washington's reasoning on this, his first strategical problem, is given fully in his journal, 1 *Diaries*, 77, and in his letter of April 23/24 to Governor Dinwiddie, *ibid.*, 77–78. For the storehouses at Red Stone Creek, see *Penn. Gazette*, Apr. 4, 1754.

[8] See *supra*, p. 355.   [9] See *infra*, p. 415.

[10] The bridle and saddle were lost. George's charge, including these items, was £2, 10s. See Toner, ed., *op. cit.*, 181.

[11] See *supra*, p. 317. The speech to Half King is in 1 *Diaries*, 77. Washington's letter to Governor Sharpe is to be found in 1 *G. W.* 43; that to Hamilton, of similar import, appeared in 2 *Sparks*, 11–13. The Indian name of Washington is spelled Caunotaucarius in 29 *G. W.*, 37.

Interrogating Ward, holding the council of war, preparing the speech to Half King, starting work on the road,[12] writing to the three Governors, and getting the messengers on the way to Williamsburg took five days.[13] The time was long, but more decisions of larger importance had to be made during that time than ever the twenty-two-year-old Virginian had faced in a similar span of days. As if stimulated by his difficulties, he continued in a certain exaltation of mind. For the first time he wrote emotionally, with warmth and freedom, of the manner in which loyalty to King and the self-interest of colonists were part of the same fabric of duty: ". . . I know," he told Governor Sharpe, "you are solicitous for the public weal and warm in this interesting cause, that should rouse from the lethargy we have fallen into, the heroic spirit of every free-born English man to attest the rights and privileges of our King (if we don't consult the benefit of ourselves) and rescue from the invasions of a usurping enemy, our Majesty's property, his dignity and land." [14]

It was earnestly if awkwardly expressed, but for the time it was in in vain. Washington's troubles multiplied. First had come the disappointment over transportation and Trent's failure to provide pack horses. Next was the staggering news that the forks of the Ohio had been seized by a vastly superior force of French. Now there drifted back to Wills Creek the men whom Ward had led out of the stockade and then had left on the trail while he hurried to report. It developed that Trent had enlisted these men, approximately forty of them, as militia, not as volunteers, though Dinwiddie had intended some of them, at least, to be volunteers.[15] Trent, moreover, had promised the recruits 2s a day, though the allowance made the troop under Washington was 8d daily.[16] The idle hands of these men from the Ohio, Washington wished to put to work on the road, along with those of his own detachment; but when he undertook to have them do this, Trent's soldiers insisted that they be paid at the rate originally allowed them. George could not do this, of course, without demoralizing his own in-

---

[12] 1 *Ford*, 58.

[13] That is, from Ward's interrogation on the 23rd to the date of the letters to Sharpe and Hamilton, Apr. 27, 1754.

[14] Washington to Sharpe, Apr. 27, 1754; 1 *G. W.*, 44.

[15] The inference from all that Dinwiddie wrote of Trent's Company is that he looked on the men as volunteers, but this was not set forth explicitly in the instructions and commission sent Trent. Cf. 1 *Din.*, 55–56 and *supra*, p. 329. Washington was under the impression that Governor Dinwiddie had directed that the men be enlisted as militia (1 *Diaries*, 79).

[16] 1 *Diaries*, 79. For the pay of Washington's men, who victualled at public expense, see Dinwiddie to Governor De Lancey, Mch. 21, 1754, and *supra*, p. 334, n. 49.

fantry, whose pay was set by his instructions at a third of the figure demanded by the men from the Ohio.

To make bad conditions worse, the newcomers to the camp were, in the main, hard adventurers, traders' helpers and the like, and they probably would have balked at nothing. George did not fear them but he could not reason with them. He compromised, at first, by saying he would await the Governor's instructions, which Ward would bring back from Williamsburg. Meantime, he realized that if Trent's men were correct in their contention that they were militiamen, he could not invoke martial law against them.[17] Postponement of the issue did not settle it. In a few days the defiant idlers around the camp became so much of a nuisance that George separated them from his troops and gave them orders to remain at Captain Trent's until the pleasure of the Governor was known. These orders the men promptly disobeyed and scattered to their own pursuits. George was more pleased to be rid of them than he was hurt by their defection.[18] The experience was disillusioning but instructive.

While Washington was dealing as best he could with these trouble-makers,[19] a number of wagons arrived from the South Branch of the Potomac and some of the cannon from Alexandria.[20] As soon as the vehicles could be loaded and the cannon put temporarily in a place of safety, Washington started the advance of his men from Wills Creek along the road which a detachment had been attempting since April 25 to put in order.[21]

Progress was hideously slow. Everywhere the trail had to be widened and repaired; at some points a new and less arduous route had to be found. Even when the wagons could be pulled over the steep road, George was not sure the artillery could be.[22] On the 1st of May he put all his men to work in an effort to make the stumpy ground as smooth as nature and implements permitted. Effort availed scarcely at all. Never was the column able to advance more than four miles a day. When conditions were at their worst, night found the wagons no farther

---

[17] The governing provisions of law for the punishment of recalcitrant militia are set forth in 5 H 18 and 91.

[18] 1 Ford, 59, 63.   [19] The date of their departure is not known.

[20] 1 Ford, 57. The cannon arrived April 28, and the wagons probably on the 29th, the fourth day, presumably, after Ward left for Williamsburg; but latitude of perhaps two days has to be allowed because of doubt concerning the date of the letter of April 23–25 to Dinwiddie. Several days may have been spent on the composition of this letter before it was entrusted to Ward, who reached Williamsburg on the 4th of May (1 Din., 148).

[21] 1 Washington to Dinwiddie, May 9, 1754; 1 Ford, 58.

[22] Ibid.

than two miles from their starting point.[23] The rains were almost incessant; every little stream, swollen far beyond its banks, was a barrier.[24] About twenty miles from Wills Creek, George and his men reached on May 7, a watercourse so deep that it was past fording, and, as it remained high, the troops had to spend more than two days bridging it.[25]

After the crossing, as the men chopped and tugged, one English trader after another would arrive at camp from the West with his skins and his goods. He would explain that he was fleeing from the French and he would have dark tales to tell of the strength of the force that had come down from Lake Erie. Eight hundred reenforcements, the merchants said, recently had reached the Ohio. Some of these dealers in fur merely repeated rumor that had been swollen by much telling; but one of them, Robert Callender, a man of intelligence, reached Washington's detachment on the 9th with exciting information of a nearer potential enemy: At Gist's new settlement, Callender had encountered a party of five French under Commissary La Force. The number was trifling; their proximity was suspicious. Ostensibly, they were searching for deserters; but actually, in Callender's opinion, they were reconnoitring and studying the country.

That news was enough to give a faster beat to any young officer's heart, especially when Callender had brought word that Half King had received George's speech and had found satisfaction in it. The Chief was marching with fifty men to join the English detachment, though the French, as always, were doing their utmost to win over the Indians.[26] On the strength of Callender's information, George determined to send out a party of twenty-five men under Captain Stephen on the 11th of May to reconnoitre and to meet Half King. This detachment was to ascertain, also, if it would be possible to move any supplies by water to the vicinity of Red Stone Creek. Pending Stephen's return, George again used the main body of his men on the improvement of the trail.[27]

There followed a week of rain and of conflicting and discouraging

[23] *Ibid.* For a description of the old road for a few miles West of Cumberland or Wills Creek, see *Lowdermilk,* 51–52.
[24] 29 *G. W.,* 38.
[25] 1 *Ford,* 58. The distance from "New Store" on Wills Creek suggests that this stream was an upper stretch of Casselman's River.
[26] 1 *Ford,* 58–59.
[27] 1 *Diaries,* 80. Captain Stephen (*loc. cit.*) stated that his mission was to apprehend the French detachment, but Washington's account indicates that he directed Stephen to retire if the English met this party of French. In event the English came upon a Frenchman separated from his companions, they were to seize him and bring him in for questioning.

reports, brightened by dispatches from Williamsburg. An express brought letters in which George was informed that Colonel Fry had reached Winchester with more than 100 men and soon would march to join the advanced contingent. Fry had been delayed, as Washington had been, by lack of transport. He had been compelled, at last, to leave Alexandria with a train that would have made regulars roar with laughter—five wagons and a cart. These vehicles were all he had been able to hire or impress, though, in the hope of procuring others, he had left a few men in the town.[28] Better perhaps than anyone else, Washington understood what Fry had been called upon to endure, and he felt relief that the Colonel had been able to advance even to Winchester.

Other troops, George learned, were coming, too. North Carolina was to send 350 men; Maryland was to supply 200; although Pennsylvania would furnish no soldiers, she would contribute £10,000; from New England, Governor Shirley was to march 600 troops to harass the French in Canada. When George read this he had not learned how readily hopes and half-promises were accepted as assurances and guarantees. He took all the reports at face value and rejoiced, in particular, over the prospect of a demonstration against Canada. "I hope," he confided in his journal, "that will give [the French] some work to do, and will moderate their zeal in sending so many men to the Ohio . . ."[29]

This warming hope was chilled on the 16th of May by two more traders who were returning to the settlements to escape French parties that had been seen in the district beyond Gist's. These traders, knowing Chestnut Ridge,[30] were surprised to find George trying to clear a road across it to Red Stone Creek. It could not be done, they said. Other traders previously had spoken in much the same strain, but the young Virginian had disregarded their predictions of failure. Now George began to study in more detail the practicability of a water route. He had reached the swollen great crossing of the Youghiogheny,[31] which ran northwestward through Laurel Hill, thence across Great Meadows and through Chestnut Ridge to the junction with the Monongahela South of Turtle Creek. Might it not be feasible, as most of the traders

[28] He began his march, almost certainly, on May 1 and attributed his delay entirely to "the want of carriages" (5 E. J., 468).

[29] 1 *Diaries*, 81. [30] *Ibid.*

[31] Near Somerfield, Penn., see *supra*, p. 284. A "great crossing" was a principal or a generally used ford or ferry. On a long river there might be several "great crossings" which easily become confused in a narrative.

affirmed, to send the heavy supplies down the Youghiogheny to the falls [32] of the Ohio or to a point opposite Red Stone Creek?

George resolved that he would find out and, to do so, he procured a canoe and made plans for building others; but before he could act, Ensign Ward came back to camp on the 17th with a letter from Governor Dinwiddie and with much gossip from Williamsburg.

The letter [33] told of the arrival in Virginia of the Independent Company from South Carolina and of the expectation that the two similar Companies from New York would reach Virginia waters within about ten days. These Companies, as George knew, were part of the British military establishment and were commanded by regular officers who held the direct commission of the King. The adjective "independent" was used to describe them because they were not attached to any Regiment. Besides these regulars, the North Carolina contingent was believed to be on the march. In acquainting George with this information the Governor wrote that the Council approved of George's caution in planning to halt at Red Stone Creek until reenforcements arrived.[34] As for Captain Trent and Lieutenant Frazier, said Dinwiddie, they should be court-martialed for quitting the forks of the Ohio without leave. Somewhat deliberately in this same letter, George and the other Virginia officers were admonished not to let "some punctillios about command" interfere with the expedition.

Ward probably supplemented this with news that a committee controlling pay of the officers and men had limited to £1, 6s the allowance for enlisting each soldier, and had not raised the scale of compensation of officers or added to the ration previously allowed, which merely was that of the private soldier.[35] This had been a sore subject with the

[32] Washington to Dinwiddie, May 18, 1754; 1 G. W., 47–48.

[33] May 4, 1754; 1 Din., 149.

[34] The Council's action, May 4, 1754, is recorded in 5 E. J., 468–69.

[35] It may have been that this information previously had reached the officers of the expedition, but action so soon after Ward's arrival indicates that he conveyed verbally, or brought some letter containing, information of the committee's failure to change pay or to enlarge rations. The incident, which is obscure in Washington's and in Dinwiddie's letters, is not clarified by the publication of the Executive Journal of the Council for the spring of 1754. No mention of these matters appears there, but in 1 Hamilton, 28, there are summary "Minutes of Council," Feb. 23, Apr. 27 and July 18, 1754. The Executive Journal does not show the Council to have been in session February 23 or April 27. It follows that the Executive Journal either is incomplete, or else the summary minutes are not of the Council but of the committee named in the act (6 H 418) for raising and expanding the £10,000. Further, in Charles Carter's letter of June 5, 1754, in 1 Hamilton, 2–3, reference is made to "some late resolve of the committee," which certainly is the "resolve" in question. Carter added: "While I was at the committee, I can aver there was the greatest readiness to promote and encourage the officers and men . . ." Reference to the act shows that Carter was one of the members named to supervise expenditures. It consequently would seem probable, but it cannot be stated positively, that a subcommittee of this special committee of ten Burgesses and four Councillors was the one against which George and his brother officers directed their verbal fire in the manner presently to be described in the text.

other officers, as it had been with George at the time he had threatened
to resign.[36] Now the officers knew they were to have no allowance to
supplement their ration. They learned, too, that they soon would be
serving with Captains, Lieutenants and Ensigns of Independent Companies who would be receiving higher pay. This prospect combined
with hard work, wet weather and poor fare to produce near-mutiny
among the Virginia officers. For the time they forgot the French, the
ridge, the road, and, under the chairmanship of Captain Stephen, they
drafted a formal protest to the Governor. They asserted, as George had,
that their pay was discriminatory; they complained that they had been
compelled to recruit virtually at their own expense; they denounced
committee action that gave them no subsistence beyond that of the
private soldier; and, reviewing their hardships, they concluded with at
least a threat of resignation en masse. This remarkable document they
duly signed and brought to George for transmission to the Governor.[37]

His officers' written protest confronted the inexperienced young
Lieutenant Colonel with a dilemma. If he considered at all the possibility of refusing to accept the paper on the ground that it was in-
subordinate, he put that idea aside, perhaps with the reflection that
officers had a right to present their grievances through channels. Besides, he regarded the protest as just, and he noted that in one respect—
a stupid and stinting limitation on the number of non-commissioned
officers—the Virginia committee was guilty of a blunder the officers had
not pointed out. George felt the sting of poor pay as sharply as they
did, but resignation was a different matter. He did not want to leave
the expedition or to lose his commission. Much as he missed good
food and the comfort of a dry bed and clean sheets, he was loving more
and more the distinction and honor of a soldier's life. Although he
would not fail to stand his ground against discrimination, he wished
to do this in a manner that would not jeopardize his continuance as a
Lieutenant Colonel.

Reflection suggested a means of achieving both ends. On the 18th
of May, while the rain kept the streams high and made road-building
impossible, George sat down and wrote the Governor a letter that was
at once boyish, wrathful and shrewd. He confessed his sympathy with
the protest, which he doubtless enclosed, and he went on to explain
that the officers would have resigned their commissions had they not

[36] See *supra*, p. 341.
[37] The text of the protest has been lost, but its content can be reconstructed easily, point by
point, from Dinwiddie to Washington, May 25, 1754; 1 *Din.*, 172–73.

felt themselves obligated by the nearness of danger to remain on duty till their successors were at hand.

Then George deliberately began a new paragraph to distinguish their intentions from his own: "Giving up my commission is quite contrary to my intention. Nay, I ask it as a greater favor, than any amongst the many I have received from your Honor, to confirm it to me. But let me serve voluntarily; then I will, with the greatest pleasure in life, devote my services to the expedition without any other reward than the satisfaction of serving my country; but to be slaving dangerously for the shadow of pay, through woods, rocks, mountains—I would rather prefer the great toil of a day laborer, and dig for a maintenance, provided I were reduced to the necessity, than serve upon such ignoble terms; for I really do not see why the lives of his Majesty's subjects in Virginia should be of less value than of those in other parts of his American dominions, especially when it is well known that we must undergo double their hardship."

George elaborated all this, pointed out the impossibility of operating with the few non-commissioned officers allowed each Company, and then he resumed: "Upon the whole, I find so many clogs upon the expedition that I quite despair of success; nevertheless, I humbly beg it, as a particular favor, that your Honor will continue me in the post I now employ, the duty whereof I will most cheerfully execute as a volunteer, but by no means upon the present pay. I hope what I have said will not be taken amiss; for I really believe, were it as much in your power as it is your inclination, we should be treated as gentlemen and officers, and not have annexed to the most trifling pay that ever was given to English officers, the glorious allowance of soldier's diet— a pound of pork, with bread in proportion, every day. Be the consequence what it will, I am determined not to leave the Regiment, but to be amongst the last men that quit the Ohio, even if I serve as a private volunteer, which I greatly prefer to the establishment we are now upon." [38]

This letter George dispatched to the Governor. He was angry; he was resolved. Whether Dinwiddie confirmed him in his commission or relieved him and sent out an entirely new group of officers, he would remain, but he would not accept pay lower than that of British officers of corresponding rank.

This did not entirely dispose of the business created by Ward's return.

[38] Washington to Dinwiddie, May 18, 1754; 1 G. W., 49–51.

The Ensign brought, also, a message from Dinwiddie to Half King, whom the Governor was anxious to have with him at the conference soon to be held in Winchester. George decided to notify Half King by the Indian messenger who had accompanied Ward to Williamsburg, but George did not forward the message itself. He reasoned that Half King and the other Chiefs, possessing full measure of Indian curiosity, would proceed more quickly if informed that a speech from the Governor was at the headquarters of the English. Then, when Half King arrived, George hoped to prevail on him to go to Winchester.[39]

Speed in all this seemed the more imperative, in spite of high water, because two friendly Indians who came to camp now reported that French on reconnaissance had been within six or seven miles of the English force five days previously. George did not know, as yet, whether Stephen and his party had captured these scouts, but George continued to hope he himself would be able to bag some of the French. To do this he would need the assistance of Half King, and he consequently took much pains with the "speech" of invitation to the Chiefs.

When this was written acceptably and was dispatched by the Indian messenger,[40] George completed his preparations to explore the Youghiogheny. On the morning of May 20, as he was making ready to start, he observed that the river had fallen far enough for the troops to get across. He consequently ordered them to ford the stream and to proceed along the trail as far as they could in the direction of Red Stone Creek so that, if he found the Youghiogheny impassable for transportation of supplies by water, the column would not have lost the time he would have spent on the river.[41]

This done, George set out downstream in a canoe on the morning of May 20, with a Lieutenant, three soldiers and an Indian guide. Before they had gone more than about half a mile, circumstance compelled them to go ashore where, luckily, they met a trader who professed to know the Youghiogheny. He discouraged George's attempt to descend it. Washington accepted this counsel to the extent that he changed a plan he had conceived of building canoes,[42] but, as always, having resolved to go on, he went. By wading and canoeing and con-

---

39 Washington to Dinwiddie, May 18, 1754; 1 G. W., 47, a letter not to be confused with the one of the same date, quoted *supra*.

40 1 *Diaries*, 82.

41 Washington to Joshua Fry, May 23, 1754; 1 G. W., 52.

42 See *supra*, p. 360.

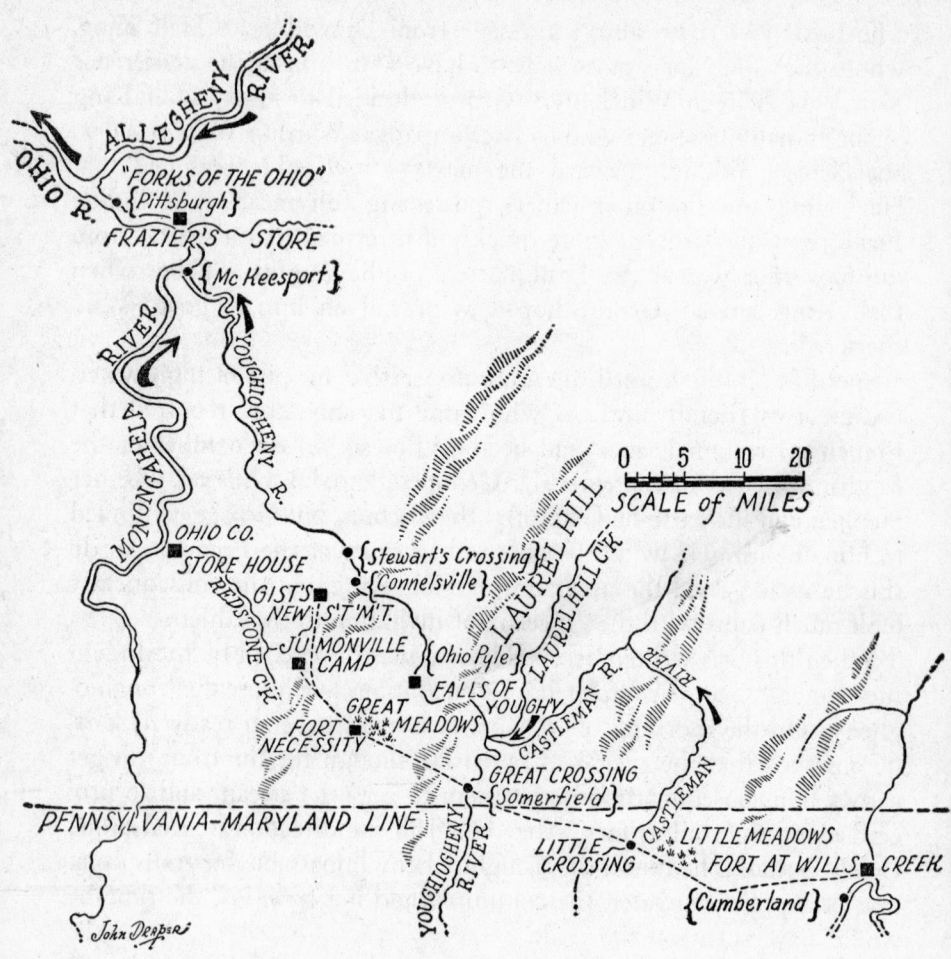

THE REGION OF WASHINGTON'S "CAMPAIGN OF 1754"

In his attempt to establish an advance base for operations to recover the "forks of the Ohio," Washington in 1754 retraced his route of 1753 as far as Gist's New Settlement. Andrew Lewis went farther westward to some undetermined point on Red Stone Creek. News of the approach of the French in superior numbers compelled Washington to withdraw to the Great Meadows.

structing a raft,[43] the party proceeded approximately ten miles to the point where Laurel Hill Creek and Casselman's River empty into the Youghiogheny.[44] There the Indian guide balked. George argued but the savage would not go farther.

[43] The retranslated English word is "boat," but Washington's journal shows that the time spent at the task would have sufficed only for the building of a raft.

[44] Near the town of Confluence. These ten miles of the Youghiogheny follow a bewildering, contradictory course and, on one stretch or another, flow in every direction except due South.

Fortunately, by this stage of his adventure, George knew that white men usually could break down Indians' resistance by making gifts; but, being thrifty, he did not commit himself lavishly in advance. He negotiated and, after a time, struck a bargain whereby the Indian agreed to remain with the party in return for a ruffled shirt and a match coat. It was possible, no doubt, for George to provide the match coat from the supplies of the expedition, but the only way to furnish the savage with the shirt was to take it, on return to camp, from the meagre personal stock the young Lieutenant Colonel had brought from Wills Creek when he deliberately had lightened his baggage to speed the march. Discommoding the Virginia officer was no bar to the sartorial ambitions of the Indian. He explained only that the French always paid well for service and therefore had guides in the woods. George was reenforced, by this remark, in a conviction he already had formed —that presents for the Indians, especially clothing and wampum, should be sent to his headquarters. Four or five hundred pounds' worth of goods, he told himself, would accomplish more on the frontier than as many thousand pounds of presents delivered in bulk when a treaty was made.[45]

Attended again by the Indian who soon was to be adorned with a ruffled shirt, George and his companions established their bivouac for the night. On the whole, as he reviewed the day's experiences, George was of opinion that if the water did not fall below the level then prevailing, the greater part of the river would afford passage for canoes. In this hopeful spirit he examined the ground at the forks the next morning and decided it was so admirable a site for a fort that he proceeded forthwith to draw a sketch of a proper structure on the most advantageous ground. Although the fort might never be constructed, his innate carefulness and his acquired precision as a surveyor prompted him to make his plan as accurate as he could without instruments.[46] The sketch completed, he went on down the river with his party until, as he subsequently wrote, "we came to a fall, which continued rough, rocky and scarcely passable, for two miles, and then fell, within the space of fifty yards, nearly forty feet perpendicular." [47] Hope of using a waterline ended at that cliff.

45 Washington to Joshua Fry, May 23, 1754; 1 G. W., 52–53. The day's adventures are recorded in 1 Diaries, 83.   46 1 Diaries, 83.

47 Washington to Joshua Fry, May 23, 1754; 1 G. W., 52. Cf. 1 Diaries, 52. These must have been the Ohio-Pyle Falls of the Youghiogheny, about eight and a half miles Northwest of Confluence.

There was nothing to do, of course, except to go ashore, rest, and then start back to rejoin the column in the knowledge that another defeat had been sustained. First had been the failure of transport, then Ward's news of the loss of the fort on the Ohio, then bad weather, swollen streams, wilderness that would not yield to road-making, a government that did not seem to know how to treat "gentlemen and officers"—and now a natural barrier that denied the little expedition a speedier passage to Red Stone Creek!

On the 23rd, George returned to his starting point, the Great Crossing of the Youghiogheny, whence he had sent his troops forward so that no time would be lost in the advance to Red Stone. At the crossing, Washington met Capt. Adam Stephen and the party of twenty-five who had been scouting for almost two weeks.

Stephen had a strange report to make. By building rafts and by killing game for food, the Captain and his men had reached the Monongahela not far from Red Stone Creek, and there they had met Indian traders whom the French had permitted to return toward the English settlements. All that these men could tell Stephen was that some French soldiers under a young officer styled Jumonville had been reconnoitring along the Monongahela, but, because of unfavorable weather, had gone back the previous day to the fort at the forks of the Ohio, Fort DuQuesne as it now was styled.

This negative intelligence was so unenlightening that Stephen had not been willing to accept it as the best that could be had. By promising a hanger-on £5, Stephen prevailed on him to go down the Monongahela and to spy on the French. Within five days, the man was back with—to quote Stephen—"the most satisfactory and accurate account of everything at Fort DuQuesne, the number of French at that post, the number employed daily on the works, the number sick in the hospital and what accidents had happened since their arrival at that place, the dimensions of the fort, the breadth and depth of the ditch, the thickness of the ramparts, in what places it was stockaded with only the length of the stockades." [48] The spy's report, indeed, was entirely too good. If it was authentic, it could only have been procured, Stephen reasoned, by giving the French full information about the English reconnoitring party. In other words, the spy might be a double traitor who was working for both sides. Fearful of this, Stephen prudently had

[48] *Stephen's "Life," Rush Papers.*

concluded that the best thing he could do at the moment was to rejoin the main force. So—there he was.[49]

In a sense, this was still another reverse for George: Twenty-six men had been out for twelve days and had learned scarcely anything except that a spy might be a traitor! Without further waste of time or words, George swallowed his disappointment and set out from the crossing to catch up with the main party on the road over Laurel Hill. He found that the badness of the road, as usual, had delayed the march,[50] but the next day he had better luck in one particular: some small information of a reliable, if not of a precise character began to arrive from the country ahead. The Indian previously sent to Half King returned with a companion who had a message from the Sachem. As written in English by John Davison, this read as follows:

"To the forist, His Majesties Commander Offiverses to hom this meay concern: On acc't of a freench armey to meat Miger Georg Wassiontton therefore my Brotheres I deesir you to be awar of them for deisin'd to strik ye forist English they see ten days since they marchd I cannot tell what nomber the half-King and the rest of the Chiefs will be with you in five days to consel, no more at present but give my serves to my Brothers the English

"The Half King

"John Davison." [51]

This was a clear warning and at the same time a definite encouragement: If the French in undetermined number were advancing to fight, Half King was coming to counsel. Besides this, little that was specific could be learned from the Indians who brought the letter. They said that parties frequently were in the woods but that they did not know of any considerable number moving in the direction of the English.[52]

[49] Ibid.
[50] Washington to Joshua Fry, May 23, 1754; 1 G. W., 52. For a contemporary description of the approaches and the difficult crossing of Laurel Hill, see Lewis Evans's analysis of his map in L. H. Gipson, Lewis Evans, 167, 190.
[51] Washington copied this literatim in his letter to Dinwiddie, May 27, 1754; 1 G. W., 53–54. The translator manifestly had difficulty in turning Davison's bizarre Irish-English into idiomatic French, and in the process he probably misinterpreted or misplaced the unpunctuated clause "I cannot tell what nomber." It seems reasonable to accept this as a reference to the reconnoitring French, rather than to Half King and his Chiefs.
[52] 1 Diaries, 84–85. Although it is most unsatisfactory to be unable to say whether these "parties" were French or Indian, the doubt cannot be resolved. The antecedent of "parties" in Washington's journal undeniably is "Indians," but the general tone of his references to the approach of Half King does not indicate that Washington expected any large reenforcement of Indians and certainly no more than the fifty mentioned in Robert Callender's report of May 9, in 1 G. W., 46. Washington understood, also, by May 27, or earlier, that Half King "purposed to settle his people to planting" (1 G. W., 57) before joining the English. The dispatches of Washington suggest that his particular reason for desiring the presence of Half King and the

The two Indians' knowledge of the situation at the French fort was somewhat more detailed, but not of immediate bearing on George's situation. From other passers-by George had heard a vague report of the departure of 50 per cent of the French garrison on some secret mission. He thought this rumor improbable, but he awaited further details.[53]

Later in the day of the 24th, after the column had reached the Great Meadows between Laurel Hill and Chestnut Ridge, there came news more detailed and exciting. An Indian trader arrived from Gist's new settlement and reported that he had seen two Frenchmen there the previous day. He was certain that a strong hostile detachment was on the march.[54] This information appealed to George as accurate and, if accurate, as calling for immediate defensive preparation. He sought out favorable ground in the Meadows and at length found two gulleys that were close together and, to his inexperienced eye, adequate as natural trenches. These he promptly manned and then he placed his wagons between them.[55]

An anxious night passed without incident. The next morning, May 25, the young commander felt the soldier's habitual campaign need of further information concerning the enemy. To get it quickly, he decided to utilize his wagon horses, which would not be needed at their normal task so long as the column remained behind the "natural entrenchments."[56] Without saddles, some of the men rode off in small reconnaissance parties to get a glimpse, if possible, of the French. George sent out other detachments on foot to scour the woods. Soldiers not required for either of these purposes George employed to cut down the bushes and other undergrowth around his camp in order to open an unobstructed field of fire. As the untrained commander of 22 went about these and the other preliminaries of what promised to be his first field engagement, his spirits rose. When all the bushes had been cleared away, George felt that he had, as he phrased it, "a charming field for an encounter."[57]

other Sachems was to get their counsel and information about the French, and then to have the natives go on to Winchester for the conference with Governor Dinwiddie.

53 Washington to Joshua Fry, May 23, 1754; 1 G. W., 52.

54 1 Diaries, 85. This probably is the same report as that mentioned in Washington to Dinwiddie, May 27, 1754 (1 G. W., 54) to the effect that the French were at the crossing of the Youghiogheny, distant about eighteen miles. This crossing evidently was the one on the trail from Fort DuQuesne to Gist's new settlement, via Frazier's; see supra, p. 285.

55 1 Diaries, 85.

56 Ibid.

57 Washington to Dinwiddie, May 27, 1754; 1 G. W., 54.

The reconnaissance was negative. As the scouts came back, one group after another, they had to confess they had found no indication of the presence of the French. A like report was made by parties that returned on the 26th after almost two days in the woods. Although some of these mounted scouts had penetrated close to the district where the French were supposed to be, not one armed white man of alien tongue had been seen.[58]

At the camp, all was quiet until the night of the 26th–27th. Then, about 2 A.M., a sentry sounded an alarm. Soon he and others fired their pieces. The whole force was aroused and put under arms. Discovery then was made that six men were missing in circumstances that indicated desertion. As soon as George learned of this, he reasoned that the deserters might have been responsible for the noise that provoked the sentry's challenge; but it was almost sunrise of the 27th when he felt safe in dismissing the troops who had been waiting with weapons in hand.[59]

Morning brought the most explicit information George had received of the movements of the French. Christopher Gist rode into camp and, after greeting his companion of the mission to Fort Le Boeuf, described how the previous noon Commissary La Force and fifty soldiers had come to the new settlement, which he had left in the charge of two Indians. The French were in ugly mood. They made ready to kill Gist's cow and they threatened to break up all his belongings, but the Indians pleaded so hard that the French forbore. Gist then hurried off to warn Washington.[60] En route, about five miles from camp, Gist found the tracks of numerous white men whom he took to be those who had been at his place on the 26th.[61] The canoes of this advance party, Gist had learned, were at Red Stone Creek.[62]

If the Frenchmen were far from their landing place, and close to his camp, George thought he had an excellent chance of cutting them off. Almost immediately after Gist had finished his story, Washington called Capt. Peter Hog, told him the news, and directed him to take seventy-five men and find the French.[63] When Hog got his soldiers

[58] In his journal (1 *Diaries*, 85), Washington wrote as if all the parties came back on the 25th, but in his letter of May 27, 1754, to Dinwiddie (1 *G. W.*, 54), he spoke of "those who returned yesterday without seeing anything" of the French.

[59] Washington to Dinwiddie, May 27, 1754; 1 *G. W.*, 54.

[60] Although it nowhere is so stated, Gist probably was in hiding near his new settlement while La Force was there. [61] 1 *Diaries*, 86; 1 *G. W.*, 54.

[62] 1 *G. W.*, 54. Washington did not report that this information about the canoes came from Gist, but he scarcely could have learned it on the 27th from any other source.

[63] *Ibid.*

ready and marched away with them, there remained in the camp only
a few more troops than the Captain took into the woods. If George's
military reading had carried him at that time to the doctrine of the con-
centration of force, he did not think it was involved. Opportunity was
offered; he would seize it. Besides, his judgment led him to believe
the French were not as numerous as they were supposed to be.[64] Instead of wondering whether he had been guilty of a dangerous division
of his few men, George fixed his thought on writing quickly a letter to
Dinwiddie, whom Gist was going to Winchester to advise during the
expected conference with the Indians.

In writing the Governor, George described briefly the message from
Half King, the alarm of the previous night and the dispatch of Hog
after the French. Gist, said Washington, had been an eyewitness of
part of what had happened and would be able to supply details. Then
George reverted to the subject that had distressed him when he had
been compelled to promise the Indian guide a ruffled shirt in order to
get the savage to continue down the river. In a careful paragraph
Washington explained that the Indians had to be paid for their services
and that the wares they liked most should be sent out for that purpose.
He repeated what he already had written Fry—that a few hundred
pounds' worth of goods sent to him "would tend more to our interest
than so many thousands given in a lump at a treaty." Then George
added seriously: "I have been obliged to pay shirts [65] for what [the
Indians] have already done, which I cannot continue to do." [66]

After Gist started toward Wills Creek with this letter, rain settled
down on the Meadows. Night was bringing the blackest of darkness
when, about 9 P.M., an Indian runner subsequently known as Silver-
heels [67] came to the camp with stirring news from Half King. The
Chief sent word that he was about six miles away and that he had seen
footprints of two Frenchmen who had crossed the trail. Half King
believed that these men belonged to the party of fifty who had passed
Gist's. All of them, the Chief thought, were near by.[68]

George resolved immediately to join Half King and to attack the

[64] 1 G. W., 55.

[65] In 1 Ford, 73, this was wrongly transcribed "spirits."

[66] 1 G. W., 55. From Washington to Dinwiddie, May 18, 1754 (1 Din., 48) it would appear
that George had been compelled to give shirts as presents even before he went down the
Youghiogheny with the Indian who coveted ruffles. George's books do not show that he ever
charged these garments against the Colony.

[67] Stephen's "Life," Rush Papers,

[68] At this point, for the reasons given in Appendix I-9, the narrative is based on Washington to Dinwiddie, May 29, 1754 (1 G. W., 63 ff), and not on the journal.

French. Although he had scarcely more than eighty men, he called up forty of them and, within an hour, started for the bivouac of the friendly natives. Black and rainy as was the night, obscure as was the road, he would push on and surprise the intruders. The advance was begun easily, but, in the utter darkness of the wilderness, guide and soldiers often lost the road. Sometimes they would have to feel their way along the sodden ground and among the bushes for fifteen minutes or longer before they could be sure they were on the trail again. Everything the men touched in the woods was dripping wet. Weapons became so damp that if the French had been encountered they could not have been given a shot.

Day was breaking when the guide stopped at the crude shelter of Half King. The Chief was there and had with him Monakatoocha, two armed braves and two boys with rifles.[69] In addition, Half King was accompanied by six or seven other Indians who possessed no firearms. It was a contingent far smaller than Robert Callender had reported the Half King was bringing,[70] but the Indians at least were on the track of the French.

The inevitable council was brief. Eloquence did not waste the moments on which successful surprise of the French might depend. Without argument or even hesitation, Half King and the others agreed to make common cause and to join the English in attacking the enemy. Quickly the Virginians and the natives went to the spot where the foot-prints of the two Frenchmen had been seen. Then Half King told two of his Indians to follow the trail and to ascertain where the French were encamped. Off stalked the Indians, their eyes on the tracks white strangers had left. George, Adam Stephen, Half King, Monakatoocha and the others, slightly more than forty in the aggregate, waited quietly in the woods.[71]

At length the two Indian scouts returned: They had found their quarry! About half a mile from the trail, in a bower well concealed

69 One of these boys was Dinwiddie's godson (1 *G. W.*, 73), and probably the only son of Monakatoocha. This youth, who participated honorably in the skirmish of the 28th, had been christened at Winchester, Sept. 16, 1753. His sponsor was Christopher Gist (P.R.O., C.O. 5: 1328, f. 117). For his good behavior in action, the Governor's namesake was rewarded by Dinwiddie from the treaty goods of 1754 with "equipment agreeable to his merit" (Dinwiddie to Washington, n.d. [June], 1754; 1 *Din.*, 229). As will appear *infra*, Half King was given the English "Dinwiddie" shortly before June 10, 1754, but he was not baptized. Cf. 1 *Hamilton*. 21.

70 See Washington to Dinwiddie, June 3, 1754; 1 *G. W.*, 73; George Washington to John Augustine Washington, May 31, 1754; *ibid.*, 70. For Callender's report of the coming of fifty men with Half King, see *supra*, p. 358.

71 Washington to Dinwiddie, May 29, 1754; 1 *G. W.*, 64.

among rocks, was a body of French troops. Questions by Half King and by George sufficed to make plain how the hiding place of the intruders stood with relation to the points of the compass, and how the party best could approach. The situation was ideal. By proceeding carefully, George's men could surround the French and could attack on all sides.

The English and the Indians advanced silently through the woods until they were close enough to see stretches of ground the Indian scouts had not been able to describe. Then it was apparent that most of the attacking party would have shelter but that the men on the right would be exposed before a circle could be formed. George at once said that he would assume charge of the right. Stephen, as senior Captain, took the left.[72] Beyond Stephen's soldiers were the Indians.[73]

Between 7 and 8 A.M.[74] unobserved deployment was completed. The Virginians and the Indians crept nearer and nearer until they were within a little more than 100 yards of the unsuspecting French. The next few steps would bring the men on the right into the open, where they would be seen, challenged and fired upon. George doubtless waited until he was sure everything was in order. Then he stepped forward and gave his command.

Almost on the instant his tall youthful figure was under the eyes of Frenchmen. As fast as they could, these soldiers ran back to their bower [75] to get their rifles.[76] A moment later, shots rang out. So nearly simultaneous were they that Adam Stephen averred afterward it was impossible to say which side fired first.[77] Men began to fall. Lieutenant Waggener sustained a wound. George heard the whistle of passing bullets as they cut the air, and somehow he felt exhilarated. It was "charming"—that was the word that came to him then or in retrospect.[78] English missiles were whistling, too, and were taking toll. Stephen had closed in with his platoon and had captured an officer. Some of the French gave ground, made off, and then, at a shout from their commander, came running back with uplifted hands. These men had seen the Indians in their rear and, knowing what their fate would be at the

---

[72] Although Stephen himself, *loc. cit.,* is the source of this bit of information, which George nowhere mentioned, there is no reason for doubting that Stephen led the left.

[73] 2 *Sparks,* 452, but without citation of authority.

[74] Druillon to Dinwiddie, n.d. [June, 1754]; 1 *Din.,* 225.

[75] Druillon, *loc. cit.,* called it a cabin.

[76] Washington to Dinwiddie, May 29, 1754, *loc. cit.;* Dinwiddie to the Lords of Trade, June 18, 1754; 1 *Din.,* 206.

[77] *Stephen's "Life," Rush Papers.*

[78] George Washington to John Augustine Washington, May 31, 1754; 1 *G. W.,* 70.

hands of the savages, preferred to surrender to the British.[79] Behind them came half a dozen Indians who fell upon the wounded, brained them and scalped them.[80] Half King demanded that the unwounded prisoners, too, be delivered to him to be scalped and slain, and once again he cried that he must be avenged on the French who had killed, boiled and eaten his father. George interposed and, with some difficulty, kept Half King from snatching the prisoners.[81]

By this time, firing had ceased. All the twenty-one unwounded French survivors had thrown down their weapons. On the ground were ten dead and a wounded man who somehow had escaped the hatchet of the Indians. One other French soldier, Mouceau by name, had been seen to make off.[82] An Englishman was dead. Besides Lieutenant Waggener, the wounded on Washington's side numbered only one or two.[83] From first shot to last surrender, not quite fifteen minutes had elapsed.[84] The surprise had been complete; George's first skirmish had achieved the ideal of the soldier, the destruction of the adversary as a fighting force. The commander of the French party, Joseph Coulon, the Sieur de Jumonville, had been killed by Half King, or at least the Chief so boasted.[85] Jumonville's second in command, Druillon, and two cadets were among the captured; but the most valuable of the prisoners by far was Commissary La Force, whom Washington described as "a bold, enterprising man and a person of great subtlety and cunning," [86] a master of the Indian tongue.[87]

While the English were counting and identifying their prisoners, the Indians plundered the French camp but found little there. Of provisions, the French had only bread.[88] On Jumonville's body or among

[79] This incident is not mentioned either by Washington or by Stephen but it was conspicuous in the account published in the *Va. Gazette* of July 19, 1754, and subsequently reprinted as set forth in Ambler, *Washington and the West*, 67–68. This account is substantially correct in all other determinable details and is to be accepted in this particular. It fits, moreover, the deployment and the combat practices of the Indians. Washington's failure to mention this detail does not invalidate it. He would not be apt to dwell on the savagery of the Colony's allies, though, as stated in the next sentence of the text, he reported to Dinwiddie that the Indians killed and scalped the wounded.

[80] Cf. Washington to Dinwiddie, June 3, 1754; 1 *G. W.*, 73: "There were five or six Indians who served to knock the poor, unhappy wounded in the head and bereiv'd them of their scalps."

[81] *Va. Gazette*, July 19, 1754, as cited in *Ambler*, supra.

[82] He is identified in Contreccœur to Du Quesne, June 2, 1754; 2 *Sparks*, 449. For the casualties, see Washington to Dinwiddie, May 29, 1754; 1 *G. W.*, 64.

[83] 1 *G. W.*, 66.

[84] *Ibid.*, 64.

[85] Parkman, *Montcalm and Wolfe*, v. 1, p. 151.

[86] Washington to Dinwiddie, May 29, 1754; 1 *G. W.*, 64.

[87] *Penn. Gazette*, July 11, 1754.

[88] Druillon to Dinwiddie, June 17, and [June] n.d., 1754; 1 *Din.*, 226, 227.

his belongings were a few papers, which were delivered to George. As soon as he could, Washington marched his prisoners under guard to Half King's camp and there held a second and more deliberate council at which he told the Chief of Dinwiddie's wish to have the Indians come to Winchester. The Sachem's answer was that he had to secure his people from French attack and had to assemble all the allied warriors. His visit to the Governor would have to be delayed. Meantime, he asked horses and a guard to go with him to Christopher Gist's and to help bring some of the Indian families to the English camp.[89]

George did not wish to divide his force any further, but, of course, he could not decline this request and he arranged, with no further bargaining, to send a detachment the next morning to assist the Chief. Then Washington started the prisoners and his own men back to the camp in the Meadows. On the way, the captured French officers, Druillon in particular, began to protest that they had come as an embassy to serve notice on the English to leave the domain of the French King. They insisted they should be treated as attendants of an ambassador, not as prisoners of war, and should be returned with an escort to Fort DuQuesne, precisely as the French had treated Washington the previous winter.[90] If George made any comment at the time, it was that he would so have treated the French had they come openly in small number.[91] Later, he had van Braam examine and translate Jumonville's papers, and then he conferred with the Dutchman, with his other officers and with Half King.

One of the documents of Jumonville proved to be a *sommation* over the signature Contrecœur,[92] dated at Fort DuQuesne, May 23, 1754. This was addressed to the commandant of the English troops on the lands of the King of France, and was an order to retire under penalty of forcible ejectment, though the desire of the French was to preserve the peace between the two Kings.[93] Another paper of the same date covered instructions given Jumonville by Contrecœur at Fort DuQuesne: With specified officers, an English interpreter and twenty-eight men, Jumonville was to find the road that communicated with the one the English had opened. These British were said by the Indians to wish to attack the French, but this seemed unbelievable in a time of

[89] I *Diaries*, 88. [90] I *G. W.*, 64–65.
[91] Druillon to Dinwiddie, n.d. [June], 1754; I *Din.*, 225. It is not certain whether this remark was made on the 28th or later.
[92] His full name was Claude Pierre Pécaudy, Sieur de Contrecœur.
[93] MS original, VSL.

peace. Should Jumonville discover such a movement on the part of the English he was to communicate the summons to them. Before doing this, Jumonville was to notify Contrecœur when he was to deliver the summons, and was later to inform the commander at the fort of the English reply. If Jumonville found that the redcoats were East of the Great Mountain, he was not to disturb them so long as they maintained peace. Jumonville was to guard against surprise and, if he met Indians, was to treat them as friends.[94]

Such were Jumonville's instructions. George and his companions unhesitatingly interpreted them to mean that Jumonville and his men were spies, and that the summons was to be a ruse for ascertaining where the English were. Then the French were to send back for reenforcements who were to come up quickly and were to fall on the English.

Moreover, the officers argued, if the French were an embassy, why were they so numerous and why so careful to hide themselves? Why did they not come boldly out and declare their presence and their mission? There was evidence, in fact, that the French had been two miles closer to the camp than when they were discovered, and that they had moved back and had sent off runners to report to Contrecœur the strength and position of Washington's party.[95]

Behind this reasoning was conviction that the French seizure of the fort at the forks had been an act of war. In the minds of Washington and the other Englishmen, the French already were the enemy. Half King was wholly of this view. The French, he said, never intended to come otherwise than in hostility: if the English were fools enough to let them go, he never would assist in taking another Frenchman.[96] Besides, if the English had La Force, they had better keep him. George agreed on this point. "Loosing [La Force]," said Washington, "would

---

94 P.R.O., C.O. 5: 14, p. 401–04. The accepted French view was that after the English opened fire, Jumonville signalled he had a message to deliver. Thereupon, firing having ceased, the English were alleged to have crowded around Jumonville. When he had read the summons once and had started to read it a second time, he was shot (Contrecœur to DuQuesne, June 2, 1754, Arch. du Seminaire de Quebec; Moreau, *Mémoire,* 21). In Rostaing's *Histoire* (Arch. du Min. de la Guerre, 236, p. 100), the assertion simply is that the Indians gave notice of Jumonville's approach, that the French received a surprise attack, and that Jumonville perished without fulfilling his mission: A "cry of horror went up from the French colonies; even the Indians were indignant."

95 This report of the dispatch of runners may have been true. If Jumonville left Fort DuQuesne with the number of men assigned him, the party would have numbered thirty-five. Casualties and the man who escaped early in the skirmish numbered thirty-three. This leaves two men "unaccounted for."

96 To repeat, this summary, for the reasons stated in Appendix I–9, is based not on the journal but on Washington to Dinwiddie, May 29, 1754; 1 *G. W.,* 64–65.

tend more to our disservice than 50 other men . . ." [97] La Force himself at first was quite candid. He said that as soon as he saw the summons and the instructions of Jumonville he believed there would be trouble,[98] though he professed not to think the French "had any other but a good design." [99] Some of the other captives talked, also, but principally in justification of their professed character as an embassy. They denied flatly that they had sent spies forward to reconnoiter the English camp.[100]

George announced no decision after this discussion of the 28th. The next morning he was told that the French wished to know if they might see him. When he consented, they formally asked him in what manner he regarded them: were they to be treated as prisoners of war or as attendants on an ambassador? They were prisoners, said George, and he gave his reasons for his decision.[101]

La Force and Druillon had been wearing few clothes when they were surprised; what they had in their shelter, the Indians doubtless had taken. Washington gave them some of his own apparel, "by which," he took pains to say, "I have disfurnished myself," [102] and at their request he supplied them, likewise, with a letter of introduction to the Governor.[103] This was personal; officially, they were to march on foot under guard to Winchester, where Dinwiddie was assumed to be. In a second letter to the Executive, written later that day, George cautioned His Honor against listening to the "smooth stories" of the Frenchmen concerning their alleged embassy. ". . . In strict justice," he said, "they ought to be hanged as spies of the worst sort . . ." [104]

[97] *Ibid.*
[98] Washington's phrase (*ibid.*, 66) was not "trouble" but "some such tendency" as developed.
[99] *Ibid.*
[100] *Ibid.*, 65.
[101] 1 *Diaries*, 89–90.
[102] *Ibid.*, 67.
[103] Washington to Dinwiddie, May 29, 1754; 1 *G. W.*, 68.
[104] Washington to Dinwiddie, n.d., but endorsed May 29, 1754; 1 *G. W.*, 69.

CHAPTER XI

"I WENT OUT, WAS SOUNDLY BEATEN, LOST THEM ALL . . ."
(June, 1754–July 4, 1754)

NOT FOR an instant did young Lieutenant Colonel Washington permit the protests of the French prisoners to divert him from two other matters of much concern—his answer to the Governor on the sore question of pay, and his preparations to meet the attack he expected in retaliation for the defeat of Jumonville's party.

The Governor's reply to the protest George had forwarded on the 18th of May was a sharp letter written from Winchester, May 25. Dinwiddie took up, one by one, the complaints of Captain Stephen and the other officers. Where the Governor thought the complaint justified, he promised such correction as he could make; where he believed the officers wrong, he said so, and reminded them that other men, applicants for commission, had "approved of the terms and were desirous to serve on those conditions."

When the Governor had disposed of the protest, he turned his attention to George and gave the commander a verbal spanking: ". . . I must begin by expressing both concern and surprise to find a gentleman whom I so particularly considered, and from whom I had so great expectations and hopes, appear so differently from himself, and give me leave to say, mistakenly, as I think, concurring with complaints in general so ill-founded." The Governor professed his understanding of George's difficulties and assured the young man that merit would not "pass unnoticed." In the course of an exhortation to stand fast, Dinwiddie remarked that he hoped the importance of the task "would sweeten the toils; that you will hereafter reflect on [this] with pleasure, and engage you to think of nothing less than resigning your command, or countenancing in any sort the discontent that could never be more unreasonable or pernicious than at present." [1]

[1] Dinwiddie to Washington, May 25, 1754; 1 *Din.*, 173.

There was more to the same effect, but this was the part of the letter that disturbed George. It touched his pride and his pocket, concerning both of which he was sensitive, and it raised, vaguely, the question of his continuance in command. So important did it appear to him that, on the 29th, the day after the fight with Jumonville, he sat down and wrote Dinwiddie an answer that displayed his youth and his ambition. "I shall begin," he wrote the Governor, "with assuring you that nothing was further from my intention than to recede, though I then pressed, and still desire that my services may be voluntary, rather than on the present pay." [2] Like Dinwiddie, he argued the issues in detail and not unskillfully, and, in respect to what he considered discriminatory pay, he reviewed all that had been said on the subject from the first discussion in Williamsburg.[3] He was bold enough in the first part of his observations on the Governor's remark about the number of men who would have been glad to serve at the designated pay and under the conditions Washington had to face. If, said George, those zealous gentlemen had known the country, they would not "so troublesomely [have] solicited" commission; but from this statement George went on somewhat uneasily: "Yet I do not offer this as a reason for quitting the service. For my own part I can answer I have a constitution hardy enough to encounter and undergo the most severe trials, and, I flatter myself, resolution to face what any man durst, as shall be proved, when it comes to the test, which I believe we are on the borders of." With this he resumed his general argument and promised to do what he could "to reconcile matters"; [4] but he could not forbear stating in detail how he figured he was receiving almost 10s less per day than an officer of like rank on the regular establishment would, to say nothing of the fact that he had no prospect of half-pay on retirement.

Once again, after penning that, George came back to the question of serving as a volunteer. This time he could not quite bring himself to say that he would decline 12s 6d *per diem* and serve as a volunteer. He wrote: "I would not have your Honor imagine from this that I have said all these things to have the pay increased, but to justify myself, and show your Honor that our complaints are not frivolous, but founded upon strict reason: for my own part, it is a matter almost indifferent whether I serve for full pay, or as a generous volunteer; indeed, did my

[2] Washington evidently used the verb "recede" in the sense, then general, of a withdrawal from an agreement, bargain, commission, etc.
[3] See *supra*, p. 335.
[4] See *infra*, p. 385.

circumstances correspond with my inclination, I should not hesitate a moment to prefer the latter; for the motives that led me here were pure and noble. I had no view of acquisition, but that of honor, by serving faithfully my King and Country."[5] There George left it. As he did not consider his circumstances permitted, he would not insist on serving without pay and would continue to accept the *per diem* of 12s 6d. Not until he made this completely, indeed tediously, plain, did he even announce to the Governor the victory he had won.

The effect of that success on his state of mind was what might have been expected in the case of an inexperienced but intelligent young soldier: It increased his self-confidence and created an unwarranted contempt for the enemy at the same time that it admonished him to prepare against an attack by a force that was certain to be numerically much superior to his own. "If the whole detachment of the French," he wrote the Governor, "behave with no more resolution than this chosen party did, I flatter myself we shall have no great trouble in driving them to the d Montreal;"[6] but, even before George indulged himself in this, he assured Dinwiddie that he would do his utmost to avoid a surprise by the enemy.[7] Washington, moreover, called immediately on Fry for reenforcements[8] and gave his Colonel virtual guarantee that the advance of the next English column would not be interrupted by the French. "If," George wrote, "there does not come a sufficient reenforcement, we must either quit our ground and retreat to you, or fight very unequal numbers, which I will do before I will give up one inch of what we have gained."[9]

In this resolution, which bespoke his inexperience, he began on the 30th of May, the second day after the skirmish, to strengthen the ground where he had found the "natural entrenchments" between which he had placed his wagons.[10] The next day he assured his brother "Jack"[11] in a letter: "We expect every hour to be attacked by superior force, but, if they forbear one day longer, we shall be prepared for them . . . The Mingoes have struck the French and I hope will give

---

5 Washington to Dinwiddie, May 29, 1754; 1 *G. W.*, 59–63.
6 Letter of June 3, 1754; 1 *G. W.*, 73. L'Abbé Robitaille (*Washington et Jumonville,* 27) declared this remark lacking in courtesy to a brave enemy.
7 Washington to Dinwiddie, May 29, 1754; 1 *Din.,* 63.
8 Captain Hog's scouting party doubtless had returned on the evening of the 28th or the morning of the 29th but the time is not given by Washington in his journal or in any of his letters.
9 Washington to Joshua Fry, May 29, 1754; 1 *G. W.*, 58–59.
10 See *supra,* p. 368; 1 *Diaries,* 90.
11 I.e., John Augustine Washington.

a good blow before they have done. I expect forty odd of them here tonight, which, with our fort and some reenforcement from Colonel Fry, will enable us"—and then he added with a combination of boyish pride and rhetoric—"to exercise our noble courage with spirit." [12]

Actually none of these things happened as he expected: The French did not approach; the fort was not finished in reasonably defensible form until June 3 and then was by no means as strong as its young engineer believed.[13] As for Indians, the English escort brought in, late on the 2nd of June, eighty or more, but that total included women and children.[14] Half King, who headed the party, must have been conscious that he was making a poor reenforcement, because he talked much of what was being done to unite the natives in support of their brothers, the English. Monakatoocha, he said, had been sent to arouse all the warriors on the Ohio and to bring them to Washington's camp.[15]

Badly as George needed more men, the arrival of the squaws and the children along with the warriors gave new seriousness to a condition that had troubled the young commander for several days: Food had become scarce; flour, in particular, was almost exhausted. There would, in fact, already have been a period of four days during which the entire detachment would have been without provision, had not a trader from the Ohio reached the camp, on his way eastward, with some flour. George bought it, though his thrift was outraged at the price, 21s 8d per hundredweight.[16]

There now were many more persons in camp to eat, and to eat heartily, too, because every Indian demanded as much as the white men received. George felt that he had either to comply or, as he phrased it, set them "adrift," [17] which was impolitic and dangerous. All he could do at the time to reduce the heavy requisition on a frail commissary was to propose that the women and children be sent to the English settlements. Half King's reply was that he would consider this and would give an answer when Monakatoocha reached the camp.[18] Meantime, few provisions, if any, were coming from Wills Creek. George's

[12] 1 G. W., 70.

[13] Washington to Dinwiddie, June 3, 1754: "We have just finished a small palisado'd fort in which, with my small numbers, I shall not fear the attacks of 500 men" (1 G. W., 73).

[14] 1 Diaries, 90; Washington to Dinwiddie, June 3, 1754; 1 G. W., 71. Journal and letters are at variance one day in their statement of the arrival of some of these savages.

[15] Washington to Dinwiddie, June 3, 1754; 1 G. W., 72.

[16] Washington to Dinwiddie, June n.d. [12], 1754; 1 G. W., 76. It is impossible to fix the date of this purchase with any certainty beyond the fact that it was prior to June 6.

[17] 1 G. W., 72.

[18] Ibid.

appeal for the hire of more wagons to forward food and artillery was met with the despairing assurance that the vehicles could not be hired for five times what their service was worth.[19] Faced with this, Washington did not know how to procure food himself or how to stir his distant commissary to get and to deliver it.

Every issue brought lower the supply of flour until on June 6, the sergeant came to the bottom of the last sack. Until the arrival of more, there would be no bread with which hungry soldiers and grumbling savages could make their tough fresh beef less unpalatable.[20] Officially, the blame rested on John Carlyle, back in Alexandria, to whom Washington had sent several expresses,[21] though George believed the prime fault was with the deputies of his friend the Commissary. Carlyle himself attributed failure both to lack of cash with which to pay for food and to the failure of contractors, George Croghan especially, to make the deliveries they had promised.[22]

In the wretched crisis this shortage of food presented him, George had new responsibility placed on his tall shoulders: Christopher Gist, arriving from Wills Creek on the very day of the exhaustion of the flour, brought news that Joshua Fry was dead. The Colonel had sustained a fall from his horse, several days prior to May 29,[23] and had succumbed on the 31st.[24] As a result, George now had the chief command of the expedition, to which he had not dared to aspire a few months previously.[25] At twenty-two years and three months, he became senior field officer of the small military establishment of the Colony. Ambitious though he was, he scarcely could have asked a more rapid rise.

As if to exemplify his extension of command, George received on the 9th the first reenforcements, probably, aside from Indians, that had joined him after he had left Wills Creek.[26] These were the remaining

---

19 Washington to James Innes, Aug. 12, 1754; 1 *G. W.*, 96.
20 Washington to Dinwiddie, June 12, 1754; 1 *G. W.*, 76.
21 *Ibid.*
22 John Carlyle to Washington, June 17, 1754; 1 *Hamilton*, 4–5.
23 Dinwiddie to Joshua Fry, May 29, 1754; 1 *Din.*, 184; *Lowdermilk*, 71 n.
24 1 *Diaries*, 91; *Lowdermilk*, loc., cit.; *Penn. Gazette*, July 11, 1754.
25 See *supra*, p. 335.
26 This is not quite certain because the French editing of the journal eliminated all entries not considered important. No mention is made there of any accession of strength from the beginning of the expedition to the 9th of June except for Stephen's Company and "some pieces of cannon" (1 *Diaries*, 74, 80). These guns presumably were forwarded under military guard. In addition, there is a possibility that one or another of the three Companies to be mentioned in the next sentence of the text was received at Cresap's, or at Wills Creek, though the vague reference to the disposition of "the detachment" (1 *Diaries*, 75) probably concerns the men Washington himself brought from Alexandria and Winchester.

three Companies of the Virginia Regiment under Capts. Robert Stobo and Andrew Lewis and Lieut. George Mercer, who had been advanced slowly by their temporary commander, Maj. George Muse.[27] All three of these officers and some of the Lieutenants were interesting men, but, at the moment, the most popular of them probably was Capt. Robert Stobo, another of the Scotsmen that Dinwiddie had favored.

Stobo, the only surviving son of a Glasgow merchant, had been sent to Virginia by his guardians to learn the business, but he had become so fond of the life of the Colony that he had gone home, had sold some of his real estate, and with a stock of goods, had come back to the Old Dominion in the expectation of remaining there for several years at least. Virginia society made a larger appeal to him than had the buying of tobacco and the sale of cloth. He had been enjoying a high life when the organization of the force to guard the Ohio had re-awakened a military impulse that had been strong in boyhood. After he had received Dinwiddie's commission as Captain, he had recruited a personal force of ten servant mechanics and had provided himself with a covered wagon to protect his equipment and supplies. First and most cherished among his possessions was a butt of Madeira, which, needless to say, made him on arrival at camp both popular and envied. Twenty-seven years of age, he made the most of his asset and dispensed convivially what was left of the 125 gallons of wine, or thereabouts, with which he had started westward.[28]

Stobo's fellow Captain, Andrew Lewis, was a colonial of no previous military experience, but he had, as Washington soon discovered, both courage and capacity. Mercer, not quite twenty-one, was a son of John Mercer of Marlborough, Stafford County, and was careful, intelligent

[27] For the slowness of Muse's marches, see Dinwiddie to Muse, June 2, 1754 (1 *Din.*, 187). Small as was Muse's command, it could have been styled a Battalion according to the terminology of that period of British organization. It was not until after the French and Indian War that a Battalion usually consisted of ten Companies, of which one was "light" and one was grenadier. See Thomas Simes, *A New Military, Historical and Explanatory Dictionary*, Phila. ed. 1776. "Regiment" likewise was in 1754 a vague descriptive noun. As late as 1780, the *Complete System of the Military Art* explained: "The number of troops, or Companies, that are to form a Regiment has never been ascertained, no more than the number of men that are to form a Troop or Company . . . In England our Regiments are generally from 10 to 13 Companies, one of which is always grenadiers. Regiments of horse are most commonly six Troops, but some of them nine. Dragoon Regiments are generally in time of war eight Troops, and in time of peace but six." Regardless of enlisted strength, the name "Regiment" was given to any organization of foot or horse that had a Colonel, a Lieutenant Colonel and a Major.

[28] *Memoirs of Major Robert Stobo* (Pittsburgh, 1854), p. 13–16. This odd and boastful little volume is to be used cautiously but, aside from possible exaggeration of Stobo's wealth and hospitality, it probably is accurate in its references to his antecedents and equipment. The plan of Fort DuQuesne that prefaces the *Memoirs* is a finished redraft, on a slightly enlarged scale, of Stobo's original sketch, for which see illustration preceding p. 438. An authoritative study of Stobo by George M. Kahrl will be found in 49 *V* 141 ff, 254 ff.

and versatile.[29] In the charge of Stobo and Lewis and Mercer, were approximately 181 soldiers,[30] few of whom had ever fired a rifle at any other target than game. These men brought scant supplies,[31] but with the convoy there arrived nine small guns and the swivels on which to place them so that they could be fired horizontally in any direction. These were the first swivel guns George had received and they were to be the principal armament of the little stockade.

More interesting than Stobo or swivels or anything else that Major Muse brought with him was a warrior emissary and interpreter whom George probably had never seen previously, though this strange individual was the subject of endless campfire description. Andrew Montour was the son of an Oneida chief, Carondawana or "Big Tree," whose wife was the daughter of a Frenchman named Montour, by a Huron squaw. "Big Tree" had been killed in battle about 1729, but his widow, Andrew's mother, had become renowned as "Madame Montour," a consistent friend of the English and a frequent visitor in Pennsylvania towns. Although Andrew thus had no French blood except that of one grandfather, he had much of the appearance of a European and spoke good French and English, as well as several Indian tongues. Styled by Quebec officials a "French Canadian deserter," he had lived nearly all his life among the Six Nations and served as interpreter and agent for the English of Pennsylvania and as an independent trader also. He was mild-mannered, quiet and of unchallengeable courage. "His cast of countenance," a missionary wrote in 1742, "is decidedly European and had not his face been encircled with a broad band of paint applied with bear's fat, I would certainly have taken him for one." Montour's garb on that occasion fitted both his paint and his European features: "He wore a brown broadcloth coat, a scarlet damaskin lappel waistcoat, breeches over which his shirt hung, a black cordovan neckerchief decked with silver bugles, shoes and stockings and a hat. His ears were hung with pendants of brass and other wires plaited together like the handle of a basket."[32]

So unusual a personage naturally received varying appraisals. In the judgment of some English colonials, Montour was the ablest and most honest of frontier traders; others regarded him as a dubious character

29 See the sketch in Toner, ed., *op. cit.*, 78 ff.
30 The returns are in *ibid.*, 172, 176, 180.
31 Cf. 1 *Din.*, 187.
32 This is Count Zindendorf's familiar description, many times reprinted. It appears in the fullest of all the sketches of the Montours, that of Darlington, *op. cit.*, 152–75. See, also, Parkman, 1 *Montcalm and Wolfe*, 58; 4 *Penn. Mag.*, 218; 14 *West. Penn. His. Mag.*, 55.

who had less influence with the tribes than he professed.[33] At the time he arrived George thought he would prove to be an invaluable assistant in dealing with the savages, whose sensibilities sometimes puzzled the young commander.[34] Specifically, Montour was commissioned to enlist, organize and command 200 Indians.[35]

Along with Montour and the English reenforcements, or on their heels, George received dispatches that contained much information. In three letters of separate date, June 1, 2 and 4, Governor Dinwiddie sent congratulations on the victory over Jumonville and gave assurance that provisions, rum and other presents for the Indians would be forwarded promptly. "I doubt not your continuing to act with prudence and resolution," Dinwiddie wrote, "and you may depend on my duly representing your merit and that of your officers and faithful soldiers to His Majesty and our next General Assembly to consider of." [36] Medals were sent for George, Colonel Fry, Half King, Monakatoocha and other Indian Chiefs, to wear "as tokens of His Majesty's favor." [37]

The remainder of the Governor's budget of instruction and announcement was of conflicting appeal. To the subject of the previous dispute over the pay of colonial officers, the Governor devoted one paragraph only, and that one primarily an expression of regret that "uneasiness" had been caused at a time of deep concern over the long delay in the march of reenforcements.[38] Then, in a letter written after receipt of the news of the death of Joshua Fry, the Governor informed George that he was to take Fry's place with the rank of Colonel.[39] George Muse was to be Lieutenant Colonel; the senior Captain, who was Stephen, was to be made Major. The executive went on immediately to say that Col. James Innes, "an old, experienced officer," was expected daily and "is appointed Commander-in-Chief of all the forces, which I am very sensible will be very agreeable to you and the other officers."

Dinwiddie already had written George that the Independent Companies were on their way to the fort, and now the Governor renewed his admonition that controversy with the commanders of these troops

[33] Croghan's opinion is in 2 *Penn. Arch.*, 118, Governor Sharpe's in 1 *Sharpe*, 151, that of Governor Dinwiddie in 1 *Din.*, 426. These judgments, except Croghan's, were expressed subsequent to this expedition.

[34] Cf. Washington to Dinwiddie, June 3, 1754; 1 *G. W.*, 72.

[35] 1 *Diaries*, 91.

[36] Letter of June 2, 1754; 1 *Din.*, 189.

[37] *Ibid.*

[38] *Ibid.*

[39] The letter of June 4, 1754, in 1 *Din.*, 193, did not specifically mention the new rank, but the Governor enclosed a commission and referred to the advancement of Muse to Lieutenant Colonel, and of the senior Captain to Major, etc.

be shunned. Specifically, Dinwiddie wrote: "The Captains and officers of the Independent Companies having their commissions signed by His Majesty imagine they claim a distinguished rank, and being long trained in arms expect suitable regards. You will therefore consult and agree with your officers to show them particular marks of esteem, which will avoid such causes of uneasiness as otherwise might obstruct His Majesty's service, wherein all are alike engaged, and must answer for any ill consequences of an unhappy disagreement." [40]

These were ponderous words, but their vagueness did not escape George. He was entirely willing to serve under Innes because he felt he could learn much from "an experienced officer and man of sense." [41] So far as the direct controversy over pay was involved, George decided to drop the argument temporarily for the dual reason that he had new responsibility and that Dinwiddie had gone on record as saying the *per diem* would have been higher if the supply bill of the General Assembly had carried a larger amount. [42] Even before receiving that admission, it will be remembered, George had resolved to do what he could to discourage further argument over inequities of compensation. Now the coming of the Independent Companies might renew heart-burnings and most certainly would raise the vexatious issue of rank and command. [43] George himself was a Virginia Colonel; the officer in charge of the nearest Independent Company was James Mackay, a Captain by royal commission. Was rank so to be disregarded that the Captain would command the Colonel, or—what was more probable— would the Captain be exempt from the orders of a man three grades his senior?

George asked himself the question in manifest disturbance of spirit, but in a determination to control his feelings. As soon as he found opportunity, he wrote the Governor with much care and restraint: "Your Honor may depend I shall myself and will endeavor to make all my officers show Captain Mackay [44] all the respect due to his rank and merit; but [I] should have been particularly obliged if your Honor had declared whether he was under my command or independent of it; however, I shall be studious to avoid all disputes that may tend to the

[40] Letter of June 4, 1754; 1 *Din.*, 193-94.
[41] Washington to Dinwiddie, June 10, 1754; 1 *G. W.*, 74.
[42] 1 *Din.*, 189.
[43] "Rank and command" was the phrase used in the royal orders of Nov. 12, 1754; 1 *Hamilton*, opposite p. 56.
[44] George spelled it McKay; 1 *G. W.*, 74.

public prejudice, but as far as I am able, I will inculcate harmony and unanimity."

Washington continued: "I hope Captain Mackay will have more sense than to insist upon any unreasonable distinction, though he and his have commissions from His Majesty; let him consider though we are greatly inferior in respect to profitable advantages, yet we have the same spirit to serve our Gracious King as they have, and are as ready and willing to sacrifice our lives for our country's as them; and here, once more and for the last time, I must say that this will be a cancer that will grate some officers of this Regiment beyond all measure to serve upon such different terms when their lives, their fortunes and their characters are equally, and I dare say as effectually exposed as those who are happy enough to have King's Commissions. I have been solicitous on this head, have earnestly endeavored to reconcile the officers to their appointment, and flatter myself I have succeeded, having heard no mention thereof lately. I considered the pernicious consequences that would have attended a disunion [and] therefore was too much attached to my country's interest to suffer it to ripen after receiving your advising letters." [45]

Righteous resolution and correspondence alike were interrupted that 10th of June by reports of the approach of a party of French. George at once sent out Indian scouts and made ready to receive the enemy. Just before twilight there came an alarm and the prospect of a night attack, but no French appeared, and no fire was opened. The next day, Washington pushed out another detachment to find the foe. Two of these scouts returned on the 12th, with news that they had seen a small number of French in the woods. Other Indians brought reports which George understood to indicate that ninety Frenchmen were not far distant. Thereupon Washington ordered Muse to enter the crude fort, to mount the swivel guns, and to hold the defences while he took 130 white men and about thirty Indians and went out to capture the entire party. To his disappointment, the young Colonel soon learned that the message of the Indian scouts had been misinterpreted: Instead of ninety French soldiers, nine French deserters were making their way to the English camp.

Washington left a few Indians to bring in these deserters,[46] and him-

<hr>

[45] Washington to Dinwiddie, June 10, 1754; 1 G. W., 74–75.
[46] For the fate of these deserters, some of whom ultimately reached Boston, see Md. Gazette. Oct. 12, 1754.

self went back to camp to wrestle once more with a nearer and more dreaded foe—hunger that might become starvation.[47] The troops and the Indians now had been without flour for six days. Such other provisions as remained in camp would be exhausted on the 14th. George had sent repeated expresses to Wills Creek and to Major Carlyle in Alexandria,[48] and he had hired fifty or sixty horses to bring up provisions from Wills Creek, if food reached that station. In the event it did not, the returning animals were to carry ammunition.[49] In George's opinion, the advance to the Monongahela depended now entirely on food. He could wait at Red Stone for powder and shot but he could not get there unless he had sufficient provisions for the march.[50] His hopes were not high, though his purpose was firm. As far as he could learn from those riders who had been at Wills Creek, no flour was being forwarded. Captain Mackay's company was known to be on the march, but he was said to be moving without the artillery he was expected to bring with him. The reason was the old one—no wagons.[51]

Probably on the 14th of June, or about that date, Captain Mackay arrived with the Independent Company from South Carolina.[52] His orders had come even farther than he had. On the 1st of March, 1754, Governor Dinwiddie had received an answer, dated January 18, to the plea he had made for help in protecting the Ohio. Lord Holderness had enclosed a letter to the Governor of New York with instructions

[47] 1 *Diaries*, 92; Washington to Dinwiddie, n.d., 1 *G. W.*, 78. This letter as printed in 2 *Sparks*, 40 ff is dated June 10, but manifestly is a combination of a letter written on that date and one begun on June 12 and finished probably on June 15. In 1 *Ford*, 99, the letter of June 10 is separated properly from that of June 12, but the letter of the 12th–15th is not divided, though a note, p. 106, gives the editor's view of where the writing of the 15th began. The text in 1 *G. W.*, 82, is marked to show the point at which the MS version in VHS starts. Examination of the MS completely justifies that editorial decision. The two papers are not even in the same hand. It would seem probable that the letter of the 12th ended with the P.S. on p. 80, and that the addendum of June 15 begins with: "Since writing the aforegoing" etc. The reason for fixing the date as June 15 is the reference to the prospective march "tomorrow" toward Red Stone. In the journal, 1 *Diaries*, 93, the date of that advance is given as June 16. The circumstantial evidence concerning the time of Mackay's arrival at Washington's camp is reviewed below, n. 52.
[48] Washington to Dinwiddie, June 12–15, 1754; 1 *G. W.*, 76.
[49] Washington to Dinwiddie, June 10, 1754; 1 *Ford*, 99.
[50] Washington to Dinwiddie, June 12, 1754; 1 *G. W.*, 76.
[51] Washington to Dinwiddie, June 10, 1754; 1 *Ford*, 99.
[52] Mackay was certainly at the fort by June 15, for the reasons given above, n. 47. He had not left Wills Creek June 10. See 1 *Din.*, 221. The extent of the exchanges between him and Washington concerning command, as set forth in the text, indicates that Mackay had been at the front a day or two when Washington wrote Dinwiddie the part of the undated letter believed to have been penned on the 15th. If Mackay received on the 10th or on the 11th the flour for which he had been waiting (1 *Din.*, 221), he probably started on the 11th. As his march to Great Meadows was slightly under forty miles over a road that had been put in as good condition as the ground permitted, he could have covered the distance in four days. This would have put him with Washington on the 14th.

for two Independent Companies to be dispatched from that Colony to Virginia. Another letter to the Governor of North Carolina contained similar orders to send one such Company. As Dinwiddie knew there were regulars in South Carolina, and none in North Carolina, he assumed that the directions were intended for Governor Glen of South Carolina and not for Governor Dobbs of the adjoining province.[53] Glen had taken the same view and had acted promptly. By approximately May 1, Capt. James Mackay with his full Company of 100 had disembarked from the *Jamaica*[54] at Hampton, Virginia.[55] Thence, by Dinwiddie's order, he and his men had proceeded aboard a sloop to Alexandria, and had marched to Wills Creek, where, as explained already, they had been delayed a long time for lack of wagons.[56] When Mackay at length was able to start his advance to Great Meadows, he drove sixty beeves with his Company, but he brought only five days' flour and little ammunition.[57]

George had kept in touch with the movements of Mackay and knew, in general, when the Captain would reach the camp, but he did not know how painfully the perplexed Governor had sought to assure cooperation between the regulars and the colonials without attempting to settle in person the delicate question of rank. Dinwiddie had been confident of his authority to issue orders to the Independent Company under the instructions sent him from England;[58] he was not sure whether Fry or Washington could give orders to the Captain. In frank avoidance of that issue, Dinwiddie had written Fry much as he had Washington: "You are by me appointed Commander-in-Chief on the expedition, but as it is not usual to have the regular forces under His Majesty's immediate commission to be under the command of an officer in America appointed by any of the Governors; yet, that there may be no misunderstanding or delay in the expedition, I recommend you to show a due regard to these troops of His Majesty, and show this officer and the others in that station as much indulgence as is in your power."[59] Somewhat less vaguely, in the same letter, the Governor had

---

[53] Dinwiddie to Holderness, Mch. 12, 1754; 1 *Din.*, 97; Dinwiddie to Glen, Mch. 5, 1754; 1 *Din.*, 90.

[54] The entry in 5 *E. J.*, 465 reads "Jamaica Snow Man of War," without any punctuation; but as a snow, which resembled a brig, was used often as a warship, it is probable that the punctuation should have been "Jamaica, snow, man of war."

[55] The exact date is not determinable but it was prior to May 4 (cf. 1 *Din.*, 147). The vessel had been expected early in April (5 *E. J.*, 465).

[56] *Ibid.*, 149–50.

[57] Washington to Dinwiddie, June 12–c. 15, 1743; 1 *G. W.*, 84.

[58] Dinwiddie to Mackay, May 4, 1754; 1 *Din.*, 149.

[59] Dinwiddie to Fry, May 4, 1754; 1 *Din.*, 146.

reiterated: "As the officers of the Independent Companies are gentle-men of experience in the art military, have served in several campaigns, are jealous of their own honor, and are well recommended, I hope you will conduct yourself towards them with prudence and receive their advice with candor, as the most probable means of promoting His Majesty's service and the success of the expedition." [60] To Mackay the Governor had written: "On your arrival . . . you are to join Col. J. Fry, who is appointed Commander-in-Chief of this expedition. And as unanimity are [61] proper rules for success, I doubt not you will promote the same to the utmost of your power." [62]

George, for his part, realized that his own instructions did not settle the main issue. He was at a loss how to act or what to do concerning the use of the Independent Company, but he was determined to receive Mackay as a gentleman and a comrade. When, therefore, he saw Mackay ride up, he greeted him in friendly manner and gave him no orders. The newcomer proved to be a Scotsman, one of four sons of Capt. Hugh Mackay, laird of Scoury. Accompanied by his brothers, James Mackay had migrated to Georgia with Governor Oglethorpe, had engaged in border warfare, and had acquired a property which he had named Strathy Hall, after the family seat in Scotland. [63] He was in carriage and in manner a gentleman, and most distinctly a soldier who was fully conscious that he had a commission from the King.

Mackay picked his own camp site; George did not go to the Com-pany or inspect it. [64] The first test came when Washington, as com-mander, sent the Captain the parole and countersign. Mackay replied that he did not think he should receive these from the colonial Colonel. The Captain talked frankly, when George brought the matter to a direct interview; but Mackay insisted that his command was a separate force and he maintained that the Governor could not issue a commission that would command him. [65] All this Mackay said so frankly and with so favorable a countenance that George scarcely could have taken offence even had not the young commander been resolved to show the "respect" that Dinwiddie had enjoined. The Virginian offered to

60 *Ibid.*, 147.
61 A word or two may be missing here.
62 Letter of May 4, 1754; 1 *Din.*, 149.
63 The most detailed sketch, lacking in detail of age, etc., is in 1 *Ga. His. Quar.*, 77 ff.
64 Washington to Dinwiddie, June 12–c. 15, 1754; 1 *G. W.*, 81.
65 What he meant probably was that the Governor could not give any colonial officer au-thority over a regular. See *infra*, n. 66.

consult and to advise, but the regular was inflexible: his force was separate.

Another and a most irritating complication arose over the duty the Independent Company was to perform. The colonials were working on the road to Red Stone. Would Mackay have his troops share in this labor? No—that was to say, not unless Colonel Washington was prepared to allow the men the regular pay of 1s sterling per day for such special service. George, it will be remembered, was alloted 8d daily for his own soldiers; he could not give more to the Independent Company. Mackay's answer was that he did not have authority to compel the men to work for less. That, he added, was not peculiar to his Company. It applied to all regulars who were subject to martial law.

At first, George did not know what to do when he came to this impasse. In spite of his need of reenforcements, he wished that Mackay were somewhere else.[66] As the Virginia Colonel could not detach the Independent Company, he concluded by the 15th—after the regulars had been with him not more than twenty-four hours—that he would himself leave: He would take his own men and their part of the remaining provisions, and would start for Red Stone Creek; Mackay could remain at the Meadows with the Independent Company. In addition, George decided that before moving, he would review the facts for the information of the Governor and would ask for new instructions.

So, on the 15th, George added some earnest paragraphs to a letter he had written the Governor three days previously. He related the incident of the parole and countersign and explained that Mackay did not think the colonial commander should give it to the Independent Company. Washington asked: "Then who is to give it? Am I to issue these orders to a Company? Or is an independent Captain to prescribe rules to the Virginia Regiment? This is the question. But its absurdity is obvious." One or the other, he or Mackay, must have authority because "two commanders are so incompatible that we cannot be as useful to one another, or the public, as we ought."

Then George reported the refusal of Mackay to have the regulars work on the road unless they got 1s a day. In a burst almost emotional, young Washington went on: "I, therefore shall continue to complete the work we have begun with my poor fellows; we shall have the whole

---

[66] Cf. Washington to Dinwiddie, June 12–c. 15, 1754: "[Mackay] thinks you [Dinwiddie] have not a power to give commissions that will command him. If so, I can very confidently say that his absence would tend to the public advantage" (1 G. W., 82).

credit, as none others have assisted. I hope from what has been said your Honor will see the necessity of giving your speedy orders on this head, and I am sensible you will consider the evil tendency that will accompany Captain Mackay's commanding for I am sorry to observe this is what we always hoped to enjoy"—then, in complete self-revelation he explained what that was—"the rank of officers, which to me, sir, is much dearer than the pay." [67]

In that spirit, George assembled his Virginia troops on the morning of June 16 and prepared to start for Red Stone Creek. In the march-off, he was anxious, of course, to have his men make a good impression on the Independent Company, but fate and the cunning of the planters of Frederick defeated him. That is to say, fate interposed many rough places on the route George selected for road-building; the planters on the South Branch and around Winchester had supplied such feeble wagons that when stone and wheel came together, the vehicle was apt to collapse. "[We] were extremely embarrassed," George had to confess, "our wagons breaking very often." [68] This was risky, as well as humiliating, because George was moving the nine swivel guns with the column. Injury to their mountings could not be repaired easily in the wilderness.

By persistence and in spite of many obstacles, George reached Gist's new settlement [69] and from that point sent back all except two of his wagons and teams to haul provisions. At this advanced post, the Colonel had to return to a diplomatic role similar to the one he had been compelled to undertake during his first visit to the Ohio. On the 12th of June, George had heard that the Delawares and the Shawnees had taken up the hatchet against the English. Doubtless on the advice of Half King, the young commander had sent messengers and wampum to those tribes and had invited them to a council at Gist's new settlement. Washington felt himself better equipped now for negotiations with the savages because he had as his counsellors not only Andrew Montour and Half King but also the famous trader, Indian diplomatist and interpreter, George Croghan. [70]

[67] *Ibid.*, 83.   [68] 1 *Diaries*, 93.
[69] The date has not been determined.
[70] In his letter of June 1, 1754, to Washington (1 *Din.*, 186–87), Dinwiddie said he was sending Croghan as interpreter to the Commander-in-Chief, James Innes, who was expected soon on the frontier; but nowhere in Washington's journal is the date of Croghan's arrival given. The first reference to him is in the entry of June 21 (1 *Diaries*, 100), but the "speeches" delivered to the Indians by Washington on and after the 18th show an acquaintance with Indian usage that suggests the counsel of someone who had such special knowledge of the natives as Croghan possessed. George scarcely could have prepared these "speeches" without more assistance than Andrew Montour and Half King could have given him.

The Delawares, under Chief Shingiss, and several Shawnee emissaries came promptly, but before Washington could employ Croghan's arts on these Indians, there arrived from Logstown eight Mingoes who seemed curiously in a hurry. Instead of resting and eating and waiting on formalities, they asked to see Washington without delay and, when admitted, told him they had a commission that required an immediate council. Surprised by this haste, the Colonel brought some of his advisers together and let the Mingoes explain themselves. The visitors said they had been anxious to see their friends' armed forces in the field, as if this were the reason for the visit; but they went on with so many expostulations in discussing the French, that George and his companions became suspicious: These Mingoes might be spies! Because of this possibility, George proceeded to act with appropriate caution and told the Mingoes that he could not receive their speech until Half King could be present. Delaware spokesmen similarly were asked to wait until that friend of the English could sit with the white men.

After Half King reached the camp, the English and about forty Indians—men of the Six Nations, Delawares and Shawnees—opened a council.[71] It lasted three days and, in the slow preparation and translation of long speeches, it must have been exceedingly tedious, but to George it must have been educational, also, because it showed him how the supposed masters of Indian statecraft and diplomacy maneuvered. He had to make the decisions and to deliver the speeches that Croghan and the others probably helped him fashion, but he had time to observe the nuances of Indian relations, as, for example, when it became proper for the Delawares to address the Six Nations as "Uncles" and the Shawnees as "Grandsons." [72] George could follow, also, the sort of argument that was thought effective, though it differed little from that which he had employed at Gist's instance in his first exchanges with Half King and the other chieftains en route to Fort Le Boeuf.

The substance of the speeches George made the Indians was that he and his men had come to fight by the side of the Six Nations and the Delawares, who were invited to send their women and children to safety in the English settlements. All other Indians of the Ohio were put on notice to choose between French and English and to take the consequences. Because of this warning, and as a result of their own

[71] In the French original as well as in the English translation of the journal, "Delawares" and "Loups" are mentioned as if they were separate "nations." In this particular entry, "Loups" and not "Delawares" are named, though, in reality, Loup (Wolf) was the name the French usually gave the Delawares.
[72] Cf. 1 Diaries, 98.

direct exchanges, the Delawares and Shawnees renewed their alliance, and professed willingness to join with the Six Nations in amity toward England.[73]

The council, terminating on the 21st of June, was held under the eyes of the eight Mingoes, whose behavior confirmed the suspicion that they were spying on the force and were spreading false information concerning the strength of the French. To verify or disprove the statements of the Mingoes regarding the dispositions of the enemy, Washington sent out friendly natives as counter-spies. "I left off working any further on the road," George explained later, "and told [the Mingoes] that as we intended to continue it through the woods as far as the fort, felling trees, etc., that we were waiting here for the reenforcements which were coming to us . . . But as soon as they were gone, I set about making out and clearing a road to Red Stone." [74]

In spite of this deception of the enemy and the encouragement of friends, George discovered promptly that the council had been a failure. Shingiss and his Delawares could not be induced to go to the camp in the Meadows with their families, though Shingiss told George the warriors might be persuaded, by the dispatch of a great war belt, to declare for the English. The Shawnees silently vanished. These were not the only disappointments. When Half King and his warriors had come from Great Meadows, George had assumed that they would remain with the troops who were opening the road toward Red Stone Creek. Instead, when the council was over, Half King and all his people started back to the camp. Nor could they be deterred by anything that Washington or Andrew Montour said to them. George was puzzled by this. He did not realize, perhaps, that as he had offered the natives the hospitality of the camp, they intended to accept it with no service in return. When told that Half King might come back to the front if wampum and a speech were sent him, Washington dispatched George Croghan with a string of wampum and an appeal to Half King to rejoin him in order to share in the welcome of Chief Monakatoocha, who was believed to be on the trail to join the English and the Indian allies.

Not until the next evening did George know the result of this appeal. Then three, and only three warriors put in their appearance. They brought a note in which Croghan explained that he had encountered much difficulty in finding any natives who were willing to join the

[73] 1 Diaries, 94–99.   [74] 1 Diaries, 101.

detachment. Half King was inclined to come but was said to have received an injury that hindered his movements. As a consequence of this defection, George had to use his own inexperienced men as scouts to prevent surprise by the French.

This failure shook the faith of Washington in Montour and Croghan, who, as he subsequently wrote, never were able, in spite of all their boasting, to bring into camp more than thirty Indians, and not more than half of the thirty serviceable.[75] Deeper than this reason for the Indians' reluctance to fight was the meagreness of the presents George could offer. In his speech to the Six Nations, he had been compelled to apologize that the gift he tendered them was "not so considerable as I could wish." [76] More Indian goods were coming but they had not arrived when most needed—a fault that seemed common to all supplies of the expedition. Still another reason why the Indians had begun to hold back undoubtedly was their belief, not openly voiced, as yet, that the forces of the English were inferior to those of the French.

The zeal of the Indians was dampened, further, by the shortage of provisions. All the flour and the bacon of the advanced party had been consumed by the 23rd of June. Nothing was left but a few steers, the milch cows and their calves.[77] George Croghan had contracted to supply 10,000 lbs. of flour [78] immediately after June 2, and later had agreed to furnish 200 horses to transport it; but he had delivered no flour and had not assembled more than twenty-five of the animals.[79] The Indians observed all this. There was sarcasm as well as the prospect of early hunger in the question they asked George—did he intend to starve them as well as the English? [80]

Thus, while the advanced detachment continued to work on the road and waited vainly for flour from the rear, the whole Indian support of the expedition was in danger of falling apart: Not one Cherokee or Catawba ally had appeared in Virginia. Though Governor Dinwiddie had been confident 1000 would come; [81] the Delawares had declined to go to the English camp; the Shawnees had disappeared;

[75] Washington to Col. William Fairfax, Aug. 11, 1754; 1 G. W., 92. The allowance finally made Montour was for the daily pay of eighteen men (1 Sharpe, 139).

[76] 1 Diaries, 96.

[77] Minutes of Council of War, Gist's house, June 28, 1754; MS return of stores, 1 Papers of G. W., LC.

[78] Dinwiddie to Washington, June 2, 1754; 1 Din., 189.

[79] It is not certain that even this number had been brought together by June 23. See Washington to William Fairfax, Aug. 11, 1754; 1 G. W., 95. Cf. Dinwiddie to John Carlyle, June 27, 1754; 1 Din., 220.

[80] Ibid.

[81] See 1 Din., 60, 61, 62, 79, 94, 106.

those of the Six Nations who were encamped at Great Meadows were indisposed to fight or even to act as scouts; Half King was injured and unable to assist if, indeed, he was not feigning illness. The only cheerful news about the Indians was an unconfirmed report that Chief Monakatoocha had burned his village, Logstown, and had started with his people up the Monongahela in canoes to Red Stone, where he was expected in two days.[82] George hoped that this able leader would come with his warriors from Red Stone Creek to the camp and would assist the few Indians who were scouting along the line of the expected French advance. The larger the number of trustworthy scouts, the less, of course, would be the chance of a coup by the force from the Ohio.

The record was poor, the prospect grim. In fact, George might have said that from the time he had left Winchester, everything except the skirmish with Jumonville had gone against him. Ill fortune in procuring transport, adverse weather on the march from Wills Creek, the shameful failure of Croghan to deliver flour and horses, the stiff attitude of Mackay and the Independent Company, the humiliation of losing the active support of the Indians because he had so little to give them, the intolerable and inexplicable delay in the arrival of promised reenforcements, the exhaustion of the supply of flour and of bacon, the threat of starvation and the scarcity of ammunition—all this had been encountered. Part of it had been overcome; part of it had to be endured. Until more provisions arrived, the English and their Indian guests would have to subsist on a little parched corn and on the unsalted fresh meat of cattle.

George did not hesitate in the face of that contingency: He had resolved that he would go to the mouth of Red Stone Creek, build a fort there, and hold it until the arrival of a force large enough to advance to the Ohio. Once again he steeled himself to carry through what he had undertaken. He reasoned that the French in their advance either would come up the Monongahela and thence up Red Stone Creek, or else they would follow the trail from Fort DuQuesne to Gist's settlement. To protect the troops and the line of supply against surprise, while building the fort, George had to adapt his force to his necessities in these two particulars: First, on their meagre fare, the English could not progress rapidly in felling trees and in dragging them out of the way so that the swivel guns and the few wagons might be moved toward Red Stone. Second, if the French were close at hand, it would be dangerous to spread out the men, snakelike, in opening the way. In this situation, it appeared to George that the best attainable result was to be had by dispatching Capt. Andrew Lewis with a few officers and sixty men to clear a road to the mouth of Red Stone Creek.[83] The remaining troops must remain at Gist's new settlement.

Such were George's orders and such his plans on the morning of June 27.[84] Off went Lewis and his threescore men; Washington and the remainder of the Virginia contingent stayed at Gist's with the wagons and the swivels. Nothing was heard from Mackay and the Independent Company, who, presumably, still were at Great Meadows.

That night or the next morning, June 28,[85] there arrived a message from Monakatoocha,[86] a most startling message: The Chief had been at Fort DuQuesne two days previously, had witnessed the arrival of reenforcements there, and had heard the French say they were going to march forward and attack the English with 800 white troops and 400 Indians.[87]

In Washington's judgment, the fact that this report came from so experienced and trustworthy a man as Monakatoocha gave it credibility that lifted it above the general level of frontier rumor repeated by ignorant or designing men. Besides, French deserters had stated earlier that reenforcements were expected at Fort DuQuesne. Two English

[83] 1 *Diaries,* 102.

[84] The orders are summarized in the entry of that date in the journal; the plan is reconstructed easily from the known situation and from the subsequent developments, except as respects the distance from Gist's at which Lewis was to work. As will be plain in a later paragraph, the slow return of Lewis suggests, though it does not prove, that he was some miles from camp on the 28th.

[85] This provoking, if relatively unimportant doubt is raised by the conflict between the minutes, in Washington's autograph, of the council of war said to have been held on June 28, at Gist's (1 *Hamilton,* 16–18), and Stephen's account (as reprinted in the *Md. Gazette,* Aug. 29, 1754, and reproduced in *Ambler,* 214–15). Stephen, beginning his narrative as of June 29, manifestly was one day late in the first part of his chronology. Washington, on the other hand, must have predated some of the proceedings of the council if, first, he was correct in saying that Lewis's departure was on June 27, and if, second, all the events described by Stephen occurred after the arrival of the message to be mentioned in the next clause of the text. It would have been impossible for Mackay and his Independent Company to have reached Gist's in time for a council on the 28th, had the decision to send for Mackay been reached, as Stephen averred, at a preliminary conference of officers. Such a meeting could not have been held earlier than the evening of the 27th or the morning of the 28th, because, when the officers were deliberating, Lewis's detachment, which left on the morning of the 27th, already was some distance from Gist's. The simplest and most probable reconciliation of dates is had by assuming Stephen one day behind and Washington at least half a day ahead in his chronology. George may have confused in his journal the first and second council, or else he may have assigned the date of the 28th to events that began on the night of the 28th–29th.

[86] The minutes of the war council (1 *Hamilton,* 17) may be interpreted to mean that Monakatoocha himself brought the news, but if a chieftain of high reputation had shared in the events that followed, he almost certainly would have been mentioned in one or another of the narratives.

[87] 1 *Hamilton,* 17. Stephen (*op. cit.*) gave the number as 300 French and 300 Indians.

soldiers, moreover, had disappeared a short time previously. These men might have joined the French and traitorously might have told the enemy where Washington was, how many troops he had, and how meagre were the supplies of the English.[88] If the French had that information, they of course would advance as rapidly as they could.

So reasoned young Colonel Washington in his first serious study of important, cumulative intelligence reports. His conclusion was that an early attack by a greatly superior force was altogether probable, almost certain indeed. How and where to meet the attack were questions on which he immediately sought the counsel of the few officers with him. Common judgment, quickly voiced, was that the scattered parts of the little force, Mackay's Independent Company, Lewis's detachment and Washington's own contingent, should be united as soon as possible. This would have to be done at Gist's because that settlement was about midway between Lewis's assumed position and the fort at Great Meadows where Mackay was waiting. Another reason for this choice was that nine of the swivels had been placed at Gist's. They could be used in defence, if a stand had to be made there; and, if a withdrawal was to be ordered, they had to be guarded until they could be escorted by a force strong enough to protect them from capture.

George accordingly wrote Mackay a dispatch, in which he requested the Captain to bring the Independent Company to his assistance. Lewis was ordered to halt his road-making and to return immediately to Gist's, where manifestly a stockade should be erected.[89] As no other or better material was at hand for quick use, George took nearly all Gist's fencing and employed it as palisades.[90]

Doubtless work on this stockade had been suspended in the darkness when Captain Mackay rode up. He had understood the plight of his colonial comrade and, as became a good soldier,[91] he had hurried forward with his troops.[92] Lewis, too, pressed his detachment and, by the forenoon of the 29th,[93] was at Gist's.[94] In spite of this successful reunion of the scattered forces, the Indian allies became more and more alarmed. Some of them had scouted around Fort DuQuesne; some

---

[88] Minutes of war council, 1 *Hamilton*, 17.

[89] *Md. Gazette*, Aug. 29, 1754.

[90] See Gist's petition, *Journ. H.B.*, 1752–58, p. 223.

[91] "A brave and worthy officer," Washington later pronounced him (29 *G. W.*, 39).

[92] The promptness of his arrival over thirteen miles of bad road suggests that his troops were behind him.

[93] Subject to the reservation of date in n. 85, *supra*.

[94] 1 *Hamilton*, 16.

had heard exaggerated stories of the overwhelming strength of the French. All the natives soon gave warning that they would leave the English unless Colonel Washington returned to the fort in the Great Meadows.[95]

In this atmosphere, George called a second council of war. All the evidence concerning the probable early arrival of the enemy was reviewed. Account was taken of the provisions. For the subsistence of 400 men at Gist's there was no bread, no bacon and only twenty-four cattle, most of them cows, with barely one quart of salt left for saving meat or making it less unpalatable. The French, moreover, might try to compel Washington to surrender by intercepting the convoys that would undertake to bring provisions to him at Gist's. It was reasoned, too, that the numerically superior French could so narrow the ground left to the English that the cattle would die for lack of grazing before they were devoured. If, on the other hand, the French chose the impatient and expensive course of direct attack, then the English would have to destroy a force three times as large as their own. Otherwise, if a partial English victory were followed by an unavoidable withdrawal, the weakened column almost certainly would be destroyed in the woods by the Indians.

The alternative was a retreat to the fort at Great Meadows before the arrival of the French. Once there, the English would be more accessible to supplies and the French less so. The enemy might be able to paddle his canoes up the Youghiogheny within five miles of Gist's; but if he got as far as the new settlement and then had to feed himself at Great Meadows, he would have to traverse with few horses thirteen miles of bad road in a mountainous country. In addition, at Great Meadows, both the routes of French advance converged—the one southward from Gist's and the one southeastward from the mouth of Red Stone Creek. Because of this, it should not be difficult at the Great Meadows to get an early report of a French advance, whereas, at Gist's, there always was the possibility that the French would slip eastward from Red Stone and lie in wait across the English line of supply.[96] In favor of the strategy that would avoid this possibility there was, finally, the insistence of Indians on a withdrawal. Unless this was

[95] 1 *Hamilton,* 17.

[96] The term "lines of communication" appears to have been used at this time primarily in the sense of lines of communication within a trench system, but occasionally the words were employed as in the nineteenth and twentieth centuries, "Lines of supply" were more frequently mentioned. See the Introduction to this volume.

done, they manifestly would carry out their threat and abandon their allies. Loss of the Indian scouts might be fatal in that difficult, wooded country.

These considerations[97] led George and his brother officers to decide unanimously that the column should retreat forthwith to Great Meadows. It was not an easy task. Besides the mountainous character of the country and the badness of the road, George had once more to contend with the lack of transport that had cramped and cursed the expedition from the day it reached Winchester. The teams that had brought the swivels and the supplies to Gist's had been sent back, it will be remembered,[98] to haul the provisions that were expected at Great Meadows. Only two teams—"very indifferent" in Stephen's opinion[99]—a few odd horses and the officers' mounts remained with the troops. These animals and the men themselves were all the resources George had for moving the nine swivels, the ammunition and the baggage.

Here again, there was no hesitation. The soldiers must draw the swivels; the ammunition and as many as possible of the other articles must be carried in the wagons and on the pack horses. Drovers could care for the cattle. Private baggage that could not be conveyed to Great Meadows must perforce be sacrificed. It was agreed! George himself drew up the minutes of the council almost in the order in which the arguments were advanced, and he prepared the "resolves" for final signature by the officers.[100]

The loading of the wagons then began, but it soon was apparent that the two vehicles would not suffice even for the ammunition. Immediately George ordered his own riding horse to be loaded with powder and shot. He would walk those thirteen terrible miles to Great Meadows before he would leave behind a single round that could be saved. The other officers, emulating him, at once tendered their mounts for the same purpose. When all had been offered, George proceeded to bargain in his private capacity with some of the soldiers to carry his baggage on their backs to the Meadows for the stiff price of four pistoles.[101]

[97] They are stated fully in the minutes of the Council, 1 *Hamilton*, 16–18.
[98] See *supra*, p. 391.
[99] *Md. Gazette*, Aug. 29, 1754.
[100] According to a note in 1 *Hamilton*, 18, the original in Washington's autograph has no signature attached, though the last lines read: "For all these considerations this Resolves was signed by."
[101] *Md. Gazette*, Aug. 29, 1754.

The retreat commenced—an ordeal that men endured only because the alternative was death in the woods from the bullet or war hatchet of an Indian. Adam Stephen said afterward that the road was "the roughest and most hilly of any on the Allegheny Mountains," [102] and doubtless at the time he found many companies who agreed emphatically and profanely. There was nothing to eat except parched corn [103] and lean beef slaughtered, cooked and swallowed in the same hour. This ration did not give the Virginians the strength they required to drag the swivels easily up the hills and over the rocks and stumps. Every grade was a despair, every furlong a torture.

Worst of all was the attitude of the men of Mackay's Independent Company. They had refused to help in getting the ammunition ready for transportation and, once the march began, they would not lend a hand in dragging the swivels or in removing obstacles from the road. These, said the regulars, were not the duties of soldiers, and could not be required of them. So far as they were concerned, they would leave the swivels in the road and be damned to them! The Virginians observed and wondered and then asked, in effect, If this is not proper work for soldiers, why should we do it? "They became as backward as the regulars," Stephen narrated afterward. All the exhortation and appeal of their officers [104] were required to keep them to their duty.

It was the first day of July when the exhausted men pulled the swivels into their feeble fort in the Great Meadows. [105] For these staggering, half-starved men, George had hoped to get provisions from the wagons and pack animals that should have reached the fort during his absence. Instead, he found the commissary almost as bare as his own. When a convoy finally did arrive, it brought a few bags of flour only. [106] This posed still another problem. The council of war at Gist's had re-

---

102 *Ibid.*

103 *Stephen's "Life," Rush Papers.*

104 *Md. Gazette,* Aug. 29, 1754.

105 *Ibid.* As Stephen did not state when the retreat began or at what hour the men reached their last position, it is impossible to fix the time of departure from Gist's. A prudent commander, accustomed to difficult marches and not fearing immediate attack, would have started, if possible, on the 29th and would have bivouacked that night by the roadside. As he had to call on his men to pull their cannon over the ridges, he would not have attempted a continuous march unless he knew his foe was at his heels. The probability therefore is that the column left Gist's on the afternoon of the 29th. If it covered two miles that day and six through difficult country on the 30th of June, it would have reached the Great Meadows, over the last five miles of the road, late in the afternoon of the 1st of July. No mention is made of a night march. At that season of long days, such a march could have been rendered unnecessary by an early start. The final determinative, of course, is the unknown one, the sharpness of the spur that keeps retreating men on their feet, namely, the fear of being overtaken.

106 *Md. Gazette,* Aug. 29, 1754. The inference, though not the certainty, is that the convoy arrived July 1 or 2.

solved that the column "return to the fort . . . and wait there until supplied with a stock of provisions sufficient to serve us for some months."[107] If there were not even provisions enough for the temporary subsistence of the troops and their Indian guests, a farther withdrawal had to be considered by Washington. Some of the men were anxious to put more miles between themselves and the French, and fewer between their stomachs and the abundant food of home; but George decided against further retreat. He thought the troops were too worn and weak to drag the swivel guns he was anxious to save. Besides, he had learned [108] that the two Independent Companies from New York had disembarked at Alexandria about three weeks previously and he reasoned that these troops and the other reenforcements promised by Governor Dinwiddie soon would reach him. If that was the prospect, duty demanded what the physical condition of George's troops dictated—that the retreat end at Great Meadows as originally planned,[109] and that the country West of Allegheny Mountain and Laurel Hill be held. An express was sent to Wills Creek to report the situation and to ask that more men and supplies be hurried forward.[110]

The fort must be strengthened so that it would be safe until the enlarged force was able to take the offensive against the French. Tired as were the men, those who had the mettle and the muscle must clear a longer field of fire, or fell trees, or work on the stockade, or dig trenches outside. The position did not now appear to be the "charming field for an encounter" that Washington had thought it when he first had sheltered his wagons behind "natural entrenchments." It was possible, George quickly perceived, to carry his crude trench beyond a small branch, so that his men could be sure of getting water. Moreover, part of the ground around the fort was so marshy that a direct assault by infantry probably could be made from one direction only, the South. It might be possible, also, to complete the little stockade in the middle of the entrenchments and to secure there the powder and provisions. This was the measure of advantage. For the rest, the fort was in a damp "bottom"; woods came within easy musket range of it; high ground surrounded it.[111]

Time did not permit the selection of a stronger, more defensible

---

[107] 1 Hamilton, 16–17.
[108] Doubtless from the teamsters of the convoy.
[109] Md. Gazette, Aug. 29, 1754.
[110] Ibid.
[111] The crest of Hager Hill, less than 700 yards from the fort, has an elevation of 2061 feet.

site.[112] The best had to be made of a weak position. George extended
the embankment beyond the brook and he had some of the men raise
higher the low parapet, outside which, on the South and West, he had
a fire trench dug. Another detachment felled timber for the palisades
of the small structure inside the earthworks. As the enlarged fort took
final form, it became a curious quadrilateral. Its long axis from Northwest to Southeast was 160 feet; the four sides varied in length from
approximately sixty to about 100 feet; the projection over the stream
was at the northeastern end of the fortification. The whole and the
parts were not a design of engineering art but of frontier necessity.
Wherefore, George gave it the name, Fort Necessity.[113]

If the improvement of this frail fort gave Washington any feeling
whatsoever of security on the 2nd of July, it must have been slight. At
nightfall, not even the little stockade had been finished.[114] An observant
enemy, disposing his riflemen with care, could rake part of the interior.
At least as serious as the weakness of the position was a circumstance
that must have angered and humiliated the Colonel. Silently, almost
mysteriously and with no explanation or word of farewell, the Indians
disappeared from their camp near the fort. Squaws and children and
warriors, even Half King himself, slunk away. George did not know
whither they went but he knew why: They had become terrified by the
reports of the great strength of the French and they had concluded their
English "brothers" were to be defeated. In the Indians' eyes, desertion
was discretion.[115] Such reconnaissance as George could arrange for the
night of July 2–3 had to be conducted by white soldiers who knew
little or nothing of the art of trailing men in the woods. The young
commander tried to make up for the inexperience of his troops by
stationing them on all the probable lines of the enemy's advance. Senti-
nels were assigned to numerous posts from which they could hear if
they could not see an approaching foe. These detachments weakened

112 Cf. Stephen in *Md. Gazette*, Aug. 29, 1754.

113 In the absence of any plan or adequate contemporary description, the design of Fort
Necessity has been the subject of a discussion almost amusingly heated. Washington said of it
only that there was "a small temporary stockade in the middle of the entrenchment called
Fort Necessity, erected for the sole purpose of [the] security [of the powder] and of the few
stores we had" (29 *G. W.*, 40). All the other evidence and all the theories were expounded in
Washington's Road (171–81), by A. B. Hulbert. That writer's conclusions are accepted in the
present account, with the reservation that it is impossible to say where the trenches ran or how
much of the ground was covered by the "small temporary stockade."

114 Stephen's "Life," *Rush Papers*.

115 Washington in 29 *G. W.*, 40. Cf. Col. James Innes to Gov. James Hamilton: "We had
not one Indian to assist when the engagement commenced or ended" (*Md. Gazette*, Aug. 1, 1754;
Ambler, 214).

greatly the defenders of the entrenchments. The entire force numbered about 400 only.[116] A hundred and more of these were sick or exhausted. George's effective total of fighting men was 284.[117]

About daybreak on the 3rd of July, a single shot rang out. A moment later, a sentinel shouted for the guard. Soon word was passed that the man had been wounded in the heel. Ordinarily, such a casualty would have been attributed to a prowling Indian, for pursuit of whom it would be foolish to arouse the camp; but this time, the shot might be a warning of early attack. The troops accordingly were ordered to get under arms.[118] Sleepy soldiers scarcely had made ready for action when a steady rain began to fall. The low ground around the fort seemed to be a veritable catch basin; in a short time the space within the entrenchments seemed almost afloat.[119] For five hours, the unsheltered men had rain, rain, rain and nothing besides. Then, about 9 o'clock, reports began to reach George from his reconnaissance parties. One story was that French and Indians in great strength, and all of them naked, were within four miles.[120] Another report, less sensational, was that 900 French were on the march from the Monongahela to attack the English.[121] In preparation for the enemy's arrival, George could do almost nothing except to urge the men to keep their powder dry. Mud already was deep inside the fort; water was rising in the trenches.

About 11 o'clock, an alert sentinel caught a glimpse of armed men and sounded a new alarm by firing his musket.[122] It was a challenge the French accepted. Although their commander subsequently admitted that he incautiously presented his flank to the English,[123] George observed no blunder. Instead, he saw the French emerge from cover and move forward [124] in three columns.[125] The shout of the white men

---

[116] Col. James Innes to Gov. James Hamilton; *Md. Gazette*, July 12, 1754.

[117] *Stephen's "Life," Rush Papers.*

[118] Stephen in *Md. Gazette*, Aug. 29, 1754. This incident of the early morning is not mentioned in any of Washington's four incomplete accounts of the action. These four are: The one published anonymously in the *Va. Gazette* of July 19, 1754, a copy of which is in 165 *Newcastle Papers*, 231, Br. Mus.; a second quoted indirectly by Dinwiddie to the Lords of Trade, July 24, 1754, 1 *Din.*, 239 ff; a third in George's comment on the publication of his journal, 2 *Sparks*, 463 ff; and, last, the one in his notes on Humphreys' proposed biography, 29 *G. W.*, 39. Omission by Washington of this detail of an alarm at dawn scarcely can be regarded as depreciation of Stephen's contemporary account, though Stephen's memory was not always accurate. His "Life" in the *Rush Papers*, was not written until 1775 and, for that and other reasons, has to be subjected to a severe critique.   [120] *Md. Gazette*, Aug. 29, 1754.

[119] *Stephen's "Life," Rush Papers.*   [121] *Va. Gazette*, July 19, 1754.

[122] *Ibid.* There is a difference of one hour in reports of this "opening shot." Washington, a year or two after the event, said the fire began at 10 A.M. (1 *Ford*, 122n); but narratives more nearly contemporaneous give the hour as 11.

[123] Villiers' account in the *Précis*, 150.

[124] 1 *Din.*, 239.   [125] *Stephen's "Life," Rush Papers.*

and the wild yell of the Indians told the garrison to expect the utmost in soldierly skill and the worst in savage cruelty.[126] George met valor with vigor. He moved his troops into the open and formed them to repel a charge. They dressed their line in good order. When the French halted and opened fire at approximately 600 yards, there was no wavering by the English and, fortunately, no loss. George did not let the men return the fire at that distance. They must wait for nearer targets and not permit the enemy to intimidate them by mere noise.[127]

Now the French began to advance again as if they intended to press their attack home. At the word of command, the English slipped back immediately into their trenches, which were deeper than ever in water. From the low parapet of these defences, the Virginians and the regulars prepared for a volley that would repulse the onslaught, but before they got the order, the charging soldiers dropped to the ground. Some of the French, as close as sixty yards, scattered and almost disappeared. "They then," wrote Washington, "from every little rising, tree, stump, stone and bush kept up a constant, galling [128] fire upon us . . ." [129] He saw, too, that it was not directed against his men only. The French deliberately shot every horse, every cow and even the dogs around the camp, until, while the engagement still was young, the English realized they had lost already their transport and their meat.[130]

If this was to be the battle, the Virginians and Carolinians must warm to it and must give as well as take. George still did not order any futile volleys, but he told his troops to fire whenever they saw a Frenchman lift head above a rock or peer from behind a tree. The colonials and the regulars were glad to hit back. They felt sure they killed many a Frenchman and kept the others from pressing closer,[131] but they themselves now were losing steadily and were having more and more difficulty in keeping their weapons and their cartridges dry enough to use. George's men, a concentrated target, exposed themselves every time they tried to pull a trigger; the French had so many trees behind which to hide that they had much the better of the exchange.[132]

The unequal fight continued into the late afternoon and rose in the fury of fire [133] until the rain gods threw in their reserves against the

---

126 29 G. W., 40.
127 Dinwiddie to the Lords of Trade, July 24, 1754; 1 Din., 239–40; Va. Gazette, July 19, 1754.
128 Washington wrote "galding."
129 29 G. W., 40.
130 Va. Gazette, July 19, 1754.
131 29 G. W., 40.
132 Cf. 1 Din., 240.
133 Villiers said (Mémoire, 151) that the fire was heaviest between 6 and 8, but English accounts do not bear this out. It is probable, also, that Villiers exaggerated the use the English made of the swivel guns.

garrison. There fell, in Washington's words, "the most tremendous rain that [could] be conceived." It filled the trenches, got into the men's cartridge-boxes,[134] wet their firelocks and reached even the powder that had been placed carefully in what was thought to be the driest spot inside the stockade. Amid the deluge, half-drowned and more nearly floating than standing on their feet, few of the English troops had any effective weapon left except the bayonet, and some did not have even that.[135] The fire of the English fell off; so, in a short time, did that of the attacking force. Observant soldiers thought this meant that the ammunition of the French was getting low, but they were surprised and puzzled that the enemy had been able to keep his powder dry.[136]

About 8 o'clock,[137] just as twilight began to gather, there came a cry from the French, *"Voulez-vous parler?"*[138] When the words were translated to the tall young Colonel he refused. No, he would not parley. The French merely wished to get to the fort and to see how the trenches were sited so they could make a new and better attack.[139]

There was a wait and then another shouted question from beyond the trenches: Would the commander send out an officer to receive a proposal, an officer who could speak French? The messenger would, on word of honor, be permitted to return unhurt.[140] George had to decide: His powder was wet; about a third of his effectives were dead or wounded; all the horses and cattle had been killed; to keep his men from hunger, he had only two bags of flour, a little bacon [141] and barely enough other food to make the whole equal three days' rations.[142] Even if, by luck, the powder could be dried quickly in uncertain weather, the wet and fouled muskets scarcely could be put in order because, in the entire command,[143] there were only two screws with which to remove the wet charges.[144] Besides these reasons for accepting the French proposal for a parley, there was another of which George may not at the moment have been aware: In some fashion, soon after dark, the soldiers got into the rum supply that had been forwarded for presents to the Indians and for issue to men on hard duty.[145] Many of the wet and

---

[134] Among different armies of the time the cartridge box, which was of wood or turned metal, contained as few as twelve or as many as thirty charges.
[135] 29 *G. W.*, 40.
[136] 1 *Sharpe*, 198; *Penn. Gazette*, Sept. 19, 1754.
[137] 1 *Din.*, 240.
[138] *Stephen's "Life," Rush Papers.*
[139] Washington in 1 *Ford*, 122n.
[140] 1 *Din.*, 240.
[141] *Md. Gazette*, Aug. 29, 1754.
[142] See *infra*, p. 409.
[143] *Md. Gazette*, loc. cit.
[144] *Ibid.*
[145] Cf. Dinwiddie to Gov. James Hamilton, Mch. 21, 1754; 1 *Din.*, 118. See *ibid.*, 124.

chilled soldiers had started drinking; some already were getting drunk; about half of the entire force soon were to be undependable.[146]

Whether or not George knew at nightfall of this condition, the other reasons for a parley with the enemy were compelling. Washington, heavy-hearted, but convinced of his duty, called two French-speaking officers, Jacob van Braam and William La Peyroney, and sent them out between the lines to ascertain what the French proposed.[147] They soon brought back assurance that the French were willing to permit the English to leave the fort and to return to Virginia without becoming prisoners of war. Probably because of the vagueness of these terms,[148] Washington rejected them and instructed his representatives to return for further parley. La Peyroney either had been wounded earlier in the day and collapsed about this time, or else he received a shot that dropped him now.[149] Van Braam was left as the one French-speaking officer to carry on the negotiations.

The Dutchman left the entrenchments and returned, after a time, with a folded sheet. On the first page were the badly penned opening paragraphs of a *Capitulation*, in French, accorded by M. de Villiers, commanding the troops of His Most Christian Majesty, to the English troops *dans le fort De Necessité*. The second page of the sheet was blurred with the ink that came through the damp paper from the first page, and was covered with scarcely legible script. Near the bottom of the sheet was a blank space in which, as subsequent scrutiny showed, the names of two English Captains were to be inserted. These men were to be hostages. As best van Braam might, by the light of a candle that scarcely could be made to burn in the rain, he undertook to translate the difficult handwriting into his own limping English. No other officer even attempted to decipher the text; van Braam probably would not have been able to do so, even blunderingly, if the capitulation had not been read aloud to him by the French officer who gave him the paper.[150] In the Dutchman's own poor English, the document set forth that it never had been the intention of the French to disturb the peace

146 *Md. Gazette*, Aug. 29, 1754. In this reference, Stephen did not say where the men procured the liquor but, in the conditions existing, there was one source only. Villiers (*Mémoire*, 152) on the morning of the 4th found in the fort some "casks of liquor" which he broke open in order to keep his men and the Indians from imbibing.

147 *Va. Gazette*, July 19, 1754; 1 *Din.*, 240.

148 The confused events of the evening of July 3 and the conflicting evidence regarding them are reviewed in a brief critique, Appendix I–10.

149 Cf. *Md. Gazette*, Aug. 29, 1754; *Ambler*, 215. See also 1 *G. W.*, 96.

150 *Md. Gazette*, Aug. 29, 1754.

and *bonne harmonie* that subsisted between the two princes, "but only to avenge . . ."

There van Braam came to a word over which he probably hesitated as at least one other translator did subsequently. In the flickering light it may have looked as if it were *l'assailir*, which did not make sense where a noun and not a verb was required by the sentence structure. Van Braam finally translated it as "death," or "loss" or "killing"—there later was some doubt which word he used. The text then went on *"qui a été fait sur un de nos officiers,"* which of course was easy. Washington and others believed the language meant that the French said they sought to avenge the death of one of their officers, who, of course, was Jumonville.

At the moment, less thought was given to this than to the specific terms, which van Braam proceeded to translate. First, the English commander could retire with his entire garrison to his own country. No insult would be offered by the French, who would do all they could to restrain their Indians. Second, the English could carry with them all their belongings except their artillery and "munitions of war," which the French "reserved" to themselves. Third, the defenders of the fort would receive the honors of war and could march out of the entrenchments with drum beating and with one small cannon. Fourth, as soon as the terms were signed, the English were to strike their colors. Fifth, at daybreak, a detachment of French would see that the English marched off and left the French in possession of the fort. Sixth, as the English had no horses or cattle left, with which to remove their effects, they could put these *en cache* until they could send draft animals for them; and to this end they could leave a guard, on condition that they should not work on any establishment in that vicinity or on that side of the mountains for one year. Finally, as the English held prisoners taken at the—again that word van Braam translated "loss" or "death" or "killing" of Jumonville—they must liberate and deliver these men, under escort, at Fort DuQuesne. As surety for this and for the general agreement—then came the blank in the text—two Captains were to be left as hostages until the arrival of the French and Canadian prisoners. The victors offered to provide a guard for these hostages, who promised return of the French prisoners in two and a half months at latest.[151]

Several of these terms were of awkward construction which was over-

---

[151] MS Capitulation, Archives of the District of Montreal; the first page and the signatures of this are reproduced as the frontispiece of Volume II.

looked or variously interpreted at the moment. The main provisions were what counted, and these were honorable. George balked at one stipulation only: the English ought not to be compelled to surrender their "munitions of war," because that phrase would include ammunition. If the troops started back without powder and ball, every man of them might be killed and scalped by the Indians before they could reach Wills Creek. Van Braam must return to the French and insist on the elimination of that phrase.

Back once more into the rain and blackness went the Captain. If he did not win M. de Villiers' consent that the English retain their ammunition, it would be better to accept the status of prisoners of war. To attempt to return unarmed to the Potomac would be self-murder in a country where the French Indians would be mad for loot and scalps. If speculation on this point was aroused, it was ended quickly. Van Braam soon returned: The French had been reasonable. From the capitulation the words *et munitions de guerre* had been stricken by a penstroke.

There remained the question of hostages. Who of the Captains should be the two delivered to the French? Hog was a man of affairs who had a new wife at home; Andrew Lewis had a family and many responsibilities as a leader in Augusta; George Mercer was young and not burdened with domestic cares but his Company had no Lieutenant and was to leave its own Ensign at the fort to look after the wounded.[152] Van Braam and Stobo, young, unmarried and unattached, thus were by elimination the most available hostages. As van Braam spoke French, he could make known his rights and wants and those of Robert Stobo, during the two months and a half they would be in the hands of the French while the prisoners taken in the skirmish with Jumonville were being returned.

The French commander was so informed. Van Braam's and Stobo's names were written in the blank left on the second page. Thereupon George signed the capitulation in a hand that showed neither excitement nor exhaustion. Mackay, too, attached his name because he would not recognize the authority of a colonial to act for his troops. Intentionally or not, he wrote "James Mackay" slightly above George's name. The French commander scrawled "Coulon de Villiers" on the sheet and completed the capitulation. It was then about midnight of July 3-4,

---

[152] See the return of Mercer's Company, July 9, 1754; Toner, ed., *Washington's Journal of 1754*, p. 180.

both of them dates thereafter to be renowned in American history.[153] All firing of course had ended. Soon the rain ceased to fall.[154] Weary men who could find a resting place in the engulfing mud stretched themselves out. The loudest sound after that was of pick and shovel as if the French were burying their dead.[155] This grim sound was audible till dawn, when a French detachment came into the trenches [156] and into the stockade. That structure must have looked smaller and even less martial than ever, because Major Stephen the previous afternoon had torn down some of the palisades to give him a field of fire for his swivels.[157]

The new garrison was under discipline. None of the French interfered with the Englishmen who surveyed their scant stores and their feeble equipment in order to decide what to destroy and what to attempt to carry away. As not one horse remained, to bear a man or a pack, George had little choice except among the light articles that could be carried on the shoulders of the troops who did not have to assist the ambulant wounded. The three days' poor rations could be divided, but the surplus powder had to be scattered. Even some of the private baggage must be left,[158] in the dim hope that it could be protected by the guard the French authorized in the capitulation. For the care of the wounded who could not be removed, as well as for the safe custody of the baggage, a total of eleven privates, under an Ensign and a Sergeant, were named from the different Companies.[159]

Major Stephen, all this while, was trying to get the men under arms and ready to march out of the fort. He was a strange figure. Wet, and muddy halfway up his thighs, he had on no stockings. With face and hands red from powder, he bore scant resemblance to an officer and carried no insignia of rank.

"Major," his servant suddenly cried out, "a Frenchman has carried off your clothes!"

Stephen turned and, by good fortune, recognized the corner of his portmanteau on the shoulder of a Frenchman who was running into a

---

[153] The French text, without the heading and the concluding dates, etc., is in 1 *Ford*, 120–21. Contemporary English translations will be found in 1 *Sharpe*, 78; 2 *Penn. Arch.*, 146. Later translations are numerous. An early MS text, mentioned in Appendix IX, remains in the archives of Virginia.

[154] None of the accounts mentions any rain after van Braam brought back the terms of capitulation.

[155] *Va. Gazette*, July 19, 1754.

[156] Villiers, in *Mémoire*, 153.

[157] *Stephen's "Life," Rush Papers.*

[158] 1 *Ford*, 122n.

[159] Toner, ed., *Washington Journal of 1754*, p. 172–80.

crowd of soldiers. Instantly the red-faced, mud-covered Major pursued, overtook the soldier, seized the case, kicked the Frenchman, and started back to his line. Two French officers stopped him: If, said they, an Englishman struck a soldier and behaved in that fashion, they could not be answerable for the capitulation. Stephen's "pertness," as he afterward styled it, evidently made the Frenchmen ask next if he were an officer. In answer he told his servant to open the portmanteau. When this was done, Stephen had the man take out what he described as a "flaming suit of laced regimentals" and this he put on, dirty as he was.[160] Instantly, and without show of amusement, the French officers changed their manner and said no more of the kick administered the soldier of His Most Christian Majesty. Instead, they jestingly asked why the English had not demanded hostages while giving two. They were themselves most desirous of going to Virginia, where, they had been told, there were a great many fair young ladies.[161]

George, like Stephen, had fine apparel which he did not wish to wear that day and could not hope to carry back to Wills Creek with him. Jacob van Braam, on the other hand, was going into the French lines as a hostage and, for the honor of King and cause, must make a good appearance. So a bargain was struck: For £6, Jacob was to have George's superfine broadcloth coat with silver fringe, and for an additional £7, he was to become possessor of a fine scarlet waistcoat, full laced. Already Jacob was in George's debt about £16 on account of a servant George had procured for him from Col. Philip Lee; but as Jacob was willing to assign George two months' pay, due the end of July, the risk was not too great. Van Braam got the finery; George would not lose the entire value of the garments.[162] It was a good bargain for a bad day.

Destruction of other belongings took some hours. It was close to 10 o'clock that 4th of July when the survivors marched out of the fort. They stepped to beat of drum; their colors were flying; they carried their arms; they received the honors of war; but they could not keep the Indians[163] from plundering what they left behind or anything else they did not guard vigilantly while they carried it with them. Not even the surgeon's chest escaped the savages.[164] Some of the redmen

---

160 *Stephen's "Life," Rush Papers.*
161 *Ibid.*
162 *Ledger A,* folio 13. In the end, it would appear, George had to write off a loss of £3, 11s.
163 The French maintained afterward that these Indians arrived on the morning of the 4th— *Va. Gazette,* July 19, 1754.
164 *Md. Gazette,* Aug. 1, 1754.

even came up to the English, gave them their names and blandly professed friendship. Among these, Virginians thought they recognized Delawares whose chieftains scarcely a fortnight previously had talked of an alliance with England.[165]

Harassed by these Indians and too exhausted to pull even the one swivel not surrendered,[166] George and his men had marched about a mile when they missed two or three of the wounded, who had expected to go with the column. George immediately sent back a party whom an Indian compelled to go to the French commander. Villiers returned them to Washington along with the wounded.[167] That night all the survivors bivouacked three miles from the fort they had lost. They were weary but they were relieved.[168] Eighteen years later, in days still darker, George was to write of the anniversary of the capitulation, "I did not let the 3rd . . . pass off without a grateful remembrance of the escape we had . . . The same Providence that protected us . . . will, I hope, continue his mercies . . ."[169]

[165] *Ibid.*
[166] Villiers in *Mémoire*, 153.
[167] *Ibid.*, 463; Washington in 1 *Ford*, 122 n.
[168] Cf. *Md. Gazette*, Aug. 29, 1754, with specific reference to the feeling of the men on receipt of the terms of capitulation.
[169] Washington to Adam Stephen, July 20, 1776; 5 *G. W.*, 213

CHAPTER XII

"And Had My Commission Taken from Me or . . ."
(July 5, 1754–November 15, 1754)

WHEN THE SURVIVORS of Fort Necessity were counted at the bivouac on the morning of July 5, 1754, they numbered 293 officers and men.[1] By the time it reached Wills Creek on the 8th or 9th,[2] the Virginia Regiment had been reduced by death, wounds, detachment, lameness and desertion to 165 rank and file.[3] George's dead numbered thirteen and his wounded fifty-four. Besides the eleven uninjured men detached at the scene of the capitulation to care for those who could not be moved, twenty-nine had been left footsore on the road. Nineteen were missing and either had deserted or had lost their lives while straying from the column.[4] Total killed finally were counted at thirty and the wounded at seventy for the entire force,[5] which, at the beginning of the expedition, had consisted of about 400 of all ranks.

George and most of his officers soon recovered from the physical strains of the battle and the retreat, but the surviving private soldiers of the Virginia Regiment less quickly responded to rest and full rations. This exhaustion manifestly might lead to demoralization, but, in retrospect, there had been little in the conduct of the men that should shame them or their Colonel. Until the evening of July 3, when they had broken into the rum, the soldiers of the colonial command had behaved well and had fought with courage. The men of Mackay's Independent

---

[1] MS morning return; 1 *Papers of G. W.,* LC.

[2] They were there July 9, because the "return" of the various Companies was made at Wills Creek. To get there on the evening of the 8th, the men would have been compelled to march seventeen miles a day on the 5th–8th. Arrival on the 9th would have presupposed a daily march of thirteen miles. The number of lame men left on the road indicates a swift march, which was possible for men who had no wagons, but the doubt concerning the exact dates has not been resolved.

[3] Returns of July 9, 1754 in Toner, ed., *Washington's Journal of 1754,* p. 172–80. Cf. 1 V 278 ff. The return of July 23, 1754, in 1 *Hamilton,* 29, included a total of 240.

[4] *Ibid.* One man was reported a prisoner in addition to the two hostages.

[5] Dinwiddie to the Lords of Trade, July 24, 1754; 1 *Din.,* 241. As the fatalities in the Virginia Regiment were thirteen and the wounded fifty-seven, it is highly improbable that Mackay's Independent Company should have had seventeen killed and only thirteen wounded. This disproportion suggests that some of the figures given by Dinwiddie were estimates. According to later terminology, the figure thirty probably represented the total of "killed and died of wounds." Loss of Washington's papers in the confusion and plundering of Fort Necessity (Toner, ed., *op. cit.,* 181) made an accurate return difficult to prepare.

Company had asserted their rights stubbornly and unworthily prior to the day of battle, but when the attack had come, they had done their full duty in the trenches.

Cowardice there doubtless had been, as always there was in battle; but the only notorious display of lack of mettle had been by an officer, not by a private. Lt. Col. George Muse had shown himself unable to endure the dangers of combat and, of course, had lost the respect of his companions-in-arms.[6] He later offended them still more by admitting his cowardice and by alleging that the others were "as bad as he."[7] Muse's speedy resignation was acceptable.[8]

This was individual humiliation. General distress was created in the command when some officer with a reading knowledge of French scrutinized in good light the text of the capitulation George Washington and James Mackay had signed with de Villiers at Fort Necessity. The word that van Braam had translated "loss" or "death" or "killing"[9] proved to be in one place *l'assassin* and in the other *l'assassinat*. For the first time it was plain to the young English officers that they unwittingly had made an acknowledgment—it might be termed a confession—that they had assassinated Jumonville, *"porteur d'une sommation."* George, Mackay, Stephen and doubtless other officers were willing to swear that van Braam had not once used the word "assassination" in translating the paper;[10] but there the word was—not once but twice—and over the signatures of the two English commanders. They did not know whether the mistranslation was due to design on van Braam's part, to the circumstances of the receipt of the document, or to the Dutchman's ignorance of their language. In their wrath, they suspected the worst and denounced van Braam as treacherous.[11]

[6] By June 25, Dinwiddie had subordinated Muse to four other officers, two of whom are presently to be introduced, but he had not deprived Muse of the rank of Lieutenant Colonel (1 *Din.*, 218). Landon Carter, who was in Williamsburg during August, heard that Muse had led the Virginia troops into the stockade for safety and had left the Independent Company to defend the trenches (*MS Diary*, entry of Aug. 22, 1754). If Carter was correctly informed, most of the Virginians must have been returned promptly to the trenches, because it scarcely is probable that the unsupported defence of the trenches by the Independent Company would have been unrecorded.

[7] La Peyroney to Washington, Sept. 5, 1754; 1 *Hamilton*, 40.

[8] 1 *Din.*, 233.

[9] See *supra*, p. 407.

[10] See Washington in 1 *Ford*, 122n; Stephen, *Md. Gazette*, Aug. 29, 1754; Mackay to Washington, Sept. 28, 1754; 1 *Hamilton*, 50. Stephen's memory was at fault when he subsequently wrote in his MS "Life" (*Rush Papers*) that he refused to sign the capitulation because that document contained the word "assassination." He would not have signed the paper in any event, because he was not a commanding officer. Had Washington or Mackay known that "assassination" was in the document—and they would have known it if Stephen had—they would of course have refused to attach their signatures.

[11] *Ibid.* See also Appendix I–10, *infra* and Sharpe to Lord Bury, Nov. 5, 1754; 1 *Sharpe*, 116,

Their indignation would have burnt even more deeply had they realized with what satisfaction the French regarded the entire operation against Fort Necessity, especially as the authorities in Quebec had been under orders to exercise stern economy.[12] Sometime prior to June 26, the commander at Fort DuQuesne, Claude Pierre Pécaudy, Sieur de Contrecoeur, had drawn up a plan for an expedition against the English and had designated for it 500 French and eleven Indian scouts. The day before this column had been due to begin its march, there had arrived at the fort Coulon de Villiers, one of the six brothers of the dead Jumonville.[13] As Villiers was furiously anxious to avenge his brother's death and was senior to any of the subordinate officers at the fort, Contrecoeur had given him the command.[14] At a conference on the 27th of June, Contrecoeur had issued specific orders. Villiers was to expel the English from French territory. Their leader was to be taken. After that, if the interlopers agreed to leave, hostilities were to cease, the English were to be treated as friends, and an exchange of prisoners was to be arranged. If the troops refused to withdraw, they were to be regarded as enemies, and their buildings were to be destroyed.[15]

Under these instructions, Villiers had moved on the 28th, via Gist's new settlement, which he had reached on the 30th. Precisely as Washington had anticipated they might, the French had found one of the English deserters and, on the basis of the information given by this creature, had pressed on. The resulting fight, according to Villiers, had cost him two killed and seventeen wounded, exclusive of those so slightly injured that they did not need a surgeon.[16] After the English had marched off on the 4th of July, Villiers had demolished the stockade, had broken up the swivel guns, including the one the English had not been able to haul away, and then he had retired before nightfall. The return march was by way of Gist's new settlement, which was burned. At 4 P.M. on the 7th, de Villiers had reported to his commander at Fort DuQuesne.[17] Then and thereafter the victory was the subject of much approving correspondence[18] in which the

12 Minister of Colonies to DuQuesne, Mch. 31, 1754: "Unless the excessive costs of the up-keep of the colonies are reduced, the French government will abandon them." (Paris: Arch. Nat., Colonies, B99, 199; LC photostat).
13 See Villiers' journal in Paris: Aff. Etr., Mém. et Docs., Amér. 10:1, 97–109.
14 Villiers' narrative, partly printed by various authorities, appears in full in the MS cited in the preceding note.
15 Declaration of Contrecoeur, June 27, 1754, ibid., 110–13.
16 Ibid., 108.   17 Ibid.
18 Cf. Varin to Intendant, n.d., 1754; Can. Arch. C, 11, A, v. 99, p. 446–48.

principal theme was the extent to which the British home government
had been cognizant of the operations the colonials had undertaken
on the Ohio.[19] When Villiers' comment subsequently appeared in
print, it was not lacking in self-praise or in derogation of his adversaries: "We made them consent to sign that they had assassinated
my brother in his camp; we had hostages for the security of the French
who were in their power; we made them abandon the King's country;
we obliged them to leave their cannon, nine pieces; we destroyed their
horses and cattle and made them sign that the favors granted were
evidence that we wanted to use them as friends."[20]

There was nearer and more informed criticism of George's conduct
of the campaign, though some of it was not known to the young
commander at the time. As he was a beginner in the art of war,
allowance was made for his numerous and obvious mistakes. One of
the wisest of all contemporary Englishmen in dealing with the Indians,
William Johnson, wrote privately: "I wish Washington had acted with
prudence and circumspection requisite in an officer of rank, and the
trust at the same time reposed in him, but I can't help saying he was
very wrong in many respects and I doubt his being too ambitious of
acquiring all the honor or as much as he could before the rest joined
him: and giving too much credit to the reports or accounts given him
by the French deserters (which did not show him at all the soldier)
was the rock on which he split. He should rather have avoided an
engagement until all our troops were assembled, for march in such a
close country and by detachments will never do . . ."[21]

Another critic who knew the Indians perfectly and the white men
well had a different point of view. Half King told Conrad Weiser that
Washington was good-natured but inexperienced and would not take
advice from the Indians, whom he commanded as if they were slaves.
George had erred greatly, Half King said, in building "that little thing
upon the Meadow, where he thought the French would come up to
him in open field." Too much had been lost—a full month—before

19 Thomas Robinson to Albemarle, Sept. 2, 1754; memo. without docket, Sept. 18, 1754;
Br. Mus., 165 Newcastle Papers, f. 191, 337. DuQuesne to Ministre (Rouille), Oct. 12, 1754;
Paris: Arch. Nat., C: 11, A, v. 99, p. 284–85; DuQuesne to Le Garde des Sceaux, Oct. 28, 1754:
Paris: Aff. Etran.: Mém. et Docts. Amér. 24, p. 184; Le Garde des Sceaux, Nov. 6, 1754; Paris:
Arch. Nat.: C., 11, A, v. 99, p. 323–26. Cf. Premiere Relation de Rouillé to Mirepoix, Dec. 31,
1754; Paris Aff. Etran. Mém et Docts, Amér. 10, 92–96.
20 Villiers' narrative, loc. cit. This extract from the Mémoire did not reach Washington's
eye until 1757. See notes in Appendix I–10. His comments, often quoted here as one of his
few narratives of the capitulation, appear conveniently in 2 Sparks, 463–65, and 1 Ford, 121–23 n.
21 Johnson to Goldsbrow Banyar, July 29, 1754; 1 Johnson Papers, 409.

starting any defences. Had the proper type of fortification been made in time, Washington could have beaten off the French. Such was the judgment of Half King.[22]

Dinwiddie was balanced in his criticism, and was relieved, in a sense, that the disaster had not been worse. He wrote the merchants Hanbury, who were both his sponsors and his confidants: "What a glorious situation is His Majesty's most ancient dominion in. There is nothing more certain than that the French could have cut off every one of our men and might have marched to Hampton without the least danger[;] and within these eight months not three men in Virginia would believe a syllable of the danger that threatened them if ever [the French] got a foot of land there. Again they must purchase it with blood. What a prospect of freedom appears to the slaves and servants on the frontier. It is not to be doubted they will meet with proper encouragement from the French whenever they choose to visit them, and how readily might all these evils have been remedied had our neighbors done their duty in lending their assistance." [23]

More particularly, from what Dinwiddie knew of George and from what he read in the ambitious young Colonel's letters, the Governor had feared that Washington might be reckless, and he had warned the commander not "to make any hazardous attempts against a too numerous enemy." [24] Later the Governor had written: "I wish you had suspended your going to Red Stone Creek till you was joined by the other forces, being much afraid of a surprize." [25] Not unnaturally, when Dinwiddie learned of the disaster, he attributed it, in part, to neglect of this advice, and he soon persuaded himself that he explicitly had ordered George not to attack until "the whole forces were joined in a body." [26]

Although the Governor blamed George to this extent, Dinwiddie adhered to his belief that larger responsibility rested on the other Colonies and, among Virginians, first on those who, having contracted to deliver flour promptly, had failed to do so.[27] George Croghan was as much condemned at Alexandria and in Williamsburg as he had been at Fort Necessity. It developed that when Dinwiddie was at Win-

---

[22] Weiser's journal, cited in 1 *Ford*, 124n.
[23] Letter of July 23, 1754, to John and Capel Hanbury; Br. Mus., 165 *Newcastle Papers*, f. 229.
[24] Letter of June 1, 1754; 1 *Din.*, 186.
[25] Letter of June 27, 1754; 1 *Din.*, 222.
[26] Dinwiddie to Gov. Horatio Sharpe, July 31, 1754; 1 *Sharpe*, 76; Dinwiddie to Horace Walpole, Sept. 23, 1754; 1 *Din.*, 344.
[27] 1 *Din.*, 219–20, 321.

chester, Croghan had contracted to deliver 50,000 lbs. of flour in fifteen days and had asserted that he already had 40,000 lbs. of this. "By what I can learn," John Carlyle wrote despairingly, "he had not 400 lbs, but has sent his brother to purchase." [28] George's own experience with the Indian traders had convinced him their promises could not be relied upon. Croghan, said Washington, "was an eye-witness to our wants, yet had the assurance, during our sufferings, to tantalize us and boast of the quantity [of flour] he could furnish . . ." [29] Croghan's spirit in the whole transaction apparently was one of pretence, rather than of performance, just as it had been when he and Montour had talked much about their influence with the Indians but, in George's words, had "involved the country in great calamity, by causing dependence to be placed where there was none." [30]

Criticism was not limited to the Colonies in general, to Washington, to Croghan and to other traders who did not meet their contracts for provisions or transport. Gradually, after George came back to the settlements, he learned how and why the Governor had been disappointed, most of all, in the failure of the North Carolina contingent and of the two New York Independent Companies to reach Great Meadows.

Col. James Innes had been told by Governor Dinwiddie as early as Mch. 23, 1754, that the position of Commander-in-Chief of the expedition to the Ohio had been intended for him. [31] Innes was a Scotsman, an old friend of Dinwiddie's, and had been in command of the Cape Fear Company in the Cartagena expedition, [32] during which he had known Lawrence Washington. [33] Some delay had attended the organization of the North Carolina troops whom Innes was to bring to Virginia, [34] but the Colonel himself had proceeded to Williamsburg

---

28 Letter to Washington, June 17, 1754; 1 Hamilton, 5. Cf. William Fairfax to Washington, July 10, 1754: "If Mr. Croghan had punctually fulfilled his engagement with the Governor at Winchester, you would not have wanted flour lately" (1 Hamilton, 26).

29 Washington to William Fairfax, Aug. 11, 1754; 1 G. W., 95.

30 Washington to Dinwiddie, Aug. 11, 1754; 1 G. W., 92. Cf. supra, p. 394 for reference to the fact that Croghan and Montour had never been able to induce more than thirty Indians to join the force at Great Meadows. See also Croghan to Governor Hamilton, May 14, 1754 (2 Penn. Arch., 145): "I have about £200 worth of provisions now half way to Ohio . . . I can dispose of them to the Virginia forces, but if your Honor should have occasion of them for the use of this government, I will not engage to Virginia . . ."

31 Dinwiddie to Innes, 1 Din., 125.

32 The fullest sketch is in 2 Biog. His. N.C. See also Toner, ed., Washington's Journal of 1754, p. 55, and 1 Thwaites, 98, n. 59. Innes's will of July 5, 1754, admitted to probate Oct. 9, 1759 (N.C. Wills, 265), indicates that he probably was a native or one-time resident of Cannesby, Caithness, Scotland. James's wife, Jean, outlived him, married Francis Corbin as her second husband in 1761, buried him, and died in April, 1775 (ibid., 134, 482).

33 Cf. William Fairfax to Washington, July 5, 1754; 1 Hamilton, 24. See also 1 Din., 246.

34 Thomas Robinson to Pres. Council N.C., July 5, 1754; 5 Col. Rec. of N.C., 131.

and thence to Winchester. He had arrived in the Valley town on June 30 [35] and had begun to exercise command under orders and commission of Dinwiddie.[36] As Innes held also an old commission as Captain in the regular establishment, he seemed well chosen. He could give orders to the young Captains of Independent Companies and thereby could escape the disputes over rank that George had encountered.[37]

Because their Colony had no magazine,[38] Innes's men had no arms except those that private individuals chose to bring along with them. Two of his five North Carolina Companies [39] had disembarked at Alexandria late in June,[40] but they found no weapons there. To procure arms was difficult; to determine the men's rate of pay was scarcely less so. When North Carolina undertook in March to raise recruits for service in Virginia, she had agreed to pay them while in their own colony 3s a day in "Proclamation Money," a paper issue that had been authorized to a total of £40,000.[41] For the expedition, including pay, £12,000 of this currency had been set aside.[42] As recruits soon numbered between 300 [43] and 400,[44] and showed themselves in no hurry to go to Virginia, a considerable part of the "supply" of funds was exhausted before the contingent arrived at Alexandria.[45] Once there, the question was, Should the men continue to receive the 3s previously allowed them daily or the 8d paid the Virginia volunteers? Dinwiddie had foreseen in March that this would be a perplexity: "I wish," he had written President Rowan, "you could prevail with the officers and soldiers to be at the same pay with our forces, but I fear if they know the pay, they will be backward in coming, but this I must leave to your prudence." [46] The officers, it would appear, had hesitated to cut the men's pay after coming to the Potomac. Although the figure may later have been re-

---

[35] Innes to Governor Hamilton, n.d., *Md. Gazette*, Aug. 1, 1754.

[36] Dated June 4. See 1 *Din.*, 194–96.

[37] Cf. *Thwaites*, loc. cit.

[38] 1 *Sharpe*, 198–99; cf. 1 *Din.*, 125.

[39] For the number, see 1 *Din.*, 149.

[40] They were there June 28. See John Carlyle to Washington, June 28, 1754; 1 *Hamilton*, 20. The other Companies arrived at Hampton. Two of them left for Alexandria about July 15. The remaining Company re-embarked later. See Dinwiddie to President Rowan, Aug. 5, 1754; 1 *Din.*, 277. Some of these troops may have come overland to Virginia and may have marched through Dinwiddie County (5 *E. J.*, 465–66).

[41] For the law, see 23 *Col. Rec. N.C.*, 392 ff. See also 1 *Din.*, 232. Details of the compensation are given in 1 *Din.*, 287, 304, 323.

[42] 1 *Din.*, 126.

[43] *Ibid.*, 134.

[44] Mathew Rowan to the Lords of Trade, Aug. 29, 1754; 5 *Col. Rec. N.C.*, 137.

[45] See, also, *supra*, p. 359.

[46] Letter of Mch. 23, 1754; 1 *Din.*, 124.

duced, in theory, to the Virginia level,[47] the "Proclamation Money" was losing its voice.

The other reenforcements on which Dinwiddie had relied for months were the long-awaited [48] two Independent Companies from New York. These troops had received in March orders to move to Virginia, but they had not reached Norfolk until the 16th of June,[49] and then proved to be such poor human material, so feebly equipped, that they had shocked the Virginians.[50] Said Dinwiddie, "these two Companies had nothing fit for a march or an engagement; had only one barrel of powder, very old and not fit for use." Physically, the Governor explained, the soldiers were "indifferent men," [51] some of them too advanced in years for a long march, and the whole "burthened with thirty women and children." The Governor fairly exploded to his colleague De Lancey of New York: "no provisions, which your former letters gave me reason to expect; no tents, which obliges me to make new tents; or any blankets, &c.; in short much worse than new raised forces." [52] Nor would the Governor have been consoled later to hear Thomas Penn's remark that "the wretched condition of the Independent Companies of New York had been long known in London." [53] To add the final discouragement, the Captain in command, Thomas Clarke, had shared Mackay's lofty view of the relationship of the King's officers to the colonial service,[54] and, when satisfied on this score, had fallen most inconveniently sick at Alexandria.[55] From first to last, every act of the Captain and the men had appeared to Dinwiddie as slovenly and slow.

In summary, then, when blame for the capitulation at Fort Necessity was apportioned, Dinwiddie and Washington and all their friends could point to the number of idle troops: of the eight Companies, approximately 550 men, who had been expected to support the Virginia Regiment, only Mackay's Company had joined Washington.[56] None

[47] Dinwiddie's remark of Aug. 5, 1754 to Mathew Rowan on this score is somewhat equivocal: "The high pay (I understand that was allowed them while in Carolina) is the reason" [for the approaching exhaustion of funds]. The inference obviously is that 3s were allowed during the period they were in Carolina and not afterward, but positive proof of this has not been found.
[48] Cf. Md. Gazette, June 27, 1754.
[49] 1 Din., 200, 205, 241.
[50] See 1 Din., 200, 213.
[51] Dinwiddie to Sec. at War, July 24, 1754; 1 Din., 245.
[52] Letter of June 20, 1754; 1 Din., 217.
[53] Letter to Governor Morris, n.d., 1755; 2 Penn. Arch., 255-56.
[54] 1 Din., 213, 218.
[55] 1 Hamilton, 20. Cf. Dinwiddie: "He was sick, and kept his company to attend him, whereas he should have directed them to march, and he might have followed, when recovered" (1 Din., 271).
[56] 1 Din., 241. Innes wrote Washington or Mackay on the 5th of July that his Regiment and the New York Companies were on the march to Winchester (1 Hamilton, 20-21).

of the others arrived in Winchester until about the 9th of July when two
unarmed North Carolina Companies, approximately 150 men, put in
their appearance.[57] The New York Companies reached there on the
11th or the 12th.[58] Dinwiddie soon was to satisfy himself that "if these
two [New York] Companies had joined our forces at the time they
should, the French would not have attacked us, or if they had, if these
Companies had behaved with the valor and resolution of the others, in
all probability, we should have defeated them." [59] The delay of the
regulars and of the North Carolinians, the Governor told some of his
official correspondents, had been "monstrous." [60] Dinwiddie did not
once suggest that, as conditions were, the more men Washington had,
the sooner they would have gone hungry. The Governor never seemed
to appreciate fully the part that feeble transportation played in the slow
progress and complete defeat of the expedition. He continued rightly
to blame the contractors; he did not realize, or at least he did not admit,
that he had been culpably over-optimistic in his assumption of the
speed with which vehicles could be assembled and men and supplies
moved to the Ohio over the rough, mountainous road George slowly
had reopened.

Such was the first appraisal of the campaign—that George had been
guilty of many of a beginner's mistakes and had been reckless and
perhaps ambitious in pushing as far as Gist's new settlement before
the arrival of reenforcements, but that the larger fault was that of
the apathetic Colonies, of the incompetent or disreputable contractors
who had failed to deliver provisions, and of the slow-moving officers of
New York and of North Carolina troops whose delay had forced
Washington and Mackay to fight against crushing odds. The humiliating admission that Jumonville had been "assassinated" by the English
was charged against von Braam and not against the commander of the
expedition.

This detailed judgment of the misadventure had not been formulated
fully by the time George and Mackay, after brief rest at Wills Creek,
hurried to Winchester, where they reported to Colonel Innes, their

[57] 1 *Sharpe*, 198–99. Sharpe must have been mistaken in saying that Innes himself arrived
that day. In *Md. Gazette*, Aug. 1, 1754, Innes stated that he reached Winchester June 30.
Cf. *supra*, p. 418.
[58] See 1 *Din.*, 241.
[59] Dinwiddie to the Lords of Trade, July 24, 1754; 1 *Din.*, 241.
[60] Dinwiddie to Sec. at War, July 24, 1754; 1 *Din.*, 245; Dinwiddie to President Rowan,
Aug. 5, 1754; *ibid.*, 277.

Commander-in-Chief,[61] whom neither of them had met previously. In Winchester, too, they saw Captain Clarke, though his New York Independent Companies had not then arrived.[62] Doubtless with Innes's permission and perhaps by his orders, George and Mackay left Winchester on the 11th of July [63] to ride to Williamsburg to report in person to the Governor. If they took the shortest road, which was by Fredericksburg, and if they stopped in that town long enough for George to visit his mother, they probably found her well. In June, one of George's friends had written that he saw Mrs. Washington frequently and had danced with her not long previously.[64]

It was the 17th of July, 1754, precisely a fortnight after the bloody day at Fort Necessity, that the two young officers reached Williamsburg.[65] The little town had been the scene of much unpleasantness for the Governor during the weeks that had elapsed since George last had seen him. Dinwiddie had left Williamsburg May 13 [66] and, with several members of the Council,[67] had gone to Winchester in high hopes of winning in conference the full support of the Indians.[68] He had waited vainly for sixteen days [69] in the Valley town and, while there, had carried on with Washington the correspondence concerning rank and operations. In the end, the Governor had accepted with disappointment but at face value the assurance of the Indian chieftains that they could not come to Winchester at that time. "They sent me a message," Dinwiddie reported, "that as the French had invaded and taken possession of their land, they did not think it proper to meet me . . . for fear their people would not remain steady." [70] In that belief he returned to Williamsburg on the 16th [71] of June and there received the news of the capitulation of Fort Necessity.

The old Scot's first impulse then had been to call on the Governors of the other Colonies for assistance,[72] a task that overwhelmed him with letter-writing.[73] He became satisfied, as he argued his case, that

61 Innes to Governor Hamilton, *Md. Gazette*, Aug. 1, 1754.
62 *Va. Gazette*, July 19, 1754; 1 *Din.*, 241.
63 *Va. Gazette*, loc. cit.
64 Daniel Campbell to Washington, June 28, 1754; 1 *Hamilton*, 15. There is no record of where George hired the horse or horses he used on this journey. Some of his mounts were fed and given pasturage at Dr. Green's in Alexandria during July (*Ledger A*, folio 17).
65 *Va. Gazette*, July 19, 1754.
66 If he held to the date indicated on May 10 (1 *Din.*, 167).
67 *E. J.*, 469. 68 1 *Din.*, 131 ff. 69 1 *Din.*, 201.
70 Letter of June 18, 1754, to the Lords of Trade; 1 *Din.*, 205. 71 *Ibid.*
72 Sharpe to Lord Baltimore, Aug. 8, 1754; 1 *Sharpe*, 79-80.
73 Dinwiddie to Governor Glen, Aug. 5, 1754; 1 *Din.*, 276.

the expedition would not have failed if the Colonies had given support;[74] but he equally was convinced that help would not be forthcoming in the early future. About the time the Mingoes were arriving at George's camp and the road toward Red Stone Creek was being cut, Dinwiddie had written despairingly: ". . . every government except North Carolina has amused me with expectations that have proved fruitless, and at length refuse to give any supply, unless in such a manner as must render it ineffectual."[75]

He concluded that troops had to be sent from home[76] and should be supported by a poll tax of half a crown levied on all the provincials and paid as Parliament should direct.[77] "Without some such thing," he soon was to write, "these obstinate people will do nothing."[78] In larger consciousness of the complexity of his task, Dinwiddie already was shaping a resolution to recover the forks of the Ohio.[79] He wrote London friends: "This affair gives me very great concern, but what can be done after such monstrous delays, few men and no money? It's of great consequence to the nation and these Colonies, that I think no time is to be lost, for if [the French] have a quiet settlement for two years, we shall never be able to root them out."[80]

In this spirit the Governor received George, heard the details of what had happened, and began even more vigorously to make his preparations for the next phase of the struggle. His new orders to Colonel Innes were for the building at Wills Creek of a log fort to receive six months' provisions. ". . . I think it's not prudent to march out to the Ohio," the Governor wrote, "till you have a sufficient force to attack the enemy, and that you be properly provided with everything for that purpose."[81] This policy was accepted as sound and fixed.

George found, of course, that his expedition was the theme of every man's talk in Williamsburg. He was himself conspicuous, not to say already famous. The victory in the skirmish with Jumonville had been much applauded. Public men shared his humiliation at having signed a document that admitted the "assassination" of the young French officer, but this word was attributed more violently than ever to

[74] Dinwiddie to James Abercromby, July 24, 1754; 1 *Din.*, 236.
[75] Dinwiddie to Sir Thomas Robinson, June 18, 1754; 1 *Din.*, 203.
[76] Dinwiddie to Lord Albemarle, July 24, 1754; 1 *Din.*, 248.
[77] Dinwiddie to the Lords of Trade, July 24, 1754; 1 *Din.*, 241. The Governor at first had proposed that the tax be 1*s*, but he had decided this was too low (*ibid.*, 204).
[78] Dinwiddie to Lord Granville, July 24, 1754; 1 *Din.*, 250.
[79] Dinwiddie to James Abercromby, July 24, 1754; 1 *Din.*, 236.
[80] Dinwiddie to J. and C. Hanbury, July 24, 1754; 1 *Din.*, 253–54.
[81] Dinwiddie to Col. James Innes, July 20, 1754; 1 *Din.*, 233.

treachery on the part of van Braam. "The only unpardonable blunder that Washington made," Landon Carter soon was to record in his diary, "[was in] making a confidant of him, for he was a poor juggling servant but by understanding French and having attended the Colonel on his embassy made in the Spring to the fort he became a favorite and was preferred." [82]

No blame was attached to Washington for the capitulation itself. The indignant judgment voiced in the *Virginia Gazette* two days after George's arrival in the capital undoubtedly was that of the Colony: "Thus have a few brave men been exposed, to be butchered, by the negligence of those who, in obedience to their Sovereign's command ought to have been with them many months before; and it is evidently certain, that had the Companies from New York been as expeditious as Captain MacCay's [sic] from South Carolina, our camp would have been secure from the insults of the French, and our brave men still alive to serve their King and country. Surely, this will remove the infatuation that seems to have prevailed too much among our neighbors . . ." [83]

Later, George was to learn that his encounter with Jumonville had been described in the *Gentleman's Magazine* [84] and had been the subject of remark by the King himself. Reading Washington's letter to his brother "Jack," as it appeared in the *London Magazine,* His Majesty noted George's assurance that there was "something charming in the sound" of the bullets. The King observed: "He would not say so if he had been used to hear many." [85] Exalted representatives of His Royal Highness were to concern themselves with the charge that Colonel Washington had attacked a diplomatic mission, and they were to demonstrate, to their own satisfaction, that this was not true,[86] but they were by no means convinced that he was a good soldier. Privately, the Earl of Albemarle, titular Governor of Virginia and British Ambassador to France, wrote the Duke of Newcastle: "Washington and many such may have courage and resolution but they have no

---

[82] Landon Carter's *MS Diary,* Aug. 22, 1754. Needless to say, Carter used the word "juggling" in a sense then common, of deceit or cheating. See *supra,* p. 277, n. 20.

[83] July 19, 1754.

[84] July, 1754, v. 24, p. 322.

[85] 1 Walpole's *Memoirs,* 346. Walpole mistakenly associated this remark with the action of July 3, 1754. In the same passage, Walpole spoke of the fight at Fort Necessity as "a trifling action, but remarkable for giving date to the war."

[86] *Egerton MSS,* 2694, 28. See also *London Gazette,* Sept. 2, 1754; *Md. Gazette,* July 4, Oct. 3, 1754; Lord Albemarle to Sir Thomas Robinson, Aug. 21, 1754; Br. Mus., Add. MS 33027, f 27.

knowledge or experience in our profession; consequently there can be no dependence on them. Officers, and good ones, must be sent to discipline the militia and to lead them on as this nation; we may then (and not before) drive the French back to their settlements and encroach on them as they do at present upon us . . ." [87]

This letter, needless to say, never came under George's eye. Those leaders nearer him were more generous than critical. Among many congratulations were, indirectly, some proud words from Joseph Ball, head of the family of George's mother. Ball professed himself much pleased over the "first victory" in the clash with Jumonville, especially as Colonel Washington "is my nephew." [88]

Otherwise than by Dinwiddie, official commendation of George and the other officers could not be expected immediately in Virginia because the General Assembly was not in session; but the Governor and Council did have authority to make a grant to the men from the money voted at the previous session. When, therefore, Washington started back to his command, he had in his baggage 300 pistoles for distribution among the men of his Regiment and of the South Carolina Independent Company "as a reward for their bravery in the recent engagement with the French." [89]

On reaching his station,[90] George found the survivors of the expedition in worse condition than they had been at any time. The Independent Companies remained at Wills Creek; his own men had come—or soon came—to Alexandria. They were demoralized, half naked, without hats or blankets, and were in resentful temper because they had not been paid.[91] Some had created disorder at Winchester;[92]

---

[87] Letter of Sept. 11, 1754; Br. Mus., Add. MS 32850, f 289, with the erratic capitalization revised and the punctuation changed slightly to clarify the meaning. This is among the last of Albemarle's letters that contains detailed reference to Virginia. He died the following December.

[88] To Benjamin Waller, Aug. 31, 1754; *Ball Letter Book*.

[89] *Council Minutes*, July 18, 1754; 1 *Hamilton*, 28. George's own expenses for this journey, £10, 15s, were charged against the Colony and were paid ultimately. (Toner, ed., *Washington's Journal* of 1754, p. 181.)

[90] George probably returned to Wills Creek briefly and, after distributing the money and inspecting the troops, made a voyage down the Potomac, at the special request of Charles Carter, to ascertain what the obstacles to navigation were. This episode, which cannot be dated accurately, is mentioned in 1 *G. W.*, 100. See also, Toner, ed., *Washington's Journal* of 1754, p. 181, and Evans's "Analysis" in L. H. Gipson, *Lewis Evans*, 167. If George went to Wills Creek, he probably was back in Alexandria by August 1, because Dinwiddie on that date directed him to consult with Major Carlyle, as if the two were at the same station. On the 3rd of August, Dinwiddie wrote of plans for George "to join the other forces" at Wills Creek (1 *Din.*, 263, 269). Mackay remained temporarily at Wills Creek. The New York Companies were there later (1 *Hamilton*, 33).

[91] 1 *Din.*, 261; 1 *G. W.*, 94.

[92] 1 *G. W.*, 93.

others had deserted and had carried their arms with them.[93] Miserable as was their plight, George could do little to relieve it, except to appeal to the Governor to remit funds with which to pay them.[94] George learned, also, that the North Carolina troops were close to dissolution because the fund for their support was almost exhausted. The soldiers were demanding for continued service the daily 3s of "Proclamation Money" allowed them in North Carolina; but Virginia could not have granted this, even if money had been available, because the per diem of 8d allotted Washington's Regiment had not been increased. The Independent Companies, especially Mackay's, remained under discipline and in fair condition, but they were numerically weak.[95]

While most of the English troops were in this plight, George learned in a strange manner that if they were stronger and were equipped to move, a great opportunity would be theirs. During the first week of August, Washington received through the hands of George Croghan a letter that had been delivered to the trader by an Indian who said he had received it at Fort DuQuesne, with instructions to take it to the English commander at Wills Creek, where he would be well rewarded for the risk he had undergone. Croghan had opened the letter, which he should not have done,[96] but he had forwarded it promptly. It proved to be from Capt. Robert Stobo, at Fort DuQuesne, and it bore date as recent as July 29. In the letter, Stobo referred to a communication he had written and had dispatched the previous day. He said there were only 200 troops at the fort and that another 200 were expected in a few days.

It was a great but an unattainable opportunity. George knew that. So, doubtless, did every other officer of the expedition. Lamentable though it was, the men who had been engaged at Fort Necessity were incapable of another effort that year. Clarke's and Innes's troops were

---

[93] 1 *Din.*, 268. [94] 1 *Din.*, 268.

[95] The evidence for this is negative, the lack of any statement that they were demoralized.

[96] Governor Sharpe to Governor Morris, Dec. 27, 1754; 1 *Sharpe*, 153; cf. 1 *Hamilton*, 49; 6 *Penn. Col. Rec.*, 141. The approximate date of the receipt of Stobo's letter may be fixed by the publication in *Md. Gazette*, Sept. 12, 1754 of a dispatch from Williamsburg, August 9, that contained unmistakable references to Stobo's message, though nothing is said concerning the source of the information. The communication reached Croghan about August 2 (see 6 *Penn. Col. Rec.*, 140). Stobo's missive of July 28 was not received by Croghan until August 28 (*Ibid.*, 161). In this letter, which contained a sketch of Fort DuQuesne, Stobo said: "Strike this fall as soon as possible. Make the Indians ours. Prevent intelligence. Get the best, and 'tis done. One hundred trusty Indians might surprise the fort." The French, Stobo disclosed, most diligently were trying to win the Indians, but the general tone of his letter was encouraging in its reference to the natives. "I assure you," he said, "there was not any of those Indians we call ours at the battle except six or seven" (MS in the Archives of the District Montreal. Cf. *Stobo*, 19–20; 1 *The Olden Time*, 59). Part of Stobo's letter is reproduced between p. 437 and p. 438.

not equipped or seasoned for the attempt. Even if they were, they lacked adequate transport, without which advance was self-murder.

Colonel Washington, for these reasons, was stunned when he opened, a few days later, a dispatch from Dinwiddie dated August 3, before Stobo's communication from Fort DuQuesne could have reached Williamsburg. The Governor told of the receipt of George's appeal for money with which to pay the troops. By the messenger, His Honor sent £600, which, he said bluntly, "is all can be got." [97] There followed some observations on the demoralization of the forces and then these sentences:

I sent you orders to recruit your Regiment with all possible diligence that you may be ready to join the other forces at Wills's Creek, to execute the scheme sent by Colonel Innes. I repeat my orders now, and am in hopes you will meet with little difficulty in complying therewith, and that with expedition, as the season of the year calls for it, and I am convinced of your hearty inclinations, which I desire you will now exert. I have [done], and will do all in my power, in prosecuting the affair in hand, and I hope in a short time we shall have our hands better strengthened with money, and I expect to hear your Regiment is completed and will soon march for Wills's Creek.[98]

George had not received the previous orders to which Dinwiddie referred and he did not know what was "the scheme sent by Colonel Innes," but the inference plainly was that another attempt was to be made forthwith to drive the French from the Ohio. It seemed incredible to Washington that such a thing could be considered by a Governor who a fortnight previously had been content to talk of building a fort at Wills Creek and of victualling it for six months' supply of troops who were not to start westward until they were equipped and concentrated.

The reason for this complete change of plan probably never was explained in its fullness to George, but it was this: Dinwiddie was unwilling, as he frankly told correspondents in England, "that the soldiers in pay should eat the bread of idleness." [99] He believed that Innes had 350 to 400 men, that George could recruit to 300, and that a total force of 1010 would be available.[100] Maryland, moreover, was expected to

---

[97] Again and again, Dinwiddie complained of the hampering shortage of money for the support of the expedition. See 1 *Din.*, 108 ff.

[98] 1 *Din.*, 268–69.

[99] 1 *Din.*, 284; cf. *ibid.*, 281.

[100] 1 *Sharpe*, 77; 1 *Din.*, 261.

vote £6000 and was to construct a magazine for provisions at Wills Creek.[101] Pennsylvania would care for the Indian women and children.[102] On these assurances and assumptions, Dinwiddie had decided to organize a new offensive. The first suggestion of this may have come from Colonel Innes.

George did not undertake immediately to answer Dinwiddie's proposal, but he sent an express to Colonel Innes,[103] and he awaited the delayed orders the Governor mentioned. These came in circumstances of ill omen. A Swedish resident of Virginia, Carolus Splitdorph,[104] who had accompanied the expedition for a time during the spring, appeared again at Washington's headquarters four days after the receipt of Dinwiddie's dispatch of August 3. Splitdorph brought the missing instructions and, unfortunately, knowing their content, incautiously stated that the troops in Alexandria soon would move. That night, six of George's men deserted.[105]

In detail, George's orders were that he was to proceed as soon as possible to Wills Creek with the troops he had. The Council, Dinwiddie explained, the previous day had decided that as the French probably would be stronger in the spring of 1755, it would be wise to recross the Alleghenies at the earliest possible moment and either to capture Fort DuQuesne or to construct defences at some point selected by a council of war. Washington was to join Innes for this purpose.[106] The Governor added: "Pray consider if [it is] possible or practicable to send a party of Indians &c. to destroy the corn at the fort and Logstown. This would be of great service and a very great disappointment to the enemy. I can say no more but to press dispatch of your Regiment to Wills Creek . . ."[107]

In his youthful pride, George had said two months previously that he had "resolution to face what any man durst,"[108] but he stood aghast at Dinwiddie's plan. It seemed to him so surely the counsel of madness, that, at the moment, he did not trust himself to address

---

[101] 1 Din., 261; 1 Sharpe, 56, 62, 104.

[102] 1 Din., 258.

[103] 1 G. W., 95. The nature of the dispatch sent by the express is not established.

[104] The index to G. W. gives the full name as Carolus Gustavus de Splitdorph.

[105] 1 G. W., 93.

[106] Dinwiddie to Washington, Aug. 1, 1754; 1 Din., 262–63. Innes's instructions were to concentrate at Wills Creek and to advance to Red Stone Creek or to some other selected position. Andrew Montour was to raise 100 Indian scouts; John Carlyle was to send to Wills Creek four months' provisions for 1200 men (1 Din., 261, 265).

[107] Ibid.

[108] 1 G. W., 60; see supra, p. 378.

the Governor.[109] He reflected and, as soon as he could muster his arguments and discharge his temper, he sat down and wrote William Fairfax a long critique of Dinwiddie's plan. To move the Regiment forthwith to Wills Creek, George told his mentor, was as impracticable as it was to dispossess the French of Fort DuQuesne. Both were "morally impossible" with existing means. Available troops were far less numerous than those of the French; the winter would be upon the men before they could achieve anything; horses could not then get over the mountains; the soldiers could not live outdoors unless they had a better defence against the cold than tents offered; food and provender could not be carried as far as Dinwiddie wanted the column to go.

When he came to discuss His Honor's plan to burn the corn at Logstown, George barely avoided sarcasm and lack of respect for the Governor: "At this question I am a little surprised, when it is known we must pass the French fort and the Ohio to go to Logstown;[110] and how can this be done with inferior numbers, under the disadvantages we labor, I see not; and, of the ground to hope we may engage a sufficient party of Indians for this undertaking, I have no information, nor have I any conception . . ."[111] George went on to explain why his own Regiment was in no condition to fight. It could not be recruited without money. Supply of its more pressing needs, including ammunition, would, "I believe, advance us into that season when it is usual, in more moderate climates, to retreat into winter quarters but here, with us, to begin a campaign."[112] The disgusted young Colonel added a paragraph on the irresponsibility of Indian traders, and another on the necessity of ample presents for the Indians, and then, without asking a change of orders or any intervention by Colonel Fairfax, he closed his letter.

George, in short, tore Dinwiddie's plan to bits and, in doing so, gave himself an excellent drill in military analysis. If he realized, when he finished it, how much he had learned since the previous November concerning the management of troops and preparation for war, he did not drop a boastful word. The subject was too grim for self-

[109] In his n.d. letter 1 *G. W.*, 102, assigned by Fitzpatrick to September but more probably of August, Washington mentioned that he had written fully to Dinwiddie by William Polson. That letter, which has been lost, may have been of the approximate date of the one to William Fairfax, mentioned in the text.

[110] Washington here spelled it Log-town.

[111] Letter of Aug. 11, 1754; 1 *G. W.*, 90–92.

[112] *Ibid.*

praise. Study of a theoretical military problem was not enjoyable when he might be required to attempt an impossible solution.

His duty was not done in writing an honest criticism of an indefensible plan. He was a soldier and he was schooling himself in discipline. The next day he wrote Innes that he was withholding the letter "to Williamsburg," [113] until he heard from the North Carolinian, so that he might "write nothing inconsistent with what" his immediate superior proposed. Then George recorded explicitly: "If you think it advisable to order me in the shattered condition we are in to march up to you, I will, if no more than ten men follows me (which I believe will be the full amount) . . ." [114]

Events of the next few days made this prediction almost a probability. Desertion continued. Every night or so, some of the ragged men of the Virginia Regiment would slip away.[115] On the 25th of August, while most of the officers were at church, twenty-five soldiers collected and undertook to make off, but before they could do so, they were arrested and locked up.[116] To deal with them vigorously was difficult not only because the troops were desperate but also because there was doubt whether they were subject to martial law.[117] George advertised deserters [118] and offered rewards for their apprehension and return; [119] Maryland authorities cooperated; [120] in spite of all effort, the strength of the Regiment dropped steadily toward a minimum of 150.[121] The officers became restive and unhappy over the demoralization of their troops and over changes in the form of new commissions which, George reported, they considered to have the savor of militia.[122]

Among the North Carolina soldiers, conditions were even worse. Some of the officers of this contingent appeared to know nothing of their duties.[123] The men persisted in their demand for the 3s per day

---

[113] It is not certain whether this referred to the letter written Fairfax or to the lost one sent Dinwiddie by William Polson, as explained in n. 109. Files of *Va. Gazette* for this period are almost blank. As the *Executive Journal of the Council* for July and August, 1754 has not yet been located (see 5 *E. J.*, ix), there is no way of determining the possible presence of Col. William Fairfax in the colonial capital prior to the meeting of the General Assembly, August 22. He was there during the session. See 3 *L. J.*, 1121.

[114] Letter of Aug. 12, 1754; 1 *G. W.*, 95–96. Captain Mackay was of like mind with Washington concerning the folly of an attempted advance with the forces then available. See Mackay to Washington, Aug. 27, 1754; 1 *Hamilton*, 33–34.

[115] 1 *G. W.*, 98.   [118] *Ibid.*, 98.

[116] *Ibid.*, 97.   [119] *Md. Gazette*, Sept. 5, 1754.

[117] *Ibid.*   [120] 31 *Md. Archives*, 47.

[121] Dinwiddie (1 *op. cit.*, 304) gave this figure in a letter of Sept. 6, 1754 to Governor Sharpe, but he did not state when the low total of 150 was reached. The return of Aug. 15, 1754 (1 *G. W. Papers*, LC) showed a total of 189 on the roster. Present for duty at that date were 150 officers and men.

[122] 1 *G. W.*, 97.   [123] 1 *Din.*, 270–71, 277.

that had been allotted them before they came to Virginia. Certain
North Carolina barrelled pork, offered for sale in order to supplement
their vanishing funds, had few takers at low prices.[124] One Company
mutinied in Augusta County; a like spirit was said to prevail among
the others.[125] With alarming speed, Companies disbanded for lack
of money with which to provide pay or to purchase subsistence.[126] By
the end of August barely twoscore or, at most, fifty North Carolinians
remained as an organized force in Virginia.[127]

The irritations of preparing a disintegrated command for an impossible task were aggravated now in the mind of George, whose Adjutancy had been changed to the Northern Neck. On the 20th of August
Colin Campbell arrived at Alexandria. He had received appointment
from Dinwiddie to act as Deputy Adjutant of the Northern Neck
during George's absence on other duty and he already had arranged
for musters in some of the Counties. For the service he was to render,
in addition to that already performed, he informed George he expected
£65 per annum of the £100 allowed the regular Adjutant by the
Council. Washington's sense of fair dealing was outraged. He knew
that other District Adjutants paid their deputies £40 or less annually;
and in a prompt letter to the Governor he cited the figures and made
this direct appeal: "I hope, if your Honor is kind enough to continue
me in that office, you will not oblige me to give such an exorbitant
allowance to a person who by all accounts knows nothing of the duty
he has undertaken." Washington then explained that he could get
an individual, trained by himself, to serve as deputy at the price the
other Adjutants paid. "I will engage," George said, "that it shall turn
out more to the public advantage . . ."[128] It was a matter, likewise,
of at least £10 and perhaps of £25, a sum for which, when honestly to
be had, George would contend not only with a hard-bargaining deputy
but also with a Scotch Governor who was the champion of all his co-
patriots.[129]

The experience with Campbell pained George, as every unreasonable
monetary dealing did, and it probably led him to doubt whether
Dinwiddie was as firm a friend as in earlier months; but the affair
of the deputy was swallowed in more important events that occurred

[124] 1 Din., 297.   [125] Ibid., 270, 277.
[126] Williamsburg dispatch of August 23 in Md. Gazette, Sept. 12, 1754. Cf. 1 Din., 297,
304, 323.   [127] 1 Sharpe, 98.
[128] 1 G. W., 99. The date of Washington's transfer from the Southern to the Northern Neck
District has not yet been established.
[129] Cf. Landon Carter's MS Diary, Aug. 22, 1754.

while Washington's Regiment was dwindling and the disbanded North Carolinians were tramping homeward. On the 22nd of August the General Assembly of Virginia met to consider the Governor's plea for a new supply with which to contest the French advance to the Ohio. In a little more than a fortnight, George learned that the Burgesses had voted £20,000 from a poll tax, but had insisted that £2500 of this be used to reimburse the Speaker and several other gentlemen who had advanced that sum to pay the expenses of Peyton Randolph, Attorney General, when he had been sent to England to present the Colony's side of the controversy with Dinwiddie over the pistole fee.[130] The Governor would not consent to this diversion of funds, and, on the 5th of September, he angrily prorogued the House to the 17th of October.[131] Partly in retaliation, the Burgesses refused, before adjournment, to pay the subsistence of the Independent Companies, and did not even reach agreement on a bill to punish desertion.[132] "The news of your engagement and rout at the Meadows," William Fairfax wrote Washington at the close of the session, "did not give the public more affecting concern than the unhappy ending of our present meeting." [133]

Soon George heard at Alexandria that Dinwiddie had declared the plans for an offensive "entirely defeated" by the "obstinacy of our Assembly," the disbanding of the North Carolinians and the reduction in the strength of the Virginia Regiment. The Governor argued stubbornly that if the Burgesses had provided the money, he could have raised 600 troops and thereby could have offset the loss of the Carolinians. ". . . I am now persuaded," he wrote Governor Sharpe, "that no expedition can be conducted here with dependence on American Assemblies." [134] Plans for an offensive in the autumn of 1754 were suspended. New alarm seized frontier families who expected Indian attacks.[135]

About the 15th of September, marching orders reached Washington but they opened with the statement by the Governor, "I fear we are not numbers sufficient to attack the fort taken from us by the French." [136] George was to proceed to Wills Creek with such men as he could muster

[130] See Koontz, *Dinwiddie*, 222 ff; Sharpe to Calvert, Sept. 15, 1754; 1 *Sharpe*, 98.
[131] *Journ. H.B.*, 1752–58, p. 189–90, 192, 196, 200, 201, 202, 203, 205; 3 *L.J. Council*, 1125 ff; 1 *Din.*, 298, 303; Francis Jerdone to Hugh Crawford, Sept. 12, 1752; 14 *W* (1) p. 144.
[132] *Journ. H.B.*, 1752–58. p. 204; 1 *Hamilton*, 38.
[133] Letter of Sept. 5, 1754; 1 *Hamilton*, 37.
[134] Letter of Sept. 6, 1754; 1 *Din.*, 304; cf. *ibid.*, 308.
[135] 1 *Sharpe* 94: Jerdone to Crawford, *supra*, n. 131; 2 *Penn. Arch.*, 173.
[136] Letter of Sept. 11, 1754; 1 *Din.*, 315.

after detaching forty or fifty, who were to go to Augusta County as a guard against incursions of small bodies of Indians and perhaps of French. At Wills Creek, George and the remnant of the Regiment would receive further orders. Lord Fairfax was told, though Washington was not, that these instructions would be to join in fitting up [137] the store of the Ohio Company as a magazine and in erecting works to make it secure.[138] Everything was to be done with economy and in the spirit of Dinwiddie's determination not to permit the men to remain idle. When the young Colonel was admonished to send the Governor the pay account of his Regiment, Dinwiddie wrote, almost with gusto, "As the pay was ordered for the whole number, there must be great saving from the dead and deserters." [139] Simultaneously, the Governor was instructing John Carlyle, now a Major, to feed the troops on Indian meal "which is a hearty food and comes much cheaper than flour." [140]

In all these dealings with the Governor there was one consolation only: The General Assembly, before prorogation, had voted thanks to George and Mackay and to their respective officers, except George Muse and Jacob van Braam, "for their late gallant and brave behaviour in the defence of their country." [141] Captain Peyroney, writing from Williamsburg, told George, "Thank God, I meet always with a good wish for you from every mouth." [142] That was something in which Washington could find satisfaction when ordered back to a frontier post where, for a time, with much construction to be undertaken, there were not tools for so simple a thing as digging a trench around the commander's tent.[143]

As it eventuated, circumstances and sickness probably relieved George of the unnecessary march to Wills Creek that autumn.[144] The loss of

---

[137] As printed the word is "filling," but "fitting" seems more probable.
[138] 1 Din., 305, 313, 315.
[139] Ibid., 317.   [140] Ibid., 319.
[141] Journ. H.B., 1752–58, p. 198. See infra, p. 438 for the reception by Washington of formal notice of this.
[142] Sept. 5, 1754; 1 Hamilton, 40.
[143] Innes to Washington, Sept. 18, 1754; 1 Hamilton, 41–42. By September 27, Innes had some tools which he took from persons who said they had found them at Great Meadows and had brought them to the settlements (ibid., 48).
[144] He certainly had not reached Wills Creek by September 28, because Mackay sent him a letter that day from the station (1 Hamilton, 50–51). On October 1, Governor Sharpe wrote as if George still were at Alexandria (ibid., 52). By October 18, as will appear presently, George was on his way to Williamsburg. As he wrote c. October 10 of going shortly to the capital (1 Hamilton, 53), it consequently would appear that if he had been at Wills Creek, his tour of duty there would have been a matter of a few days only. In the absence of all positive evidence that he was at Wills Creek early in October, the circumstantial evidence is almost conclusive that he remained at or near Alexandria until he set out for Williamsburg.

health he attributed to the hardships he had endured; the hampering circumstances were the preparations for the departure of Capt. Andrew Lewis's for Augusta,[145] and, doubtless, Washington's inability to get the other men equipped for a winter on the Upper Potomac.

Avoidance of that dull service was not escape from all annoyance. On the contrary, there were new irritations, regrets and further humiliation. George learned, for one thing, that Gov. Horatio Sharpe of Maryland had made criticisms of the affair at Fort Necessity in a manner that showed misunderstanding of what had happened. In self-defence, Washington wrote the Governor an account which Sharpe accepted in a handsome and friendly letter.[146] Although this swept the slate clean, it was of course unpleasant to have lost even temporarily the good opinion of the Governor of the Colony across the Potomac.

The principal regret of this period of inaction was over news of the death of Half King. The Chief, it will be remembered, had disappeared from the Meadows at the time the French approached[147] and later he had expressed a poor opinion of George's leadership.[148] Even so, Half King had been the most loyal of the supporters of England in the realm of the Six Nations and, with the exception of Andrew Montour, probably was the ablest of the savages Washington had met. It was distressing to learn that Half King had arrived at Paxton, Pennsylvania, on the 1st of October in ill health which he and his friends attributed to French witchcraft. Three days later he died—one of the most intriguing figures of his day on the frontier.[149]

George's new humiliations of September and of the first days of October were over the prospect that if he went back to Wills Creek, he no longer would be commander of the forces. Instead, he would be subordinate to Innes and would be in unpleasant relationship to the Captains of the Independent Companies. Besides Mackay, with whom George now had a satisfactory personal *modus vivendi,* Captain Clarke was at Wills Creek. Another officer with a King's commission, Capt.

[145] Lewis left between September 19 and October 2 at a date not determinable from surviving records. See Washington's account with "the Country" in Toner, ed., *Washington's Journal of 1754,* p. 184.
[146] 1 *Hamilton,* 51–53. Sharpe is sketched in *DAB* and in the preface to his *Correspondence,* which is cited many times in these notes. See also Giddens in 32 *Md. Hist. Mag.,* 156–64, 215–25. Sharpe was said to have made a good impression on his visit to Wills Creek in November. See *Penn. Gazette.* Dec. 5, 1754. As Washington's relations with him never became as close as it appeared in the autumn of 1754 they might be, Sharpe is not treated in detail here.
[147] *Supra,* p. 402.
[148] See *supra,* p. 415.
[149] 2 *Penn. Arch.,* 177, 178; 6 *Penn. Col. Rec.,* 184. Cf. Dinwiddie: ". . . he was a steady friend and a brave man" (1 *Din.,* 369. See *ibid.,* 395).

John Rutherford, had arrived there from England to assume command of the New York Company that had no Captain.[150] He of course had stood with the other officers of the regular establishment in demanding seniority over all the colonials except Innes, whose old royal commission antedated Rutherford's, as it did those of the other Captains.[151] George had no such advantage. His high pride rebelled because either he would have to remain entirely separate from these officers, or else he would have to recognize their authority as superior to his. Innes offered to permit George to do separate duty, so that there could be no clash with the proud Captains, but this was not enough. It was as unsoldierly as it was personally unacceptable. For that matter, George's spurring ambition may have led him to wonder why Innes, and not he himself, was at the head of the forces on the frontier. Innes's troops had disbanded and gone home: what title had he to remain in command? [152] He knew nothing of frontier fighting.

While ambition and pride of rank were gnawing George's vitals, there came still another affair that may have involved humiliation. At Fort Necessity, it will be recalled, George had agreed to two conditions the French commander imposed for the future: Washington had promised, first, that "they" would work on no building at Fort Necessity or anywhere West of the mountains for a year from the date of the capitulation. Second, George had given two hostages for the redemption of his promise to return within two months and a half the prisoners taken in the Jumonville affair.[153] The Council of Virginia had decided that Washington had no right to negotiate on this subject because he had no authority over the prisoners. As for the specific terms, Dinwiddie had interpreted "they" not to mean the English as a whole but only the eleven men left behind to care for the wounded at Fort Necessity, though he admitted that the French probably thought the word "they" inclusive [154] of all the troops.

On the basis of this reasoning, Dinwiddie never intended the English to remain East of the mountains for a year, or even for a day longer than numerical weakness kept them there; but at first he was willing to carry out the promised exchange of French prisoners for the English hostages.[155] On August 22, the captives started under guard from

<hr />

[150] I *Din.*, 349.

[151] I *Hamilton*, 48, 50.

[152] Jealousy on Washington's part cannot be demonstrated but it cannot be ignored as a possibility. There is a vague hint of it in William Fitzhugh to Washington, Nov. 4, 1754; I *Hamilton*, 54.

[153] See *supra*, p. 407–08.

[154] I *Sharpe*, 77; 2 *Din.*, 228.

[155] I *Din.*, 233.

Williamsburg for the long journey to Fort DuQuesne,[156] via Winchester, and they had reached the Valley town when the contents of Stobo's letter of July 29 became known generally.[157] In this secretly dispatched message, Stobo had spoken of the extent to which the French missed the services of La Force, who was one of the men to be returned to Fort DuQuesne.

This was enough for Dinwiddie. He was so much impressed by Stobo's words that he ordered La Force sent back to Williamsburg where he was imprisoned again. Then, on the ground that the French had themselves violated the capitulation by taking prisoners and by offering them for sale,[158] Dinwiddie undertook to negotiate through Colonel Innes an exchange that would release Stobo and van Braam in return for all the French officers except La Force.[159] The commander at Fort DuQuesne suspected that Lieutenant Lyon, the officer sent to submit this exchange, was a spy and he confined the Virginian until he could write formal rejection of the proposal.[160] Because of this, the other French prisoners taken in May remained in Winchester or in Fairfax jail.[161] Throughout these vain negotiations, Dinwiddie held to the position taken by the Council that the French prisoners were not in Washington's hands at the time of the capitulation of Fort Necessity, and that the Colonel consequently could not covenant to deliver them [162]—a statement legally correct but morally a repudiation of the terms Washington had signed. If George felt this was in any sense personal, he said nothing of it.[163]

Regardless of this incident, George had an accumulation of discontent and humiliation weighing on his mind when he started for Williamsburg about October 17, the date to which the House of Burgesses had been prorogued by the Governor.[164]

156 *Md. Gazette,* Sept. 12, 1754; 1 *Din.,* 293.
157 1 *Din.,* 298, 313; *Md. Gazette,* Oct. 3, Oct. 10, 1754.
158 *Md. Gazette,* Sept. 12, 1754.
159 1 *Din.,* 298; *Penn. Gazette,* Oct. 24, 1754.
160 Paris; Arch. Nat., C, 11, A, 99, f 318–22. For the substance of Lyon's report on his return, see *Md. Gazette,* Oct. 28, 1754.
161 1 *Din.,* 313, 347; 1 *Sharpe,* 142.
162 1 *Din.,* 347; 2 *Din.,* 228; 2 *Sparks,* 467.
163 Sparks, *loc. cit.,* maintained that Dinwiddie's acts were "a subject of mortification" to George, but he gave no authority for his statement. In August, 1756, when La Force escaped from Williamsburg jail, George expressed himself as "extremely concerned" over the "accident" (1 *G. W.,* 443), and said nothing about any injustice to the prisoner. For the escape and recapture of La Force, see 3 *Burk,* 192–93; *Md. Gazette,* Aug. 26, 1756.
164 It is possible that George made the journey to settle his accounts, for which see Toner, ed., *Washington's Journal* of 1754, p. 180 ff. It may have been, on the other hand, that the settlement was prompted by the events presently to be described in the text.

The young Colonel rode by way of Taylor's Ordinary[165] and then by Todd's at the crossing of the Mattapony on the boundary between King and Queen and King William Counties. Thence George continued southward, West of the Mattapony and through King William Court House,[166] until he reached Claiborne's on the Pamunkey. Passing that stream, he kept close to the meridian and spent the night of October 20 at Chiswell's.[167]

The next day, October 21, George was in Williamsburg.[168] He found the Governor busy in the entertainment of distinguished men and in the planning of a larger war with greater means. On the 7th, the Governor of North Carolina, Arthur Dobbs, had arrived in Williamsburg after a dismal, almost interminable voyage from Spithead of no less than twelve weeks aboard the man-of-war *Garland,* which had lost a mainmast in a fearsome storm off the Virginia coast. Dobbs had brought from the home government £10,000 in specie for Governor Dinwiddie's use in securing the defence of the Colony, and he had delivered also a crown credit for a like sum and notice that 2000 stands of arms were to be sent to Virginia.[169] Important dispatches had been in Dobbs's hands for Horatio Sharpe, Governor of Maryland, whom Dinwiddie in His Majesty's name was to summon to Williamsburg for conference with the Governors of Virginia and North Carolina. Obediently, Sharpe had been able to reach the Virginia town on the 19th,[170] and

[165] Fitzpatrick, *Colonial Traveler,* 61, located this ordinary in Stafford County. If that was the place at which George stopped, one questions why he did not proceed to Fredericksburg and spend the night at his mother's or at his sister's house. It seems more probable that George's first day's journey was to Fredericksburg and his second to Taylor's Ordinary in Hanover. There were two inns of that name in Hanover, one at Taylorsville, the other near Fork Church. Both were on the route George would have followed from Fredericksburg, but he rested at the second of the two. See Rosewell Page, *Hanover County,* 43.

[166] He was there the night of October 19 and was following the route recommended to travelers in the *Virginia Almanac* for 1756.

[167] He spelt it as it was pronounced, Chizzel's. It was at or near the present Toano (*Ledger* A, folio 10). Mention already has been made of "Washington's Burgess Route," with a map, published by Rev. Arthur P. Gray in 46 *V* 299 and separately reprinted.

[168] He boarded for the whole or a part of the time at Mrs. Coulthard's. She probably was the daughter of Richard Booker and the wife of John Coulthard, who, in the *Va. Gazette* (Hunter's) Apr. 25, 1751, had announced the removal of his shop from "next door to the Printing Office to the Back Street, next door to the house of Mr. Walter King." The second of these sites is not positively identified. Coulthard's estate at the time of his death was small. Mrs. Coulthard may have had to conduct a boarding house to maintain the family. See 7 *V* 97–99. George entertained at Finnie's Ordinary and may have lodged there some of the nights he was in Williamsburg. See *Ledger A,* folio 10.　　　[169] 1 *Din.,* 353 ff, 371.

[170] He so affirmed in separate letters, 1 *Sharpe,* 103, 109. Dinwiddie's statements of later date that he was awaiting the arrival of Sharpe (1 *Din.,* 350, 366) can mean only that Dinwiddie either had the habit of starting a letter one day and finishing and dating it several days later or else he gave a letter the date on which it was copied or mailed. Dates of his letters cannot always be trusted, for this reason, and must be checked if important conclusions of any nature depend on precise timing. All the details of Dobbs's coming and of Sharpe's visit will be found in 1 *Sharpe,* 103 ff.

had been closeted with Dinwiddie and with Dobbs, a man of sixty-five who had large experience as a public servant.[171]

George found, also, that the General Assembly had met according to the prorogation and that members were discussing on the very day of his arrival a resolution to raise £20,000 "for the protection of His Majesty's subjects against the insults and encroachments of the French." [172] The temper of the Burgesses was said to be better than when they had been prorogued without passing any supply. Prospects now were that the entire £20,000 would be voted unconditionally. That sum, added to what the King had sent, would provide money for a much larger expedition than the one George had commanded. Other Colonies might increase still further the war chest of the English,[173] though Dinwiddie was convinced that the total of colonial funds and men would not suffice. There must be more gold and more troops from England.[174]

The most exciting news of all was that among the papers brought from England by Dobbs had been a Lieutenant Colonel's commission for Horatio Sharpe.[175] With it were the King's orders for Sharpe to take charge of the forces that were to "be raised on this part of the continent to protect His Majesty's Dominions from the encroachments and devastations of his presumptuous enemies." [176] By Sharpe's direction and with Dinwiddie's approval, Innes was to be "Camp Master General" at Wills Creek [177]—that and no more. Dinwiddie, of course, would continue to organize the Virginia troops according to his own plans; but Sharpe would have authority over the forces Dinwiddie raised and over all the others, whether colonial or Independent Companies. This new arrangement the Governor of Virginia took in good part, because he believed it would advance the King's cause and would end strife between the regular and the colonial officers.[178] At the same time, this honor for Sharpe reawakened the martial ambitions Dinwiddie had cherished earlier and then regretfully had put aside.[179]

171 He is sketched in *DAB*.
172 *Journ. H.B.*, 1752–58, p. 214.
173 1 *Sharpe*, 104; 1 *Din.*, 354; *London Gazette*, Dec. 17, 1754.
174 1 *Din.*, 355, 365.
175 1 *Sharpe*, 72, 73.
176 The language is Sharpe's. See his letter to Lord Baltimore, Oct. 25, 1754 (*ibid.*, 102). Walpole stated (1 *Memoirs*, 347) that Sharpe owed his commission to the recommendation of the Hanbury firm.
177 1 *Din.*, 352; William Fitzhugh to Washington, Nov. 4, 1754, 1 *Hamilton*, 54.
178 1 *Din.*, 354, 365; 1 *Sharpe*, 111.
179 In the earliest of the correspondence there is no explicit statement that Sharpe's appointment was limited to the period prior to the arrival of troops from England; but Sharpe's

STOBO'S LETTER THAT CAME BACK

No wonder the story of Robert Stobo has become a favored theme of fiction! It has all the elements ready-made. A writer need not trouble himself to ask whether an imaginary episode had verisimilitude. Stobo did everything and suffered everything that a hero should.

In the spring of 1754, he came to Washington's little command, with a most popular letter of introduction, to wit, a pipe of Madeira, and he endeared himself to his new comrades by dispensing it generously.

Later, when the French required at the surrender of Fort Necessity that two hostages be given for the return of the prisoners captured in the affair with Jumonville, it was unpleasant, of course, to have to give up anyone, but Stobo and Jakob van Braam seemed the men who would be least inconvenienced by what promised to be a brief period of easy captivity.

Stobo undertook to make the best of it. Taken to Fort DuQuesne, he discovered that the place was weakly held. He secretly sent that information back to the English settlements in two letters that separate Indian runners carried. In one of these communications he drew a careful sketch of the fort.

The colonials could not undertake in the fall of 1754 the attack on Fort DuQuesne that Stobo advocated. Nor would the Governor of Virginia honor the promise Washington made in the capitulation of

(Continued on third page following)

...to arms one hundred & twenty Indians might Surprise this fort, they
... across all day & night lodge themselves so that they might return...
... Lucia with their families ... the Sally gate & the Forts door...
... the Guard of Contre ... stay in the Fort at night. The Guard
... exceeds 60. all the rest are in the Cabins round the Fort. ...
... ... communicate this but to few & them you can trust, as Intelligence
comes here unaccountably. if they should know I have wrote ...
at least lose the little liberty I have, I should be glad to ...
... but take no notice of this in your ... ...
... I believe me to be ...

                                                Your
                                                Rob.t Hobs

... be kind to this Indian
... ... Delaney George
have been here _____

a Envoijer aut legeneral pirie que a ... est ...
Exacte qu'il est ... ...
qu'il ... est ... ... qu'il fait fait

parafé le 23 ... 1756

Langloiſerie

parafé le ...

Langloiſerie

Fort Necessity for the release of the prisoners taken when Jumonville was killed. Those prisoners, said the Governor, were not Washington's but the Colony's. Washington had no right to bargain for their return.

Stobo consequently was detained by the French and was sent to Quebec. There, one day in 1756, he was confronted with the original of the letter in which he had drawn the ground plan of the fort on the Ohio. That document, he subsequently learned, the colonials had preserved and had delivered to Braddock before the General started for the Ohio. After his defeat, the paper was found in his baggage.

It was evidence on which the French based a charge of treason against Stobo. As markings on the reproduction show, the letter was used as an exhibit in the trial of Stobo. He received a sentence of death, but, because this had to be approved by the government in Paris, he was not executed immediately. While he was in close captivity he escaped with invincible daring and reached the British who were preparing an advance on Quebec. The rest of the story, as relates to Washington, will appear in Volume III.

This original of Stobo's incriminating letter is in the archives of the District of Montreal.

Quickly, on arrival in Williamsburg, Washington learned of these happenings. Before he heard the details of what was planned for the future, he discharged a pleasant duty. Some time prior to his departure from Alexandria, he had received the letter in which the Speaker of the House transmitted the formal thanks of the Burgesses to Washington and all his officers except Muse and van Braam.[180] George felt it proper to acknowledge this resolution and, on the second day after he reached Williamsburg, he wrote the Speaker in what he considered the most appropriate style:

Sir,

Nothing could give me and the officers under my command, greater satisfaction, than to receive the thanks of the House of Burgesses, in so particular and public a manner, for our behavior in the late unsuccessful engagement with the French, and we unanimously hope, that our future proceedings in the service of our country, will entitle us to a continuance of your approbation. I assure you, sir, I shall always look upon it as my indispensable duty to endeavor to deserve it.

I was desired by the officers of the Virginia Regiment to make their suitable acknowledgments for the honor they have received in your thanks; I therefore hope the enclosed will be agreeable and answer their, and the intended purpose of,

Sir,

Your most obedient humble servant,

George Washington.

The letter from the officers, "signed for the whole corps" by Washington, was to the same effect. Both papers were entered in the journal of the Burgesses.[181]

This duty having been performed, courtesies and friendly words probably were exchanged by George at Finnie's Ordinary with members of the House and of the Council. From these worthies, from other friends and probably from the Governors themselves, Washington

---

observations to Sir Thomas Robinson, Oct. 25, 1754 (1 *Sharpe*, 105–06), show that he did not expect to retain command if forces were sent from the home country. Apparently, Robinson's first official announcement of the dispatch of Halket's and Dunbar's Regiments, and of plans to send a "General Officer of rank and capacity" was under date of Oct. 26, 1754. See *Sharpe*, 107. An Edinburgh dispatch in the *London Gazette* of Dec. 17, 1754, would leave the impression that Braddock's appointment and the temporary nature of Sharpe's commission were known in Virginia by October 24. Dinwiddie's letter of October 25 to the Lords of Trade indicates that he anticipated the dispatch of two Regiments but knew nothing of the commander of the expedition (1 *Din.*, 365).

[180] 1 *Hamilton*, 45. The letter was dated Sept. 15, 1754.

[181] *Journ. H. B.*, 1752–58, p. 219–20.

learned at least something of what was contemplated. Together, the three executives were working on a plan similar in every way to the one Dinwiddie had formulated in August and then had abandoned when money ran out and the North Carolina troops scattered. The information of the Governors was that the French force on the Ohio was so reduced that a new opportunity was offered the English.[182] If practicable, Sharpe was to raise 700 men who, with the Independent Companies, were to proceed forthwith to the Ohio and were to capture Fort DuQuesne before the French could reenforce it.[183] As George already had assailed Dinwiddie's design as impractical, when two months and more of open weather prevailed, he probably was not consulted during the discussion revived after the frost had come to Laurel Hill and to Chestnut Ridge.

Amazement over this rash scheme was effaced almost immediately by news for which Washington was altogether unprepared. Welcome had been accorded him, thanks had been voted him, satisfaction had been expressed with his handling of the troops, "honor" of the sort he most coveted, the praise and good opinion of responsible men, had been showered on him—and now he was to be told, of all things, that the Virginia Regiment was to be broken into Independent Companies!

From William Fitzhugh, who had come with Sharpe to Williamsburg, Washington received the impression that the change to Independent Companies was to be made under peremptory orders from England.[184] When George sought further explanation, he was told that the Home Government would be petitioned to send King's commissions for company officers in blank to Dinwiddie. The Governor then could fill in the names and distribute the commissions to colonials who immediately would become Captains and Lieutenants of the

---

[182] The reason for reconsideration of the offensive was not set forth in detail by Dinwiddie or by Sharpe, but it almost certainly was the report made by Lieutenant Lyon, on his return late in September from his mission to Fort DuQuesne. He was said to have affirmed that the French at that station did not exceed 100 men, who were poorly supplied with provisions (*Md. Gazette,* Oct. 28, 1754). The vagueness of Du Quesne's references to the location of his troops makes it difficult to say how wide of the mark Lyon's estimate was. It will be remembered that Du Quesne had been warned by the Ministry at the end of May, 1754, that unless the excessive cost of the upkeep of the colonies were reduced, the government would abandon them (Paris Arch. Nat., Colonies, B 99, 199). On Oct. 7, 1754, Du Quesne had reported that he felt justified in not reducing the garrison to 800 men, because 1600 had difficulty in holding the English on one hand and the Indians on the other. He did not make plain how large was the region this "garrison" was supposed to control (Can. Arch., C, 11, A, 99, p. 260, Cor. Gen.). As of October 29 (*ibid.,* 245), Du Quesne reported that Villiers had 200 regulars who set a fine example for the Canadian troops.

[183] 1 *Sharpe,* 105; text of the plan, 1 *Din.,* 351.

[184] See Washington to Fitzhugh, Nov. 15, 1754; 1 *G. W.,* 106.

regular military establishment. Thereafter no difference other than that of date of commission would exist between the officers of the old Independent Companies and the new. Such an arrangement had been made at the time of the Cartagena expedition; the Governor was pressing for it now;[185] Sharpe approved;[186] the Burgesses were requesting Dinwiddie, who assented heartily, to recommend to His Majesty's favor those officers who had distinguished themselves in the expedition to the Ohio.[187]

This was logical enough on its face, and, as Dinwiddie explained, it was one means of assuring the cooperation of regulars who insisted on their authority over colonials who would not submit.[188] From George's point of view, it meant that he would cease to be a Colonel and would become a Captain, and at that not even on the King's commission, unless and until His Majesty approved Dinwiddie's recommendation that the colonials be on the regular establishment. "In short," George said indignantly, "every Captain bearing the King's commission, every half-pay officer, or other, appearing with such a commission, would rank before me."[189]

His pride rebelled against such a thing, and the more so because he had a suspicion that conspiracy had been hatched at Wills Creek[190] by men inimical to him and ambitious to outstrip him. Dinwiddie did nothing to placate him. Most particularly the Governor did not confide that in the letters regarding the changes in the Regiment, he had sought commission for himself as Colonel of the new force and had not so much as mentioned Washington.[191] Nor did the Governor relieve George of the impression, wrongly received, that orders to reduce the Regiment to Independent Companies had arrived from England.[192]

Sharpe was more considerate. He formed a good opinion of the young Virginian and tried to prevail on George, through William

---

[185] The development of the plan may be followed in Dinwiddie's letters to Sir Thomas Robinson, to the Lords of Trade, and to Lord Halifax. See 1 *Din.*, 354, 355, 356 and 369.
[186] 1 *Sharpe*, 106.
[187] 1 *G. W.*, 105; *Journ. H.B.*, 1752–58, p. 219, 221.
[188] 1 *Din.*, 365.   [190] *Ibid.*, 106.
[189] 1 *G. W.*, 105–06.   [191] 1 *Din.*, 355, 372–73.
[192] See 1 *G. W.*, 105, for his continuing impression, as late as Nov. 15, 1754, that such instructions had been sent by the Secretary of State for War. Nothing is said on the subject in Robinson's instructions of July 5, 1754 to Sharpe (31 *Md. Council Proc.*, 53); no acknowledgment of such orders appears in *Din.* or in *Sharpe*. The familiar royal "Orders for settling the Rank of the Officers of His Majesty's Forces," reproduced in 1 *Hamilton*, opposite p. 56, bore date of Nov. 12, 1754. The first reference to the subject of colonial rank in *Pargellis*, p. 36, is Nov. n.d., 1754. Earliest discovered mention of the plan to reduce the Virginia Regiment to Independent Companies is in Dinwiddie's letter of Oct. 25, 1754 to the Lords of Trade (1 *Din.*, 365). This letter does not indicate with whom the suggestion originated.

Fitzhugh, to serve with the troops he was to raise. When George declined, Sharpe asked that Washington at least promise to consider any proposition he might be able to make after he returned to Maryland.[193] George could not refuse this but he did not believe Sharpe could tender a position he could accept. "I think," he said later, "the disparity between the present offer of a company and my former rank too great to expect any real satisfaction or enjoyment in a corps where I once did, or thought I had a right, to command . . ." [194]

In that spirit, proud and indignant but not openly wrathful, Washington tendered his resignation as Colonel of the Virginia Regiment. Dinwiddie accepted it. George turned decisively to other matters and completed his shopping in Williamsburg by purchasing new fittings and horse furnishings of the sort a planter of station required. He had been less careful than usual with his money while in Williamsburg and, when he came to count it, found to his distress that he was short £1, 6s, which he concluded he either had lost or unwittingly had contributed to some light-fingered person. His next act was to settle with Colin Campbell, the gentleman whom Governor Dinwiddie had imposed on him as Deputy Adjutant for the Northern Neck. George had no intention of giving up that position or any larger part of the salary of £100 a year than honest bargaining required. He found Campbell willing, in the final negotiations, to accept £50 per annum but not as little as the £40 allowed the other deputies. George accordingly paid him £25 for half a year's service, £5 more than he thought proper, but £7, 6s less than he had feared he might be compelled to give up.[195] This arranged, George settled his board bill of £1, 7s 6d with Mrs. Coulthard and paid the somewhat formidable account of £5, 9s 6d he had accumulated while entertaining at Finnie's.[196]

Then on the 2nd of November, he left the colonial capital and started home.[197] Governor Sharpe already had departed on the 29th of October; [198] the General Assembly was about to adjourn. When the Burgesses first had met on the 17th, the Governor had thought them "extremely obstinate and self-opinionated," [199] but he had addressed

[193] Although not set forth explicitly in the surviving correspondence, this is plainly to be inferred from Fitzhugh to Washington, Nov. 4, 1754; 1 *Hamilton*, 54.

[194] 1 *G. W.*, 104–05.

[195] See *supra*, p. 430.

[196] *Ledger A*, folio 10. Cf. 1 *Din.*, 316.

[197] The date is fixed by his account that night at Armistead's Ordinary and, the next night, at King William Court House (*Ledger A*, folio 17).

[198] 1 *Sharpe*, 113. The Governor reached Annapolis on the 1st of November.

[199] 1 *Din.*, 323.

them deferentially [200] and had refrained wisely from pursuing the advantage he had gained by a final settlement in his favor of the controversy over the pistole fee.[201] Moreover, the Governor had appealed to the legislators' sense of fair play by dwelling on the "distinguished marks of His Majesty's paternal care" [202] in sending £10,000 specie, in granting a credit for a like amount, and in shipping 2000 stands of arms.[203] Without abashment the Governor had concealed from the legislators the fact that the money had to be repaid the Crown from the Colony's export tax on tobacco, unless he was successful in prevailing on the government to waive or at least to delay collection.[204]

On these representations, the Burgesses had risen to their conception of their duty and had remained throughout their session in the friendly spirit of which George had evidence when he arrived on the 21st of October. In the end, the Assembly voted £20,000 for the defence of the Colony through two successive poll taxes of 2s 6d. This money was to be spent by a designated committee "with the consent and approbation of the Governor or Commander-in-Chief for the time being"—an arrangement that Dinwiddie this time accepted without formal protest.[205]

The General Assembly passed, also, an act for the conscription of vagrants between the ages of twenty-one and fifty for a term of one year.[206] In short, all that the Governor desired or the emergency required of the Assembly, it had done. While George was riding northward that 2nd of November, Dinwiddie was telling the Council and Burgesses, "Your example, gentlemen, will be great encouragement to others; and, I hope, for the future, generous benevolence will incite every member of the community to a due and just regard for the happiness and peace of the whole." [207] By the time George reached home,[208] the Burgesses were scattering under a welcome prorogation to March, 1755.[209]

[200] *Journ. H.B.*, 1752–58, p. 209–10.
[201] 1 *Din.*, 362 and *supra*, p. 171. See also 1 *Din.*, 137, 153; *Md. Gazette*, May 9, 1754.
[202] 1 *Journ. H.B.*, 1752–58, p. 209.
[203] *Ibid.*
[204] 1 *Din.*, 353, 356, 369, 402, 410.
[205] 6 H 435 ff.
[206] 6 H 438–40.
[207] *Journ. H.B.*, 1752–58, p. 227. For his improved opinion of the Burgesses, see 1 *Din.*, 372, 380, 402.
[208] He was at Belvoir Nov. 15, 1754 (1 *G. W.*, 104), but on November 20 he paid John Carlyle £8 for board over an unspecified period (*Ledger A*, folio 11).
[209] *Journ. H.B.*, 1752–58, p. 227.

George, for his part, had no rendezvous except with his own lands, to which he had given little attention during the year that had elapsed since he had undertaken to carry Dinwiddie's message to Fort Le Boeuf. On the 15th of November, 1753, George had been at Wills Creek and had been engaging Christopher Gist as a guide for his first great adventure in the wilderness. Now, Nov. 15, 1754, he was sitting at a desk in Col. William Fairfax's home, Belvoir. Within twelve months had come, first, the journey almost to Lake Erie and the struggle in the snow as George hurried back to warn Dinwiddie that the French were preparing to descend to the Ohio. They had done so quickly enough and had driven off Ward before Washington could reach the Monongahela. The responsibilities and excitement of acting as leader of the advanced column, the anxieties and disappointments of command, promotion to the rank of Colonel after the death of Fry, the difficulties with Mackay, the doubtful conferences with the Indians, the affair with Jumonville, the attempt to cut a road to Red Stone Creek, the shameless delay of contractors, the hunger of the soldiers, the disappearance of the red warriors, the blood and the mud of the 3rd of July, the humiliation of retreat and of that word "assassination," the journey to Williamsburg, the thanks of the House of Burgesses, and then the blow, almost the insult, of dropping from the first post of field command to the rank of Captain subordinate to every half-pay officer who might come from England—all this had been hard, hard, hard. George had given his every energy to his duty and had endured more of hardship than any Virginian of his day had been called on to suffer in the public service. It had been shabbily rewarded, he thought. He himself had been repudiated and humiliated. Now the whole of it was behind him. In front of him, there on the desk, was the single sheet [210] on which he was to accept or decline the offer Governor Sharpe had extended on the 4th of November through William Fitzhugh in accordance with the promise made at Williamsburg.

Sharpe had done his best: If George would reconsider his resignation, Colonel Innes would be no obstacle to his service, because the North Carolinian was merely to exercise post command at Wills Creek. When Sharpe himself was not afield, Fitzhugh would see to it that George would not be required to take orders from those who had been his juniors when he was on the frontier. A letter from Sharpe to Dinwiddie, written to give assurance of this, was enclosed with the Mary-

[210] 1 G. W., 107.

lander's invitation and could be forwarded to Williamsburg if George accepted the offer. Fitzhugh added his personal advice "by no means to quit." He said George would "hold" his "post"—did that mean his rank as Colonel?—and, when the Regiment was reduced, George would be assigned separate duty.[211]

No! He would not accept it. Sharpe and Fitzhugh deserved, of course, the best and most polite answer he could pen, because they had been considerate and generous; but the decision stood—no, no, no. Col. George Washington, now nearly twenty-three years of age, would not submit to loss of rank which Sharpe did not have authority to change. George so wrote Fitzhugh, gravely and politely, and, in the course of the letter, came to the suggestion that he might "hold" his "post." The answer was: "You make mention in your letter of my continuing in the service, and retaining my Colonel's commission. This idea has filled me with surprise; for if you think me capable of holding a commission that has neither rank nor emolument annexed to it, you must entertain a very contemptible opinion of my weakness, and believe me to be more empty than the commission itself."

George could not refrain, next, from mention of those Captains "bearing the King's commission" and those half-pay officers who would rank him. Rather than subject himself to that and to the risk of a second disappointment, he would endure fatigue and loss of property and of health. Pride rose again as he wrote on: "I shall have the consolation of knowing that I have opened the way when the smallness of our numbers exposed us to the attacks of a superior enemy; that I have hitherto stood the heat and brunt of the day, and escaped untouched in time of extreme danger; and that I have the thanks of my country for the services I have rendered it."

There followed a hint that George knew and might expose the methods by which the breakup of the Regiment had been accomplished. As for the plan of operations, "it is to be hoped the project will answer; it shall meet with my acquiescence in everything except personal services."

The large hand of the former Colonel was nearing the end of the sheet. He explained that as he could not use it, he was returning Sharpe's letter to Dinwiddie. Of the Maryland Governor, George wrote: ". . . assure him, sir, as you truly may, of my reluctance to quit the service and of the pleasure I should have received in attending his

211 Fitzhugh to Washington, Nov. 4, 1754; I *Hamilton*, 54–55.

fortunes. Also inform him [212] that it was to obey the call of honor, and the advice of my friends, I declined it, and not to gratify any desire I have to leave the military line."

Then he added, in regret and in confession, in memory of stirring days and perhaps in vague thought of the future: "My inclinations are strongly bent to arms." [213]

[212] The original reads: ". . . in attending his Fortunes, also inform him . . ."
[213] 1 G. W., 104–07.

APPENDIX I–1

THE NORTHERN NECK PROPRIETARY TO 1745

THE ROOTS of the Northern Neck proprietary [1] ran back to the early autumn of 1649, eight months after the execution of Charles I, when his older son, Charles II, was at St. Germain-en-Laye, near Paris. War in England had gone against the Royalists, but Montrose in Scotland and Ormonde in Ireland had armies that still would fight for the Stuarts. In both countries Charles II had been proclaimed King. With him in France, urging him to raise again the royal standard, were men who had fought at Edgehill and at Bradock-down, at Stratton and at Landsdown, at Adwalton Moor and at Lostwithiel. Some of them remembered all the bitterness of Marston Moor and Naseby and Preston. On the strength of what Montrose had achieved at Inverlochy and at Auldearn, they still hoped for new victories in Scotland and for the restoration of the monarchy, but at the moment some of them were selling or pawning their jewels to buy food and to pay for shelter.[2]

In a knowledge of their sacrifices for him, Charles decided that before he left France he would allot to a few of his most faithful supporters some of the unoccupied lands of Virginia, where, as in Ireland and in Scotland, the people were loyal to him. Such an act would have numerous precedents. Virginia colonials themselves had said, more than a decade previously, that the award of frontier lands to deserving soldiers was "the usual custom and policy of all Nations, but in more especial manner of the state of England." [3] This principle, Charles might have reasoned, he could apply in behalf of none more justly than for those defenders of the throne he named in his grant.

The first of these "right trusty and well-beloved companions" of the exiled King was Ralph Lord Hopton, Baron of Stratton, then about fifty-one years

---

[1] At the outset, acknowledgment must be made of the extent to which this appendix is based on the researches of Fairfax Harrison, who died in 1938. In his *Virginia Land Grants* and in his *Landmarks of Old Prince William*, Mr. Harrison published much of the essential material, which he had collected with great assiduity. Contributions to the *Virginia Magazine* included additional facts that were obtained through expensive investigation in England. Although he concerned himself little with the lower Northern Neck, Mr. Harrison gathered many more data than he used and he most thoughtfully placed in the VHS the copies of the transcripts of the *Gooch Papers* which are in the Library of Congress.

[2] This continued a chronic state until the Restoration. Cf. Sir Edward Nicholas, Oct. 5, 1659: "We are [in Brussels] for want of money due H. M. The creditors are importunate and the necessities of the family incredible" (*Cal. State Papers, Dom.*, 1659–60, p. 223).

[3] Patent of July 6, 1636, quoted in *Va. Land Grants*, 51.

of age. He had fought in the Thirty Years' War and, according to some reports, had been the escort of the Queen of Bohemia in her flight after the Battle of Prague. During the English civil struggle, General Hopton had been among the staunchest of Charles's commanders. To him, in large measure, was credited the victory in the engagement at Stratton. After the undependable Goring retired, Hopton was Commander-in-Chief of the royal forces in the West of England—"as faultless a person, as full of courage, industry, integrity and religion" as any man of Clarendon's acquaintance.[4]

Hopton's Commissary General in the Stratton campaign, Sir John Berkeley, was another beneficiary of the grant. He, too, had shared in the Thirty Years' War, though as a diplomatist and not as a warrior. A third rewarded officer was Sir William Morton, a lawyer turned soldier, who had been captured at the surrender of Lord Chandos's castle of Sudeley in Gloucestershire. "His mettle," wrote Clarendon, "was never suspected and his fidelity as little questioned"; his years of imprisonment were "sustained with great firmness and constancy."[5] As much, no doubt, could be said of a fourth grantee, Sir Dudley Wyatt, who served on occasion during the Civil War as confidential messenger between King Charles and Queen Henrietta in France.[6] Still another individual listed in the grant, Thomas Culpeper, Esq., may have owed recognition to the part a man of this name had borne in the grim siege of Colchester, June, 1648; but there is equal probability that Thomas Culpeper gained his place on the list of honor through the influence of a cousin presently to be introduced.[7]

One of the two remaining beneficiaries of the grant of Virginia lands was a notorious figure at the court of the two Charles—Henry Jermyn, Baron of St. Edmundsbury and later Earl of St. Albans.[8] He had not failed in the field of action, but he had been far more conspicuous as the Master of Horse and the favorite of Charles's mother. At heart an intriguer, he subsequently was suspected of having dared to contract a private marriage with Henrietta.[9] Almost beyond doubt, Jermyn was included in the Virginia proprietors at the instance of the Queen Dowager.[10] He certainly would not have been on the list by the choice of the members of the exiled court, because they complained three years later that he maintained a fine table and ample

[4] Clarendon, *History of the Rebellion,* v. 4, p. 1681, 1715. In the Oxford edition of 1827 (cited hereafter as *Clarendon's Rebellion*), the pagination is continuous.

[5] 4 *Clarendon's Rebellion,* 1729.

[6] See Fairfax Harrison, *Proprietors of the Northern Neck,* 33 *V* 347. This study by Mr. Harrison, which is one of the basic authorities concerning the proprietary, was printed separately in a small, private edition but it most readily is consulted in 33 and 34 *V.*

[7] All the evidence concerning this Thomas Culpeper is summarized by Fairfax Harrison in 33 *V* 343 ff. Thomas was the father of Alexander Culpeper (1631–94), who will appear in a later paragraph as owner of one-sixth of the proprietary. For him see *ibid.,* 353 ff. See also *Cal. State Pap., Dom.,* 1659–60, p. 68, 223.

[8] Contemporary grants spell the latter title St. Edmunds Bury.

[9] See the references cited by Firth in *DNB; Cal. State Pap., Dom.,* 1650, p. 320.

[10] Cf. 1 *Nicholas Papers,* 152.

equipage while many of them had to walk the streets of Paris in quest of board at one pistole a week.[11]

The other beneficiary of the patent, the one whose descendants influenced the history of Virginia, was the suave and turbulent, the paradoxical and distrusted John Lord Culpeper. Born about 1600,[12] he was the son of Thomas [13] Culpeper of Wigsell, and after some schooling at Hart Hall,[14] Oxford, he was admitted to the Middle Temple. His stay there must have been brief, for he soon was a soldier on the Continent.[15] He attained to no distinction [16] until after he was named to the Long Parliament in November, 1640, as Knight of the Shire from Kent.[17] "When he came thither," recorded Clarendon,[18] "he might very well be thought a man of no very good breeding; having never sacrificed to the muses or conversed in any polite company." [19] What Culpeper lacked of acquaintance with the Muses, he quickly made up in mastery of parliamentary art. He was plausible, persuasive, skillful in obstructing what he opposed,[20] and so deft in confusing the Commons by his shifts of position [21] that during one debate he was put in the chair, when the House went into committee, in order to keep him silent.[22]

A servant of this versatility in the royal cause did not lack recognition. Less than two years after Culpeper entered the Commons, he was Chancellor of the Exchequer and a member of the Privy Council.[23] Before Charles I left Whitehall—to return no more until the time of his execution—Culpeper shared with Falkland and Clarendon the management of royal interests in Parliament.[24] Readily enough, Culpeper entered the thickest of legislative contention,[25] though he soon was at odds with Clarendon.[26] Still worse

[11] 5 *Clarendon's Rebellion*, 2647. This was in 1652, after the grant was made.

[12] He was baptized August 7 of that year; 33 *V* 238.

[13] *DNB* incorrectly said John.   [14] See Foster, 1 *Alumni, Oxonienses*, 303.

[15] *The Life of Edward Hyde, Earl of Clarendon, written by himself* (cited hereafter as *Clarendon's Life*), v. 1, p. 106.

[16] For his two marriages, 1628 and 1631, see 33 *V* 245, 246.

[17] John Rushworth, *Historical Collections*, (cited hereafter as *Rushworth's Collections*), v. 4, p. 4.

[18] Cf. 2 *Nicholas Papers*, 101: "A sworne enemy to Sir E[dward] H[yde] even to death."

[19] 1 *Clarendon's Life*, 107.

[20] Sir Simonds D'Ewes' *Journal* is crowded with references. See also S. R. Gardiner, *History of England*, v. 9, p. 238, 281, 287, 289, 358. In 4 *Rushworth's Collections*, 33, appears a somewhat famous speech of Culpeper's against monopolies.

[21] 1 *Clarendon's Life*, 107.

[22] See Gardiner, *op. cit.*, 377. For some of Culpeper's other activities, see *ibid.*, v. 10, p. 2, 14, 75, 97, 127, 205.

[23] *Ibid.*, 10, 127; 1 *Clarendon's Life*, 170, 199.

[24] 1 *Clarendon's Life*, 101–03, 114, 133. Cf. 1 *Nicholas Papers*, 107, Oct. 1, 1648: "None of the King's affairs which of late have been left wholly to the conduct of Lo[rd] Culpeper have been managed with any advantage to His Majesty." See *ibid.*, 293, letter to Sir Edward Hyde, 18 April, no year.

[25] 2 *Clarendon's Rebellion*, 924; 3 *ibid.*, 1070–72; 4 *Rushworth's Collections*, 627; Whitelock's *Memorials*, 61.

[26] 1 *Clarendon's Life*, 170, 199.

contention developed around Culpeper when, taking the field, he insistently urged the futile siege of Gloucester. Although he previously had ridden neck to neck with Prince Rupert at Edgehill,[27] he gave unwise counsel regarding Gloucester and brought on himself the wrath of Rupert and of the army. Wrote Clarendon: "All conspired to lay the whole reproach on the Master of the Rolls, who spoke the most in those debates and was not at all gracious to the soldiers." [28]

The King did not share that feeling. In October, 1644—the year of Marston Moor—Charles made Sir John a peer as first Baron of Thoresway,[29] and later entrusted to him, among others, the custody of the Prince of Wales in the event the young man [30] ever was in danger of falling into the hands of the Parliamentary troops.[31] The new baron did not take his new duties so seriously that he denied himself a drunken brawl with a fellow Royalist,[32] but after the Prince went to France,[33] Culpeper was as useful as any member of the contentious Court [34] and doubtless as quick to seek rewards.[35]

To these seven, then, the grant was made: Ralph Lord Hopton, Baron of Stratton; Henry Lord Jermyn, Baron of St. Edmundsbury; John Lord Culpeper, Baron of Thoresway; Sir John Berkeley; Sir William Morton; Sir Dudley Wyatt; Thomas Culpeper, Esq. Their patent, which was dated Sept. 18, 1649,[36] covered the entire Northern Neck of Virginia, "bounded by and within the heads" of the Potomac and the Rappahannock Rivers.[37] Of the magnitude of the territory covered by the grant, certainly the King and probably the beneficiaries had little knowledge. Had the maps been accurate, it would have appeared that the absolute minimum was 1400 square miles, or close to 1,000,000 acres.[38] The maximum might be much larger.

[27] 3 Clarendon's Rebellion, 1538, 1540.

[28] 3 ibid., 1487; 4 ibid., 1559. Culpeper was Master of the Rolls after the Restoration, not when the grant was made.

[29] 4 ibid, 1814, 1839. Clarendon admitted that Culpeper deserved the honor but added that both Court and army were displeased.

[30] Prince Charles, later Charles II, was then fifteen.   [31] 4 Clarendon's Rebellion, 1819.

[32] Sir Richard Grenville, writing Lord Ormonde, Apr. 9, 1646, reprinted in 33 V 241 n., described the adversary as "Mr. Slingsby." The circumstances make it quite probable Sir Walter Slingsby was meant. See Cal. State Pap., Dom., 1644–45, p. 478, 520. A curious drunken bout of Culpeper's with a Dane at The Hague is mentioned in 3 Nicholas Papers, 14.

[33] For his wanderings, see Whitelock's Memorials, 200, 343; 1 Clarendon's Life, 316.

[34] See Whitelock's Memorials, 343, 466; 3 Clarendon State Papers, 112.

[35] Tradition always has been that Culpeper was included in the grant as compensation for losses sustained in the royal cause. This probably was true, at least in theory. The sequestration of his largest property, Leeds Castle, was voted by Parliament in 1649. See Cal. State Pap., Dom., 1649–50, p. 39, repeated in Cal. State Pap., Dom., 1651, p. 197, 309. 2 Acts and Ordinances of the Interregnum, 520. Neither act recognized the peerage of Culpeper. Both mentioned him as Sir John Culpeper, late of Hollingbourn, in the County of Kent, Knight.

[36] Br. Mus., Additional Charter 13585. A copy of this first patent, which does not appear to have been printed previously, will be found in Appendix I–2, Part I.

[37] For the later controversy concerning the western limits of the proprietary see infra, p. 489.

[38] That is, from the falls of the Potomac to the forks of the Rappahannock: one-third of the present Fairfax County, one-third of Prince William, two-thirds of Stafford and the whole of King George, Westmoreland, Richmond, Lancaster and Northumberland. As will be seen, infra, p. 499, the commissioners of 1737 estimated the minimum total as 1,476,000 acres.

Within this domain, the owners of the patent were to possess all the rights of any court baron of England, "and all and whatsoever doth belong or appertain to a court leet or view of frank pledge." They could build towns, castles and forts, could create and endow colleges and schools, and were to enjoy the patronage of churches. All the fines, forfeitures and strays within the jurisdiction of the types of court authorized by the patent were to be the property of the favored courtiers. It would be their right to "give, grant, or by any other way or means sell or alienate" acreage within the proprietary. Lands sold or leased in any such manner were to be held "in free and common socage by fealty only, and by suit of court, or by any other lawful tenure or tenures used within our Kingdom of England, rendering and paying rents and other lawful reservations as should seem fit and convenient" to the Proprietors. Any defects in the patent the King promised to correct. The grant was in perpetuity at an annual rent, payable in Jamestown, of £6, 13s 4d, "in lieu of all services and demands whatsoever."

Had he given any thought to the justice or equity of this grant, Charles scarcely could have considered it unfair to those who lived in settled parts of the Dominion of Virginia. The land of the Colony had been given, in the first instance, by Charles's grandfather, James I, to a stock company, which had exercised the powers of a Proprietor until its dissolution. In part, too, the New England Council of 1620 was proprietary.[39] To Lord Baltimore, in 1632, had been given a proprietorship of a type almost feudal. Sir Ferdinando Gorges's patent for Maine had been proprietary.[40] The Virginia grant was wholly in accord with a colonial policy which still was experimental but was taking form.[41]

As for the conditions under which the Proprietors might grant lands, the underlying principle was the familiar one, *nulle terre sans seigneur*. In Virginia, as in all the Colonies except Massachusetts, Rhode Island and Connecticut, some phases of medieval land tenure survived. "This tenure," to quote one who studied it thoroughly, "was commonly styled free and common socage or tenure in fee-simple, the terms of which were fealty and a fixed rent." To continue this essential explanation: "Feudally speaking, fealty was the bond between lord and man, which survived only in the oath of allegiance to the Crown; rent was the bond between the lord and the land, the symbol of territorial ownership, and was usually called the quit-rent, or sometimes . . . the chief rent. In addition there were other incidents, such as alienation fines and escheats. The quit-rent was originally a commutation in money of certain medieval villein obligations, such as

---

[39] Its corporate aspect must not be overlooked.

[40] See Charles M. Andrews, *The Colonial Period of American History* (cited hereafter as Andrews, *Colonial Period*), v. 1, p. 405. The patent to William Penn, covering the largest of all the proprietaries, was not issued until Mch. 4, 1680/81.

[41] This is one of the major theses of Andrews's rewarding study.

APPENDIX

laboring for the lord of a manor a number of days in the week and paying
to him a portion of the produce. . . . In very early times in England, the
payment of money rent seems to have been the privilege of a class of
sokemen (whence the name of the tenure), the free peasantry, who in considerable numbers survived the Norman Conquest, and as a commutation
to have been applied first to those of the unfree who held 'uncertainly,' or
at the will of the lord, that is, the future copyholders as contrasted with the
freeholders. But later the quit-rent was used to designate any form of payment, which absolved or made quit the tenant, whether vassal, freeholder,
copyholder, or leaseholder, in respect of personal service or other similar
obligation to the lord. The tenure thus evolved became the 'freest' of all
the English land tenures, and because of its easy adaptability to a changing
land system, which was gradually throwing off its medieval fetters, was
widely employed to meet the need of a simpler and more flexible method
of acquiring landed property. . . . As there were no copyholds in America,
[socage tenure] applied only to freeholds and leaseholds, the prevailing types
of land in the colonies, and unless the payment of the rent were waived, as
in the case of the corporate colonies, all colonial freeholders and leaseholders
were under obligation to recognize in one form or another the higher title
of some landed proprietor. The payment in no way hampered the freeholder
in the control of his land, for though actual ownership remained elsewhere,
he was free to alienate or bequeath this real estate according to the law of his
colony and to exercise all the rights of possession, provided he conformed to
the terms of his tenure." [42]

The patent to Culpeper and the others was, therefore, in the spirit of the
most liberal existing tenure. If the Proprietors saw fit to exercise their right
to make grants "in free and common socage by fealty only," they could
relieve the purchaser of all obligation to pay quit rent.

When the royal bounty thus was shown in 1649, Virginia still was governed
by loyalists. There as in Scotland and in Ireland, Charles II had been proclaimed King on receipt of the news of his father's death. The lawmakers
of the Colony had gone further and had included among treasonable utter-
ances any statement by any person that called into question the "undoubted
and inherent right" of the new monarch "to the Colony of Virginia and all
other his Majesty's dominions." [43] Tradition has it, moreover, that the
Virginians sent Richard Lee to the Continent to invite Charles to make his

[42] C. M. Andrews in his introduction to B. W. Bond, Jr., *The Quit-Rent System in the
American Colonies*, 15–17.

[43] 1 H 360. A brief review of this period will be found in T. J. Wertenbaker, *Virginia under
the Stuarts* (cited hereafter as Wertenbaker, *Va. under Stuarts*), 95 ff. The speech of Governor
Sir William Berkeley to the Assembly, March, 1651, and the declaration of the Assembly are
reprinted in 1 V 75 ff. A MS copy is in the VSL.

home with them.[44] A like invitation is said to have been extended to Charles's followers. Three hundred and thirty of them, according to the later interpretation of a familiar story, were said to have come to Virginia on a single vessel. While this figure doubtless represented the entire ship's company and not Royalists only, a number of the unemployed officers of the scattered army of Charles reached Virginia during the period of the Commonwealth and resided there for varying lengths of time.[45] Among those who had some thought of making the voyage was one of the beneficiaries of the grant to the Northern Neck, Sir Dudley Wyatt, who probably was attracted both by his interest in the proprietary and by the fact that he had one or perhaps two sisters in the Colony. His end came before he could undertake this new adventure.[46] Although he left a will and heirs in 1651, his interest in the grant of the Northern Neck was well-nigh forgotten.

Another of the Proprietors, Thomas Culpeper, almost certainly immigrated to Virginia in 1650 and brought with him a wife, a daughter of twenty, another daughter of sixteen, and two sons. Death overtook him in 1651 or 1652, but both his daughters remained in the Colony.[47] One of them, Frances, was to have subsequently the distinction of marrying a Governor of North Carolina, and, after his death, a Governor of Virginia. Her third husband was another colonial Governor of Virginia.[48] Thomas Culpeper's heir, his son Alexander, inherited his share of the Northern Neck proprietary.

No part of the grant appeared to have any value after Mch. 22, 1652. On that date, the Colony surrendered to Parliamentary Commissioners,[49] who brought with them a naval squadron to enforce their demands. Sir William Berkeley, the royal Governor, went into retirement. In this sudden revolution, young Alexander Culpeper's land claims might have proved more incriminating than enriching. Sometime in 1652, probably, he went with his mother to England.[50]

For some years after the death of Sir Dudley Wyatt and of Thomas Culpeper, no further change occurred in the proprietary. It remained a paper and a promise, no more, through the period of Oliver Cromwell's rule in England. During the years 1650–59, the exiled Charles took one action only of special importance to Virginia. That was Sept. 22, 1650, when at

---

[44] See the references in D. S. Freeman, 1 *R. E. Lee,* 168. None of the references justifies the tradition.

[45] See Col. Henry Norwood's narrative in 3 *Force's Tracts.* No. X. Norwood reached Virginia in 1650 with two brother officers. At Ralph Wormeley's plantation he found four other cavaliers.

[46] 33 V 347 n. A document in 2 *Cal. Clarendon Papers,* 33, implies that Wyatt was dissuaded from going to America.

[47] The elder, Anne, who married Christopher Danby, subsequently returned to England (33 *V* 349).

[48] For Frances's husbands, see *infra,* p. 459, 485–86.   [49] 1 *H* 363–65.

[50] All these details, most painstakingly developed by Fairfax Harrison's research, will be found in 33 *V* 353 ff.

Governor Berkeley's instance,[51] the King named one of his Colonels, Henry Norwood, as Treasurer of the Colony.[52] Norwood, who was a cousin of the Governor, doubtless collected what he could before the Parliamentary Commissioners took over the government. After that, there was little in Virginia for him or for any other Royalist. The appointees of Cromwell of course ignored the grant of the Northern Neck, if, indeed, they knew of its existence. Small effort was made to collect the quit rents, which nominally were 2s per 100 acres. By an old order of Charles I, these quit rents were not required for the first seven years of the settlement of new land; [53] the colonials paid only when they were compelled to do so.

The return of Charles II to England in 1660 [54] ended this first, inactive period of the Northern Neck proprietary and opened the initial phase of the second period, which was one of resistance and contention. Courtiers returning with the monarch believed that their King should and could compensate them for all they had suffered and for everything they alleged they had lost by their adherence to him. In the front rank of the importunate was John Lord Culpeper, whose experience had perhaps been typical. After Parliament had confiscated Culpeper's estates, Cromwell had stipulated in his treaty with France that Mazarin expel Culpeper from that country.[55] The baron accordingly had gone to The Hague where he had resided uneasily when he was not traveling restlessly in Charles's interest.[56] After the Restoration, Culpeper went to England in the suite of the King and took his place again in the Privy Council as Master of the Rolls.[57] So heavily had he lost in the service of the Crown, Culpeper confided to friends, that he had fallen into the hands of the money-lenders. "The usurer and I," he said

[51] 33 V 5.

[52] Transcript of Latin grant, VHS. Norwood succeeded William Claiborne, for whose activities see 1 V 314 ff and J. H. Claiborne, Life of William Claiborne. In addition, B. C. Steiner's Beginnings of Maryland, and the Archives of Maryland, Proceedings of the Assembly, v. 1, include much information on Claiborne. The grant to him was £500 from the quit rents, with the stipulation that anything above that amount was to be reported to the Governor and Council and was to be disbursed by the Assembly (1 H 307). In 1671 Berkeley reported, "there is no revenue arising to His Majesty but out of the quit rents" and this, said Berkeley, a kinsman of Norwood's, "he hath given away to a deserving servant, Col. Henry Norwood" (2 ibid., 517). It is impossible to say whether this meant that all the quit rents were allowed Norwood at the time of Berkeley's report, or whether they did not exceed £500 per annum. In 1681, when William Blathwayt undertook to get an accounting from Norwood for 1669 (Cal. Am. & W. I. 1681–85, No. 202 and 1 Blathwayt Journal, 130) Norwood replied that the quit rents of that year properly were his (cf. Va. Land Grants, 177). For Norwood's financial arrangements with Culpeper, after the grant of 1673, see 1 Blathwayt Journal, 17, where the statement was made, June 15, 1680, that the terms of the grant of the quit rents to Arlington and Culpeper "had not yet been put into execution." The essential facts about Norwood will be found in 1 V 453 and in 33 ibid., 1 ff.

[53] See Lord Culpeper's comment at the time of his dismissal from office, infra, p. 478.

[54] Norwood evidently went back to England in 1661. Cf. Council Minutes, 492, 493, 507.

[55] Guizot, History of Oliver Cromwell, v. 2, p. 468; 2 Nicholas Papers, 197.

[56] For his frequent missions during these years, vide Cal. State Pap., Dom., 1649–50, p. 505, and ibid., 1659–60, p. 223; see also 1 Nicholas Papers, 182, for an account of Culpeper's arrival in Moscow, 1650.

[57] 1 Clarendon's Life, 316. See supra, p. 450.

grimly, "are not yet even; for I have only scratched the usurer, the usurer has stabbed me." [58] Skillful representation of the case led Culpeper's King to promise him £12,000, but before the peer could collect any of it, he died on the 11th of July, 1660.[59] His place in the history of Virginia was negligible, except through his descendants, but he had one distinction: he valued so little his share of the Virginia proprietary that in his will [60] he did not even mention it.

Other beneficiaries of the grant were less indifferent. Soon after the Restoration—and probably Sept. 29, 1661—the patent issued at St. Germain-en-Laye was enrolled,[61] and then was put on the market. In 1662, Sir Humphrey Hooke and two other well-to-do men of Bristol became interested in a lease of the proprietary, where, it would appear, they hoped to settle new adventures.[62] This enterprise King Charles warmly approved in a letter of Dec. 5, 1662, to Governor Berkeley, whom he instructed to assist the lessees.[63]

The royal order served a purpose precisely the reverse of that which the King intended. It aroused the opposition of Governor and Council to the proprietorship and to the lease of it. A total of 576 grants of "headright" lands in the Northern Neck had been made in the King's name by the Governor of the Colony prior to 1661.[64] Title to these lands would be clouded and might be lost if the grant to the King's favorites stood. For the protection of settlers, Virginians of legal mind or training may have gone so far as to maintain that the King could not alienate the land.[65]

Feeling against the patent was the sharper because economic discontent prevailed in the Colony. The low price of tobacco, the only staple, had convinced many of the growers that the crop could not be profitable, under existing laws, unless there was a halt of a year or more in production. This "cessation" depended on the cooperation of Maryland and of North Carolina.

[58] 67 *Gentleman's Magazine*, 477, and here changed from third to first person. See 1 *Nicholas Papers*, 235. There seems little doubt from these papers that Charles was deeply in debt to Culpeper for advances the baron had made to him or on his account. Cf. *Cal. Treas. Papers,* 1676–79, p. 542, 843.

[59] 33 *V* 243.

[60] *Ibid.*   [61] See *supra*, p. 450 and *infra*, p. 456, n. 74.

[62] *Cal. Am. & W. I.,* 1661–68, No. 391, 520; 18 *V* 411, 412, 413, 414. It is probable that the two entries of the same date (p. 411, 412) are different drafts of the same document. No positive statement has been found that Hooke himself was ever in Virginia, though the inference is to that effect. Hooke was Alderman and later High Sheriff of Bristol. His associates were John Fitzherbert and Robert Vickaredge, Merchant. See *Cal. State Pap., Dom.,* 1625–49, p. 744; *ibid.,* 1661–62, p. 170.

[63] Abstract in 18 *V* 412.

[64] *L.O. Records,* 2, 3 and 4. For "headrights," the allowance of land made those who brought persons to Virginia, see *infra*, p. 1 and *infra*, n. 76.

[65] Harrison in his *Land Grants,* 63, asserted that this argument was advanced but a more cautious statement is indicated by the fact that almost the identical language used by Harrison appears in the Burgesses' protest of June 30, 1730 (*Journ. H. B.,* 17). That protest is remarkably inaccurate and evidently was the work of men who did not know the facts. If this was the source of Harrison's statement, it cannot be accepted without reservation.

In futile efforts to procure action by their northern neighbor, the Virginia provincials became wrathful with Lord Baltimore, the Proprietor of that Colony,[66] and not unnaturally assumed that a master of a large part of their soil would be similarly autocratic. With this fear before them, the Virginians prepared an address to the Crown,[67] and named one of their ablest citizens, Col. Francis Moryson, to go to England with the paper and to act there as agent for the Dominion. He was to ask that Lord Baltimore be ordered to accede to a cessation. A second instruction to Moryson was that he seek the revocation of the lease to Hooke and the Bristol merchants.[68]

Almost before Moryson could reach England and begin to make friends there, Hooke and his associates procured from the King another letter in support of the lease.[69] In addressing the Governor of Virginia this time, Charles politely assumed, in the familiar fiction of the throne, that the previous failure of the colonials to desist from their obstruction of the lease was due to their non-receipt of his previous letter. The Virginians now were told not only to forbear further "interruption" of the plans of Hooke but also to protect his agents and to give them encouragement.[70] Perhaps in a suspicion that even these repeated orders could be evaded, the Privy Council directed that Moryson be supplied with a copy of a renewed petition of the Proprietors and that he return an answer to it.[71] Despite this rebuke, Moryson's activities and the continued resistance of Virginia achieved the prime object: After 1664, nothing more was heard of Hooke and the Bristol lease.[72]

This was the first victory of the colonials in the war with the Proprietors and it was followed five years later by another. Moryson, working shrewdly, convinced the Proprietors that they could achieve more if they demanded less, and he promised on Virginia's behalf to consent to a new patent if the objectionable features of the old one were abandoned.[73] Out of these negotiations came an agreement which was confirmed by a renewed and modified royal grant, May 8, 1669.[74]

That was a landmark in the history of the proprietorship and of Virginia

[66] *Beverley*, 57.

[67] Text in Neill's *Virginia Carolorum*, 308–13.

[68] See the abstracts cited in 18 *V* 413 and the note by W. G. Stanard.

[69] In all probability this was written at the instance of Lord St. Albans, *et al.*, but of this there is no positive evidence. See *infra*, p. 459.

[70] 18 *V* 414; *Cal. Am. & W. I.*, 1661–8, No. 520.

[71] 1 *Acts Privy Council*, No. 611.

[72] Cf. Charles Calvert to Lord Baltimore, Apr. 27, 1664; 17 *V* 310.

[73] See undated petition of St. Albans, *et al.*, doubtless of late 1669 or 1670, abstracted in *Cal. Am. & W. I.*, 1669–74, No. 145; a poor transcript is in LC.

[74] Abstracted in *Cal. Am. & W. I.*, 1669–74, No. 63; full text in 1 *DeJarnette Transcripts*, No. 86, p. 302–13. DeJarnette dated this May 8, 1667, but quoted at the end of the document, "the one and twentieth year of our reign," which would be 1669. In *Journ. H.B.*, June 30, 1730, p. 92, the year likewise was given wrongly as 1667. See Close Roll 4720, 21 Charles 11, pt. 7, no. 10, 1667, June 29, for surrender of the first patent.

land titles. It may be said to have ended the first phase of the second period.[75] For the relief of early residents of the Northern Neck, the patentees agreed to recognize all land titles issued in their domain prior to Michaelmas, 1661. In actual fact, much the greater part, if not all, of these grants were "head-rights," that is to say, lands patented and planted, at least in theory, by persons who had received them for coming to America or for bringing other individuals to Virginia.[76] This agreement consequently was recognition by the Proprietors of royal grants in the Northern Neck, but it was subject to the definite and important proviso that the holder of these royal grants had to be in "actual possession" of the land as of May 8, 1669. Another proviso was that the usual quit rents were to be paid thereafter[77] and that all reversions and escheats were to be the Proprietor's—a compromise that later created disputes.

In this historic grant, moreover, the King restricted in two important particulars the authority of the Proprietors. First, in place of a grant in perpetuity, they were limited in their rights to such tracts as they "possessed, inhabited or planted" in twenty-one years, i.e., before May 8, 1690. After that date, all remaining land was to be at the King's disposal. Second, the political authority of the Proprietors was subordinated to that of the colonial government. The revised patent specified that the Proprietors ". . . shall not act or intermeddle with the military affairs or forces in this tract of land hereby granted, or any part therein, or any forts or fortresses, or castles thereof, without the order and authority and consent of the Governor and Council of Virginia, and that the Governor and Council of Virginia shall have full power and authority to lay and levy any tax or imposition in and upon the said territory . . . and all and every the possessors and inhabitants thereof for the public and common defence of the said Colony of Virginia and the territory and lands thereby granted as upon other parts of Virginia, proportionable, and the [Proprietors] shall be in all subject and obedient to such

[75] Study of the various periods of the proprietorship may be facilitated by the outline, infra, p. 510–11.

[76] The legal or customary basis of headrights is set forth in Va. Land Grants, 16 ff, and in 1 Andrews, Colonial Period, 125. A typical grant of 1626, cited by Andrews, will be found in 25 V 338. The number of these grants is not known. Those of 1662 numbered ninety-three, those of 1663 were 121, and those of 1664 reached a total of seventy-eight. Northern Neck grants of 1665 were thirty-four in number, of which it would appear that ten only were seated. In 1666, there were forty-four grants. Six of these were seated. Four were for headrights. The total for 1667 was thirty-eight, though two only may be said with certainty to have been seated. Nine were headrights. Of the thirty-eight grants of 1668, practically all were headrights, several were to ship captains, and scarcely one was seated. All but one of the nineteen grants of 1669 were made by the Governor. That exception, a grant of 6160 acres in Lancaster, was in Berkeley's name, but a note signed by Philip Ludwell states that this was a regrant, written by him. Eighteen of these nineteen grants of 1669 were headrights. Thus in 1665–69, an aggregate of 174 grants, to a total of 185,857 acres, appear on the records. This land, where not in the form of regrants, lay in the back country of the Northern Neck.

[77] For the quit rents of the Northern Neck—2s for 100 acres, with graduated "fines" for acreage above 100—see supra, p. 12.

laws as are and shall be made by the said Governor and Council and Assembly for or concerning the said Colony or government thereof." [78] Concerning all of this, the implied argument of Moryson was sound: the rights of the Proprietors were stronger because they were more reasonable.

Within these prudently accepted limitations, which scarcely would affect their profits, the men who held the patent began in 1670 a halfhearted effort to collect quit rents and to develop the Northern Neck. The one task was more formidable than the other. Earlier experience was repeated. Original settlers of the Northern Neck had not returned quit rents to the Crown with any regularity, if at all; they had no intention of paying the Proprietor unless they were compelled to do so. Patenting new lands and promising to pay quit rents in the future was a less serious matter.

This soon was discovered by Thomas Kirton, kinsman of an individual who had bought Lord Hopton's share. Kirton came to Virginia in 1670 and opened a land office in Northumberland, one of the eastern Counties of the proprietary.[79] With him was to be associated Edward Dale, then prominent in Lancaster County.[80] In due course, Apr. 5, 1671, Kirton presented to the General Court a copy of the amended letters patent and of his and Dale's power of attorney. Action was prompt. ". . . the said letters patent being read in court, the Governor and Council did fully and unanimously yield humble obedience thereunto and did so declare and did order the said submission . . . to be recorded . . . And it is further declared by the Court that the rents and profits . . . within the said tract, which by the said letters patent do belong to the said patentees, the Sheriffs of the Counties within the said precincts shall forbear to demand until further order." [81]

This acceptance, though complete, was not without resentment. In reporting to the Council for Foreign Plantations, June 26, 1671, the Secretary of the Colony said there was thankfulness for the limitations, but that the grant to the Proprietors of lands taken up nine years previously by settlers had created "infinite discontents." Never, he went on, had he observed anything so much move the grief and passion of the people as uncertainty whether they were to "make a country" for the King or for the Proprietors.

[78] *DeJarnette Transcripts*, loc. cit. An abstract appears in *Cal. Am. & W. I.*, 1669–74, No. 63.
[79] *Va. Land Grants*, 80; 4 *W* (1) p. 39; 6 *ibid.*, 222–24. *Westmoreland Orders*, 1676–89, entry of June 13, 1677, "Mr. Thomas Kirton enters a Caveatt against the estate of Capt. Jno. Appleton's that no debts be paid till his Mats. hath the Quit rents in his hands." In June, 1672, Kirton was in Northumberland (Orders, 1666–78, p. 77). His own home in Westmoreland was very near the Northumberland boundary.
[80] He was appointed Sheriff Apr. 18, 1670, but in September, 1671, he was mentioned as Clerk (*Council Minutes*, 206, 267). Many references to Dale will be found in *Swem*. As stated, *supra*, Kirton married Anna, widow of the notorious "Dick" Cole. In 1686, Kirton informed the Westmoreland Court that its records were "somewhat decayed and the transfers through time and carelessness scarcely legible," whereupon, the Court directed him to transcribe all the records in one book. For this he was to have 2000 lbs. of tobacco and cask, provided he finished this work by 1688 (*Westmoreland Orders*, 1676–89, p. 529).
[81] *Council Minutes*, 247; *Cal. Am. & W. I.*, 1661–68, No. 1513.

Already, the Secretary protested, the agents of the patentees were slighting the government further than was warranted. Their aim, he believed, was to get themselves wholly free from the government of the Colony, a course that would ruin the country and render it incapable of defending itself. The Council for Foreign Plantations was besought to save Virginia from further encroachments by the Proprietors until the Assembly could make representations. Meantime, would the President of the Council [82] conceal the protest from the fury of Mr. Justice Morton of the King's bench, before whom some of the causes of the colonists might be heard? The Secretary did not have to add that the judge, in civil life Sir William Morton, was one of the Proprietors of the Northern Neck. [83]

When the Virginia Assembly met in September, 1671, the lawmakers directed that a petition to the throne be prepared against the "alteration" of the tenures of residents of the Northern Neck, and "alienation from their immediate dependence upon his Majesty." Maj. Gen. Robert Smith was designated to go to England and was empowered "to negotiate there the public affairs" of the Colony according to instructions that would be given him. [84]

Those "public affairs" now more directly concerned the Culpeper family, because of a most unusual incident. The revised grant that Kirton and Dale had laid before the General Court on the 5th of April, 1671, had named four Proprietors only. These were Henry Jermyn, Earl of St. Albans; second, Sir John Berkeley, who had become Lord Berkeley; third, Sir William Morton; and fourth, John Trethewy, who had acquired the interest of Lord Hopton. As noted already, the name of Sir Dudley Wyatt had disappeared from the grant. Lord Culpeper and Thomas Culpeper were not mentioned. In the case of the peer, this was because he had shown no interest in the grant. Thomas Culpeper, like Wyatt, had died; but, as it chanced, Thomas's son Alexander was in Jamestown when the letters patent were presented in court. Moreover, through the marriage of his sister Frances, he now was brother-in-law of Governor Berkeley, who, as always, was alert to the interest of his connections. [85] Alexander Culpeper consequently learned at once of the content of the papers. The next day he appeared before the Court and informed the members that he and Lord Culpeper had never surrendered their rights in the Northern Neck. He asked that their claim be entered, which the minutes of the Court record tersely, "is accordingly granted." [86] In circumstances a trifle different, the Culpepers might have lost their rights

[82] The Earl of Sandwich; see John Evelyn's *Diary*, v. 2, p. 65.

[83] *Cal. Am. & W. I.*, 1669–74, No. 572.

[84] *Journ. H. B.*, 1659/60–1693, p. 57.

[85] Virtually all that is known about Alexander Culpeper is summarized by Fairfax Harrison in 33 *V* 353 ff.

[86] *Council Minutes*, 250.

in Virginia. Among the results might have been a changed beginning to the career of George Washington.

Shortly after Alexander Culpeper thus reestablished in Virginia his title and that of his cousin, he went to England [87] to solicit the office of Surveyor General of Virginia and of course acquainted Lord Culpeper with the manner in which they so narrowly had escaped the technical loss of their rights in the Northern Neck proprietary. The nobleman to whom Alexander told this story was Thomas, second Baron of Thoresway, then thirty-six years of age,[88] who had succeeded in 1660 to his father's title and importunities. Thomas's first recorded public act was to petition for the payment of the £12,000 Charles had promised the first Lord, but, at the outset, he had meagre success. All that a hard-pressed sovereign could do at the time was to restore the landed estate of Culpeper which, it will be remembered, the Commonwealth had confiscated.[89] To this relief was added in 1661 the office of Governor of the Isle of Wight, a post that young Culpeper seems to have administered with a combination of indifference, arrogance and autocracy.[90] These qualities were condoned [91] or, at least were not considered a barrier to the appointment of Culpeper, Mch. 20, 1671, as a member of the Council of Foreign Plantations.[92] He was holding this position when Alexander Culpeper returned from Virginia. Lord Culpeper may have had his interest aroused by Alexander's description of opportunities in the Colony or else he may have had his cupidity fired by observing, as a member of the Council, how Lord Baltimore was reaping a harvest from Maryland.[93] For either or both these reasons, Lord Culpeper now looked to Virginia for the fattening of a fortune that seems to have been chronically undernourished. He and his fellow-Proprietors decided that they would undertake to collect quit rents formerly paid the Crown within the area granted them, and that they would

[87] See 33 V 355.

[88] He was baptized at Hollingbourn, near Leeds Castle, Mch. 2, 1636. See 33 V 252.

[89] For the return of the property, see 12 Car. II, c. 8 private, cited by Fairfax Harrison in 33 V 253. Cf. 34 ibid., 19–24. Apparently Leeds Castle was restored also, but it was scarcely habitable. Evelyn leased it as a detention camp for prisoners of war. 2 Evelyn 10, 15, entries for Oct. 17, 1665, May 8, 1666. See also Cal. State Pap., Dom., 1649–50, p. 486–87; ibid., 1650, p. 140, 147, 436; ibid., 1665–66, p. 3.

[90] Cal. State Pap., Dom., 1665–66, p. 350. Culpeper also was promised a chancery position as soon as a vacancy occurred, but it never was given though often sought. See ibid., 1661–62, p. 580 et passim.

[91] For some of his acts and for the movements of himself and family, see Cal. State Pap., Dom., 1661–62, p. 46, 131, 290; ibid., 1664–65, p. 109; ibid., 1665–66, p. 350, 479, 504; ibid., 1666–67, p. 70, 355; ibid., 1664–65, p. 109.

[92] He soon was Vice President. See 2 Evelyn, 65; Cal. Am. & W. I., 1669–74, No. 992.

[93] This was Fairfax Harrison's theory (33 V 254), but it probably was formulated before the Minutes of the Council and General Court were published. The articles by Mr. Harrison on the Proprietors of the Northern Neck began to appear in the issue of 33 V, April, 1925. The Minutes were published only the year preceding. It is not thought that Mr. Harrison had ascertained the circumstances that had preceded Alexander Culpeper's visit to England. On the contrary, the belief of Mr. Harrison apparently was that Lord Culpeper as well as his cousin had been responsible for the reassertion of their rights in the proprietary. See ibid., 255.

insist upon a resurvey of all lands taken up in the Northern Neck as "head-rights." The cost of this resurvey they believed they could make the tenants pay.

Inasmuch as Alexander Culpeper now had received the solicited appointment of Surveyor General of Virginia [94] and would profit by resurvey, he probably was the author of this second demand. It was forwarded soon to Thomas Kirton, the Proprietors' agent in Virginia, and, on the 25th of March, 1672, was presented to the General Court in the form of instructions to Kirton from the Proprietors. The Court again asserted that the rights of the Proprietors would not be obstructed, though appeal to the throne would be reserved. Then the members went on to say: "But the Court doth think it very hard, that the tenants who have been long seated and peaceably enjoyed their estates should pay that rent which they have formerly paid to his Majesty's treasurer or deputy according to his Majesty's instructions, or that the said tenants should be recharged to a new survey their lands after so long time of possession." [95]

The Virginians did not let the issue end with a protest. They resolved to acquire for the Colony, if possible, the rights granted the six Proprietors, and by the autumn of 1673, the colonials had reason to believe that three of the owners could be bought out for £400 each. So exigent did the situation appear, and so large the opportunity, that Governor Berkeley himself offered to lend the Colony £1200 with which to make the purchase. The Assembly accepted gratefully, promised to pay him 8 per cent interest, and authorized him to proceed.[96] For reasons not plain, the sale of this half-interest in the proprietary failed.[97] Perhaps the non-execution of the proposal was due to the activity of Lord Culpeper, who apparently made an effort that year to acquire the rights of the other Proprietors of the Northern Neck.[98]

Before negotiations for the Northern Neck were concluded, one way or the other, there came startling news from England. Major General Smith, the Colony's agent at St. James's, reported that he had seen in the Signet Office

---

[94] 8 V 409; Cal. Am. & W. I., 1669–74, No. 644. He was reappointed Apr. 24, 1686, 19 V 6.

[95] Council Minutes, 296.   [96] Journ. H.B., Oct. 20, 1673, p. 61.

[97] It has been assumed that the offer of £1200 was for the entire proprietary and that the failure of the transaction was due to the demand of the Proprietors for double the authorized amount. See 6 W (1) p. 224. Actually, the "order" stated that the loan was to "buy out three of the patentees of Rappahannock Neck." Authority had been given the previous June to purchase as many shares as possible (Council Minutes, 347).

[98] The agreement of May 20, 1675 by certain of the beneficiaries (3 Randolph MS, 334) and the formal deed of July 21, 1681 (cited from Conway Robinson's Notes in 9 V 309, make it reasonably plain that if Culpeper undertook in 1673 to buy out his fellow-Proprietors, he did not complete the transaction. In 6 R. Lancaster Deeds, 25, 1683, May 25, is the appointment of David Fox as steward of Lancaster County. Culpeper there speaks of himself as: "I, Thomas Lord Culpeper, Baron of Thoresway, sole owner and proprietor of the Northern tract of land lyeing between the two great Rivers of Rappahannock and Potomack, by several mean purchases . . ." See 8 V 177; Close Roll, 4568, 33 Charles 11, pt. 14, No. 19. 1684, July 21 (rec.); Court D.B. 3;3. Note by Conway Robinson in 9 V 304.

a document, dated Feb. 25, 1673, under which all land in the Colony, not previously patented, had been assigned by the King to Thomas Lord Culpeper and to Henry Earl of Arlington for a term of thirty-one years. The two Proprietors were given (1) all arrears of quit rents for the whole of Virginia due after May 8, 1669; (2) all future quit rents and escheats for the term of the patent; (3) the right to confirm previous land grants; (4) exclusive authority to issue new grants, and (5) substantially all the "regalities" that had been allowed other Proprietors in America under grants from the Crown [99]—to establish Counties, name local officials, organize courts and discharge many functions previously vested in the Governor, the Assembly or the freeholders.

All this was set forth for any man's reading in a copy of the patent, which reached Virginia from General Smith probably in the summer of 1674.[100] As the colonials in astonishment studied this paper, they may or may not have known that Arlington was a member of "the Cabal" at the royal court, that he had no personal interest in Virginia, and that he was under suspicion of seeking to make a separate peace with the Dutch, who probably had bribed him.[101] As for Culpeper, the provincials' recent experience with the demand for resurveys of Northern Neck holdings was not of a sort to make them relish closer relations with men of that name. Besides, the Virginians' dealing with Lord Baltimore, in the matter of the cessation of tobacco-growing, had led them to think a Proprietor stubborn, cunning and autocratic. The personalities, in short, were not encouraging; but as the Colony's interest went beyond personalities, Governor Berkeley immediately called the Assembly to meet in September.

When the Burgesses convened and read the patent, the second phase of the second period of the proprietary began. If the years from 1649 to 1661 might be called the period of inaction, the span that ended with the grant of 1673 was preliminary of contention. It ushered in a decade and a half of

[99] Text in 2 H 569 ff; abstract in *Cal. Am. & W. I.*, 1669–74, No. 769. The grant was, in its plain terms, for the unpatented land in the whole of Virginia, but the document may implicitly have assumed that the earlier St. Albans-Culpeper grant covered the whole of the Northern Neck and that, in consequence, only unpatented lands South of the Northern Neck were given Arlington and Culpeper. Several abstracts in *Randolph MS* refer to the "northern" (e.g., v. 3, p. 324), and to the "southern" grants (e.g., *ibid.*, 401). See also the explicit statement of Lord Howard, Feb. 20, 1685, in *Cal. Treas. Papers*, 1685–89, v. 8, pt. 1, p. 507. Beverley, *op. cit.*, 61, noted that "those grants were distinguished by the names of the northern and southern grants of Virginia, and the same men were concerned in both." This distinction between a northern and a southern proprietary would seem to be borne out by the maintenance of separate offices during the joint agency of Daniel Parke and Nicholas Spencer, as recorded *infra*, p. 470. Culpeper himself, in discussing quit rents in 1683, spoke separately of the "southern grant." See *infra*, p. 479 and *Cal. Treas. Papers*, 1689–92, p. 1504; P.R.O., C.O., 1, 51, p. 105, LC trans. Whether the Arlington-Culpeper grant actually superseded the St. Albans-Culpeper grant, or merely complemented it in Southern Virginia, the Courts were not called upon to decide.

[100] See *Journ. H. B.*, May 20, 1684, p. 237. See also *Historical MSS Commission*, 11th Report, App. 7, p. 10, Berkeley's letter to Thos. Osborne, Earl of Danby, Feb. 1, 1675 regarding the grant.

[101] Pepys's *Diary*, v. 9, p. 247, entry for Apr. 28, 1669.

struggle over the "regalities." Earnestly and promptly the Burgesses called for the drafting of "an address and supplication" to the King for the revocation of the Arlington-Culpeper patent, and they expressed their fear that "grievous pressures [were] likely to grow" upon them by reason of the "late grants to the Lords." His Majesty was besought to confirm by royal charter the "liberties, privileges, immunities, rights and properties" of the Colony. To meet the expenses of negotiations in England by a commission of three, the members of the Assembly did not balk at imposing a tax of 120 lbs. of tobacco per tithable.[102]

Governor and Council concurred. Berkeley had tried his hand at drama while a young man, and he had some pride in composition. He now sought to outdo himself in a letter that asked a hearing of the reasons why, as he wrote, "we are unwilling and do conceive [we] ought not to submit to those to whom His Majesty (upon misinformation) hath granted the dominion over us who do most contentedly pay to His Majesty more than we have ourselves for our labour and do wish we could yet be more advantageous to the King and nation for which we hope to find his Majesty's most royal favour and protection from such impositions as will ruin us and consequently his Majesty's revenue . . ."[103]

This was the basis of the appeal the three agents of Virginia made in England. They did not despair of acquiring the Northern Neck. While they pursued that negotiation, they pressed for a compromise with Arlington and Culpeper as the practical alternative to an appeal to the King for a revocation of the grant to the two Lords. In approaching this task, the Virginia agents found themselves confronted by interlocked relationships. Arlington was Lord Chamberlain; Culpeper had many powerful connections; Mr. Justice Morton, as already noted, was in a position to protect his sixth interest in the Northern Neck proprietary; Col. Henry Norwood, who had a royal grant of Virginia quit rents and had been Treasurer until 1673, had just entered into an arrangement by which he was to receive one-third of the profits of the new proprietary; as stated earlier, Alexander Culpeper, Surveyor General and owner of one-sixth of the Northern Neck grant, was cousin of Lord Culpeper and brother-in-law of Governor Berkeley.

In spite of this entangling opposition, which was apt to trip them at any step, the colonials made some progress toward the revision of the Arlington-Culpeper grant. Lord Arlington, who conducted most of the exchanges, did not seem averse to forgoing the objectionable regalities.[104] He sought, and the Virginia agents were willing to accept, an arrangement by which he and

---

[102] 2 H 313; *Journ. H. B.*, 1684, p. 237.

[103] 3 *Randolph MS*, 319; 2 *Burk*, Appendix xxxiii.

[104] Memorandum of the Virginia agents, 3 *Randolph MS*, 321. The dating of the various items of the *Randolph MS* at this period is so confused that a precise reconstruction of the chronology is impossible.

Culpeper would receive the quit rents in return for a surrender of everything else covered by their letters patent. As the negotiations developed, the issue became that of the price of the tobacco in which the quit rents were to be settled, because the colonials did not have in Virginia sufficient coin to tender payment in that medium. The agents offered, at length, to pay the quit rents at a price of 12s per hundredweight of tobacco. This, said the spokesmen for Virginia, "we conceive to be reasonable and as low as we can submit to since there is at least as much above that rate as there is [below] it." [105]

Arlington's counter-proposal was ambiguously worded. It stipulated that the quit rents should be "payable in tobacco *ad valorem*," [106] that is, on the nominal monetary value of the quit rents, regardless of the amount of tobacco that had to be sold to produce that sum. Further, Arlington insisted that he and Culpeper have the escheats "by certain compositions where tolerable titles shall appear as is limited by the act of Assembly in such cases." [107]

These terms the Virginia agents rejected and forthwith proceeded to carry out their instructions to petition the King. They asked that they be not taxed without their consent, and that "those regalities divested from His Majesty may again be invested in him." All land grants and escheats, they besought the King to entrust to the Governor and Council. The quit rents assigned the Proprietors under the two grants were solicited for the Colony. [108]

It probably was at this stage of the Virginians' appeal that they were faced with another coup. On June 19, 1675, the King granted Lord Culpeper succession to the office of Governor of Virginia when the incumbent, Sir William Berkeley, died, surrendered or forfeited the post. The salary was to be that paid Berkeley, £1000 a year out of money raised in the Colony for the support of the government. [109] Berkeley was then sixty-nine, [110] and,

[105] *Ibid.*, 322. An error of copying made the bracketed word "above." [106] *Ibid.*, 322.

[107] *Ibid.*, 322–23. Apparently this was dated Apr. 26, 1675. Certain "propositions by the Governor and Secretary" in 1660–61 are presented in 2 H 136–38, as the substance of the law of escheats. These concern persons who died intestate as well as those who died without heirs. It should be added that Virginia had a system of "deserts" that had some of the legal aspects of escheated property. A person patenting land was required to occupy and to plant part of it within a given time. In the event he failed to do this, or abandoned the property after having attempted to occupy and plant it, the land was said to have been "deserted" and then was subject to new grant by the Crown, by the Colony or by the Proprietor as the case might be. Numerous instances of this are to be found in the *Council Minutes* after 1670. See p. 207, 215, 221, 225. The last of these cited entries was for the grant to Maj. John Washington of 450 acres of land at the head of Nomini River in Westmoreland County. It does not appear from the records that Arlington and Culpeper sought the "deserts."

[108] Neither the date nor the text of the petition is available but the "heads" are given in 3 *Randolph MS*, 324. Further information concerning the petition may be had from the "Notes Explanatory" of "Mr. Attorney," *ibid.*, 328. See also P.R.O., C.O., 1, 34, No. 99.

[109] 2 H 565; *Cal. Am. & W. I.*, 1675–76, No. 599. Berkeley had complained much over the meagreness of the salary, out of which, he said, he had to "maintain the port of my place, and one hundred intervening charges that cannot be put to public account." There was, he said, "no government of ten years settlement but has thrice as much allowed him" (2 H 516. Cf. *Cal. Am. & W. I.*, 1675–76, No. 968).

[110] *DNB* gave no date of birth, but Philip Alexander Bruce in *DAB* put it in 1606.

after the Cromwellian wars, had shown a violence of temper that threatened soon to end his days. With that prospect plain, Culpeper could afford to let the salary await upward adjustment so long as he had assurance that the office would be his. If he succeeded Berkeley at an early date and could execute his plan to buy out the other grantees of the Northern Neck, he would be in a position excelled by that of no American Proprietor: he would be Governor, sole owner of all the country between the Potomac and the Rappahannock, and, with Arlington, patentee of all unoccupied lands in the remainder of Virginia. In the event Culpeper acquired the rights of Arlington, he would be, in all except title, the King of Virginia, a dominion he had never seen.

Grant to Culpeper of the succession to the governorship probably increased the difficulties of the Virginia agents. They renewed their negotiations with him and with Arlington, when they could get no action on their petition to the King, but they reached no agreement.[111] Once more they returned to the throne for authority, which probably had been challenged, to acquire the Northern Neck by purchase. The device they submitted for approval was the establishment of a corporation, owned by the Colony, to buy and to hold the Northern Neck. To this, in November, 1676, royal assent was given,[112] but that was the sum of achievement at the time.

If anything more could have been accomplished by persistent negotiation or reiterated petition, the opportunity was lost in the confusion of the rebellion of 1676 in Virginia. Its leader, Nathaniel Bacon, scarcely could have won followers in any considerable number if discontent had not been stirred by the arbitrary government of Berkeley, by the low price of tobacco, and by the weight of the taxes imposed to combat the proprietorship.[113] Bacon died of disease, while still in arms against Berkeley, but the strain of the uprising was more than the ageing Governor could endure. Before the end of 1676 he had to ask for retirement,[114] and, reluctantly and with some delay, he left Virginia May 5, 1677. Shortly after his arrival in England, he died.[115] This brought Culpeper's commission into operation. A change of Governor would, in best conditions, have delayed action on so complicated a matter as the establishment of a corporation to buy the Northern Neck. When the new Governor was himself the principal Proprietor, agreement on terms might be immensely more difficult. If he proved to be a hard trader, negotiations might as well be dropped. Logically, then, there followed a period during which the Burgesses and Council studied and tested their

[111] 3 *Randolph MS*, 334.
[112] *Cal. Am. & W. I.*, 1675–76, Nos. 403, 696, 834.
[113] Cf. *Journ. H. B.*, 1684, p. 237; *Beverley*, 64.
[114] 5 *McDonald Transcripts*, 61–62.
[115] Wertenbaker, *Va. Under the Stuarts*, 211.

Governor before they renewed their effort to restore the old and cherished land tenure.

Culpeper's administration as Governor was, for these reasons, most particularly a part of the history of the proprietorship. It was not an administration opened with zeal for Virginia. On July 20, 1677,[116] Culpeper took the oath, but he showed no disposition to cross the Atlantic and to assume his duties. He remained in England, drawing his salary, until after the death, in November 1678, of his Lieutenant, Herbert Jeffrey.[117] As long previously as Feb. 28, 1674, the King had promised the office of acting Governor, in the event of Jeffreys's death, to Sir Henry Chicheley, a member of the Council long resident in Virginia. Chicheley claimed his post on Nov. 30, 1678,[118] and labored to allay the bitterness aroused by the vindictive rule of Berkeley, but he came to the office too late in life and had too many entanglements, social and political, to be successful.[119] Misgiving probably was felt in London concerning his ability to direct affairs in Virginia and, in particular, to deal with conditions that had arisen from Bacon's Rebellion. Accordingly, Apr. 1, 1679, the King notified the Council that Culpeper would be sent out as Governor by the first ship, and that all suits relating to the uprising were to be held until Culpeper arrived and could pass on the wisdom or unwisdom of prosecuting them sternly.[120]

The next month, returning shipmasters, who had left Virginia during January, reported in England that Chicheley was "very old, sickly and crazy." [121] This should have hastened Culpeper's departure for his post, but he was engaged at the time in a new effort to collect some of the money due him on account of his father.[122] Moreover, Culpeper was told that he need not leave until September and that his stay in the Colony would not have to be prolonged. He made the most of this assurance. In fact, he delayed his sailing so long that the King had to threaten him with forfeiture

116 5 *McDonald Transcripts*, 130. *Cal. Am. & W. I.*, 1677–80, No. 360.

117 *Cal. Am. & W. I.*, 1667–80, No. 878; *Col. Papers*, 43, No. 13, VSL. Cf. Wertenbaker, *Va. Under the Stuarts*, 221. The use of the terms Governor, Deputy Governor and Lieutenant Governor represents an evolution. From the early days of the Colony, if the Governor left Virginia, he named a Deputy Governor who, by custom, was the senior member of the Council. The title Lieutenant Governor has not been found in *Cal. State Papers Am. & W. I.* prior to 1676. In that year Chicheley was named as Berkeley's Deputy and was commissioned to act as Governor in Chief. Capt. Thomas Fox was appointed Lieutenant Governor. Other records mention both Chicheley and Jeffreys as Deputy Governor. Culpeper was called Governor; Jeffreys was termed his Lieutenant. Lord Howard of Effingham was Governor and was represented by a Lieutenant. Nicholson in 1690–92 was styled Lieutenant Governor. In 1698, he became Governor and held that title until his recall in 1705. Then, from 1705 to 1768, the resident "Governor" actually was the Lieutenant Governor.

118 *Council Minutes*, 522.

119 His administration is sketched briefly in Wertenbaker, *Va. Under the Stuarts*, 221 ff. See also 17 *V* 144 ff.

120 *Cal. Am. & W. I.*, 1667–80, No. 951.

121 *Ibid.*, No. 996.

122 *Cal. Treas. Papers*, 1676–79, No. 1440, 1453.

of office if he did not go to Virginia.[123] Even then, on one pretext and another, Culpeper lingered until Feb. 13, 1680.[124]

His instructions covered many subjects.[125] Among other things, the new Governor was to see to it that in the future, before legislation was offered in the Assembly, it was formulated by Governor and Council and was sent to England for the approval of the King. Not until this approval was given and the bills returned to Virginia, could the Assembly be convened to pass the measures.[126] In accordance with this new policy, which destroyed all colonial right to initiate laws, three bills were given Culpeper. These he was to "offer unto the next Assembly that they may be assented to, and enacted as originally coming from us." [127] One of them was a pardon for nearly all the participants in Bacon's Rebellion; the second was a naturalization measure; the third was a bill to establish a permanent revenue.

On his arrival in Virginia,[128] Culpeper did not see fit to explain this part of his instructions. Not a word did he say of the decision of the Crown to pass judgment on all proposed legislation before it was submitted to the Assembly. In his opening speech to the Burgesses, June 9, 1680, he thus explained his delay in coming to his post: "It is now almost three years since it first pleased his Majesty . . . to commission me his Lieutenant and Governor General of this his great and most considerable Colony, though to me the time has seemed much longer, having been contrary to my inclinations detained from you on other services by the King's express commands, for nothing less should have hindered me." [129] Of Bacon's uprising, Culpeper said: ". . . as his Majesty hath forgot it himself, he doth expect this to be the last time of your remembering the late rebellion and . . . he shall look upon them to be ill men that shall rub the sore by using any future reproaches or terms of distinctions whatever." [130] In outlining the fiscal legislation the home government desired, Culpeper was deliberately vague: "The third [measure] is an additional act about the two shillings per hogshead &c which must necessarily improve the revenue by preventing frauds and abuses in the payment thereof." [131] After boasting of what he had accomplished in England for the Colony and what he would do from his own salary to lighten the expense of providing for the garrisons on the

---

[123] *Cal. Am & W. I.*, 1677–80, No. 1112, 1138, 1201, 1217, 1231.

[124] *Ibid.*, 1681–85, No. 319.

[125] *Ibid.*, 1677–80, No. 932, 1207. The instructions are in 2 *DeJarnette Transcripts*, p. 436 ff. Parts of them are printed in the introduction (p. xxix ff), of the *Journ. H. B.*, 1659/60–1693.

[126] *Journ. H. B.*, 1659/60–1693, p. xxix. Exception was allowed "in case of invasion, rebellion or some very urgent necessity" (2 *DeJarnette Transcripts*, 440, 441).

[127] *Ibid.*, 440, 448.

[128] Lyon G. Tyler in the Richmond *News Leader*, July 24, 1931, published an interesting review of political conditions in the Colony at that time.

[129] *Journ. H. B.*, 1680, p. 147.

[130] *Ibid.*, 148.

[131] *Ibid.*

rivers,[132] Culpeper proceeded: "The other part of the [King's] letter concerns the quit rents, which I had also long since represented unto his Majesty, wherein as soon as he shall be fully informed of the state you are in, and your readiness and cheerfulness for his own service and your own good [,] I doubt not but such measures will be taken both for the past and future as will be satisfactory to all interests (that I have therein shall never stand in competition to yours) and conduce to his Majesty's service, and the good of this Colony, to which my utmost endeavors shall be always ready." [133]

Suavity did not fulfil its purpose. The Assembly passed promptly two of the three bills submitted by the Governor, but it balked at imposing a permanent tax in place of the levies previously laid at each session to meet the expenditures of the ensuing year.[134] In seeking to advance this revenue bill, Culpeper had to combine threats and half-promises. He hinted that resistance to the King would "make the exercise of Assemblies . . . wholly impracticable . . ." Almost in the next breath he suggested that if the bill were accepted, the King might consent to a "cessation" of tobacco-planting in order to raise prices that overproduction had lowered.[135] The Governor pointed, also, to a clause in the bill which provided that the revenue from the proposed permanent tax was "to and for the better support of this, his Majesty's Colony of Virginia in such manner as is hereinbefore expressed, and to and for no other use [,] intent and purpose whatsoever." [136] Said Culpeper: " 'Twas with no small difficulty I did in your behalves and in some sort my own too (for my interest is considerable) obtain the inserting those words . . ." [137]

The Burgesses were not convinced. Before accepting the tax measure, they insisted that previous special revenue acts be repealed and that tobacco shipped in Virginia vessels be exempt from the tax.[138] On these points, Culpeper had to yield. Even then, he might not have procured the passage of the bill, as amended, had he not bargained secretly to secure the appointment of a prominent Burgess, Col. Isaac Allerton, to the Council of Virginia in return for Allerton's vote and influence in favor of the revenue bill.[139]

Despite this unworthy toll, the legislative fruits of the session were considerable,[140] and were evidence of the skill of Culpeper's husbandry, though

132 These were two small Companies of infantry stationed at the heads of navigation to guard against Indian raids.   133 Ibid., 149.

134 The "permanent tax" was to be at the same rate as the annual export levy, viz., 2s on each hogshead or 500 lbs. of tobacco shipped in bulk (2 H 466).

135 Address of June 24, 1680; Journ. H. B., 130.

136 Ibid.

137 Ibid.   138 Ibid., 133.

139 Ibid., xxiv, with citation of 6 McDonald Transcripts, 117.

140 In 2 H 458–89, are seventeen acts and four declarations or orders of the Assembly. Many other orders appear in Journ. H. B., 1680, p. 150–53, but these are local or private. Hening remarked (op. cit., 458 n) that in most of the records this session brought the first use of the term General Assembly to describe a legislative body previously styled the Grand Assembly.

they scarcely could be regarded as a tribute to his character. Still less to his credit was Culpeper's manipulation of the rate of exchange. If the colonial historian Beverley stated the facts correctly, Culpeper drew colonial funds for the pay of two Companies of garrison troops about to be dismissed. With this money in hand, the Governor decided that Spanish pieces of eight should be exchanged at six shillings instead of five, ostensibly in order that the Spanish coin might be kept in Virginia and not drained to other Colonies. Before he took any public action in raising the rate of exchange, Culpeper is alleged to have bought up privately at a low rate "light"—that is worn—pieces of eight. This coin Culpeper held when he issued a proclamation that increased exchange. After the Spanish coin commanded six shillings, Culpeper is said to have paid off the two Companies of disbanded garrison troops in the light coin at the new rate with substantial profit to himself.[141]

After Culpeper had completed this smooth operation, he adjourned [142] the Assembly. On the 2nd of August he called for the general payment of quit rents due the Crown but chronically in arrears; [143] and then, before he could feel the pulse of colonials who were angered by that document, he prepared to return home via New England. He left on August 11 [144] in a self-satisfied state of mind. From Boston he wrote his sister: "I have taken all the care that man can do, but 'tis God Almighty that only can give a blessing and success to my endeavors: If I return in safety, I doubt not of giving account both as the public, as well as private, but especially the first." He went on: "I intend to return shortly into these parts again, for I think in my conscience the country and climate is better than old England." [145]

Although Culpeper did not so confide to his sister, he had another reason for planning to voyage at intervals to America, a reason that was related, first of all, to changes in the administration of the proprietary. The demand for a resurvey of private holdings between the Potomac and the Rappahannock [146] had raised so many angry, threatening protests that the matter had been dropped. Thomas Kirton and Edward Dale, the agents for the Northern Neck, had quarreled.[147] Dale ceased to act as agent; Kirton retained his position but did not remit for the quit rents he collected during

---

[141] Beverley, 73–74. In the absence of any substantiating record, the circumstances described by Beverley have to be stated with some reservations.

[142] This, and not "prorogued," is the term used in the journal, 143, entry of July 7, 1680. In 1682 and thereafter, the journal usually stated that the General Assembly was prorogued or dissolved, though the entries of some sessions end with the mere statement that the Burgesses waited on the Governor at a designated place.

[143] See infra, p. 478, 488.

[144] In a letter cited in Cal. Am. & W. I., 1681–85, No. 319, Culpeper reported that he sailed for England on this date, but Nicholas Spencer wrote (ibid., 1677–80, No. 1486) that Culpeper went to New England. The letter quoted immediately infra shows that Spencer's report was correct.

[145] To Judith Culpeper, Oct. 5, 1680 (3 R 192).

[146] See supra, p. 460–61.

[147] Council Minutes, 314, 335.

the later years of his service.[148] In 1673, and perhaps before that time, he was ousted and was succeeded early in 1674 by William Aretkin, who probably continued to operate a land office that Kirton had opened in Northumberland County.[149] Aretkin held his post for less than three years but he began the issuance of Northern Neck land grants,[150] few of which, apparently, had been allowed under Kirton and Dale.[151] It was during the agency of Aretkin, though on Culpeper's direct order, that the grant was made to John Washington and to Nicholas Spencer of the 5000 acres previously held by Richard Lee, under royal grant, nearly opposite the Indian village of Piscataway. By signing this grant for the Proprietors, Aretkin escaped oblivion, but after the summer of 1677 his name disappeared from the records.[152]

That year, probably about the time he became Governor, Culpeper chose as his agents two of the most conspicuous men in Virginia. Daniel Parke, Secretary of the Colony, was named to operate at Yorktown an office for lands in the Arlington-Culpeper proprietary. Nicholas Spencer, a member of the Council, was designated agent for the Northern Neck.[153] This arrangement for two agents was upset in March, 1679, by the death of Parke, but Culpeper and the other Proprietors decided that Spencer should be sole agent under both patents.[154]

When Culpeper first came to Virginia as Governor in 1680, he doubtless conferred often with Spencer, who had succeeded Parke as Secretary of the Colony. It must have been, to some degree, on the basis of what Spencer reported concerning quit rents that Culpeper renewed a decision that changed the history of the proprietorship: He determined, more ambitiously than ever, to acquire the rights of the other participants in the two basic grants and to exploit Virginia lands for his own exclusive benefit. On investigation, after returning to England in 1680, Culpeper established in

148 *Ibid.*, 440, entry of Mch. 15, 1676. The court minute is to the effect that he presented "an account too long for the Court to examine every article." This of course suggests that his collections of quit rents may have been numerous.

149 4 *W* (1) p. 38–39. For Aretkin's appointment, see *Va. Land Grants,* 80, 154; *W* (1) p. 224 n.

150 In *Va. Land Grants,* 80, Mr. Harrison stated that during the period of the Arlington-Culpeper patent, two grants only were made in the Northern Neck, but the Northern Neck Land Books show in 1673–77, the period of Aretkin's agency, the following grants: Lancaster Co., three grants, 779 acres; Northumberland, two grants, 2200 acres; Westmoreland, 10 grants, 9295 acres.

151 Thirteen grants, all signed by Berkeley, appear to have been made in the Northern Neck during 1672–73. The number in 1674 was thirty-five.

152 He is not mentioned in *Swem.*

153 They presented to the General Court, Oct. 6, 1677, their power of attorney (9 *V* 306). For a sketch of Parke, who was Treasurer as well as Secretary, see 14 *V* 174–75. He must not be confused with his son, Col. Daniel Parke, aide to the Duke of Marlborough. Nicholas Spencer, the other agent, appears many times on the official scene and in dispatches. Perhaps the best view of him is through his letters, etc., in *Cal. Am. & W. I.,* 1677–80. He is well-sketched in *Va. Land Grants,* 81.

154 9 *V* 306.

detail the rights of his fellow-Proprietors of the Northern Neck. Several of the owners had died after the renewal of the patent in May, 1669, but the interest of most of them had been kept alive. Sir Dudley Wyatt's rights may have been reasserted.[155] All these shares, except that of his cousin Alexander, Lord Culpeper undertook to obtain, and by July 21, 1681, he succeeded in doing so. Apparently he borrowed from two friends some of the money for the transaction, and he consequently had to include them among the purchasers, but he paid them off or satisfied them otherwise within a short time. Neither of them appears at any subsequent time in any land grant issued by the Culpepers.[156] How much Culpeper and his temporary partners paid for the four-sixths or five-sevenths of the proprietary, the records do not show. In 1675, it will be recalled, the agents of Virginia had procured options on three of the sixth interests at £400 each.[157]

With control of the Northern Neck thus securely in his family, Culpeper proceeded to negotiate with his partner in the grant of Southern Virginia. Lord Arlington was then sixty-three, embittered, without further influence at court, and in retirement. His surviving passions were hate and house-building. Culpeper apparently had no great trouble in prevailing on the Earl to sell at an unrecorded figure his half of the southern proprietary, in which Arlington never appears to have had any other than a monetary interest. The formal transfer was made Sept. 10, 1681.[158]

Sole Proprietor of Southern Virginia, five-sixths owner of the Northern Neck, Governor of Virginia—Culpeper would prosper with the Colony. His prospects never had seemed so bright when, at his sunny noon, there

[155] The reason for suggesting this possibility is that the indenture of July 21, 1681, to be mentioned presently, accounts for all the former owners except Thomas Culpeper and Sir Dudley Wyatt. It is known that Thomas Culpeper's share was in the hands of his son, Alexander Culpeper. Although Wyatt's interest was assumed to have lapsed (see *supra*, p. 459), those listed as sellers in 1681 include "Anthony Guidott of Lincoln's Inn," a person who has not appeared previously in any of the transactions. The punctuation and language of the indenture separate Anthony Guidott from the other grantors and do not explain his interest. It is difficult to account for the inclusion of his name otherwise than on the supposition that he claimed the interest of Wyatt, which Culpeper bought, though the purchaser was unwilling to admit, by specific reference to Wyatt, that Guidott's claim was valid.

[156] These two men are mentioned as "Hon. Henry Brouncker of Sheene Abbey in the parish of Richmond in the county of Surrey, Esq., Cofferer of the household of the said Majesty, and Thomas Panton of Piccadilly in the County of Middlesex, Esq." (P.R.O., Close Roll, 33 Charles II, 54, 4568, 19, part of it obliterated by a fold in the vellum but easily understood from the context.) Brouncker, a famous chess player and a brother of the mathematician of the same name, is readily and none too favorably identified. He married the widow of the brother of the Earl of St. Albans, one of the Proprietors, and he appears often in *Pepys* (v. 3, p. 67, 166, 231–32; v. 4, p. 344, 346; v. 7, p. 200, 312; v. 8, p. 264; v. 9, p. 61, 180, 262), and occasionally in *Evelyn* (v. 2, p. 65, 125, 150). Brouncker's position of cofferer was that of one of the treasurers of the household or wardrobe. In the reign of Edward I, when the office first took on importance, it corresponded to that of head book-keeper and cashier. The post was abolished in 1782. Thomas Panton, the other purchaser of Northern Neck interests, must have been the notorious ex-gambler who, after incredible skill and good luck as a card-player, became a real estate speculator. A sketeh and bibliography will be found in *DNB*.

[157] 3 *Randolph MS*, 344 and *supra*, p. 461.
[158] 9 *V* 309. The text is in 2 *H* 578 ff.

came vexing clouds. The King had not been pleased, it would appear, at Culpeper's haste in returning to England from Virginia. In November, 1680, before the Governor's arrival at court, orders in Council were issued that may have been directed at Culpeper, though they were general in terms: Under pain of the King's highest displeasure, no Governor of His Majesty's plantations was to come to England on any pretence whatsoever without formal leave from the King in Council. Verbal permission would not be a sufficient warrant.[159]

If these orders were not designed as a rebuke to Culpeper, he soon had another and a sharper proof of the truth of a statement written in his grandfather's time concerning the wretchedness of those who hang on "princes' favors." William Blathwayt in June, 1680, had become Surveyor and Auditor General of Plantation Revenues and, as was usual in the case of that remarkable man, had taken his duties seriously.[160] In particular, the arrears of quit rents and the dissipation of that source of revenue by grants to favorites stirred Blathwayt to an inquiry that reached far. The King directed Culpeper to inform the Assembly of Virginia that these rents would be better managed. At the same time Culpeper was directed to report on what had been received by him.[161] As a third reform, King Charles was induced to promise that he would make no further grant of quit rents in Virginia or anywhere else in America but would reserve that revenue for the support of the colonial governments.[162] A fourth move by Blathwayt was to bring Colonel Norwood to book for the quit rents he had collected as Treasurer of Virginia.[163] Culpeper received, in addition, the call usually made on retiring Governors for a report and general accounting.[164] The extant answer to this would indicate that Culpeper did not take either Blathwayt or Blathwayt's prodding seriously. The Governor casually, almost condescendingly explained that while in Virginia, he had issued, Aug. 2, 1680, a proclamation for the payment of all quit rents but that he had received no accounting. He feared the low price of tobacco and the cost of collection would create a large difference between what was expected and what was paid.[165] That was all.

About that time, Culpeper's salary began to fall in arrears. Whether this was by way of punishment for his apparent indifference to his duties, or whether it was circumstantial, the Governor himself apparently did not

---

159 *Cal. Am. & W. I.*, 1677–80, No. 1573. For some comment on the residence of Governors in colonial Virginia, see P. A. Bruce, *Institutional History of Virginia in the Seventeenth Century*, v. 2, p. 332 ff.

160 See Gertrude A. Jacobsen, *William Blathwayt*, 150 ff; 1 *Blathwayt Journal*, 1.

161 3 *Randolph MS*, 397; 1 *Blathwayt Journal*, 43, 47, 56–58.

162 2 *Acts Privy Council, Col.*, No. 43.

163 *Cal. Am. & W. I.*, 1681–85, No. 202, 232; *Cal. Treas. Papers*, 1681–85, pt. 1, p. 62, 304, 1 *Blathwayt Journal*, 16.

164 6 *McDonald Transcripts*, 105–12.   165 *Cal. Am. & W. I.*, 1681–85, No. 319.

know.[166] The next year, Culpeper's insistence on what he termed his "rights" brought him a sharp command. Conditions in Virginia had taken a most unhappy turn for the worse. Warning was given that a second uprising might occur; [167] the troops in the Colony seemed more inclined to mutiny than to serve the King.[168] It was imperative that the Governor take the reins of authority from Chicheley, whose helpless bewilderment was apparent in his correspondence.[169] On June 17, Culpeper was notified that he must embark for the Colony August 1.[170] A new commission was drawn for him but when he claimed it, he was assessed with fees of £70. He was loath to leave England and perhaps he hoped that this episode would create another delay. Instead, upon his refusal to pay, he was ordered almost peremptorily to depart anyway. His salary was suspended until he settled for the papers.[171]

It was on Dec. 17, 1682, that Culpeper arrived in his domain for the second time.[172] He brought with him several Portuguese, whom he probably disposed of as indentured servants. In the words of the complaining Captain of the frigate, "he filled the ship as much as if she had been a merchantman," [173] but the discontent Culpeper left aboard the vessel [174] was mild in comparison with that which he found ashore.

A new law concerning the establishment of wharves had created much confusion.[175] The price of tobacco was ruinously low. Planters again had been demanding a "cessation." When the Deputy Governor had failed to approve suspension of all growing of the leaf for a year, men had gone through Gloucester County in the late spring of 1682 and had destroyed the plant beds or, later, the tobacco in the ground.[176] With some difficulty this "plant cutting" had been stopped in Gloucester but it then had been taken up in New Kent and in Middlesex.[177] "I know," wrote the Secretary of the Colony, Col. Nicholas Spencer, "the necessities of the inhabitants to be such . . . their low estate makes them desperate . . . If they go forward the only

---

[166] The date is not known, but on Oct. 6, 1682, Culpeper wrote that his salary was in great arrears, and on Sept. 20, 1683, he said "£4000 are due me" (*Cal. Am. & W. I.*, 1681–85, No. 1258). For the certificate of Auditor Nathaniel Bacon to this effect, May 29, 1683, see 6 *McDonald Transcripts*, 177.

[167] *Cal. Am. & W. I.*, 1681–85, No. 275, 524.

[168] *Ibid.*, No. 494.

[169] Chicheley's letter of May 8, 1682, cited in the preceding note, well illustrated his confusion. [170] *Cal. Am. & W. I.*, 1681–85, No. 567.

[171] *Ibid.*, No. 612, 678, 742, 763, 830; 1 *Acts Privy Council*, Col., No. 1320. Cf. 16 *V* 201.

[172] *Cal. Am. & W. I.*, 1681–85, No. 944, 983. From 1 *L. J.*, 54, it appears that the Speaker and the Burgesses welcomed the Governor on the 18th.

[173] *Cal. Am. & W. I.*, 1681–85, No. 983.

[174] Captain Tyrrell to the Commissioners of the Admiralty: "[Lord Culpeper] has been very unkind in several respects." (*Ibid.*)

[175] *Ibid.*, No. 1063; for the act of 1680, see 2 *H* 471 ff.

[176] Most of the destruction was of plant beds at too late a date for growing more plants in time to "make a crop" before frost. See *Beverley*, 74.

[177] *Cal. Am. & W. I.*, 1681–85, No. 495, 524, 561, 652.

destroying tobacco plants will not satiate their rebellious appetites who, if they increase and find the strength of their arms, will not bound themselves." [178] A member of the Council went so far as to declare, "If care be not taken for cessation, we must all go plundering with others." [179]

The instigator of this "plant cutting" was suspected to be Maj. Robert Beverley, Clerk of the Assembly, though in reality no positive evidence was found against him. His arrest, confinement on a warship, and subsequent release on high bail increased his popularity.[180] In dealing with Beverley, the Deputy Governor had been stern to the limit of the law, but in the treatment of other alleged participants in the "plant cutting," Chicheley had been lenient. Pardons had been granted to many. Moreover, in the spring of 1682, when the agitation over a cessation was at its peak, he had been prevailed upon to convene the Burgesses, but before the House had assembled, he had received instructions from England not to have it meet before November 10, by which time Culpeper was expected in Virginia.[181] Chicheley had not felt that he could cancel his call, and he consequently had permitted a brief session of Assembly during which he had limited the indignant members to the discussion of the single question of retaining in Virginia the two Companies of British troops the Crown no longer was willing to support. This restriction on lawmaking had created much resentment among Burgesses who had planned to pass an act that would forbid the planting of tobacco in 1682.

When, in November of that year, Chicheley again had summoned the Burgesses to Jamestown, in anticipation of Culpeper's coming, he had found them in contentious mood. From the opening of the session, November 10, until December 6, there had been labored controversy over the proper title of the Clerk of the House of Burgesses and over the assignment of members of the Council to sit with the Burgesses and thereby to preserve the judicial function of the House.[182] Robert Beverley represented a continuing subject of dispute. His supporters, who apparently were a majority of the Burgesses, did not attempt to name him Clerk of the new Assembly, but they voted to pay him 20,000 lbs. of tobacco for his services at the April session. The sum [183] was regarded by the Deputy Governor and Council as far too much. They

---

178 Quoted in Wertenbaker, *Va. Under the Stuarts*, 235. Wertenbaker's is the best brief account of the plant cutting. The quoted dispatch appears also in *Cal. Am. & W. I.*, 1681–85, No. 495. 179 *Ibid.*, No. 1042.

180 1 E. J., 25 ff; *Cal. Am. & W. I.*, 1681–85, No. 492, 563, 574, 704, 776.

181 This is substantially the language of Wertenbaker, *op. cit.*, 233. See *Cal. Am. & W. I.*, 1681–85, No. 548, 649.

182 1 L. J., 26, 29, 30–32, 37, 39. Both these were questions of interest, which one is tempted to elaborate, but the controversy is not a part of the history of the Northern Neck patent. Nor does there appear to be anything material to add to the explanation given by the learned H. R. McIlwaine in his introduction to *Journ. H. B.*, 1659/60–1693, p. xx, xxiii, xxxiv–xxxvi, xxxxvii.

183 Correctly speaking, the word should be "weight," but in 2 H 507 *et passim* "summe" is used in a manner to indicate it was the term commonly employed.

suggested 6000 lbs. as a proper figure, only to find the Burgesses reluctant to accept so low a compromise.[184]

Such was the situation, confused and explosive, that Culpeper faced on his arrival, Dec. 17, 1682. He met it with a combination of vigor, brusqueness, deception, mercy and delay. In the matter of Major Beverley, he scarcely waited a day. When the public claims and allowances were laid before him on the 19th of December, after the Burgesses had passed them, the Governor disapproved even the compromise of 6000 lbs. of tobacco. "I shall not consent," Culpeper wrote, "[Beverley] being represented to His Majesty as a principal fomenter and encourager of the late disorders of plant cutting and other disorders . . ."

This much plain, beyond further argument or adjustment, the Governor insisted on reviewing the bills passed during the session, prior to his arrival, and he returned some of them to the House for amendment.[185] In all of this, he proceeded with a speed and a decision which might have led the Burgesses to marvel at his industry, or else to conclude that he was taking his cues uncritically from the Secretary of the Colony, his cousin,[186] Nicholas Spencer. The lawmakers did not yield subserviently. In some instances they made the desired amendments; in others they asked for further consideration by the Governor. He, in turn, compromised or with equal readiness evaded. Most particularly, Culpeper found, on arrival, that the Burgesses were about to pass, in the usual form, a resolution for the levy to support the government[187] and an order for disbursing the funds so raised. His instructions, as previously, were that this no longer should be done, because the home government believed this a loose and imprudent system of raising and expending revenue. The King held to the instructions formerly given that a permanent tax be imposed by act of Assembly. Instead of announcing this to the Burgesses, Culpeper merely maintained that the various "orders," which were the appropriation items, could not be reviewed by him within the time the House should remain in session. Claims, therefore, must be deferred: only the general levy could be passed.[188]

As soon as this was settled, Culpeper summoned before him the Speaker and the House, on the sixth day of his presence at Jamestown. He had come to Virginia, he said, with the King's "especial commands, not to call any Assembly at all, till the dignity of the government should be first asserted by the punishment of the offenders" in the "plant cutting"; but, he explained, he had approved with needful amendment the acts passed before his arrival.

---

[184] 1 *L. J.*, 47, 48, 51, 52, 53.   [185] 1 *L. J.*, 56.
[186] So identified in *Beverley*, 76.   [187] 1 *L. J.*, 53, 54.
[188] This was the conclusion of McIlwaine in *Journ. H. B.*, 1659/60–1693, p. xxxvii–xxxviii, though he admitted that the entries in *L. J.* scarcely sufficed to explain the incident. There is no Journal of the House of Burgesses for the session of November–December. 1682. The tax law appears in 2 *H* 507–08.

The Burgesses, he pointed out, had failed to pass any bill for the proper punishment of "plant cutting." They must compensate for this by showing on their return home their "indignation and detestation" of such methods.[189] With no more ado, he dissolved the House.

Culpeper's own attitude toward the "cessation" was more to be condemned than was the tenderness of the lawmakers toward the rioters. Because of earlier protests by the Virginians, Culpeper had been empowered before he left England to grant a suspension of tobacco planting and he even had been given a letter which required the Maryland Proprietor, Lord Baltimore, to take similar action. Culpeper went to see Baltimore[190] but apparently could procure no assurance that Maryland would halt planting or even reduce the crop.[191] Returning to Jamestown, the Governor insisted publicly that a "cessation" would do no good, but in a private dispatch to Sir Leoline Jenkins he confided: "I so encouraged the planting of tobacco that if the season continue to be favorable . . . there will be a greater crop by far than ever grew since its first seating. And I am confident that Customs next year from thence will be 50,000 hhds."[192] He confessed that "the great crop then in hand would most certainly bring [Virginia] into the utmost exigencies again." Then he grimly gave assurance that he would be prepared to deal with any disorders that might arise.[193]

The best preparation, he coldly reasoned, was punishment of past offenders. In March, 1683, he wrote a friend: "I shall in April make an example of some plant cutters now indicted for treason, for terror to others, if their juries find them guilty. The greatest rogue of all was pardoned by Sir Henry [Chicheley] on condition to build a useful bridge near his house, for performance thereof his son-in-law,[194] being one of His Majesty's Council also, and Mr. Beverley was security. The next great rogue was let out on bail. I have issued out a proclamation under the seal of the Colony for him to deliver himself up by a day for trial, and am now sueing the bail; and Sir Henry promised the Lord knows who, all that were in the fields without taking a list of them, which so embarrasses me that the lot of severity will fall on the least guilty or least malicious."[195] In this resolution Culpeper persisted. Three of the plant cutters were convicted; two of these were

189 1 L. J., 61; P.R.O., C. O. 5, 135. L. C. Trans.

190 It is entirely probable that Culpeper had his first and only view of the Northern Neck while on the voyage up Chesapeake Bay to visit Lord Baltimore. See infra, p. 502.

191 Cal. Am. & W. I., 1681–85, No. 1007, 1258.

192 Ibid., No. 1007, 1018.

193 Wertenbaker, Va. Under the Stuarts, 238–39, with references to MSS in P.R.O.

194 This was Ralph Wormeley, the stepson, not the son-in-law of Chicheley. "'Son-in-law" was then used in the sense that "stepson" now is. The Governor did not state and perhaps did not know that the construction of a useful public work was a penalty frequently imposed by the General Court. Numerous such instances will be found in the Council Minutes.

195 To Lord Dartmouth, March 18, 1683; Hist. MSS Com., 11th Report, pt. 5, v. 3, p. 80, Earl of Dartmouth Papers. See also Cal. Am. & W. I., 1681–85, No. 1258.

hanged. Of the third, Culpeper wrote: "He was extremely young, not past 19, merely drawn in and very penitent, and therefore . . . I thought fit to mingle mercy with justice and reprieved him . . . to the end the whole country might be convinced that there was no other motive in the thing but purely to maintain Government." [196]

These things were done quickly. Then, about the end of May, 1683,[197] Culpeper left Virginia and returned to England. He explained later, for the second time, that he knew the large tobacco crop of the year "would certainly plunge the country into further difficulty next year" and that he wished "to consult as to the measures to be taken." [198] A month before his departure he had written, in contrast: "Tobacco now bears a good price, and will be of tolerable value all next year, if not longer." Concerning the reasons for his proposed voyage to England, he wrote in March that he wished "to prepare certain things of great consequence in the future, which cannot be well understood by letter." [199] As his actual reason for leaving his post probably was a desire to see his mistress—a reason of a sort not unfamiliar to his King [200]—he might have excused himself at court but for one circumstance. Before he had left England, the previous year, he had received a copy of the order, already mentioned, to the effect that without the King's consent "no Governor of his Majesty's Plantations do come into England from his Government." [201] Apparently it had been understood that a Governor would be allowed to leave if he had a Deputy Governor or named one,[202] but Culpeper had not protected himself in this manner. Although Chicheley had died February 5, much to the relief of Culpeper,[203] the Governor had appointed no temporary successor.[204]

It proved to be a costly omission. On August 2, soon after Culpeper's arrival in London, a committee of the Privy Council was named to ascertain whether he had forfeited his office of Governor by absenting himself from the Colony for three months without appointing a deputy.[205] Either then or soon after,

[196] Quoted in Wertenbaker's *Va. Under Stuarts*, 238; *Cal. Am. & W. I.*, 1681–85, No. 1258, P.R.O., C.O.: 1: 51, p. 113.

[197] He was present at the meeting of the Council May 22. See 1 *E. J.*, 44.

[198] *Cal. Am. & W. I.*, 1681–85, No. 1258.

[199] The paraphrase is that of 20 *V* 82.   [200] See *infra*, p. 481.

[201] Wertenbaker's *Va. Under Stuarts*, 239, *Cal. Am. & W. I.*, 1681–85, No. 676. This was in August, 1682.

[202] Cf. *Cal. Am. & W. I.*, 1681–85, No. 1172.

[203] 20 *V* 82.

[204] It may be this should read "no lawful temporary successor." The reason for suggesting "lawful" is a clause in *Cal. Am. & W. I.*, 1681–85, No. 1208, Aug. 24, 1683, for the validation of acts of the Council of Virginia on the ground that Culpeper, contrary to instructions, had appointed Nicholas Spencer, instead of Nathaniel Bacon, the senior member of Council, to act in Culpeper's absence. There may have been involved a neat question of colonial law whether the acting President of the Council was, *ipso facto*, acting Lieutenant Governor. During the time Spencer headed the Council, he is mentioned in the *Executive Journal* (v. 1, p. 49 ff) simply as "Nicholas Spencer, Esq. President." Bruce, in his *Institutional History*, etc., v. 2, p. 307, referred to the authority of a Governor to name a deputy, during temporary absence, unless the King had done so.   [205] *Cal. Am. & W. I.*, 1681–85, No. 1172.

Culpeper was arrested and confined.[206] He made his excuses with some adroitness and a show of indifference: "No doubt another Governor of greater ability will outdo my poor endeavors; but what the wit of man can expect from a Governor beyond peace and quiet, and a large crop of tobacco, I know not. I have done my duty, and my conscience does not accuse me. But the load of Government is so heavy that I am as contented to be eased of it as to take it up. I hear that there is to be new Governor. I beg that my dues and concerns may not suffer thereby." [207] On this plea or on grounds not recorded, Culpeper· was released; [208] but four days later, Sept. 28, 1683, he was deprived of his post in favor of Lord Howard of Effingham.[209]

Although ousted, Culpeper was required, against his will, to prepare a written report on the execution of his instructions.[210] In doing this, the retiring Governor had something to say about quit rents. During the time of Charles I, it will be recalled, these rents had been suspended in Virginia for the first seven years of settlement. Culpeper's instructions had been to terminate this concession and, also, to restrain the practice of procuring grants of more land than could be cultivated.

His comment was: "The unvaluable payment of quit rents heretofore hath contributed much to the remote and scattered seating of the country and consequently all the other mischiefs mentioned in the instructions and many more. But how to vacate any grants legally passed I know not. And besides there are such vast tracts of land taken up already by the omission of former governors that it is to no purpose to make any restraint therein now. And the only remedy . . . is to cause the quit rents reserved in the respective grants thereof to be paid in specie . . . by such as have above 1000 or 1500 acres and by the rest in tobacco or other commodities *ad valorem,* for that will cause a great many to fling up such part of their lands as they cannot employ to present advantage, and so to make room for others and cause nearer seating."

In general review of what was amiss in the government, Culpeper wrote: "The wants and defects are great, but poverty is the greatest. There is no one product of value but tobacco, no need, no improvement that can be considerable, (for some time) but flax and hemp . . . I see no advantage at present but by sending beef, pork, corn and provisions to the . . . West Indies . . . Without being money out of purse (H.M. can help most by seeing there is) the habit of full government, the keeping peace and quiet . . . and the encouragement of building towns and shipping that there may be a market and a vent for the same." [211]

[206] 1 *Sainsbury,* 86; *Cal. State Pap., Dom.,* 1683, p. 107, 124, 331; P.R.O., C.O. 5: 1356, p. 103, 109.
[207] *Cal. Am. & W. I.,* 1681–85, No. 1258.   [208] 1 *Sainsbury,* 86.
[209] *Cal. Am. & W. I.,* 1681–85, No. 1274; *Cal. Treas. Papers,* 1681–85, pt. 2, p. 1132.
[210] *Cal. Am. & W. I.,* 1681–85, No. 1209, 1270, 1279, 1280, 1290.
[211] Article 81 of Instructions; see 6 *McDonald Transcripts,* 169–70.

This, so to say, was abstract and impersonal. Culpeper's own interest he put on a different footing. His forty-seventh instruction had expressed the King's intention of "taking in" the patents that had permitted favored subjects to issue land grants or to receive the revenue from quit rents. Consequently, Culpeper had been told to see that "the quit rents which shall hereafter become due to us (the respective patentees being first fully satisfied) also the escheats, fines and forfeitures be applied to public use." On this Culpeper's comment was sharp: "The patentees not having been treated with, much less satisfied, there is no occasion to do anything with either of these instructions. However I caused the same to be collected by the Sheriffs and the returns to be made of the number of acres, especially of the southern grant, etc. But as to such fines and forfeitures only as are due his Majesty . . . you will see some good beginning by the auditor's next account." Culpeper had noted in comment on another instruction that the escheats "are not due the King, but to the respective patentees." [212]

At the very time that Culpeper thus was asserting his rights, the Council was petitioning Charles to compensate the owners of the patent to Southern Virginia.[213] Culpeper, for his part, was willing to sell to the Crown. His "asking price" was £7000 cash.[214] In the end, he received, on June 24, 1684, the promise of £700 cash and a pension of £600 per annum for the remaining life of the patent, twenty-one years. Half this pension was in payment for Culpeper's "pretensions," that is, his "regalities," in Virginia.[215]

The colonials were notified that the patent to all Virginia except the Northern Neck had been purchased by the Crown and that it was the intention of the King to "apply all the profits and advantages" from the recovered grant to the benefit of the Colony; but there was one change, an important one: future quit rents, escheats, fines and forfeitures must be paid in coin, not in tobacco.[216] For the time, of necessity, the Virginians had to accept this arrangement, but before the receipt of the news of agreement between King and patentee, they had shown that they did not intend to be compliant in dealing with Culpeper. In April, 1684, Colonel Spencer presented to the House of Burgesses, then in session, a copy of the King's grant

---

[212] Article 17 of Instructions, 6 McDonald Transcripts, 123. For the argument over the escheats and the settlement of Culpeper's salary, etc., see Cal. Treas. Papers, 1685–89, v. 8, pt. 1, p. 507; pt. 3, p. 1293, 1588; 1 Blathwayt Journal, 372.

[213] 6 McDonald Transcripts, 222. The petition was received Sept. 29, 1683.

[214] Cal. Am. & W. I., 1681–85, No. 1395; Close Rolls, 4615, 36 Car. 11, pt. 1, No. 16, L. C. trans.; 1 Blathwayt Journal, 172, 174; Cal. Treas. Papers, 1681–85, p. 1175.

[215] Cal. Am. & W. I., 1681–85, No. 1771. Other sources are cited in Andrews, Colonial Period, v. 2, p. 235 n. The unfinished term of the Southern Virginia proprietary must not be confused with that of the Northern Neck. Under the revised patent of May 8, 1669, all ungranted lands of the Northern Neck reverted to the Crown after twenty-one years, i.e., in 1690. The term of the grant of Feb. 25, 1673, for the remainder of Virginia, was thirty-one years, i.e., until 1704.

[216] Cal. Am. & W. I., 1681–85, No. 1815; Orders of the Lords of the Treasury, July 25, 1684, 22 V 344–45. At this time, Lawrence Washington the first was a Burgess.

of Feb. 25, 1673, to Arlington and Culpeper.[217] This was, apparently, the first time the document had been entered of record in Virginia, though an unofficial copy of it had been received in 1674.[218] Almost simultaneously with the presentation of the paper, Secretary Spencer submitted a claim by Culpeper for 90,000 lbs. of tobacco to recompense him for advances made to keep troops at the heads of the rivers.[219] The tobacco, it was contended, was spent in the service of Virginia from quit rent leaf that properly belonged to Lord Culpeper as Proprietor.[220]

The Burgesses assailed the basis of this contention by denying that the grant had been validated or that the quit rents ever had belonged to Culpeper.[221] Their new Governor, Lord Howard, took the opposite view.[222] Culpeper, said Howard, had a valid claim to the quit rents and to repayment for the advances to the soldiers. The Burgesses had to acquiesce, but the controversy doubtless was one of the reasons the Council of Virginia, Apr. 25, 1685, petitioned the King "in some way to compensate the Lord Culpeper as his Majesty shall see fit, for the Northern Neck," so that the inhabitants of that region could "hold their lands immediately from his most sacred Majesty."

In urging this, the Council asserted that the difference in tenure discouraged settlement of the proprietary. "No grants or patents," said the Council, "[have] issued for lands there surveyed and seated, for the last past twelve years, whereby that as would be, as flourishing a part, as is in the Government, is but thinly peopled, and thereby exposed, more openly to the attempts and incursions of the Indians . . ."[223] This was an argument that had weight even at Whitehall, but nothing was done for a reason all-sufficient: At the very next meeting of the Council of Virginia, the Governor announced the death of Charles II, which had occurred more than two months prior to the adoption of the petition.[224] The fourth of the Stuart Kings, and the last, James II, had succeeded his brother. It meant for England that a bigot had taken the place of a prodigal.

The change of Kings came when Culpeper's patent of the Northern Neck was within five years of termination. Although Culpeper had sold to the Crown his rights in Southern Virginia, he either wished to retain permanently his interests in the Northern Neck, or else he reasoned that if he had to give up that patent also, he could get more for it if it had a long life. He accordingly undertook to get a renewal of the grant to the region between the Potomac and the Rappahannock. This was a task not readily or quickly performed, but it was not beyond the skill of a courtier long trained in the

[217] *Journ. H. B.*, Apr. 25, 1684, p. 201.
[218] See *supra*, p. 462.
[219] *Journ. H. B.*, anno cit., 230–31.
[220] *Ibid.*
[221] *Ibid.*, 238.
[222] *Ibid.*, 242, 244.
[223] 1 E. J., 69; *Cal. Am. & W. I.*, 1685–88, No. 140. Needless to say, the Council was mistaken about the land grants in the Northern Neck. Approximately forty grants are of record for the twelve years in question. See *supra*, p. 470.
[224] 1 E. J., 70. Charles died Feb. 6, 1685.

art of wringing concessions from a reluctant debtor monarch. At length, on September 27 in the fateful year of revolution, 1688, Culpeper succeeded in procuring from James what was, ostensibly, a renewal in perpetuity of the grant to the Northern Neck—its forests, its rivers and all its riches—at an annual rental of £6, 13s 4d.[225]

Actually, a change destined to multiply the area of the proprietorship was made so quietly and so speciously that it may have escaped notice altogether. The previous grants, it will be remembered, had fixed the western boundaries at the "heads" of the Rappahannock and Potomac; this new grant read: "first heads or springs." [226] Culpeper and his heirs ultimately were to be immensely the gainers by this, but he never confessed, so far as the records indicate, that acceptance of this favor at the hand of James was not in keeping with the part he was playing at that very time in the councils of the King's adversaries who had invited William of Orange to come to England. When James fled, Dec. 11, 1688, Culpeper was a member of the commission that assumed temporary charge of the government until William and Mary arrived and Parliament tendered the Crown to them.[227] It was another "double or quits" in a gambler's life and it won.

Culpeper did not enjoy long his extended domain. His end came Jan. 27, 1689, in circumstances singularly scandalous. He had married at The Hague, almost thirty years previously, Margaretta van Hesse, aged 24, daughter of a man of wealth and station. By her, about 1670, Culpeper had a daughter, Catherine. No other children were born of his wife. As early as 1671, and perhaps before 1670, Culpeper had a mistress in London, Susannah Willis by name, alias Welden, alias Laycock. She became the mother of two daughters, Susannah, born 1672, and Charlotte, five years younger. Both these children Culpeper acknowledged and supported. About ten days before his death, he made a will which confirmed a trusteeship he had created the previous October for the benefit of these illegitimate daughters. Lady Culpeper and his heiress, Catherine, were left with the Northern Neck proprietorship and with his British real property, most of which, though chargeable with his debts, had been purchased chiefly with the dowry of his wife. Virtually everything else possessed by him went to Susannah Willis and her two children. As Culpeper died in the house he kept in London for his second family, Mrs. Willis, it seems, had him buried privately and without delay. Then she proceeded skillfully to secure the estate he left her. In self-protection Lady Culpeper had to institute legal proceedings against her dead husband's mistress. Long contention, bills in Parliament and suits in

225 The text will be found in 15 V 392 ff. Mention of the rent is on p. 397. VSL has a photostat of the first printed text of the grant, London, 1688.

226 See infra, p. 489; 15 V 396.

227 Hist. MSS Commission, 11th Report, pt. 5, v. 3, Earl of Dartmouth Papers, 229. See also Burnet's History of his Own Times, v. 1, p. 819.

chancery kept alive for years this ugly chapter in the unlovely career of Thomas Lord Culpeper.[228]

The death of Culpeper and the renewal in perpetuity of an enlarged grant ended the second period of the proprietary. To recapitulate briefly, the first phase of that period, beginning with the restoration of the Stuarts in 1660, had ended in 1669 with the recognition of the validity of all grants made on the Northern Neck prior to Michaelmas, 1661, if these tracts actually were occupied on May 8, 1669. That agreement, opening a second phase, had relieved the fears of settlers that they would lose their property, but it did not end dispute. On the contrary, the award of "regalities" to Culpeper and Arlington in Southern Virginia shifted and extended the controversy. Culpeper's behavior as Governor doubtless added so much to strife that the final surrender of his semi-feudal rights in 1684 did not silence the Burgesses. Their aim was to secure clear real estate titles and to pay neither to Crown nor to Proprietor any larger or more regular quit rents than they were compelled to tender to William and Mary or to Culpeper's heiress.

Catherine Culpeper, inheritor of five-sixths of the renewed proprietorship,[229] is mentioned once only in the available correspondence of her father. When he was about to return to England after his first service as Governor, he wrote from Boston, Oct. 5, 1680: "I shall now marry Cate as soon as I can, and then shall recognize myself to be a free man without clogge or charge." [230] As "Cate" was then about ten years of age, her father's professed wish to see her mated scarcely could be regarded as an expression of parental love, though he was credited with saying, even while living with his mistress, "that he would not do anything in reference to his estate to the prejudice of his wife and child." [231] No echo lingers of the comment of mother or of daughter on this unredeemed pledge. They lived at Leeds Castle, reduced the family debt if and as they could and, no doubt, gave some measure of thought to the deferred enterprise Lord Culpeper had avowed for "Cate" in 1680.

At this point, the history of the Culpepers and of the Northern Neck proprietorship blends with the line of the renowned Thomas, third Lord Fairfax, who admittedly had been second only to "Old Nol" among the Roundhead Generals. In character no less than in accomplishment, General

---

[228] As this incident in the story of the Northern Neck proprietorship was treated fully by Fairfax Harrison in 33 V 262 ff, it merely is summarized here. The essential documents, some of which are cited but not quoted by Harrison, are: The petition of Lady Culpeper to the Lord Commissioners of the Great Seal, n.m. 20, 1688; the petition of Catherine Culpeper, n.m. 20, 1688, and the plea of Susannah Willis, als. Weldon, n.m., n.d., 1689, all in P.R.O., C 7, 671, 9. Susannah's plea is so tattered that it scarcely is legible.

[229] The remaining sixth was held by Alexander Culpeper. See *infra*, p. 486.

[230] 3 R 193.

[231] Lady Culpeper's bill of Jan. 15, 1690 in *Hist. MSS Commission*, 12th Report, App. 6, MSS of the House of Lords, 1689–90, p. 434. See also Fairfax Harrison in 33 V 265.

Fairfax was conspicuous. His chief weakness probably was his excessive consideration for his ambitious wife. Lady Fairfax had been born Anne Vere, daughter of Fairfax's early commander in the Low Countries, Sir Horace Vere. She had one daughter, Mary Fairfax, born in 1638. As Mary grew toward young womanhood, she seemed to have abundant prospects, because her father's estates, which were by no means small, had been increased by a grant he had received from Parliament as pension and arrears of pay.

This grant included part of the property of George Villiers, second Duke of Buckingham,[232] who was then twenty-three and was aspiring ambitiously to the hand of the widowed Princess of Orange. Mocked by the exiled court for so impudent a suit, Buckingham soon afterward lost the favor of Charles II. By 1657, the Duke probably had spent most of the money he had raised in Holland by the sale or pawn of a collection of pictures and jewels one of his servants had succeeded in bringing from England. To most men, there seemed no way of recovering any part of the family fortune otherwise than by the restoration of Charles, but to the intriguing young Duke, disaster was challenge. Faced with continuing adversity, Buckingham decided to go to England and to recoup at least a part of his losses by marrying the daughter of the Parliamentary General to whom his confiscated property had been granted! Without apparent hesitation he undertook the gamble, only to find, when he reached England, that Mary Fairfax was engaged to marry the Earl of Chesterfield. That did not deter Buckingham. He exercised his wiles, won the support of Mary's grandmother, Lady Vere, broke up the engagement, and pressed his suit. About three months after his arrival in England, he was the son-in-law of General Fairfax.

Suspicions were aroused in the exiled court of Charles as a result of this matrimonial coup; tension was created between Cromwell and Fairfax; but these are part of the story of the Commonwealth, not of the proprietary of Virginia. For her share in the financial maneuver—it scarcely can be called a romance—Mary Fairfax, Duchess of Buckingham, was rewarded by her husband with disdain, a title and no more. After the Restoration, the Duke formed a notorious liaison with the Countess of Shrewsbury, by whom he had a son. When the child died, Buckingham had him buried in Westminster Abbey as Earl of Coventry. For a time after this, the Duke made a pretence of living with his wife and of attending church in her company, but he soon became involved in new intrigues. By the time he was fifty-eight, a plain-spoken contemporary described him as "worn to a thread with whoring."[233] The next year he died without issue. So wasteful had been his life

232 The act of confiscation which included Buckingham's holdings was that of July 16, 1651. See *supra*, p. 450. Under this act Fairfax received Helmsley Castle and York House in the Strand.
233 1 *Ellis Correspondence*, 64, 276.

that after the Restoration his income of £26,000 per annum had not sufficed. He had dissipated the whole of his own estate and left his widow little more than her dower and her prospective inheritance from her father.[234] As the Duchess insisted on maintaining a separate establishment, her father had to assist her. In doing so he attempted in 1666 by methods of doubtful legality to divide his entailed property.[235] His will was based on this conveyance.

The heir to the title of General Lord Fairfax was a cousin, Henry Fairfax of Oglethorpe. He died without incident of historical importance and left a son, Thomas, who was born in 1657. The income this Thomas, fifth Lord, received from the Fairfax estate was small, because the Duchess of Buckingham was still alive. He was her heir at law, and he could have disputed his grandfather's will, but so long as the Duchess did not undertake to sell property he regarded as entailed to him, he did not resort to litigation.[236] Peace with the Duchess was more profitable, if practicable, because his own tastes were extravagant.[237] His need of money sent him on curious trails. Doubtless it would be unfair to say that his quest of the pound sterling prompted his marriage, but money or no money, in 1690, about two years after Thomas succeeded his father in the peerage, he married Catherine Culpeper. He was then thirty-three; she was about twenty.

Through this marriage, the Culpeper interests in the Northern Neck passed under control of the Fairfaxes. The proprietary itself in time became known as the Fairfax Grant, and in Washington's youth was supposed by uninformed colonials to have been made originally to the Fairfax family.

At the outset the fifth Lord had his hands full of troubles nearer than the Northern Neck. As the husband of Catherine, he had to undertake to rescue as much as possible of the Culpeper property, and in particular, he had to guide Lady Culpeper's action against her dead husband's mistress. Parliament refused to pass a bill to revoke the settlement Culpeper had made in favor of his illegitimate daughters, but a compromise was not precluded. Fairfax negotiated and at length arranged a bargain to this effect: Culpeper's settlement was to be cancelled; for one of the natural daughters, both of whom had married by that time, an annuity of £100 was to be made a charge on certain of the Culpeper lands; the other illegitimate daughter was to be paid £4000 cash for a complete release. As this agreement was a revision of Culpeper's will, and of the settlement which had been admitted to probate and to record, approval of the compromise called for an act of

---

[234] This sketch of Buckingham's marital and financial adventures is based on the excellent article of Sir Charles Harding Firth in *DNB*.

[235] See Fairfax Harrison's analysis in 34 *V* 61–62.

[236] For the details of ultimate settlement, which do not appear to be germane to the history of the proprietorship, see 4 *Fairfax Correspondence*, 254 ff and 34 *V* 62.

[237] The principal cause of his heavy expenditures was the improvement of Denton Hall. See Ralph Thoresby, *Diary*, v. 1, p. 381, 396.

Parliament. When Fairfax sought this, he found himself opposed by Lady Catherine's uncle, John, third Lord Culpeper, who had succeeded to the title.[288] Culpeper protested that the agreement with Mrs. Willis's heirs disregarded certain annuities already charged against the Culpeper estates.[239] Further, he insisted that the compromise cancelled, to his disadvantage, the general provisions of inheritance under the will of his brother, the second Lord. In the resulting contest between the two peers, the Commons decided for Lady Fairfax, but the Lords again refused to upset the arrangements Thomas Lord Culpeper had made for the children of his mistress.[240] In the interest of Lady Catherine, Lord Fairfax had to institute proceedings in chancery, a slow and unprofitable course for a man who wanted more money than he could get from his farms and from the West Indian wrecks, flotsam and jetsam for which he had a crown grant in 1702-07.[241]

As for the Northern Neck proprietary, it proved as much of a bother as Fairfax would let it be, under agents who changed too frequently for the convenience of a landlord who was indisposed to bestir himself. Lord Culpeper's apparent shrewdness in naming Daniel Parke and Nicholas Spencer as his agents [242] for his proprietaries had failed of its purpose. Parke had died Mch. 6, 1679. Spencer remained sole agent until his end came Sept. 23, 1689.[243] His most historic service was in issuing a grant, which Culpeper himself seems to have arranged, for 30,000 acres to be used as a refuge for Catholics. This Brent, Brent Town or Brenton grant, as it subsequently was styled in Virginia, had raised hopes of extensive settlement because James II encouraged the project by guaranteeing freedom of worship to all residents of the tract.[244] The flight of James and the death the next year of Culpeper as well as of Spencer put an end to the enterprise. Settlement in the upper stretches of the proprietary continued to be slow. On the Land Books of the Lords of the Northern Neck only 292 grants, of every sort and size, antedated 1669. By 1690 the total had not reached 1200.[245]

In succession to Spencer as agent of the Proprietors, Philip Ludwell was named. An interesting man he was. Born in Somerset, he had come after 1660 to Virginia, where his brother Thomas was Secretary of the Colony. Following the death of Governor Berkeley, July 9, 1677, Ludwell married the widow who, it will be remembered, had been Frances Culpeper, daughter

[238] He was the sixth child and third son of John, first Baron Thoresway, by his second wife and cousin Judith, daughter of Sir Thomas Culpeper of Hollingbourn. See 33 *V* 246-48.

[239] 33 *V* 267.   [240] *Ibid.*

[241] *Cal. Treas. Papers*, 1704-5, p. 100-1. Cf. 34 *V* 63.

[242] See *supra*, p. 470; 2 *Westmoreland Wills and Deeds*, p. 13. Thomas Kirton held lands granted him by Ludwell, Feb. 28, 1690.

[243] *Cal. Am. & W. I.*, 1689-92, No. 505.

[244] 17 *V* 309. The royal grant was dated Feb. 10, 1687.

[245] To be precise, the total was 1197. Most of these were in Lancaster and Westmoreland. These figures assume that surviving Land Books cover all the grants that were made and "taken up," that is, occupied or seated permanently.

of Thomas Culpeper, Esq. and cousin of the second Lord. Although Ludwell thus placed himself on the side of the proprietary interests, he won popularity with the people for a time by opposing Governor Howard.[246] In 1689, he was named Governor of North Carolina and, in 1691, had South Carolina added to his care.

This experience apparently disposed Ludwell as agent to handle the Culpeper-Fairfax domain with the same autocracy he was free to display in public office. Among the proprietary "rights" Ludwell sought to establish on the Northern Neck were that of escheats and that of estrays. The Council of Virginia promptly protested that Ludwell had appointed a "Ranger General who he impowers to make deputies with divers unusual powers to take up horses, cattle, etc., which should it be put in execution, would so disturb the inhabitants, and indeed take from them their horses, cattle, etc., that it would hazard the peace of this Their Majesties' country."[247] Sheriffs and other officers first were directed by the Council to return Ludwell's papers and then were forbidden to execute any of them.[248]

Several times previously, it will be recalled, in disputes over the proprietary, the Burgesses had petitioned the Crown to take over the Northern Neck. They now proposed that this be done on the basis of the negotiations of 1675–76.[249] Alarmed by the action of the lawmakers, Ludwell counselled the Proprietors to procure from the Crown a confirmation of their title. Lady Culpeper and other interested persons accordingly petitioned on May 21, 1691. As the fifth Lord Fairfax had been among the supporters of William in 1688, the King was well disposed to him. The patent to the Northern Neck was confirmed, Dec. 15, 1692,[250] to the definite advantage of Fairfax and to the reassurance of his tenants. Applications for grants increased so heavily that Ludwell was assailed for absenteeism because he maintained no establishment to which applicants could go. At length, in 1693, he opened an office, but at this promising moment in the history of the Northern Neck he received orders to proceed to Charleston, South Carolina, and to hold an assembly there as Governor.[251]

If this was unfortunate for the Proprietors, they gained by the next twist of fate. In 1694, Alexander Culpeper died. His sixth of the Northern Neck proprietary, inherited from his father, Thomas Culpeper, Esq., he bequeathed to Lady Culpeper, widow of his cousin, the second Lord.[252] She and her

---

246 1 *V* 176; 6 *W* (1) p. 222; *Va. Land Grants,* 82; *Cal. Am. & W. I.,* 1689–92, No. 1154.
247 1 *E. J.,* 132, Oct. 23, 1690. Culpeper instituted the rangers (*Landmarks,* 79).
248 *Ibid.,* 131; *Cal. Am. & W. I.,* 1689–92, No. 1132; 4 *V* 184; *Westmoreland Orders,* 1690–98, p. 10; *Lancaster Orders,* 1686–90, p. 78, entry of Feb. 11, 1690.
249 *Journ. H. B.,* 1659–93, entry of May 21, 1691, p. 371.
250 Petition of Margaret Lady Culpeper, VHS photostat of LC trans.; original in P.O.R., C.O. 5: 1306, p. 21; the confirmation of the charter, *ibid.,* 1358, p. 319–20; *Journ. H. B.,* 1659–93, p. 371; *Cal. Am. & W. I.,* 1689–92, No. 1514.
251 1 *V* 177; Hawks, *History of North Carolina,* v. 2, p. 492 ff; 1 *Col. Rec. N. C.,* 363; *Va. Land Grants,* 155.   252 See his will, proved Jan. 5, 1695, in 33 *V* 357–78.

daughter Catherine, Lady Fairfax, thus became sole Proprietors and wisely sought and gained from the Crown, Jan. 11, 1693, still another confirmation of their title,[253] a decisive event in the history of the grant. Thereafter, in all the controversies between the Colony and the Proprietors, no effort was made by Virginia to buy the patent to the Northern Neck on her own account, though the King was to be asked to purchase it.[254]

For another reason, also, the confirmation of 1693 was historic: It led to a succession of somewhat contradictory shifts of policy, the result of which was the more rapid development of the middle and then of the western part of the Northern Neck. Ludwell's deputy having shown lack of needful ability, Capt. Roger Jones, a London agent, recommended William Fitzhugh and George Brent, two Virginians of station, to issue land grants and to collect quit rents.[255] The two men accepted the appointment and soon bestirred themselves, but Brent was inclined to be high-handed. He asserted vigorously the alleged title of the Proprietors to all escheats, and when he had difficulty in getting the holders of headrights to accept tenancy under the new Proprietors,[256] he threatened to double their quit rents.[257]

This aroused the General Assembly again. Among the leaders of that body was Robert Carter, who later was to be one of the most important persons in the annals of the proprietary. Carter in 1695 was more or less an advocate of popular rights, and, being already one of the largest landowners of the Northern Neck, was interested, immediately and substantially, in the Proprietors' plans. He accordingly prevailed on the Burgesses to appoint a committee to prepare a protest against the methods Fitzhugh and Brent were employing. This committee promptly submitted and the Burgesses approved a paper that doubtless was Carter's own handiwork. It complained that as many as 50,000 acres of the Northern Neck might be taken by one person under a single grant and held without any actual "seating" or occupation of the land.[258] Surveys, said the committee, were not correct; patents were changed to conveyances; lands were "sold" at too high a figure; the traditional procedure in respect to escheats was violated.[259]

The members of the Council of the Colony, deliberating as the upper house of the General Assembly, refused to approve this protest, but the legislative upstir alarmed Fitzhugh, who was more conciliatory than Brent. It was necessary, Fitzhugh believed, for the Proprietors to exert themselves

[253] *Cal. Am. & W. I.,* 1693–96, No. 34; *Wilmington Papers,* 111; *Cal. Treas. Papers* 1689–92, p. 1097.

[254] See the Burgesses' protest of 1730, *infra,* p. 498.

[255] See Fitzhugh to Jones, n.d. [1694], 4 *V* 183–84. 5 *Westmoreland Wills and Deeds,* 63, for land regranted by Fitzhugh and Brent, Oct. 24, 1694.

[256] That is, legally speaking, to attorn.

[257] *Va. Land Grants,* 89.   [258] See *supra,* p. 7.

[259] *Journ. H. B.,* 1695–1702, p. 27–29, address of May 10, 1695. Cf. *Cal. Am. & W. I.,* 1693–96, No. 1871. For a sketch of Brent, see 17 *V* 309.

in England and to offset the hostility they were encountering among the colonials. In an elaborate metaphor he wrote Capt. Roger Jones: "You will see . . . what a hard game we have to play, the contrary party that is our opposers having the best cards and the trumps to boot, especially the honours, yet would my Lord Fairfax there take his turn in shuffling and dealing the cards, and his Lordship with the rest would see we were not cheated in the game, I question not but we should gain the set, though the game is so poorly played, but if we be not, as we have now and always urged, supported from thence not only our master's money will be lost, but we shall hardly be able to keep our just and legal standing." [260]

For the time being, Fitzhugh wrote in vain; but he and Brent and their friends beat off the attack of Robert Carter. Left free to do much as they pleased in Virginia, they soon began the practice that changed substantially the settlement of western lands and set off a long process of land speculation. Brent and Fitzhugh, as agents, became "consistently their own best customers," [261] and took out grants for large and desirable tracts. In this, strictly speaking, there was nothing illegal. The two men paid as others did for the patents and they pledged themselves in the same way for the quit rents; but they were in position to select the best lands and, by the magnitude of their new plantations, to discourage independent settlement by the purchasers of small farms in the western part of the Northern Neck.

This was a policy of evil potentialities. At the time it gave Fairfax no real concern. If he knew of it at all, he probably felt that Fitzhugh was cancelling this debit by a credit of many digits. Like all his predecessors, Fitzhugh had been defied, or at least resisted, by those who had occupied tracts in the Northern Neck prior to the revised patent of 1669. Those landholders insisted that their quit rents, if due at all, should go to the Crown and not to the Proprietors. Against this view Fitzhugh argued with persistence and, no doubt, with an exhibit of formal documents. Finally he convinced Richard Lee, the second of the name in Virginia, that his contention was valid. Lee privately made composition and thereby recognized the rights of the Proprietors.[262] Slowly afterward, other planters effected compromises by which their titles were cleared and the receipts of Lord Fairfax moderately increased.

Brent became a great landowner, but before he could develop his tracts, he died in the spring of 1699.[263] Fitzhugh followed in October, 1700.[264] In choosing a successor to these men who had laid the foundations of a new policy in the proprietorship, there apparently was sloth or difficulty. At length, in 1702, the powerful London agent, Micajah Perry the elder, who

[260] Letter of May 11, 1697; 6 V 61–62.   [261] Va. Land Grants, 88–90.

[262] Va. Land Grants, 87 ff. This important change in the proprietary, though doubtless authentic, is described nowhere in contemporary documents. The only authority is Beverley, op. cit., 76.

[263] Va. Land Grants, 92; cf. 17 V 309.   [264] Ibid., 93.

acted for many planters, recommended Robert Carter of Corotoman, Lancaster County, as agent. The Proprietors accepted him.[265]

Carter, then forty years of age, was the son of a Royalist who had come to Virginia in 1649. Born in Lancaster County, he had been schooled in England, but in all of his sympathies he was a colonial. At the time he became agent for the proprietary he already had some distinction and was rising in fortune. He was the man, it will be recalled, who had framed the remonstrance when George Brent had threatened to double the quit rents of those who were slow to recognize the new Proprietors.[266] After Carter became the representative and not the antagonist of the proprietary,[267] he showed diligence in its interest—and to his own profit. He quickly increased the number of those who followed the example of Richard Lee in settling for past-due quit rents. Deputies promptly collected current accounts. More and more grants were issued in the western, unoccupied parts of the Northern Neck. Carter did not deny himself what he granted others. Soon after he became agent, he had two friends patent about 13,500 acres, which were transferred to him. In 1709 he "took up" 912 acres of choice land on the Occoquan in the name of a three-year-old son.[268]

In the opening of these fine lands Carter began a long and famous controversy over boundaries. To recapitulate, the original grant of the Northern Neck described the confines of the proprietary as "the heads of the Rivers of Tappahanocke als Rappahanock and Quiriough or Patawomecke River, the courses of the said rivers as they are commonly called and known by the inhabitants, and all the islands withe the banks of those rivers." [269] This language was repeated in the patent of 1669, but, it will be recalled,[270] there was different phrasing in the grant of 1688, which was issued when Lord Culpeper had become the sole Proprietor. Some steward of King James II negligently or by persuasion changed the western boundaries to "the first heads or springs."

At the time the first patent was issued in 1649, the "heads" of the rivers did not call for exact demarcation. There was land enough and to spare between the long tidal stretches of the Potomac and the Rappahannock. Two genera-

[265] *Ibid.*, 102. Perry's influence was resented by Governor Alexander Spotswood. In 1714, apropos of the appointment of a member of the Council of Virginia through the influence of Perry, the Governor wrote: ". . . it is doing little honour to the Government to have its Council appointed in the Virginia Coffee House, and I believe a Governor who has a power under the Great Seal . . . is as capable of judging of the qualifications requisite for persons in that post as an merchant in London who has no other rule to judge of a man's merit than by the number of his tobacco hogsheads" (2 *Spotswood's Letters*, 79). For Robert Carter's power of attorney, granted Apr. 28, 1702, see 3 *Westmoreland Deeds and Wills*, 95–97.

[266] See *supra*, p. 487.

[267] His first grant is dated June 2, 1703 (*L.O. Records, N.N.*, 3); his last, Aug. 7, 1712 (*ibid.*, 4).

[268] *Landmarks*, 198.

[269] British Mus., Additional Charter, 13,585.

[270] See *supra*, p. 481.

tions later, settlement had extended upstream. On the Potomac, no issue had yet been shaped, but the southern boundaries of the proprietary were disputed. About ten miles above the falls of the Rappahannock near Fredericksburg, two streams joined in what became known as the "forks of the Rappahannock." One of these streams, later called the Rapidan, extended westward and northwestward about sixty miles toward the mountains subsequently renowned as the Blue Ridge. The other, or northern branch on its lower stretches was styled the Rappahannock and, upstream, was known as the Hedgeman River. Although the length and source of these two watercourses had not been determined in 1706, the northern stream manifestly had its sources much closer to the Potomac than did the southern fork. If, therefore, the northern fork was the one from the "head" of which the patent extended to the Potomac, the proprietary would be perceptibly smaller—none knew precisely how much smaller—than if the "head" of the southern fork was the limit. Actually, as later maps were to show, the difference was approximately 900 square miles, or 576,000 acres, nearly the area of the three present Counties of Culpeper, Madison and Rappahannock.[271] Much of this was excellent land.

In issuing grants in the region of the "forks of the Rappahannock," the Governor and Council assumed that the Rapidan was no more than a creek and that the upper Rappahannock was the stream the source of which fixed the southern limits of the proprietary. According to this view, land between the "forks" was royal domain, to be assigned on the usual terms. In 1706, a grant of 4,000 acres in that area was brought before the Virginia Council for ratification. Carter challenged it. He insisted that the grant of the Proprietors covered "all the lands bounded by and within the first heads or springs" of the Rappahannock and Potomac, and that the land within the forks belonged to the Proprietors. Later it was asserted that confusion had arisen because, at the time of the original grant, the existence of the lower fork was not known.[272]

The Council did not attempt to deny these contentions without seeking to determine the facts by actual examination. It ordered "the breadth and courses of the said branches measured," to determine which was the larger. In event the difference was so slight that a conclusion was impossible, the controversy was to be referred to Queen Anne. Meantime, no patent of land within the forks was to issue either from the Crown or from the Proprietors.[273] Inspection accordingly was made in the late summer by a joint

[271] The actual area of the three Counties is 982 square miles. Deduction of 82 square miles for the districts not within the river boundaries is a rough basis of estimate. Half a million acres is a fair round figure. For later estimates of the area of the proprietary within the different boundaries, see the report of the commissioners, quoted in 28 V 315–16. See, also, *infra*, p. 507.

[272] Edward Jenings to the Lords of Trade, June 24, 1708; P.R.O., C.O., 5, 1316, p. 20, LC Trans.

[273] 3 E. J., 85–86; Jenings to the Lords of Trade, *loc. cit.*

board of eight men with a surveyor in attendance. Unanimous judgment was that the streams seemed of equal magnitude. Carter and the Proprietors gained a point in the testimony of one of the members of the board that "by report of the Indians the southern branch is reputed the main stream." [274] This evidence the Council of Virginia admitted to the record, but there the issue rested.[275] The Lords of Trade took no part in this controversy except to notify the Governor, under date of Mch. 26, 1707, to be "very watchful that H. M. lands be not invaded under any pretence of a grant to any Proprietor." [276] Under this authorization, which he may have misinterpreted, Gov. Alexander Spotswood began in 1710 [277] to renew the grant of land within the disputed region.[278] In the absence of instructions from the Proprietors, Robert Carter could do nothing.

For that matter, Carter might have complained during the early stages of this contest that he had received no encouragement from Fairfax. The Proprietor spent what Carter forwarded through the London office, but Fairfax scarcely kept any accounts. Like most of the earlier patentees, he put no adequate valuation on property he never had seen. In 1708, when Carter had been agent less than five years, a change of attitude occurred. Fairfax became interested in a proposal to trade the Northern Neck for an hereditary office in Derbyshire,[279] and before making the exchange, he had the common sense to ascertain and to compare the return from the two. He found that he had received no less than £684 that year from Carter as the revenue of the Northern Neck. Promptly and positively, Fairfax broke off negotiations [280] for the exchange.

Doubtless the Proprietor would have looked thereafter with larger interest to Virginia, but his books were being closed. In December, 1709, oppressed by debt, he came to London to see if he could find relief. He must have discovered, instead, that his creditors intended to arrest him. His attendants consequently took him to a hiding place where, on Jan. 5, 1710, he died.[281] Inheritance of the great military name had made him useful to William III, who had conferred on him in 1701 the rank of Brigadier General. In other respects, the life of Fairfax had been martial only in a losing battle with extravagance and debt. He never saw Virginia.

Before the tangled affairs of the fifth Lord could be set down on a balance sheet, another change in the ownership of the proprietary occurred: In May,

274 Jenings to the Lords of Trade, *loc. cit.*
275 3 *E. J.,* Oct. 17, 1706, p. 130–31.
276 Gooch to the Lords of Trade, June 29, 1729; 1 *Gooch MSS,* 119–20.
277 He took the oath June 23, 1710; *ibid.,* 247.
278 Robert Carter to William Cage, July 26, 1723, *Carter Transcripts.*
279 Mentioned as the "lott and cope and office of berg-master in the wapentake of Wicksworth," which, translated from the interesting localisms of Derbyshire, means "the mining taxes assigned to the administrator of the hundred of Wicksworth."
280 *Dabney Papers,* VHS, MSS, v. 83, No. 32.
281 34 *V* 31; R. Clayton to Lady Fairfax, 4 *Fairfax Correspondence,* 241.

1710, Margaret, Lady Culpeper, the Dowager Baroness of Thoresway, reached the stumbling end of her seventy-five years.[282] From her husband, Thomas, second Lord Culpeper, she had received much woe and little wealth, but it will be remembered that under the will of her husband's cousin, Alexander Culpeper, she was bequeathed in fee a sixth interest in the proprietary.[283] This she left to her grandson, Thomas Fairfax, who had become sixth Lord on the death of his father.[284] The new Lord Fairfax had, by his own admission, nothing beyond this,[285] and, as he was then only sixteen, he required guardians at law.[286]

Control of the Northern Neck, therefore, was in the keeping of the owner of the five-sixths interest, his mother, Lady Fairfax, née Catherine Culpeper, widow of the fifth Lord. She, like most of the earlier Proprietors, was in chronic financial distress. Almost two years after her husband's death she had to write her son from Leeds Castle: "I have done all I can in business in London now; but it is very bad. Your father hath destroyed all that can be for you and me both; but I will do all that is in my power to get something again, and I do hope you will deserve it of me in time." [287]

As often is the fate of widows, Lady Fairfax had friends who believed new men and new methods would assure larger income for her. Even before Lady Culpeper's death, Lady Fairfax's agent, R. Clayton, had affirmed that the Proprietors were poorly served in London and in Virginia. Confidently he wrote: "That Mr. [Micajah] Perry is a sharp man, and I fear you are but very indifferently dealt with by him and his friend [Robert Carter] in Virginia, and if I don't help you to a chapman for it [288] (which you will soon hear further from me about), I doubt not of putting your Ladyship and your lady mother in a way to make more of it yearly than hath been made since Mr. Perry and his friend's management thereof." [289] This was argument of a sort that appealed to the financially embarrased Lady Fairfax. Notice was given Robert Carter that he no longer was needed.

At the instance of Clayton and on the recommendation of Thomas Corbin,[290] who was a Virginia agent in London, Lady Fairfax approved a major change in the management of the proprietary. In the place of an

---

[282] She was born Jan. 12, 1635. See 33 V 261–62.

[283] See *supra*, p. 486.

[284] For her will, see 33 V 262.

[285] Cf. his letter of July 7, 1710, quoted in 34 V 60: "All I have during my mother's life is what my grandmother Colpeper left me."

[286] These were Admiral Robert Fairfax and Bryan Fairfax the younger; 34 V 60.

[287] Letter of Dec. 15, 1711, 4 *Fairfax Correspondence*, 243.

[288] This is an interesting use of the word "chapman." Conceivably, Clayton meant "broker," which was a contemporary definition of "chapman"; but the context suggests that he meant "purchaser" or "lessee," a definition of "chapman" not frequent before the end of the eighteenth century.

[289] Letter of Feb. 23, 1710, 4 *Fairfax Correspondence*, 241.

[290] In *Landmarks*, 153, Fairfax Harrison suggested the possibility that Philip Ludwell, also, might have had a hand in the appointment.

agency, she effected a lease of the proprietary to Edmund Jenings for a term of years, on a basic payment of about £425 per annum.[291] Other provision must have been made for patent fees, or escheats, or delinquent quit rents. Had this not been so, Lady Fairfax scarcely would have accepted £425 for property that had been yielding her husband £684 yearly at the time of his death.

Whatever these details, Corbin's counsel was not devoid of self-interest. Jenings was his brother-in-law. In addition, Corbin had his nephew, Thomas Lee, made Jening's deputy.[292] Lee, then twenty-one years of age, was full of promise and was destined for a large career.[293] Jenings, who possessed more of reputation than of vigor, had been born in 1659, had been Attorney General of Virginia at twenty-five, and later had served for years as a member of the Council. In 1706–10, he had acted as Governor and had the prestige of that position when he went to England. He was residing there when, in 1711 [294] or 1712, he was named agent for the proprietary.[295] The appointment was not in every respect as advantageous to the lessee as it appeared to be, because Jenings was burdened by debt and ill health and, in addition, had to face the persistent hostility of Micajah Perry and of Robert Carter, both of whom were offended at the change of agents.[296] Perry, it appears, was a heavy creditor of Jenings; [297] Carter was at the time a mem-

[291] It has not been thought that Jenings was a lessee, but in letters of Feb. 24, and July 5, 1720, Robert Carter specifically mentioned the lease, and in a communication of June 30, 1724, he sought to reduce by "odd £20" his payment, because it exceeded by that amount the sum Jenings had paid (*Letters*, 113). It is known that Carter's offer for his first lease was £450 yearly. See *Va. Land Grants*, 102. For the agency of Jenings and the resulting struggle with Carter, see Maurer Maurer, "Edmund Jenings and Robert Carter," 55 *V* 20 ff.

[292] *Va. Land Grants*, 99 ff. Fairfax Harrison was of opinion that Lee was named deputy in appreciation of the fact that Thomas Lee's father, Richard, as noted *supra*, p. 488, had been the first early landowner of the Northern Neck to make composition for quit rents. The probability is equally strong that the Corbin connection, rather than the father's service, was responsible for Thomas Lee's appointment. For Thomas Lee's power of attorney, dated Dec. 11, 1711, "rec[orde]d, Sept. 16, 1712," see 5 *Westmoreland Deeds*, 56.

[293] This remarkable man, one of the greatest of Virginia colonials, is known in the genealogy of the family as "President" Thomas Lee. His mother was Laetitia Corbin. For a sketch, see *Lee of Virginia*, 103 ff.

[294] In *Landmarks*, 146, Fairfax Harrison noted that Thomas Lee's power of attorney bore date of Dec. 11, 1711, though he did not begin to sign grants until Sept. 1, 1713. If Jenings was named lessee and agent at the same date in 1711, he was then in Virginia, as the Journals of the Council show. There appears to be no certainty regarding the date of Edmund Jenings's return to England. Harrison ascertained (*Landmarks*, 152) that in 1713 the Privy Council was informed that Jenings was residing in England "to recover his health and settle his private affairs" and that he did not intend to go back to Virginia. The last entry of a Council meeting attended by him bears date of July 21, 1712. See 3 *E. J.*, 317.

[295] Few names occur with greater frequency in the records of Virginia at the end of the seventeenth century. Much useful material concerning him appears in an article by Maurer Maurer, "Notes on the Honorable Edmund Jenings," 52 *V* 249 ff.

[296] *Landmarks*, 152. Lee had anticipated this. Writing Lady Fairfax he said: "I cannot tell you whether Col. Carter will believe that sufficient proof to enable me to discharge him on account of your Ladyship when he has paid the money due, but this is a business that I shall hardly transact until I have more particular instructions from your Ladyship" (copy in back of *Account Book* of sixth Lord Fairfax; LC).

[297] *Ibid.*

ber of the Council of Virginia and had large influence. So long as Jenings, in England, undertook to manage the proprietary, Perry could harass him there while Carter made trouble for him in Virginia.

In spite of all this, during the time Thomas Lee was deputy and acting agent in Virginia, Lady Fairfax was well served. Lee had an interest in topography and a zest for accuracy. Where earlier agents had been content to describe in the text of a grant the lets and bounds, Thomas Lee inserted the surveyor's plat in the Land Books and by so doing clarified records that might otherwise have become confused beyond comprehension. In addition, young Lee had both his curiosity and his imagination fired by the little-known inland reaches of the proprietary. He went on tours of observation up the beautiful Potomac and through the "back country." Increasingly, too, he issued grants for lands in the western parts of the older Counties of the Northern Neck.[298] Lee was encouraging the settlement of the frontier when, in the winter of 1715–16, Jenings came back to Virginia [299] and undertook the direct administration of the proprietary. To young Thomas Lee was assigned nothing more than the office work. The assumption is that Jenings shouldered the heavier task in the hope of a larger return from the lease.[300] He was, in any event, most active, and during 1719 he issued no less than fifty patents. This was a larger total than had been signed in any previous year of the agency, with one exception.[301]

On May 31, 1719, Lady Fairfax, the former Catherine Culpeper, breathed her last.[302] Her passing brought about the fourth partial change of ownership in a little more than nine years. Thomas, sixth Lord Fairfax, became the sole Proprietor of the Northern Neck, but his mother, for some reason, had been unwilling to vest in him anything more than a life interest in her five-sixths of the property. She named trustees for the payment of the specific bequests she made, and she elaborately entailed the lands.[303] Fairfax, then twenty-six years of age, resented this, but at the outset he was little interested in the Virginia property. He left the direction of it to William Cage, the trustee named by his mother, and he devoted his own energies to attempting to make for himself a public career.

As trustee, Cage soon ascertained, if he did not already know, that Jenings was delinquent in payment on the lease, which then was expiring.[304] Con-

[298] Va. Land Grants, 99; Landmarks, 143 ff.

[299] He took the oath as a member of the Council Feb. 22, 1715/16. See 3 E. J., 421. Thereafter his name is entered as that of senior Councillor. In December, 1715, he was elected Lieutenant of York County, which would indicate that he had returned or intended soon to do so (ibid., 419).   [300] Va. Land Grants, 100.

[301] Year by year, the grants during this agency and lease were as follows: 1713, grants 2; 1714, grants 12; 1715, grants 88; 1716, grants 26; 1717, grants 39; 1718, grants 14; 1719, grants 50; 1720, grants 1.

[302] She probably was forty-nine years of age. 34 V 21, 27.

[303] Her will is in ibid., 27.

[304] See letter of Robert Carter, Feb. 13, 1721; Carter Letters, 69.

sequently, Cage decided to change representatives and, for counsel, turned to Micajah Perry, who suggested that Robert Carter again be engaged. This proving agreeable both to Carter and to Cage, a lease, probably for five years, was negotiated at £450 per annum, with the proviso that Carter was to undertake the collection of the money due the Proprietor by Jenings.[305]

This lease opened the second agency of Carter, which covered perhaps the most important years in the entire life of the proprietary.[306] In experienced knowledge of what the last patent gave the Proprietors, Carter insisted not only that quit rents be forthcoming but also that felons' goods and deodands [307] be delivered him as lessee.[308] The claim against Jenings was prosecuted by Carter with a zeal the debtor may have considered spiteful.[309]

Larger matters were handled in larger spirit. Carter believed, in particular, that failure to make an adequate survey of the Brent Town grant [310] was delaying settlement in Stafford County, which was a part of the proprietary. Although Mrs. Brent and the residents of the tract threatened to waylay the Surveyor, Carter had the lines drawn so swiftly and so quietly that the work was done before the inhabitants knew of it. "Now," he reported to Cage, "I cannot conclude this private survey will be binding either to you or to the Proprietors of the Brenton grant; however, it will have this good effect: to lay open a large quantity of back land toward the mountains that people have been hitherto afraid to meddle with, being kept in awe by that grant." [311]

As a second large service to the Proprietor, Carter renewed the dispute over the boundaries of the Northern Neck.[312] In doing so, he had to cope with so much apparent indifference on Fairfax's part that he later complained to Perry: ". . . I never had one line from the Proprietors about this matter, and if they do not think fit to bestir themselves in support of their own estate I shall have little reason to give myself any trouble in throwing myself into the frown of Governors. As their trustee I have done my duty in hanging out the light for them." [313] Carter did not mention a circumstance sub-

305 As no copy of the lease is known to be in existence, its terms have to be reconstructed from references in Carter's letters, which are not always explicit. From the accounts of Edmund Jenings, it is evident that his agency terminated Sept. 29, 1719 (*Carter Letters*, 131). As Carter himself was negotiating a new lease in June, 1724, the two dates would suggest that his first lease was for five years (*ibid.*, 113).

306 On the basis of land grants bearing Carter's name, Fairfax Harrison dated this second agency from 1722, but Carter's letter of Jan. 27, 1721 (*Letters*, 63), mentioned the fact that he had received his lease some months previously.

307 That is, personal chattels forfeited to the Crown because they had been responsible for the death of some person. P.R.O., C.O. 5, 1344, Apr. 20, 1726.

308 Letters of July 4, 22, 1723, to William Cage—Carter Transcripts; Gooch to Lords of Trade, July 23, 1730; 1 Gooch MSS, p. 174.

309 Letters of July 4, 1723, *Carter Letters*, 111; July 9, 1724, *ibid.*, 114.

310 Carter styled it Brenton. For its establishment, see *supra*, p. 485.

311 Letter of July 9, 1724, to William Cage, *Carter Letters*, 115.

312 See *supra*, p. 489.

313 Letter of July 26, 1723, *Carter Transcripts*.

sequently urged against him—that he had insured himself doubly and would gain personally no matter who lost. Besides taking out large patents for lands of the proprietary, he had procured grants from the Crown for tracts within the "forks of the Rappahannock," a district which he continued to claim for the Proprietor.[314]

However the ethics of that might be adjudged, there was no denying the value of Carter's third major labor, which was that of seating small farmers on the frontier. He had much to do in providing tracts for Scotch-Irish who had come to Virginia as indentured servants and, in 1723–25, were completing their "time." [315] New controversies there were, too, over the disposition of fines and the property of felons,[316] controversies that Carter faced with resolute mind and stern hand.

In 1724, a new lease of the property had to be negotiated. Carter proceeded to this task with much bargaining and with protests that he was not getting from the property as much as he was paying for it.[317] On the strength of this assertion, he possibly got a reduction of about £30 a year in the rent he paid,[318] "very hard terms" he styled them.[319] While Carter doubtless felt this and told the truth about the lack of profit on the lease, he must have entered a heavy charge for his own services.[320] During his first agency, he had followed in moderate measure the example of Brent and Fitzhugh in taking out grants for desirable lands within the proprietary. As early as 1709, it will be remembered, Carter had patented more than 14,000 acres.[321] Now, in 1723, he had in his lease a clause that permitted him specifically to grant unpatented land [322] and on this basis he embarked on more extensive land speculations to any persons—a term that of course included his family.

These were facilitated by the Treaty of Albany. The promise made in 1722 under that agreement by the Five Nations, it will be remembered,[323] was that they would not come South of the Potomac nor East of the "great ridge of mountains" without the consent of the Governor of Virginia. In return, Spotswood promised that the Virginia Indians would not invade the "Long House" of the Iroquois League. Although this treaty left in doubt whether the Blue Ridge or the Alleghenies fixed the line, the Albany agree-

---

[314] See *infra*, p. 490–91.   [315] See *Landmarks*, 232 ff.

[316] *Carter Letters*, 116, 120, 121; *Transcripts*, Letter of July 23, 1723.

[317] Carter insisted, Aug. 1, 1721 (*Letters*, 108), that he had not made more than £100 from the agency in 1720.

[318] From £450 to £420 per annum (*ibid.*, 113, 123, and *Va. Land Grants*, 100, 102), though Gooch stated in 1730 that Carter paid £450 a year (*Gooch MSS*, 174). See *infra*, p. 501.

[319] Letter of July 19, 1725, *Carter Letters*, 119. The duration of the lease is not certain. During the negotiations, Carter spoke of seven, eight and ten years as the term (*ibid.*, 113, 116).

[320] See *infra*, p. 498, for Governor Gooch's estimate in 1730 of Carter's actual profit from the lease.

[321] *Landmarks*, 198, and *supra*, p. 489.

[322] Cf. John, Charles and Landon Carter to Alderman Perry, [no month] 10, 1736. ". . . let me have a lease . . . with the same power of granting unpatented lands that my father had . . ." (*Carter-Plummer MSS*, 9).

[323] See *supra*, p. 13. All the essential facts and the basic references are summarized in *Landmarks*, 86 ff, and in many familiar reference works.

ment gave to the frontier a partial security of which Carter eagerly availed himself. In the Brent Town tract and in a settlement that Governor Spotswood was attempting on the Rapidan River, Carter saw possibilities that appealed to his business sense and no less to his imagination. He reasoned that by the exercise of good judgment, he could patent lands ahead of the migration, and that he either could establish the Virginia equivalent of English manors [324] for his children, or else, at a profit, could transfer the lands in small tracts to adventurous settlers.

Carter was neither precipitate nor dilatory. He waited until he thought the treaty was as firm as an Indian agreement ever was, and then, in 1724, he took out grants of 89,937 acres. Thereafter, as he saw good land, located along the line of pioneers' advance, he granted it, in the Proprietor's name, to his children or to his own representatives.[325] The total of these grants during Carter's second agency was about 200,000 acres [326] in an aggregate of approximately 1,310,000 acres to all applicants and on all accounts.[327] From inheritance of so vast a personal estate, with lands on all the rivers and at many a future crossroads and town site, there was a prospect of continued economic advantage and of further enrichment, even, for Robert Carter's children and grandchildren.

During 1724, Carter perhaps felt that he might come under criticism for these grants or on some other account,[328] but in his extant letters, the sole explanation of the magnitude of his acquisition of land is an indirect one: "I have . . . often inculcated to you," he wrote Perry, "the meanest of the plans, how much the lands were overstocked with slaves, how impossible it was to make tolerable crops with them and how absolutely necessary it was to find more lands for the better half of these slaves . . ." [329] In self-protection he sought to procure broad powers of attorney from Fairfax [330] and he doubtless found reassurance—if ever he admitted the need of it—in the reflection that the practice of patenting thousands of acres to be subdivided into small holdings was defended by others besides himself. Governor Gooch summed up the argument for vast grants when he wrote the Lords of Trade in 1729: "Without taking up these large tracts upon which great improvements were necessary to be made, these counties would not have been settled so speedily as they have been, and much of that land which has been seated in small parcels would in all probability have remained to this day desolate . . ." [331]

[324] For the distinction, see the admirable note in *Landmarks*, 249.
[325] *Landmarks*, 241 ff, and particularly n. 7, p. 251.
[326] *Ibid.*, 241–45. The present writer's recheck of the *Land Office Records* puts the figures for all Carter grants after 1703 at 186,674, but it is entirely probable that some grants to agents of Carter were not identified as "Carter lands."
[327] Computed from the *Land Office Records*.
[328] Cf. his letter of Oct. 6, 1724, to William Cage, *Carter Letters*, 116.
[329] *Carter Transcripts*, letter of Apr. 15, 1729.
[330] *Carter Letters*, 61, 64.
[331] To the Lords of Trade, November 8; quoted in *Landmarks*, 242.

Sound or unwise, this policy of developing "manors" probably aroused new antagonism to the proprietorship and sharpened the dispute over the geographical limits of the Fairfax Grant. The first issue was the old one of the "forks of the Rappahannock." On Carter's petition for a determination of the "great or main stream," the Council of Virginia resolved to send a full statement of the case to the Lords Commissioners for Trade and Plantations. Pending a decision, the Governor was to continue free to make grants within the "forks." [332] Carter had to content himself with entering a caveat in each case. This was in June, 1729,[333] at a time the General Assembly was not in session. When it met the next year, it displayed vigorously the resentment Virginians increasingly felt over the rights Carter was asserting in the name of the Proprietors. On the appeal of citizens of Westmoreland County, the General Assembly approved a paper which was, in effect, a protest against substantially all the terms of the proprietorship—quit rents, manorial authority, boundaries and titles. In respect to certain fines and forfeitures in the Northern Neck, the Burgesses said: "We humbly hope that this part of the grant is illegal as it is destructive of [the Colony's] rights and privileges." The King was petitioned to take such action as would "relieve your subjects whose estates lie within the said territory against the exorbitant and unwarrantable powers contained" in the final grant of the Northern Neck. A suggested alternative was the familiar one of royal purchase of the grant.[334]

This petition Governor Gooch supplemented with a letter in which he contended that the "heads" of the rivers, as set forth in the original patents, were the "heads of navigation," that is, the falls of the Rappahannock and the Potomac. He submitted, too, that the purchase of the proprietary might be a good investment for the Crown. Carter, said the Governor, was supposed to pay £450 annually to Fairfax and to receive £700.[335]

Within the fortnight that witnessed the adoption of the appeal by the General Assembly, still more serious controversy arose over the boundaries of the Northern Neck. Several bold settlers of German and Swiss origin, then living in New York and West Jersey, undertook to procure grants of 50,000 acres of land in the Shenandoah Valley. The Council agreed with the sole proviso that the grants be in proportion to the number of families seated there in two years.[336] A similar order for 100,000 acres was issued in October, 1730, for 100 families from Pennsylvania.[337] In all these cases, Carter

---

[332] For the Governor's previous decision to issue such grants, see *supra*, p. 491.

[333] 4 *E. J.*, 205, 206.

[334] *Journ. H. B.*, 1730, 93 ff. Cf. *ibid.*, 82, 83.

[335] 1 *Gooch MSS*, 174, July 23, 1730. Cf. *ibid.*, 121-22, June 29, 1729; 28 *V* 301 ff. Doubtless by "receive" Gooch meant "collect," which would indicate a profit, or a personal compensation, of £250 per annum.   [336] 4 *E. J.*, 223-24.

[337] *Ibid.*, 229. All these settlements are described in Kercheval, *History of the Valley*, 48-59. In 16 *L.O. Surveys*, 276, 306, 307, 310, 311, 312, 314, 318, 322, 324, 329, 330, 342, are records of tracts purchased by Jost Hite "of Isaac and John van Meter who had obtained orders in council from the Lieutenant Governor and the Council." For the van Meters, see *supra*, p. 220.

made his protest a matter of record: [338] The lands allotted these settlers, he said, were within the proprietary and could not be transferred by the Governor.

In taking this position, Carter was asserting, in effect, that the Potomac, as such, did not end at the point [339] where it received the waters of the Shenandoah.[340] Coupled with his contention over the limits of the southern river had its "first head or spring" beyond the mountains west of the Shenandoah.[340] Coupled with his contention over the limits of the southern boundary, this assertion of title to the upper Potomac, if sustained, would extend the area of the proprietary to a total of 5,282,000 acres as compared with the 1,476,000 acres included within the limits the Colony conceded, namely, from the forks of the Rappahannock to the mouth of the Shenandoah.[341]

Carter stated the issue and prepared for the contest, but he did not wage the final battle. On Aug. 4, 1732, he died at Corotoman, his home estate in Lancaster County. His friends lamented; his enemies did not withhold their last, harsh judgment. Governor Francis Nicholson long previously had denounced Carter for "his extraordinary pride and ambition," his "covetousness and cowardice," his "haughtiness and insolence." [342] All this was revived no doubt in the year of George Washington's birth and of Robert Carter's death, but the descendants of "King" Carter were a refutation of calumny. Robert E. Lee, the two Presidents Harrison of the United States, six Governors of Virginia and a vast company of able men and women had Carter's blood in their veins. It is doubtful if any American was blessed with progeny of more notable achievement.

At the time of Carter's death, talk was not of his daughters who were to bear eminent sons, but of his regal living, and of his ownership of unreckoned thousands of acres of land, and of slaves and goods in proportion.[343] Gossip in the Northern Neck perhaps exaggerated his wealth, but he was, in any event, the largest individual landowner of his time in Virginia and the most renowned exemplar of an economy, if it deserves the name, that did not perish with him. He became a mythical figure and he remained a land

[338] 4 E. J., 223.   [339] Now Harpers Ferry.

[340] This, needless to say, was the substance and not the exact language of Carter's contention. His argument was well summarized in a letter from Governor Gooch to the Lords of Trade, July 10, 1731 (*Gooch MSS*, 241 ff). Cf. same to same, Feb. 18, 1733; 2 *ibid.*, 321 ff.

[341] Report of Commissioners, 28 V 315–16. This maximum figure exceeds by more than 1,000,000 acres the area as shown on modern maps.

[342] Memorandum, presumably of 1705, in 8 V 56.

[343] In *Gentleman's Magazine*, v. 2, November 1732, p. 1082, he was credited with the ownership of 300,000 acres but for a more realistic estimate, see *supra*, p. 14. His will and an inventory of his personal effects appear in 5 V 408–28; 6 *ibid.*, 1–22, 145–52, 260–68. In 32 *ibid.*, 18–22, is a long note by W. G. Stanard on Carter. An analysis of Carter's library, with many useful references to the man himself, appears in *Wright*, 248–85. Much information concerning the Carters will be found in T. A. Glenn, *Some Colonial Mansions*, 1st ser., 217–60, though much material has come to light since the publication of that work in 1898.

speculator's ideal. Robert Carter's opportunities of increasing his fortune arose, in large part, from his advantageous position as agent for the proprietary, but all his gobbling up of desirable lands did not cancel or even diminish perceptibly the service he rendered the Fairfaxes. One of the most distinguished of their line spoke by the record when he said: "Any reader of the council minutes (not to speak of Col. Carter's own letters) between 1723 and 1732 can testify that it was to Carter's prudent caveats and alert interest that Fairfax owed the ultimate prevalence of his claims in his litigation with the Virginia government." [344]

In criticism of Carter's management, and of the entire period of the leases, it could be said, first, that the accepted policy might do more to perpetuate a landed class than to settle the frontier. If the professed aim of the speculators was realized in the ultimate subdivision of large holdings into small farms, leased on fair terms, the promoters of the "manors" would earn the profit of the middleman. Should the speculators demand too much for their lands or find pride and position in the ownership of unoccupied fields and forests, then settlement might be delayed. Immigration, especially the new movement from Pennsylvania, might be diverted westward. Time would be the arbiter between these two possible trends. One view was as tenable as the other in 1732.

More positive was the effect of the agents' policy in arraying the proprietary against the colonial government. From the time of the brief Hooke lease of 1662–64, every assertion by the Proprietors of extended or enlarged "rights" had aroused the Burgesses,[345] but usually the lawmakers who petitioned the King to recover the Northern Neck were men whose economic interest and class sympathy was with the holders of large estates acquired under the patent of Culpeper or of Fairfax. A different situation was created when Carter asserted, in the Proprietor's name, a title to a considerable part of the royal domain, a region in which many future plantations were directly on the line of easiest settlement and least arduous communication. This claim to the farthest headwaters of the Rapidan and of the Potomac placed in opposition to Fairfax even those members of the Council who supported the view that large grants facilitated settlement. Although the issue was not so stated at the time of Carter's death, events were shaping themselves toward a contest between the speculators who wished to develop the royal domain and those who sought to do the same thing within the proprietary.

Carter's sons did not know whether he held a lease of the proprietary at the end of his life.[346] They collected and remitted what was due and they

---

[344] Fairfax Harrison in *Landmarks*, 254.

[345] Cf. the general conclusions, *infra*. p. 512.

[346] See John, Landon and Charles Carter to Alderman Perry, Aug. 27, 1732: ". . . we shall refer you to the Secretary [John Carter], to whom my father has bequeathed the lease in case one is subsisting" (*Carter-Plummer MSS*, p. 57). The natural supposition, of course, is

made some halfhearted proposals for a new agreement at £500 per annum and the right to grant unpatented lands;[347] but their indifference and the state of the dispute over the boundary at last compelled Lord Fairfax to take a hand in the administration of his Virginia domain. It was time he was bestirring himself to make a success of a frustrated life. He had been embittered toward both his mother and his grandmother, according to tradition, because he had thought they had treated him unjustly in the handling of his estate.[348] With no other career open to him, he procured a commission in the army. In politics a Whig, he found more or less of a welcome at the court of George I, where he was made Treasurer of the Household, on the staff of the Lord Chamberlain.

The next stage was a humiliating misadventure, which Archdeacon Burnaby thus recorded: "Early in life [Fairfax] had formed an attachment to a young lady of quality; and matters had proceeded so far as to induce him to provide carriages, clothes, servants and other necessary appendages for such an occasion. Unfortunately, or rather let me say fortunately, before the contract was sealed a more advantageous or dazzling offer was made to the Lady who thought herself at liberty to accept it; and she preferred the higher honor of being a Duchess to the inferior station of a Baroness. The disappointment is thought to have made a deep impression on Lord F[airfax]'s mind . . ."[349] Either this or the loss of his office on the triumph of Sir Robert Walpole caused young Fairfax to retire to Leeds Castle. There he was living quietly when word reached him that Robert Carter was dead and that the western boundaries of his proprietary were being challenged by the government of Virginia.[350]

The first moves of Lord Fairfax were wise. He evidently became alarmed over the size of the "manors" that were being carved from the proprietary,

---

that Robert Carter's lease expired in 1732. This fits into what is known concerning the duration of the lease Carter renewed in 1724. He spoke then of seven, eight, or ten years' renewal. See *supra*, p. 496. In his will (6 *V* 2), Carter bequeathed the lease of the proprietary to John, but the will was drawn in 1726 (*ibid.*, 7), when the lease had some years to run.

[347] John, Landon and Charles Carter to Alderman Perry, Aug. 1, 1733, and n.m. 10, 1736; *Carter-Plummer MSS*, 9, 78. For their own payments of quit rents, see *ibid.*, 10, 18, 20, 45. In the letter of Aug. 1, 1733, the Carter brothers made this most interesting reference to the payment of Northern Neck quit rents: "The profits arising from the quit rents of the Northern Neck are upon a precarious foot. The tenants by their leases are to pay a shilling stirling for every fifty acres, but by custom, or I know not by what rule, they are like to discharge this in tobacco at the rate of 1*d* a pound. When tobacco is worth little or nothing there is not any money to be got; when it bears a price, then they will pay money and no tobacco is to be had. But as it does not advance in price but upon a very short crop, the poorer sort, who have but little tobacco or money must have time given them till again it becomes worth nothing."

[348] This is the story set forth by Archdeacon Andrew Burnaby. As noted *supra*, p. 494. Fairfax Harrison in 34 *V* 58 ff disproved most of the allegations of Burnaby, but it is not improbable that the Archdeacon was correct in saying that the sixth Lord was alienated from his mother and from Lady Culpeper.

[349] Burnaby, *loc. cit.*

[350] Most of these facts are paraphrased from Fairfax Harrison's article in 34 *V* 35-36. See also *Journ. Trade and Plant.*, 1729-34, p. 256, 368; LC trans.

and he stopped the grant of lands as soon as he could.[351] For the further protection of his interests, he contrived to have his cousin William Fairfax transferred from Massachusetts to the South Potomac, as Collector of Customs, in order that this trusted kinsman might serve also as agent for the proprietary.[352] William Fairfax, who appears many times in these pages, was forty-three years of age in 1734 and was the second son of Lord Fairfax's uncle Henry, brother of the fifth Lord.[353] A man of no shining abilities, William Fairfax was kindly, diligent, conscientious, politically experienced, and content to be his cousin's agent, not his rival, though he, like Fitzhugh, Brent and Robert Carter, was to face the lure of large purchases of land.

As soon as Lord Fairfax secured himself in this manner against the swift dissipation of his domain, he petitioned the Privy Council to determine the limits of the proprietary and, meantime, to order the Governor of Virginia to cease issuing land grants within the disputed areas.[354] This petition was referred to the Lords of Trade and, after examination and report, was approved.[355] On Nov. 29, 1733, the Privy Council directed the Lords Commissioners for Trade and Plantations to have the "marks and boundaries" of the proprietary "surveyed and settled" by a joint commission. Three to five members were to act for Lord Fairfax; a like number were to represent Virginia. These men were to complete their work within two years after these instructions were received in Virginia. During the period of the survey, the Governor was to withhold grants in the disputed areas.

Fairfax had been well advised in asking that a time limit be prescribed, because colonial authorities, learning from the home government, had made an art of procrastination. In this instance, by no means all the delay was on one side. Fairfax decided in the late winter of 1734–35 to go to Virginia and to ascertain for himself the state of his affairs and the prospect of winning the boundary case. Aboard a man-of-war, he arrived early in May, 1735,[356] and had warm welcome at the hands of Governor Gooch, but the Proprietor did not linger near the colonial capital. Instead, he proceeded to the Northern Neck, where William Fairfax already had established residence.[357] When at length the peer stepped from the skiff that brought him ashore, he probably was the first owner of the Northern Neck ever to set foot there, though the grant in one form or another had been in effect for almost two-thirds of a century.[358]

[351] Landmarks, 271–72.
[352] Ibid., 340; Va. Land Grants, 104; Burnaby, Appendix IV.
[353] Burnaby, loc. cit.; Landmarks, 340–41.   [354] 3 Acts Privy Council, Colonial, 385.
[355] Ibid., 386. Journ. Trade & Plant., 1729–34, p. 368. LC trans.
[356] Gooch's letter of Jan. 8, 1737, fixes the date, which usually has been put in 1736 (2 Gooch MSS, 462. Cf. Landmarks, 246).
[357] Cal. Treas. Papers, 1731–34, p. 524. As of Aug. 27, 1734, William Fairfax became Collector of the South Potomac, in loco Henry Moryson, deceased. See Westmoreland Orders, 1731–39, p. 148; see also supra, Chapter IV, p. 182.
[358] For Culpeper's probable glimpse of the Northern Neck in 1683, see supra, p. 476.

Riding around his cousin's abode, Fairfax was pleased with the beauty of the wide, silent rivers, with the abundance of game, and with the verdure of the far-spreading forests; but, as his knowledge of conditions was broadened, he became concerned over the manifest popular opposition to the proprietary. Apparently, also, the alarm that Fairfax had felt before leaving England assumed a new form. He took a pessimistic view of the former lessees' policy and he grew fearful that Robert Carter already had put the dead hand of inactive ownership on immense tracts of choice land.[359]

In ascertaining these facts and perhaps in adjusting himself to the heat of an unfamiliar climate, Fairfax passed six full months. Then, in the sparkling weather of early autumn, he went to Williamsburg and on the 14th or 15th of October [360] presented Gooch the text of the order in Council for the determination of the boundary line. In addition, Fairfax delivered to the Governor a letter from the Duke of Newcastle. "I must desire," Newcastle wrote, "you will do him what service you can . . . by preventing as much as may be any unnecessary difficulties or delays in the dispatch of [Fairfax's] business and by assisting him with your good offices whenever his Lordship shall have occasion for them." [361]

Gooch was much impressed by this letter, but the General Court was about to convene, and the approach of winter precluded any survey until 1736.[362] The most that Gooch thought possible at the time was to name on behalf of the Colony the commissioners to execute the order from England. On Dec. 10, 1735, three members of the Council—William Byrd II, John Robinson and John Grymes—were empowered to take depositions, to prepare maps and to make a report "in order to the final determination" of the boundaries "in such manner as His Majesty shall hereafter direct." [363] Fairfax was at that time Gooch's guest [364] and seemingly was content with this action. His attorney, Edward Barradall, went even further: he appeared before the Council and said that Lord Fairfax was "well satisfied of the candor and integrity" of the Councillors who had just been named and was willing to have them act for him also.[365] Although Governor Gooch believed Fairfax could gain little land West of the Blue Ridge through establishment of the

---

359 *Landmarks,* 247, and n. p. 254. Burnaby later thought that Fairfax believed Carter had "abused" the Proprietors' "confidence" and had "enriched himself and family . . . at the expense of his employer" (*op. cit.*). Fairfax Harrison concluded (*op. cit.*) that Fairfax's dissatisfaction sprang from the belief that where lands were taken up extensively, they were not apt to be developed soon or properly.

360 Gooch's letter of Nov. 5, 1735, and of Jan. 8, 1737, in 2 *Gooch MSS,* 416, 462.

361 Letter of Mch. 18, 1735; 2 *Gooch MSS,* 384. This Duke of Newcastle, a title much confused in the seventeenth and eighteenth centuries, was Thomas Pelham Holles, 1693-1768, Minister of State for thirty years.

362 All these details were explained to the Lords of Trade in Gooch's letter of Jan. 8, 1737 (2 *Gooch MSS,* 462 ff).   363 4 *E. J.,* 366.

364 Gooch's letter of Jan. 8, 1737, cited *supra.*

365 4 *E. J.,* 366. Barradall was Attorney General in 1737-43 and was a legal draftsman of some skill. Cf. *30* V 256 n. For a sketch, see 10 *W* (1) p. 34.

boundary,[366] he did not think the Proprietor should have the same commissioners, and he so informed Fairfax.[367] The peer gave no indication of a change of mind as a result of anything Gooch told him.[368] On the contrary, in April, 1736, Fairfax placed in Gooch's hands a memorial which apparently was in accordance with Barradall's previous statement.[369] Similar views were expressed in England by Fairfax's solicitor,[370] but neither in Virginia nor "at home" were written powers of attorney given to his own boundary commissioners by Fairfax. If remarked at all, this was not regarded as a serious omission in view of what he and Barradall had said. No action of any official sort seemed necessary until August, 1736, when the commissioners were completing their preparations to make the survey. Gooch then had counsel prepare for Fairfax's signature a promise to accept the commissioners' findings. Fairfax similarly was supplied with a copy of the instructions delivered to the men who were to supervise the determination of the boundary.

The papers arrived in Westmoreland on the 14th of August. Fairfax studied them and the next day wrote at length to Gooch. "If," said the Proprietor, "I should assent in the manner expressed, to have the Northern Neck which I claim, run out, marked and ascertained, immediately after the survey of the same by commissioners I should give up the benefit which I have always expected of having their said survey reported first to the Governor and to be by him transmitted home to His Majesty, for as the main dispute is concerned in the constructions of the words in the several grants, what is there meant and understood to be the first heads or springs of the two rivers Rappahannock and Potomac, it seems most equitable to have the same determined by His Majesty in Council, before whom the case may be fairly argued on both sides . . ." Fairfax went on to insist that "the affair is of too great consequence to have it ended here without reserving the liberty of appeal . . . I have all the just confidence in the honor and integrity of the commissioners appointed, but can't submit that they should finally determine till His Majesty's pleasure be further known." [371]

This letter was brought back to Williamsburg and was followed by Fairfax himself in September. In conference with him, the Governor passed over the fact that the Lord's insistence on the right of appeal was in accord with the first resolution of the Council, which had itself reserved to the Crown the "final determination" of the boundaries.[372] All Gooch's argument was directed to having Fairfax withdraw from his position and validate the assurance given by Barradall the previous December that the Proprietor

366 Gooch's letter of May 19, 1736 (2 *Gooch MSS*, 427).
367 Gooch's letter of Jan. 8, 1737 (2 *Gooch MSS*, 462 ff).
368 *Ibid.*, 2 *Gooch MSS*, 463.
369 2 *Wilmington Papers*, 112. LC trans.   370 *Ibid.*
371 1 *C* 226.   372 See *supra*, p. 498.

would accept the Virginia commissioners as his own. The Governor later reported: "When I reasoned with His Lordship upon this surprising change he told me notwithstanding what had been done in England by his solicitor, of which His Lordship declared himself ignorant, though I put his Lordship in mind of the memorial to me . . . he absolutely refused giving any other authority." [373] He would consent only, Fairfax said, to a survey and report. Gooch, of course, had no alternative to laying this statement before the Virginia Council. That body voted promptly to sign the instructions of the men who, it carefully stipulated, were to act as "His Majesty's commissioners." The implication was that they were not merely the representatives of the Colony. These gentlemen were directed to ascertain "in what manner his Lordship proposes to have his boundaries settled conformable to the said order of His Majesty in his Privy Council." [374]

Fairfax's reply this time was that he would accept the commissioners of the Virginia Council and would agree to have them examine and report their opinion of the boundaries. More than that, Lord Fairfax reiterated, he would not authorize commissioners to do, even if he appointed them himself. This was unacceptable to the Council, which resolved that "His Majesty's commissioners" must execute the royal order "in the manner most agreeable to His Majesty's pleasure signified" in the original instructions.[375] On receipt of notice of this, Fairfax decided to name Charles Carter, William Beverley and William Fairfax to act for him.[376]

While the commissioners prepared in September to begin the survey, the House of Burgesses made an interesting move. Its members knew that many of the grants previously issued in the proprietary had been defective either in naming the Proprietors or in asserting for the agents an authority that had not been given them in legal form. Correction of these flaws was imperative and should long previously have been made. The Burgesses may have felt in 1736 that the time was auspicious to force action by Fairfax; the Proprietor, on the other hand, may have suggested legislation in the belief that this would allay resentment.

Whatever the inspiration of the measure, Fairfax's counsel, Edward Barradall, drew with the peer's consent [377] a bill which recited at length the various royal patents and then confirmed en masse, "all and every grant and grants heretofore duly and regularly made and passed by any of the agents or attornies of the Proprietors of the said territory." [378] This language,

373 Letter of Jan. 8, 1737 (2 *Gooch MSS*, 463).

374 4 *E. J.*, 377. 375 *Ibid.*, 378.

376 From this point, the principal source on the boundary dispute is William Byrd's familiar "Report of the Commissioners to lay out the bounds of the Northern Neck." The edition used is that of J. S. Bassett, *Writings of William Byrd*, 401 ff.

377 Gooch to Lords of Trade, Dec. 5, 1736 (2 *Gooch MSS*, 452).

378 4 *H* 514 ff. The quotation is *ibid.*, 522–23. For the various legislative stages of the bill, see *Journ. H. B.*, 1736, p. 295, 300, 304, 306, 309, 315; 2 *L. J.*, 851, 852, 853, 855.

according to the historian of Old Prince William, "was not only immediately effective but kept the Virginia courts busy for a century." [379] The Council, for its part, was so well satisfied of the gain to the Colony from the confirmation of titles that it particularly requested the Governor to seek the King's approval of the act. [380]

On Sept. 25, 1736, two days after the adjournment of the Burgesses who passed this measure, the commissioners of both parties to the boundary dispute met in Fredericksburg, but they found their instructions greatly at variance. Fairfax's representatives were authorized only to ascertain the head springs of the southern fork of the Rappahannock and of the main branch of the Potomac, and to run the appropriate lines. Said William Byrd later: "We made the proper objections thereto as being inconsistent with His Majesty's order. But were answered that His Lordship would by no means leave the decision of the controversy to any commissioners whatsoever: when we understood this, we found ourselves then under a necessity either to return home without doing anything . . . or else by the latitude which our commission gave us to drive the nail that would go, and join with them in obtaining a full and faithful state of the facts in order to be laid before His Majesty. Thus far we yielded to act in conjunction with the Lord Fairfax's commissioners, although they were not required by their commissions to act in conjunction with us." [381]

Surveying parties were named accordingly. Provision was made for dividing the expenses. [382] All the commissioners then went to the forks of the Rappahannock, measured both streams, and prepared the necessary deposition. Thereupon, as William Byrd reported later, it was "agreed on both sides, that until the surveyors should have made their returns, nothing further could be done in this affair." [383]

While the lines were being run, the Governor refrained from issuing land grants in the disputed area, [384] but Fairfax took precisely the opposite tack. He reopened his land office [385] for his own benefit. In the fertile areas most apt to be affected, one way or the other, by the outcome of the boundary dispute, he took out three patents in his own name for about 162,000 acres. Doubtless he was advised by counsel that if grants to this land were issued in legal form prior to a settlement of the controversy, the property would in any issue be securely his. In event the Colony won its case and recaptured the land, Fairfax could pay the quit rents to the King. If His Lordship prevailed in the

[379] *Landmarks*, 172.

[380] 4 *E. J.*, 383; Gooch to the Duke of Newcastle [?], Jan. 11, 1737 (2 *Gooch MSS*, 466). Royal approval was given and was recorded by the Virginia Council Apr. 21, 1739 (4 *E. J.*, 437).

[381] *Byrd*, 402.

[382] 4 *E. J.*, 394, 397, 405, 420.   [383] *Byrd*, 404.

[384] 4 *E. J.*, 402. For the progress of the settlement, see *Proceedings of Lords of Trade, 1738–39*, v. 48, p. 32–128, LC trans.

[385] The office had been closed from approximately the time of Robert Carter's death in 1732.

litigation, he would have to do no more than transfer the rents on his own account books.[386]

While Fairfax thus was fortifying his position as landlord, the Virginia commissioners' report, with the maps and depositions, was completed by William Byrd, Aug. 10, 1737, and was transmitted promptly to the Lords of Trade.[387] Both of Fairfax's contentions were denied in this document. The north branch of the Rappahannock was held to be the southern boundary of the Northern Neck; a point opposite the mouth of the Shenandoah was declared to be the head of the Potomac. "We therefore humbly conceive it could never be the intention of the late King James II," the commissioners asserted, "to bound the territory granted to the Lord Culpeper by two streams one of which runs more than two hundred miles higher than the other." [388] If, said the commissioners, Fairfax's domain ran from the forks of the Rappahannock to the mouth of the Shenandoah, the grant contained at least 1,470,000 acres. By fixing the boundaries at the headwaters of the North Fork of the Rappahannock (the Hedgeman River) and at the mouth of the Shenandoah, the area was 2,033,000 acres. Acceptance of Fairfax's claims from the first springs of the southern fork of the Rappahannock to the head of the farthest branch of the Potomac,[389] would give Lord Fairfax a minimum of 5,282,000 acres. This, the commissioners concluded, "is as much land as at present pays quit rent to His Majesty in all the rest of Virginia." [390] Fairfax's commissioners filed their report the day after the Colony's representatives did. They vindicated the Proprietor in full and insisted that the "head spring" of the Potomac was deep in what is now West Virginia. No compromise was offered.

The next move was one scarcely to be expected of a man who at first had been indifferent to his own interests and then had been most leisurely in opening his case in 1735: Fairfax closed his land office and, about the end of September, 1737, abruptly left Virginia for England, in order to appeal to the Privy Council for the acceptance of the boundaries his commissioners had set. Gooch protestingly wrote: "Lord F . . . very privately embarked in the Rappahannock River in the very latest ship bound for London, leaving behind a letter to be sent me notifying me of his departure; but without communicating the report drawn up by his commissioners or giving me or the King's commissioners a view of the map of his boundary prepared by his surveyors, tho' in point of decency I expected it . . . I would not be misunderstood if I desired his Lordship should not be admitted to a hearing on his pretensions

[386] *Landmarks*, 246–47, 272–73.

[387] 28 *V* 314. No record of the submission of the report to the Council of Virginia appears in *E. J.* The *Gooch MSS* include a letter (v. 2, p. 479) that covers the dispatch of the report to the Lords of Trade (Aug. 19, 1737).

[388] *Byrd*, 409.

[389] The commissioners were careful to call it the Cohungorooton [Cohongoronton].

[390] *Byrd*, 409.

without a previous communication made to me of his commissioners' report and their map. I hope I shall be excused if I caution Your Lordships against giving too easy credence in points where the reports and maps differ because it is doing justice to those doing service to H.M. to allow them an opportunity of vindicating their conduct." The Governor asked, further, that if Fairfax obtained the boundaries proposed by the commissioners of the proprietary, due regard should be had for the rights of those settled there on lands granted by the Crown.[391]

As always, there was long delay in prevailing on the Privy Council to take up the case. In the summer of 1738, a date was set for a hearing, but the Treasury intervened for an examination of the facts.[392] Not until Jan. 12, 1739, could Fairfax get his petition referred by the Privy Council to the Lords of Trade.[393] It was July 27 when they made a report which a committee of the Privy Council decided to check by such maps as existed at the time of the grant by James II.[394] Thereafter the case dragged on until, in December, the record temporarily lapsed through the failure of the Secretary to make the proper entries.[395]

By that time—more than two years after Fairfax's departure—pressure had risen in Virginia for resumption of grants in those parts of the upper Northern Neck that were not involved in the boundary dispute. Fairfax thought it wise to accede to those demands for westward extension of the cultivated territory of Virginia, but in most instances he limited the area of all land granted. In this he followed a policy which, on Nov. 9, 1738, the Governor and Council had reaffirmed to the effect that "the several surveyors within this Colony do observe as a general rule to admit of no entries for any greater quantity of His Majesty's lands lying contiguous to one another than four hundred acres for any person whatsoever, nor survey any entries already made for any greater quantity without the licence of this board." [396] Adventurous men were beginning to think of the lands beyond the mountains, but until the boundaries of the proprietary were determined, there was hesitation. William Fairfax, the Proprietor's cousin and agent, bought up land that early patentees had not developed. Tracts of at least 17,000 acres were set aside for his children and members of his family.[397] His intimates and kinsmen of his

---

[391] Gooch to the Lords of Trade, Nov. 8, 1737 (2 *Gooch MSS*, 502).
[392] *Ibid.*, 512.
[393] 3 *Acts Privy Council, Col.*, 386–87. During the years 1738–47, Lord Fairfax was present at the meetings of the Commissioners for Trade and Plantations. See *Journals* for these years, LC trans.
[394] *Ibid.*   [395] *Ibid.*
[396] 4 *E. J.*, 431. Apparently there was no effective prohibition on the number of 400-acre grants of non-contiguous lands that might issue to any individual.
[397] Some of these grants were larger than might be inferred from *Landmarks*, 272–73. George William Fairfax patented 5724 acres that can be traced, Brian and William Henry 1500, William himself, 4350, Hannah 1000, Thomas 640, Anne and Sarah 3900. There may have been other grants.

wife fared even better. A favored patentee was William Beverley, one of Fairfax's commissioners in determining the boundary line. By persistence, flattery and service rendered the Proprietor, Beverley added extensively to the grant he and his associates had received of 118,000 acres near the Shenandoah.[398]

Surveyors ran the lines of great estates and of frontier farms; Fairfax in England patiently continued, through counsel of manifest ability, to have his farthest boundaries confirmed. Legal obstacles were added to the inertia of the Privy Council. Attorneys for the Crown were inquiring about the quit rents, current and delinquent, on grants that had been made in the King's name by the Governor, within the domain that would be Fairfax's if his contentions were upheld. Conceivably, the King and the Colony might be in debt to Fairfax for all the quit rents that had been collected in the extended proprietary. Titles covered by royal grants in the disputed region might be clouded or annulled.

Fairfax and his solicitor approached these obstacles shrewdly and in a spirit of compromise the peer had not displayed in Virginia. Lesser interests were relinquished in order that the larger might be confirmed. After coaxing and maneuvering for years, Fairfax finally received permission in 1745 to appear in person before a committee of the Privy Council and to make this proposal: In return for recognition of the boundaries he maintained were his, he would (1) confirm all royal titles issued in disputed areas, (2) waive all past quit rents due him within the extended proprietary, and (3) yield to the Crown all arrearages of such rents due under royal grants, provided (4) he was allowed all these rents for the future.[399] Law officers were to draw up such papers as might be necessary to make this agreement binding and effective.[400]

On this basis, Apr. 6, 1745,[401] the Privy Council decided Fairfax *vs* Virginia by granting the petitioner every foot of ground for which he had contended.[402] Permanent boundary lines were to be extended along the Rapidan to its head-waters, and westward from the mouth of the Shenandoah to the most remote spring of western Virginia that flowed into the stream that became the Potomac.

Virginia perforce acquiesced. Governor Gooch made no comment in papers that have been preserved, and subsequently he appeared anxious only that the Crown pay promptly the bills for the £1200, Virginia currency, spent in running the final boundaries.[403] The General Assembly did not meet between

[398] Orange County Grants in 15 *L.O. Records,* 15. See also *supra,* p. 218, and William Beverley's letters to Fairfax, 3 *W* (1) p. 227–30. Cf. Kegley, *Virginia Frontier,* 148.

[399] 3 *Acts Privy Council, Col.,* No. 281; P.R.O. Treas. 1, p. 320. LC trans.

[400] 3 *Acts Privy Council,* 281.

[401] The decree was dated April 11. See *Landmarks,* 624; 1 *Wilmington Papers,* 111; *Journ. Com. for Trade & Plant.,* LC trans., Va. Miscel., 1606–1772, p. 3, 18, C.

[402] The interesting maps in this controversy are described in *Landmarks,* 618 ff. Details of the final survey are in *ibid.,* 624.

[403] 3 *Gooch MSS,* 908; Letter of June 10, 1747.

October, 1744, and Feb. 20, 1746, and when it did convene it made no protest. At Belvoir and at Mount Vernon, kinship and marital ties may have prompted rejoicing that Lord Fairfax had won.

The arrival of Lord Fairfax himself in 1747 made some changes in the management of the proprietary, but for a time these merely strengthened the direct family control that had been begun in 1733 when William Fairfax had become agent. Soon after Lord Fairfax took up permanent residence in Virginia, the operation of the Treaty of Lancaster opened new regions beyond the western boundary of his domain.[404] Demand for land within the proprietary continued, but most of the speculators looked now to the Ohio and even to the Mississippi.[405]

From 1649 to 1745, the years covered by this review, the history of the proprietary may be summarized in five periods, as follows:

I. Inactive period (From the grant of Sept. 18, 1649, to the enrolment of this grant, Sept. 29, 1661).

II. The period of contention (From the enrolment of Sept. 29, 1661, to the confirmation of the Fairfax title, Jan. 11, 1693).

Phase A: (Sept. 29, 1661–May 8, 1669)
  Protest against the Hooke lease (1662–64)
  Confirmation of the grant and acceptance of royal grants in the Northern Neck (May 8, 1669).

Phase B: (May 8, 1669–Jan. 11, 1693)
  Contest over resurveys (1671–73)
  Effort of Virginia to purchase the proprietary (1672 *et seq.*)
  The Arlington-Culpeper regalities of Feb. 25, 1673
  The Culpeper administration of Virginia (1680–83)
  Settlement of June 24, 1684 and the cancellation of the regalities
  Revision of the patent and perpetual grant to "first heads or springs," Sept. 27, 1688.
  Death of Culpeper (Jan. 27, 1689)
  Confirmation of Fairfax title (Jan. 11, 1693).

III. The period of successful agencies (From the confirmation of the Fairfax title, Jan. 11, 1693, to the conclusion of the first agency of Robert Carter, 1711).

The Brent-Fitzhugh agency and first large grants to the agents (1694–1700)

The Burgesses' protest of 1695

404 See *supra*, p. 186 ff.

405 For the later years of the proprietary and the succession to the title of Fairfax, see Fairfax Harrison in 34 *V* 37 ff. The act of October, 1785, for the cancellation of the proprietorship and the abolition of quit rents is in 12 *H* 111–13.

Settlement with Richard Lee (1699) and acceptance of the proprietorship
by persons having royal grants to Northern Neck lands

First agency of Robert Carter (1702–11)

Initial dispute over boundaries (1706).

IV. The period of leases (From the lease to Edmund Jenings, 1711, to the
death of Robert Carter, Aug. 4, 1732).

Phase A: The Jenings-Lee lease (1711–19)

Thomas Lee's survey plats

Jenings' direct administration (1715/16–19)

Thomas, sixth Lord Fairfax, sole Proprietor, May 31, 1719.

Phase B: The lease and second agency of Robert Carter (1719–32)

Treaty of Albany (September, 1722)

Renewal of the boundary dispute (1723)

Negotiation of second lease (1724)

Carter's vast grants to himself and his family

Development of the "manors."

V. The period of family management of the proprietary (From the death
of Robert Carter, Aug. 4, 1732, to the decree in the boundary dispute,
Apr. 6, 1745, and thence, though not treated here, to the cancellation of
the proprietorship, 1785).

Appointment of William Fairfax as agent (1733)

Temporary suspension of grants (1733)

Fairfax's visit and boundary negotiations (1735–37)

The confirmation of defective titles (1736)

Fairfax's appeal and victory in establishing extended boundaries (1737–
Apr. 6, 1745).

Nothing in the curious story covered by this outline is more remarkable
than the ignorance of most Virginians concerning the terms of the proprietary
in which many of them lived. This was due partially to the secrecy that
attended the various renewals and changes. Nearly all these revisions increased the authority or the domain of the Proprietors, but the Burgesses, the
Council and even the Governor often were in the dark for years regarding
some of the essential conditions under which the Culpepers and the Fairfaxes
held their lands from the King.

For example, discovery of the "regalities" under the Culpeper-Arlington
grant produced a convulsion in Virginia and led to a virtual demand for the
cancellation of the special privileges. While this is plain, the records are so
confused in their references to the scope of the grant that one is forced to
conclude some of the colonials never knew precisely what lands were given
the two Lords. Nearly all of the later protests of the colonials concerning the
proprietary are incorrect in some statements respecting its history.

Next to the grant of regalities under the Arlington-Culpeper patent—to cite another example of the colonials' lack of information—the largest amendment of the proprietary was that of 1688, when the patent was rewritten to include the "first springs" along with the "heads" of the Rappahannock and the Potomac as the western boundaries of the proprietary. One searches in vain for any evidence that the Virginians sensed the significance of this language or even knew that the words had been added, until controversy arose over the grant of lands in the forks of the Rappahannock.

Perhaps, in a small measure, it was because of ignorance regarding the background of the proprietary that no Virginian of 1745 seems to have regarded the land system of the Northern Neck as an experiment in government or as an example of the slow change in the relationship of Crown and Colony. The Virginians' struggle with the Proprietors was in no real sense a preliminary of revolution. From the beginning, the right of the Crown to do as it pleased with the royal domain was taken for granted. In England there had been a fumbling effort to be just in the patenting and administration of these lands, but the courtiers, the peers, the lawyers and the London merchants had all the advantage over the colonials. Resistance to the extension of the proprietary in Virginia had been continuous on the part of the people and, in the main, on the part of the Governors, but the appeal was for the exercise of the royal authority, not for the freedom of the Colony. Resistance of a lesser sort existed to the payment of quit rents, though this was because the rent had the character of a tax and not because the quit rent was contrary to the colonial theory of property right. The gradual development of a craving for direct ownership is to be observed during this period only in the steady insistence on clear titles.

It is as easy to overstate the effect of the leases as it is to read into the struggle against the Proprietors an unreal connection with the preliminaries of the Revolution. In actual fact, prior to the Treaty of Albany, none of the larger grants made by agents to themselves or to their friends had any lasting effect on the proprietary or on the Colony. The second agency of Robert Carter had larger importance for the reasons given in Chapter I. Had Carter lived ten years longer, he might have captured the proprietary by the magnitude of the grants of excellent land that he issued members of his family on the authorized terms. In addition, Carter put on the lower Shenandoah Valley and on the rich lowlands of the upper Potomac the impress of the Tidewater slave economy. Critics might have said that he transferred latifundia to the frontier; Carter might have replied that he encouraged settlement by giving assurance it would have much the same stamp as the life to which residents of Tidewater were accustomed. Had the words been in use then, he could have boasted that he was advancing "civilization westward" by opening lands in a manner that would have been impossible with small farmers. Carter's policy was pursued in slightly different ways by William Fairfax, by William Beverley, and by Lord Fairfax himself. Patents for small tracts became more numerous. Side by side with this movement was a continuance of the grant or consolidation of large estates by men who loved wide acres and combined the ambitions of a baron with the greed of a land speculator. The system tended to stratify the society of Virginia, but before this was accomplished, the Revolution came and overthrew both the system and the society based on it.

APPENDIX I-2

PART I

THE FIRST PATENT OF THE PROPRIETARY

CHARLES R.

CHARLES THE SECOND by the grace of God King of England Scotland France and Ireland Defender of the faith &c. TO ALL to whome these presents shall come Greeting.WHEREAS wee have taken into Our Royall Consideracon the great propagation of the Christian faith, and the manifold benefitts arising to the Church of God,together with the wellfare of multitudes of Our Loyall Subiects by the vndertakings and vigorous prosecution of Plantations in fforeign parts, and particularly in our Dominions of America AND whereas wee are informed by Our Right trusty and welbeloved Raph Lord Hopton,Baron of Stratton, Henry Lord Jermyn Baron of St Edmunds Bury,John Lord Culpeper Baron of Thoresway, Sr John Barkeley,Sr William Norton [sic] Sr Dudley Wyatt & Thomas Culpeper Esqr.That all that intire Tract of Land,portion and Teritory lying in America, and bounded by, and within the heads of Tappahannocke als Rappahanocke and Quircough or Patawomecke Rivers, the Courses of the said Rivers and Chesapayoake Bay, the said Rivers themselves, and all Islands within the said Rivers togeather with the ffishing of the same are in Our free guift and disposicon, and that wee are intitled to the same, and every part and parcell thereof KNOWE ye therefore that wee for and in Consideracon of many faithfull services donne to Our late Royall ffather of blessed memory, and to Our selfe by the said Lord Hopton,Lord Jermyn,Lord Culpeper,Sr John Barkeley, Sr William Mortin [sic], Sr Dudley Wyatt and Thomas Culpeper HAVE of Our especiall grace, certeyne knowledge, and meere motion, given granted and confirmed, and by these Our Letters Patents for Vs,Our heires and Successors doe give,grant and confirme vnto the said Raph Lord Hopton,Henry Lord Jermyn,John Lord Culpeper, Sr John Berkeley Sr William Morton, Sr Dudley Wyatt, and Thomas Culpeper, their heires and assignes for ever All that entire Tract,Territory, or porcon of Land situate,lying and beeing in America, and bounded by and within the heads of the Rivers of Tappahanocke als Rappahanock and Quiriough or Patawomecke Rivers, the Courses of the said Rivers as they are comonly called and knowen by the Inhabitants, and discriptions of those parts, And Chesapayocke Bay, togeather with the Rivers themselves, and all the Islands within the Banks of those Rivers; And all Woods Vnderwoods,Tymber and Trees,wayes,waters,Rivers ponds,pooles, water Courses, ffishing streames,Havens,ports,Harbours,Creeks,wrecks of Sea, ffish Royall,Deere,wild beasts and fowle of what nature or kinde soever, Mynes of Gold and Silver,Lead,Tynne,Iron, and Copper, and Quarryes of Stone and Coale which now are, or at any tyme hereafter,shall bee had, comeing,beeing,ariseing,reneweing,accrewing, found or taken within the Bonds of prcincts aforesaid,Togeather with the Royaltyes of Hawking and Hunting for themselves,their heires and assignes,servants and Tenants, in and vpon the Lands and prmisses aforesaid, and in and vpon every part and parcell thereof,Saveing,excepting and reserveing to us,Our heires and Successors.One full ffift part of all Gold Mynes,or Gold Oare, and One full Tenth part of all Silver Mynes,or silver Oare hereafter to bee had or found within the said entire Tract or Territory of Land TO HAVE hold and enioy all the said Tract Territory,or portion of land, and all and singular other the prmisses with their and every of their appurtenncs hereby granted,or mencond or intended to bee granted (except as before excepted) to the s id Raph Lord Hopton, Henry Lord Jermyn,John Lord Culpeper,Sr John Barkeley, Sr William Morton, Sr Dudley Wyatt and Thomas Culpeper their heires and assignes for ever, to their onely vse and behoofe, and to no other vse intent or purpose whatsoever YEILDING and paying therefore yearely at the feast of St John the Baptist to vs,Our heires and Successors the sume of Sixe pounds Thirteene shillings and ffower pence at Our Receipt of James Towne in Our Dominion of Virginia in lieu of all services and demands whatsoever.AND wee doe further by these prsents of Our especiall grace, certeyne knowledge and meere motion give and grant vnto them the said Lord Hopton, Lord Jermyn,Lord Culpeper,Sr John Berkeley, Sr William Morton,Sr Dudley Wyatt, and Thomas Culpeper their heires and assignes and every of them full power,licence and authority to divide the said Tract or Territory of Land into Countyes,Hundreds,parishes,Tythings,Towneshipps,Hamletts and Boroughs, and to erect and build vpon such part or parts of the said Tract or Territory of Land as shall vnto them and every of them seems fitt and convenient Citties,Townes, Parish Churches,Colledges,Chappels, ffree schooles, Almeshouses and Houses of Correction, and to endowe them with Lands, Tenements,goods and Chattells at their free wills and pleasures.AND wee doe hereby give and grant for Vs,Our Heires and Successors vnto the said Lord Hopton,Lord Jermyn,Lord Culpeper, Sr John Berkeley, Sr William Morton, Sr Dudley Wyatt, and Thomas Culpeper their heires and assignes and every of them that they shall be full and perpetuall patrons of all and every Church and Churches to bee built and endowed as afor said, and shall nominate and prsent able and fitt persons to bee Incumbents of such Churches, and vpon the avoydance of such Churches or any of them whether it shall bee by death, cession, resignacon,deprivacon, or otherwise, to nominate and prsent such other fitt person or persons to such Churches or Chappells so happeing(sic) to bee voyd as to them shall seem fitt and convenient, And that they and every of them have and enioy, and may have and enioy full faculty,power and authority of electing nominateing and presenting any fitt person to the Office or place of Master of any Colledge, or Schoole Master of any Schoole to be founded and endowed by them or by any other person or persons whatsoever in and vpon the said Tract or Territory of Land or in or vpon any part or parcell thereof AND wee doe further for Vs Our heires and Successors give and grant vnto the said Lord Hopton,Lord Jermyn, Lord Culpeper, Sr John Berkeley,Sr William Morton Sr Dudley Wyatt, and Thomas Culpeper their heires and assignes by these presents, that they the said Lord Hopton,Lord Jermyn,Lord Culpeper, Sr John Barkeley, Sr William Morton, Sr Dudley Wyatt, and Thomas Culpeper their heires and assignes shall and may divide any part or parts of the said Tract Territory or porcon of Land by these presents given granted and confirmed,or thereby menconed or intended to bee given granted and confirmed into Mannors and that they may call such Mannors after their owne, or any of their names, or by any other name or names whatsoever.And that they their heires and assignes and every of them may at all or any tyme or tymes hereafter have and hold within and vpon every such Mannor and within the limitts and prcincts of the same Mannor a Court of the nature of a Court Baron to enquire, he re,determine, and execute all and singular such things and matters, and in such manner and forme as hath at any tyme heretofore beene,now is, or of right ought to bee vsed in any Court Baron within Our Kingdome of England, to bee holden before a Steward or Stewards from tyme to tyme to bee nominated constituted and appointed by the said Lord Hopton,Lord Jermyn,Lord Culpeper,Sr John Berkeley, Sr William Morton, Sr Dudley Wyatt, and Thomas Culpeper their heires and assignes, and before the free suitors of the said Mannors respectively, in the same manner and forme as hath been vsed and accustomed in any other Court Baron or Court of the natore of a Court Baron within Our Kingdome of England,

and in such severall and respective Courts to hold pleas of all and singular actions,trespasses,covenants,accompts, contracts, detinewes, debts and demands whatsoever where the debt,or thing demanded exceede not the value of fforty shillings of currant money of England. And that they and every of them their and every of their heires and assignes shall and may from tyme to tyme, and at all tymes hereafter have receive and take all and singular amercements ffines,comodityes,advantages,perquisits, and emolumts whatsoever to such respective Court Barons belonging or any way apperteyneing, without any Accompt or other profitt to bee made or rendered to Vs Our heires or Successors AND further wee of Our especiall grace certeyne knowledge and meere motion for Vs,Our heires and Successors have given and granted and doe by these prsents for Vs ,Our heires and Successors give and grant to the said Lord Hopton,Lord Jermyn,Lord Culpeper, Sr John Berkeley,Sr William Morton, Sr Dudley Wyatt, and Thomas Culpeper their heires nd assignes and every of them,that they and every of them, their and every of their heires and assignes shall and may at all tymes hereafter have hold and enioy within the aforesaid respective Mannors and within the limits and prcincts of the same Mannors a Court Leete and Viewe of ffrancke Pledge of all the Tenants,residents,and inhabitants of the Hundred or Hundreds within which such respective Mannor or Mannors shall lye or bee, to bee there holden twice in every yeare that is to say,once within the space of a Moneth next following the ffeast of St Michael the Archangell, and againe within the space of a Moneth next prceding and goeing before the feast of Easter to bee holden from tyme to tyme at such places ,and vpon such dayes as to the said Lord Hopton,Lord Jermyn, Lord Culpeper, Sr John Berkeley, Sr William Morton, Sr Dudley Wyatt, and Thomas Culpeper their heirs and assignes shall seeme most fitt,convenient and necessary, according to the Lawes,vsages, and Customes of Our Kingdome of England before the Steward or Stewards of the said Lord Hopton,Lord Jermyn, Lord Culpeper, Sr John Berkeley, Sr William Morton, Sr Dudley Wyatt and Thomas Culpeper their heires and assignes for the tyme being.And also all and singular goods and Chattells wayved, and all Estrayes happening,found, beeing, and taken within the limitts or prcincts of the said Leets, or Viewes of ffrancke pledge, and all and whatsoever doth belong or apperteyne to a Court Leete or View of ffrancke Pledge,As also all and singular Amercemts ffines, for feitures,paynes, penaltyes,perquisits rights and Jurisdictions whatsoever belonging to a Court Lette or Views of ffrancke Pledge, or which doe, or may belong or apperteyne vnto Vs Our heires and Successors for or by reason of any such Court Leete or View of ffrancke Pledge AND further Our will and pleasure is, and Wee for Vs,Our heires and Successors by these psents doe grant and give Licence to the said Lord Hopton, Lord Jermyn, Lord Culpeper, Sr John Berkeley,Sr William Morton, Sir Dudley Wyatt, and

Thomas Culpeper their heires and assignes,That they and every of them may have and hold within the said respective Mannors so to bee made as aforesaid and within the Libertyes and prcincts of the said Mannors and within any part of the Tract or Territory of Land by these prsents granted on every Saturday in every weeke One Markett, as also Two ffaires every year to bee kept on such dayes, for so long tyme, and at such places within the said Tract or Territory of Land as to the said Lord Hopton,Lord Jermyn, Lord Culpeper, Sr John Berkeley,Sr William Morton, Sr Dudley Wyatt, and Thomas Culpeper their heires and assignes shall seeme most meete and convenient. Togeather with a Court of Py-powders in every of the said severall ffaires and with all Libertyes ffree Customes,Tolls, Stalladge,Piccadge,ffines, Amercemts and all other profitts comodityes, advantages, and emolumts whatsoever belonging or apperteyning to any Markett ffaire or Court of Pyepowders holden or to bee holden within our Kingdome of England, and this without the molestacon,perturbacon, or contradiction of Vs,Our heires or Successrs AND Wee have given and granted, and wee doe further by these prsents for Vs,Our heires and Successors give and grant to Lord Hopton, Lord Jermyn, Lord Culpeper, Sr John Berkeley, Sr William Morton, Sr Dudley Wyatt and Thomas Culpeper their heires and assignes full faculty, power and authority at all tymes hereafter, and in such place or places as to them shall seeme fitt and convenient (the same place or places beeing parcell of the premisses hereby granted) to erect One or more Parke or Parkes for the breeding,feeding and sustentacon of Deere and other wild beasts of Chase And that they may enclose, imparke, and impale such Parke or Parkes with walls,payles,rayles,or such materialls as to them shall seeme fitt and convenient. And beeing so imparked and inclosed may have and Hold and enioy such Parke and Parkes forever without any molestacon perturbacon or interruption of Vs Our heires or Successors or any of our Justices, Ministers or Officers. And that they their heires and assignes may have hold and enjoy within the Parke and Parkes to bee erected,enclosed and impalled as aforesaid, and in all other Lands and prmisses granted by these prsents ffree Chase, and ffree warren, and whatsoever privilege and freedome besides that doth belong or apperteyne to the Libertyes of Parkes,Chases and Warrens so that no other person or persons whatsoever may prsume to enter into the said Parke or Parkes,or into any other part or parcell of the prmisses before these prsents granted, to hunt,chase, or kill any of the deere, wild beasts, or other beasts of chase and warren beeing within the said Parke and Parkes and other the Lands aforesaid without the leave and License of the said Lord Hopton, Lord, Jermyn, Lord Culpeper, Sr John Berkeley, Sr William Morton, Sr Dudley Wyatt and Thomas Culpeper, their heires and assignes. AND wee doe further for Vs Our heires and Successors by these prsents grant and give license to the said Lord Hopton,Lord Jermyn,Lord Culpeper, Sr John

Berkeley, Sr William Morton, Sr Dudley Wyatt and Thomas Culpeper their heires and assignes freely and without the molestacon of Vs Our heires and Successors to give, grant,or by any other way or meanes sell or aliene all and singular the premisses by these prsents granted and every part and parcell thereof to any person or persons, beeing willing to contract for and buy the same.To bee holden of the said Lord Hopton,Lord Jermyn, Lord Culpeper, Sr John Berkeley, Sr William Morton, Sr Dudley Wyatt, and Thomas Culpeper their heires and assignes as of any of their aforesaid Mannors in free and comon soccage by fealty onely, and by suite of Court, or by any other lawfull tenure or tenures vsed within our Kingdome of England Rendering and paying such Rents, and other lawful reservacons as shall seemes fitt and convenient to the said Lord Hopton,Lord Jermyn, Lord Culpeper, Sr John Berkeley, Sr William Morton, Sr Dudley Wyatt, and Thomas Culpeper their heires and assignes NOTWITHSTANDING the Statute comonly called Quia Emptores terrarum, or any other statute,Act Ordinance,or provision,or any other thing cause or matter whatsoever to the contrary notwithstanding AND for the better Plantation and security of all and singular the prmisses before by these prsents granted, and for suppressing such of Our Subiects as shall Rebell against Vs,Our heires and Successors and for the better resisting of forreigne force, and for the encouragement of such of our good Subiects as shall inhabite and reside vpon any part or parcell of the said Tract Territory or porcon of Land hereby granted, wee doe will and Comand the said Lord Hopton, Lord Jermyn, Lord Culpeper, Sr John Berkeley, Sr William Morton, Sr Dudley Wyatt, and Thomas Culpeper their heires and assignees. And wee doe hereby for Vs Our heires and Successors give and grant to them, and every of them, free leave, and full license and authority at their owne proper costs and charges to found erect and build in and upon some part of the prmisses One or more Castell or Castells, together with as many fforts and places defensible as to them shall seeme fitt and convenient; which said Castles fforts and places defensible shall be built of Lyme and Stone,or other materialls, with Battlements, fflanckers, Loopeholes, and fortifyed with walls,LynesBullwarks,false brayes,Graffs wett or dry, and all other warlike fortificacons as they shall thinke fitt to resist an enimy, and this without perturbacon molestacon or disturbance of Vs,Our heires or Successors or any of our officers or Ministers whatsoever. AND Wee doe for Vs,our heires and Successors for the Consideracons aforesaid convenant grant and agree to and with the said Lord Hopton,Lord Jermyn,Lord Culpeper, Sr John Berkeley, Sr William Morton, Sr Dudley Wyatt, and Thomas Culpeper their heires executors and assignes, and to and with every of them by these prsents that at any tyme hereafter vpon humble suite made vnto vs by the said Lord Hopton, Lord Jermyn.Lord Culpeper, Sr John Berkeley, Sr William Morton, Sr Dudley Wyatt and Thomas Culpeper their heires and assignes, Wee, Our heires and Successors shall enlarge and confirme these Our prsent Letters Patents by granting vnto them and their heires,other new Ones, with such favourable concessions and grants as may supply any defect herein conteyned. AND further Wee of our especiall grace certeyne knowledge and meere motion, doe grant vnto the said Lord Hopton,Lord Jermyn, Lord Culpeper, Sr John Berkeley, Sr William Morton, Sr Dudley Wyatt, and Thomas Culpeper their heires and assignes and every of them by these prsents That these shall bee to all intents and purposes firme valid good effectuall and Sufficient in the lawe against Vs, Our heires and Successors in all the Courts of Vs Our heires or Successors hereafter to bee procured or obteyned by the said Lord Hopton, Lord Jermyn,Lord Culpeper, Sr John Berkeley, Sr William Morton, Sr Dudley Wyatt,and Thomas Culpeper their heires or assignes NOTWITH-STANDING the ill nameing,or ill reciteing,or not nameing or not reciteing, any parcells of Lands Mannors, Castells, Boundarys,limits or prcincts of Lands hereby granted,or intended to bee granted. And notwithstanding the not finding an Office or Inquisition of the prmisses or of any part or parcell thereof by which Our Title or the Title of any of Our Progenitors or Antecessors of in and to the prmisses, or of,in or vnto any part or parcell thereof ought to have been found before the makeing and granting of these our Letters Patents AND our will and pleasure is and wee doe hereby grant vnto the said Lord Hopton,Lord Jermyn, Lord Culpeper, Sr John Berkeley, Sr William Morton, Sr Dudley Wyatt, and Thomas Culpeper their heires and assignes, that they shall have these Our Letters Patents made, and Sealed with Our Great Seale of England without giveing or paying any fee great or small to Vs, or to Our vse into the Hamper(sic) or elsewhere IN WITNES whereof Wee have caused these Our Letters to bee made Patents .Witnes Our selfe at St Germayne en Lay the Eighteenth day of September in the ffirst Yeare of Our Reigne [1]

Endorsed

      patent for lands
      in Virginia

[1] Br. Mus.: Add. charters 13585. The front of the original text is reproduced, *supra,* following p. 35.

PART II

The Final Boundaries of the Proprietary

Order in Council

At the Court at St. James's the 11th day of April 1745.

PRESENT

The Kings most Excellent Majesty in Council.

Upon reading at the Board a Report from the Right Honourable the Lords of the Committee of Council for Plantation Affairs dated the 6th of this Instant in the words following—Viz^t "Your Majesty having been pleased by Your Order in Council of the 21st of December 1738 to referr unto this Committee the humble Petition of Thomas Lord Fairfax, Setting forth that the Petitioner and his Ancestors by Letters Patent under the Crown made by King Charles the Second the 8th day of May in the 21st Year of his Reign and by King James the Second the 27th of September in the 4th Year of his Reign is and have been intitled to the Inheritance of all that Entire Tract or Territory or Parcel of Land Scituate in Virginia in America and bounded by and within the first heads or Springs of the Rivers Tappahannock alias Rappahannock and Quiriough alias Pattawomeck Rivers the Courses of the said Rivers from their said first Heads or Springs as they are commonly called and known by the Inhabitants and Descriptions of those parts and the Bay of Chesapeyock together with the said Rivers themselves and all the Islands within the Outermost Banks thereof and the Soil of all and Singular the Premises and all Lands Woods Underwoods Timber Waters Rivers Havens Ports Harbours Bays Creeks Ferrys Advowson Royalties and Hereditaments That the Petitioner in the Year 1733 preferred a Petition to Your Majesty in Council Setting forth as above and that there had been divers disputes between the Governor and Council in Virginia and the Petitioner and his Agent Robert Carter Esqr touching the Boundarys of the Petitioners said Tract of Land and that the Governor and Council of Virginia had from time to time actually taken upon them to issue Grants of several parcels of Land part of the Petitioners said Tract and had actually run out Surveys of several other Parcels of Land though the same as the Petitioner apprehends were clearly within the Bounds of the Lands so granted from the Crown as aforesaid under which the Petitioner Claims the Petitioner therefore prayed that Your

Majesty would be pleased to Order a Commission to issue for running out marking & ascertaining the Bounds of the Petitioners said Tract of Land, that Your Majesty having taken the said Petition into Consideration together with a Report of the Lords Commissioners for Trade and Plantations and also of the Committee of the Lords of Your Majestys Privy Council thereupon was pleased by Your Order in Council of the 29th of November 1733 to Direct that the Lieutenant Governor of Virginia should Nominate three or more Commissioners not exceeding five who in Conjunction with a like Number to be Named and Deputed by the Petitioner were to Survey and Settle the Marks and Boundarys of the said District of Land agreable to the Terms of the Patents under which the Petitioner Claimed And Your Majesty further directed that in the meantime the Lieutenant Governor should not presume to make any Grants of Lands within the abovementioned Tract. That pursuant to the said Order three of the Council of Virginia were appointed Commissioners by the said Lieutenant Governor and the Petitioner appointed three Commissioners on his behalf that the said Commissioners appointed Surveyors on each side who Surveyed the said Disputed Boundary, That after the said Surveys were made the Petitioner Proposed to the Virginia Commissioners to meet together and to agree on one General Plan and to join in a Report thereof but which the Virginia Commissioners refused to Comply with so that as no General Plan or Report could for this reason be Settled between them the Commissioners for Virginia on the 10th of August 1737 made their Separate Return and Report Directed to the Lords Commissioners for Trade and Plantations transmitting here with a Plan or Survey of the Disputed Boundarys with several other Papers mentioned in and referred to by their Report and the Pet^{rs} Commissioners the next day made their Separate Return and Report likewise Directed to the said Lords Commiss^{rs}: for Trade and Plantations also Transmitting therewith a Plan or Survey of the Disputed Boundarys together with several Papers mentioned in and referred to by their Report both which Reports and Surveys are now lying before their Lordships. The Petitioner therefore humbly prayed that Your Majesty would be graciously pleased to take the said Surveys into Your Royal Consideration and that the said Report of the Petitioners Commissioners and the said Survey so returned by them as aforesaid might be both of them Confirmed and Approved by Your Majesty and that Your Majesty would be pleased to Order and Direct the Dividing Line between the Petitioners said District of Land and the said Province of Virginia to be run out and the Boundarys thereof fixed and ascertained agreable to the said Plan and Survey thereof so returned by the Petitioners said Commissioners within a time to be limited for that purpose And that the Petitioner might have all such further and other Relief in the Premises as the Nature and Circumstances of his case shall require. The Lords of the Committee in Obedience to Your Majestys said Order of

Reference did some time since take the said Petition into their Consideration and thought proper to Order the Lords Commissioners for Trade and Plantations to Examine into the several Reports Returns Plans or other Papers transmitted to them by the Commiss^rs appointed on behalf of the Crown as likewise of the Petitioner for Settling the said Boundaries and to report a State of the Facts as they should appear to them upon such Examination together with such Observations as should Occur to them which they having accordingly done—The Lords of the Committee have met several Days to Examine into this Affair and have likewise Examined into the said Returns Plans and other Papers relating thereto. And the Question being only concerning that Boundary which ought to be drawn from the first head or Spring of the River Pattawomeck alias Powtomack The Committee do Agree humbly to Report to Your Majesty as their Opinion that within the Words and meaning of the Letters Patent Granted by King James the 2^d bearing date the 27th day of September in the 4th Year of his Reign the said Boundary ought to begin at the first Spring of the South Branch of the River Rappahannock now called Rappidan which first Spring ought to be the Spring of that part of the said River called Rappidan as is called in the Plans returned by the name of Conway River and that the said Boundary be from thence drawn in a Streight Line North West to the Place in the Alagany Mountains where that part of the River Patawomeck alias Potowmack which is now called the Cohongoroota alias Cohongoronton first Arises the other Boundarys being the said Rivers themselves as they run from their said respective Heads till they fall into Chesapeyock alias Chesapeak Bay And that Your Majestys Governor of Virginia should be directed to Nominate three or more Persons not exceeding five who in Conjunction with a like Number to be named and Deputed by the Lord Fairfax are without Delay to run and mark out the Boundary and Dividing Line between the said Province and the Petitioners Land from the said first Spring of the said South Branch of the said River Rappahannock now called Rappidan and to be from thence drawn in a Streight Line North West to the said Place in the Alagany Mountains where that part of the said River Pattawomeck alias Potowmack which is now called Cohongoroota alias Cohongoronton first arises and to make a Plan from those drawn by the said former Commissioners Copys whereof were returned with their Reports as before mentioned and therein to Describe the said Boundary or Dividing Line by Metes and Marks and also the Courses of the said Rivers as they run from their said respective Heads till they fall into the Chesapeyock alias Chesapeak Bay aforesaid and to transmit the same to Your Majesty in Council in Order to its being preserved among the Records of Your Majestys Privy Council And that the said Governor should be further Directed not to make any Grants of Lands lying within the said Boundarys nor Molest or Disturb the Petitioner in the Quiet Possession and Enjoyment of the Lands

to be Subject to the Grants made of any parts thereof by Your Majesty or any
of Your Royal Predecessors and so as the said Lord Fairfax do comply with
his proposal hereinafter mentioned And the Committee do further humbly
Report to Your Majesty that the Petitioner the Lord Fairfax hath appeared
in Person before this Committee and proposed and Consented that all the
Grantees of Lands under the Crown within the Boundarys aforementioned
shall quietly enjoy their Lands according to their respective Grants and likewise to do and Consent to all such Acts as shall be thought necessary by Your
Majesty to Confirm and Secure such Grantees in the quiet Possession of their
said Lands pursuant to their Grants and to Discharge Your Majesty from all
Demands of the said Lord Fairfax on Account of Quit Rents that have been
received by Your Majesty And to Yield up to Your Majesty all Arrears thereof
that have hitherto become due upon Express Condition nevertheless that the
said Lord Fairfax shall for the future be intitled to all the Advantages Profits
and Emoluments whatsoever to arise from Grants made by the Crown of
Land within his Boundarys which the Crown would or might have been
intitled unto by the Terms or in Consequence of the said Grants, and where
upon such Grants Quit rents are reserved that the said Lord Fairfax shall be
intitled to Demand and receive the same from the Grantees to his own use
and benefit from the time that Your Majestys Pleasure to be signified here-
upon shall be made known to the Governor and Receiver General of Your
Majestys Quit Rents in that Province Whereupon the Lords of the Committee
are humbly of Opinion that what is so Proposed by the Lord Fairfax is
reasonable and proper to be complied with and that in Order to make the
same effectual it may be advisable for Your Majesty to Direct Your Attorney
and Solicitor General to Consider of and lay before Your Majesty what they
conceive necessary to be done either on the part of the said Lord Fairfax to
Confirm and Secure the said Grantees in the Possession and Enjoyment of
their Lands as likewise to Discharge Your Majesty from all Demands of the
said Lord Fairfax on Account of the said Quit Rents that have been received
by Your Majesty and to Yield up to Your Majesty all Arrears thereof that
have hitherto become due or on the part of Your Majesty to Enable the Lord
Fairfax for the future to receive the Quit Rents or any other benefit reserved
by or which may arise from the Grants under the Crown of Lands within
his Boundarys

His Majesty this day took the said Report into Consideration and was
pleased with the Advice of His Privy Council to Approve thereof and to Declare and Order as it is hereby Declared and Ordered that within the words
and meaning of the Letters Patent granted by King James the Second bearing
date the 27th day of September in the Fourth Year of his Reign the Boundary
of the Petitioners Land doth begin at the first Spring of the South Branch
of the River Rappahannock now called Rappidan which first Spring is the

Spring of that part of the said River called Rappidan as is called in the Plans returned by the name of Conway River And that the said Boundary be from thence drawn in a Strait Line North West to the place in the Alagany Mountains where that part of the River Patawomeck alias Potowmack which is now called Cohongoroota alias Cohongoroton first arises the other Boundarys being the said Rivers themselves as they run from their said respective Heads till they fall in Chesapeyock alias Chesapeak Bay. And His Majesty doth hereby further Order that the Governor or Commander in Chief for the time being of His Majestys said Province of Virginia Do Nominate three or more persons (not exceeding five) who in Conjunction with a like Number to be named and deputed by the Lord Fairfax are, without Delay, to run and mark out the boundary and Dividing Line between the said Province and the Petitioners Land from the said first Spring of the said South Branch of the said River Rappahannock now called Rappidan in a Strait Line North West to the said Place in the Alagany Mountains where that part of the said River Patawomack alias Potowmack which is now called Cohongoroota alias Cohongoroton first arises and to make a Plan from these drawn by the said former Commissioners (Copys whereof were returned with their Reports as before mentioned) and therein to Describe the said Boundary or Dividing Line by Metes and Marks and also the Courses of the said Rivers as they run from their said respective Heads till they fall into Chesapeyock alias Chesapeak Bay aforesaid and To transmit the same to His Majesty at this Board in Order to its being preserved among the Records of His Majestys Privy Council—And that the said Governor or Commander in Chief do not make any Grants of Lands within the said Boundarys nor Molest or Disturb the Petitioner in the quiet possession and Enjoyment of the Lands contained there in but the said Lands to be Subject to the Grants made of any parts thereof by His Majesty or any of his Royal Predecessors and so as the said Lord Fairfax do Comply with his proposal mentioned in the aforegoing Report And His Majesty doth hereby likewise Signify His Royal Pleasure that the Lord Fairfax shall for the future be intitled to all the Advantages Profits & Emoluments whatsoever to arise from Grants made by the Crown of Lands within his Boundarys which the Crown would or might have been intitled to by the Terms or in consequence of the said Grants and whereupon such Grants Quit Rents are reserved that he the said Lord Fairfax shall be entitled to demand and receive the same from the Grantees to his own use and benefit from the time that the Order shall be made known to the said Governor and to His Majestys Receiver General of the Quit Rents in that Province and that with respect to the several matters proposed by the above Report to be referred to the Consideration of His Majestys Attorney and Sollicitor General His Majesty hath this day Ordered the necessary Directions to be given to them thereon accordingly—and the Governor Lieutenant Governor

or Commander in Chief of His Majestys said Province of Virginia for the
time being, The Receiver General of His Majestys Quit Rents in the said
Province for the time being or his Deputy and all others whom it may
concern are to take Notice of His Majestys Pleasure hereby Signified and
Yield due Obedience thereto

A true Copy
W Sharpe

Endorsed   Virginia
                Copy of an Order of Council dated
                the 11th of April 1745 determining
                the bounds of the Ld Fairfax's Lands
                in Virginia and fixing the Tenure
                of those Lands within his Grant
                that have been settled under Grants
                from the Govr of Virginia
                Recd June the 17th   1745
                Read July the 25th [1]

[1] P.R.O., C.O. 5, 1326, f. 293–304.

APPENDIX I-3

TYPICAL NORTHERN NECK KINSHIP

THE NAMES cited *supra* in the text, p. 2, are typical of scores so connected
by intermarriage that the full art of the professional genealogist is challenged.
A few examples will show the intricacy of the relationship developed in three
generations. To begin with the Turbervilles, George of that name, son of
an immigrant, first married Frances Ashton of Hickory Hill, through whom
he acquired that estate.[1] After her death, George Turberville married Lettice
Fitzhugh,[2] daughter of a lady whose name epitomized Northern Neck
eminence and fecundity—Ann Lee Fitzhugh McCarty. When Lettice
Turberville expired and a decent period of mourning had elapsed, George
Turberville married Martha, daughter of Richard Lee, resident in England.[3]
Within two or three generations, the lines of the Tubervilles were so inter-

[1] For her, see 7 *W* (1) p. 95.
[2] Her pathetic memorial inscription is *ibid.*
[3] *Lee of Virginia*, 93.

twined with those of Lees, Corbins, Tayloes and Fitzhughs [4] that few understood the precise degree of kinship among them.[5]

Another tangled and interesting connection developed from the marriages of the Bushrods and the Corbins. The first John Bushrod died in 1729 and left a widow, who subsequently married Willoughby Allerton,[6] a descendant of the New England Brewsters, and a planter of widely linked grandchildren. John Bushrod II, owner of the beautiful Potomac estate Bushfield,[7] won the hand of Jane Corbin, daughter of Gawin Corbin.[8] That family's home was Pecatone, said to have been architecturally the finest residence on the Potomac.[9] Jane's aunt Laetitia had married Richard Lee; her aunt Alice's husband was Philip Lightfoot; her aunt Frances was Mrs. Edmund Jenings; her aunt Anne accepted William Tayloe; her aunt Winifred took the name of Leroy Griffin—a bewildering connection.[10] New ties were made a generation later when Hannah Bushrod, daughter of John II and Mildred Corbin Bushrod, married John Augustine Washington, whose family and kinship were large.[11] Similarly, the Steptoes were connected with the Allertons, the Washingtons, the Eskridges, the Ayletts and the Lees.[12] The Ashtons of Nominy Plantation, besides their link with the Turbervilles, were blended with the Lees, the Ayletts, and many besides.[13] Still again, Daniel McCarty married a daughter of Humphrey Pope, who was the widow of James Payne. Survivors among her four children by Payne and her eight by McCarty married widely. The second wife of Daniel has

[4] For George Turberville, see *Westmoreland Orders*, 1721-31, p. 343; *ibid.*, 1731-39, p. 134. His will is in 9 *Westmoreland Deeds and Wills*, 200. A later generation of Lee-Turbervilles appears in the frequently-quoted *Journal of Philip Fithian*, p. 120, 255. Some of the odd perplexities of the task of curbing young George Lee Turberville in England are described in William Lee to Richard Henry Lee, Apr. 27, 1772, *Lee Papers*, VHS.

[5] Numerous references to them will be found in Chapter IV.

[6] *Eaton*, 7.

[7] Fithian, *op. cit.*, 89, wrote that this property had "the most agreeable situation of any I have yet seen in Maryland or Virginia." See also *Eubank*, 50. For the antecedents of the Bushrods, consult the register of St. Stephen's parish in 17 *W* (1) p. 237, and Charles Arthur Hoppin, *The Washington Ancestry*, v. 1, p. 377.

[8] Some authorities give her name as Mildred. Cf. 29 *V* 521. The origins of the Virginia Corbins are explained in 4 *W* (1) p. 30.

[9] *Lee of Virginia*, 84. The house was destroyed by fire in 1886. *Magazine of the Society of Lees of Virginia*, v. 2, p. 44.   [10] *Lee of Virginia*, 84.

[11] The richest of the early Corbins was Gawin the second, who married Hannah Lee. His will is preserved in 13 *Westmoreland Deeds and Wills*, 265. Reference to his inventory, which has many unusual items, will be found in Chap. IV. The original appears in 4 *Westmoreland Records*, 111. For Hannah Lee, see Ethel Armes, *Stratford Hall*, 204.

[12] See 13 *Westmoreland Deeds and Wills*, 95; Hardy's *Colonial Families*, 484; *Virginia Heraldica*, 86.

[13] The Ashton descent was through Col. Henry Ashton, 1671-1731, son of John Ashton. For the memorial inscriptions of Henry Ashton and his wife, see 7 *W* (1) p. 94. A description of Nominy Plantation will be found in *Eubank*, 47. The connection of the Aylett family with that of the Washingtons through Augustine Washington the second (see *supra*, p. 78), is sketched in *Lee of Virginia*, 172. William Aylett's marriage contract with Elizabeth Eskridge, Mch. 30, 1738, is recorded in *Westmoreland Records and Inventories*, 1723-46, p. 164. His will, Mch. 29, 1744, is in 10 *Westmoreland Deeds and Wills*, 51. It is one of the few wills of the time and locality in which there is no profession of religious faith.

been introduced already—Anne Lee Fitzhugh, daughter of the second Richard Lee.[14]

These, to repeat, are a few only of the many crossing lines of Northern Neck kinship. The most surprising aspect of it all is the small number of marriages outside the dominant caste.

[14] See M. J. O'Brien, *The McCarthys in Early American History*, and 2 W (2) p. 125. The will of Daniel McCarty, Mch. 29, 1724, is in 8 *Westmoreland Deeds and Wills*, 17. His inventory, June 15, 1724, appears in *Westmoreland Records and Inventories*, 1723-46, p. 28.

APPENDIX I-4

WASHINGTON'S ENGLISH ANCESTORS OF THE DIRECT PATERNAL LINE

CONCERNING HIS ancestors, George Washington knew scarcely anything. All he remembered at sixty was that in youth he had been told the family had come from one of the northern Counties of England. He was not sure whether it was Lancashire or Yorkshire or a region still farther North.[1] Two brothers, John and Lawrence Washington, he understood, had settled in Virginia about 1657. His ancestor was John, whose son Lawrence was his grandfather.[2] George was acquainted in youth with many of his cousins, but with them both interest and information ended. Genealogy seemed to him as of "very little moment."[3] Inquirers later traced his male line to Lawrence Washington, whose name appeared in the records of the town of Northampton in 1530/31. By the assumption of kinship that seems probable, though unprovable in at least five instances, the ancestors of Lawrence of Northampton can be carried back ten generations to the second half of the thirteenth century when a family of de Wessington was residing near the border of Lancashire and Westmorland.[4] As far as can be ascertained from scanty records, none of the early members of the de Wessington or Washington family was either notable or notorious. Lawrence, born about 1500, apparently became a successful wool merchant, who in 1532 was Mayor of Northampton. Seven years later, after the dissolution of the monasteries, he acquired St. Andrew's Priory, one of the three estates of Sulgrave Manor.[5]

[1] Letter to Sir Isaac Heard, May 2, 1792; 32 G. W., 32-33.
[2] Letter to William Augustine Washington, Nov. 14, 1796; 35 G. W., 281.
[3] 36 G. W., 173.
[4] The evidence is amassed, with much ingenuity and after long research, in 1 Hoppin, 1-247. Attention again is directed to the briefer genealogy, containing more information concerning Washington's nearer kin and immediate generation, in Washington C. Ford, *The Washington Family*. See *supra*, p. 15 ff.
[5] 1 Hoppin, 56, 57, 61-64, 70.

There, in comfort, he and his wife, Amy Pargiter,[6] reared those of his four sons and seven daughters who survived childhood.[7]

On Lawrence's death, Feb. 19, 1583/84, his son Robert, who was then forty-four, succeeded to the Sulgrave property. After the demise of Robert's first wife, Elizabeth Light,[8] he married Anne Fisher, thirty years his junior.[9] His surviving children by his first wife were still numerous and included an heir; but when his issue by his second spouse raised the total of his offspring to fifteen, his mate not unnaturally sought to advance the interest of her own brood. Probably at her instance, but with the consent of Lawrence, who was his oldest son, Robert Washington, in 1610, sold the landed property subject to life tenancy of the manor house.[10] On his passing in 1619, the eighty-year occupancy of Sulgrave by the Washington family ended.

Lawrence, Robert's heir, in 1616 had predeceased his father, but had begotten no less than eight sons and nine daughters [11] by his wife, Margaret Butler of Tighes, Sussex.[12] In spite of adversity, she and her husband were the most successful of the English Washingtons in the training of their children.[13] Their fifth son, the second Lawrence Washington, was born in 1602,[14] and was the first member of his family known to have graduated at Oxford. A bachelor of arts of Brasenose, 1623, he was named Fellow on the Darbie Foundation eleven days later. After he won his M.A. on Feb. 1, 1626, he remained at the university. In time he became lector of Brasenose and then one of the proctors of Oxford.

Marriage to Amphillis Twigden in 1631 compelled him, under the regulations of Oxford, to resign his fellowship within a year or a little more. When he left the university, he owed it 17s 6d and had liability for £9, 5s 6d of his pupil's battels. Apparently he did not settle promptly. On the margin of the account book remains the entry, "Mr. Washington to be sued." [15] If action ever was entered, it was after he had taken holy orders and, in March 1632/33, had become rector of All Saints, Purleigh Parish, Essex.[16] His ministry there does not appear to have been conspicuous for anything more remarkable than his defence of the perquisites of his office. Twice, at least, he

---

[6] He had no issue by his first wife, Elizabeth, widow of William Gough (1 Hoppin, 56).

[7] 1 Hoppin, 69.

[8] She died at an undetermined date prior to 1599, the year of Oliver Cromwell's birth.

[9] 1 Hoppin, 75, 81–82.   [10] 1 Hoppin, 75, 81.

[11] Hoppin, 100.

[12] It is through her line that the assumed descent of the later Washingtons from early English kings is traced. See the family tree in 1 Hoppin, 54–55.

[13] Cf. 1 Hoppin, 105.

[14] Hoppin stated (1 op. cit., 110), that Lawrence may have been born at Sulgrave, but that he could not have been there more than four years.

[15] The Brazen Nose, v. 2, no. 10, May, 1919, p. 473; ibid., v. 4, no. 1, Nov., 1924, p. 15. "Battels," in English college speech, are a student's accounts for provisions or, less accurately, for all institutional charges. A reproduction of part of the page of the Bursar's book, showing Lawrence Washington's debt, appears between pages 35 and 36.

[16] For a description of the church there, see 15 V 314–15.

was plaintiff in suits.[17] He probably was convivial, besides, and not averse to sitting over a pot of ale at an inn table.

Disaster came in 1643. Triumphant Puritans ousted Rev. Lawrence Washington from his rectorship and justified their action by charging him with being a "common frequenter of Ale-houses, not only himself sitting daily tippling there, but also encouraging others in that beastly vice." In fact, the rector was said to have been "oft drunk."[18] Against these charges, some of the parishioners and other friends vigorously defended their minister. Through their help he was allowed to preach at Little Braxted, Essex, but financially he must have been a ruined man.[19] He died in defeat, January, 1652, when he was fifty-four.[20]

Apparently, Rev. Lawrence Washington had made an effort to give good schooling to his two sons, John, born about 1632, and Lawrence, born 1635.[21] In some manner an appointment to Sutton's Hospital,[22] later Charterhouse, was procured in 1640 for John, but it was contingent on a vacancy that did not occur. John went elsewhere for such instruction as he received, and by the time he was twenty-three or twenty-four he had learned something of shipping and of seamanship. In 1656, on invitation of Edward Prescott, owner of the ketch *Sea Horse of London,* he journeyed to Danzig, joined the vessel, sailed with her to Lübeck and Copenhagen and, at Elsinore, agreed to a partnership voyage with Prescott to Virginia.[23] It is impossible to say whether Virginia happened to be the vessel's destination or whether John Washington bargained with Prescott because he wanted to go there. The Washington family had no previous direct association with the Colony, so far as is known; but John doubtless had some secondhand acquaintance with the province through his mother's brother-in-law, William Roades, who had managed an estate there.[24] Interest in Virginia may have been aroused in John Washington's mind, also, by the fact that Warham Horsmanden, a kinsman of a former rector of All Saint's, Purleigh, had gone to Virginia during the civil war.[25]

[17] 1 *Hoppin,* 116–17.
[18] Quoted in 1 *Hoppin,* 124.
[19] 1 *Hoppin,* 124, 125.
[20] 1 *Hoppin,* 126. He, dying intestate, was buried in the parish churchyard at Maldon, near Braxted Parva. His widow followed him within two years.
[21] In addition, he had a third son, William, and three daughters, Elizabeth, Margaret and Martha (1 *Hoppin,* 128–29).
[22] Strictly speaking, the Hospital of King James.
[23] 1 *Hoppin,* 147–48 where the unusual records from Westmoreland County are quoted.
[24] 1 *Hoppin,* 146.
[25] 15 *V* 315. Events after the arrival of John Washington in Virginia are described *supra,* p. 15 ff.

APPENDIX I-5

THE AMERICAN ANCESTRY OF MARY BALL

WHEN WILLIAM BALL reached Virginia in 1657,[1] he was different from most immigrants in that he was a mature man [2] who then or thereafter "transported" at his own expense his wife, two children and a number of servants, free or indentured.[3] It was not often that so large a household was brought over by a man past his youth. Equally unusual was it for so many to enter the Colony otherwise than at the cost of some resident planter or trader.

If family records are accurate, the immigrant was a son of William Ball of Lincoln's Inn, one of the four attorneys of the Office of Pleas and Exchequer. While still living in England, the younger William married Hannah Atherold,[4] and by her he had at least four children, all of whom were born in the "home country." After he came to Virginia he established himself on a neck of land he called Millenbeck, at the mouth of Corotoman Creek, Lancaster County, and there he bettered his fortune as a planter and, still more, as a trader. When King Charles had gone back to England, Ball claimed the "headrights" of himself and household.[5] Other lands he acquired, also,[6] along with the honors and offices of a gentleman of the County. By 1677 he was Major of the county militia;[7] twice at least he was Burgess;[8] in the defence of Lancaster against the Indians and in the turmoil of Bacon's Rebellion, he was conspicuously useful.[9] When he sat down in August, 1677, with John Washington and others to lay a levy on the Northern Neck for the expenses of suppressing the uprising, William Ball was in the company of his peers.[10] He had risen as high and as fast as his neighbors had.

---

[1] *Hayden*, 49, gave the date as 1651, but in the back cover of the *Letter Book* of Joseph Ball second was found "a history of the Ball family from a Downman MS." This may have been prepared by Joseph Ball, who interested himself in genealogy during his long residence in England. The date of the immigration of William Ball is given in this document as 1657. No reference to him is found in Virginia records prior to 1659 when he is listed among the Justices of Lancaster County (3 *Lancaster Orders*, 77).

[2] Born, according to Hayden, in 1615 and consequently 36, if migrating in 1651, or 42 if migrating in 1657.

[3] See the grant of "headright lands," Mch. 14, 1666/67; 3 *Lancaster Orders*.

[4] Nothing is known of her except that she came to Virginia, headed the household of William Ball and died in 1694; but from the interest taken in her by her grandson Joseph Ball second, it is manifest that she was a person of honor in the traditions of the family. Joseph's interest was not diminished by the fact that he was uncertain of her name. See letters of Joseph Ball second to Joseph Chinn, July 17, 1745, May 23, 1747 (*Ball Letter Book*).

[5] Mch. 14, 1666/67; 3 *Lancaster Orders*, 366.

[6] Cf. 5 *L.O. Records*, 270. [7] Cf. *Journ. H.B.*, 1659–93, p. 49.

[8] 1668–76, 1676–77; *ibid.*, unpaged list. [9] *Ibid.*, 111; 2 H 329.

[10] See *supra*, p. 29; *Westmoreland Deeds*, 1665–77, p. 349.

About three years later his life closed. It was marred only by his bitter estrangement from his daughter Hannah, who had married David Fox. In his will he gave her 5s sterling which, said he, "is an overplus of her portion or deserts." The father took precautions, also, to keep the mother from leaving the daughter any part of her estate,[11] but in this he did not altogether succeed. When Hannah Ball died in 1694, she bequeathed to her "loveing daughter Hannah Fox, wife of Col. David Fox, a suite of red curtains, valens and counterpane and bolster, a pewter cistern to set bottles in, a pewter custard pan, a cabinet that stands next the kitchen, a silver sugar dish, mustard pot and 3 spoons, a silver trencher." The mother made an effort, too, to have her daughter inherit the "negro and mulatto girl given me by my husband to dispose of as I please."[12]

Of the four children of William and Hannah Ball, the youngest was Joseph,[13] who was born in England, presumably in 1649.[14] Surviving records do not show when he came to Virginia but he was in the Colony at the time of his father's death. As the Northern Neck developed, Joseph prospered moderately. His "tithables" over a period of years never rose above fifteen or declined below nine;[15] his residence, though located at some distance from Morattico Creek, was a comfortable abode and bore a name reminiscent of old England, Epping Forest;[16] he held the usual offices of Justice of the County Court, vestryman and Burgess;[17] in 1699 he was appointed Lieutenant Colonel of the militia of the County.[18] His first marriage[19] yielded five daughters[20] and a son, Joseph second.

Evidently the affection of the first Joseph Ball for these children was unusually strong. From 1703 onward he deeded to them or to their husbands much of his real estate,[21] and in 1706 he made reservation of house room and

[11] Oct. 5, 1680; 5 *Lancaster Wills*, 70.

[12] R 8 *Lancaster Wills*, 52. Her principal will, which bears date of Dec. 5, 1694, follows in the records an incomplete testament of June 25, 1695, in which Hannah Ball undertook to leave the two slaves to her daughter. It is not plain whether the later document was admitted to probate.

[13] Richard, the oldest, died in Maryland in 1677 (7 V 440; 8 *ibid.*, 80). William Ball the second of Virginia was the next son. (See his will of Nov. 4, 1694; R 8 *Lancaster Wills*, 45.) Hannah, the third child, has been mentioned.

[14] *Hayden*, 61.

[15] CD 4 *Lancaster Orders*, 1696–1702, p. 7; *ibid.*, 1702–13, 138, 232.

[16] Although the name had kindled much romance, little is known of the house. To judge from Joseph Ball's inventory, the residence was not large. In a deed of June 1, 1706 (9 R *Lancaster Deeds*, 163), Joseph Ball spoke of "the great house which is now building." Mention of the ruinous condition of the "old building" is made in the *Letter Book* of Joseph Ball, about 1750, and this may refer to the main house.

[17] He served in 1698, 1700, 1702 and possibly at other sessions.

[18] 1 *E. J.*, 444.

[19] To Elizabeth, whose family name is given as Rogers or Romney. She perhaps died by 1703 and certainly before 1707.

[20] The number usually given is four, but the mention of a fifth, Frances, in Miller, *Descendants of Thomas Carter*, 271, indicates that she was the oldest and was born in 1681. She died Sept. 3, 1699, "three hours after she was delivered of a son."

[21] 9 R *Lancaster Deeds*, 211, 245, 246, 277.

pasturage as if he were retiring,[22] but he soon made other plans. He fell in love with Mary Johnson, the widowed mother of two children; and, after making still another deed of gift, which perhaps was intended to placate his sons and daughters, he married Mrs. Johnson. Of her history, prior to that time, nothing is known except that she had witnessed a deed of Joseph Ball's as early as 1703 and, in doing so, had made her mark.[23] Joseph, when re-married, was fifty-eight; Mary was not past the child-bearing age. Sometime in 1708 or 1709 she bore him a daughter, whom they named after her. This child's infancy was spent with her parents on the property her father had reserved when he had made his gifts to his children by his first marriage. The second family lived comfortably, though not luxuriously. There were nine Negroes or more, an indentured white servant and a sufficiency of live-stock. For approximately three years and a half Joseph enjoyed this life of quiet domesticity. Then, in the early summer of 1711, he died.[24] He had a measure of deserved happiness in his children, but he had lived long enough to see them have their share of distress and misery.

The oldest daughter of the first marriage, Anne Ball, married Col. Edwin Conway, who was brother of Francis Conway. A time was to come when Francis's daughter was to have a son who was to be christened James Mad-ison. Anne Ball's children by Col. Edwin Conway numbered nine. The youngest of these married James Gordon, whose diary was to give him a place in many a footnote of Virginia history.[25] Nothing is known of Anne Ball Conway's marital life. It may have been happy. In later years, after her death and his remarriage, Colonel Conway was notoriously irascible.

Elizabeth Ball, second daughter of Joseph and Elizabeth Ball, married Rev. Joseph Carnegie.[26] If the volume of his litigation is a gauge of the conten-tiousness of his character, he could not have been an easy man with whom to live.

Neither Anne nor Elizabeth had so tragic a life as their sister Esther or Easter,[27] the third daughter of Joseph Ball's first marriage. Presumably in

---

[22] *Ibid.*, 163.

[23] *Ibid.*, 113, 211. It has been argued that her maiden name was Bennett and that she may have been Joseph Ball's housekeeper (15 W (2) p. 176). With equal vigor it has been maintained that she was Mary Montague before her marriage and that from her Washington received the Montague seal he used. The only inferential evidence of any possible value is the fact that in his will Joseph Ball remembered Elizabeth, Mary Johnson's daughter by her former husband. As Joseph's life with his second wife was brief, it may be maintained that he perhaps had known Elizabeth as a girl on the plantation or "around the house" before he married the mother. The whole of the sensitive or sarcastic argument about the Johnson marriage of Joseph Ball is futile. As is set forth in the text, the care Mary Ball received at the hands of the Johnson connec-tion is ample proof of their gentility and kindness.

[24] His will is dated June 5, 1711; it was probated July 11, 1711 (R 10 *Lancaster Wills*, 88). The facts given in the text concerning his possessions during the infancy of Mary are taken from this will.   [25] He is quoted scores of times, *supra*, Chapter IV.

[26] He was licensed to preach Oct. 26, 1700.

[27] It is probable that the name was Esther, which until recent years was pronounced Easter in some Counties of Virginia.

1703, Esther became the wife of Rawleigh Chinn. Their mismating was un-recorded until 1721/22. Then began a succession of difficulties that scandal-ized the Northern Neck. The husband became engaged in brawls with his wife's brother Joseph [28] and even with a blacksmith.[29] Esther had to go into court with a complaint that Rawleigh abused her and denied her subsistence until actually she was compelled to leave home in order to be delivered safely of a child.[30] The next year, she had to ask that Chinn be put under bond as she feared he would injure or kill her.[31]

When this petition was denied, after a hearing in court, Esther Chinn in-stituted against one of her husband's witnesses an action for perjury.[32] From her estranged mate she won at length an annual separation allowance of £25 sterling or 4000 pounds of tobacco.[33] Free to this extent, Rawleigh Chinn in time had an affair with Margaret Downman, a daughter of the second Wil-liam Ball and herself the widow of Rawleigh Downman. By the widow Margaret Downman, Rawleigh Chinn was believed to have had three chil-dren. Both he and Margaret were cited several times before the grand jury and before the church wardens on a charge of living in adultery.[34] As neither party answered any summons, jury and wardens obligingly dropped the charge. Rawleigh shared in land speculation as well as in affairs of the heart [35] and he made a few gifts of small tracts to a son and a daughter.[36] When he died in 1742/43 he left a considerable part of his property to his illegitimate children, and nothing to his wife beyond the allotment given her by court order.[37]

The fourth daughter of Joseph Ball by his first marriage was Hannah, whose life was in unsensational contrast to that of Esther. At an unde-termined date and age, Hannah married Rawleigh Travers the second.[38] In 1730 or about that year Rawleigh died.[39] The inventory of his estate suggests that he was a well-to-do farmer rather than the owner of a great plantation.[40] Beyond this, scarcely anything is known of his life. Hannah remarried, but

[28] H 7 *Lancaster Orders*, 20, 21, 51, 107, 111, 113, 116, 121, 137.
[29] *Ibid.*, 102.   [30] *Ibid.*, 51, 60.
[31] *Ibid.*, 107.   [32] *Ibid.*, 186.
[33] See Rawleigh Chinn's will in 13 *Lancaster Deeds and Wills*, 253–54.
[34] 10 *Richmond Co. Orders*, 13, 330 *et passim*.
[35] Cf. his patents of 3800 acres in 1731–32; *L.O. Records, N.N.*, D, 73, 79.
[36] H 7 *Lancaster Orders*, 235; 13 *Lancaster Deeds and Wills*, 1735–43, p. 253.
[37] 13 *Lancaster Deeds and Wills*, 253–54. Esther Chinn's pathetic will is in 15 *ibid.*, 32; the will of Margaret Downman is in 6 *Richmond Co. Wills*, 1 & 2.
[38] His father's name appears in Lancaster County as early as 1654. See 5 *V* 160. In 1661–67 the first Rawleigh Travers was Burgess for the County, and in 1665 he was patentee of 3650 acres of land on Potomac Creek (5 *L.O. Records*, 521). Part of this land subsequently was ac-quired by Col. George Mason the second (1 Rowland's *Mason*, 88). In 1687 Travers was one of the justices of the County (3 *Lancaster Orders*, 33). It is probable that the Col. William Travers the first, mentioned as at Kinsale in 1662–63 (2 *H* 330) was the brother of Rawleigh Travers the first, whose home for some years was at Morattico and then in Stafford County.
[39] 22 *T* 42.
[40] *Stafford Wills*, 1729–48, p. 107.

her second husband, Simon Pearson, did not long survive.[41] The widow, in fact, had the extraordinary experience of filing in court on the same day the inventory of her first husband and the will of her second.[42] The total left her by two mates was not large. On her death, which did not occur until at least twelve years after that of Simon Pearson, her personal effects were reckoned at £314.[43]

If Anne, Elizabeth, Hannah and even Esther Ball are shadowy figures, scarcely more than names, their brother Joseph is a known and understandable person. The reason is the fortunate survival of his Letter Book in which he wrote and then corrected the first draft of his communications during a long period of residence in England. There are several such Virginia records of equal or greater length but none that more clearly and candidly discloses the personality of its writer. His characteristics, already sketched in part,[44] included an interest in his family stock and a pride in those of his kinsmen who attained distinction. He was generous, too, on occasion,[45] but was careful in choosing the occasion. Joseph had absolute confidence in his own judgment and full assurance of his rectitude. He was most exact in money matters and as careful to pay what he owed as he was to collect his due,[46] but he was litigious,[47] domineering and disinclined to ask advice even on matters of which he had no knowledge. This cost him late in life much of what he had accumulated by saving and sueing. He decided, about 1758 or 1759, that he could make money by erecting houses in London and he began the enterprise without seeking the counsel of those who knew the values and the building methods of the city. The venture put him heavily in debt and perhaps contributed to his death, Jan. 10, 1760.[48]

[41] *Ibid.*, 101.

[42] This probably was due to the fact that she had delayed putting into the records of the court the inventory of Rawleigh Travers's property which she and her second husband used jointly. After the death of Pearson, who left children by a previous marriage, it became important for her to distinguish her effects from those of the younger Pearsons.

[43] *Stafford Deeds*, O, p. 30. Some details of the children of Rawleigh and Hannah Moore Travers will be found in *Hayden*, 295 and in Culbertson, *Hunters of Virginia*, 145. The will of Rawleigh Travers the third is in *Stafford Deeds*, O, p. 76.

[44] See *supra*, p. 190 ff.

[45] For his gift of a tea-set to Betty Washington, see *supra*, Chapter IV.

[46] Cf. Joseph Ball to Charles Arnold, Oct. 25, 1744. As an example of his insistence on being paid, his *Letter Book* shows that he did a little genealogical research in England for a friend in Richmond County and billed him for 6s 3d—one half for the official inquiry and the other half for "my trouble" (Letter to Luke Milner, Mch. 19–20, 1743/44, *loc. cit.*).

[47] Cf. Joseph Ball to Joseph Chinn, Feb. 18, 1743/44, n.d., 1746, and Apr. 11, 1748, *loc. cit*.

[48] Rawleigh Downman to Mrs. Ellen Chichester, n.d., 1760, *Ball Letter Book*. This Rawleigh was the son of Rawleigh Downman, who married the second William Ball's daughter Margaret, the same Margaret who later figured in the unhappy affairs of Rawleigh and Esther Chinn. When the younger Rawleigh Downman sought to marry Frances Ball, daughter of Joseph Ball, her father refused his consent. Persuasion finally wrung from him a "yes," but not until Frances was 30 years old. Even then, Joseph stipulated that she should not leave England during the lifetime of her mother. That lady, Frances Ravenscroft Ball, expired in May, 1762. See Rawleigh Downman to Joseph Chinn, Aug. 12, 1762 (*loc. cit.*). Within approximately three years, Rawleigh and Frances Ball Downman were in Virginia. Cf. Rawleigh Downman to Edward Athawes and Son, Dec. 20, 1765 (*loc. cit.*).

APPENDIX I–6

The Cost of Washington's Birthplace
Washington Vs the Jones Estate

Decd is Dr from Aprill 1722 till 1723				pr Contra				
	Tobo	L	s	d		Tobo	L	s	d
Paid him in money & Goods		33		9½	By building the round hill church	6000	40		
To Do that year in Tobo by Orders .	9004				By your rent twice charged		3		
from 1723 to 1724									
To pd him in money & goods		24	16	6	By my house when finished	5000	1		
					By 1 L of Tee [?]			14	
from 1724 to 1725									
To pd him in money & goods		9	18	11	By 2 bedsteads		1		
To ditto in Tobacco	188½				By 1 cradle			7	6
To the not finishing my house	500				By 2 mantle pieces .		2	10	
To his sickness & burial if allowed Maj Eskridge ...	500				By Mr. DeButts ...	200	2		
						11200	49	11	6
To Clks fees Admr 150 & oath to account order & record	183				By making a small poplar table			6	
						11200	49	17	6
	13961	67	16	2½	By ball due AW	2761½	17	18	8½
						13961	67	16	2½

Errors excepted by Augustine Washington

This account was produced into Court by Augustine Washington Gent. upon oath and was allowed by the Court payable at 16 shillings 8 pence p Cent And ordered to be recorded

Recordat 8vo die Aprils 1726

Test Thos Sorrell

ClCom

pr Eundum Cluum [1]

[1] *Westmoreland Records and Inventories,* 1723–46, p. 20. Cf. *Westmoreland Orders,* 1721–31, p. 102. The late Charles Arthur Hoppin filed in the Westmoreland County Museum, Montross, Va., a number of deeds, leases and miscellaneous legal papers that related directly or indirectly to the affairs of Augustine Washington. Through the courtesy of Mrs. A. E. Carver, President (1948) of the Women's Club of Montross, these records have been made available for the present study. In his MS notes on the document here printed, Mr. Hoppin wrote: "This account was occasioned by the death of the said David Jones before he had completed his agreement regarding the said building and the account against the said Washington was made up by the administrator of the estate of the said David Jones dec'd and delivered to Capt. Wn. The latter copied the Jones statement unto another paper and then added his own account of what he had previously paid to Jones for labour and materials (excluding the brick for the walls of the house, which brick was made by Capt. AW and his slaves etc. from clay on his estate). The joint minutes were then submitted to the Co. Court of Westm'd for judgment. The Court awarded Capt AW the sum of 276½ pounds of tobo and £17.18 s. and 5½ pence as being what he had paid prior to Jones's death in 1725. The total amount as paid by Capt Wn to said Jones for labor and certain materials was 13961 pounds of tobo and also in money £67:16:2½ between Apr, 1722 and the death of Jones in 1725. Evidently the brick for the house had been made by Capt. Wn as well as the foundations for the house before Jones began the general woodwork construction, much of the timber being supplied by the sd Wn. from the woods on his estate, cut, hauled and sawed by his slaves. The account reveals that in his sickness David Jones was cared for by AW and after his death Wn buried him. Also it reveals that Capt Wn employed Jones to build the Round Hill Church west of Oak Grove and paid him for labour etc., 6000 pounds of tobo and £40 in cash. The services of Jones would amount, reckoned by the present standard of money, to approximately $5000, tobo being reckoned at approximately 10 to 12 cents a pound originally." On the last point, it is necessary to point out that the figure of $5000 given by Mr. Hoppin as the cost of David Jones's service includes the account for Round Hill Church, which was 6000 pounds of tobacco. The statement of Augustine Washington shows that Jones's charge for the residence was 5000 pounds of tobacco, which the court valued at 16s 8d per hundred weight, or two pence a pound. Jones's bill for the dwelling, therefore, was about £41 sterling par, or, assuming a purchasing power ten times that of the present time, slightly under $2000. This is the maximum figure. As for the making of brick and the sawing of timber by Augustine's servants, separately from the contract, this is possible, but there is no evidence whatsoever that brick were used, nor is it by any means certain that a young planter of the moderate estate of Augustine would have had slaves capable of making brick or, indeed, of sawing house-timbers. Augustine's son George as late as 1773 had to hire a white man, Joseph Hagan, to burn brick for Mount Vernon (*Ledger B,* folio 77), though his servants were more numerous and certainly no less skilled than those of Augustine half a century before. The best testimony Mr. Hoppin could adduce to support his statement concerning brick was a letter of William Lanier Washington, written Apr. 14, 1926. In this letter Mr. Washington said that his father, James Barroll Washington, told him that his (i.e., J. B. Washington's) grandfather, who was born in 1789, informed him (J. B. W.) in boyhood that the brick for the birthplace were made on the premises (8 *T* 85). W. L. Washington and his father of course transmitted accurately the tradition they received; but the gentleman to whom the tradition is credited—the great-grandfather of William Lanier Washington—himself was born nine years after the burning of a Wakefield which undoubtedly had brick foundations. That structure never has been proved to have been the original house on the site. The inventory of Augustine ("Austin") Washington, (*Westmoreland Records,* No. 4, 1756–67, p. 178 ff) was that of a man abundantly able, judging from his household effects, to have built a handsome new house on Pope's Creek or to have done as his brother Lawrence did at Mount Vernon, in the enlargement of an existing residence.

APPENDIX I-7

Schooling Under Hobby

THE FIRST place of education to which George was ever sent, was a little "old field school," kept by one of his father's tenants, named Hobby; an honest, poor old man, who acted in the double character of sexton and schoolmaster. On his skill as a grave-digger, tradition is silent; but for a teacher of youth, his qualifications were certainly of the humbler sort; making what is generally called an A. B. C. schoolmaster. Such was the preceptor who first taught Washington the knowledge of letters! Hobby lived to see his young pupil in all his glory, and rejoiced exceedingly. In his cups—for though a sexton, he would sometimes drink, particularly on the General's birth days—he used to boast that " 'twas he, who, between his knees, had laid the foundation of George Washington's greatness."—M. L. Weems, *Life of George Washington,* edition of 1860, p. 12.

The Cherry Tree

The following anecdote is a case in point. It is too valuable to be lost, and too true to be doubted; for it was communicated to me by the same excellent lady to whom I am indebted for the last.

"When George," said she, "was about six years old, he was made the wealthy master of a hatchet! of which, like most little boys, he was immoderately fond, and was constantly going about chopping every thing that came in his way. One day, in the garden, where he often amused himself hacking his mother's pea-sticks, he unluckily tried the edge of his hatchet on the body of a beautiful young English cherry-tree, which he barked so terribly, that I don't believe the tree ever got the better of it. The next morning the old gentleman, finding out what had befallen his tree, which, by the by, was a great favorite, came into the house; and with much warmth asked for the mischievous author, declaring at the same time, that he would not have taken five guineas for his tree. Nobody could tell him any thing about it. Presently George and his hatchet made their appearance. "George," said his father, "do you know who killed that beautiful little cherry tree yonder in the garden?" This was a tough question; and George staggered under it for a moment; but quickly recovered himself: and and looking at his father, with the sweet face of youth brightened with the inexpressible charm of all-conquering truth, he bravely cried out, "I can't tell a lie, Pa; you know I can't tell a lie. I did cut it with my hatchet."—Run to my arms, you dearest boy, cried his father in transports, run to my arms glad am I, George, that you killed my tree; for you have paid me for it a thousand fold. Such an act of heroism in my son is worth more than a thousand trees, though blossomed with silver, and their fruits of purest gold."—*Ibid.*, 15-16.

George as a Youthful Peacemaker

A very aged gentleman, formerly a school mate of his, has often assured me, (while pleasing recollection brightened his furrowed cheeks,) that nothing was more common, when the boys were in high dispute about a question of fact, than for some little shaver among the mimic heroes, to call out, "well boys! George Washington was there; George Washington was there. He knows all about it: and if he don't say it was so, then we will give it up."— "Done," said the adverse party. Then away they would trot to hunt for George. Soon as his verdict was heard, the party favoured would begin to crow, and then all hands would return to play again.

About five years after the death of his father, he quitted school for ever, leaving the boys in tears for his departure; for he had ever lived among them, in the spirit of a brother. He was never guilty of so brutish a practice as that of fighting himself; nor would he, when able to prevent it, allow them to fight one another. If he could not disarm their savage passions by his arguments, he would instantly go to the master, and inform him of their barbarous intentions.

"The boys," said the same old gentlemen, "were often angry with George for this."—but he used to say, "angry or not angry, you shall never, boys, have my consent to a practice so shocking! shocking even in slaves and dogs; then how utterly scandalous in little boys at school, who ought to look on one another as brothers. And what must be the feelings of our tender parents, when, instead of seeing us come home smiling and lovely, as the joy of their hearts! they see us creeping in like young blackguards, with our heads bound up, black eyes, and bloody clothes! And what is all this for? Why, that we may get praise!! But the truth is, a quarrelsome boy was never sincerely praised! Big boys, of the vulgar sort, indeed may praise him: but it is only as they would a silly game cock, that fights for their pastime: and the little boys are sure to praise him, but it is only as they would a bull dog—to keep him from tearing them"—*Ibid.*, 23-24.

APPENDIX I–8

Outline of Section of Chapter IV

"Virginia During the Youth of Washington"

APPENDIX I–9

CRITIQUE OF WASHINGTON'S JOURNAL OF 1754

PART OF A French translation of Washington's journal for the period Mch. 31–June 27, 1754, appeared in a book published in Paris during 1756 under the title, Mémoire contenant le précis des faits, avec leurs pièces justificatives pour servir de résponse aux observations envoyées par les ministres d'Angleterre dans les cours de l'Europe.

Issued to vindicate French occupation of the Ohio and to portray the British as the aggressors there, the Mémoire contained Pièces Justificatives in two divisions. Sixteen documents, French and British, constituted the first part, and thirteen made up the second. Journal du Major Washington was No. VIII of the first part. A copy of this pamphlet was found on a French prize ship, was brought to New York, and in 1757 was published in several editions. A London version of the same year was entitled The Conduct of the Late Ministry. This was reprinted as The Mystery Revealed.[1]

Washington said of the journal, as published: "I kept no regular one during that expedition; rough minutes of occurrences I certainly took and find them as certainly and strangely metamorphosed; some parts left out, which I remember were entered, and many things added that never were thought of; the names of men and things egregiously miscalled; and the whole of what

[1] See Francis Parkman's note on the copy of the French original, now in the Harvard Library, given him by Jared Sparks. The copy of the same French text, owned by Thomas Jefferson, is among the treasures of the Library of Congress.

I saw Englished is very incorrect and nonsensical; yet I will not pretend to say that the little body, who brought it to me, has not made a literal translation, and a good one." [2]

The text, for these reasons, is suspect in all that concerns British policy and Washington's behavior in the Jumonville affair. Unfortunately, too, an English translation of a French text based on an English original is a difficult document to which to apply the usual tests of internal evidence. These do not yield many of the things one could wish to know concerning the general accuracy of the narrative or the circumstances in which Washington's "rough minutes" were revised.

Comparison of events described in the journal with those set forth in Washington's letters to Dinwiddie shows some errors of date in the journal but nothing factual that is greatly at variance with Washington's known communications prior to May 27, 1754. A somewhat different approach is offered by the footnotes of the French text. These appear most conveniently in the Toner edition and they raise the question whether the journal was edited in Canada or in Paris. As numbered by Toner, notes d, p. 37; f, p. 39; h, p. 48; k, p. 52; o, p. 67; p, p. 71, and dd, p. 99, suggest a knowledge that an official in Paris might not possess regarding conditions in Pennsylvania and individuals named by Washington. On the other hand, note rr, p. 118, discloses lack of information concerning the treaty of Logstown, with which a Canadian official probably would have been familiar. Most of the remaining notes read as if they were the work of the men who edited the other documents of the Mémoire.

Another bit of collateral evidence is presented in a letter from Du Quesne to the Keeper of the Seals, Oct. 28, 1754: [3] "The Governor of New England could not make a levy to raise troops without the King's consent and you have seen by the journal of G. Washington that all the provinces have furnished their detachments." This would indicate that the journal had been transmitted from Canada to France at a date sufficiently in advance of Oct. 28, 1754, for the Governor of Canada to assume that it had been received and read by that time. While this is not convincing evidence, it gives reason for believing that as it left Canada the journal was in a form to justify that term and was not merely a collection of minutes and other papers.

The one demonstrable instance of French editing is in the entry of May 27–28, 1754. This manifestly includes the substance of Washington's letter of May 29, 1754, to Governor Dinwiddie, a rough draft of which doubtless was found at Fort Necessity. The original of this communication is in 1 Din., 176 ff. A few comparisons will be informative:

---

[2] Washington to unidentified correspondent, presumably in 1757; 2 Sparks, 463.
[3] Paris: Aff. Etrang.: Mém. et Docts. 10, 47–153.

Text of original in 1 Din., 179 ff	*Translation of Mémoire in 1 Ford, 74 ff*
. . . about 9 o'clock the same night [May 27] I received an express from the Half King, who was incamped with some of his people about 6 miles off . . .	About 8 at night, received an express from the Half King, which informed me that as he was coming to join us . . .
I set out with 40 men before 10.	That very moment I sent out forty men, and ordered my ammunition to be concealed, fearing a stratagem of the French to attack our camp.
When we came to the Half King, I councilled with him and got his assent to go hand in hand and strike the French.	. . . about sunrise we arrived at the Indian camp, where after holding a council with the Half King, it was concluded to attack them together.
I thereupon, in conjunction with the Half King and Monacatoocha, formed a disposition to attack them on all sides, which we accordingly did . . .	. . . we formed ourselves for surrounding them and took up our march one after the other, in the Indian manner: we were advanced pretty near to them, as we thought, when they discovered us: whereupon I ordered my company to fire . . .
. . . and after an engagement of about 15 minutes, we killed 10, wounded one and took 21 prisoners, amongst those that were killed was Monsieur De Jumonville, the commander . . .	. . . [my company] was supported by that of Mr. Waggener, and my company and his received the whole fire of the French, during the greater part of the action, which lasted only a quarter of an hour before the enemy was routed. We killed Mr. de Jumonville, the commander of that party, with nine others; we wounded one, and made twenty-one prisoners.
	The Indians scalped the dead and took most of their arms . . .

These [captured] officers pretend they were coming on an embassy, but the absurdity of this pretext is too glaring as Your Honor will see by the instructions and summons enclosed. These instructions were to reconnoitre the country, roads, creeks, &c., to Potomack, which they were about to do.

After that I marched on with the prisoners. They had informed me that they had been sent with a summons to order me to depart—a plausible pretence to discover our camp, and to obtain a knowledge of our forces and our situation! It was so clear that they had come to reconnoitre, that I admired their assurance, in telling me that they were come as an embassy; for their instructions mentioned that they should get what knowledge they could of the roads, rivers and of all the country as far as Potomack.

These enterprising men were purposely choose [sic] out to get intelligence, which they were to send back by some brisk dispatches with mention of the day that they were to serve the summons, which could be through no other view than to get sufficient reinforcements to fall upon us immediately after; this, with several other reasons, induced all the officers to believe firmly that they were sent as spies rather than as anything else, and has occasioned my sending them as prisoners, though they expected, or at least had some faint hope of being continued as ambassadors.

They finding where we were incamped, instead of coming up in a publick manner, sought out one of the most secret retirements, fitter for a deserter than an ambassador to in-

And instead of coming as an ambassador publicly and in an open manner, they came most secretly, and sought after the most hidden retreats, more fit for deserters than an ambas-

camp in, stayed there two or three days, send spies to reconnoitre our camp, as we are told, though they deny it.

Their whole body moved back near two miles, sent off two runners to acquaint Contrecoeur with our strength, and where we were incamped, &c.

Now 36 men would almost have been a retinue for a princely ambassador, instead of petit. Why did they, if their designs were open, stay so long within 5 miles of us without delivering his embassy or acquainting me with it. His waiting could be with no other design than to get [a] detachment to enforce the summons as soon as it was given; they had no occasion to send out spies, for the name of ambassador is sacred among all nations, but it was by the track of these spies they were discovered, and we got intelligence of them. They would not have retired two miles back without delivering the summons, and sought a skulking place (which to do them justice, was done with great judgment), but for some special reason besides.

sador; in such retreats they remained hid for whole days together being no more than five miles from us. From thence they sent spies to reconnoitre our camps;

the whole force retraced their steps two miles; they sent the two messengers spoken of in the instructions to acquaint M. de Contrecoeur of the place we were in, and of our dispositions, that he might send his detachments to enforce the summons as soon as it should be given.

Besides, it was a suite worthy of a prince that this ambassador had; whereas he was merely a petty French officer. An ambassador has no need of spies, his character being always sacred: and since their intention was so good, why did they tarry two days, five miles from us, without acquainting me with the summons,

or at least, with something that related to the embassy? That alone would be sufficient to raise the strongest suspicions, and we ought to do them the justice to say that, wishing to hide themselves, they could not pick out better places than they have done.

In any analysis of these parallel passages, due allowance must be made for the natural inclination of the unknown translator to employ a smooth, idiomatic French. Some of the discrepancies between the original to Dinwiddie and the retranslated text are to be explained on this ground. There remain differences of sufficient importance to suggest that Washington's draft of his letter to Dinwiddie was revised after it was captured, to stress facts that sustained the French point of view and to eliminate facts derogatory of the French mission. This theory must not be carried too far, because of the possibility that the first draft of Washington's letter may have been changed substantially by him before it was dispatched to the Governor.

Fact and probability, therefore, can be fitted together to no firmer conclusion than this: Colonel Washington kept a rough but continuous and measurably coherent journal, perhaps in a blank book, along with his daily notes and the draft of letters he later wrote out in "fair copies" for his correspondents. One such draft was the first form of part of a letter subsequently sent to Governor Dinwiddie under date of May 29, 1754. This journal, possibly with other papers, fell into the hands of the French at Fort Necessity. The document was transmitted to France soon after it was captured and, before the end of October, 1754, it was assumed by the Governor of Canada to have been read in Paris. Some unidentified French editor either believed that the draft of the letter to Dinwiddie was part of the journal, or else he deliberately incorporated it into the journal.

The editor, in addition, emphasized facts that gave color to the allegation of an attack on a French embassy, and he eliminated some items that indicated a purpose on the part of the French to employ force, if the English did not withdraw. Items that disparaged the Indian allies of Britain, Half King in particular, were enlarged out of proportion to the place given them in the letter. Prior to publication of the journal in a justificatory memoir, footnotes were added. These were intended to make the English appear as the aggressors and Washington as the assassin of Jumonville. It is not possible to say whether the redaction was in Paris, in Canada, or in both. The treatment of the account of the Jumonville affair somewhat strongly suggests the hand of someone familiar with the incidents. Other parts of the journal indicate, on the whole, that the editorial treatment was in Paris.

As an historical document of value in the biography of Washington, the translated and retranslated journal is not to be accepted as literally correct, and in some of its dates it demonstrably is in error. There is no reason for challenging its general trustworthiness prior to the events that culminated in the death of Jumonville and the assertion by the French survivors of their alleged right to diplomatic immunity. Concerning these events, which are by far the most important in the journal, there fortunately exists, in Washington's letter of May 29, 1754, to Dinwiddie, an adequate, contemporary first-hand narrative.

APPENDIX I–10

THE CAPITULATION OF FORT NECESSITY

OBSCURITY OF detail and conflict of evidence make the capitulation of Fort Necessity a fascinating historical puzzle in three particulars: Were the preliminary negotiations conducted by Jacob van Braam alone or by him and William La Peyroney? What were the conditions Washington rejected? Did van Braam deceive Washington concerning the terms and, especially, concerning the admission that Jumonville had been "assassinated"?

The available evidence consists of: (1) various references in the four accounts, direct and indirect, for which Washington was responsible, as mentioned, *supra,* p. 403, n. 118; (2) the letter of Maj. Adam Stephen in the *Md. Gazette* of Aug. 29, 1754; (3) Stephen's mention of the circumstances in his "Life," prepared for Benjamin Rush; (4) Villiers' observations in the *Précis* that included Washington's journal, conveniently translated in 2 *Sparks,* 461 ff; (5) van Braam's testimony at the trial of himself and Captain Stobo in Canada in 1756, *Rapport de l'Archiviste de la Prov. de Quebec, 1922–23,* p. 304 ff; (6) the text of the capitulation itself as given in the original at Montreal and in the early copy in the Virginia archives; and (7) van Braam's memoir and the action of the General Assembly of 1760–61, in his case.

Governor Dinwiddie is the first witness on the question whether van Braam alone or van Braam and La Peyroney together conducted the preliminary negotiations. In the Governor's letter of July 24, 1754,[1] the statement is made that "the commander [Washington] sent two officers, to whom they [the French] gave their proposals . . ." The *Virginia Gazette,* July 19, 1754, on the indirect authority of Washington and Mackay, quoted the two officers as saying: "We then sent Captain van Braam and Mr. Peyronee [sic] to receive their proposals, which they did . . ." This would leave no doubt of the circumstances were there not (1) numerous references to the action of van Braam alone and (2) the statements of Adam Stephen that "Mr. van Braam was sent to speak to them," and that "Mr. Peyroney was dangerously wounded, and we much regretted to the loss of his services on this occasion."[2] From the context, it is clear that Stephen meant to say La Peyroney, an intelligent and well-educated Frenchman, was missed in the translation of the terms. It is not clear when La Peyroney was injured,

---

[1] 1 *Din.,* 240.
[2] *Md. Gazette,* Aug. 29, 1754; *Ambler,* 212. The name is spelled Peyronee, Peyronie and in various other ways, but Peyroney is the signature to one of his autograph letters in 1 *Hamilton,* 40.

though the statement that he did receive a wound is verifiable. In these circumstances, the solution given in the text appears to be the only one that reconciles the evidence: La Peyroney probably began the negotiations in company with van Braam and, during the course of them, either received a wound or collapsed because of a wound sustained earlier in the day.

Regarding the rejection of conditions originally imposed by the French commander, Washington wrote later: ". . . we looked upon his offer to parley as an artifice to get into and examine our trenches, and refused on this account until they desired an officer might be sent to them, and gave their parole for his safe return . . . We absolutely refused their first and second proposals and would consent to capitulate on no other terms than such as we obtained." [3] The narrative in the *Virginia Gazette* reads, in part: ". . . when the French called to parley: from the great improbability that such a vastly superior force and possessed of such an advantage, would offer a parley first, we suspected a deceit and therefore refused to consent that they should come among us; on which they desired us to send an officer to them, and engaged their parole for his safety; we then sent . . . to receive their proposals . . . and about midnight we agreed . . ." [4] Adam Stephen testified: [5] "Upon our insisting on it they altered what was more material to them [than the admission that Jumonville had been assassinated] the article relating to ammunition, which they wanted to detain; and that of the cannon, which they agreed to have destroyed, instead of reserved for their use." Part of this last assertion can be discarded. The capitulation specifically stated that the English could carry off all their belongings, *a l'exception de l'artillerie, que nous nous* [sic] *réservons.* [6] Stephen could not have been correct about the artillery unless the French agreed informally to destroy what they "reserved" officially. This is most improbable, but the original text of the capitulation shows that Stephen was correct in saying the French yielded on the matter of ammunition. From the MS, the words *munitions de guerre* had been struck out, apparently by the same pen with which the names of van Braam and Stobo were written into the space left in the paragraph on hostages.

Fitting together these bits of evidence is not easy, nor does any arrangement quite carry conviction. The first decision of Washington manifestly was to refuse parley, but that "no" may not have been counted as formal. If, as the evidence indicates, van Braam and La Peyroney then went out to meet the French, and van Braam later brought back the text, the proposals with which the two returned from the French lines must have been rejected because they were verbal. The alternative is to assume that La Peyroney

[3] 2 *Sparks,* 464.
[4] *Va. Gazette,* July 19, 1775; *Ambler,* 211–12.
[5] *Md. Gazette,* Aug. 29, 1754; *Ambler,* 215–16.
[6] 1 *Ford,* 120 n.

was wounded on the first visit to the French lines and that van Braam consequently read the terms after that same visit. Almost beyond question, the final rejection was of the term that called on the English to surrender their munitions of war. The statement in the text is based on this interpretation of the circumstances.

Both the preceding questions are of no great moment except as literal accuracy of statement is to be desired. The third, concerning the alleged treachery of van Braam, is historically of more importance. At the time, as explained in the text, George and other officers [7] felt that they had been duped by van Braam, who was denounced as a poltroon and traitor and was not included in the thanks voted by the General Assembly to the officers and men of the expedition.[8] After the publication of the *Mémoire* it was humiliating to read that Villiers boasted he had "made the English consent to sign that they had assassinated my brother in his camp." [9]

The capitulation itself attests that the English signed to that effect; but these five circumstances should be mentioned:

First, the original of the capitulation was badly written. The words *l'assassin* in one place and *l'assasinat* in the other were so scribbled that the long "s's" might readily have been confusing. In both instances the "a" of the antepenult was dotted as if it were an "ie." Van Braam was not the only man who had difficulty in understanding what the word was. When some translator—the chirography shows he was not van Braam—sat down to make what may have been the official "fair copy" for the Virginia authorities, he wrote "assault" and then scratched that out and wrote "killing." [10]

Second, the conditions under which the paper was passed and signed, as recorded by Adam Stephen, would have made accurate translation difficult by any man, however familiar with the language. Stephen wrote: "When Mr. van Braam returned with the French proposals, we were obliged to take the sense of them by word of mouth: It rained so heavily that he could not give us a written translation of them; we could scarcely keep the candle light to read them; they were wrote in a bad hand, on wet and blotted paper so that no person could read them but van Braam who had heard them from the mouth of the French officer." [11]

Third, in the trial by the French of van Braam and Stobo, Oct. 23, 1756, after van Braam was asked one or two questions in English, "he begged us to question him in French, which he understood better than English, which the accused asked of himself, in French." [12] His knowledge of

[7] *Md. Gazette*, Aug. 29, 1754; *Ambler*, 415.
[8] See *supra*, p. 438.   [9] 2 *Sparks*, 462.
[10] MS "Articles of Capitulation granted to Col. Washington by the French Command'r"; VSL.   [11] *Md. Gazette*, July 29, 1754; *Ambler*, 415.
[12] *Rapport de l'Archiviste de la Prov. de Quebec*, 1922–23, p. 309.

French, therefore, must be assumed to be good. It will be recalled, also, that he had advertised for pupils to study French under him in Annapolis. Both Washington and Stephen attested van Braam's limited knowledge of English. "The interpreter," George wrote, "was a Dutchman little acquainted with the English language." [13] It is almost certain that in oral translation of a badly written document, van Braam had to change the French to his native Dutch and render that into English. This process, needless to say, lent itself to error, in spite of van Braam's adequate knowledge of French.

Fourth, van Braam had no discoverable motive for treachery. Stephen's charge of further instances of deceptive translation by van Braam [14] is shown by the text of the capitulation to be unfounded and to be due not to van Braam but to Stephen's own misunderstanding of the terms. If, in the same connection, van Braam was a traitor, he scarcely would have bought a British uniform waistcoat from George when going into the French lines as a hostage.

Fifth, and conclusively, the Virginians themselves realized, in time, that they had done van Braam an injustice and that his erroneous translation was due to ignorance of the English language. On his return from hostageship, the General Assembly of Virginia in 1760–61 by successive "resolves," voted him his accumulated back pay of £828 [15] and £500 besides,[16] and asked the Governor to "take [van Braam] . . . into his special favor and protection and recommend him for promotion in His Majesty's service." [17] This last action was by unanimous vote of the Burgesses and, though not formally so stated, evidently was intended to right the wrong done van Braam by the suspicions cast on him in 1754. If the other considerations listed here did not apply, this final vote of the Burgesses would be a definite verdict of "not guilty" in the case of the young Dutchman. He duly received commission in the Royal American Regiment, later the Sixtieth Foot, and his allotment of 9000 of the 200,000 acres of western land granted by the Governor and Council to participants in the campaign of 1754. Although van Braam had difficulty in procuring this land, because of his absence from the Colony, he finally established title with Washington's assistance, sold the tract and devoted the proceeds to the purchase of a farm in Wales. He was placed on Captain's half pay after the peace of 1763 but, in October, 1775, he was appointed to one of the Battalions of his old Regiment and was sent to East Florida. In July, 1779, when he resigned, he held the rank of Major.[18]

[13] Letter to unnamed correspondent, n.d., 2 *Sparks*, 464.

[14] *Md. Gazette*, Aug. 29, 1754; *Ambler*, 215–16.

[15] *Journ. H.B.*, 1758–61, p. 162, 166.

[16] *Ibid.*, 227, 232.

[17] *Ibid.*, 238, 245–46.

[18] See the summary by E. Alfred Jones, 30 *V* 394–95, of a MS memoir by van Braam in P.R.O.: C.O., 5–166, 43–49.

KING DEFENDED CONSTITUTION IN '76, SAYS BRITON

Gives New Motives for War with Colonies

[Chicago Tribune Press Service]

LONDON, April 22—A British historian, writing on the American Revolution, suggests that King George III was not intent upon suppressing the American colonists, but concerned solely with Britain's "constitutional" rights. The historian relates that George feared the loss of America would bring the gradual end of the British empire.

The historian, Eric Robson of Manchester university, says the king in no way planned to "defeat the political progress of the [American race." Robson contends that manuscripts of the king's reign contradict many conclusions that George was to blame for the struggle between the American colonies and Britain.

Rather than allow himself to become "imbued with a grossly inflated idea of the legitimate powers of the monarchy," the king used his authority in defense of the constitution, Robson wrote in an article in the magazine, History Today.

War to Uphold Parliament

"The conflict with the American colonies," Robson says, "was conducted by the king and his ministers to uphold the supremacy of parliament in Westminster, and the rights of the crown were not at stake." Only when it was found impossible to subdue the colonies did the king abandon "the battle of the legislature," as he described it, Robson said.

[Britain has no written constitution. Acts of parliament are the supreme law of the land.]

Robson suggests there was a wider background to the American Revolution than has been appreciated by the king's contemporaries, or later by his critics.

The historian quotes a letter from Francis Bernard, governor of Massachusetts Bay colony, to the British secretary of war Nov. 23, 1765. The governor said: "All the political evils in America arise from the want of ascertaining the relation between Great Britain and the American colonies. In Britain the American governments are considered as corporations empowered to make by-laws, existing only during the pleasure of parliament, who hath never yet done anything to confirm their establishment, and hath at any time a power to dissolve them. In America they claim . . . to be perfect states, no otherwise dependent upon Great Britain than by having the same king."

Feared End of Empire

Britain, for the first time, was faced with the problem of a rapidly maturing country determined to manage its own affairs. Britain refused to recognize the American colonies as an equal since that would have been contrary to the views held in Britain on the relative position of mother country and dependent colonies.

The Americans were convinced that independence was a good thing for America. The British were convinced such a step meant the destruction of the British empire. The British grievance can therefore be considered a commercial as much as a political concern, Robson says.

Blames British "Snobbery"

In his own words, King George feared that "the West Indies must for its own interest be dependent on North America. Ireland would soon follow the same plan and be a separate state. Then this island [Britain] would be reduced to itself, and soon would be a poor island indeed, for reduced in her trade, merchants would retire with their wealth to climates more to their advantage, and shoals of manufacturers would leave the country for the new empire."

Human motives of selfishness and jealousy also affected the British attitude, Robson asserts. "It was a question," he said, "of whether Britain would continue as the head of the greatest empire on earth, or return to her original station as one of the lesser European powers."

The historian contends that the American colonies might never have challenged British authority had Britain not been so convinced of its own social superiority.

The move towards independence indicated Britain's failure in colonial statesmanship, Robson says. "In contrast to the majority of the majority of the Americans, who knew what they wanted, from 1763 until 1774 English ministers fumbled and failed to adhere to any one policy," he says.

N. Y. LIBRARY GIVEN APPEAL OF COLONISTS TO KING FOR PEACE

New York, Dec. 28 (Special)— The Olive Branch Petition—a final, somewhat appeasing appeal for peace to King George III. of England, delivered by the American colonists in 1775—has been obtained by the New York public library, it was announced today.

The seven page manuscript, one of the two original drafts of the original petition, was the gift of Lucius Wilmerding, library trustee and stockbroker. At its only public sale, 16 years ago in the depth of the depression, the petition brought $53,000.

Paul North Rice, reference department chief, said it was the most important historical document acquistion by the library in a generation. The second draft is in the London public record office, where George III. tossed it without bothering to acknowledge receipt or make any reply—one of history's best bad guesses.

SCALE of MILES

0 10 20 30 40 50

DELAWARE

PHILADELPHIA
CHESTER

RIVER

PENNSYLVANIA

MARYLAND

SUSQUEHANNA

WEST BRANCH

JUNIATA RIVER

CARLISLE

SHIPPENSBURG

POTOMAC R

OPEQUON CREEK

SLEEPY CREEK

CACAPON RIVER

LITTLE CACAPON RIVER

WINCHESTER

RAYSTOWN

FORT LOUDON

ALLEGHENY MOUNTAINS

CUMBERLAND

FORT

SOUTH BRANCH

PATTERSON CREEK

MOUNTAINS

WILLS CR

LAUREL HILL

LOYAL HANNON

CONEMAUGH RIVER

RIDGE

CHESTNUT

FORT DUQUESNE

VENANGO

FRENCH CREEK

To FORT LE BOEUF

ALLEGHENY RIVER

TURTLE CR.

YOUGHIOGHENY

RIVER

REDSTONE CREEK

OHIO R.

MONONGAHELA